Psychological Perspectives on Risk and Risk Analysis

Martina Raue • Eva Lermer • Bernhard Streicher
Editors

Psychological Perspectives on Risk and Risk Analysis

Theory, Models, and Applications

Foreword by Paul Slovic

Springer

Editors
Martina Raue
AgeLab
Massachusetts Institute of Technology
Cambridge, MA, USA

Bernhard Streicher
Institute of Psychology
UMIT - Private University for Health Sciences, Medical Informatics and Technology
Hall in Tyrol, Austria

Eva Lermer
Department of Experimental Psychology
University of Regensburg
Regensburg, Germany

FOM University of Applied Sciences for Economics and Management
Munich, Germany

ISBN 978-3-030-06440-2 ISBN 978-3-319-92478-6 (eBook)
https://doi.org/10.1007/978-3-319-92478-6

Softcover re-print of the Hardcover 1st edition 2018

This Springer imprint is published by the registered company Springer Nature Switzerland AG
The registered company address is: Gewerbestrasse 11, 6330 Cham, Switzerland

Foreword

I have been fortunate to study psychological aspects of risk since 1959. At that time, this was a topic of interest to only a handful of researchers, far from the mainstream of psychological inquiry. Risk and decision making then was the province of economists and mathematicians, building on a rich intellectual heritage going back centuries and based around formal models such as utility theory.

Only a few years earlier, in 1954, a psychologist named Ward Edwards, son of an economist, had written a brilliant review that eventually sparked a revolution. Titled "The Theory of Decision Making," it sought to educate psychologists about economic theories and concepts, e.g., "utility," and the potentially rich psychological issues underlying them. Edwards used his own research on probability and variance preferences among gambles as an example of how experimental psychology could be brought to bear on understanding human behavior in the face of risk. A few philosophers and mathematical psychologists joined the effort and a new field of study was born.

Now, more than half a century later, many hundreds of researchers have created a legacy of thousands of articles contributing to a complex, multifaceted, and fascinating portrait of risk perception, risk communication, and risk management. Even economists, long resistant to psychological approaches, have now joined the parade as champions of "behavioral economics."

Readers of this book have, in one place, an up-to-date and authoritative overview of the important ideas and findings generated by these decades of empirical and theoretical research. Employing this knowledge won't rid the world of risk, but it will make the world a safer place.

Decision Research and University of Oregon
Eugene, OR, USA

Paul Slovic

Preface

Risk is not out there, waiting to be measured! Risk is subjective, danger is real.

—Paul Slovic

A firefighter can make a life-or-death decision under time pressure without thinking much about it. A child can cross a busy street without knowing facts about velocity or braking distances. Some people decide to go base jumping or free climbing, while others—or even the same people—get nightmares from the thought of having to fly in an airplane. Most people agree that measles pose a much greater risk than the vaccination against them, but a minority still refuses to have their children vaccinated. People fear terrorist attacks, but not heart attacks, despite the fact that more people die from heart attacks than terrorist attacks. Some companies grow and expand in the face of changing markets, new technologies, and emerging regulations, while their competitors fall into bankruptcy around them. These examples demonstrate that people, either for themselves or as members of an organization, are good at judging risk in certain situations, but fail in other situations. Different people judge risks differently than others, and some seem to take more risks than others. Psychology offers explanations for these observations, strategies to communicate risk effectively, and practical implications for industry and policy. This volume bundles many of these insights.

"Risk is subjective, danger is real," but nevertheless, risk is often stated in numbers, mostly probabilities. How likely is it to die from an airplane crash? How likely are complications from a measles infection? How likely is a terrorist attack? How likely is it to die from a heart attack? How likely is it to win the lottery? How likely is heads over tails? Every decision situation that can be expressed in probabilities is a decision under risk. When I choose heads over tails, there is the "risk" of being wrong or losing when the coin flips to tails. The odds of the coin flip are clear; the chance of heads or tails is 50%. The chance of winning the lottery is about 1 in 175,000,000. But what are the chances of death or serious injury while base jumping? While experts can provide us with probabilities based on mathematical models or research data for some situations, high uncertainty still reigns in many others. How should I weigh the pros and cons of one medical treatment over another? How do I make investment decisions without knowledge of future developments on the stock market? How threatening is climate change? Can I trust genetically modified food or additives? In the real world, we usually deal with situations of high uncertainty. But even when people are given numbers such as the likelihood of side effects for a medical treatment or of winning in a gambling situation, some uncertainty remains, and one's reasoning may not be "rational" in a mathematical sense.

Psychological aspects of risk and risk analysis were first systematically studied in the 1950s and 1960s, a time when economists treated people as rational decision-makers or "economic men" who make choices based on cost-benefit analyses. For decades, economic theories on human risk taking behavior were based on the assumption that human beings behave logically. However, most people do not engage in statistical analyses when they judge risks in their daily lives, instead relying on more "human tools." From the experienced firefighter who trusts his intuition based on years of learning to the child who is able to cross a busy street by using a simple rule of thumb, human beings have amazing abilities which guide them through the uncertainties of life. Consider the development of self-driving cars. This technology can make our streets safer and dispense with human cognitive limitations that are often the cause of accidents. At the same time, however, it is extremely challenging for the developers to integrate all possibilities inherent to the road environment and teach the car what to do in unusual situations. While a machine can easily learn how to judge the speed of approaching cars or to remain alert for bikes and pedestrians, it fails to make judgments in unclear situations that may ask for a small violation of traffic rules (e.g., in construction zones). In situations of uncertainty, humans have developed adaptive strategies that are sometimes better than machine-based algorithms—but may in other instances lead them astray.

When investigating human risk judgments, it makes a difference whether one looks at subjective risk perception or risk taking behavior. A base jumper might judge the risk of the activity at hand as high, but still jump; a person who is afraid of flying might judge the risk of flying as low, but not enter an airplane. Likewise, most smokers are well aware that smoking can cause cancer, but this awareness does not seem to prevent them from smoking. Psychological research has identified several factors that influence the perception and judgment of risks as well as risk taking behavior. This volume highlights how individual differences (Part I) and situational circumstances (Part II) influence risk perception and risk taking behavior. Behavioral models of human decision making under risk and the challenge of integrating different approaches and theories are discussed in Part III. This volume also gives an overview of practical implications for risk communication (Part IV) and in the areas of industry, policy, and research (Part V). This book aims at a broader audience beyond the field of scientific psychology; therefore, the chapters include many vivid examples to illustrate theoretical concepts. Each chapter also gives practical implications.

Individuals or groups of people differ in the way they perceive risk and in their willingness to take risk, which is the focus of Part I. The authors of Chap. 1, Marco Lauriola and Joshua Weller, review numerous studies on the relationship between risk taking and personality traits. This chapter gives a systematic overview on why some people take more risks than others. The authors discuss different approaches of measuring risk taking, from self-reported behaviors to choice-based tasks. They also distinguish between risk-related personality traits such as sensation-seeking or impulsivity and general personality traits such as those included in the Big 5 personality inventories. They further include different domains such as recreational risks, social risks, ethical risks, health and safety risks, and gambling and financial risk taking. The chapter concludes with the argument that there is no single risk taking personality trait, but rather risk taking can be explained by the interplay of various traits and emotional states. The author of Chap. 2, Bruno Chauvin, reviews studies on the influence of sociodemographic characteristics, cultural orientation, and level of expertise on the judgment of risks. Based on a large body of research, he discusses the influence of sex and race, phenomena such as "the white male effect," and the role of power in decision making. Further, Chauvin introduces studies on culture and risk perception, which has especially received attention in the literature within the *cultural cognition theory of risk*, and differences between experts and laypeople's risk judgments. In Chap. 3, Vivianne Visschers and Michael Siegrist also look at the perceptions of experts versus laypeople, but focus specifically on differences between hazards as laid out in a *psychometric paradigm*. The authors discuss how potential hazards are sometimes perceived as more dangerous by the public than experts and how the public's risk perception is often shaped by factors such as perceived benefit, trust, knowledge, affective associations, values, and fairness. Based on studies in various areas such as gene modification or climate change, they offer practical implications for risk management and communication.

In Part II, cognitive, emotional and social influences on human risk perception and risk taking are considered. In Chap. 4, Rebecca Helm and Valerie Reyna take a cognitive perspective on risk taking and also consider developmental and neurobiological research. The authors discuss *Prospect Theory*, dual process theories, *Fuzzy Trace Theory*, and *Construal Level Theory*. They point out how framing and mental representations of risk influence judgment and behavior and consider neural underpinnings of risk taking. Chapter 5, by Mary Kate Tompkins, Pär Bjälkebring, and Ellen Peters, gives an overview of current research on the role of affect and emotion in risk perception. The risk perception literature makes a primary distinction between risk as feelings and risk as analysis, and psychologists have pointed out the importance of feelings when judging risks. The authors thereby focus on the *affect heuristic* and the *appraisal-tendency framework*. Chapter 6, by Eric Eller and Dieter Frey, is centered around social influences on risk perception and risk behavior. Group influences, which have long been studied in social psychology, also affect decisions under risk, especially in professional contexts such as teamwork. The chapter points out how groups may hinder adequate risk identification, risk analysis, and decision making. The authors end the chapter with a set of recommendations to overcome these group barriers.

Part III especially focuses on observed human behavior, which is described in behavioral models of risk taking. In Chap. 7, Martina Raue and Sabine Scholl point to the challenges of considering many pieces of information or deciding under time pressure. As a result of these limitations, people simplify decision processes and use rules of thumb or heuristics. The authors thereby focus on two approaches: the *heuristics and biases* program and the *fast and frugal heuristics*. In Chap. 8, Michael Birnbaum gives a systematic overview of behavioral models of risk taking, which are theories that describe human behavior in decisions that involve risk. While a normative model describes behavior as it ought to be in relation to an observed risk, a behavioral model describes behavior as it has been observed. In Chap. 9, Cvetomir Dimov and Julian Marewski discuss the challenges of theory integration. The authors argue that psychological researchers often aim at explaining the human mind without crossing the borders of their individual subdisciplines. They therefore call for more attention to theory integration. Readers may become aware of this issue when reading through the chapters of this volume that discuss sometimes competing approaches and theories. In this chapter, a method—*cognitive architectures*—is introduced to systematically integrate existing theories and empirical findings. The authors use two competing theoretical approaches of decision making under uncertainty—the heuristics and biases program and fast and frugal heuristics (introduced in Chap. 7)—to demonstrate how cognitive architectures work. In Chap. 10, Bernhard Streicher, Eric Eller, and Sonja Zimmermann point out limitations of existing approaches to handling risk and uncertainty. To overcome these limitations, they introduce a model of risk culture, which serves as an integrative framework for different theories of risk perception and behavior, as a reference point for holistic measurements, and as a starting point for evidence-based interventions.

Part IV is centered around risk communication and starts with Chap. 11, in which Ann Bostrom, Gisela Böhm, and Robert O'Connor discuss principles and challenges of communicating risks. They describe key components of risk information processing, including exposure and attention, understanding, evaluation, and behavioral response. The authors explore influences on each of these components and focus on the roles of uncertainty, mental models, choice architecture, and habits. In Chap. 12, Ulrich Hoffrage and Rocio Garcia-Retamero note that "risks are unavoidable, but poor risk communication and misunderstanding are really unnecessary." The authors make several suggestions on how to improve risk communication in the health sector and focus on the interpretation of test results, the use of natural frequencies and visual aids, the difference between relative and absolute risk reduction, and the meaning of survival rates. In Chap. 13, Tamar Krishnamurti and Wändi Bruine de Bruin also focus on health risks and summarize four lessons learned for effective health risk communication on an organizational level. The four lessons include accessibility, appropriate delivery methods, pre-tests of communication practices, and the collaboration of interdisciplinary teams. All chapters in Part IV point to the importance of matching the risk communication strategy to the target audience's goals, attributes, and mental model of the world they live in.

While all the chapters include a section on practical implications, the chapters in Part V are specifically centered around this aspect. In Chap. 14, Eva Lermer, Bernhard Streicher, and Martina Raue give an overview of recent research on measuring subjective risk estimates. It is of high practical importance for both researchers and practitioners to understand how risk perception can be measured and especially how it may vary depending on the measurement used. In Chap. 15, insights on risk and uncertainty in the insurance industry are given by Rainer Sachs. This chapter is an overview of the professional work of risk managers. The author outlines how their methods and tools have developed historically from experience-based methods to mathematical models. He describes the limits of these models and challenges in the face of emerging risks and uncertainty. This volume closes with Chap. 16, in which Ortwin Renn summarizes implications of psychological aspects of risk perception for policy and government. He stresses that human risk perception may differ from statistical assessment of risks, but needs to be valued as an indicator for individual and societal concerns that require attention.

Theory integration is often challenging in scientific research (see Chap. 9 for a discussion), but the reader will notice that the chapters of this volume often overlap, demonstrating that various aspects, findings, and theories in the field of risk are integrated and acknowledged by the authors. The chapters also nicely complement one another. In that line, most chapters include cross-references within the book that can be used to gain a deeper understanding of concepts, models, and research findings.

It was a pleasure for us to work with outstanding authors who have shared their excitement about this book. All of them have been extremely motivated, dedicated, and open-minded. We cannot thank our contributors enough for making this book a very rewarding and successful project. We would also like to thank our wonderful editor at Springer, Morgan Ryan, who was exceptionally supportive during every step of this project.

Cambridge, MA, USA — Martina Raue
Munich, Germany — Eva Lermer
Hall in Tyrol, Austria — Bernhard Streicher

Contents

Contributors

Michael H. Birnbaum Decision Research Center, California State University, Fullerton, CA, USA

Gisela Böhm Department of Psychosocial Science, Faculty of Psychology, University of Bergen, Bergen, Norway

Department of Psychology, Inland Norway University of Applied Sciences, Lillehammer, Norway

Pär Bjälkebring Department of Psychology, University of Gothenburg, Gothenburg, Sweden

Department of Psychology, The Ohio State University, Columbus, OH, USA

Ann Bostrom Daniel J. Evans School of Public Policy & Governance, University of Washington, Seattle, WA, USA

Wändi Bruine de Bruin Centre for Decision Research, Leeds University Business School, University of Leeds, Leeds, UK

Department of Engineering and Public Policy, Carnegie Mellon University, Pittsburgh, PA, USA

Bruno Chauvin University of Strasbourg, Strasbourg, France

Cvetomir M. Dimov Department of Organizational Behavior, Faculty of Business and Economics, University of Lausanne, Lausanne, Switzerland

Department of Psychology, Carnegie Mellon University, Pittsburgh, PA, USA

Eric Eller Department of Psychology, Ludwig-Maximilian University Munich, Munich, Germany

Dieter Frey Department of Psychology, Ludwig-Maximilian University Munich, Munich, Germany

Rocio Garcia-Retamero Department of Experimental Psychology, University of Granada, Granada, Spain

Rebecca K. Helm University of Exeter Law School, Exeter, UK

Ulrich Hoffrage Department of Organizational Behavior, Faculty of Business and Economics, University of Lausanne, Lausanne, Switzerland

Tamar Krishnamurti Division of General Internal Medicine, University of Pittsburgh School of Medicine, Pittsburgh, PA, USA

Department of Engineering and Public Policy, Carnegie Mellon University, Pittsburgh, PA, USA

Marco Lauriola Department of Social and Developmental Psychology, University of Rome "Sapienza", Rome, Italy

Eva Lermer Department of Experimental Psychology, University of Regensburg, Regensburg, Germany

FOM University of Applied Sciences for Economics and Management, Munich, Germany

Julian N. Marewski Department of Organizational Behavior, Faculty of Business and Economics, University of Lausanne, Lausanne, Switzerland

Robert E. O'Connor Social, Behavioral and Economic Sciences Directorate, National Science Foundation, Alexandria, VA, USA

Ellen Peters Department of Psychology, The Ohio State University, Columbus, OH, USA

Martina Raue AgeLab, Massachusetts Institute of Technology, Cambridge, MA, USA

Ortwin Renn Institute for Advanced Sustainability Studies, Potsdam, Germany

Valerie F. Reyna Human Neuroscience Institute, Cornell Magnetic Resonance Imaging Facility, Cornell University, Ithaca, NY, USA

Rainer Sachs Munich Reinsurance Company, Integrated Risk Management, Munich, Germany

Sabine G. Scholl School of Social Sciences, University of Mannheim, Mannheim, Germany

Michael Siegrist Institute for Environmental Decision Making, Consumer Behavior, ETH Zurich, Zurich, Switzerland

Bernhard Streicher Institute of Psychology, UMIT - Private University for Health Sciences, Medical Informatics and Technology, Hall in Tyrol, Austria

Mary Kate Tompkins Department of Psychology, The Ohio State University, Columbus, OH, USA

Vivianne H. M. Visschers School of Applied Psychology, University of Applied Sciences and Arts Northwestern Switzerland (FHNW), Olten, Switzerland

Joshua Weller Department of Developmental Psychology, Tilburg University, Tilburg, Netherlands

Sonja Zimmermann Institute of Psychology, UMIT - Private University for Health Sciences, Medical Informatics and Technology, Hall in Tyrol, Austria

About the Editors

Martina Raue is a Research Scientist at the MIT AgeLab in Cambridge, Massachusetts and an Instructor in the Department of Psychology at Harvard University. She studies risk perception and decision making over the lifespan, with a focus on the roles of time and emotion. She applies theories from social psychology to challenges and risks of longevity and examines ways to improve planning and preparing for later life. Dr. Raue received her Ph.D. in social psychology from the Ludwig-Maximilian University Munich in Germany and her master's degree in psychology from the University of Basel in Switzerland.

Eva Lermer is a Professor of Business Psychology at the FOM University of Applied Sciences for Economics and Management in Munich, Germany, and a Research Scientist at the Department of Experimental Psychology at the University of Regensburg, Germany. Her research interests include subjective risk assessment, decision making, and de-biasing strategies. In addition to her scientific research, Professor Lermer works as a consultant for profit and nonprofit organizations. She received her academic degrees from the University of Salzburg in Austria and the Ludwig-Maximilian University Munich in Germany.

Bernhard Streicher is a Full Professor of Social and Personality Psychology and Head of the Department of Psychology and Medical Sciences at the University for Health Sciences—UMIT in Hall, Tyrol, Austria. His research interests include the psychological mechanisms of decision making under risk and uncertainty and the question of how to enhance the risk competencies of people and organizations. In addition to his scientific research, Professor Streicher works as a lecturer and consultant regarding the topic of "risk" for profit and nonprofit organizations. Professor Streicher received his academic titles from the Ludwig-Maximilian University Munich in Germany.

Martina Raue, Eva Lermer, and Bernhard Streicher jointly founded the *Risikolabor* (risk lab) at the Ludwig-Maximilian University Munich in 2011. While currently based at different institutions, they continue to collaborate on various research projects investigating human perception of risk and influences on risk taking behavior. In addition, they offer consulting and workshops on the topic. More about their work can be found at www.risikolabor.org.

Part I
Individual Differences in Risk Perception and Risk Taking Behavior

Chapter 1
Personality and Risk: Beyond Daredevils—Risk Taking from a Temperament Perspective

Marco Lauriola and Joshua Weller

Abstract We reviewed studies relating risk taking to personality traits. This search long has been elusive due to the large number of definitions of risk and to the variety of personality traits associated with risk taking in different forms and domains. In order to reconcile inconsistent findings, we categorized risk taking measures into self-report behavior inventories, self-report trait-based scales, and choice-based tasks. Likewise, we made a distinction between specific risk-related traits (e.g., sensation seeking, impulsivity) and more general traits (e.g., the Big Five). Sensation seeking aspects like thrill and experience seeking were more strongly associated with recreational and social risks that trigger emotional arousal. Impulsivity was associated with ethical, health safety, gambling, and financial risk taking, due to disregard of future consequences and to lack of self-control. Among the Big Five, extraversion and openness to experience were associated with risk seeking; whereas conscientiousness and agreeableness had more established links with risk aversion. Neuroticism facets, like anxiety and worry, had negative relationships with risk seeking; other facets, like anger and depression, promoted risk seeking. We concluded that the notion of a unidimensional "risk taking" trait seems misleading. The interplay of many traits encompassed in an overarching temperament model best represented personality-risk relations. Positive emotionality traits promoted risky behaviors that confer an emotionally rewarding experience to the person. Negative emotionality traits lead to heightened perceptions of danger, primarily motivating the avoidance of risk. The last disinhibition affected risk taking as a result of differences in self-control control acting upon momentary feelings and in self-interest. Potential applications for practitioners are also discussed.

M. Lauriola (✉)
Department of Social and Developmental Psychology, University of Rome "Sapienza", Rome, Italy
e-mail: marco.lauriola@uniroma1.it

J. Weller
Department of Developmental Psychology, Tilburg University, Tilburg, Netherlands

M. Raue et al. (eds.), *Psychological Perspectives on Risk and Risk Analysis*,
https://doi.org/10.1007/978-3-319-92478-6_1

For decades, the construct of risk taking has captured the attention of researchers from a multitude of disciplines, including clinicians, psychologists, and economists. Understanding *who* is more likely to take a risk has clear implications for one's financial, social, and personal well-being, as well as society in general. For instance, conceptualizing how individuals who engage in risky behaviors arrive at decisions can help to pinpoint identifying the underlying mechanisms that mediate maladaptive decision making processes. Additionally, identifying who is more likely to take a risk can improve risk communication efforts by means of tailored messages highlighting goals and values that are important to them.

However, the notion of a "risk taker" appears to be more complex than a singular category that can apply to behaviors spanning across a variety of different contexts. In fact, there has been some disagreement reflecting the degree to which risk taking tendencies are dispositional in nature. For those who indeed consider it to be dispositional, scholars have been divided about whether risk taking is better conceptualized as a unitary trait or as a domain-specific phenomenon. On the one hand, traits like sensation seeking and impulsivity were long thought to represent the personality basis of risk taking across different types of behaviors and situations (e.g., Enticott & Ogloff, 2006; Zuckerman & Kuhlman, 2000). On the other hand, supporters of a domain-specific approach suggest that risk behaviors may be qualitatively different from one another (e.g., Anderson & Mellor, 2009; Hanoch, Johnson, & Wilke, 2006; Soane & Chmiel, 2005; Weber, Blais, & Betz, 2002). Subsequently, different personality variables may uniquely account for variance across specific risk domains. For instance, Weller and Tikir (2011) found that dispositional honesty/humility predicted ethical and health risk taking, but not social or recreational risk taking. From this lens, a domain-specificity account of risk neither precludes the possibility that broader dispositional factors are associated with specific risk domains, nor does it necessarily rule out that stable overarching preferences for risk taking exist. Domain-specific risk taking studies often yield positive intercorrelations among risk propensity in different domains, as well as significant correlations between risk propensity and personality (e.g., Dohmen et al., 2011; Highhouse, Nye, Zhang, & Rada, 2016; Nicholson, Soane, Fenton-O'Creevy, & Willman, 2005; Weber et al., 2002; Weller, Ceschi, & Randolph, 2015a; Weller & Tikir, 2011). Additionally, test-retest correlations for risk taking demonstrate considerable temporal stability, up to 2 years (e.g., Chuang & Schechter, 2015, Table 1). These findings suggest that not only do stable individual differences in risk behaviors exists but also that broader personality traits may be associated with these behaviors.

Acknowledging that risk behaviors may be both domain-specific and multiply-determined, the current chapter proposes that individual differences in risk propensity can be best understood within the context of a broader, hierarchical personality framework, with each broad personality trait influencing some aspect of risk taking. Based on its theoretical ties to emotional and cognitive control processes, we organize our discussion around a "Big Three," or temperament-based, framework (e.g., Clark & Watson, 2008; Tellegen & Waller, 2008). Adult temperament models stress that the broadest dimensions, extraversion/positive emotionality (extraversion), neuroticism/negative emotionality (neuroticism), and disinhibition vs. constraint (disinhibition), are affect-relevant traits. Because of this theoretical link, temperament models converge with advances in the behavioral decision literature that highlights the interplay between affective and cognitive processes, in the appraisal of risk and decision making in general (e.g., Loewenstein, Weber, Hsee, & Welch, 2001; Rusting, 2001; Slovic & Peters, 2006; Weber & Johnson, 2009).

The aims of this chapter are threefold. First, we address the issue of differences in conceptual definitions of risk taking and their corresponding operational definitions across disciplines, we believe, have hindered reaching common ground in this area (cf. Fox & Tannenbaum, 2011). Second, we briefly review the literature on traits that has demonstrated a link between personality and risk taking. Specifically, we examine the constructs of sensation seeking and impulsivity, as well as broad, higher-order trait dimensions (i.e., Big Five). Finally, we propose that these findings might be partly reconciled by framing the reviewed studies in terms of a Big Three model, linking personality traits to risk behaviors.

Definitions of Risk and Construct Validity of Risk-Related Traits

Like many constructs, the risk taking literature is no stranger to numerous theoretical and, therefore, operational definitions. Many different measures may exist, but it is unclear whether they assess the same construct. At best, research would yield moderate to strong correlations across different assessments; at worst, there would be no convergence across the different paradigms, suggesting that these variables may all assess different processes and perhaps constructs.

Choice-Based Experimental Tasks

One straightforward definition of risk taking, from an economic and financial perspective, is *the tendency to choose an option that has a greater outcome variance* than another option. From this perspective, a risky choice may not necessarily be associated with a negative outcome or a problem behavior. One of the first methods to quantify risk taking involved using *one-shot, hypothetical gambles*, eliciting a choice between a small number of options – usually between an uncertain, or risky, option (50% chance to win $10, otherwise win $0) and a certain option (100% chance to win $5 for sure). Proponents of this method assert that it provides an analogue for how individuals use and integrate specific contextual information about a risky decision (e.g., the magnitude of the outcome and the probability that the outcome will be realized. These studies have been instrumental in demonstrating a gap between how people actually approach risky choices (e.g., prospect theory) and how a normatively rational actor would approach them (cf., Goldstein & Weber, 1995; Lopes, 1995, see also Birnbaum, Chap. 8).

Hypothetical gambles still are common in behavioral economics, based on the assumption that financial risk taking, and risk taking in general, can be modeled almost exclusively as maximizing the expectation of some individual utility function that maps on a cardinal scale the subjective value of each available choice option (cf., Friedman, Isaac, James, & Sunder, 2014; Takemura, 2014). Unfortunately, however, expected utility assessments of risk attitude have demonstrated limited predictive validity outside the laboratory or field context in which they were elicited (Anderson & Mellor, 2009; Dohmen et al., 2011; Friedman et al., 2014; Schonberg, Fox, & Poldrack, 2011; Weber et al., 2002). Moreover, the average risk taking pattern elicited by hypothetical gambles for which outcomes and probabilities are clearly stated before making a decision (i.e., a description-based decision) can differ from the pattern resulting from situations for which outcomes and probabilities are learned by experience (e.g., offering the decision makers a probability sampling or providing them with a feedback on their choices; Barron & Erev, 2003; Hertwig, Barron, Weber, & Erev, 2004; Hertwig & Erev, 2009; Schonberg et al., 2011). This knowledge has motivated researchers to develop behavioral paradigms that more adequately capture the psychological experience of risk. New paradigms have become increasingly popular, especially within the clinical neuropsychological literature (Schonberg et al., 2011; Weber & Johnson, 2009). Though not an exhaustive list, representative examples include the *Iowa Gambling Task* (IGT; Bechara, Damasio, Damasio, & Anderson, 1994), the *Balloon Analogue Risk Task* (BART; Lejuez et al., 2002), and the *Columbia Card Task* (CCT; Figner, Mackinlay, Wilkening, & Weber, 2009).

Tasks like IGT, BART, and CCT involve making repeated decisions in the face of uncertainty and directly experiencing the consequences of their choices. For instance, participants taking the IGT are asked to draw cards from four available decks differing in payoff size and structure. Two risk disadvantageous decks confer higher rewards on most trials but also very big losses on some trials, with a negative long-term expected value. The other two decks are risk advantageous, conferring lower rewards on most trials but only occasional small losses, with a positive long-term expected value. In order to perform well on this task, the participants must learn which decks are more advantageous, indeed drawing more cards for them than from disadvantageous decks. Another prominent task used to assess risk taking tendencies is BART. On this task participants are asked to inflate a virtual balloon displayed on a computer screen by pressing a pump button. Each click inflates the balloon and transfers $0.05 to a temporary account. Participants are informed that the balloon can explode after each pump, erasing the money earned on the trial. However, if they stop pumping, they earn all of the points accrued for that balloon. As each pump is a gamble, which confers an additional reward but also involves increased risk (i.e., the chance of the balloon popping becomes greater), participants must learn about the stochastic structure of the task in order to perform well. The last risk task that we briefly review is the CCT. On this task participants take repeated trials in which they are presented with 32 cards presented face down and they are instructed to sequentially turn over them. Like BART pumps, every choice is rewarded, unless one turns a loss card. Different from IGT and BART, the CCT offers to the decision precise information about the magnitude of gains, losses, and the associated probabilities. Indeed, the effect of learning is more limited for this task, and this perhaps makes the CCT a more refined and decomposable measure of risk taking tendencies than IGT and BART.

Although such paradigms differ in the types of decisions that are made, they collectively represent a major step toward developing a body of literature that appreciates the nuanced processes that may operate in guiding decision making across different risk contexts. Inspired by the pioneering work using the IGT to explicate decision making deficits in patients with neurological damage to the prefrontal cortex and amygdala, researchers have demonstrated the promise of showing differences between individuals with clinical diagnoses (e.g., substance use disorder) and healthy comparisons, as well as age-related differences in decision making (e.g., Bornovalova, Daughters, Hernandez, Richards, & Lejuez, 2005; Brevers, Bechara, Cleeremans, & Noël, 2013; Coffey, Schumacher, Baschnagel, Hawk, & Holloman, 2011; Kräplin et al., 2014). Specifically, these tasks also have led to insights into the neural correlates of risk behavior and how the development of these systems may impact risk taking tendencies over the lifespan (e.g., Bechara, Damasio, Damasio, & Lee, 1999; Gladwin, Figner, Crone, & Wiers, 2011; Paulsen, Carter, Platt, Huettel, & Brannon, 2011).

Self-Report Behavior Approaches

In contrast to a financial-based definition of risk taking based on variance, self-report methods define risk taking largely as *problem behaviors* that have the potential for negative consequences for the person (e.g., externalizing, addiction, gambling, unhealthy habits, etc.). One method involves directly asking individuals about their present or past risk behaviors, perceptions of risks, or the likelihood that one would engage in a behavior in the future. Some researchers have used a single survey question, asking about risk taking globally (e.g., "Are you generally a person who is fully prepared to take risks, or do you try to avoid taking risks?"; Dohmen et al., 2011), or have included global assessments across risk taking domains, such as recreation or health (e.g., "Please could you tell us if any of the following risks have ever applied to you, now or in your adult past?"; Dohmen et al., 2011; Nicholson et al., 2005). More refined measures have expanded on the behavioral self-report approach, including multi-item scales that are designed to provide more precision in the measurement of domain-specific risk taking. For instance, the *domain-specific risk taking* (DOSPERT; Blais & Weber, 2006; Weber et al., 2002,) provides a multidimensional measure across six broad risk domains: social (e.g., asking an employer for a raise), recreation (e.g., skydiving), investment (e.g., investing in a speculative stock), gambling (e.g., betting a portion of income on a sporting event), health/safety (e.g., drinking too much alcohol at a party), and ethics (e.g., cheating on a tax return). Another domain-specific inventory, the *passive risk taking scale* (PRT; Keinan & Bereby-Meyer, 2012), assesses one's acceptance of risk due to inaction or omission of control across three domains: resource inaction (e.g., checking the credit card statements monthly), medical (e.g., flu vaccinations), and ethical domains (e.g., not say anything when receiving too much change at the store). Although these self-report measures tend to better predict outcomes than do one-shot experimental gambles, some skepticism remains on whether this difference reflects common method variance and redundancy between scale and outcomes in survey research (e.g., Anderson & Mellor, 2009; Charness, Gneezy, & Imas, 2013; Lönnqvist, Verkasalo, Walkowitz, & Wichardt, 2015; Nicholson et al., 2005).

Self-Report Trait-Based Approaches

Personality researchers interested in better understanding individual differences in risk taking have developed constructs, and corresponding scales, that are believed to represent the affective, cognitive, and behavioral indicators that predispose one to engage in risk behaviors. These indicators often include elements of preferences toward uncertainty, thrill and excitement seeking, harm avoidance, impulsiveness, and even the engagement in specific risk behaviors. For example, risk taking scales from the *Jackson Personality Inventory* (JPI; Jackson, 1994) and the *Personality Inventory for DSM-5* (PID-5; Krueger, Derringer, Markon, Watson, & Skodol, 2012) provide a total score that assumes variation on a single underlying factor. In contrast, scales like the *Stimulating-Instrumental Risk Inventory* (SIRI; Zaleskiewicz, 2001) or the *RT-18* (de Haan et al., 2011) are based on personality items akin to existing sensation seeking and impulsivity measures and consider risk taking tendencies as a multidimensional phenomenon.

It should be noted that personality-like items are sometimes included in risk taking inventories, and risk-related trait scales elicit endorsements of engaging in specific risk behaviors (e.g., "I have tried marijuana, or would like to"; "I would like to go scuba diving"; Zuckerman, Eysenck, & Eysenck, 1978), or conversely, some items ask whether a person likes to take risks but does not clearly define what a risk is. Nonetheless, no current broad-based personality model considers risk taking as a broad, orthogonal dimension, per se. Rather, several lower-order traits presumably related to risk taking appear in larger-scale personality inventories, like the *NEO-PI-R* (i.e., excitement seeking, impulsiveness, anxiety, anger, openness to actions; Costa & McCrae, 2008), the *Multidimensional Personality Questionnaire* (i.e., harm avoidance; Tellegen & Waller, 2008), the *Temperament and Character Inventory* (i.e., exploratory excitability, impulsiveness, harm avoidance; Cloninger, Przybeck, Svakic, & Wetzel, 1994), and the *Hogan Personality Inventory* (i.e., thrill seeking, experience seeking, impulse control; Hogan & Hogan, 1995). Additionally, items related to sensation seeking, impulsiveness, and risk taking also appear in the extraversion scale on the *Eysenck Personality Inventory* (Eysenck, Eysenck, & Barrett, 1985). Other personality inventories like the *HEXACO-PI* (Lee & Ashton, 2004) also include facets, such as unconventionality, social boldness, prudence, or anxiety, along with the higher-order honesty-humility dimension, which may also contribute to risk taking, especially in the social, ethical, and health risk taking domains (e.g., Weller & Tikir, 2011).

Risk-related traits like impulsivity or sensation seeking have been long and extensively studied as predictors of a variety of real-world problem behaviors, such as reckless driving, health-risking sexual behaviors, gambling, alcoholism, and unethical behaviors (e.g., Chambers & Potenza, 2003; DeAndrea, Carpenter, Shulman, & Levine, 2009; Dahlen, Martin, Ragan, & Kuhlman, 2005; De Wit, 2009; Gullone & Moore, 2000; Hittner & Swickert, 2006; Hoyle, Fejfar, & Miller, 2000; Nelson, Lust, Story, & Ehlinger, 2008). Likewise, the degree to which different traits are associated with risk taking as a function of domains has recently been addressed using the DOSPERT or other multidimensional domain-specific measures (e.g., Gullone & Moore, 2000; Romero, Villar, Gómez-Fraguela, & López-Romero, 2012; Soane, Dewberry, & Narendran, 2010; Weller & Tikir, 2011; Zaleskiewicz, 2001).

Personality and Risk Taking

Because economists and psychologists from different subdisciplines have defined and measured risk in varied ways, mixed findings have arisen from using the same label (i.e., risk) for entirely different variables assessed in empirical studies (i.e., behavioral decision paradigms, behavioral self-report, or trait-based approaches). However, emerging from this lack of consensus is an increasing awareness that a unidimensional risk taking trait may not adequately explain individual differences in risk taking. As we will demonstrate in the following sections, research has strongly provided evidence that suggests that personality traits are correlated with specific types of risks. Moreover, these findings provide the foundation for considering risk taking within the context of a broader personality framework.

In this section, we briefly review some of the most commonly used personality indicators of risk behaviors. Specifically, we focus on two constructs, sensation seeking and impulsivity, as well as broader personality dimensions. Both sensation seeking and impulsivity are often deemed the traits that best represent a generalized latent disposition capable to motivate risk taking across domains and situations (e.g., Enticott & Ogloff, 2006; Zuckerman & Kuhlman, 2000). Though often treated as unidimensional constructs, the multidimensional nature of these constructs can help to better place dispositional risk taking tendencies within the context of a temperament model of personality. For instance, facets of both sensation seeking and impulsivity are similar to other narrow traits in commonly used personality inventories and belong to broader and relatively orthogonal personality dimensions (Anusic, Schimmack, Pinkus, & Lockwood, 2009; Markon, Krueger, & Watson, 2005; Sharma, Markon, & Clark, 2014).

A temperament approach offers researchers several advantages. First, research has increasingly recognized that self-reports in temperament reflect underlying neurobiological mechanisms that are responsible for an individual's experience of positive and negative affect (e.g., Derringer et al., 2010; DeYoung, 2010; Munafo, Clark, & Flint, 2005; Reuter, Schmitz, Corr, & Hennig, 2007). Second, temperament is proposed to have a developmental history. Research has suggested that childhood temperament is linked to individual differences in temperament as an adult (e.g., Rothbart & Ahadi, 1994). Last, self-reported adult temperament has been found to be stable over time (Bazana, Stelmack, & Stelmack, 2004, for a meta-analysis of the stability of temperament traits). Thus, the temperament dimensions can be said to be enduring, stable dispositions, a feature that matches nicely with the search for stable risk preferences (cf. Fox & Tannenbaum, 2011).

Sensation Seeking and Risk Taking

Personality psychologists' interest in risk taking dispositions has grown due to the seminal work of Zuckerman and colleagues, who defined the sensation seeking trait as individual differences "in the seeking of varied, novel, complex, and intense sensations and experiences, and the willingness to take physical, social, legal, and financial risks for the sake of such experience" (Zuckerman, 1994, p. 27). From this perspective, risk taking is not a primary trait characteristic, but rather a reflection of seeking situations that satisfy one's need for arousal, excitement, novelty, and change, which often, but not necessarily, involve elements of risk.

Versions of the *Sensation Seeking Scale* (currently SSS-V is the most popular; Zuckerman et al., 1978) have been extensively used in personality-risk research (see Roberti, 2004 for a review). The SSS-V not only provides a global score that characterizes relative levels of overall sensation seeking but also includes four subscales: thrill and adventure seeking (e.g., involvement in risky sports), disinhibition (e.g., involvement in wild parties or uncontrolled situations), experience seeking (e.g., involvement in novel, strange, or unusual activities), and boredom susceptibility (e.g., constant need for arousal).

Before reviewing specific facets of sensation seeking, it is worth noting that people scoring high on the SSS-V total score typically approach risky situations with more self-confidence and good feelings compared to people who report lower scores on these scales (Horvath & Zuckerman, 1993; Zuckerman, 1994). Thus, beyond the popular view that sensation seekers are involved in risk taking for the mere sake of stimulating experiences, the literature also suggests that they place greater hedonic value on exciting activities. Consistent with an "affect heuristic" account, those who have good feelings toward a hazard or activity situation tend to perceive it as safer and expect greater benefits from it, thus increasing the likelihood of engaging in risk taking (e.g., Finucane, Alhakami, Slovic, & Johnson, 2000; Hanoch et al., 2006; Slovic, Finucane, Peters, & MacGregor, 2004; Weber et al., 2002). According to Zuckerman (2007), sensation seekers are likely to take risks across different domains (e.g., physical, social, legal, and financial risks). In one study, Zuckerman and Kuhlman (2000) tested the generality of sensation seeking-risk relations across six types of behaviors (smoking, drinking, drugs, sex, driving, and gambling), each assessed by self-reported direct measures of risk taking. Higher overall sensation seeking scores were significantly correlated with all risky behaviors, except gambling and risky driving. In terms of construct validity, the study showed that a common personality factor linked sensation seeking tendencies to different types of risk. Roberti (2004) carried out a comprehensive review of the risky behaviors for which sensation seekers typically engage. Effect sizes tended to be medium to large for overall sensation seeking scores with substance use, gambling, reckless driving, and risky sexual experiences (e.g., multiple partners, unprotected sex, younger age for the first sexual intercourse, etc.), though were only considered medium in size for involvement in risky sports (e.g., extreme sports).

Because the need for arousal and stimulating experiences is a linchpin of the construct, risky choices that are more emotionally engaging are believed to demonstrate stronger correlations with sensation seeking. Supporting this assertion, Zaleskiewicz (2001) found that sensation seeking predicted self-reported "stimulating" risk behaviors (i.e., motivated by the need for arousal, e.g., skydiving, bungee jumping, or scuba diving), but "instrumental" risk behaviors (i.e., risks needed to reach some important future goal, e.g., business or financial decisions) were less strongly associated with sensation seeking. Similarly, decisions from description (e.g., hypothetical one-shot gambles, no experience of consequences) might lack the necessary element of arousal that rewards the decision maker and, thus, lower observed correlations between risk taking and sensation seeking (Zuckerman, 2007). However, as the activity or task becomes more of a decision from experience (e.g., BART, the affective or "hot" version of the CCT), sensation seeking would be predicted to demonstrate stronger correlations with behavior, corresponding with increases in autonomic arousal (Schonberg et al., 2011). Consistent with this view, Figner et al. (2009) found that the need for arousal scores, a construct closely related to sensation seeking, predicted risky choices on the affectively laden, experiential version of the CCT, but not on the more deliberative, non-feedback version of the task. In keeping with the view that sensation seeking tendencies are more related to risk taking on behavioral risk tasks that provide immediate feedback and trigger emotional arousal, de Haan et al. (2011) found that the risk taking subscale of the RT-18, which included items ostensibly related to sensation seeking, was more strongly associated with risk taking on the *Cambridge Gambling Task* (CGT, Rogers et al., 1999), an experienced-based risk taking task, than was the risk assessment subscale of the RT-18 (de Haan et al., 2011), which included more items ostensibly related to impulsiveness (vs. deliberation).

Sensation Seeking from a Temperament Perspective

Although these findings suggest that sensation seeking is broadly related to risk taking across a number of domains, only considering sensation seeking total scores may obfuscate specific contributions of unique facets specifically related to temperament. In this regard, Glicksohn and Abulafia (1998) reconsidered sensation seeking as a trait that spans across the Eysenckian temperament dimensions of extraversion and psychoticism and, hence, proposed two major components. First, the non-impulsive, socialized mode of sensation seeking is most likely involved in seeking stimulating situations characterized by minimal or no risk; when risk is present, premeditation, intense training, or careful planning may be required (e.g., travel to exotic or unusual new places, perform in front of a big audience, sky or cycle downhill at high speed; see also Hansen & Breivik, 2001). For example, a mountaineer or a scuba diver might deliberately take risk facing variable conditions or hostile environments and yet adopt precautions to control the risk, such as checking weather forecasts or up-keeping air cylinders and equipments (Woodman, Barlow, Bandura, Hill, Kupciw, & MacGregor, 2013). Furthermore, sensation seeking is only one of the motives that drive people to engage in high-risk sport activities, and not all risky sports are equally appealing for sensation seekers (e.g., skydiving vs. mountaineering; Barlow, Woodman, & Hardy, 2013). In terms of SSS-V subscales, thrill and adventure seeking may be more strongly aligned with this component. In contrast, a second dimension, the impulsive, unsocialized mode, is most likely involved in engaging in stimulating experiences for which the risk of personal and social harm is high (e.g., gambling, bullying others, attending "wild" parties). Disinhibition and boredom susceptibility subscales may be especially strong markers of this component. Accordingly, Glicksohn and Abulafia (1998) suggest that the former component is more strongly associated with extraversion, whereas the latter component is more strongly tied to psychoticism, a construct similar to disinhibition in a Big Three temperament framework.

As anticipated, de Haan et al. (2011) developed a brief risk taking measure that included items tapping into sensation seeking tendencies from different personality inventories. The analysis yielded a first factor, labeled *risk taking*, characterized largely by items describing enjoyment or involvement in a variety of stimulating risky situations; whereas a second factor labeled *risk assessment* included items reflecting the tendency to deliberate over choices compared to acting impulsively. Furthermore, the two factors were moderately intercorrelated, and the group of people scoring higher on the risk taking subscale and lower on the risk assessment ones included more risk takers, such as recreational drug users, that not only sought for stimulating experiences but also, but less so, were less likely to approach decisions in a reasoned, deliberative manner. Likewise, Woodman et al. (2013) developed a *Risk Taking Inventory* for high-risk sport participants.

Given these insights, we can reconsider Zuckerman and Kuhlman's (2000) findings that overall sensation seeking did not correlate with risky driving and gambling. In fact, if only some facets of a multifaceted trait can predict a specific target variable, using the total trait score for prediction can be misleading because non-predictive facets might dilute the predictive relationship of other facets more closely tied to the target variable of interest. In keeping with this view, research has suggested that separate SSS domains may more or less strongly be associated with specific types of risk behavior, which may attenuate total score correlations with the criterion. For instance, Jonah (2001) found that the thrill and adventure seeking subscale showed stronger correlations with risky driving than did the other subscales. Conversely, Fortune and Goodie (2010) found mean-level differences between pathological and non-pathological gamblers for the disinhibition and boredom susceptibility subscales, but not the experience seeking or thrill and adventure seeking subscales.

More broadly, we can consider these results within a temperament perspective. Specifically, thrill and adventure seeking involves seeking and positively appraising arousing and stimulating events, which may be more strongly associated with positive emotionality. By contrast, disinhibition and boredom susceptibility, relate to the impulsive, unsocialized mode, may be more strongly aligned with disinhibition (vs. constraint). As we will explain in a later section, this distinction may have important implications for understanding the personality antecedents of domain-specific risks.

Impulsivity and Risk Taking

Like sensation seeking, impulsivity is a trait that has been extensively associated with real-world risk taking (e.g., Chambers & Potenza, 2003; Dahlen et al., 2005; De Wit, 2009; Hoyle et al., 2000). Real-world risky behaviors often involve a choice between an immediate reward associated with a bad habit (e.g., taking drugs, gambling, or smoking) and a delayed greater reward that might be obtained by ending that habit (cf., Chapman, 2005; Critchfield & Kollins, 2001). Therefore, it has been hypothesized that impulsive individuals are inclined to engage in maladaptive risky behaviors to the extent that they value the immediate positive consequences of their actions (e.g., the exhilaration of gambling) to be larger than delayed advantages deriving from abstaining from those actions.

Impulsivity is a construct that has been conceptualized in a multitude of ways, including present time orientation, inability to delay gratification, reward sensitivity, impaired cognitive control, quick decision making, lack of premeditation and planning, and even behavioral disinhibition, sensation seeking, and risk taking (Bari & Robbins, 2013; Enticott & Ogloff, 2006). For purposes of the current chapter, we follow a recent definition offered by Moeller, Barratt, Dougherty, Schmitz, and Swann (2001), who argue that a description of impulsivity needs to incorporate an individual's tendency to demonstrate decreased sensitivity to less favorable behavioral consequences both in the short- and long-term and fast responses based on incomplete information processing. Moeller et al. (2001) also note that, based on these definitional components, impulsivity involves risks but suggest that impulsive risk taking may be distinguished from sensation seeking risks.

The impulsivity literature is voluminous, and a full review of methodologies span beyond the scope of the chapter. However, we describe several methods by which impulsivity is measured, both from self-report and behavioral perspectives, to highlight personality processes linking impulsivity with risk taking.

Self-Reported Impulsiveness

Several measures of impulsiveness have been developed but tend to include different dimensions. For instance, Dickman (1990) categorized impulsivity as dysfunctional or functional, depending on whether one's tendency to make quick decisions was associated with the choice of disadvantageous or advantageous options, respectively. Other measures are distinguished between different forms of impulsivity, including motor (e.g., acting on the spur of the moment), non-planning (e.g., doing things without thinking), and inattention (e.g., distractibility; Patton, Stanford, & Barratt, 1995). Likewise, Whiteside and Lynam (2001) made fine-grained distinctions among (lack of) premeditation (e.g., acting without deliberation), urgency (e.g., acting hastily under positive or negative mood states), (lack of) perseverance (e.g., easily being distracted), and sensation seeking. Collectively, impulsivity facets in self-report scales are related to risk taking with a small-medium effect size (i.e., $0.20 < r < 0.50$). However, research has also shown that specific facets account for unique portions of risk taking variance, thus potentially affecting risk taking through specific pathways or processes (e.g., Sharma, Kohl, Morgan, & Clark, 2013; Stanford et al., 2009).

Behavioral Paradigms

A variety of behavioral measures have been used to measure impulsivity, often focusing on either inter-temporal choice paradigms or testing attentional components of impulsivity. Inter-temporal choice, or delay discounting, tasks have been used to describe how people trade off between smaller sooner rewards and later larger ones (for a review of inter-temporal choice research and discount rate elicitation methods, see Green & Myerson, 2004). Conceptually, these tasks measure how much a reward loses subjective value based on the delay to the reward being received. For example, the *Monetary Choice Questionnaire* (MCQ; Kirby, Petry, & Bickel, 1999) includes 27 items, each requiring a choice between a smaller immediate monetary amount and a larger delayed one (e.g., "Would you prefer $33 today or $80 in 14 days?"; Kirby et al., 1999, p. 81). Individuals are said to be more impulsive the more quickly a reward loses its value as a function of its delay; that is, the higher their discount rate. Sometimes, they are even referred to as *impulsive decision makers*, a term that denotes the close link between impulsivity and decision making processes (cf., Green & Myerson, 2004). These preferences have been shown to have considerable temporal stability, in some cases up to many years (e.g., Kirby, 2009; Odum, 2011; Ohmura, Takahashi, Kitamura, & Wehr, 2006).

Converging evidence supports the claim that these impulsive decision makers show higher instances of engaging or persist in risky behaviors than those with lower discount rates. For instance, research has demonstrated greater levels of average discount rates between clinical samples of, for example, substance users and problem gamblers and healthy comparison groups (e.g., Alessi & Petry, 2003; Bornovalova et al., 2005; Coffey, Gudleski, Saladin, & Brady, 2003; MacKillop et al., 2011; Reynolds, 2006). Delay discounting rates are significantly correlated with self-report measures of impulsivity, especially with factors relating to impatience when delaying the experience of hedonic activity or reward (Cyders & Coskunpinar, 2012; Duckworth & Kern, 2011; Kirby & Finch, 2010).

Taken together, the literature supports the hypothesis that discounting of future consequences, and the associated increased sensitivity to present rewards, may be a process links impulsivity to risk taking behaviors. However, because delay discount rates are calculated as a function of both the rewards and the period of delay, one can presumably conceptualize that both reward sensitivity and some form of deliberation occur that weight the value of the immediate and future reward. In support, Figner et al. (2010) found that participants randomly assigned to receive repetitive transcranial magnetic stimulation (rTMS), a neuroscientific method that temporarily disrupts neural activity for a short duration by means of low-frequency magnetic waves, to the left dorsolateral prefrontal cortex (DLPFC), an area related to self-control and deliberation. Participants who received the rTMS treatment to the DLPFC displayed greater impatience than those who received rTMS treatment in regions not implicated in self-control. Additionally, when both the smaller and larger options were presented in the future, but with the same delay interval as the smaller now/longer later condition, the effect of rTMS disappeared. These findings provide strong evidence of the link between impulsiveness (in the form of self-control) and delay discounting, rather than affecting reward sensitivity.

Given the theoretical links between risk taking and the components of impulsiveness relating to self-control and delay of immediate rewards, impulsivity is often implicated in risk taking. For instance, performance on the IGT (Bechara et al., 1994) is believed to reflect a bias in recognizing long-term negative consequences associated with one's choices. Compared to healthy comparison groups, clinical groups known to exhibit risky or impulsive tendencies, such as problem gamblers and substance users, predominantly choose from the two high reward decks, demonstrating a "myopia for the future" (e.g., Bechara, 2005; Brevers et al., 2013; Cunha, Bechara, de Andrade, & Nicastri, 2011; Fridberg et al., 2010; Kräplin et al., 2014). Similarly, deciding where to stop in order to maximize winnings on BART (Lejuez et al., 2002) may be related to the diminished sensitivity to a negative consequence, as well as to disregard for future consequences. Like the IGT, clinical groups known to exhibit risky or impulsive tendencies, including crack or cocaine users, marijuana smokers, and alcohol- or tobacco-dependent people, exhibit a disadvantageous strategy on the BART, revealing concern for potential rewards and disregard for potential losses (Bornovalova et al., 2005; Coffey et al., 2011).

Other operative definitions of impulsivity have focused on response inhibition (see Bari & Robbins, 2013) or the ability to suppress preplanned or ongoing responses in the face of changing internal or external situations (e.g., being able to stop an action for which one has received extensive training). For instance, in the stop-signal task, the participant is first trained to press a specific key in response to a "go" signal in a reaction time task. Then, on some trials, a "stop" signal precedes the "go" signal, and he/she is asked to suppress the impending response, e.g., pressing a different key (for details, see Verbruggen & Logan, 2008). The time taken by the person to suppress the inappropriate motor response on "stop" trials is believed to be a reliable and valid measure of response inhibition ability (Congdon et al., 2012; Weafer, Baggott, & De Wit, 2013). Evidence suggests that response inhibition in laboratory tasks is associated with the inhibition of socially undesirable or restricted behaviors, a temperamental characteristic (i.e., disinhibition) involved in risk taking, self-control, as well as externalizing psychopathology (Young et al., 2009). Problem gamblers and addicted individuals perform worse than healthy controls on stop-signal tasks, as well as on temperament measures of disinhibition (e.g., Goudriaan, Oosterlaan, de Beurs, & Van Den Brink, 2006; Lawrence, Luty, Bogdan, Sahakian, & Clark, 2009; De Wit, 2009). Moreover, interventions designed to train self-control on go/no-go tasks (i.e., a class of tasks alike to the stop-signal paradigm) show some effectiveness for improving self-regulation across a variety of health behaviors (for a recent review, see Allom, Mullan, & Hagger, 2016).

Impulsivity from a Temperament Perspective

Sharma et al. (2014) published two comprehensive studies that shed light on the common and distinct factors that distinguish impulsivity from risk taking. Each study was based on a factor analysis of meta-analytic correlations. The first study addressed the phenotypic structure of self-reported impulsivity; the second study examined the underlying common factors to different behavioral measures of impulsivity, including delay discount and stop-signal tasks, IGT, and BART. Briefly, the self-report study maintained that impulsivity is best represented as a multidimensional construct, resembling the Big Three temperament structure: extraversion/positive emotionality, disinhibition vs. constraint, and neuroticism/negative emotionality (see also Sharma et al., 2013). The behavioral meta-factor analysis also yielded a multidimensional structure, revealing four underlying factors, each reflecting a specific cognitive process, inattention, inhibition, impulsive decision making, and shifting, respectively. Stop-signal reaction time and delay discount rates were among the factor markers for inhibition and impulsive decision making factors, respectively. In contrast, IGT scored loaded on multiple factors, whereas the BART did not load at all on the impulsivity factors. It follows that disadvantageous risk taking on the IGT was associated with a combination of response inhibition and impulsive decision making, whereas risk taking on BART was unrelated to other behavioral assessment factors in the meta-analysis, suggesting that different processes may be involved. These findings clarified that impulsivity should not be considered equivalent to risk taking, at least in terms of behavioral risk tasks. However, impulsive processes, especially response inhibition and impulsive decision making, might play a role in risky decision making. Additionally, Sharma et al. (2014) reported meta-regression analysis results aimed to disentangle the relative contribution of impulsivity factors that emerged from self-report and behavioral assessments. A first finding was that self-descriptive and behavioral factors were only weakly correlated. A second finding was that each type of factors significantly contributed to the prediction of problematic daily-life impulsive behaviors. Thus, the joint use of personality scales and behavioral tasks was recommended for future research in this domain.

The Big Five and Risk Taking

Since the 1980s, the five-factor model of personality, or the Big Five (i.e., neuroticism, extraversion, openness to experience, agreeableness, and conscientiousness), contributed to the resurgence of the trait approach in personality psychology and attracted research interest across a variety of disciplines, including economics and behavioral decision making (e.g., Borghans, Duckworth, Heckman, & Ter Weel, 2008). The organizing, hierarchical model (i.e., having a general factor at the top, narrow facets at the bottom and intermediate major aspects between the two levels) has been vastly influential in promoting a common framework by which to examine the associations between dispositions and actual life outcomes (e.g., DeYoung, Quilty, & Peterson, 2007).

Relating to Big Three models, extraversion and neuroticism are common to both frameworks, whereas disinhibition vs. constraint can broadly be thought as a factor superordinate to conscientiousness and agreeableness (Anusic et al., 2009; Markon et al., 2005). Specifically, with respect to temperament models, extraversion is believed to be strongly associated with positive emotionality or being dispositionally inclined to experience positive affect. Conversely, negative emotionality lies at the core of the neuroticism dimension, a disposition to experience negative affective states such as worrying, anxiety, and vulnerability. The third primary dimension, disinhibition (vs. constraint), reflects broad individual differences in the tendency to behave in an undercontrolled versus an overcontrolled manner. The dimension measures behavioral style of pursuing stimulating experiences or acting on immediate thoughts and feelings with little regard for safety, social responsibility, or legality versus a behavioral style that emphasizes order and rules, conservative and conventional behavior, responsibility and respect for others, and taking action only after consideration of the broad consequences for oneself and others (Clark & Watson, 2008; Tellegen & Waller, 2008). Although not directly related to either positive or negative affect, disinhibition is believed to regulate emotional experience by interacting with the two other dimensions and has been widely implicated in a variety of risk taking behaviors. In terms of Big Five dimensions, Markon et al. (2005) proposed a model in which agreeableness and conscientiousness form specific, lower-order factors of disinhibition. Openness to experience does not easily tie into the Big Three, but it also is the factor that is the least replicable across cultures, suggesting that it may not represent temperament.

The multifaceted structure of the Big Five has important implications for understanding how each broad trait dimension may promote or prevent risk taking behaviors. In fact, subsumed under each broad trait domain, there may be facets that are associated with particular behaviors. Adding to the complexity, it is possible that not all facets within a specific broad-based trait dimension are equally associated with risk taking, potentially resulting in the attenuation of validity coefficients when a composite score of the higher-order trait is used in correlation analyses (i.e., a total score approach; Chen, Hayes, Carver, Laurenceau, & Zhang, 2012).

For instance, extraversion (vs. introversion) has an agentic aspect (e.g., assertiveness, excitement seeking, and activity level facets) that is believed to represent active pursuit of rewards as well as a more affiliative aspect (e.g., gregariousness, friendliness) that promotes involvement in social relations (e.g., Depue & Collins, 1999). Others stressed the importance of positive affect, or cheerfulness, as an additional core aspect (e.g., Tellegen, 1985). Additionally, facets like excitement seeking are theoretically tied to sensation seeking and certain types of risk taking, whereas other facets like gregariousness, assertiveness, or activity level are not such clearly linked with risk taking. In this regard, Sharma et al. (2014) showed that a general personality dimension anchored by extraversion/positive emotionality emerged in a meta-factor analysis of commonly used measures of impulsivity and related Big Five extraversion scales, including scales such as the excitement seeking and venturesomeness facets, as well as sensation seeking, thus showing that personality characteristics ostensibly related to sensation seeking tend to merge into a common construct.

Research examining the associations between broad-based extraversion and risk taking has been mixed. Paralleling sensation seeking studies, extraversion was most strongly associated with recreational and social types of risks (e.g., Gullone & Moore, 2000; Nicholson et al., 2005; Skeel, Neudecker, Pilarski, & Pytlak, 2007; Romero et al., 2012). In contrast, null or mixed results emerged when relating extraversion to self-reported risk taking, experimental risk paradigms, or perceived risk attitude scales, all findings that might be potentially explained by construct breadth (Lauriola & Levin, 2001; Weller & Tikir, 2011). For instance, using the extraversion scale of the HEXACO Personality Inventory (i.e., a six-factor, alternative structural model of personality based in the lexical tradition; Lee & Ashton, 2004), which notably does not include sensation seeking-related facets, both Weller and Tikir (2011) and Weller and Thulin (2012) found no coherent patterns of associations between extraversion facets and risk taking tendencies.

Openness to experience is another Big Five trait dimension that may promote some forms of risk taking behavior. Some authors argue that openness to experience is not an entirely independent personality dimension due to medium-large correlations with both extraversion and sensation seeking, especially with the experience seeking subscale of the SSS-V (e.g., Aluja, Garcıa, & Garcıa, 2003; García, Aluja, García, & Cuevas, 2005). Moreover, its multifaceted structure long has been debated, recently coming to a reconciliation, which views two major aspects (i.e., intellect and culture) and six facets (i.e., fantasy, aesthetics, feelings, actions, ideas, and values; DeYoung et al., 2007; Woo et al., 2014). Among those facets, openness to actions, ideas, and fantasy seem especially germane to a discussion of risk taking. Openness to actions represents behavioral preferences for novelty and variety; openness to ideas represents a cognitive style, similar to need for cognition, tolerance for ambiguity, and epistemic curiosity (Mussel, 2010; see also Lauriola et al.,

2015). Both these facets are associated with a range of behaviors that may expose people to risks in order to achieve new knowledge or experiences, such as active exploration of the environment, discovery, innovation, entrepreneurship, novelty, change, thrill, and adventure seeking (Kashdan, Rose, & Fincham, 2004; Schweizer, 2006; Woo et al., 2014). Moreover, some authors found that fantasy, a facet that describes people who have a vivid imagination and get lost in thought, is also correlated with personality characteristics that promote risk taking, like impulsivity, psychoticism, and trait hostility (García et al., 2005). In turn, research largely suggests that openness, like extraversion, is associated with risk taking through a process of both the active exploration of the environment and a general proclivity to seek out new experiences (e.g., Lauriola & Levin, 2001; Nicholson et al., 2005; Romero et al., 2012; Terracciano, Löckenhoff, Crum, Bienvenu, & Costa, 2008; Weller & Tikir, 2011). These results suggest that individuals who show higher levels of extraversion and openness often take risks to enhance and expand their perspective of the world by experiencing novel and uncertain situations, as opposed to risks that violate social norms.

Whereas both higher levels of extraversion and openness facilitate the behavioral expression of risk taking and share common variance with sensation seeking, positive affect, and perhaps impulsivity (De Vries, de Vries, & Feij, 2009; Kashdan et al., 2004; Sharma et al., 2014), high levels of conscientiousness and agreeableness may attenuate risk behaviors. In the NEO-PI-R, conscientiousness includes facets such as competence, order, dutifulness, achievement, striving, self-discipline, and deliberation, which may be further sorted into industriousness and orderliness aspects (DeYoung et al., 2007; Roberts, Lejuez, Krueger, Richards, & Hill, 2014). Conscientiousness represents a general dimension of cognitive and behavioral control (vs. more reckless and careless behaviors; Markon et al., 2005; Samuel & Widiger, 2008; Sharma et al., 2014). As such, the range of risky health (e.g., alcohol/substance use, risky driving, sexual behavior) behaviors with which is inversely correlated resembles those typically associated with impulsivity (Bogg & Roberts, 2004). Other meta-analytic studies confirmed the association between low conscientiousness and both antisocial and unethical behaviors (Berry, Ones, & Sackett, 2007; Jones, Miller, & Lynam, 2011; Ruiz, Pincus, & Schinka, 2008). Both the total score and the facet-level analysis yielded small-medium correlations (i.e., $-0.20 < r < -0.50$), although deliberation (i.e., the tendency to think things through before acting or speaking) often had more sizable relations than other facets (Jones et al., 2011; Ruiz et al., 2008). Independent studies that used domain-specific risk taking indicators corroborated these findings, showing that low conscientiousness was more strongly associated with risk taking in health/safety and ethical domains (e.g., Gullone & Moore, 2000; Nicholson et al., 2005; Weller & Tikir, 2011).

In Big Five models, agreeableness reflects compassion and emotional affiliation with others (e.g., trust, altruism, tender-mindedness), as well as a politeness aspect that reflects consideration for others in terms of mutual respect (e.g., modesty, compliance, straightforwardness). Similar to low conscientiousness, lower levels agreeableness has been associated with a greater incidence of risk taking behaviors. Low agreeableness typically characterizes people who place their self-interest above all, in turn being unconcerned toward others' needs or feelings and likely to express hostile, antisocial tendencies and violate societal norms (e.g., DeYoung et al., 2007).

Compared to conscientiousness, agreeableness often yields larger correlations with risky behaviors, especially ones that include unethical behaviors, social deviance, and antisociality (Berry et al., 2007; Jones et al., 2011; Ruiz et al., 2008). A closer look to agreeableness facets reveals that straightforwardness (i.e., directness and frankness in dealing with others vs. deceitfulness or manipulativeness) is the most closely associated with problematic behavioral tendencies, like physical aggression or interpersonal violence, criminal behaviors (e.g., stealing, stalking, bullying), and conduct and antisocial personality disorder (Jones et al., 2011; Ruiz et al., 2008). In contrast, tender-mindedness (i.e., extent to which a person is compassionate and sympathetic) and modesty (i.e., one's tendency to be humble and other-focused), although negatively associated with antisocial behaviors, resulted in more modest correlations and, in some cases, null effects (see also Weller & Tikir, 2011, for a similar argument concerning the honesty-humility dimension using the HEXACO personality framework).[1]

Neuroticism (vs. emotional stability) can be defined as a dispositional tendency to experience negative emotional states. Individuals reporting greater levels of neuroticism tend to experience more intense negative emotions, worry, experience sadness, and respond more extremely to stressors. In Big Five models, neuroticism includes facets related to negative affect (e.g., anxiety, depression, self-consciousness, and vulnerability), which typically are associated with amplified perceptions of risk/danger (e.g., Chauvin, Hermand, & Mullet, 2007). On the other hand, anger-irritability (e.g., quick to anger, easily agitated) and immoderation-impulsivity (i.e., overindulgence, regret of prior decisions, etc.) are also often considered facets of neuroticism, and these might promote risk taking through behavioral disinhibition or poor behavioral control under negative emotional states (e.g., Cyders & Smith, 2008; Dindo, McDade-Montez, Sharma, Watson, & Clark, 2009; Lerner & Keltner, 2001). In this regard, Sharma et al. (2014) pointed out that neuroticism/negative emotionality provides the ground for a variety of impulsive behaviors, such as inability to control cravings and tendency to rash action in response to negative mood states.

Consistent findings that link neuroticism facets to risk aversion come from studies of trait anxiety. Not only high-trait anxious individuals exhibit a variety of cognitive biases, such as intolerance of uncertainty, higher sensitivity to threat, and greater attribution of negative valence to ambiguous information (for a review see Hartley & Phelps, 2012), but also consistently demonstrate greater risk aversion in framing experiments (e.g., Kowert & Hermann, 1997; Peng, Xiao, Yang, Wu, & Miao, 2014), hypothetical gambles or decision scenarios (e.g., Raghunathan & Pham, 1999), health decisions (e.g., Lauriola, Russo, Lucidi, Violani, & Levin, 2005), and perceived risk attitude scales (e.g., Lorian & Grisham, 2010; Weller & Tikir, 2011). With respect to behavioral risk taking tasks, results are somewhat

[1] Some debate exists regarding the orthogonality of agreeableness and honesty-humility. Please see Ashton, Lee, and de Vries (2014) for a comprehensive look at this question.

mixed. Although some studies have found that greater trait anxiety was related to less risk taking (e.g., Maner et al., 2007; Peters & Slovic, 2000), other studies, exclusively based on the Iowa Gambling Task, have reported disadvantageous decision making for both high-trait and low-trait anxious individuals (e.g., De Visser et al., 2010; Miu, Heilman, & Houser, 2008). More research using multiple behavioral risk tasks and multiple indicators of neuroticism need to be conducted to further understand these inconsistencies.

"Not all negative moods are equal" was the incipit of Raghunathan and Pham (1999), who showed that trait anxiety promoted a tendency to avoid risks in hypothetical gambling and decision scenarios, whereas sadness promoted risk seeking. Others have reported divergent correlations for anxiety and anger with risky decision making. For instance, trait anxious individuals make more pessimistic appraisals of future events, whereas trait anger individuals make more optimistic appraisals, presumably leading to a discounting of perceived dangers (Lerner & Keltner, 2001). Likewise, trait anger predicted financial risk taking (i.e., investing vs. not investing, amount of invested money, confidence in predictability of a stock trend), whereas anxiety had just an opposite effect (Gambetti & Giusberti, 2012).

These findings suggest that different emotions convey distinct types of information to the decision maker and, perhaps, can motivate different risk attitudes. For instance, anxiety focuses on one's attention on potential threats and motivates risk aversion; in contrast, anger may decrease risk perceptions, thus setting the stage for risk taking; likewise, sadness might trigger a sense of reward replacement, which in turn may promote impulsive decision making and risk taking (Lerner & Keltner, 2001). Largely, the above findings reinforce the view that facets encompassed in broad domain may have different predictive relations with risk taking. In fact, it is not uncommon to find studies of personality and risk taking that yielded null results or small effect sizes when using a total score approach that combines individual facets, each of which might have different predictive relations to risk taking (Gullone & Moore, 2000; Romero et al., 2012; Skeel et al., 2007).

Conclusion

Throughout this chapter, we have highlighted the wide variety of traits that correlate with risk taking tendencies, both inside and outside the laboratory setting. In doing so, we have integrated, but by no means exhaustively reviewed, a broad array of research domains, some of which are voluminous in scope. First, our review suggests that the notion of a unidimensional "risk taking" personality construct seems to be a less tenable alternative in search of dispositional tendencies that may predict stability and consistency of risky behaviors. Instead, this chapter reinforces the view that risk taking is a multiply-determined phenomenon and confluence of different traits may impact such behaviors.

Second, we noted that personality researchers have developed several constructs, like sensation seeking, impulsivity, or other traits in the five-factor model, to reveal

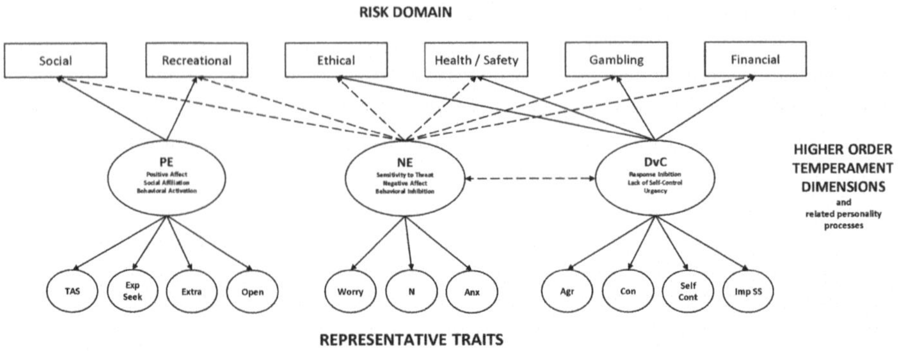

Fig. 1.1 Proposed conceptual model. This figure represents a conceptual model that links specific traits to domain-specific risk taking, by means of broad temperament dimensions. Note that lower-order traits for each dimension are not exhaustive. Moreover, some traits that are considered "representative" might be considered subordinate to other traits at the same level, indicating that an empirical study may not precisely replicate this structure. *DvC* disinhibition vs. constraint, *NE* negative emotionality, *PE* positive emotionality, *Agr* agreeableness, *Con* conscientiousness, *Self Cont* self-control, *ImpSS* impulsive unsocialized sensation seeking, *Worry* trait worry, *Neur* neuroticism, *Anx* trait anxiety, *TAS* thrill and adventure seeking, *Exp Seek* experience seeking, *Extra* extraversion, *Open* openness

and ultimately account for the underlying processes predisposing people to take more or less risk. However, whether the operative definitions of these constructs capture a unitary generalized risk taking disposition or reflect the joint effect of a limited number of higher-order risk-related temperament dimensions still bears some ambiguity and added further complexity to our current understanding of personality-risk relations.

Taking into account these issues, we propose a broad conceptual model that integrates a hierarchical temperament-based model with domain-specific risk taking (see Fig. 1.1). Working from the bottom of the figure upward, we illustrate how superordinate temperament dimensions, and associated personality processes, may account for common variance among more specific traits. For the sake of simplicity, we omitted more narrow traits in some cases, such as some Big Five facets, that may be accounted for by the lower-order traits.[2] At the top of the model are instead some common domains of risk behaviors considered in the literature. The solid arrows indicate that these dimensions have more direct associations with specific risk domains, indicated at the top of the figure. Dotted lines refer to primarily indirect associations between the broad trait dimensions and risk taking (and the proposed correlation between disinhibition and negative emotionality in higher-order structural models; e.g., Digman, 1997; Markon et al., 2005).

[2] For brevity, we only refer to representative examples in the current model, rather than a comprehensive diagram.

Risk-Related Constructs Within a Temperament-Based Model.

Positive Emotionality

A number of social and recreational risky behaviors, spanning from adventure sports to visiting exotic or unusual places to performing in front of a big audience, not only are believed to be a direct manifestation of sensation seeking tendencies (e.g., Roberti, 2004), but also they are often associated with extraversion and openness to experience (e.g., Aluja et al., 2003). Moreover, personality research shares the notion that overlapping variance between the aforementioned traits may be accounted for by a higher-order temperament dimension recognized as positive emotionality.[3] In a Big Three temperament framework, positive emotionality is characterized by both chronic experience of positive affect and seeking out social interaction and affiliation with others (Clark & Watson, 2008; DeYoung et al., 2007; Markon et al., 2005; Tellegen & Waller, 2008). Moreover, positive emotionality has strong links with specific aspects of the behavioral activation system in reinforcement sensitivity theory, such as stronger pursuit of appetitive goals and high responsiveness to rewards (e.g., Corr, DeYoung, & McNaughton, 2013; Depue & Collins, 1999; DeYoung, 2010). Thus, consistent with an affect heuristic account (e.g., Finucane et al., 2000), people high on positive emotionality traits, such as sensation seeking and extraversion, tend to chronically experience positive affect and to overestimate the likelihood of positive future consequences of their actions (e.g., Borkenau & Mauer, 2006; Horvath & Zuckerman, 1993). Taken together, our review suggests that a higher-order positive emotionality temperament promotes actions such as novelty seeking, exploration, adventurousness, entrepreneurship, and seeking social dominance or approval by others. By definition, these actions may confer a rewarding experience to the person but also can bear negative consequences, especially if they are appraised with good feelings and self-confidence (e.g., Roberti, 2004; Zuckerman, 2007).

Negative Emotionality

Increased sensitivity to punishment and greater anticipated, or experienced, negative affect associated with potential losses are likely personality processes that may account for lesser risk taking among people high on the second superordinate temperament dimension in our model, namely, negative emotionality. It has long been established that traits related to the experience of chronic negative affect, especially trait anxiety, worry, and neuroticism, are related to the activation of a behavioral inhibition system (e.g., Corr et al., 2013). Hence, negative emotionality traits may lead to heightened perceptions of danger associated with an activity (e.g., Hartley & Phelps, 2012). Consequently, lower-level traits that comprise the broad negative

---

[3] This broad factor also has been referred to by other names, such as "agency" or "plasticity" (Anusic et al., 2009; DeYoung, 2010).

emotionality dimension may primarily motivate the avoidance of risk (or harm avoidance) by means of an overly pessimistic appraisal of the potential negative outcomes associated with one's choices. This finding appears to be robust across risk domains and operational approaches. However, our review of facet-level results raises interesting questions about the degree to which the findings connecting negative emotionality-related traits are generalizable to other traits. Specific negative emotions have been found to differentially impact risk taking and decision making in general (Gambetti & Giusberti, 2012; Lerner & Keltner, 2001; Raghunathan & Pham, 1999), consistent with an appraisal tendency approach.

The differences in findings may possibly be reconciled based on research investigating higher-order factors of broad personality dimensions. In two independent studies, Digman (1997) and Markon et al. (2005) found that neuroticism is inversely correlated with both agreeableness and conscientiousness, suggesting that a superordinate factor, abstractly referred to as β, may account for common variance between these three dimensions (indicated by a bidirectional arrow in our model). Incidentally, there is an ongoing debate about whether trait hostility/anger is a marker of neuroticism or agreeableness. Although typically considered a negative affect in both state and trait inventories (Costa & McCrae, 2008; Tellegen & Waller, 2008; Clark & Watson, 2008), some models place trait anger/hostility as being more closely aligned to agreeableness (Ashton et al., 2014) or psychoticism (Eysenck et al., 1985), which would suggest that this trait is a stronger marker of disinhibition. Trait anger is often characterized by low frustration tolerance, and the expression of anger may indicate diminished abilities to exert control over one's emotions. Although the correlations between trait anger and risk taking appear to be more consistent with this latter view, we defer to the structure that emerges in current temperament scales. However, this is an area that could benefit from additional research.

Disinhibition (vs. Constraint)

Eysenck et al. (1985) maintained that a third broad temperament dimension, independent from both extraversion/positive emotionality and neuroticism/negative emotionality, accounted for individual differences in aggressive, antisocial tendencies, tough-mindedness, and impulsive actions. This trait, originally called psychoticism, shows relations with traits in the five-factor model, namely, low agreeableness, low conscientiousness, and other minor facets of the other Big Five, including anger, impulsivity, and fantasy (see also Lynam & Widiger, 2001; Markon et al., 2005). Although many researchers have moved toward the label, disinhibition (vs. constraint), and more refined measures of this construct, the core of Eysenck's psychoticism dimension endures in Big Three personality models. This broad dimension is believed to account for common variance in both agreeableness and conscientiousness and is believed to be a primary vulnerability factor for externalizing disorders, such as substance use disorder and antisocial personality disorder (see Markon et al., 2005). Beyond the two broad Big Five dimensions, other constructs including impulsivity (Sharma et al., 2014) and the impulsive unsocialized mode of sensation seeking, which includes SSS-V disinhibition and boredom susceptibility scales (Zuckerman, 2007), may be associated with the broad dimension. Collectively, these constructs demonstrate robust associations with problem behaviors, such as antisociality, unethical behaviors, addiction, and other health risks (Berry et al., 2007; Bogg & Roberts, 2004; Jones et al., 2011; Ruiz et al., 2008). In this regard, we speculate that this broad temperament dimension may directly affect risk taking as a result of differences in cognitive and emotional control. When experiencing high levels of positive or negative affect, a disinhibited individual may be more likely to act upon these feelings, acting in self-interest to remove a negative emotional state or increase or extend a positive one. Although more research needs to be conducted in this area, this assertion is close to the definition of negative and positive urgency (i.e., the tendency to act hastily when distressed or excited) offered by Whiteside and Lynam (2001).

Risk Taking Dispositions and Domain-Specific Risk Taking

A widely accepted notion is that risk taking in different domains varies within individuals to a larger extent than it varies between individuals in the same domain (Blais & Weber, 2006; Hanoch et al., 2006; Weber et al., 2002). This view is seemingly incompatible with simplistic single-trait approaches, which aimed to explicate a general risk taking disposition. Not surprisingly, extant reviews of the literature recognize that decision making behavior depends on the interplay of task, environmental, and person characteristics and conclude that a greater focus on person-domain interactions rather than on the main effects of personality traits is needed (Appelt, Milch, Handgraaf, & Weber, 2011; Mohammed & Schwall, 2009).

Moving beyond a single-trait approach, our review has shown that the three superordinate temperament dimensions, as depicted in Fig. 1.1, may influence the behavioral expression of risk taking tendencies. Broad patterns emerge that suggest that certain domains may preferentially be associated with certain types of risks. Specifically, positive emotionality may be more strongly associated with recreational and social risk taking because extraverted individuals may be more likely to be socially intrepid and seek out novel and stimulating experiences. This view is consistent with Depue and Collins (1999) who speculated that both willingness to actively pursue incentives in the environment and greater sensitivity to rewards are vital to enjoying relationships with others, building large networks of friends and being socially dominant. In contrast, disinhibition appears to be more strongly linked to ethical, health/safety, and financial (especially gambling) risk taking behaviors which often, but not exclusively, involve some kind of planning, forethought actions, ability to delay gratification, and/or inhibition of maladaptive responses that may violate social norms or laws. However, negative emotionality appears to be the dimension associated with risk taking across the broadest range of risk domains, though this association may be an indirect one, mediated through amplified perceptions of danger for those who exhibit greater levels of the trait (e.g., Gullone & Moore, 2000; de Haan et al., 2011; Hansen & Breivik, 2001; Nicholson et al., 2005; Roberti, 2004; Romero et al., 2012; Soane et al., 2010; Weller & Tikir, 2011; Zaleskiewicz, 2001).

Conceptually, the three broad temperament dimensions can be considered relatively orthogonal factors and theoretically are tied to specific neurobiological mechanisms, such as the functions of the prefrontal cortex for disinhibition (vs. constraint) or differences in endogenous dopamine and serotonin levels for extraversion and neuroticism, respectively (Clark & Watson, 2008; DeYoung, 2010; Tellegen & Waller, 2008; Zuckerman & Kuhlman, 2000). Given their presumed functional and structural independence, it is possible that trait × trait interactions may exist that increase or decrease the likelihood of risk taking across multiple domains. For instance, it is possible that a personality profile characterized by high negative emotionality and high disinhibition might indicate global risk taking preferences. For instance, this configuration of traits was found to be more frequent among those who takes health risks as well as among those who takes high risks in sport (Castanier, Scanff, & Woodman, 2010; Vollrath & Torgersen, 2002). Taken to the extreme ends of the distributions and extending into maladaptive levels of these traits, such a constellation of traits may be associated with borderline personality disorder (e.g., Markon et al., 2005; Samuel & Widiger, 2008). Such individuals tend to engage in problem behaviors, such as substance use, simultaneously discounting the potential risks and unrealistically overestimating the expected benefits, and would also fail to self-control themselves in the presence of a strong emotional response, both positive and negative. Conversely, other extreme profiles, such as high negative emotionality and high constraint, might be relatively frequent among the adult population, thus promoting extreme more caution in the face of uncertain choices.

Implications for Future Research

Before concluding, we discuss some implications of our review that may assist future researchers. First, when considering broad, superordinate traits as predictors, we must also consider a bandwidth-fidelity tradeoff, which states that broad traits can best predict global outcomes very well, but specific outcomes only moderately so. More specific traits, on the other hand, are better suited to predict specific behaviors which are more directly associated with that construct. Consistent with this reasoning, higher-order temperament factors may demonstrate lower predictive validity for specific risk behaviors, compared to more global outcomes. Therefore, we encourage researchers interested in such research to include lower-order traits that offer greater "fidelity," in addition to broad superordinate dimensions when selecting constructs that they believe to influence risk behaviors. Following standards for establishing construct validity, this approach should be directed and informed by the proposed nomological network, rather than adopting a "kitchen sink" approach (Appelt, Milch, Handgraaf, & Weber, 2011). On a related note, we encourage researchers interested in constructs such as sensation seeking and impulsivity to include and interpret subscale scores, due to apparent heterogeneity across different temperament dimensions.

Second, although some researchers have specified particular risk domains, the phenotypic structure of risk taking from a behavioral self-report perspective remains unclear. Though purported to be independent domains, moderate to large correlations have been observed between DOSPERT risk taking scales, for instance (Weller et al., 2015; Weller & Tikir, 2011). A recent study (Highhouse et al., 2016) has shown that a nested factor model with one general risk taking factor and six group factors fitted DOSPERT data better than any other competing factor model based on five or six relatively independent risk domains. Additionally, other research questions emerge, such as the degree to which passive risks are subsumed in broader domains along with active risks, or if these behaviors represent an independent construct, with unique personality antecedents (Keinan & Bereby-Meyer, 2012). Moreover, behavioral self-report risk scales predominately involve negative behaviors, consistent with lay perceptions of risks. However, many risks involve opportunities for personal growth and enlightenment. Integrating these behaviors into a risk framework would be beneficial. Efforts applying best practices in scale construction and factor analytic techniques may help to clarify an underlying simple structure.

Third, we encourage more research that integrates experimental paradigms of risk taking, behavioral self-report, and personality traits. Investigating decision processes and specific vulnerability factors that may increase disadvantageous decision making have the potential to better conceptualize problems that may be opaque from a behavioral self-report of risk taking. Ultimately, such investigations may help to inform prevention and intervention efforts designed to decrease the incidence of problem behaviors (see Weller, Kim, Leve, 2016 for an example).

Final Remarks

In closing, we offer some final remarks that may suggest potential applications for practitioners based on core ideas and results of this chapter, such as identifying the traits that are most commonly associated with specific risk domains. On this subject, personality and clinical research suggest that low disinhibition (vs. constraint) is a prominent protective factor for preventing a variety of real-world risk behaviors, especially in the ethical, health/safety, financial, and gambling domains. Although disinhibition (vs. constraint) and other temperament dimensions are expected to be relatively stable and strongly heritable, they are also malleable and may gradually change through targeted interventions. For instance, improving self-control through directed trainings has demonstrated some promise in promoting health behaviors (see Allom, Mullan, & Hagger, 2016). In addition to disinhibition (vs. constraint), negative emotionality traits also need attention in the prevention of risk taking. Our literature review has shown that facets like anxiety, worry, and fear can lead to amplified risk perceptions. Although there is a general tendency to reduce or eliminate risk in western society, one must be mindful that increased worry can lead to overreactions such as market panics and taking costly actions against hazards that may be rare events (see Hartley & Phelps, 2012; Sunstein, 2002). Additionally, greater negative emotionality is commonly viewed as a gateway to nearly all psychopathologies, including ones that are related to risk behaviors such as substance use disorders (Kotov, Gamez, Schmidt, & Watson, 2010; Markon et al., 2005). Moreover, amplified stress reactivity, also associated with negative emotionality, has been associated with increases in risk behaviors (e.g., Mather & Lighthall, 2012). More research needs to be conducted to understand why high negative emotionality is associated with amplified risk perceptions, yet also related to greater engagement in substance use and other health outcomes like obesity (Sutin, Ferrucci, Zonderman, & Terracciano, 2011). Consistent with Kotov, Gamez, Schmidt, and Watson (2010) who report that substance use disorder has a stronger link with disinhibition than neuroticism, we speculate that interactions between negative emotionality and disinhibition may impact risk taking and encourage future research in this area. Last, positive emotionality traits also are regarded as directly linked with risk taking in social and recreational domains. If one equates general risk taking tendencies solely with activities in these domains, it could yield an inappropriate risk communication message for the domains (e.g., health or ethical risk taking) that may bear direr long-term consequences for individuals and society in general, such as substance use and committing criminal acts.

Instead of treating risk taking as a unitary construct, our hope is that practitioners and researchers alike will increasingly appreciate that not all risks are created equal. From there, communication efforts, both prevention- and promotion-oriented, may be crafted to encourage health-effacing behaviors. Coupled with behavioral tasks that can decompose how individuals make suboptimal long-term choices, decision aids potentially may be crafted to help promote the engagement of risks that offer the potential for personal growth and abate behaviors that may yield deleterious long-term effects. These insights may be especially important for vulnerable populations. As an example, Weller and colleagues (Weller, et al., 2015b) speculated that adding training for decision skills to programs designed to promote goal setting and self-control may optimally improve health outcomes for maltreated adolescent girls, a population that demonstrates high rates of substance use and health-risking sexual behaviors (see also Weller, Kim, & Leve, 2016).

In sum, we believe that this chapter offers researchers with a broad, organizing framework in which results from disparate fields may be better understood. Such communication is a hallmark of scientific progress as it breaks down barriers caused by a variety of conceptual and operational definitions. By collectively engaging in this process, researchers and practitioners can come closer to better understanding intricate associations between neurobiological processes, dispositional tendencies, and risk behavior.

Acknowledgments The authors equally contributed to the preparation of this chapter.

References

Alessi, S. M., & Petry, N. M. (2003). Pathological gambling severity is associated with impulsivity in a delay discounting procedure. *Behavioural Processes, 64*(3), 345–354.

Allom, V., Mullan, B., & Hagger, M. (2016). Does inhibitory control training improve health behaviour? A meta-analysis. *Health Psychology Review, 10*(2), 168–186.

Aluja, A., Garcıa, Ó., & Garcıa, L. F. (2003). Relationships among extraversion, openness to experience, and sensation seeking. *Personality and Individual Differences, 35*(3), 671–680.

Anderson, L. R., & Mellor, J. M. (2009). Are risk preferences stable? Comparing an experimental measure with a validated survey-based measure. *Journal of Risk and Uncertainty, 39*(2), 137–160.

Anusic, I., Schimmack, U., Pinkus, R. T., & Lockwood, P. (2009). The nature and structure of correlations among Big Five ratings: The halo-alpha-beta model. *Journal of Personality and Social Psychology, 97*(6), 1142–1156.

Appelt, K. C., Milch, K. F., Handgraaf, M. J. J., & Weber, E. U. (2011). The decision making individual differences inventory and guidelines for the study of individual differences in judgment and decision-making research. *Judgment and Decision making, 6*, 252–262.

Ashton, M. C., Lee, K., & de Vries, R. E. (2014). The HEXACO honesty-humility, agreeableness, and emotionality factors: A review of research and theory. *Personality and Social Psychology Review, 18*, 139–152.

Bari, A., & Robbins, T. W. (2013). Inhibition and impulsivity: Behavioral and neural basis of response control. *Progress in Neurobiology, 108*, 44–79.

Barlow, M., Woodman, T., & Hardy, L. (2013). Great expectations: Different high-risk activities satisfy different motives. *Journal of Personality and Social Psychology, 105*(3), 458–475.

Barron, G., & Erev, I. (2003). Small feedback-based decisions and their limited correspondence to description-based decisions. *Journal of Behavioral Decision Making, 16*(3), 215–223.

Bazana, P. G., Stelmack, R. M., & Stelmack, R. M. (2004). Stability of personality across the life span: A meta-analysis. In R. M. Stelmack (Ed.), *On the psychobiology of personality: Essays in honor of Marvin Zuckerman* (pp. 113–144). New York, NY: Elsevier.

Bechara, A., Damasio, A. R., Damasio, H., & Anderson, S. W. (1994). Insensitivity to future consequences following damage to human prefrontal cortex. *Cognition, 50*(1), 7–15.

Bechara, A., Damasio, H., Damasio, A. R., & Lee, G. P. (1999). Different contributions of the human amygdala and ventromedial prefrontal cortex to decision-making. *Journal of Neuroscience, 19*, 5473–5481.

Bechara, A. (2005). Decision making, impulse control and loss of willpower to resist drugs: A neurocognitive perspective. *Nature Neuroscience, 8*(11), 1458–1463.

Berry, C. M., Ones, D. S., & Sackett, P. R. (2007). Interpersonal deviance, organizational deviance, and their common correlates: A review and meta-analysis. *The Journal of Applied Psychology, 92*(2), 410–424.

Blais, A. R., & Weber, E. U. (2006). A Domain-Specific Risk-Taking (DOSPERT) scale for adult populations. *Judgment and Decision making, 1*(1), 33–47.

Bogg, T., & Roberts, B. W. (2004). Conscientiousness and health-related behaviors: A meta-analysis of the leading behavioral contributors to mortality. *Psychological Bulletin, 130*(6), 887–919.

Borghans, L., Duckworth, A. L., Heckman, J. J., & Ter Weel, B. (2008). The economics and psychology of personality traits. *Journal of Human Resources, 43*(4), 972–1059.

Borkenau, P., & Mauer, N. (2006). Personality, emotionality, and risk prediction. *Journal of Individual Differences, 27*(3), 127–135.

Bornovalova, M. A., Daughters, S. B., Hernandez, G. D., Richards, J. B., & Lejuez, C. W. (2005). Differences in impulsivity and risk-taking propensity between primary users of crack cocaine and primary users of heroin in a residential substance-use program. *Experimental and Clinical Psychopharmacology, 13*(4), 311–3181.

Brevers, D., Bechara, A., Cleeremans, A., & Noël, X. (2013). Iowa Gambling Task (IGT): Twenty years after—Gambling disorder and IGT. *Frontiers in Psychology, 4*, 665.

Castanier, C., Scanff, C. L., & Woodman, T. (2010). Who takes risks in high-risk sports? A typological personality approach. *Research Quarterly for Exercise and Sport, 81*(4), 478–484.

Chambers, R. A., & Potenza, M. N. (2003). Neurodevelopment, impulsivity, and adolescent gambling. *Journal of Gambling Studies, 19*(1), 53–84.

Chapman, G. B. (2005). Short-term cost for long-term benefit: Time preference and cancer control. *Health Psychology, 24*(4), S41–S48.

Charness, G., Gneezy, U., & Imas, A. (2013). Experimental methods: Eliciting risk preferences. *Journal of Economic Behavior and Organization, 87*, 43–51.

Chauvin, B., Hermand, D., & Mullet, E. (2007). Risk perception and personality facets. *Risk Analysis, 27*(1), 171–185.

Chen, F. F., Hayes, A., Carver, C. S., Laurenceau, J. P., & Zhang, Z. (2012). Modeling general and specific variance in multifaceted constructs: A comparison of the bifactor model to other approaches. *Journal of Personality, 80*(1), 219–251.

Chuang, Y., & Schechter, L. (2015). Stability of experimental and survey measures of risk, time, and social preferences: A review and some new results. *Journal of Development Economics, 117*, 151–170.

Clark, L. A., & Watson, D. (2008). An organizing paradigm for trait psychology. In O. P. John, R. W. Robins, & L. A. Pervin (Eds.), *Handbook of personality: Theory and research* (pp. 265–286). New York, NY: Guilford Press.

Cloninger, C. R., Przybeck, T. R., Svakic, D. M., & Wetzel, R. D. (1994). *The temperament and character inventory: A guide to its development and use*. St Louis, MO: Center for Psychobiology of Personality.

Corr, P. J., DeYoung, C. G., & McNaughton, N. (2013). Motivation and personality: A neuropsychological perspective. *Social and Personality Psychology Compass, 7*(3), 158–175.

Coffey, S. F., Gudleski, G. D., Saladin, M. E., & Brady, K. T. (2003). Impulsivity and rapid discounting of delayed hypothetical rewards in cocaine-dependent individuals. *Experimental and clinical psychopharmacology, 11*(1), 18–25.

Coffey, S. F., Schumacher, J. A., Baschnagel, J. S., Hawk, L. W., & Holloman, G. (2011). Impulsivity and risk-taking in borderline personality disorder with and without substance use disorders. *Personality Disorders: Theory, Research, and Treatment, 2*(2), 128–141.

Congdon, E., Mumford, J. A., Cohen, J. R., Galvan, A., Canli, T., & Poldrack, R. A. (2012). Measurement and reliability of response inhibition. *Frontiers in Psychology, 3*, 37.

Costa, P. T., & McCrae, R. R. (2008). The revised neo personality inventory (neo-pi-r). In G. J. Boyle, G. Matthews, & D. H. Saklofske (Eds.), *The SAGE handbook of personality theory and assessment* (Vol. 2, pp. 179–198). Thousand Oaks, CA: SAGE.

Critchfield, T. S., & Kollins, S. H. (2001). Temporal discounting: Basic research and the analysis of socially important behavior. *Journal of Applied Behavior Analysis, 34*(1), 101–122.

Cunha, P. J., Bechara, A., de Andrade, A. G., & Nicastri, S. (2011). Decision-making deficits linked to real-life social dysfunction in crack cocaine-dependent individuals. *The American Journal on Addictions, 20*(1), 78–86.

Cyders, M. A., & Coskunpinar, A. (2012). The relationship between self-report and lab task conceptualizations of impulsivity. *Journal of Research in Personality, 46*(1), 121–124.

Cyders, M. A., & Smith, G. T. (2008). Emotion-based dispositions to rash action: Positive and negative urgency. *Psychological Bulletin, 134*(6), 807–828.

Dahlen, E. R., Martin, R. C., Ragan, K., & Kuhlman, M. M. (2005). Driving anger, sensation seeking, impulsiveness, and boredom proneness in the prediction of unsafe driving. *Accident Analysis & Prevention, 37*(2), 341–348.

de Haan, L., Kuipers, E., Kuerten, Y., van Laar, M., Olivier, B., & Verster, J. C. (2011). The RT-18: A new screening tool to assess young adult risk-taking behavior. *International journal of general medicine, 4*, 575.

De Visser, L., Van Der Knaap, L. J., Van de Loo, A. J. A. E., Van der Weerd, C. M. M., Ohl, F., & Van Den Bos, R. (2010). Trait anxiety affects decision-making differently in healthy men and women: Towards gender-specific endophenotypes of anxiety. *Neuropsychologia, 48*(6), 1598–1606.

De Vries, R. E., de Vries, A., & Feij, J. A. (2009). Sensation seeking, risk-taking, and the HEXACO model of personality. *Personality and Individual Differences, 47*(6), 536–540.

De Wit, H. (2009). Impulsivity as a determinant and consequence of drug use: A review of underlying processes. *Addiction Biology, 14*(1), 22–31.

DeAndrea, D. C., Carpenter, C., Shulman, H., & Levine, T. R. (2009). The relationship between cheating behavior and sensation-seeking. *Personality and Individual Differences, 47*(8), 944–947.

Depue, R. A., & Collins, P. F. (1999). Neurobiology of the structure of personality: Dopamine, facilitation of incentive motivation, and extraversion. *Behavioral and Brain Sciences, 22*(03), 491–517.

Derringer, J., Krueger, R. F., Dick, D. M., Saccone, S., Grucza, R. A., Agrawal, A., … Nurnberger, J. I. (2010). Predicting sensation seeking from dopamine genes a candidate-system approach. *Psychological Science, 21*(9), 1282–1290.

DeYoung, C. G. (2010). Personality neuroscience and the biology of traits. *Social and Personality Psychology Compass, 4*(12), 1165–1180.

DeYoung, C. G., Quilty, L. C., & Peterson, J. B. (2007). Between facets and domains: 10 aspects of the Big Five. *Journal of Personality and Social Psychology, 93*(5), 880.

Dickman, S. J. (1990). Functional and dysfunctional impulsivity: Personality and cognitive correlates. *Journal of Personality and Social Psychology, 58*(1), 95–102.

Digman, J. M. (1997). Higher-order factors of the big five. *Journal of Personality and Social Psychology, 73*(6), 1246–1256.

Dindo, L., McDade-Montez, E., Sharma, L., Watson, D., & Clark, L. A. (2009). Development and initial validation of the disinhibition inventory a multifaceted measure of disinhibition. *Assessment, 16*(3), 274–291.

Dohmen, T., Falk, A., Huffman, D., Sunde, U., Schupp, J., & Wagner, G. G. (2011). Individual risk attitudes: Measurement, determinants, and behavioral consequences. *Journal of the European Economic Association, 9*(3), 522–550.

Duckworth, A. L., & Kern, M. L. (2011). A meta-analysis of the convergent validity of self-control measures. *Journal of Research in Personality, 45*(3), 259–268.

Enticott, P. G., & Ogloff, J. R. (2006). Elucidation of impulsivity. *Australian Psychologist, 41*(1), 3–14.

Eysenck, S. B., Eysenck, H. J., & Barrett, P. (1985). A revised version of the psychoticism scale. *Personality and Individual Differences, 6*(1), 21–29.

Figner, B., Knoch, D., Johnson, E. J., Krosch, A. R., Lisanby, S. H., Fehr, E., & Weber, E. U. (2010). Lateral prefrontal cortex and self-control in intertemporal choice. *Nature Neuroscience, 13*(5), 538–539.

Figner, B., Mackinlay, R. J., Wilkening, F., & Weber, E. U. (2009). Affective and deliberative processes in risky choice: Age differences in risk taking in the Columbia Card Task. *Journal of Experimental Psychology: Learning, Memory, and Cognition, 35*(3), 709–730.

Finucane, M. L., Alhakami, A., Slovic, P., & Johnson, S. M. (2000). The affect heuristic in judgments of risks and benefits. *Journal of Behavioral Decision Making, 13*(1), 1–17.

Fortune, E. E., & Goodie, A. S. (2010). The relationship between pathological gambling and sensation seeking: The role of subscale scores. *Journal of Gambling Studies, 26*, 331–346.

Fox, C. R., & Tannenbaum, D. (2011). The elusive search for stable risk preferences. *Frontiers in Psychology, 2*, 298.

Fridberg, D. J., Queller, S., Ahn, W. Y., Kim, W., Bishara, A. J., Busemeyer, J. R., … Stout, J. C. (2010). Cognitive mechanisms underlying risky decision-making in chronic cannabis users. *Journal of Mathematical Psychology, 54*(1), 28–38.

Friedman, D., Isaac, R. M., James, D., & Sunder, S. (2014). Risky curves: On the empirical failure of expected utility. *Economic Review, 101*(2), 695–723.

Gambetti, E., & Giusberti, F. (2012). The effect of anger and anxiety traits on investment decisions. *Journal of Economic Psychology, 33*(6), 1059–1069.

García, L. F., Aluja, A., García, Ó., & Cuevas, L. (2005). Is openness to experience an independent personality dimension? Convergent and discriminant validity of the openness domain and its NEO-PI-R facets. *Journal of Individual Differences, 26*(3), 132–138.

Gladwin, T. E., Figner, B., Crone, E. A., & Wiers, R. W. (2011). Addiction, adolescence, and the integration of control and motivation. *Developmental Cognitive Neuroscience, 1*(4), 364–376.

Glicksohn, J., & Abulafia, J. (1998). Embedding sensation seeking within the big three. *Personality and Individual Differences, 25*(6), 1085–1099.

Goldstein, W. M., & Weber, E. U. (1995). Content and discontent: Indications and implications of domain specificity in preferential decision making. *Psychology of Learning and Motivation, 32*, 83–136.

Goudriaan, A. E., Oosterlaan, J., de Beurs, E., & van den Brink, W. (2006). Psychophysiological determinants and concomitants of deficient decision making in pathological gamblers. *Drug & Alcohol Dependence, 84*(3), 231–239.

Green, L., & Myerson, J. (2004). A discounting framework for choice with delayed and probabilistic rewards. *Psychological Bulletin, 130*(5), 769–792.

Gullone, E., & Moore, S. (2000). Adolescent risk-taking and the five-factor model of personality. *Journal of Adolescence, 23*(4), 393–407.

Hanoch, Y., Johnson, J. G., & Wilke, A. (2006). Domain specificity in experimental measures and participant recruitment an application to risk-taking behavior. *Psychological Science, 17*(4), 300–304.

Hansen, E. B., & Breivik, G. (2001). Sensation seeking as a predictor of positive and negative risk behaviour among adolescents. *Personality and Individual Differences, 30*(4), 627–640.

Hartley, C. A., & Phelps, E. A. (2012). Anxiety and decision-making. *Biological Psychiatry, 72*(2), 113–118.

Hertwig, R., Barron, G., Weber, E. U., & Erev, I. (2004). Decisions from experience and the effect of rare events in risky choice. *Psychological Science, 15*(8), 534–539.

Hertwig, R., & Erev, I. (2009). The description–experience gap in risky choice. *Trends in Cognitive Sciences, 13*(12), 517–523.

Hittner, J. B., & Swickert, R. (2006). Sensation seeking and alcohol use: A meta-analytic review. *Addictive Behaviors, 31*(8), 1383–1401.

Highhouse, S., Nye, C. D., Zhang, D. C., & Rada, T. B. (2016). Structure of the dospert: Is there evidence for a general risk factor? *Journal of Behavioral Decision Making, 30*(2), 400–406. https://doi.org/10.1002/bdm.1953

Hogan, R., & Hogan, J. (1995). *Manual for the Hogan personality inventory*. Tulsa, OK: Hogan Assessment Systems.

Horvath, P., & Zuckerman, M. (1993). Sensation seeking, risk appraisal, and risky behavior. *Personality and individual differences, 14*(1), 41–52.

Hoyle, R. H., Fejfar, M. C., & Miller, J. D. (2000). Personality and sexual risk taking: A quantitative review. *Journal of Personality, 68*(6), 1203–1231.

Jackson, D. (1994). *Jackson personality inventory-revised*. Port Huron, MI: Sigma Assessments Systems, Inc.

Jonah, B. (2001). Sensation seeking and risky driving: A review and synthesis of the literature. *Accident Analysis and Prevention, 29*, 651–665.

Jones, S. E., Miller, J. D., & Lynam, D. R. (2011). Personality, antisocial behavior, and aggression: A meta-analytic review. *Journal of Criminal Justice, 39*(4), 329–337.

Kashdan, T. B., Rose, P., & Fincham, F. D. (2004). Curiosity and exploration: Facilitating positive subjective experiences and personal growth opportunities. *Journal of Personality Assessment, 82*(3), 291–305.

Keinan, R., & Bereby-Meyer, Y. (2012). "Leaving it to chance"—Passive risk taking in everyday life. *Judgment and Decision making, 7*(6), 705–715.

Kirby, K. N. (2009). One-year temporal stability of delay-discount rates. *Psychonomic Bulletin & Review, 16*(3), 457–462.

Kirby, K. N., & Finch, J. C. (2010). The hierarchical structure of self-reported impulsivity. *Personality and Individual Differences, 48*(6), 704–713.

Kirby, K. N., Petry, N. M., & Bickel, W. K. (1999). Heroin addicts have higher discount rates for delayed rewards than non-drug-using controls. *Journal of Experimental Psychology: General, 128*(1), 78–87.

Kotov, R., Gamez, W., Schmidt, F., & Watson, D. (2010). Linking "big" personality traits to anxiety, depressive, and substance use disorders: A meta-analysis. *Psychological Bulletin, 136*(5), 768–821.

Kowert, P. A., & Hermann, M. G. (1997). Who takes risks? Daring and caution in foreign policy making. *Journal of Conflict Resolution, 41*(5), 611–637.

Kräplin, A., Bühringer, G., Oosterlaan, J., van den Brink, W., Goschke, T., & Goudriaan, A. E. (2014). Dimensions and disorder specificity of impulsivity in pathological gambling. *Addictive Behaviors, 39*(11), 1646–1651.

Krueger, R. F., Derringer, J., Markon, K. E., Watson, D., & Skodol, A. E. (2012). Initial construction of a maladaptive personality trait model and inventory for DSM-5. *Psychological Medicine, 42*(9), 1879–1890.

Lauriola, M., & Levin, I. P. (2001). Personality traits and risky decision-making in a controlled experimental task: An exploratory study. *Personality and Individual Differences, 31*(2), 215–226.

Lauriola, M., Litman, J. A., Mussel, P., De Santis, R., Crowson, H. M., & Hoffman, R. R. (2015). Epistemic curiosity and self-regulation. *Personality and Individual Differences, 83*, 202–207.

Lauriola, M., Russo, P. M., Lucidi, F., Violani, C., & Levin, I. P. (2005). The role of personality in positively and negatively framed risky health decisions. *Personality and Individual Differences, 38*(1), 45–59.

Lawrence, A. J., Luty, J., Bogdan, N. A., Sahakian, B. J., & Clark, L. (2009). Impulsivity and response inhibition in alcohol dependence and problem gambling. *Psychopharmacology, 207*(1), 163–172.

Lee, K., & Ashton, M. C. (2004). Psychometric properties of the HEXACO personality inventory. *Multivariate Behavioral Research, 39*(2), 329–358.

Lejuez, C. W., Read, J. P., Kahler, C. W., Richards, J. B., Ramsey, S. E., Stuart, G. L., … Brown, R. A. (2002). Evaluation of a behavioral measure of risk taking: The Balloon Analogue Risk Task (BART). *Journal of Experimental Psychology: Applied, 8*(2), 75.

Lerner, J. S., & Keltner, D. (2001). Fear, anger, and risk. *Journal of Personality and Social Psychology, 81*(1), 146–159.

Loewenstein, G. F., Weber, E. U., Hsee, C. K., & Welch, N. (2001). Risk as feelings. *Psychological Bulletin, 127*, 267–286.

Lönnqvist, J. E., Verkasalo, M., Walkowitz, G., & Wichardt, P. C. (2015). Measuring individual risk attitudes in the lab: Task or ask? An empirical comparison. *Journal of Economic Behavior & Organization, 119*, 254–266.

Lopes, L. L. (1995). Algebra and process in the modeling of risky choice. *Psychology of Learning and Motivation, 32*, 177–220.

Lorian, C. N., & Grisham, J. R. (2010). The safety bias: Risk-avoidance and social anxiety pathology. *Behaviour Change, 27*(01), 29–41.

Lynam, D. R., & Widiger, T. A. (2001). Using the five-factor model to represent the DSM-IV personality disorders: An expert consensus approach. *Journal of Abnormal Psychology, 110*(3), 401–412.

MacKillop, J., Amlung, M. T., Few, L. R., Ray, L. A., Sweet, L. H., & Munafò, M. R. (2011). Delayed reward discounting and addictive behavior: A meta-analysis. *Psychopharmacology, 216*(3), 305–321.

Maner, J. K., Richey, J. A., Cromer, K., Mallott, M., Lejuez, C. W., Joiner, T. E., & Schmidt, N. B. (2007). Dispositional anxiety and risk-avoidant decision-making. *Personality and Individual Differences, 42*(4), 665–675.

Markon, K. E., Krueger, R. F., & Watson, D. (2005). Delineating the structure of normal and abnormal personality: An integrative hierarchical approach. *Journal of Personality and Social Psychology, 88*(1), 139–157.
Mather, M., & Lighthall, N. R. (2012). Risk and reward are processed differently in decisions made under stress. *Current Directions in Psychological Science, 21*(1), 36–41.
Miu, A. C., Heilman, R. M., & Houser, D. (2008). Anxiety impairs decision-making: Psychophysiological evidence from an Iowa Gambling Task. *Biological Psychology, 77*(3), 353–358.
Moeller, F. G., Barratt, E. S., Dougherty, D. M., Schmitz, J. M., & Swann, A. C. (2001). Psychiatric aspects of impulsivity. *The American Journal of Psychiatry, 158*(11), 1783–1793.
Mohammed, S., & Schwall, A. (2009). Individual differences and decision making: What we know and where we go from here. In G. P. Hodgkinson & J. K. Ford (Eds.), *International review of industrial and organizational psychology* (Vol. 24, pp. 249–312). Hoboken, NJ: Wiley.
Munafo, M. R., Clark, T., & Flint, J. (2005). Does measurement instrument moderate the association between the serotonin transporter gene and anxiety-related personality traits? A meta-analysis. *Molecular Psychiatry, 10*(4), 415–419.
Mussel, P. (2010). Epistemic curiosity and related constructs: Lacking evidence of discriminant validity. *Personality and Individual Differences, 49*(5), 506–510.
Nelson, M. C., Lust, K., Story, M., & Ehlinger, E. (2008). Credit card debt, stress and key health risk behaviors among college students. *American Journal of Health Promotion, 22*, 400–412.
Nicholson, N., Soane, E., Fenton-O'Creevy, M., & Willman, P. (2005). Personality and domain-specific risk taking. *Journal of Risk Research, 8*(2), 157–176.
Odum, A. L. (2011). Delay discounting: I'm ak, you're ak. *Journal of the Experimental Analysis of Behavior, 96*(3), 427–439.
Ohmura, Y., Takahashi, T., Kitamura, N., & Wehr, P. (2006). Three-month stability of delay and probability discounting measures. *Experimental and Clinical Psychopharmacology, 14*(3), 318–328.
Patton, J. H., Stanford, M. S., & Barratt, E. S. (1995). Factor structure of the Barratt impulsiveness scale. *Journal of Clinical Psychology, 51*(6), 768.
Paulsen, D. J., Carter, R. M., Platt, M. L., Huettel, S. A., & Brannon, E. M. (2011). Neurocognitive development of risk aversion from early childhood to adulthood. *Frontiers in Human Neuroscience, 5*, 178.
Peng, J., Xiao, W., Yang, Y., Wu, S., & Miao, D. (2014). The impact of trait anxiety on self-frame and decision making. *Journal of Behavioral Decision Making, 27*(1), 11–19.
Peters, E., & Slovic, P. (2000). The springs of action: Affective and analytical information processing in choice. *Personality and Social Psychology Bulletin, 26*(12), 1465–1475.
Raghunathan, R., & Pham, M. T. (1999). All negative moods are not equal: Motivational influences of anxiety and sadness on decision making. *Organizational Behavior and Human Decision Processes, 79*(1), 56–77.
Reuter, M., Schmitz, A., Corr, P., & Hennig, J. (2007). Molecular genetics support Gray's personality theory: The interaction of COMT and DRD2 polymorphisms predicts the behavioural approach system. *The International Journal of Neuropsychopharmacology, 10*, 1), 1–1),12.
Reynolds, B. (2006). A review of delay-discounting research with humans: relations to drug use and gambling. *Behavioural pharmacology, 17*(8), 651–667.
Roberti, J. W. (2004). A review of behavioral and biological correlates of sensation seeking. *Journal of Research in Personality, 38*(3), 256–279.
Roberts, B. W., Lejuez, C., Krueger, R. F., Richards, J. M., & Hill, P. L. (2014). What is conscientiousness and how can it be assessed?. *Developmental Psychology, 50*(5), 1315–1330.
Rogers, R. D., et al. (1999). Dissociable deficits in the decision-making cognition of chronic amphetamine abusers, opiate abusers, patients with focal damage to prefrontal cortex, and tryptophan-depleted normal volunteers: Evidence for monoaminergic mechanisms. *Neuropsychopharmacology, 20*, 322–339.

Romero, E., Villar, P., Gómez-Fraguela, J. A., & López-Romero, L. (2012). Measuring personality traits with ultra-short scales: A study of the Ten Item Personality Inventory (TIPI) in a Spanish sample. *Personality and Individual Differences, 53*(3), 289–293.

Rothbart, M. K., & Ahadi, S. A. (1994). Temperament and the development of personality. *Journal of Abnormal Psychology, 103*(1), 55.

Ruiz, M. A., Pincus, A. L., & Schinka, J. A. (2008). Externalizing pathology and the five-factor model: A meta-analysis of personality traits associated with antisocial personality disorder, substance use disorder, and their co-occurrence. *Journal of Personality Disorders, 22*(4), 365–388.

Rusting, C. L. (2001). Personality, mood, and cognitive processing of emotional information: Three conceptual frameworks. *Psychological Bulletin, 124*, 165–196.

Samuel, D. B., & Widiger, T. A. (2008). A meta-analytic review of the relationships between the five-factor model and DSM-IV-TR personality disorders: A facet level analysis. *Clinical Psychology Review, 28*(8), 1326–1342.

Schonberg, T., Fox, C. R., & Poldrack, R. A. (2011). Mind the gap: Bridging economic and naturalistic risk-taking with cognitive neuroscience. *Trends in Cognitive Sciences, 15*(1), 11–19.

Schweizer, T. S. (2006). The psychology of novelty-seeking, creativity and innovation: Neurocognitive aspects within a work-psychological perspective. *Creativity and Innovation Management, 15*(2), 164–172.

Sharma, L., Markon, K. E., & Clark, L. A. (2014). Toward a theory of distinct types of "impulsive" behaviors: A meta-analysis of self-report and behavioral measures. *Psychological Bulletin, 140*(2), 374–408.

Sharma, L., Kohl, K., Morgan, T. A., & Clark, L. A. (2013). "Impulsivity": Relations between self-report and behavior. *Journal of Personality and Social Psychology, 104*(3), 559–575.

Skeel, R. L., Neudecker, J., Pilarski, C., & Pytlak, K. (2007). The utility of personality variables and behaviorally-based measures in the prediction of risk-taking behavior. *Personality and Individual Differences, 43*(1), 203–214.

Slovic, P., Finucane, M. L., Peters, E., & MacGregor, D. G. (2004). Risk as analysis and risk as feelings: Some thoughts about affect, reason, risk, and rationality. *Risk analysis, 24*(2), 311–322.

Slovic, P., & Peters, E. (2006). Risk perception and affect. *Current Directions in Psychological Science, 15*(6), 322–325.

Soane, E., & Chmiel, N. (2005). Are risk preferences consistent?: The influence of decision domain and personality. *Personality and Individual Differences, 38*(8), 1781–1791.

Soane, E., Dewberry, C., & Narendran, S. (2010). The role of perceived costs and perceived benefits in the relationship between personality and risk-related choices. *Journal of Risk Research, 13*(3), 303–318.

Stanford, M. S., Mathias, C. W., Dougherty, D. M., Lake, S. L., Anderson, N. E., & Patton, J. H. (2009). Fifty years of the Barratt Impulsiveness Scale: An update and review. *Personality and Individual Differences, 47*(5), 385–395.

Sunstein, C. R. (2002). Probability neglect: Emotions, worst cases, and law. *The Yale Law Journal, 112*(1), 61–107.

Takemura, K. (2014). *Behavioral decision theory: Psychological and mathematical descriptions of human choice behavior*. Tokyo: Springer.

Tellegen, A. (1985). Structures of mood and personality and their relevance to assessing anxiety, with an emphasis on self-report. In A. H. Tuma & J. D. Maser (Eds.), *Anxiety and the anxiety disorders* (pp. 681–706). Hillsdale, NJ: Erlbaum.

Tellegen, A., & Waller, N. G. (2008). Exploring personality through test construction: Development of the Multidimensional Personality Questionnaire. In G. J. Boyle, G. Matthews, & D. H. Saklofske (Eds.), *The Sage handbook of personality theory and assessment* (Vol. 2, pp. 261–292). Thousand Oaks, CA: SAGE.

Terracciano, A., Löckenhoff, C. E., Crum, R. M., Bienvenu, O. J., & Costa, P. T. (2008). Five-factor model personality profiles of drug users. *BMC Psychiatry, 8*(1), 1–10.

Verbruggen, F., & Logan, G. D. (2008). Automatic and controlled response inhibition: Associative learning in the go/no-go and stop-signal paradigms. *Journal of Experimental Psychology: General, 137*(4), 649.

Vollrath, M., & Torgersen, S. (2002). Who takes health risks? A probe into eight personality types. *Personality and Individual Differences, 32*(7), 1185–1197.

Weafer, J., Baggott, M. J., & de Wit, H. (2013). Test-retest reliability of behavioral measures of impulsive choice, impulsive action, and inattention. *Experimental and Clinical Psychopharmacology, 21*(6), 475–481.

Weber, E. U., & Johnson, E. J. (2009). Mindful judgment and decision making. *Annual Review of Psychology, 60*, 53–85.

Weber, E. U., Blais, A.-R., & Betz, N. (2002). A domain-specific risk-attitude scale: Measuring risk perceptions and risk behaviors. *Journal of Behavioral Decision Making, 15*(4), 263–290.

Weller, J. A., & Thulin, E. W. (2012). Do honest people take fewer risks? Personality correlates of risk-taking to achieve gains and avoid losses in HEXACO space. *Personality and Individual Differences, 53*, 923–926.

Weller, J. A., & Tikir, A. (2011). Predicting domain-specific risk taking with the HEXACO personality structure. *Journal of Behavioral Decision Making, 24*(2), 180–201.

Weller, J. A., Ceschi, A., & Randolph, C. (2015a). Decision-making competence predicts domain-specific risk attitudes. *Frontiers in Psychology, 6*, 540.

Weller, J. A., Kim, H., Leve, L. D., Bhimji, J., & Fisher, P. A. (2015b). Plasticity of decision-making abilities for maltreated adolescents: Evidence from a random clinical trial intervention. *Development and Psychopathology, 27*, 535–551.

Weller, J. A., Kim, H., & Leve, L. (2016). Losses loom larger than gains when predicting behavioral risk outcomes: An early intervention study with a sample of maltreated female adolescents. In M. Toplak & J. Weller (Eds.), *Individual differences in judgment and decision making from a developmental perspective*. Cambridge, UK: Psychology Press forthcoming.

Whiteside, S. P., & Lynam, D. R. (2001). The five factor model and impulsivity: Using a structural model of personality to understand impulsivity. *Personality and Individual Differences, 30*(4), 669–689.

Woo, S. E., Chernyshenko, O. S., Longley, A., Zhang, Z. X., Chiu, C. Y., & Stark, S. E. (2014). Openness to experience: Its lower level structure, measurement, and cross-cultural equivalence. *Journal of Personality Assessment, 96*(1), 29–45.

Woodman, T., Barlow, M., Bandura, C., Hill, M., Kupciw, D., & MacGregor, A. (2013). Not all risks are equal: the risk taking inventory for high-risk sports. *Journal of sport and exercise psychology, 35*(5), 479–492.

Young, S. E., Friedman, N. P., Miyake, A., Willcutt, E. G., Corley, R. P., Haberstick, B. C., & Hewitt, J. K. (2009). Behavioral disinhibition: Liability for externalizing spectrum disorders and its genetic and environmental relation to response inhibition across adolescence. *Journal of Abnormal Psychology, 118*(1), 117–130.

Zaleskiewicz, T. (2001). Beyond risk seeking and risk aversion: Personality and the dual nature of economic risk taking. *European Journal of Personality, 15*, 105–122.

Zuckerman, M. (1994). *Behavioral expressions and biosocial bases of sensation seeking*. New York, NY: Cambridge University Press.

Zuckerman, M. (2007). *Sensation seeking and risk*. Washington, DC: American Psychological Association.

Zuckerman, M., & Kuhlman, D. M. (2000). Personality and risk-taking: Common biosocial factors. *Journal of Personality, 68*(6), 999–1029.

Zuckerman, M., Eysenck, S. B., & Eysenck, H. J. (1978). Sensation seeking in England and America: Cross-cultural, age, and sex comparisons. *Journal of Consulting and Clinical Psychology, 46*(1), 139.

Chapter 2
Individual Differences in the Judgment of Risks: Sociodemographic Characteristics, Cultural Orientation, and Level of Expertise

Bruno Chauvin

Abstract This chapter presents a detailed overview of the risk perception research that has been conducted on some individual differences in the judgment of risks. Among the individual differentiation factors examined here are the sociodemographic characteristics of individuals (e.g., gender, ethnicity). An important finding of this first part is that sex and race are strongly related to risk judgments. White men tend to judge risks as smaller and less problematic than do women and non-white men. A variety of explanations has been developed to account for this white male effect (as well as other sociodemographic differences). To date, (1) being in advantageous positions in terms of power, control over risks, and benefit from them, in conjunction with (2) selecting risk information in a manner supportive of his/her cultural orientation, appear to be the most plausible explanations of the low (versus high)-risk sensitivity. Part 2 is devoted to another important source of individual differences in risk perception, documenting the role of cultural worldviews in shaping individual risk perceptions. In this regard, the cultural cognition thesis is outlined as one of a variety of approaches for understanding the influence of such sociocultural values on risk perception. According to this approach, individuals form risk perceptions that cohere with values characteristic of groups with which they identify. The last part is focused on the striking differences of opinion between experts and the public. Experts generally rate risk as lower and as synonymous with statistical data. Lay people tend to have a broader and more qualitative conception of risk. Both technical risk assessments and public perceptions of risk, however, are recognized as subjective and value-laden views. Accordingly, it is also argued that members of the public and experts may disagree about risk because they have different worldviews, different affective experiences, and a low versus high level of trust in risk regulatory authorities.

B. Chauvin (✉)
University of Strasbourg, Strasbourg, France
e-mail: Bruno.chauvin@unistra.fr

M. Raue et al. (eds.), *Psychological Perspectives on Risk and Risk Analysis*,
https://doi.org/10.1007/978-3-319-92478-6_2

Introduction

Studies of risk perception conducted on lay people have been aimed at answering two main questions. The first question was *why do people on average perceive some hazards as riskier than others?* The second question was *why do individuals differ in their perceptions of the same hazard?* (Slovic, 2000). The most common approach used to answer the first question is referred to as the psychometric paradigm (Slovic, 1987). Within the psychometric paradigm, people make judgments about the perceived riskiness of a variety of hazards. These judgments are then related to judgments about other properties such as the hazard's status on qualitative dimensions (e.g., voluntariness, dread, knowledge, controllability). Researchers working in this paradigm have repeatedly shown that (1) the many dimensions characterizing hazards can be grouped into a limited number of factors and (2) a substantial part of the variance of risk assessments can be explained by a combination of these factors. Most important is the dread factor. The higher a hazard's score on this factor, the higher its perceived risk (Slovic, Fischhoff, & Lichtenstein, 1980, 1985). Thus, psychometric studies grew out of an interest in understanding why *people on average* judge the risks from some hazardous activities differently from the risks of other activities (question # 1), but not why *different people* judge the same hazardous activity differently (question # 2) (with the noteworthy exception of the experts and lay people differences that psychometric studies have consistently shown—see part 3 below for details). However, there is no logical necessity that the relationships found across hazards will also be found within a single hazard across individuals (Gardner & Gould, 1989; see also Visschers & Siegrist, Chap. 3). It was then the start of a flood of research designed to answer the second question about the differences between people and the factors that explain those differences. The present chapter aims at addressing this issue. The first part of the chapter is mainly focused on sociodemographic differences in risk perception because they have been thoroughly explored in research on risk perception (Breakwell, 2007; Chauvin, 2014). Among the sociodemographic characteristics examined are gender, age, ethnicity, level of education, occupation/income level, and political orientation. This chapter also examines the differences in risk judgment that are linked to the cultural worldviews of individuals (part 2) and the differences between experts and lay people (part 3). Individuals' cultural commitments and level of expertise are reviewed in this chapter because both contribute to the understanding of risk perception (Kahan, 2012; Kahan, Jenkins-Smith, & Braman, 2011; Slovic, 2016).

Sociodemographic Differences in Risk Perception

A substantial body of research on risk perception has shown differences between men and women in their estimates of risk (e.g., Savage, 1993; Xiao & McCright, 2015). Several dozen studies conducted in the USA and around the world have indeed documented the finding that men tend to judge risks as smaller and less problematic than do women (Slovic, 1999). This is not to say, however, that men are more accurate than women in their perceptions of risk.

Other demographic differences have also been reported as additional findings in some of these studies. They relate to ethnicity, age, educational level, occupation/income level, or political orientation. For instance, ethnicity and gender are often examined in parallel (e.g., Finucane, Slovic, Mertz, Flynn, & Satterfield, 2000; Hakes & Viscusi, 2004; Macias, 2016). The dominant pattern is that males tend to perceive risks to be lower than females and that whites perceive risks to be lower than non-whites.

One of the first studies explicitly aimed at investigating demographic influences on risk perception is Savage's (1993) study. He found that US women, people with lower levels of schooling and income, younger people, and blacks expressed more dread of several common hazards like aviation accidents, fires in the home, and automobile accidents. At the same time, he found that women, people with lower levels of schooling and income, the young, and blacks also felt heightened personal exposure to risks. From that, he concluded that the most likely leading explanation of the relationship between demographic factors and dread of a hazard is the perceived personal exposure to the hazard. Gender differences in risk perception have also been reported elsewhere in the world for various hazards. In the French context, women tended to perceive the risks associated with domestic activities (e.g., home appliances) and public transport (e.g., railroads) to be higher than did men (Karpowicz-Lazreg & Mullet, 1993). An analysis of the public perception of flood risk on the Belgian coast revealed that women, older people, and people with flood experience had higher perceived levels of coastal flood risks (Kellens, Zaalberg, Neutens, Vanneuville, & De Maeyer, 2011). In Asia, such gender differences also exist. For instance, Xie, Wang, and Xu (2003) found that Chinese women perceived disease, inflation, or natural disasters as riskier than Chinese men did, even though there were smaller and fewer differences across gender in the more educated and more influential occupational groups. Compared with men, Taiwanese women felt more fearful, worried, and threatened in regard to the risk of earthquakes (Kung & Chen, 2012).

These demographic differences have been upheld in examinations of specific risk domains. Regarding technological risks, early work has shown that US women, as well as ethnic minorities and less educated people, expressed a greater concern for a variety of technological risks such as water contamination or nuclear war (Pilisuk & Acredolo, 1988). Similar data were reported by Bastide, Moatti, Pages, and Fagnani (1989) who found that French women judged industrial hazards as more risky than did men. They also indicated that less educated people, blue-collar or white-collar workers with low income, young people, and individuals in sympathy with the ideas of radical leftist groups also expressed a higher aversion to the technological risks than people with higher educational levels and incomes, older respondents, and individuals voting for conservative parties. They stressed in conclusion the importance of broad social factors (such as the general feeling of security) and the crucial role played by some ideological or ethical values in influencing individual risk perception. More recently, Morioka (2014) reported that Japanese men expressed less concern about radiation from Fukushima and perceived a greater sense of invulnerability to physical harm than women.

Research on environmental risk has yielded similar results. Women consistently report greater concern about environmental problems and have more pro-environmental views than do men (Davidson & Freudenburg, 1996; Xiao & McCright, 2015). For instance, Lai and Tao (2003) found that women, older participants, and less educated individuals perceived several hazards like acid rain, pesticides and herbicides, or radioactive fallout more threatening to the environment than did men, younger participants, and more educated individuals, respectively. Marshall, Picou, Formichella, and Nicholls (2006) similarly found that women more than men, and black people more than white people, were concerned about local pollution risks, even after controlling for age, education, and environmental attitudes (see also van der Linden, 2015).

In the same vein, accumulated research findings show that women perceive health and safety risks higher than men. For example, Dosman, Adamowicz, and Hrudey (2001) found that Canadian women were more inclined to consider additives, bacteria, and pesticides in food as health risks than men. Older and less educated participants also tended to judge health risks as high compared to their counterparts (i.e., young and well-educated people). One reason could be that women and less educated people have less power and feel less in control of the risks (see Krewski, Slovic, Bartlett, Flynn, & Mertz, 1995a, for similar results). A possible reason for the positive relation between individuals' age and their perception of risk is personal experience. It could be that younger individuals have not yet experienced the possible effects of any of these health issues and, as a result, do not yet perceive them as risks (see Lai & Tao, 2003, or Wachinger, Renn, Begg, & Kuhlicke, 2013, for similar views about natural hazards; see also Sherman, Minich, Langen, Skufca, & Wilke, 2016). More recent studies also reported similar relationships between individuals' age and level of education (on the one hand) and their perception of health risk (on the other hand) while specifying that such a relationship varied across risk domains. For instance, Bonem, Ellsworth, and Gonzalez (2015) found that, compared to young adults, older adults tended to see more risk in health behaviors such as engaging in unprotected sex or using recreational drugs. Cummings, Berube, and Lavelle (2013) observed that individuals with higher levels of education were more likely to rate risks such as street drugs, AIDS, and cigarette smoking as low health risks compared to less educated individuals. Homko et al. (2010) explored gender differences in risk perception among individuals with diabetes. They found that women with diabetes perceived their risk for cardiovascular diseases (hypertension, myocardial infarction, and stroke) to be significantly higher than did men with diabetes. Gender differences also exist for criminality: females provide systematically higher subjective ratings of crime than do males, perhaps in response to the dangers present within their early local environment (e.g., sexual assault) (Gustafson, 1998; Sherman et al., 2016).

In sum, worldwide research shows that risk perceptions are skewed across gender: women worry more than men about myriad hazards, from domestic activities to

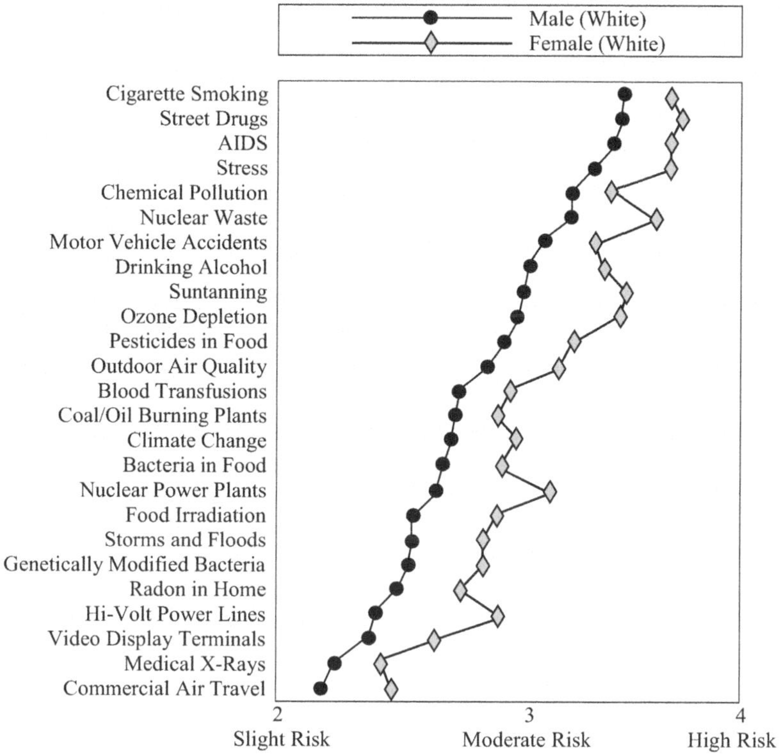

Fig. 2.1 Mean risk perception ratings by gender (originally published in Flynn et al., 1994). Reproduced with permission from the corresponding author

public transportation, from flood to earthquakes, from nuclear technology to environmental pollution, and from pesticides in food to cardiovascular diseases, and criminality. Figure 2.1 illustrates the difference between men and women for a variety of risks.

A number of hypotheses have been put forward to explain these differences in risk perception—especially the gender differences (see Davidson & Freudenburg, 1996, for a review). One of the first hypotheses suggested a lack of knowledge and familiarity with science (among women or ethnic minorities or people with lower level of education) as a basis for these differences (Pilisuk & Acredolo, 1988). This hypothesis, however, has received little empirical support when tested. Gender and ethnicity differences persist even after controlling for science literacy (Kahan, Braman, Gastil, Slovic, & Mertz, 2007). For instance, Barke, Jenkins-Smith, and Slovic (1997) have found that female physical scientists judge risks from nuclear technologies to be higher than do male physical scientists. Similar results with scientists were obtained by Slovic and colleagues (Kraus, Malmfors, & Slovic, 1992; Slovic et al., 1995) who found that female toxicologists were far more likely than male toxicologists to judge societal risks as moderate or high. As a result, the demographic differences in risk perception do not seem to be a simple matter of scientific illiteracy.

Another common explanation for these differences in risk perception, especially for the gender effect, is related to social roles and everyday activities that are socially prescribed and performed by men and women (theorized by Gustafson, 1998, as the gender perspective). During the socialization process, various socializing agents (family, school, peer groups, mass media) ascribe distinct social roles for men and for women. Men are given the role of economic provider (referred to as the *economic salience hypothesis* by Davidson & Freudenburg, 1996), while women are given the role of nurturer and care provider (referred to as the *health and safety concern hypothesis* by Davidson & Freudenburg, 1996). This socialization process continues into adulthood and influences choice of occupation, family roles, and responses to science and technology. Man's place stereotypically lies in the public or cultural sphere (which includes the arenas of business, politics, and science), whereas woman's place often still lies in the private sphere (with concern about child rearing, food production, or health). As a consequence, women are likely to have higher concern levels for the health, safety, and environment of both family and community, and men are likely to be more concerned about economic issues *only*, which in turn results in a greater overall risk perception for women. In addition, those distinct concerns may be reinforced by parenthood (according to the *parental role hypothesis* as outlined by Davidson & Freudenburg, 1996). The effect of having children would make (1) men even more concerned about economic matters because of their roles as fathers/economic providers for their children's needs and (2) women even more concerned about health, safety, and environmental issues because of their roles as mothers/caretakers. Uneven empirical support has been reported for the various hypotheses included in this explanatory framework (see Davidson & Freudenburg, 1996, or Gustafson, 1998, for details). Specifically, the economic salience hypothesis and the parental role hypothesis led to decidedly mixed results, while the health and safety concern hypothesis received more consistent support, leading Davidson and Freudenburg (1996) to argue that this hypothesis is the best explanation for gender differences in risk perception.

For some years, however, a number of researchers took a rather less enthusiastic perspective about the nurturer and care provider hypothesis, thus reducing the salience of the biological and social factors in accounting for the gender effect (e.g., Kahan et al., 2007; Slovic, 1999, 2000). Indeed, according to Satterfield, Mertz, and Slovic (2004), even though this hypothesis may be considered as a viable starting point, it does not explain accumulating evidence that non-white *men*'s perceptions of risk are very similar to those held by white and non-white *women*, while white men consistently offer the lowest risk ratings (e.g., Finucane et al., 2000; Flynn, Slovic, & Mertz, 1994; Marshall et al., 2006). Similarly, Kahan et al. (2007) argued that this hypothesis not only fails to explain variance across ethnicities (see Macias, 2016, for a recent example) but also cannot account for the relative uniformity of risk assessments among women and non-white men (e.g., African-American men, who presumably are no more socially or biologically disposed to be caring than are white men). This phenomenon, called the *white male effect*, has been first reported by Flynn et al. (1994). In their seminal work, they found that ethnicity and gender differences in risk perception could be attributed to a discrete class of highly risk-skeptical white men (who represented about 30% of the white male sample, while the remaining white males were not much different from the other groups with regard to perceived risk). When compared to the rest of the respondents, the group of white males with the lowest risk perception scores were better educated, had higher household incomes, and were politically more conservative. This subgroup also showed greater trust in authorities and institutions and more anti-egalitarian attitudes. These findings led Flynn et al. (1994, p. 1107) to put forward sociopolitical explanations to account for the white male effect: "perhaps white males see less risk in the world because they create, manage, control, and benefit from so much of it. Perhaps women and non-white men see the world as more dangerous because in many ways they are more vulnerable, because they benefit less from many of its technologies and institutions, and because they have less power and control." Interestingly, many of the studies above suggested explanations for their findings which are in line with the sociopolitical factor hypothesis. To account for sociodemographic differences in risk perception, research indeed stressed the crucial role played by some ideological or ethical values as well as the general feeling of security (e.g., Bastide et al., 1989), the sense of invulnerability (e.g., Morioka, 2014), or the feeling of power and control over risks (e.g., Dosman et al., 2001; see also Turiano, Chapman, Agrigoroaei, Infurna, & Lachman, 2014, for a more recent study that demonstrates the importance of individual perceptions of control in buffering the mortality risk among individuals low in education).

Subsequent research provided empirical support for as well as some refinements of the sociopolitical factor hypothesis suggested by Flynn et al. (1994). For instance, Finucane et al. (2000) observed the white male effect in their data from a national survey in the USA. In this study, white males were the group with the consistently lowest risk perceptions across a range of hazards, even after controlling for age, income, education, and political orientation. Moreover, compared with others, white males were more sympathetic with hierarchical, individualistic, and anti-egalitarian worldviews (see part 2 below for details about these worldviews) and were more trusting of technology managers, less trusting of government, and less sensitive to potential stigmatization of communities from hazards. Interestingly, this result is in line with the *institutional trust hypothesis* previously suggested by Davidson and Freudenburg (1996) to account for gender differences in environmental risk concerns. This hypothesis holds that men tend to be more trustful than women of institutions—particularly those involving science or technology – and that trust is negatively related to environmental concerns. The findings from Finucane et al.' (2000) study suggest that white males tend to promote individual achievement, initiative, self-regulation, confidence in experts, and intolerance of community-based decision and regulation processes. Accordingly, compared with many females and non-white males, white males seem to be in positions of more power and control, benefit more from many technologies and institutions, are less vulnerable to discrimination, and may therefore see the world as safer. However, although white males in this research again stood apart from others with respect to their judgments of risk and their attitudes concerning worldviews and trust (thus supporting the sociopolitical explanation), data also revealed that the white male effect is more complex than originally thought, both in its *expression* and in its *explanation*.

Two findings reported by Finucane et al. (2000) needed and received further investigation: (1) Asian males showed similar or lower risk perception than white males for several hazards (e.g., motor vehicles, hormones in meat). In a study specifically designed to examine risk perceptions in an ethnically diverse sample, Palmer (2003) found that both white males and Taiwanese-American males perceived health and technology risks as low compared to others and endorsed an individualist view rather than an egalitarian view. Accordingly, he concluded that *low-risk effect* may be a more suitable term than white male effect [to account for this result]. In the same vein, Olofsson and Rashid (2011) reported that there are no significant difference between Swedish men and women in risk perception and no white male effect, which, they concluded, results from the relative equality between the sexes in Sweden. As a consequence, they claimed that the *societal inequality effect* is a more proper description than the white male effect. (2) Non-white females reported the highest risk estimates for several hazards (e.g., blood transfusions, bacteria in food). A similar result has been reported by Johnson (2002) about outdoor air pollution. In his study, white men were a distinctive group (in that they reported less concern about air pollution than the rest of the sample), but less so than non-white women (who reported more concern about and sensitivity to air pollution than other groups did). As the most distinctive group, non-white women deserve at least as much attention as white men from researchers.

Additionally, further investigation of the sociopolitical factor hypothesis offered new insights as to how to explain the white male effect. For instance, in an extensive survey in the USA, Satterfield et al. (2004) found that (1) white males produced the lowest risk estimates across a range of hazards, (2a) white males rated themselves as less vulnerable (including perceived personal fragility, economic insecurity, and physical vulnerability) than did females or non-whites, (2b) white males perceived lower environmental injustice (defined herein as the belief that minority populations are disproportionately burdened by the health- and community-compromising by-products of industrialization) than did females or non-whites, and (3) those who regarded themselves as vulnerable and as a target of environmental injustice reported higher risk ratings. Taken together, these findings led Satterfield et al. (2004) to claim that the white male effect is driven not simply by the advantageous social position of white males but also by the subjective experience of vulnerability and by the perceived environmental injustice (see also Brody, Zahran, Vedlitz, & Grover, 2008). It should be noted, however, that ethnicity and gender remain robust predictors of risk perception even after vulnerability and environmental injustice are taken into account. For Kahan et al. (2007), this last finding is crucial because it means that something else (so far unexamined) must come into play to fully account for the white male effect. In their study, that *something else* is described as follows: the insensitivity to risk reflected in the white male effect can be considered as a defensive response that hierarchical and individualistic white males display when their cultural identities are threatened (see part 2 below for details about these cultural worldviews). Kahan et al. (2007) tested and provided support for this *cultural-identity-protective cognition* mechanism across various types of risks. With regard to the risk of gun violence and gun accidents, for example, they found the most skeptical attitude about asserted gun risks among individualistic and hierarchical white males, i.e., within the subgroup whose cultural identity is threatened most by regulation of guns. This result is consistent with the status of guns in the US society. Guns are associated with *hierarchical* social roles (father, protector) and with *hierarchical* and *individualistic* virtues (courage, honor, self-reliance), all of which are stereotypically *male* roles and virtues. Historically, in addition, having a gun is a *white* prerogative (see Kahan et al., 2007, for details). Congruently, (1) hierarchical and individualistic worldviews yielded less skepticism and fewer doubts among women and minorities, because guns are less important for their cultural roles; (2) egalitarian (and communitarian) respondents (whites and minorities, men and women, indistinctly) worried more about gun violence because of the positive association of guns with values such as patriarchy and racism and distrust of strangers, which are at odds with their worldviews. In short, this study showed that the respondents inclined to see guns as the safest of all were hierarchical and individualistic white men: "their stance of fearlessness is convincingly attributable to cultural-identity-protective cognition insofar as they are the persons who need guns the most in order to occupy social roles and display individual virtues within their cultural communities" (Kahan et al., 2007, p. 492). More generally, this study demonstrated that gender and race per se do not influence risk perception. The white male effect appears only in conjunction with distinctive cultural worldviews.

In sum, this brief review gives priority to the *extended* sociopolitical factor hypothesis as the most plausible explanation of the sociodemographic differences in risk perception. Indeed, those who have power and control over risks, who benefit from them, who trust in authorities and experts, and who do not see themselves as vulnerable or as a target of environmental injustice tend to perceive risks as low compared to others. This *risk skepticism* seems to be conditional on individuals' cultural orientations: it seems to occur only when hazardous activities integral to the cultural identity of individuals are challenged as harmful. These advantageous positions are mostly hold by a subgroup of white men with a high level of education, high incomes, right-wing political preferences, and hierarchical and individualistic worldviews. At the opposite end of the spectrum are non-white women. That is probably why white men consistently show the lowest risk perception across a range of hazards, while non-white women provide higher risk ratings than all others (see Table 2.1 for a summary).

Table 2.1 Summary of the potential explanations of gender and ethnicity differences in risk perception

Gender × ethnicity	Social role[a]	Social position[b]	Vulnerability[c]	Environmental injustice	Risk perception[d]
White male	−	−	− −	−	− − − − −
White female	+	+	− +	−	+ + + − −
Non-white male	−	+	+ −	+	+ + + − −
Non-white female	+	+	+ +	+	+ + + + +

Note: In this table, the symbols "+" and "−" are used for reporting information in a simplified format, and so they should not be regarded as reflecting strictly equivalent levels. Nevertheless, they provide a useful framework for highlighting, for instance, that white males and non-white females are the two most distinctive groups in terms of risk perception

[a]The symbol "+" means that socially prescribed roles bring an increased sensibility and concern about risk. It is the opposite effect for the symbol "−"

[b]The symbol "+" refers to the lack of power and control. It is the opposite effect for the symbol "−"

[c]The first symbol refers to perceived vulnerability (socially, economically speaking), and the second symbol refers to real vulnerability (physically speaking) (see Baumer, 1978)

[d]According to the cultural-identity-protective cognition mechanism (Kahan et al., 2007), individuals' risk perceptions (last column) are likely to be conditional on individuals' cultural orientations

The Cultural Worldviews and Their Relationship with Risk Perception

The Cultural Theory of Risk

The cultural theory of risk perception (Douglas & Wildavsky, 1982) asserts that individuals' perceptions of risk reflect and reinforce their commitments to visions of how society should be organized. Individuals, according to the theory, choose what to fear (and how much to fear it) in order to support their cultural way of life. Therefore, risk perception will vary systematically according to individuals' preferences for different cultural worldviews (Wildavsky & Dake, 1990). The competing positions at stake in this debate are reflected in the grid-group typology (Douglas, 1982) which is based on two cross-cutting dimensions: *group* and *grid*. The group dimension reflects the extent to which individuals are committed to social structures that foster strong social bonds, collective identity, and cooperation (high group) as opposed to emphasizing individual differences, self-reliance, and competition (low group). The grid dimension reflects the extent to which individuals are committed to role- or class-based social stratification and differentiation (high grid) as opposed to the belief that no one should be excluded from social roles on the basis of their sex, age, or ethnicity (low grid). When combined, the group and grid dimensions generate a 2 × 2 matrix reflecting four distinct cultural worldviews: hierarchism (high group/high grid), individualism (low group/low grid), egalitarianism (high group/low grid), and fatalism (low group/high grid) (Tansey & O'Riordan, 1999; Thompson, Ellis, & Wildavsky, 1990). Theoretically speaking, the cultural theory of risk has been important in emphasizing the key role of competing social and cultural structures in shaping individual risk perceptions (Wildavsky & Dake, 1990). It should be noted, however, that cultural theory suffers from some conceptual weaknesses. For instance, it is not clear from the theory how people come to adopt a particular cultural worldview. It is also not clear whether people are thought to inhabit these cultural worldviews in a transient fashion or to reside in these types for long periods. Cultural theory has also been criticized because its two-by-two classification of cultural diversity is seen as overly simplistic (Boholm, 1996).

Each cultural worldview, cultural theory posits, functions as an *orienting mechanism* that helps people navigate in an uncertain and dangerous world. Persons who have a hierarchical orientation (1) support the establishment and the traditional values of authority, order, and family, (2) promote trust in expertise, and (3) dislike social deviances (e.g., civil disobedience, crises). These are three different ideas. They regard nature as being tolerant (to the adverse effects of technologies), and so they approve technology, providing it is certified safe by experts. Those who have an individualistic orientation value individual achievement, support self-regulation (especially the freedom to bid and bargain), view risk as an opportunity, and dislike social rules that constrain individual initiative. They believe that nature is resilient and, therefore, are optimistic about technology (whose benefits are viewed as more than compensating for any environmental damage that is created). Those with an egalitarian orientation advocate equality and fairness, promote a world in which wealth and power should be widely distributed, and abhor the role differentiation characteristic of hierarchy. They claim that nature is fragile and vulnerable, and so they are afraid of technology because of their catastrophic potential (especially when these technologies are seen as maintaining inequalities that harm the society and the environment). Those with a fatalistic orientation are characterized by a high level of disengagement, favor isolation, and are resigned to strict controls on their behavior. They believe that much of what happens in the society is largely beyond their control. They see nature as capricious and, thus, uncontrollable. Given these characteristics, fatalists tend to be indifferent toward risk, except for risks that affect them personally and directly (Dake, 1991, 1992). As a result, each cultural worldview has its own typical risk portfolio which dismisses some hazards and highlights others based on whether the hazardous activity is one that defies or instead conforms to its norms. Environmental and technological hazards represent a typical case of differences among cultural worldviews. Persons who adhere to the individualistic worldview are likely to be dismissive to claims of environmental and technological risks because giving credence to such risks would lead to restrictions on commerce and industry, two aspects of modern society that they value. The same orientation toward environmental and technological risks should be expected for individuals who adhere to the hierarchical worldview and who see assertions of such hazards as challenging the competence and authority of societal elites. Individuals who adhere to the egalitarian worldview, in contrast, see commerce and industry as sources of unjust social disparities and, as such, are assumed to credit claims that environmental and technological risks associated with those activities are unacceptable (Wildavsky & Dake, 1990; Xue, Hine, Loi, Thorsteinsson, & Phillips, 2014).

The relationship between cultural worldviews and risk perceptions—as asserted by the promoters of the cultural theory of risk perception—has animated nearly three decades of empirical research aimed at testing the cultural theory of risk (Kahan, 2012). As reported by van der Linden (2015), some authors provided empirical support for the theory (e.g., Dake, 1991; Peters & Slovic, 1996), while others have fiercely criticized its use, repeatedly arguing that cultural worldviews have low explanatory power of risk perception (e.g., Sjöberg, 1997, 1998b). Others have similarly claimed that cultural theory explains little variance in perceived risk but take a less extreme position and do not dismiss the theory in its entirety (e.g., Brenot, Bonnefous, & Marris, 1998; Marris, Langford, & O'Riordan, 1998). Others still have designed new approaches to empirically test the cultural theory of risk (e.g., Kahan, 2012; Rippl, 2002).

Empirical Relationship Between Cultural Worldviews and Risk Perception

In the early 1990s, Dake and his colleagues conducted the first quantitative empirical studies aimed at measuring cultural worldviews and assessing their relations with risk judgments (Dake, 1991, 1992; Wildavsky & Dake, 1990). They developed four sets of items to form four separate scales designed to assess individuals' commitment to hierarchism, individualism, egalitarianism, and fatalism. The following are examples of items used to operationalize each cultural worldview: "I think there should be more discipline in the youth of today" (hierarchism), "in a fair system people with more ability should earn more" (individualism), "if people in this country were treated more equally we would have fewer problems" (egalitarianism), and "I don't worry about politics because I can't influence things very much" (fatalism). In Dake's (1991) study, perceptions of risk were assessed through a list of societal concerns including issues pertaining to social deviance, environmental problems, technological hazards, international threats, or market failures. Dake (1991) found that egalitarians reported strong concerns about technological and environmental threats (e.g., nuclear energy, environmental pollution), but they worried less about the various forms of social deviance (e.g., civil disobedience, loss of respect for authority). On the contrary, Hierarchists and individualists showed far less concern than egalitarians about technological and environmental threats. Forms of social deviance were the societal concerns most strongly correlated with hierarchism and individualism. Individualists also were concerned about the risks of inflation, debt, and overregulation (fatalists were not considered in this study). He concluded that "these findings lend credence to a major tenet in cultural theory—that each kind of cultural biases engenders a different ranking of possible dangers" (Dake, 1991, p. 73). Peters and Slovic (1996) reported similar results. They found that people holding an egalitarian orientation had higher perceived risk for a wide range of hazards and were particularly concerned about nuclear power. People with hierarchical or individualistic orientations had much lower perceptions of risk and more favorable attitudes toward nuclear power. For both of them, nuclear power is not a threat (hierarchists approve this technology because it is certified safe by experts, and individualists view this technology as an opportunity to improve health and social well-being).

Subsequent research using Dake's measures or refinements thereof has confirmed the existence of a pattern of relationships between cultural worldviews and risk perceptions which is consistent with the predictions of cultural theory. For instance, Brenot et al. (1998) found that the more egalitarian the individuals were, the higher was their perceived risk of technological and environmental hazards (e.g., chemicals, radioactive waste) or health-related issues (e.g., AIDS, smoking). Marris et al. (1998) reported that the hierarchical worldview was associated with a higher risk perception for social threats (e.g., mugging, terrorism). Bouyer, Bagdassarian, Chaabane, and Mullet (2001) found that people who adhere to a fatalistic orientation showed a high concern for risks associated with public transportation (e.g., planes, trains) (see also Krewski, Slovic, Bartlett, Flynn, & Mertz, 1995b; Palmer, 1996). However, in every study above, correlations between cultural worldviews and risk perceptions were low, suggesting that cultural worldviews explain only a modest variability in risk judgments.

Based on a review of empirical work on cultural theory and risk perception (including some of the introduced studies), Sjöberg (1997) agrees with that stance that cultural worldviews are not major factors in risk perception but make a minor contribution to its explanation. After collecting new data from Swedish, Brazilian, and US samples, he goes even further by stating that the cultural theory of risk is "simply wrong" (Sjöberg, 1997, p. 126; Sjöberg, 1998b, p. 150; see also Sjöberg, 2003). To draw such a different conclusion, he argues that the correlations between cultural worldviews and risk perceptions were mostly very weak (although abundant and statistically significant), resulting in a very low average proportion of explained variance in risk perception. So, part of the opposition between him and others, Sjöberg admits, may be due to different ways of using and interpreting statistics. Sjöberg's critique of cultural theory is also based on the methodological weaknesses of the measures operationalizing cultural theory. For instance, he and others (e.g., Brenot et al., 1998; Marris et al., 1998) reported that the separate scales used to assess each cultural worldview (1) failed to display satisfactory values of internal consistency (low-scale reliability) and (2) were not independent from each other (low discriminant validity). In fact, as noted by van der Linden (2015, p. 116), "it's not uncommon for subjects to have high scores on competing scales (e.g., Hierarchism and Individualism), which is problematic, since in theory, individuals cannot be characterized by mutually inconsistent worldviews". In conclusion, to Sjöberg, cultural theory as a whole should be dismissed, and other approaches are clearly called for [to account for risk perception].

Undoubtedly, these are the persistent questions about the theoretical, methodological, and empirical validity of cultural theory which have led a number of scholars to experiment with alternative measurement strategies and conceptions of cultural theory. One of them is Rippl (2002). She developed a new measurement instrument in which each cultural worldview is related to each other in a manner which is consistent to the grid-group typology (for instance, in her instrument, individualism and hierarchism are *negatively* correlated, as are egalitarianism and fatalism). Yet, the overall power of cultural types for explaining risk perception was not improved by using a more valid instrument (see Rippl, 2002, for details). More recently, Kahan and his collaborators have developed a new conceptualization and measurement of cultural worldviews known as the *cultural cognition* thesis (Kahan, 2012; Kahan, Braman, Slovic, Gastil, & Cohen, 2009; Kahan, Jenkins-Smith, & Braman, 2011; Kahan, Wittlin, Peters, Slovic, Larrimore Ouellette, Braman, & Mandel, 2011). Cultural cognition has to be considered as a *conception of, not a substitute for*, the cultural theory of risk. It is only one of a variety of competing approaches for interpreting and testing the cultural theory of risk (Kahan, 2012). Cultural cognition refers to the tendency of people to base their factual beliefs about the risks and benefits of a hazardous activity on their cultural appraisals of these activities. Specifically, individuals form risk perceptions that cohere with values characteristic of groups with which they identify. To form risk perceptions that are congenial to their cultural values, individuals would use a collection of psychological mechanisms (e.g., the *cultural-identity-protective cognition* mechanism mentioned above) that dispose them selectively to credit or dismiss evidence of risk in patterns that fit values they share with others (Kahan, 2012; Kahan, Jenkins-Smith, & Braman, 2011). One distinctive feature of Kahan's approach is the way in which cultural cognition measures cultural worldviews. Cultural cognition uses two continuous attitudinal scales. One, *hierarchy-egalitarianism*, consists of items that determine a person's relative orientation toward high or low grid ways of life (e.g., "a lot of problems in our society today come from the decline in the traditional family" versus "our society would be better off if the distribution of wealth was more equal"). The other, *individualism-communitarianism*, consists of items that determine a person's relative orientation toward weak or strong group ways of life ("the government interferes far too much in our everyday lives" versus "it is society's responsibility to make sure everyone's basic needs are met") (Kahan, 2012). Compared with Dake's measures, cultural cognition scales exhibit higher levels of reliability (e.g., Kahan et al., 2007; Kahan et al., 2009). They also avoid related problems of logical indeterminacy by providing each individual with a single score for the group dimension (low or high) and a single score for the grid dimension (low or high), while—with Dake's *separate* scales—it is possible for an individual to score high (or low) on all four cultural worldviews (Kahan, 2012). Empirically speaking, Kahan and his collaborators presented both correlational and experimental evidence confirming that cultural cognition shapes individuals' beliefs about risk. For instance, Kahan et al. (2009) found that hierarchical individualistic people—who have a pro-technology cultural orientation—are thus more likely to become exposed to information about nanotechnology and to draw positive inferences from what they discover. In contrast, egalitarian-communitarian individuals—who lack that predisposition—are less likely to become exposed to information, and when they do become exposed to it, they are significantly more likely to react negatively. Both hierarchical-individualists and egalitarian-communitarians have selected information about nanotechnology in a biased fashion that matches their cultural orientations (see also Kahan, Wittlin, Peters, Slovic, Larrimore Ouellette, Braman, & Mandel, 2011, for a study about climate-change risk perceptions). It should be noted, however, that cultural cognition approach faces some objections (e.g., De De Witt, Osseweijer, & Pierce, 2017). One is that the two cognition cultural scales generate *hybrid* cultural worldviews (e.g., hierarchical-individualists or egalitarian-communitarians), not *basic* cultural worldviews from a cultural theory perspective. Another theory-based objection to the cultural cognition scheme is that it ignores *fatalism* (see Kahan, 2012, for details).

To recap, the cultural theory of risk, since its launch in the 1980s, has been highly influential in the field of risk perception (Boholm, 1996; see also Bostrom et al., Chap. 11, and Renn, Chap. 16). Early proponents claim that cultural theory provides the best predictions of a broad range of perceived risks and an interpretive framework in which these predictions cohere (e.g., Wildavsky & Dake, 1990). Opponents claim that cultural theory is simply wrong and does not have a strong explanatory power of risk perception (e.g., Sjöberg, 1997). At the instigation of others, like Kahan (e.g., Kahan, 2012; Kahan et al., 2007), cultural theory has evolved over the past 15 years, both conceptually and methodologically. These developments provided some valuable insights into conflict over risk across individuals and groups (e.g., Kahan et al., 2009), but there is a need for further work on this theory (Kahan, 2012; Rippl, 2002).

Experts and Lay Differences in Risk Perception

Psychometric studies (i.e., studies which have employed the psychometric paradigm) contributed to better understand risk perception primarily by identifying key risk characteristics (e.g., the *dread* factor) as inherent attributes of the hazards themselves, rather than as constructs of the respondents (e.g., Slovic et al., 1985). However, psychometric studies have also proven to be well suited for identifying similarities and differences in risk perception among groups, namely, between experts *and* lay people. A consistent result from the earliest psychometric studies was indeed that experts' judgments of risk differed systematically and markedly from those of nonexperts (Slovic, 1987). For instance, in Slovic, Fischhoff, and Lichtenstein's (1979) study, a group of experts selected for their professional involvement in risk assessment (including a geographer, an environmental policy analyst, an economist, a lawyer, a biologist, a biochemist, and a government regulator of hazardous material) and various groups of lay people were asked to rate the riskiness of 30 activities and technologies. The expert group viewed electric power, surgery, swimming, and X-rays as riskier than did the groups of lay people, but nuclear power, police work and mountain climbing to be much less risky than did lay people. The perceptions of experts also reflected the vast range, from high to low risk, inherent in the statistical measures. In contrast, nonexperts' perceptions of risk were compressed into a smaller range. On the whole and on average, experts rated

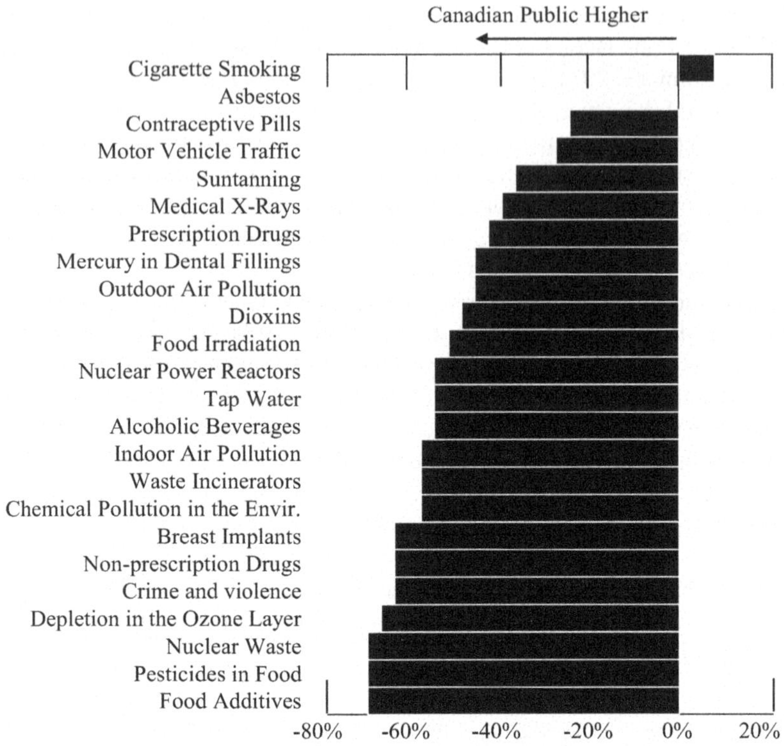

Fig. 2.2 Difference in percent experts' moderate- and high-risk responses minus percent Canadian public moderate- and high-risk responses (originally published in Mertz et al., 1998). Reproduced with permission from the corresponding author

risk as lower (see also Slovic et al., 1980, 1985). Over time, the early work was replicated and extended with diverse samples of experts and lay people worldwide (see, e.g., Purvis-Roberts, Werner, & Frank, 2007, for a study in Kazakhstan), with different sets of hazards (e.g., Sjöberg, 1998a; Slovic et al., 1995), as well as with hazards pertaining to one single domain, such as chemical substances (e.g., Kraus et al., 1992), nuclear power exploitation (e.g., Flynn, Slovic, & Mertz, 1993), ecology (e.g., Lazo, Kinnell, & Fisher, 2000), biotechnology (Savadori et al., 2004), nanotechnology (Siegrist, Keller, Kastenholz, Frey, & Wiek, 2007), or health-related issues (Dhar-Chowdhury, Haque, & Driedger, 2016). Each of these studies provided additional empirical evidence of the expert versus lay disconnect in assessing a specific risk. Figure 2.2 depicts a pattern of differences between experts and lay people with regard to the risk associated with a variety of activities, substances, and technologies.

In other words, research has consistently shown that the concept *risk* meant different things to different people, namely, experts versus lay people (Slovic, 2000). When experts judged risks, they tended to see riskiness as synonymous with probability of harm or expected mortality. Their responses correlated highly with technical estimates of annual fatalities. In contrast, the public was found to have a broader conception of risk, qualitative and complex, that also incorporates considerations such as uncertainty, dread, catastrophic potential, controllability, equity, risk to future generations, and so forth, into the risk equation (experts' perceptions of risk are not closely related to these characteristics) (Slovic, 2000; Slovic et al., 1980). In this light, it is not surprising that (1) substantial differences were observed between experts' and lay people's views of risk and (2) expert recitations of risk statistics often did little to change people's perceptions and conflicts over risk which often did occur between experts and the public (Slovic, 2016).

At first glance, the *risk as analysis* mode of thinking of experts could be seen as a more rational and then a more appropriate conception of risk than the *risk as feelings* mode of thinking of lay people. In that view, the public is needed to be better educated and informed, to rely less on emotional judgments, to be aware of the qualitative aspects of hazards that could bias its judgments, and to be open to new evidence that might alter its risk perceptions. In other words, it would be sufficient to align lay people's *misjudgments* with experts' *realistic assessments* of risk to reducing divergences among groups and the conflicts that arise from these divergences. Some observers—industrialists or scientists—held this stance for a while (see Kraus et al., 1992, or Slovic, 1987, for details). At much the same time, however, others rejected this idea and claimed that disagreements about risk should not be expected to evaporate in the presence of evidence. Definitive evidence, particularly about rare hazards, is difficult to obtain. Weaker information is likely to be interpreted in a way that reinforces existing beliefs (Slovic et al., 1979; see also Kruglanski, 2012, for a recent theory about how lay people form judgments).

Almost four decades later, our understanding of risk perception has greatly increased, and a more balanced appreciation of the strength and weaknesses of both expert risk assessments and public perceptions has evolved (Slovic, 2016). Over time, it was indeed recognized that there is coherence in public risk perception as well as some sort of rationality when evaluating hazards' riskiness. Firstly, perceived risk and acceptable risk as judged by lay people were found to be systematic and predictable (Slovic, 2000). Secondly, a large research literature in psychology has documented the importance of *affect* (a feeling that something is good or bad) in conveying meaning upon information and motivating behavior, particularly when important numerical information (e.g., numbers of deaths resulting from war or genocide) comes across as *dry statistics* that fail to spark emotion or feeling and thus fail to motivate action (Slovic, 2007, 2010). For instance, using an experimental design, Small, Lowenstein, and Slovic (2007) found that donations in response to an identified individual victim of food crisis (picture of a single human face) were far greater than donations in response to the statistical portrayal of the food crisis (numerical representations of human lives). They also measured feelings of sympathy toward the cause (the identified individual or the statistical victims). These feelings were most strongly correlated with donations when people faced an identifiable victim. More broadly, affect plays a central role in what have come to be known as *the experiential system* which relies on affect-laden images to respond rapidly and automatically to risk (Slovic, Finucane, Peters, & MacGregor, 2004; see also

Damasio, 1994; Epstein, 1994). Research now recognizes that affective and emotional processes—combined with the reason-based *analytic system*—are essential to rationality. Reliance on the feeling of risk was essential to human survival in the course of evolution (let's think about the gut feeling that told us whether an animal was safe to approach), and even today, feelings serve as a compass that guides most of our (risk) judgments, decisions, and actions (Slovic, 2016; see also Tompkins et al., Chap. 5). A critical theoretical study by Garvin (2001) provided further evidence for the rationality of public risk perceptions. She observed that the basic framework of public responses to risk was neither irrational nor unreliable but depends largely upon the personal experience, indirect experience from media sources, and perception of the trustworthiness of relevant institutions or social actors. She concluded that the public legitimizes supporting evidence for its opinion about the perceived riskiness of a variety of hazards (and dismisses conflicting evidence) by relating it to its social and cultural reality, to a received wisdom that is embedded in *social* rationality.

On the other hand, the technical foundations of scientific risk assessment also came under scrutiny, and it was recognized that there are subjectivity, biases, and value-laden issues in expert risk judgments (e.g., Merkelsen, 2011; Savadori et al., 2004). Social scientists indeed argued that the measurement of risk is inherently subjective (Slovic, 1999). The nuclear engineer's probabilistic risk estimate for a nuclear accident and the toxicologist's quantitative estimate of a chemical's carcinogenic risk are both based on theoretical models, whose structure is subjective and assumption-laden and whose inputs are dependent on judgment at every stage of the assessment process. Even the apparently simple task of choosing a risk measure for a well-defined endpoint such as human fatalities is surprisingly complex and judgmental. For example, road traffic risks can be expressed in terms of annual death rate per passenger, per mile traveled, per passenger-mile, and so on. Which measure one thinks more appropriate for decision making depends on one's point of view (Slovic, 1999, 2016). Moreover, experts' judgments appear to be prone to many of the same biases as those of the general public, particularly when experts are forced to go beyond the limits of available data and rely on intuition (Slovic, 1987). Sokolowska and Sleboda (2015) recently provided support for this view. They found that technical expertise helps physicians to avoid oversimplified judgments of consequences of health-related risks (e.g., abortion) as long as they are well known to science, but it is insufficient to protect against such judgments when they are related to emerging, poorly understood technologies (e.g., stem cell research). In such cases, they might rely on affect to make judgments. In a study involving nuclear-waste experts, Sjöberg (1998a) held a similar view by stating that it is very reasonable to assume that perceived control and familiarity account for experts' low rating of nuclear risks. Just as nonscientists, scientists have their own models, assumptions, and value-laden risk assessment techniques. They are often very different from the nonscientists' models, which may account for a number of expert-lay differences in risk perception and conflicts over risk. The *intuitive toxicology* perspective has been an important approach in this regard (Slovic, 2000). It consists in using extensive open-ended interviews to construct *mental models* depicting people's knowledge, attitudes, values, perceptions, and inference mechanisms with regard to specific hazards such as chemical or nuclear technologies. In the 1990s, several studies have used this approach to explore the cognitive models underlying the *scientific toxicology* of experts and compare these models with those that comprise lay people's *intuitive toxicology*. Such comparisons have exposed the specific similarities and differences within expert communities as well as the similarities and differences between expert views and lay perceptions. Kraus et al. (1992), for instance, have found a great divergence of opinion among the toxicologists themselves on questions pertaining to the reliability and validity of animal tests for assessing the risks that chemicals pose to humans. The public was also divided about this issue. It should be noted, however, that this issue is an isolated case. In general, toxicologists and lay people were found to differ greatly. Compared to the toxicologists, the public was found to be much less sensitive to considerations of dose and exposure, much less favorable toward chemicals, much more concerned regarding chemical risks, and much more eager to reduce chemical risks at any cost. In this study, these differences were still observed when education, ethnicity, and gender differences between toxicologists and the public were minimized (see Rowe & Wright, 2001, for a critical analysis of the failure of most studies to match expert and nonexpert samples on the basis of demographic factors). Kraus et al. (1992) also observed a strong *affiliation bias*. Compared to other experts, toxicologists who worked for industry were somewhat more confident in the general validity of animal tests (except when those tests were said to provide evidence for carcinogenicity). They also perceived chemicals as more benign than did their counterparts in academia and government (see also Barke & Jenkins-Smith, 1993). Similar results have been found in additional studies in Canada (Slovic et al., 1995), in the USA regarding the nuclear risk (Flynn et al., 1993), or in the UK (Mertz, Slovic, & Purchase, 1998). Furthermore, these studies provided some insights as to why expert risk assessments (1) vary in this way and (2) differ greatly from public risk perceptions. In Slovic et al.' (1995) study, among toxicologists, those with high average risk ratings tended to disagree with a number of hierarchical worldviews (e.g., risks are adequately regulated) and to agree with a number of egalitarian worldviews (e.g., small risks should not be imposed on people). The public agreed more with the egalitarian and fatalism worldviews and were more inclined to distrust people in positions of authority. In Flynn et al.' (1993) study, compared to the public, nuclear industry experts tended to express much more trust in the ability of authorities to manage radioactive wastes (see also Siegrist et al., 2007, for the importance of trust in regulatory authorities). In Mertz et al.' (1998) study, senior managers of a major chemical company had low-risk perceptions that were similar (if somewhat lower) to those of British toxicologists working in industry. Both groups also exhibited similar individualistic cultural worldviews. In contrast, compared to senior managers, toxicologists affiliated with academia tended to have higher perceptions of risk and dissimilar cultural worldviews (see also Sokolowska & Sleboda, 2015).

In sum, the idealized roles of scientific experts as rational and the public as capricious and misinformed present oversimplified versions of reality (Garvin, 2001). Something else comes into play to fully account for public and expert risk judgments, expert-lay differences in risk perception, and closely related conflicts over risk. Indeed, the knowledge gained from these studies of expert and lay perceptions of risk is that there is rationality as much as subjectivity and value-laden issues in both expert and public views on risk (Slovic, 2016). For both, the experiential mode of thinking (albeit mostly used by the public) and the analytic mode of thinking (albeit mostly used by experts) are at work and continually active when judging risk, interacting in what has been characterized as *the dance of affect and reason* (Finucane, Peters, & Slovic, 2003). For both, views on risk are influenced by cultural worldviews, trust in regulatory agencies, personal ideologies, and organizational values (Slovic, 1999; Slovic, 2000). Just as the public risk perception, risk expertise does not exist in an institutional vacuum (Merkelsen, 2011). Rather, risk expertise should be examined in its organizational setting, as a part of a network that fosters specific interests and values distinct from—and sometimes conflicting with—those at stake in other organizational settings. For instance, with regard to the risks of nuclear energy, scientists in industry or in business consulting are likely to give more priority to economic competitiveness and national defense, while scientists in university are likely to give more priority to environmental problems (Barke & Jenkins-Smith, 1993). Thus, similarities and differences among experts as well as between experts and lay people with regard to risk perceptions are likely to be partly due to different *frames of reference* for each of these groups.

Conclusion

Individuals do differ in their perception of risks. Indeed, factors such as gender, ethnicity, cultural views (of how society should be organized), and level of expertise are strongly correlated with risk judgments. The dominant pattern is that women worry more than men about myriad hazards and that whites perceive risks to be lower than non-whites. Risk perception also varies according to individuals' preferences for different cultural worldviews. For instance, persons with an egalitarian orientation—who claim that nature is fragile and vulnerable—see environmental and technological risks as unacceptable, contrary to persons with an individualistic orientation, who believe that nature is resilient. Another consistent finding is the significance of the differences between experts and lay people in risk perceptions. Experts generally rate risks as lower.

Why do some individuals perceive some hazards as riskier than other individuals? Answering this question is not straightforward. However, for about 40 years, research on risk perception has gradually illuminated much of this fundamental issue by demonstrating that (1) risk is inherently subjective (including for experts) and (2) its assessment is a socially constructed phenomenon that depends on social, political, cultural, and psychological factors (Slovic, 2016). White men consistently show the lowest risk perception across a range of hazards probably because they hold advantageous positions in terms of power, control over risks, and benefit from them. This insensitivity to risk of white men, as well as the sensitivity to risk of other groups (especially non-white women), seems to occur when their cultural identities are threatened, that is, when the cultural worldviews they support are challenged (Kahan, 2012). More broadly, social and cultural values held by individuals could play an important role in risk perception as orienting mechanisms, serving to guide people's responses to risk (Slovic, 2000). Members of the public and experts may disagree about risk because they define risk differently. Experts tend to give priority to technical risk assessments, while the public tend to have a more complex conception of risk that incorporates the psychological qualities of hazards as well (Slovic, 2000). This is not to say, however, that expert-lay differences in risk perception and conflicts over risk stem from the subjective and value-laden nature of public views of risk (versus the rationality of risk expertise). Similarly to the public, experts are influenced by emotion and affect, cultural worldviews, and values, particularly when they are working at the limits of their expertise (Slovic, 2016). Accordingly, divergences of opinion between experts and the public, as well as divergences among experts and among lay people, are more probably due to different affective experiences and reactions, different worldviews, and different values. A lack of trust in risk managers is also a reason why the public and the experts differ in their views of risk.

The practical implication of the knowledge gained from the research on risk perception described in this chapter is that any process of risk management which considers the public as a *monolithic* group is doomed to failure. To some extent, the same holds true for the experts. As a consequence, no matter how difficult that might be, those who promote and regulate health and safety (e.g., risk communicators, decision makers, regulatory agency representatives) need to take into account and integrate an appropriately diverse representation of the spectrum of interested and affected parties in their policies of risk management. It is a prerequisite for good decisions in the face of risk.

References

Barke, R. P., & Jenkins-Smith, H. (1993). Politics and scientific expertise: Scientists, risk perception, and nuclear waste policy. *Risk Analysis, 13*, 425–439.

Barke, R. P., Jenkins-Smith, H., & Slovic, P. (1997). Risk perceptions of men and women scientists. *Social Science Quarterly, 78*, 167–176.

Bastide, S., Moatti, J.-P., Pages, J.-P., & Fagnani, F. (1989). Risk perception and social acceptability of technologies: The French case. *Risk Analysis, 9*, 215–223.

Baumer, T. L. (1978). Research on fear of crime in the United States. *Victimology, 3*, 254–264.

Bonem, E. M., Ellsworth, P. C., & Gonzalez, R. (2015). Age differences in risk: Perceptions, intentions, and domains. *Journal of Behavioral Decision Making, 28*, 317–330.

Boholm, A. (1996). Risk perception and social anthropology: Critique of cultural theory. *Ethnos, 61*, 64–84.

Bouyer, M., Bagdassarian, S., Chaabane, S., & Mullet, E. (2001). Personality correlates of risk perception. *Risk Analysis, 21*, 457–465.

Breakwell, G. M. (2007). *The psychology of risk*. Cambridge: Cambridge University Press.

Brenot, J., Bonnefous, S., & Marris, C. (1998). Testing the cultural theory of risk in France. *Risk Analysis, 18*, 729–739.

Brody, S. D., Zahran, S., Vedlitz, A., & Grover, H. (2008). Examining the relationship between physical vulnerability and public perceptions of global climate change in the United States. *Environment & Behavior, 40*, 72–95.

Chauvin, B. (2014). *La perception des risques. Apports de la psychologie à l'identification des déterminants du risque perçu* [The perception of risk: Contributions of the research in psychology for identifying what are the determinants of perceived risk]. Bruxelles: De Boeck.

Cummings, C. L., Berube, D. M., & Lavelle, M. E. (2013). Influences of individual-level characteristics on risk perceptions to various categories of environmental health and safety risks. *Journal of Risk Research, 16*, 1277–1295.

Dake, K. (1991). Orienting dispositions in the perception of risk: An analysis of contemporary worldviews and cultural biases. *Journal of Cross-Cultural Psychology, 22*, 61–82.

Dake, K. (1992). Myths of nature: Culture and the social construction of risk. *Journal of Social Issues, 48*, 21–37.

Damasio, A. R. (1994). *Descartes' error: Emotion, reason, and the human brain*. New York, NY: Avon.

Davidson, D. J., & Freudenburg, W. R. (1996). Gender and environmental risk concerns. A review and analysis of available research. *Environment and Behavior, 28*, 302–339.

De Witt, A., Osseweijer, P., & Pierce, R. (2017). Understanding public perceptions of biotechnology through the "integrative worldview framework". *Public Understanding of Science*, 26, 70-88.

Dhar-Chowdhury, P., Haque, C. E., & Driedger, S. M. (2016). Dengue disease risk mental models in the city of Dhaka, Bangladesh: Juxtapositions and gaps between the public and experts. *Risk Analysis, 36*, 874–891.

Dosman, D. M., Adamowicz, W. L., & Hrudey, S. E. (2001). Socioeconomic determinants of health- and food safety-related risk perceptions. *Risk Analysis, 21*, 307–317.

Douglas, M. (1982). *Essay in the sociology of perception*. London: Routledge.

Douglas, M., & Wildavsky, A. (1982). *Risk and culture. An essay on the selection of technological and environmental dangers*. Berkeley: University of California Press.

Epstein, S. (1994). Integration of the cognitive and psychodynamic unconscious. *American Psychologist, 49*, 709–724.

Finucane, M. L., Peters, E., & Slovic, P. (2003). Judgment and decision making: The dance of affect and reason. In S. L. Schneider & J. Shanteau (Eds.), *Emerging perspectives on judgment and decision research* (pp. 327–364). Cambridge: Cambridge University Press.

Finucane, M. L., Slovic, P., Mertz, C. K., Flynn, J., & Satterfield, T. A. (2000). Gender, race, and perceived risk: The "white male" effect. *Health, Risk and Society, 2*, 159–172.

Flynn, J., Slovic, P., & Mertz, C. K. (1993). Decidedly different: Expert and public views of risks from a radioactive waste repository. *Risk Analysis, 13*, 643–648.

Flynn, J., Slovic, P., & Mertz, C. K. (1994). Gender, race, and perception of environmental health risks. *Risk Analysis, 14*, 1101–1108.

Gardner, G. T., & Gould, L. C. (1989). Public perceptions of the risks and benefits of technology. *Risk Analysis, 9*, 225–242.

Garvin, T. (2001). Analytical paradigms: The epistemological distances between scientists, policy makers, and the public. *Risk Analysis, 21*, 443–455.

Gustafson, P. E. (1998). Gender differences in risk perception: Theoretical and methodological perspectives. *Risk Analysis, 18*, 805–811.

Hakes, J. K., & Viscusi, W. K. (2004). Dead reckoning: Demographic determinants of the accuracy of mortality risk perceptions. *Risk Analysis, 24*, 651–664.

Homko, C. J., Zamora, L., Santamore, W. P., Kashem, A., McConnell, T., & Bove, A. A. (2010). Gender differences in cardiovascular risk factors and risk perception among individuals with diabetes. *Diabetes Education, 36*, 483–488.
Johnson, B. B. (2002). Gender and race in beliefs about outdoor air pollution. *Risk Analysis, 22*, 725–738.
Kahan, D. M. (2012). Cultural cognition as a conception of the cultural theory of risk. In R. Hillerbrand, P. Sandin, S. Roeser, & M. Peterson (Eds.), *Handbook of risk theory: Epistemology, decision theory, ethics and social implications of risk* (pp. 725–760). London: Springer.
Kahan, D. M., Braman, D., Gastil, J., Slovic, P., & Mertz, C. K. (2007). Culture and identity-protective cognition: Explaining the white-male effect in risk perception. *Journal of Empirical Legal Studies, 4*, 465–505.
Kahan, D. M., Braman, D., Slovic, P., Gastil, J., & Cohen, G. (2009). Cultural cognition of the risks and benefits of nanotechnology. *Nature Nanotechnology, 4*, 87–91.
Kahan, D. M., Jenkins-Smith, H. C., & Braman, D. (2011). Cultural cognition of scientific consensus. *Journal of Risk Research, 14*, 147–174.
Kahan, D. M., Wittlin, M., Peters, E., Slovic, P., Larrimore Ouellette, L., Braman, D., & Mandel, G. N. (2011). *The tragedy of the risk-perception commons: Culture conflict, rationality conflict, and climate change* (Cultural Cognition Project Working Paper N° 89)
Karpowicz-Lazreg, C., & Mullet, E. (1993). Societal risks as seen by the French public. *Risk Analysis, 13*, 253–258.
Kellens, W., Zaalberg, R., Neutens, T., Vanneuville, W., & De Maeyer, P. (2011). An analysis of the public perception of flood risk on the Belgian coast. *Risk Analysis, 31*, 1055–1068.
Kraus, N., Malmfors, T., & Slovic, P. (1992). Intuitive toxicology: Expert and lay judgments of chemical risks. *Risk Analysis, 12*, 215–232.
Krewski, D., Slovic, P., Bartlett, S., Flynn, J., & Mertz, C. K. (1995a). Health risk perception in Canada I: Rating hazards, sources of information and responsibility for health protection. *Human and Ecological Risk Assessment, 1*, 117–132.
Krewski, D., Slovic, P., Bartlett, S., Flynn, J., & Mertz, C. K. (1995b). Health risk perception in Canada II: Worldviews, attitudes and opinions. *Human and Ecological Risk Assessment, 1*, 231–248.
Kruglanski, A. W. (2012). Lay epistemic theory. In P. A. M. Van Lange, A. W. Kruglanski, & E. T. Higgins (Eds.), *Handbook of theories of social psychology* (Vol. 1, pp. 201–223). Thousand Oaks, CA: Sage.
Kung, Y.-W., & Chen, S.-H. (2012). Perception of earthquake risk in Taiwan: Effects of gender and past earthquake experience. *Risk Analysis, 32*, 1535–1546.
Lai, J. C., & Tao, J. (2003). Perception of environmental hazards in Hong Kong Chinese. *Risk Analysis, 23*, 669–684.
Lazo, J. K., Kinnell, J. C., & Fisher, A. (2000). Expert and layperson perceptions of ecosystem risk. *Risk Analysis, 20*, 179–193.
Macias, T. (2016). Environmental risk perception among race and ethnic groups in the United States. *Ethnicities, 16*, 111–129.
Marshall, B. K., Picou, J. S., Formichella, C., & Nicholls, K. (2006). Environmental risk perceptions and the white male effect: Pollution concerns among deep-south coastal residents. *Journal of Applied Sociology/Sociological Practice, 23*(8), 1–49.
Marris, C., Langford, I., & O'Riordan, T. (1998). A quantitative test of the cultural theory of risk perceptions: Comparison with the psychometric paradigm. *Risk Analysis, 18*, 635–647.
Merkelsen, H. (2011). Institutionalized ignorance as a precondition for rational risk expertise. *Risk Analysis, 31*, 1083–1094.
Mertz, C. K., Slovic, P., & Purchase, F. H. (1998). Judgments of chemical risks: Comparisons among senior managers, toxicologists, and the public. *Risk Analysis, 18*, 391–404.
Morioka, R. (2014). Gender difference in the health risk perception of radiation from Fukushima in Japan: The role of hegemonic masculinity. *Social Science and Medicine, 107*, 105–112.

Olofsson, A., & Rashid, S. (2011). The white (male) effect and risk perception: Can equality make a difference? *Risk Analysis, 31*, 1016–1032.

Palmer, C. G. (1996). Risk perception: An empirical study of the relationship between worldview and the risk construct. *Risk Analysis, 16*, 717–723.

Palmer, C. G. (2003). Risk perception: Another look at the "white male" effect. *Health, Risk & Society, 5*, 71–83.

Peters, E., & Slovic, P. (1996). The role of affect and worldviews as orienting dispositions in the perception and acceptance of nuclear power. *Journal of Applied Social Psychology, 26*, 1427–1453.

Pilisuk, M., & Acredolo, C. (1988). Fear of technological hazards: One concern or many? *Social Behavior, 3*, 17–24.

Purvis-Roberts, K. L., Werner, C. A., & Frank, I. (2007). Perceived risks from radiation and nuclear testing near Semipalatinsk, Kazakhstan: A comparison between physicians, scientists, and the public. *Risk Analysis, 27*, 291–302.

Rippl, S. (2002). Cultural theory and risk perception: A proposal for a better measurement. *Journal of Risk Research, 5*, 147–165.

Rowe, G., & Wright, G. (2001). Differences in expert and lay judgments of risk: Myth or reality? *Risk Analysis, 21*, 341–356.

Satterfield, T. A., Mertz, C. K., & Slovic, P. (2004). Discrimination, vulnerability, and justice in the face of risk. *Risk Analysis, 24*, 115–129.

Savadori, L., Savio, S., Nicotra, E., Rumiati, R., Finucane, M., & Slovic, P. (2004). Expert and public perception of risk from biotechnology. *Risk Analysis, 24*, 1289–1299.

Savage, I. (1993). Demographic influences on risk perceptions. *Risk Analysis, 13*, 413–420.

Sherman, A. K., Minich, S. H., Langen, T. A., Skufca, J., & Wilke, A. (2016). Are college students' assessments of threat shaped by the dangers of their childhood environment? *Journal of Interpersonal Violence, 31*, 2006–2025.

Siegrist, M., Keller, C., Kastenholz, H., Frey, S., & Wiek, A. (2007). Laypeople's and experts' perception of nanotechnology hazards. *Risk Analysis, 27*, 59–69.

Sjöberg, L. (1997). Explaining risk perception: An empirical evaluation of cultural theory. *Risk Decision and Policy, 2*, 113–130.

Sjöberg, L. (1998a). Risk perception: Experts and the public. *European Psychologist, 3*, 1–12.

Sjöberg, L. (1998b). Worldviews, political attitudes, and risk perception. *Risk: Health, Safety, and Environment, 9*, 137–152.

Sjöberg, L. (2003). Distal factors in risk perception. *Journal of Risk Research, 6*, 187–211.

Slovic, P. (1987). Perception of risk. *Science, 236*, 280–285.

Slovic, P. (1999). Trust, emotion, sex, politics, and science: Surveying the risk-assessment battlefield. *Risk Analysis, 19*, 689–701.

Slovic, P. (2000). *The perception of risk*. London: Earthscan.

Slovic, P. (2007). "If I look at the mass, I will never act": Psychic numbing and genocide. *Judgment and Decision making, 2*, 79–95.

Slovic, P. (2010). *The feeling of risk*. London: Earthscan.

Slovic, P. (2016). Understanding perceived risk: 1978–2015. *Environment, 58*, 25–29.

Slovic, P., Finucane, M. L., Peters, E., & MacGregor, D. (2004). Risk as analysis and risk as feelings: Some thoughts about affect, reason, risk, and rationality. *Risk Analysis, 24*, 311–322.

Slovic, P., Fischhoff, B., & Lichtenstein, S. (1979). Rating the risks. *Environment, 21*, 14–20; 36-39.

Slovic, P., Fischhoff, B., & Lichtenstein, S. (1980). Facts and fears: Understanding perceived risks. In R. C. Schwing & W. A. Alberts Jr. (Eds.), *Societal risk assessment: How safe is safe enough?* (pp. 181–214). New York: Plenum Press.

Slovic, P., Fischhoff, B., & Lichtenstein, S. (1985). Characterizing perceived risk. In R. W. Kates, C. Hohenemser, & J. X. Kasperson (Eds.), *Perilous progress: Managing the hazards of technology* (pp. 91–125). Boulder: Westview Press.

Slovic, P., Malmfors, T., Krewski, D., Mertz, C. K., Neil, N., & Bartlett, S. (1995). Intuitive toxicology II. Expert and lay judgments of chemical risks in Canada. *Risk Analysis, 15*, 661–675.
Small, D. A., Loewenstein, G., & Slovic, P. (2007). Sympathy and callousness: The impact of deliberative thought on donations to identifiable and statistical victims. *Organizational Behavior and Human Decision Processes, 102*, 143–153.
Sokolowska, J., & Sleboda, P. (2015). The inverse relation between risks and benefits: The role of affect and expertise. *Risk Analysis, 35*, 1252–1267.
Tansey, J., & O'Riordan, T. (1999). Cultural theory and risk: A review. *Health, Risk, & Society, 1*, 71–90.
Thompson, M., Ellis, R., & Wildavsky, A. (1990). *Cultural theory*. Boulder and San Francisco: Westview Press.
Turiano, N. A., Chapman, B. P., Agrigoroaei, S., Infurna, F. J., & Lachman, M. (2014). Perceived control reduces mortality risk at low, not high, education levels. *Health Psychology, 33*, 883–890.
van der Linden, S. (2015). The social-psychological determinants of climate change risk perceptions: Towards a comprehensive model. *Journal of Environmental Psychology, 41*, 112–124.
Wachinger, G., Renn, O., Begg, C., & Kuhlicke, C. (2013). The risk perception paradox: Implications for governance and communication of natural hazards. *Risk Analysis, 33*, 1049–1065.
Wildavsky, A., & Dake, K. (1990). Theories of risk perception: Who fears what and why? *Daedalus, 119*, 41–60.
Xiao, C., & McCright, A. M. (2015). Gender differences in environmental concern: Revisiting the institutional trust hypothesis in the USA. *Environment and Behavior, 47*, 17–37.
Xie, X. F., Wang, M., & Xu, L. C. (2003). What risks are Chinese people concerned about? *Risk Analysis, 23*, 685–695.
Xue, W., Hine, D. W., Loi, N. M., Thorsteinsson, E. B., & Phillips, W. J. (2014). Cultural worldviews and environmental risk perceptions: A meta-analysis. *Journal of Environmental Psychology, 40*, 249–258.

Chapter 3
Differences in Risk Perception Between Hazards and Between Individuals

Vivianne H. M. Visschers and Michael Siegrist

Abstract How people think about a hazard often deviates from experts' assessment of its probability and severity. The aim of this chapter is to clarify how people perceive risks. We thereby focus on two important research lines: (1) research on the psychometric paradigm, which explains variations between the perceptions of different risks, and (2) research on factors that may determine an individual's perception of a risk (i.e., perceived benefits, trust, knowledge, affective associations, values, and fairness). Findings from studies about various risks (e.g., genetically modified organisms, food additives, and climate change) are reviewed in order to provide practical implications for risk management and communication. Overall, this chapter shows that the roles of benefit perception, trust, knowledge, affective associations, personal values, and fairness are not always straightforward; different factors appear involved in the perception of different hazards. We recommend practitioners, when they encounter a new hazard, to consult previous studies about similar hazards in order to identify the factors that describe the public's perception of the new hazard.

After a terrorist attack, people are often worried about the risk of becoming a victim of such an attack, and as a result, they overestimate its likelihood. On the other hand, people may underestimate the risks associated with certain lifestyles (e.g., smoking, consumption of alcohol). The probability of dying from a given hazard is thus often only poorly related to lay people's risk perception (Lichtenstein, Slovic, Fischhoff, Layman, & Combs, 1978). Various factors have been found to explain how people perceive a hazard, such as the risk's characteristics, individual differences, the setting, society, the information provided, and how the risk is mentally processed.

Two important research lines can be identified in the field of risk perception. First, many studies have been conducted into the variations between the perceptions

V. H. M. Visschers (✉)
School of Applied Psychology, University of Applied Sciences and Arts Northwestern Switzerland (FHNW), Olten, Switzerland
e-mail: vivianne.visschers@fhnw.ch

M. Siegrist
Institute for Environmental Decision Making, Consumer Behavior, ETH Zurich, Zurich, Switzerland

M. Raue et al. (eds.), *Psychological Perspectives on Risk and Risk Analysis*,
https://doi.org/10.1007/978-3-319-92478-6_3

of different risks (i.e., the psychometric paradigm). Second, some studies aim to reveal factors that can explain an individual's perception of a risk (e.g., the perceived benefits, trust, and knowledge). In the first line of research, the focus is upon explaining differences between the perceptions of different hazards, looking at the risks' qualitative characteristics. The second line of research seeks to explain why certain people perceive hazards in certain ways and why such perceptions may vary between individuals. We will discuss both research lines in this chapter. Moreover, we aim to review and summarize the findings from studies about various risks to reveal the practical implications for risk management and communication.

The Psychometric Paradigm of Risk Perception

If the number of fatalities caused by a hazard is only weakly associated to people's risk perception, which factors influence risk perception? In an attempt to answer this question, the psychometric paradigm was developed (Fischhoff, Slovic, Lichtenstein, Read, & Combs, 1978; Slovic, 1987). The goal of this approach was to unveil why people perceive certain hazards differently.

In studies utilizing the psychometric method for analyzing risk perception, participants rated a broad set of hazards on a large number of characteristics (Fischhoff et al., 1978), for example, the newness of the hazard (e.g., are the risks novel or familiar?), the severity of consequences (e.g., how likely is it that the consequences will be fatal?), and knowledge about the risk (e.g., to what extent are the risks known to science?). In most of the studies, between 9 and 15 rating scales were used. Furthermore, a very heterogeneous set of hazards was examined (e.g., hazards ranging from nuclear power to smoking). Analyses were mostly conducted on data that were aggregated across study participants. In other words, they did not use raw data, but rather mean values across participants, resulting in a rating scale × hazards matrix.

Results of the psychometric paradigm suggest that most of the qualitative risk characteristics that can be used for describing a hazard are correlated or even highly correlated. In the majority of the studies, the correlations between the rating scales could be explained by two principal components (Slovic, 1987). The first principal component was labeled as *dread risk*. The rating scales of perceived lack of control, dread potential, and fatal consequences were highly correlated with this principal component. The second principal component was labeled as *unknown risk*. The rating scales of perceived newness, perceived scientific knowledge, and delay of the effects were highly correlated with this second component. The two factors, dread risk and unknown risk, can explain people's perceived risks associated with a hazard very well. In a *cognitive map*—the main outcome of the psychometric paradigm and one of the icons of risk perception research—the hazards are located in the space between the two principal components dread risk and unknown risk according to people's ratings on these two dimensions. This map is thus a visual representation of lay people's risk perception and the differences between the perceptions of different hazards.

The psychometric paradigm has been used to study risk perception in various countries, such as Norway (Teigen, Brun, & Slovic, 1988), Italy (Savadori, Rumiati, & Bonini, 1998), France (Karpowicz-Lazreg & Mullet, 1993), Switzerland (Siegrist, Keller, & Kiers, 2005), and China (Lai & Tao, 2003). Even though cross-cultural differences have been observed, the two-dimensional solution was replicated in most studies. There are some differences in the cognitive map of people's risk perception across the countries, but similarities among the countries outweigh the dissimilarities.

The psychometric paradigm helps to better understand why lay people are concerned about some hazards, but not about others. Nuclear power and gene technology are perceived as dreadful and unknown hazards. Therefore, they receive high risk ratings among lay people. Hazards such as alcoholic beverages or swimming are perceived as familiar and non-dreadful. As a consequence, these hazards are perceived as being not very risky.

As mentioned above, most studies in the tradition of the psychometric paradigm analyzed aggregated data (i.e., across participants), which would be justified if there were no individual differences regarding risk perception. It has been shown, however, that there are substantial differences across individuals when it comes to risk perception (Siegrist et al., 2005; Siegrist, Keller, & Kiers, 2006). Therefore, it is important to better understand the factors that explain individual differences in the perception of a hazard in order to predict people's decision making. These are discussed next.

Factors Related to Risk Perception

For the decision making practice (e.g., for policy-makers), it is more relevant to know which individual factors predict lay people's acceptance and choices regarding risks and whether particular factors are more important in some groups than in others (e.g., local residents vs. the general population). Research in this area has, in particular, focused on new and controversial technologies in order to find effective ways to communicate about them with lay people (e.g., nuclear power, carbon capture and storage [CCS], genetically modified [GM] organisms, and mobile communication technologies). A review of the literature revealed that various factors have been investigated in relation to acceptance or decision making, such as perceived voluntariness and perceived responsibility (Harding & Eiser, 1984) or personal norms (de Groot & Steg, 2010). The factors that have been investigated most thoroughly in this respect were perceived benefits, knowledge, trust, affective associations, personal values, and fairness. These will therefore be discussed in detail below.

Perceived Benefits

Man-made hazards are always coupled with some kind of benefits; there would otherwise be no reason to introduce the hazard. Nuclear power has been introduced because it is a relatively cheap and efficient way to produce electricity despite its risk of radiation. GM crops may, for example, be better resistant to pests, although they may invade in the ecosystem and damage it unintentionally (Wolfenbarger & Phifer, 2000). Artificial sweeteners are low in calories, although some of them have been associated with carcinogenic risks (EFSA, 2006). But even natural hazards, such as flooding and earthquakes, are indirectly related to benefits: we encounter them because they occur in situations that have attractive characteristics. The river delta that is part of the Netherlands, for example, drew many people to live there because it was an excellent place for trading, despite the fact that the area is vulnerable to flooding. In other words, when examining people's perception of a risk, their perception of its benefits should also be taken into account.

Research examining the association between perceived risks and perceived benefits predominantly found a negative relationship: the more benefits that are associated with a hazard, the lower its risks are considered to be (de Groot, Steg, & Poortinga, 2013; Finucane, Alhakami, Slovic, & Johnson, 2000; Harding & Eiser, 1984; Siegrist, Cousin, Kastenholz, & Wiek, 2007; Visschers & Siegrist, 2013). This consistent relationship between risk perception and benefit perception has been shown for a wide range of hazards, such as nuclear power, nanotechnology food products, artificial sweeteners, and smoking.

The perceived benefits of a hazard have been shown to be a stronger predictor of people's acceptance of this hazard than its perceived risks. This has, for example, been found in the case of GMO applications (Siegrist, 2000), nanotechnology foods (Siegrist et al., 2007), nuclear power (Visschers, Keller, & Siegrist, 2011), and CCS (Wallquist, Visschers, Dohle, & Siegrist, 2012). Perceived benefits are probably more important in these cases because the public generally agrees about the hazards' risks, but it varies about the perceived benefits. The opposite effect has been found in the case of antimicrobial usage in pig farming (Visschers et al., 2015) and acceptance of artificial sweeteners and colors (Bearth, Cousin, & Siegrist, 2014a). Here, perceived risks and concerns were found to be more important in explaining people's acceptance of the hazards than their perceived benefits. This may be because all people agreed about the benefits of these two hazards but not so much about their risks. Pig farmers generally believed that antimicrobials have large benefits for their animals (Visschers et al., 2015) and consumers generally did not seem to acknowledge the health benefits of food additives (Bearth et al., 2014a).

A longitudinal survey on the perceived risks and benefits of biotechnology applications additionally showed that both perceived risks and benefits remained stable within people over time. Moreover, perceived benefits displayed a higher stability than perceived risks (Connor & Siegrist, 2016). In other words, people did not change their opinion on the benefits of these applications, whereas they may have slightly updated their perception of the risks over time due to, for example, newly acquired knowledge. Similarly, the perceived benefits of nuclear power remained stable over time in a Swiss study, despite the occurrence of a salient event that highlighted its risks (i.e., the nuclear accident in Fukushima; Visschers & Siegrist, 2013). The nuclear accident did not change the relationship between the perceived benefits and acceptance of nuclear power nor the relationship between the perceived risks and acceptance. People's perception of nuclear power's benefits remained a stronger predictor of acceptance than their perception of its risks.

Knowledge

People need to understand the risks and benefits associated with a hazard to be able to evaluate and make an informed decision about them. Some authors even assumed that more knowledge leads to a better understanding of the negligible risks and the vast benefits, and thus to more support for hazardous technologies and events (Evans & Durant, 1995), so that various studies investigated the relationship between knowledge about a hazard and its perception (see Davidson & Freudenburg, 1996; Evans & Durant, 1995; Satterfield, Kandlikar, Beaudrie, Conti, & Herr Harthorn, 2009; Siegrist & Cvetkovich, 2000). The results of these studies were however unclear; some found a positive relationship between knowledge and attitude toward the hazard, some found a negative relationship, and others could not identify a relationship.

There are three reasons that may explain these mixed findings. *First*, the extent to which a hazard challenges moral values determines the relation between knowledge and attitudes (Evans & Durant, 1995). More knowledge has been found to be associated with more support for issues that are generally approved of and do not cause a moral dilemma (e.g., searching a cure for cancer), whereas a negative relation was found for technologies that have a moral component to them (e.g., creating human embryos for medical purposes). Hence, in the case of morally challenging hazards, more knowledge may result in a more critical view.

A *second* reason may be that knowledge has been assessed in different ways. In some studies, respondents were asked to indicate how much they believed they knew about the hazard (i.e., subjective knowledge). In others, the amount of accurate information was measured (i.e., objective knowledge). Subjective knowledge has been found to be mostly positively related to positive attitudes toward a hazard and to its acceptance, such as in the areas of GM foods (House et al., 2005), mobile phone communication (Cousin & Siegrist, 2010), and foodborne illnesses (Bearth, Cousin, & Siegrist, 2014b). On the other hand, the findings about the relationship between objective knowledge and attitudes toward a hazard were mixed. For example, in the case of mobile communication, more knowledge about how base stations interact with human activities was associated with somewhat higher perceived risks of cell phones but with lower perceived risks of base stations (Cousin & Siegrist, 2010). More knowledge about gene technology slightly decreased the perceived risks of gene technologies, whereas more general biological knowledge increased the perceived risks (Connor & Siegrist, 2010).

In the abovementioned studies in which objective knowledge was found to be related to risk perception, the assessed objective knowledge was relevant for the evaluation of the hazard, which leads to a *third* reason for the mixed results in this area of research. Relevant knowledge implies that it should clarify the risk's causes and its consequences. Indeed, in the case of CCS, having more concrete knowledge about whether and how CO_2 can leak after storage increased the perceived risks, whereas more knowledge about the properties of CO_2 was associated with a lower risk perception of CCS (L'Orange Seigo, Arvai, Dohle, & Siegrist, 2014; Wallquist, Visschers, & Siegrist, 2010). Concrete knowledge about the consequences and causes of climate change increased concern about this hazard (Shi, Visschers, & Siegrist, 2015; Tobler, Visschers, & Siegrist, 2012), while knowledge about the characteristics of greenhouse gases and general science knowledge slightly reduced concern (Kahan et al., 2012). Similarly, more knowledge about the consequences of foodborne illnesses was linked to higher perceived risk and the severity of contracting a foodborne illness (Bearth et al., 2014b).

Hence, increasing people's knowledge through communication and education is most likely to affect their perception of the hazard, whereby the direction of the change depends on the kind of knowledge that is assessed (see the example above about CCS). If the attained knowledge is relevant to evaluate the hazard, this will affect acceptance or decision making. However, in the absence of knowledge, the following two factors have been suggested to explain the perception and acceptance of a hazard: trust and affect.

Trust

When people do not have the capacities or abilities to evaluate and manage a hazard themselves, they rely on other actors to provide information about the hazard's severity and probability and to mitigate the risk effectively. Relevant actors are the producers of the hazard (e.g., the food packaging industry in the case of nanotechnology foods and the nuclear plant operators in the case of nuclear power), regulating and controlling organizations (e.g., governmental organizations), scientists working in the hazard's field, and independent nongovernmental organizations. In order to rely on other actors to manage a hazard, people have to trust them. That is, they have to believe that the actors consider the same values to be as important as they do (i.e., value similarity; Earle & Cvetkovich, 1995). The stronger people believed that responsible actors in the areas of GM food, pesticides, nuclear power, and artificial sweeteners held the same important values, goals, opinions, and intentions as they did, the more they trusted these actors to deal with the respective hazards in an appropriate way (Poortinga & Pidgeon, 2006; Siegrist, Cvetkovich, & Roth, 2000).

The findings from surveys confirm that people particularly rely on trust to judge a hazard when they have little knowledge about that hazard (Siegrist & Cvetkovich, 2000). Trust in stakeholders is then used to evaluate the hazard's risks and benefits. In other words, people use their trust evaluation—as well as their value evaluations—as a heuristic. Because trust in stakeholders is based on value similarity and values are such fundamental principles that they hardly change within individuals, the relationship of trust with perceived risks and benefits should remain stable over time. This has indeed been found in the case of nuclear power: Swiss people still relied on their trust in nuclear power operators to evaluate the risks and perceived benefits of nuclear power after the nuclear accident in Fukushima (Visschers & Siegrist, 2013). Some may think that this is a remarkable finding since the nuclear accident in Fukushima could have made the public more knowledgeable about the stakeholders' actual performances so that evaluating the stakeholders' value similarity and trust was no longer necessary to estimate the risks and benefits of this technology.

Trust in stakeholders not only influences the perceived risks and benefits of a hazard but also its acceptance. Various studies have shown that perceived risks and perceived benefits partly or fully mediate the relationship between trust and acceptance of, for example, a risky technology. That is, trust in the technology's stakeholders indirectly affects their acceptance, through risk perception and benefit perception. The indirect effect of trust on acceptance, through risk and benefit perception, has been found for nuclear power (Visschers et al., 2011; Whitfield, Rosa, Dan, & Dietz, 2009), GM applications (Connor & Siegrist, 2010; Siegrist, 2000), nanotechnology food products (Siegrist et al., 2007), and food additives (Bearth et al., 2014a). The picture is not so clear in the case of CCS: trust appeared to be related to the perceived benefits of CCS but hardly to the perceived risks (L'Orange Seigo et al., 2014; Wallquist et al., 2012). Wallquist et al. (2012) suggested that trust may have been of little importance to lay people in evaluating the risks and benefits of CCS at that time because they did not know yet whether the stakeholders' values were similar to theirs regarding CCS.

Affective Associations

In addition to lay people's reliance on trust, they have also been found to rely on affect to evaluate the perceived risks and benefits of a hazard. The affect heuristic refers to the mental shortcut in which people rely on the positive or negative valence associated with a hazard to judge its benefits and risks (Finucane et al., 2000). If positive feelings overrule, then people will associate the hazard with high benefits and low risks and vice versa if negative feelings overrule. This also explains why perceived risks and benefits are negatively related for most hazards.

As with trust, affect was found to be an indirect predictor of the acceptance of a hazard; the affect–acceptance relationship is mediated by risk and benefit perceptions (Siegrist et al., 2007; Visschers et al., 2011). Both affect and trust are based on holistic evaluations and have been found to be related (Dohle, Keller, & Siegrist, 2010). The two however have complementary effects on risk and benefit perception (Siegrist et al., 2007; Visschers et al., 2011): even if people's affective feelings are taken into account to predict their perceived risks and benefits, considering their trust in stakeholders can improve the prediction of these two perceptions. Trust in stakeholders and affect therefore seem to have different functions in the perception of hazards and should both be examined to explain the public's perception of a hazard.

People seem to be more concerned about man-made (i.e., anthropogenic) catastrophes compared with natural disasters (Baum, Fleming, & Davidson, 1983). Recent experiments demonstrated that people's general affective feeling (i.e., an instantaneous negative-positive gut feeling or affective primacy; see Zajonc, 1980) induced by the hazard may cause this difference in perception: the same negative outcome (e.g., number of birds killed by an oil spill) was associated more strongly with negative affect when caused by humans than when caused by nature (Siegrist & Sütterlin, 2014). The instantaneous gut feeling evoked by the respective hazard fully mediated the relation between type of cause and perceived risk: affect thus explained why people are more concerned about human-caused risks compared with nature-caused risks. People may be less negative about natural hazards because naturalness is linked to better quality and safety (Li & Chapman, 2012; Rozin et al., 2004). Additionally, man-made hazards may evoke higher levels of negative effect, because they can be controlled by some people (i.e., the belief that if no one had invented the technology, we would not have to experience its risks), whereas there is little control over natural hazards.

A method to investigate people's affective reaction to a hazard is to explore their affective associations with this issue. First, individuals are asked which association comes spontaneously to their mind when thinking of a hazard and to indicate how positive or negative this association is to them (Szalay & Deese, 1978). This procedure can be repeated for three or more times to calculate an average affect rating. For example, associations and affect ratings have been related to the acceptance of nuclear waste depositories (Slovic, Flynn, & Layman, 1991), to the acceptance and trust related to nuclear power plants (Keller, Visschers, & Siegrist, 2012; Peters & Slovic, 1996), to attitudes toward agricultural biotechnology and willingness to choose a GM food (Connor & Siegrist, 2011), and to the perceived risks of mobile phone base stations (Dohle, Keller, & Siegrist, 2012b).

Moreover, after a content analysis of the elicited images in the affective association method, a mental map can be formed that indicates the risks and benefits that people associate with the hazard, which is useful for communication purposes. In the case of nuclear power, we showed that *male proponents* of replacing nuclear power plants strongly associated nuclear power with its positive consequences and with the need for this energy source, whereas *male opponents* thought about nuclear waste and health risks and *female opponents* reported associations with accidents and military use of nuclear technologies (Keller, Visschers, & Siegrist, 2012). In a longitudinal survey, respondents were asked to rate an unfamiliar hazard (e.g., food irradiation [relatively unknown in 2004]) on its riskiness and to mention a hazard that reminded them of this unknown risk (some people, e.g., associated food irradiation with genetically modified food). They then rated their associated hazard on its riskiness two weeks later. Participants' perceptions of the unknown hazard appeared to significantly relate to the perceptions of their associated hazards (Visschers, Meertens, Passchier, & de Vries, 2007). Risk communication is therefore more effective when messages are tailored to the associations per consumer group than when mass communication is used. The important associations per consumer group can be identified through interviews and surveys among samples of the population.

Few researchers focused on specific emotions rather than affect, arguing that specific emotions may have differential influences on risk and benefit perception and thus on the acceptance of a hazard or behavioral responses (Keller et al., 2012; Lerner & Keltner, 2001). The negative emotions fear and anger have been related to the perception of hazards. Fear is experienced when one encounters an unpleasant situation that is accompanied with uncertainty (Lerner & Keltner, 2001). Fear, therefore, results in pessimistic perceptions of hazards and in wanting to avoid or escape the hazard. Anger is evoked when a bad situation can be blamed on someone else and results in approach behavior, optimistic evaluations of hazards, and risk seeking. Research by Böhm (2003) showed that people rated global human-caused hazards (e.g., chemical dumps) to be high on moral emotions, such as anger and contempt, whereas natural hazards (e.g., earthquakes) were rated low on moral emotions and higher on emotions related to future consequences, or so-called prospective consequential emotions, such as fear and hopelessness. Human-caused creeping hazards (i.e., slowly evolving, unobserved hazards, such as nuclear power and species extinction) were strongly associated with prospective consequential emotions but also with emotions related to retrospective consequences, such as regret and sadness. Moreover, both types of consequential emotions were associated with help and prevention responses, whereas ethical emotions induced aggressive and retaliation responses (Böhm & Pfister, 2000). Similarly, anger was found to reduce the perceived risks, benefits, and acceptance of a hazard, whereas fear was mainly associated with higher perceived risks (Dohle, Keller, & Siegrist, 2012a; L'Orange Seigo et al., 2014).

Positive emotions, such as pride and satisfaction, may also be relevant for certain types of hazards. Both positive and negative emotions were found to be related—in opposite directions—to the acceptance of different energy resources (i.e., hydro, nuclear, gas-fired, solar, and wind power; Visschers & Siegrist, 2014). Positive emotions appeared to be even more strongly linked to the acceptance of wind power than to the acceptance of the other energy resources, whereas negative emotions seemed to reduce the acceptance of solar power more than of the other energy resources.

Affect and emotions play an important role in how people perceive and to what extent they accept a hazard (see also Tompkins et al., Chap. 5). Although people could use their knowledge to evaluate a hazard, they were still found to rely on some emotions to estimate its risks and benefits (L'Orange Seigo et al., 2014). In other words, despite people's ability to cognitively deliberate about a hazard, this did not silence their instantaneous affective responses (see, e.g., Slovic, Finucane, Peters, & MacGregor, 2004; Strack & Deutsch, 2004).

People thus seem to use the affect that they experience when encountering a hazard as a heuristic. Their reliance on such simple heuristics may cause biased decisions. It has been shown, for example, that participants evaluated the same number of fatalities to be more acceptable in the case of solar power compared with nuclear power because the former is associated with positive affect whereas the latter evokes negative affect (Siegrist & Sütterlin, 2014). Identical negative outcomes were evaluated differently depending on the cause of the event (the installation of solar panels vs. the construction of a nuclear power plant). Such a biased perception of fatalities is a challenge for structured decision making approaches that have been proposed for improving people's decisions (Arvai & Post, 2012). People's reliance on the affect heuristic is also a challenge for the acceptance of cost-benefit analyses because equally negative outcomes are differently evaluated depending on the cause.

Values

Values are defined as guiding principles of decisions and behaviors (Schwartz, 1992). They thus serve as foundations for our attitudes, beliefs, intentions, and, in the end, behaviors. In the cultural theory of risk perception (Douglas & Wildavsky, 1982) and in its successor, cultural cognition theory (Kahan, Braman, Gastil, Slovic, & Mertz, 2007), individual and societal differences in risk perception are explained by differences in underlying cultural values. The latter theory defines four worldviews: hierarchy vs. communitarianism (i.e., the importance of the group) and individualism vs. egalitarianism (i.e., equality).

Values affect people's perception of a hazard in the following way: if a hazard's characteristics highlight important values in people, they will acknowledge them. People with strong communitarian and egalitarian values were, for example, found to be more worried than people with strong hierarchical and individualistic values about gun possession, environmental pollution, and climate change (Kahan et al., 2007; Kahan et al., 2012; Shi et al., 2015) because these hazards can have large negative consequences on society as a whole and thus oppose egalitarian or altruistic values. On the other hand, hierarchical people perceived more risks of having a voluntary abortion (Kahan et al., 2007) and of vaccinating teenage girls against the human papillomavirus (HPV) than egalitarian people (Kahan, Braman, Cohen, Gastil, & Slovic, 2010) because these hazards directly or indirectly defy traditional gender norms and roles, which are part of hierarchical values.

Using a different value categorization, similar results were found for nuclear power: the more people valued hierarchy, fatalism, and tradition, as well as individualism and egoism, the more support they showed for nuclear power, whereas higher egalitarianism, altruism, and biospherism (i.e., the importance of nature and the environment) were related to less support for this energy source (de Groot et al., 2013; Peters & Slovic, 1996; Whitfield et al., 2009). Similarly, environmental values were negatively associated with the acceptance of nuclear power and positively associated with solar, wind, and hydropower (Visschers & Siegrist, 2014), whereas energy security values were positively related to nuclear power and negatively related to renewable energy resources.

Values do not seem to be as important for the perception of some hazards as they are for other hazards. That is, the impact of values on the perception of nuclear power and of other energy resources seems to be lower (e.g., Peters and Slovic, 1996; Visschers & Siegrist, 2014) than on the perception of hazards such as climate change (Kahan et al., 2012; Shi et al., 2015). This may be because climate change is a more abstract risk than energy technologies or because a hazard such as climate change confirms or challenges a person's important values (see Baron & Spranca, 1997). For example, believing that climate change forms a serious risk is strongly related to intentions to mitigate climate change (Shi et al., 2015). This belief and these intentions require an appreciation of altruistic initiatives and ignoring self-enhancement, because climate change concern requires concern about other people, living in vulnerable areas but also future generations. Hydropower, on the other hand, seems acceptable for people with differing value orientations: it is highly acceptable for people with strong egoistic values because it is a secure energy source, and at the same time, it is in line with high biospheric and altruistic values because it is a climate-friendly source.

Fairness

A final factor that can explain the perception and acceptance of a hazard is perceived fairness. Fairness can concern various issues. First, people can evaluate to what extent a hazard's consequences are equally distributed over different people and regions (i.e., outcome or distributional fairness; Tyler, 2000). Second, they can judge the fairness of the decision procedure around the hazardous activity—the extent to which people are allowed to have a voice and contribute during this process (i.e., procedural fairness; Tyler, 2000). People who reported to have experienced a fair process have been found to show more acceptance of a decision, which is also called the fair process effect (Van den Bos, 2005). Third, interpersonal fairness refers to the perception that the stakeholders are trustworthy and respect the public's views (Besley, 2010). Last, there is informational fairness or justice, which is people's belief that they are well informed. Procedural, interpersonal, and informational justice all concern communication during the decision process.

Some scholars argued that procedural and outcome fairness only matter among people to whom the hazard is not morally important (Skitka, 2002). For example, those who carry a moral mandate against nuclear power will not consider the fairness of the decision procedure or of the decision outcome in their acceptance of the decision; they will only focus on their personal attitudes and perceptions of the hazard. Survey research showed that procedural and outcome fairness can increase people's acceptance of, for example, an experiment in which GM plants are tested in the field, but also of the decision to rebuild nuclear power plants (Besley, 2012;

Siegrist, Connor, & Keller, 2012; Visschers & Siegrist, 2012). This increase in acceptance however depends only to a small extent on people's moral mandate. Thus, contrary to Skitka's (2002) assumptions, fairness information seems to affect the acceptance of a hazard among all people, independent of the hazard's personal importance. Moreover, a fair decision procedure can increase the acceptance of a hazard, despite the fact that people are concerned about its risks (Tyler, 2000). This is probably because risk perception is relatively stable over time (Connor & Siegrist, 2016; Siegrist & Visschers, 2013; Verplanken, 1989). It therefore seems highly worthwhile to establish a fair and participatory decision procedure around the introduction of a hazard that affects the public.

Implications for Practice

What do these findings mean for practice? How should risks be handled in practice when considering the general public? We reviewed the findings around the psychometric paradigm of risk perception and around six factors (i.e., perceived benefits, knowledge, trust, affect, human values, and fairness) that can be taken into account when examining the public's perception of a hazard and may therefore be worthwhile to consider when communicating with the public.

Overall, our review revealed that the roles of these six factors are not always straightforward; different factors appeared involved in the perception of different hazards. For example, the perceived benefits of a hazard seemed more influential on people's acceptance of different energy sources than the perceived risks, but the former was less relevant for the acceptance of food additives. Also, trust in stakeholders was found to determine people's acceptance of various energy sources but not that of CCS. Value orientations seem worth considering when looking at people's perception of climate change but less when explaining people's acceptance of energy sources.

More precisely, we would make the following nine recommendations to practitioners in risk management and communication:

1. A method such as the psychometric paradigm can be useful for predicting the perceptions of a risk in a large group of individuals (i.e., a population) and comparing people's perceptions of different risks. Based on the cognitive map, which represents the locations of various hazards within the most important perception components (e.g., its dreadness and to what extent it is known), communicators can identify appropriate, comparable risks, which may facilitate the public's understanding of the seriousness and probability of a new hazard (Bostrom, 2008; Keller, Siegrist, & Visschers, 2009; Roth, Morgan, Fischhoff, Lave, & Bostrom, 1990; Slovic, Kraus, & Covello, 1990). One caveat of the psychometric paradigm, however, is that most studies that use this method analyze aggregated data, rather than individual cases. Consequently, the findings do not reveal

any variations in perceptions among different people, despite the fact that these variations are particularly interesting for communication purposes.

2. When examining the public's acceptance of a hazard, it is important to uncover the ways in which the public perceives the hazard's benefits, as well as its perceived risks. Indeed, the perceived benefits appear to be a more important predictor of people's acceptance of most hazards than the perceived risks. Moreover, the perceived benefits seem to remain stable across individuals, both over time and in the face of new, interfering events.
3. People's knowledge about hazards should be considered when explaining their perceptions and acceptance of a risk, but only if this knowledge is assessed objectively, using a multidimensional scale that contains concrete and relevant items, rather than using, for example, a general science knowledge scale. To find out what kind of knowledge the public needs to possess to be able to make an informed decision about a risk, the mental models approach can be applied (Morgan, Fischhoff, Bostrom, & Atman, 2002). With this method, experts and lay people are interviewed about a hazard so that their cognitive maps of the hazard can be drawn. A comparison of the two types of maps—the expert map and the lay map—reveals what lay people know correctly, what they believe falsely, and what knowledge gaps they have about the hazard. These areas can then be addressed in risk communication, thus facilitating the making of an informed decision.
4. Putting effort into being, becoming, or finding trustworthy stakeholders that are involved in managing and in communicating about the risk at hand is extremely important, as people's trust in stakeholders is a direct predictor of their perceptions of a risk, as well as an indirect predictor of their acceptance of that risk. The more a stakeholder can exhibit and emphasize values that are similar to those of an individual, the more an individual will evaluate the stakeholder as being trustworthy.
5. Similarly, spontaneous affective associations are important to consider when examining people's perceptions and acceptance of a risk. As these gut feelings are based on fundamental reactions, they are difficult to change. It is, however, still important to examine the causes of affective associations (e.g., human-made vs. natural causes) because different causes can lead to different emotions, which explains why they result in different risk perceptions and varied behavioral responses to deal with the risk.
6. Although lay people often use their trust in stakeholders and their affective associations with a hazard as heuristics in their perceptions of the risks and benefits of a hazard, affect and trust still have independent relations with risk and benefit perception. For example, even if trust in the relevant stakeholders is high, this will not result in high benefit perception and low risk perception, if the risk induces a strong negative affective association. Therefore, researchers should always consider both affect and trust when examining the public's perception and acceptance of a hazard.
7. An individual's values are important underlying determinants of the perceptions and acceptance of a risk through, for example, trust. These values are, however,

difficult to change because they are based on fundamental principles. Nevertheless, research has shown that other factors, such as one's knowledge about the hazard, still influence people's perceptions of a hazard, despite the presence of values that may be in conflict with this knowledge. Hence, although some people may hold values that hinder the acknowledgment of a hazard (e.g., in relation to climate change), it is still worthwhile informing and educating them about the hazard, as this knowledge acquisition will lead to greater concern about the risk and—eventually—to the acceptance of risk mitigation efforts.

8. Based on the fairness effect (i.e., the finding that the experience of fairness results in greater acceptance of decisions or measures), we recommend that risk managers should consider the following suggestions when introducing possibly hazardous technologies to lay people: (1) develop and follow a fair decision procedure, making clear how, when, and where the risky technology will be initiated (e.g., allowing for participatory decision making so that the public can have a voice); (2) inform the public in a timely and honest fashion; (3) assure that the stakeholders are perceived as trustworthy (i.e., that they have similar values as the public); and (4) attempt to distribute the costs and benefits of the hazardous technology evenly across the population and, possibly, over other stakeholders.
9. Last but not least, because the perceptions and acceptance of a hazard differ according to the type of hazard in question and the feelings of individuals or groups, tailored communication methods should be used to inform lay people about specific hazards. This means that the information provided ought to fit with the mental model of the individual or particular group (i.e., the knowledge, beliefs, attitudes, and current behaviors of the person/group; see Morgan et al. 2002). The more the message is tailored to the mental map of an individual, the more likely it is that the individual will feel that he/she is being addressed personally and will therefore process the offered information carefully and act accordingly (Kreuter, Farrell, Olevitch, & Brennan, 2012; Kreuter & Wray, 2003). Information tailoring is very labor-intensive, however, because individuals have to be interviewed or surveyed in order for their mental models to be identified, and then individual messages need to be created, which require careful consideration.

These are just a few recommendations that may be worth considering in risk management and communication practices; it would be incorrect to consider the six factors (i.e., perceived benefits, knowledge, trust in stakeholders, affective associations, values, and fairness) to form one absolute framework that explains people's perceptions and acceptance of all hazards. The consideration of all of these factors will not lead automatically to successful risk management. We would like to suggest, however, that our recommendations should form part of a library that can be consulted when managing a hazard in a public context. The acceptance of certain hazards can be best explained by looking at people's trust, perceived benefits, and perceived risks, whereas others are better clarified by looking at people's values, knowledge, and perceptions of risk. When encountering a new hazard in practice, first of all, practitioners should consult previous studies about similar hazards in order to identify the factors that might assist with understanding the public's perception of the new hazard.

References

Arvai, J., & Post, K. (2012). Risk management in a developing country context: Improving decisions about point-of-use water treatment among the rural poor in Africa. *Risk Analysis, 32*, 67–80.

Baron, J., & Spranca, M. (1997). Protected values. *Organizational Behavior and Human Decision Processes, 70*, 1–16.

Baum, A., Fleming, R., & Davidson, L. M. (1983). Natural disaster and technological catastrophe. *Environment and Behavior, 15*, 333–354.

Bearth, A., Cousin, M.-E., & Siegrist, M. (2014a). The consumer's perception of artificial food additives: Influences on acceptance, risk and benefit perceptions. *Food Quality and Preference, 38*, 14–23.

Bearth, A., Cousin, M.-E., & Siegrist, M. (2014b). Poultry consumers' behaviour, risk perception and knowledge related to campylobacteriosis and domestic food safety. *Food Control, 44*, 166–176.

Besley, J. C. (2010). Public engagement and the impact of fairness perceptions on decision favorability and acceptance. *Science Communication, 32*, 256–280.

Besley, J. C. (2012). Does fairness matter in the context of anger about nuclear energy decision making? *Risk Analysis, 32*, 25–38.

Böhm, G. (2003). Emotional reactions to environmental risks: Consequentialist versus ethical evaluation. *Journal of Environmental Psychology, 23*, 199–212.

Böhm, G., & Pfister, H. R. (2000). Action tendencies and characteristics of environmental risks. *Acta Psychologica, 104*, 317–337.

Bostrom, A. (2008). Lead is like mercury: Risk comparisons, analogies and mental models. *Journal of Risk Research, 11*, 99–117.

Connor, M., & Siegrist, M. (2010). Factors influencing people's acceptance of gene technology: The role of knowledge, health expectations, naturalness, and social trust. *Science Communication, 32*, 514–538.

Connor, M., & Siegrist, M. (2011). The power of association: Its impact on willingness to buy GM food. *Human and Ecological Risk Assessment, 17*, 1142–1155.

Connor, M., & Siegrist, M. (2016). The stability of risk and benefit perceptions: A longitudinal study assessing the perception of biotechnology. *Journal of Risk Research, 19*, 461–475.

Cousin, M.-E., & Siegrist, M. (2010). The public's knowledge of mobile communication and its influence on base station siting preferences. *Health, Risk & Society, 12*, 231–250.

Davidson, R. J., & Freudenburg, W. R. (1996). Gender and environmental risk concerns: A review and analysis of available research. *Environment and Behavior, 28*, 302–339.

de Groot, J. I. M., Steg, L., & Poortinga, W. (2013). Values, perceived risks and benefits, and acceptability of nuclear energy. *Risk Analysis, 33*, 307–317.

de Groot, J. I. M., & Steg, L. (2010). Morality and nuclear energy: Perceptions of risks and benefits, personal norms, and willingness to take action related to nuclear energy. *Risk Analysis, 30*, 1363–1373.

Dohle, S., Keller, C., & Siegrist, M. (2010). Examining the relationship between affect and implicit associations: Implications for risk perception. *Risk Analysis, 30*, 1116–1128.

Dohle, S., Keller, C., & Siegrist, M. (2012a). Fear and anger: Antecedents and consequences of emotional responses to mobile communication. *Journal of Risk Research, 15*, 435–446.

Dohle, S., Keller, C., & Siegrist, M. (2012b). Mobile communication in the public mind: Insights from free associations related to mobile phone base stations. *Human and Ecological Risk Assessment, 18*, 649–668.

Douglas, M., & Wildavsky, A. (1982). *Risk and culture: An essay on the selection of technical and environmental dangers*. Berkeley, CA: University of California Press.

Earle, T. C., & Cvetkovich, G. (1995). *Social trust: Toward a cosmopolitan society*. Westport, CT: Praeger.

EFSA (European Food and Safety Authority). (2006). Opinion of the scientific panel on food additives, flavourings, processing aids and materials in contact with food (AFC) related to a new long-term carcinogenicity study on aspartame. *The EFSA Journal, 356*, 1–44.
Evans, G., & Durant, J. (1995). The relationship between knowledge and attitudes in the public understanding of science in Britain. *Public Understanding of Science, 4*, 57–74.
Finucane, M. L., Alhakami, A., Slovic, P., & Johnson, S. M. (2000). The affect heuristic in judgments of risks and benefits. *Journal of Behavioral Decision Making, 13*, 1–17.
Fischhoff, B., Slovic, P., Lichtenstein, S., Read, S., & Combs, B. (1978). How safe is safe enough? A psychometric study of attitudes towards technological risks and benefits. *Policy Sciences, 9*, 127–152.
Harding, C. M., & Eiser, J. R. (1984). Characterising the perceived risks and benefits of some health issues. *Risk Analysis, 4*, 131–141.
House, L., Lusk, J., Jaeger, S., Traill, W. B., Moore, M., Valli, C., … Yee, W. M. (2005). Objective and subjective knowledge: Impacts on consumer demand for genetically modified foods in the United States and the European Union. *AgBioforum, 7*, 113–123.
Kahan, D. M., Braman, D., Cohen, G. L., Gastil, J., & Slovic, P. (2010). Who fears the HPV vaccine, who doesn't, and why? An experimental study of the mechanisms of cultural cognition. *Law and Human Behavior, 34*, 501–516.
Kahan, D. M., Braman, D., Gastil, J., Slovic, P., & Mertz, C. K. (2007). Culture and identity-protective cognition: Explaining the white-male effect in risk perception. *Journal of Empirical Legal Studies, 4*, 465–505.
Kahan, D. M., Peters, E., Wittlin, M., Slovic, P., Ouellette, L. L., Braman, D., & Mandel, G. (2012). The polarizing impact of science literacy and numeracy on perceived climate change risks. *Nature Climate Change, 2*, 732–735.
Karpowicz-Lazreg, C., & Mullet, E. (1993). Societal risk as seen by the French public. *Risk Analysis, 13*, 253–258.
Keller, C., Bostrom, A., Kuttschreuter, M., Savadori, L., Spence, A., & White, M. (2012). Bringing appraisal theory to environmental risk perception: A review of conceptual approaches of the past 40 years and suggestions for future research. *Journal of Risk Research, 15*, 237–256.
Keller, C., Siegrist, M., & Visschers, V. (2009). Effect of risk ladder format on risk perception in high- and low-numerate individuals. *Risk Analysis, 29*, 1255–1264.
Keller, C., Visschers, V., & Siegrist, M. (2012). Affective imagery and acceptance of replacing nuclear power plants. *Risk Analysis, 32*, 464–477.
Kreuter, M., Farrell, D., Olevitch, L., & Brennan, L. (2012). *Tailoring health messages: Customizing communication with computer technology*. New York, NY: Routledge.
Kreuter, M. W., & Wray, R. J. (2003). Tailored and targeted health communication: Strategies for enhancing information relevance. *American Journal of Health Behavior, 27*, S227–S232.
L'Orange Seigo, S., Arvai, J., Dohle, S., & Siegrist, M. (2014). Predictors of risk and benefit perception of carbon capture and storage (CCS) in regions with different stages of deployment. *International Journal of Greenhouse Gas Control, 25*, 23–32.
Lai, J. C.-l., & Tao, J. (2003). Perception of environmental hazards in Hong Kong Chinese. *Risk Analysis, 23*, 669–684.
Lerner, J. S., & Keltner, D. (2001). Fear, anger, and risk. *Journal of Personality and Social Psychology, 81*, 146–159.
Li, M., & Chapman, G. B. (2012). Why do people like natural? Instrumental and ideational bases for the naturalness preference. *Journal of Applied Social Psychology, 42*, 2859–2878.
Lichtenstein, S., Slovic, P., Fischhoff, B., Layman, M., & Combs, B. (1978). Judged frequency of lethal events. *Journal of Experimental Psychology: Human Learning and Memory, 4*, 551–578.
Morgan, D. L., Fischhoff, B., Bostrom, A., & Atman, C. J. (2002). *Risk communication: A mental models approach*. London: Cambridge University Press.
Peters, E., & Slovic, P. (1996). The role of affect and worldviews as orienting dispositions in the perception and acceptance of nuclear power. *Journal of Applied Social Psychology, 26*, 1427–1453.

Poortinga, W., & Pidgeon, N. F. (2006). Prior attitudes, salient value similarity, and dimensionality: Toward an integrative model of trust in risk regulation. *Journal of Applied Social Psychology, 36*, 1674–1700.
Roth, E., Morgan, M. G., Fischhoff, B., Lave, L., & Bostrom, A. (1990). What do we know about making risk comparisons? *Risk Analysis, 10*, 375–387.
Rozin, P., Spranca, M., Krieger, Z., Neuhaus, R., Surillo, D., Swerdlin, A., et al. (2004). Preference for natural: Instrumental and ideational/moral motivations, and the contrast between foods and medicines. *Appetite, 43*, 147–154.
Satterfield, T., Kandlikar, M., Beaudrie, C., Conti, J., & Herr Harthorn, B. (2009). Anticipating the perceived risk of nanotechnologies. *Nature Nanotechnology, 4*, 752–758.
Savadori, L., Rumiati, R., & Bonini, N. (1998). Expertise and regional differences in risk perception: The case of Italy. *Swiss Journal of Psychology, 57*, 101–113.
Schwartz, S. H. (1992). Universals in the content and structure of values: Theoretical advances and empirical tests in 20 countries. *Advances in Experimental Social Psychology, 25*, 1–65.
Shi, J., Visschers, V. H. M., & Siegrist, M. (2015). Public perception of climate change: The importance of knowledge and cultural worldviews. *Risk Analysis, 35*, 2183–2201.
Siegrist, M. (2000). The influence of trust and perceptions of risks and benefits on the acceptance of gene technology. *Risk Analysis, 20*, 195–203.
Siegrist, M., Connor, M., & Keller, C. (2012). Trust, confidence, procedural fairness, outcome fairness, moral conviction, and the acceptance of GM field experiments. *Risk Analysis, 32*, 1394–1403.
Siegrist, M., Cousin, M.-E., Kastenholz, H., & Wiek, A. (2007). Public acceptance of nanotechnology foods and food packaging: The influence of affect and trust. *Appetite, 49*, 459–466.
Siegrist, M., & Cvetkovich, G. (2000). Perception of hazards: The role of social trust and knowledge. *Risk Analysis, 20*, 713–720.
Siegrist, M., Cvetkovich, G., & Roth, C. (2000). Salient value similarity, social trust, and risk/benefit perception. *Risk Analysis, 20*, 353–362.
Siegrist, M., Keller, C., & Kiers, H. A. L. (2005). A new look at the psychometric paradigm of perception of hazards. *Risk Analysis, 25*, 211–222.
Siegrist, M., Keller, C., & Kiers, H. A. L. (2006). Lay people's perception of food hazards: Comparing aggregated data and individual data. *Appetite, 47*, 324–332.
Siegrist, M., & Sütterlin, B. (2014). Human and nature-caused hazards: The affect heuristic causes biased decisions. *Risk Analysis, 34*, 1482–1494.
Siegrist, M., & Visschers, V. H. M. (2013). Acceptance of nuclear power: The Fukushima effect. *Energy Policy, 59*, 112–119.
Skitka, L. J. (2002). Do the means always justify the ends, or do the ends sometimes justify the means? A value protection model of justice reasoning. *Personality and Social Psychology Bulletin, 28*, 588–597.
Slovic, P. (1987). Perception of risk. *Science, 236*, 280–285.
Slovic, P., Finucane, M. L., Peters, E., & MacGregor, D. G. (2004). Risk as analysis and risk as feelings: Some thoughts about affect, reason, risk, and rationality. *Risk Analysis, 24*, 311–322.
Slovic, P., Flynn, J. H., & Layman, M. (1991). Perceived risk, trust, and the politics of nuclear waste. *Science, 254*, 1603–1607.
Slovic, P., Kraus, N., & Covello, V. T. (1990). What should we know about making risk comparisons? *Risk Analysis, 10*, 389–392.
Strack, F., & Deutsch, R. (2004). Reflective and impulsive determinants of social behavior. *Personality and Social Psychology Review, 8*, 220–247.
Szalay, L. B., & Deese, J. (1978). *Subjective meaning and culture: An assessment through word associations*. Hillsdale, NJ: Lawrence Erlbaum.
Teigen, K. H., Brun, W., & Slovic, P. (1988). Societal risks seen by a Norwegian public. *Journal of Behavioral Decision Making, 1*, 111–130.
Tobler, C., Visschers, V. H. M., & Siegrist, M. (2012). Consumers' knowledge about climate change. *Climatic Change, 114*, 189–209.

Tyler, T. R. (2000). Social justice: Outcome and procedure. *International Journal of Psychology, 35*, 117–125.
Van den Bos, K. (2005). What is responsible for the fair process effect. In J. Greenberg & J. A. Colquitt (Eds.), *Handbook of organizational justice* (pp. 273–300). Mahwah, NJ: Lawrence Erlbaum.
Verplanken, B. (1989). Beliefs, attitudes, and intentions toward nuclear energy before and after Chernobyl in a longitudinal within-subjects design. *Environment and Behavior, 21*, 371–392.
Visschers, V. H. M., Backhans, A., Collineau, L., Iten, D., Loesken, S., Postma, M., … Stärk, K. D. C. (2015). Perception of antimicrobial usage, antimicrobial resistance and policy measures to reduce antimicrobial usage in convenient samples of Belgian, French, German, Swedish and Swiss pig farmers. *Preventive Veterinary Medicine, 19*, 10–20.
Visschers, V. H. M., Keller, C., & Siegrist, M. (2011). Climate change benefits and energy supply benefits as determinants of acceptance of nuclear power stations: Investigating an explanatory model. *Energy Policy, 39*, 3621–3629.
Visschers, V. H. M., Meertens, R. M., Passchier, W. F., & de Vries, N. K. (2007). How does the general public evaluate risk information? The impact of associations with other risks. *Risk Analysis, 27*, 715–727.
Visschers, V. H. M., & Siegrist, M. (2012). Fair play in energy policy decisions: Procedural fairness, outcome fairness and acceptance of the decision to rebuild nuclear power plants. *Energy Policy, 46*, 292–300.
Visschers, V. H. M., & Siegrist, M. (2013). How a nuclear power plant accident influences acceptance of nuclear power: Results of a longitudinal study before and after the Fukushima disaster. *Risk Analysis, 33*, 333–347.
Visschers, V. H. M., & Siegrist, M. (2014). Find the differences and the similarities: Relating perceived benefits, perceived costs and protected values to acceptance of five energy technologies. *Journal of Environmental Psychology, 40*, 117–130.
Wallquist, L., Visschers, V. H. M., Dohle, S., & Siegrist, M. (2012). The role of convictions and trust for public protest potential in the case of carbon dioxide capture and storage (CCS). *Human and Ecological Risk Assessment, 18*, 919–932.
Wallquist, L., Visschers, V. H. M., & Siegrist, M. (2010). Impact of knowledge and misconceptions on benefit and risk perception of CCS. *Environmental Science & Technology, 44*, 6557–6562.
Whitfield, S. C., Rosa, E. A., Dan, A., & Dietz, T. (2009). The future of nuclear power: Value orientations and risk perception. *Risk Analysis, 29*, 425–437.
Wolfenbarger, L. L., & Phifer, P. R. (2000). The ecological risks and benefits of genetically engineered plants. *Science, 290*, 2088–2093.
Zajonc, R. B. (1980). Feeling and thinking: Preferences need no inferences. *American Psychologist, 35*, 151–175.

Part II
Cognitive, Emotional and Social Perspectives on Risk

Chapter 4
Cognitive, Developmental, and Neurobiological Aspects of Risk Judgments

Rebecca K. Helm and Valerie F. Reyna

Abstract In this chapter, we explore the literature on the cognitive, developmental, and neurobiological aspects of risk and show how work in this area is important in explaining and understanding decisions relating to risk. We outline different theories of risk preference and risk taking, including prospect theory, traditional dual-process theories, fuzzy-trace theory, and construal level theory. We focus on how cognitive differences can account for differences in risk preference and risk taking and examine how cognitive developmental trends can explain the observation that adolescents (and young adults) are prone to unhealthy risk taking. We outline important work in this area showing that the way information is mentally represented influences decisions relating to risk, in addition to more traditional factors such as reward sensitivity and inhibition. We explain how accounting for the role of mental representation can explain and predict counterintuitive findings in the literature on risk taking. In addition, we consider the neural underpinnings of risk taking and what research into the neural underpinnings of risk taking can tell us about cognitive aspects of risk.

Research investigating cognitive, developmental, and neurobiological aspects of risk is an emerging area in which there is much new work showing an important role of mental representations in decisions regarding risk. In the first part of this chapter, we describe important traditional theories that have provided insight into the cognitive aspects of risk—prospect theory and traditional dual-process theories—and explain how these theories contribute to understanding and explaining decisions relating to risk. We then consider two theories—fuzzy-trace theory and construal level theory—that add to prospect theory and traditional dual-process theories by

R. K. Helm
University of Exeter Law School, Exeter, UK

V. F. Reyna (✉)
Human Neuroscience Institute, Cornell Magnetic Resonance Imaging Facility, Cornell University, Ithaca, NY, USA
e-mail: vr53@cornell.edu

M. Raue et al. (eds.), *Psychological Perspectives on Risk and Risk Analysis*,
https://doi.org/10.1007/978-3-319-92478-6_4

recognizing an important construct that has been shown to influence decisions relating to risk: how information is mentally represented and, hence, processed. In the second part of this chapter, we consider findings in the risk taking literature and show how these findings are explained by theories of risk that account for cognitive constructs. We show how understanding the role of mental representations can add to traditional theories and predict counterintuitive findings in the developmental and adult literatures. For example, we discuss fuzzy-trace theory's prediction that adolescents are technically more rational in their risk preferences, but are also prone to unhealthy risk taking such as participation in crime, reckless driving, and unprotected sex (Figner & Weber, 2011; Reyna, Chapman, Dougherty, & Confrey, 2012; Reyna & Farley, 2006). We mention this prediction, in particular, because it distinguishes alternative theories and because it bears directly on ways to improve risky decisions. In the final part of the chapter, we discuss the neural underpinnings of risk taking, with reference to the distinctions introduced in the earlier parts of the chapter.

Theories Providing Insight into Cognitive Aspects of Risk

Prospect Theory

Early accounts that aimed to explain people's decision making regarding risk relied on *expected utility theory* (von Neumann & Mortgenstern, 1944). According to expected utility theory, when making a decision about whether to take a risk, the most desirable course of action is to choose the option with the highest subjective value to the individual. So, if an individual is making a choice between a sure option (e.g., receiving $5,000 for sure) and a risky option (e.g., a 50% chance of $10,000; otherwise, nothing), they should pick the option with the highest value to them (the highest subjective value). The highest subjective value is different from the expected value of an option, which is calculated as the sum of each objective outcome multiplied by its probability of occurrence (e.g., 0.50 × $10,000 = $5,000). This is illustrated by the fact that most people choose the sure option in the task, despite the fact that the sure option and the risky option have equal expected values (Fox & Tannenbaum, 2011). Expected utility theory, which goes beyond expected value, can explain why people do this. That is, expected utility of outcomes is thought to be nonlinear; as outcomes (e.g., dollars) increase, their utility (or subjective value) does not increase one for one in terms of objective value. Instead, there are *diminishing returns*, so that the outcomes in a sure option (smaller numbers) are discounted less than those in a risky option of equal expected value (larger numbers), making the sure option more valuable (see Fox & Tannenbaum, 2011; Machina, 1982; Tversky & Kahneman, 1986; see also Birnbaum, Chap. 8).

Despite explaining that most adults are risk averse (they prefer the sure option over the risky one), expected utility theory cannot explain other findings in the risk taking literature—notably, the large body of research showing that superficial changes in the wording of information (e.g., wording the same options as gains or losses), known as *framing*, can have a large influence on risk preferences.

The risky-choice framing task is important to understand because it produces inconsistency in risk preference. When preferences change on the basis of superficial differences in the wording of options as gains or losses, this is known as a *framing effect* (Reyna et al., 2011; Tversky & Kahneman, 1981; 1986). In the gains version of the task, participants choose between a sure option and a gamble of equal expected value, as in the earlier example (gaining \$5,000 for sure vs. a 50% chance of gaining \$10,000); as discussed, most people choose the sure \$5,000. In the losses version, a decision-maker may be given \$10,000 but must choose between losing \$5,000 for sure or taking a 50% chance of losing \$10,000 and a 50% chance of losing nothing. Note that the gains and losses versions describe the same options (e.g., \$10,000 - \$5,000 = \$5,000). Despite these options being the same, adults change their preferences from risk aversion (choosing the sure option) when *gains* are described to risk seeking (choosing the gamble) when *losses* are described, which is referred to as a standard framing effect. Because the options are the same, shifts in choice selection across frames are viewed as a violation of a fundamental axiom of expected utility, that of preference consistency.

Prospect theory built on expected utility theory and explained framing effects. According to prospect theory, outcomes are coded as gains or losses relative to a reference point, such as the status quo (Tversky & Kahneman, 1986). Therefore, what is important is not absolute values, but changes in values. For example, for a person expecting a raise in their salary, their salary with the raise would become the reference point and not getting a raise would be considered a loss. In framing problems, in the gain frame the reference point is \$0, but in the loss frame the reference point is the initial endowment. So, in a loss frame problem where you are given \$10,000 and have to choose between losing \$5,000 for sure and a 50% chance of losing \$10,000 and a 50% chance of losing nothing, people generally code the sure loss of \$5,000 as a downward deviation from \$0 (the reference point), rather than an overall gain of \$5,000.

Framing effects are explained by the way that people value outcomes, as well as a probability weighting function that overweights small probabilities and underweights moderate to large probabilities. According to prospect theory, the valuation of outcomes changes at the reference point (\$0 in the gain frame and \$10,000 in the loss frame) and can be described by an S-shaped value function. In problems involving gains, the value function is concave (e.g., dollars become worth less as value increases, so the first \$5,000 gain is valued higher than the second \$5,000 gain). This means that people value \$10,000 less than twice as much as they value \$5,000. Therefore, when asked to pick between \$5,000 for sure and a 50% chance of \$10,000, people are likely to value \$5,000 more highly than half of \$10,000 (as the value of \$10,000 is less than twice the value of \$5,000). This leads to a preference for the sure option. In contrast, the reference point in the loss frame is \$10,000, and options are coded as losses relative to this \$10,000. In problems involving losses, the value function is convex (e.g., dollar losses become less bad as value increases, so the first $5,000 loss hurts more than the second $5,000 loss). This means that people dislike a loss of $10,000 less than twice as much as they dislike a loss of $5,000. Therefore, when asked to pick between a $5,000 loss for sure and a 50% chance of a $10,000 loss, people are likely to dislike the sure loss of $10,000 less than twice as much as they dislike the loss of $5,000. This leads to a preference for the risky option in the loss frame, as a 50% chance of a $10,000 loss is valued as less bad than a $5,000 loss for sure.

Prospect theory also explains framing effects through a probability function, where people overweight small probabilities and underweight moderate to large probabilities. This means that in cases involving moderate to large probabilities, people underweight the probability (50% in our example). This means that in the gain frame where the choice is between $5,000 for sure and a 50% chance of $10,000, people underweight the 50%, treating this option as less than 50% of 10,000. This leads to a preference for the sure option. In the loss frame where the choice is between losing $5,000 for sure and a 50% chance of losing $10,000, people underweight the 50%, treating this option as a less than 50% chance of losing $10,000. This leads to a preference for the risky option.

Although prospect theory offers an explanation of framing effects that has to do with the perception of outcomes and probabilities, it does not discuss the types of non-perceptual cognitive processes involved in decisions relating to risk. Other accounts of risk have attempted to provide such an explanation.

Traditional Dual-Process Theories and Type 1/Type 2 Thinking

Traditional dual-process theories explain risky decision making through the distinction between fast and intuitive thinking, called *Type 1* thinking, and slow and deliberative thinking, called *Type 2* thinking, replacing earlier System1/System2 terminology (Evans & Stanovich, 2013; Kahneman, 2003). According to dual-process theories, Type 1 thinking is intuitive and experiential in contrast to Type 2 thinking that involves logical and rational cognitive capacities. Type 2 thinking operates when a need to override Type 1 thinking is detected, for example, when an individual notices that gain and loss framed problems are the same, they may calculate expected value, thus attenuating framing effects (see Stanovich & West, 2008). Type 2 thinking interrupts Type 1 thinking, suppresses its default responses, and substitutes a logical or rational response (Evans & Stanovich, 2013; Kahneman, 2011). Recent extensions to dual-process theories recognize two components of Type 2 thinking—the cognitive capacities for rational judgments (such as intelligence) and cognitive propensities for reflective thinking (such as need for cognition, actively open-minded thinking, and the tendency to collect information before making up one's mind) (Evans & Stanovich, 2013).

According to these theories, reliance on Type 1 thinking can result in biases when making decisions, including those regarding risk. For example, when analyzing the risk of an environment or activity, reliance on Type 1 may lead to attribute substitution. This is where a harder to evaluate characteristic is substituted for an easier to evaluate characteristic, even when the easier to evaluate characteristic is less accurate (Evans & Stanovich, 2013; Kahneman & Frederick, 2002). For example, in judging the probability of an accident, people can substitute the vivid availability in memory of a single observed accident on a slide for a quantitative analysis of the frequency of accidents on slides (Evans & Stanovich, 2013; Kahneman, 2003). Some traditional dual-process approaches have associated framing effects with Type 1 processing (Kahneman, 2003; Stanovich & West, 2008). When the same person received both gain and loss problems (in a within-subjects design), successfully engaging in Type 2 processing has been shown to reduce framing effects, as it causes the person to notice the similarity between gain and loss frames and inhibits framing differences (Stanovich & West, 2008). In addition, neuroimaging research has provided some evidence that framing effects are caused by an initial emotional evaluation and can be reduced by suppression of this initial response (De Martino, Kumaran, Seymour, & Dolan, 2006; Kahneman & Frederick, 2007).

In addition, certain conceptions of traditional dual-process theories associate Type 1 thinking with *affective* and *emotionally charged* thinking (Epstein, 1994; Slovic, Finucane, Peters, & Macgregor, 2006). This thinking has also been associated with unhealthy attitudes to risk (see also Tompkins et al., Chap. 5). For example, Type 1 thinking has been linked to the decision to engage in smoking. Slovic (2001) suggested that young smokers gave little or no conscious thought to the risks of smoking but were instead driven by affective impulses such as wanting to do something new and exciting and have fun with their friends (but see Reyna & Farley, 2006, for a review of the role of affect and emotion in risk taking and Rivers, Reyna, & Mills, 2008, for an alternative explanation of emotion and risk in adolescent decision making).

Neurodevelopmental imbalance theories of risk taking take a similar approach to that of Slovic, associating affective thinking with unhealthy attitudes to risk, particularly in adolescents. These theories have similar intellectual roots to traditional dual-process theories and distinguish between a *hot* motivational affective system (much like Type 1 thinking) and *cold* deliberation and inhibition (much like Type 2 thinking) (Somerville & Casey, 2010; Steinberg, 2008). According to these models, risk taking in adolescence is caused by an imbalance between the development of brain regions responsible for control and *affective* brain regions. Specifically, regions implicated in control (prefrontal cortical regions) develop linearly with age and begin to stabilize by adolescence, while subcortical *affective* brain regions develop faster and are hypothesized to be hyperresponsive in adolescence (Casey, Jones, & Hare, 2008; Defoe, Dubas, Figner, & van Aken, 2015; Somerville, Hare, & Casey, 2011; Steinberg, 2008). This imbalance between cold control systems and hot affective systems is predicted to cause adolescents to become biased toward arousing rewards, leading to increased risk taking (Somerville et al., 2011; Steinberg, 2008). Dual-process approaches have been applied to explain real-life risk taking such as adolescent drug taking and addiction (Gladwin, Figner, Crone, & Wiers, 2011). These theories predict an increase in risk taking from childhood to adolescence, which then declines in adulthood (Dahl, 2004). However, a comprehensive meta-analysis of experiments on risky decision making showed that risk preference declines from childhood to adolescence, disconfirming predictions of dual-process imbalance models (Defoe et al., 2015). Theories such as fuzzy-trace theory and construal level theory are able to explain findings not explained by traditional dual-process theories by accounting for the role of mental representations in decisions relating to risk.

Fuzzy-Trace Theory: Gist and Verbatim Representations

Fuzzy-trace theory builds on traditional dual-process theories, but it adds crucial constructs that explain prior findings and that make new predictions. Consistent with traditional dual-process theories, fuzzy-trace theory distinguishes metacognitive capacities such as inhibition and reflection from motivational/affective influences such as reward sensitivity and emotion (Rivers, Reyna, & Mills, 2008). However, fuzzy-trace theory also incorporates an additional cognitive distinction between verbatim versus gist mental representations—not found in traditional theories (Reyna, 2012; Reyna, Wilhelms, McCormick, & Weldon, 2015). Therefore, fuzzy-trace theory encompasses three constructs that are important in risk taking—*hot* motivational/affective factors such as reward sensitivity and emotion (similar to Type 1), *cold* metacognitive factors such as reflection and inhibition (similar to Type 2), and gist versus verbatim mental representations.

Fuzzy-trace theory posits two types of mental representations and associated processing types—gist and verbatim. When people are faced with a decision, they encode two types of mental representations of their options—the bottom-line meaning of the options (gist) and the exact details (verbatim; Reyna, 2012; Reyna & Brainerd, 2011). Usually, people encode multiple gist representations at varying levels of precision but all simpler and more meaningful than verbatim representations. Gist and verbatim representations are encoded simultaneously in parallel and stored separately (Reyna, 2012). Gist representations of a risky-choice framing problem start with the simplest nominal-scale distinction between some quantity and no quantity. Thus, the gist of the choice in the gain frame boils down to gaining something (for sure) versus possibly gaining nothing—two outcomes that are categorically different from one another. Verbatim representations are detailed representations of the surface form of information (e.g., in a risky-choice framing problem that the choice is between $5,000 for sure and a 50% chance of $10,000). The same information is encoded at multiple levels of precision from verbatim to simplest gist, roughly analogous to scales of measurement from verbatim to gist—exact numerical values (e.g., $5,000 and a 50% chance of $10,000), then ordinal distinctions (e.g., more chance of less money vs. less chance of more money), then categorical distinctions (e.g., some money vs. chance of some money or no money; Reyna, Chick, Corbin, & Hsia, 2014; Wilhelms, Helm, Setton, & Reyna, 2014). According to fuzzy-trace theory, when making a choice, some people rely more on the gist or the verbatim representations of information—but most adults have a preference for the simplest gist-based representations. They then apply values or moral principles to choose between options (e.g., valuing some money over no money). Thus, the representations that a decision-maker relies on and the principles they apply to those representations govern their decisions regarding risk.

Unlike traditional dual-process theories (which include intuition in Type 1 processing and inhibition in Type 2 processing), in fuzzy-trace theory intuition is not associated with a lack of inhibition. As noted above, fuzzy-trace theory encompasses the role of inhibition (a metacognitive factor encompassing reflection and promoting deliberation) (an aspect of Type 2 processing) and motivational/affective processes, including emotion and reward sensitivity (some of which are akin to those in Type 1). However, unlike traditional dual-process theories, fuzzy-trace theory breaks mental representation (simple meaning-based gist vs. more specific surface-level verbatim) out into separate constructs that have been shown to be dissociated and that are not found in other dual-process theories (see Reyna, 2012). Gist-based processing is referred to as intuition as it is typically fuzzy and qualitative rather than precise and analytical but gist-based intuition characterizes advanced cognition. It is a sophisticated way of thinking based on the meaning of information rather than literal surface details (Adam & Reyna, 2005; Reyna & Lloyd, 2006). So, fuzzy-trace theory would not categorize the unconscious gist-based intuitions of experts (e.g., cardiologists diagnosing a heart attack, Reyna & Lloyd, 2006) together with impulsive choices of adolescents (e.g., the decision to go out with friends instead of studying for a test) (Reyna et al., 2015).

Fuzzy-trace theory posits that when making decisions, adults (in the types of decisions they have experience making) and experts (particularly in their area of expertise) tend to rely on gist representations (resulting in gist-based processing), referred to as a fuzzy-processing preference, and this reliance tends to increase with age and experience (Reyna et al., 2014; Reyna & Brainerd, 2008; Reyna & Lloyd, 2006; Wilhelms, Corbin, & Reyna, 2015). So, for example, when making a decision on whether to go bungee jumping or not at a particular center, an adult would be likely to process both the verbatim probability of serious injury (e.g., 10%) and the gist that the chance of injury was relatively large, but would base his or her decision on the qualitative gist. Specifically, they would rely on the fact that the chance of serious injury was relatively large, rather than trading off precise risks and rewards. Laboratory and field experiments with children, adolescents, and adults and studies with experts and novices have confirmed this prediction (e.g., Reyna, 1996; Reyna et al., 2011; Reyna & Brainerd, 1994, 1995; Reyna & Ellis, 1994; Reyna & Lloyd, 2006), as have studies of real-life decision making (Mills, Reyna, & Estrada, 2008; Reyna et al., 2011; Reyna & Farley, 2006). The prediction that reliance on gist increases with age has also been supported by recent research in the context of risk taking using eye-tracking data, showing that, prior to decisions, adolescents acquired more information in a more thorough manner compared to adults, suggesting they were engaging in a more analytical processing strategy involving trading off decision variables (Kwack, Payne, Cohen, & Huettel, 2015). In addition, this prediction is supported by literature from a large number of cognitive tasks showing that reliance on gist-based representations increases with age and expertise (e.g., Brainerd, Reyna, & Ceci, 2008; Reyna & Ellis, 1994; Reyna & Lloyd, 2006).

The idea that intuitive gist-based processing supports sophisticated and developmentally advanced reasoning has been supported by results showing that reliance on gist-based processing promotes better decision making in practical contexts, for example, when doctors make choices about treatment options for patients with cardiac risk (Reyna & Lloyd, 2006) and when individuals make decisions about whether to risk HIV by engaging in unprotected sex (Reyna et al., 2011). This idea has also been supported by research showing that manipulations designed to encourage intuitive thinking improve decision making (e.g., participants are given a distraction task rather than being asked to think carefully about their decision), compared to manipulations designed to encourage analytic/deliberative thinking (e.g., participants were told to think carefully before making decisions), on a variety of reasoning tasks (Usher, Russo, Weyers, Brauner, & Zakay, 2011).

The implication for risky decision making is that as age and experience increase, precise quantitative processing of risks and rewards is predicted to give way to mature qualitative processing that captures the bottom-line meaning (the gist) of decision options. This development is predicted to have a protective effect against unhealthy risk taking when risks are objectively low and benefits are objectively high (e.g., the risk of arrest from a single instance of drunk driving for a short distance is low, and the benefits of driving may be high). Although the verbatim representation promotes risk taking because benefits outweigh risks, the gist representation of such a choice would be that there is a non-negligible possibility of a life-altering injury or a felony drunk-driving conviction. In addition to drunk driving, many other crimes have a low risk from a single instance of risky behavior, as do many public health risks (e.g., the risk of HIV from unprotected sex; Reyna et al., 2011; Reyna & Mills, 2014). Thus, processing less information more meaningfully—the core gist—generally reduces risk taking in cases in which objective risks are low and benefits are high. In cases where objective risks are high and benefits are high, there is likely to be less of a difference between reliance on gist and reliance on verbatim, as here processing the information meaningfully and conducting a trade-off of risks and benefits would often both lead to risk avoidance.

When relying on gist-based representations and processing, an individual is more likely to make decisions based on simple bottom-line values and moral principles, for example, "avoid risk" or "better to be safe than sorry." According to fuzzy-trace theory, these principles are represented in long-term memory as vague gists and generally do not incorporate exact magnitudes of potential risks and benefits (see Helm & Reyna, 2017; Reyna & Casillas, 2009). This is because verbatim representations fade quickly and are too precisely specified to be applicable to a wide variety of decisions. These values and principles should be distinguished from the representations of options to which they are applied in order to make decisions, although they are related: That is, gist representations of values are more easily cued when an individual relies on gist representations of options because of their similarity to one another, a well-known property of retrieval cueing.

As noted above, according to fuzzy-trace theory, reliance on gist generally increases as age increases. Specifically, reliance on gist increases in decisions where an individual has some experience making that type of decision. When making decisions about risk, adults are predicted to have a fuzzy-processing preference (Reyna, 2012). This means that they have a tendency to rely on the simplest gist possible to make a decision. When two options are categorically different (e.g., win something vs. maybe win nothing or risk of death or serious injury vs. no risk of death or serious injury), adults will generally make their decisions based on this categorical difference and not more fine-grained distinctions. In contrast, many risk-takers (including many adolescents) rely on more fine-grained distinctions, operating closer to the verbatim end of the verbatim-gist processing continuum. These people, then, engage in more precise processing that supports risk-benefit trade-offs, which often results in risk taking when the benefits of risky behavior are high and the risks are objectively low.

For example, the risk of HIV infection from a single act of unprotected sex is objectively low (0.08% from one incident of unprotected sex, see Boily et al., 2009). People relying more on verbatim details (and therefore trading off risks and benefits) may choose to engage in unprotected sex (a risky behavior) (Mills et al., 2008). In contrast, those relying on gist would be likely to see their options as risking a life-threatening illness vs. not risking a life-threatening illness. The latter categorical representation is more likely to cue a categorical gist principle such as "it only takes once," so that unprotected sex would be avoided (Mills et al., 2008; Reyna et al., 2011; Reyna & Mills, 2014; Wilhelms et al., 2014).

Therefore, fuzzy-trace theory recognizes two distinct routes to unhealthy risk taking. One route is reactive and characterized by a failure to inhibit behavior, succumbing to emotion or temptation. This route is recognized in the dual-process approach of neurodevelopmental imbalance theories described above (although note that traditional dual-process theories associates this route with intuition and fuzzy-trace theory does not) and also in literature on affective and emotional aspects of risk, sometimes referred to as "risk-as-feelings" (Loewenstein, Weber, Hsee, & Welch, 2001; Weber & Johnson, 2009). Emphasized in fuzzy-trace theory, a second (and distinct) route to risk taking is the route described in the previous paragraph, a reasoned route characterized by reliance on verbatim rather than gist processing that is particularly important in groups such as adolescents who are disposed to rely more on verbatim processing, compared to typical adults (Reyna & Farley, 2006). This route involves relying on fine-grained distinctions regarding the degree of risk and amount of reward such that they compensate for one another—higher rewards compensate for higher risks (Reyna et al., 2011). Thus, the counterintuitive prediction of fuzzy-trace theory is that much adolescent risk taking is a result of reasoning rather than being reactive or impulsive, which has been supported by research in a variety of domains of risk taking.

Construal Level Theory

Another theory that provides insight into how mental representations can influence risk perception and risk taking is construal level theory. Construal level theory proposes that psychological distance changes the way that individuals represent objects and events (Trope & Liberman, 2003, 2010). Psychological distance refers to the removal of the object or event being considered from the person making the decision, distance in terms of time, space, social distance, or hypotheticality (Fujita, Henderson, Eng, Trope, & Liberman, 2006; Trope & Liberman, 2000, 2010; Wakslak, Trope, Liberman, & Alnoy, 2006). Hypotheticality (possible as opposed to actual events) is also related to probability or risk, as contrasted with certainty. According to construal level theory, objects or events at a greater psychological distance are more likely to be represented in terms of abstract features conveying the meaning of the object, event, or individual (high-level construals). In contrast, objects, events, or individuals at a smaller psychological distance are more likely to be represented in terms of concrete-specific details (low-level construals) (Trope & Liberman, 2003). For example, moving to a new house next week is likely to be described in terms of concrete, specific actions such as packing boxes, while moving next year would be described in more abstract, global terms such as a new phase of life (Bonner & Newell, 2008).

Work in this area has suggested that psychological distance can influence (and sometimes improve) decision making. For example, an increase in psychological distance has been shown to increase the weighting of central (as opposed to peripheral) features when individuals are making decisions (e.g., a central feature when evaluating a movie would be the quality of the featured film rather than the quality of the commercials; Trope & Liberman, 2000; Fukukura, Ferguson, & Fujita, 2013). Research has shown that this relationship between weighting central features and the quality of decision making is accounted for by gist memory for features, as defined in fuzzy-trace theory (see Fukukura et al., 2013; note that centrality is not sufficient to characterize gist, which has special memorial and reasoning properties; Reyna, 2012). Participants primed to think in a more abstract (psychologically distant) way had more gist memory for features of cell phones they were told about and subsequently made better decisions about which cell phones were the best. Importantly, memory for gist representations accounted fully for the relationship between psychological distance and decision quality (Fukukura et al., 2013).

Research has also examined the relationship between psychological distance and risk taking and has shown that construal level influences risk taking. Higher construal level leads to more risk taking behavior than a lower construal level (Lermer, Streicher, Sachs, Raue, & Frey, 2016; Raue, Streicher, Lermer, & Frey, 2014; Sagristano, Trope, & Liberman, 2002). For example, research on medical decision making has shown that framing risks associated with mononucleosis (a contagious viral infection) as occurring "every day" (e.g., 1 incident occurs every day) increased risk perception and reduced intentions to take risks compared to framing risks as occurring "every year" (e.g., 365 incidents occur every year), despite the fact that the risks are mathematically the same (Chandron & Menon, 2004). This effect has been explained by temporal immediacy—a more proximal risk (risks every day) seems more concrete, immediate, and threatening than a more distant risk (risks every year; see also Bonner & Newell, 2008).

Another study looking at the effect of construal level on risk used the Balloon Analog Risk Task (BART; in this task, participants accumulate money each time they pump air into a computerized balloon but lose the accumulated money if the balloon bursts; Lermer, Streicher, Sachs, Raue, & Frey, 2015). Participants were primed to think in an abstract or concrete way using categorization priming (adapted from Fujita et al., 2006); they were asked to name either a subordinate or a superordinate category for 30 items. Participants primed to think in a more abstract way took more risks than those who were primed to think in a concrete way. This influence of construal level on risk taking was shown to be mediated by game strategy, meaning whether a participant endorsed a strategy of "few pumps, consistent winnings of small amounts and little losses" more than a strategy of "many pumps, high gains but more losses." The difference between strategies was greater for concrete thinkers than for abstract thinkers, with abstract thinkers favoring the higher risk game strategy. This suggests that a concrete mind-set was linked to safer strategies (Lermer et al., 2015).

The importance of game strategy, such as "many pumps, high gains but more losses," suggests that construal level has an effect by influencing the gist that individuals rely on. These simple game strategies reflect bottom-line gist principles, rather than a focus on precise verbatim analysis (Reyna, 2008). Indeed, bursts in the BART usually occur randomly making it difficult to learn precise risk-reward payoffs. As initially indicated by Trope and Liberman (2003), studies suggest that a greater psychological distance promotes reliance on gist, although other evidence suggests that greater distance favors risk taking because risks seem distant (such as high gains but more losses), whereas a smaller psychological distance favors safe strategies because risks seem close (such as consistent winnings and little losses). Unfortunately, results from the BART are ultimately difficult to interpret because the task confounds a number of known determinants of risky decision making.

Explaining Developmental Findings in the Risk Taking Literature

In this part of the chapter, we consider findings in the risk taking literature and show how these findings can be explained by theories on cognitive aspects of risk. We focus on developmental trends in risk taking, which can provide insight into different cognitive components of decisions regarding risk. Recognizing the influence of mental representations, in addition to more traditional aspects of risk taking such as affect and inhibition, can predict and explain findings in the risk taking literature that are not explained by other theories.

Finding 1: Adults Show More Standard Framing Effects than Adolescents in Risky-Choice Framing Tasks

Research has shown that adults shift risk preferences depending on superficial wording of options whereas adolescents do so to a lesser extent and sometimes show "reverse" framing effects (choosing the risky option in the gain frame and the sure option in the loss frame—the opposite of the standard framing effect) under predictable circumstances. For example, adults show the framing effect (picking the sure option in the gain frame and the risky option in the loss frame) to a greater extent than adolescents when options and expected values are equal (Reyna et al., 2011). Because options are numerically equivalent, this result suggests that adolescents are trading off risks and benefits (leading to the same decisions in gain and loss frames), whereas adults are more influenced by superficial differences in wording that imply a different gist. Research has also shown that adolescents who take more risks score lower on measures of gist thinking and higher on verbatim measures and also are less likely to showing standard framing effects, treating objectively equivalent options similarly (see Reyna et al., 2011; Reyna & Farley, 2006). Trading off risks and benefits, a deliberative rather than impulsive way of thinking, is associated with taking more risks and having poorer outcomes.

As noted above, the tendency to be risk seeking in the loss frame and risk averse in the gain frame is explained by prospect theory (Tversky & Kahneman, 1986). As also noted above, traditional dual-process theories have associated framing (and particularly within-subjects framing) with Type 1 processing. However, these traditional theories do not explain numerous effects predicted by fuzzy-trace theory (e.g., see Kühberger & Tanner, 2010; Reyna & Brainerd, 1995), such as developmental reversals that have been shown in framing effects—specifically children and adolescents are less susceptible to framing bias than adults (Reyna et al., 2011), and less-experienced risky decision-makers are less susceptible to framing bias than experts in the experts area of expertise (e.g., experts in making risky decisions such as intelligence agents have been shown to be more susceptible to framing bias than controls; Reyna et al., 2014).

Fuzzy-trace theory a priori predicts and explains framing effects and also developmental reversals in framing effects (e.g., Reyna & Ellis, 1994). Consider the risky-choice framing problem described above: in the gain frame, a decision-maker must choose between gaining $5,000 for sure or a 50% chance of winning $10,000 and a 50% chance of winning nothing. In the loss frame, a decision-maker is given $10,000 and must choose between losing $5,000 for sure or taking a 50% chance of losing $10,000 and a 50% chance of losing nothing. Note that processing equal expected value (as happens when relying on literal objective numbers or verbatim processing) in each problem leads to indifference ($5,000 vs. $5,000). In contrast, reliance on gist leads to differing preferences between the two frames (Kühberger & Tanner, 2010). In the gain frame, the gist of the choice is definitely winning some money (choice a) or possibly winning no money (choice b), as the choices are boiled down to their simplest gist (something vs. nothing). This leads to a preference for the sure option (option a), as definitely winning money is preferable to possibly winning no money. In the loss frame, the gist is a choice between definitely losing some money (option a) and possibly losing no money (option b), as again the choices are boiled down to their simplest gist (something vs. nothing). This leads to the standard framing effect—a preference for the risky option (option b) as possibly losing no money is better than definitely losing some money.

Research has shown that adolescents show reverse framing effects when outcomes are large and, hence, differences between outcomes are large (Reyna et al., 2011; Reyna & Ellis, 1994; Reyna & Farley, 2006). This result is important theoretically and must be explained by any theory of risk preference. Literal or verbatim processing does not, by itself, produce reverse framing effects. Verbatim processing produces indifference between literally equivalent options as found in young children (Reyna & Ellis, 1994). Research suggests that it is the combination of both verbatim processing and reward sensitivity (and consequent focus on large differences in outcomes) that produces reverse framing (Reyna et al., 2011). Thus, according to fuzzy-trace theory and confirmed by empirical findings, reverse framing effects occur when people pay more attention to precise numerical differences in risks and rewards and, also, when they especially value reward (e.g., preferring a possible $10,000 over a sure $5,000 and a sure loss of $5,000 over a possible loss of $10,000). Verbatim processing and reward sensitivity, then, promote choosing the risky option (win $10,000) in the gain frame and the sure option (lose $5,000) in the loss frame. Corroborating this explanation, emphasizing the categorical nature of a framing decision increases framing effects, whereas emphasizing numerical comparisons eliminates framing effects (Kühberger & Tanner, 2010).

By including a discrete role of mental representation relied on (gist/verbatim), we can understand the development of the standard framing effect from adolescence to adulthood, but without recognizing the role of mental representation, we cannot explain the transition from no-framing effect in childhood to the reverse framing effect to the standard framing effect in adulthood. Importantly, research has shown that framing responses in risky-choice framing laboratory tasks are predictive of real-life risk taking, such as decisions to engage in unprotected sex (e.g., Reyna et al., 2011).

Finding 2: Adolescents Take Fewer Risks than Children When a Diagnostic Task Is Used (a Sure/Safe Option Is Included)

A recent meta-analysis showed that adolescents took fewer risks than children on tasks with a sure/safe option versus a risky option with the possibility of a 0 outcome (such as $5,000 for sure or 50% chance of $10,000, when $5,000 for sure is the sure/safe option; Defoe et al., 2015). This task is crucial because it allows respondents who rely on simple categorical gist to choose an option based on that strategy (Reyna et al., 2011). Other risky decision making tasks make it impossible to use gist to make a choice by eliminating categorical contrasts between options, forcing responding based on verbatim distinctions (even individuals who generally rely on gist will not be able to do so where reliance on gist does not provide a distinction between options). Therefore, tasks with options that contrast winning some money versus winning none are able to *diagnose* the use of a categorical gist strategy. Fuzzy-trace theory also makes clear predictions when two risky options are presented (i.e., two gambles), namely, that people ratchet up their level of precision in order to discriminate the options (see Reyna, 2012).

Prospect theory is not a developmental theory (so makes no prediction), and traditional dual-process theories do not predict this pivotal finding that children take more risks than adolescents when a diagnostic task is used. However, by accounting for a role of mental representations, fuzzy-trace theory can predict and explain this finding. As noted above, according to fuzzy-trace theory, reliance on gist-based representations increases with age and experience (Reyna et al., 2014). When a task has a sure/safe option and a risky option with the possibility of a 0 outcome (e.g., no money won, or no lives saved), the gist of the decision at the simplest level is no risk versus some risk (promoting reliance on the sure/safe option). When a task has two risky options (both of which have the possibility of a 0 outcome), the simplest level of gist is some risk versus some risk. Here, the simplest level of gist will not provide a choice between the two options, and so individuals have to rely on more precise representations. This is because the simplest gist will be something vs. something, forcing reliance on more fine-grained distinctions to make a decision. So, when the decision is between $5,000 and a 50% chance of $10,000, reliance on the simplest gist (something vs. something or nothing) leads to preference for the sure option, whereas reliance on verbatim ($5,000 vs. $5,000) leads to indifference. This means that increasing reliance on gist (as occurs with age according to fuzzy-trace theory) would be expected to influence individuals only in tasks with a sure/safe option (as compared to two risky options), as appears to be the case from the recent meta-analysis. Traditional dual-process theories do not predict or explain this result. Imbalance models in particular, which predict a general increase in risk taking from childhood to adolescence due to neurobiological developments, do not explain this finding, which is the opposite developmental difference.

Finding 3: Adolescents Trade-Off Risks and Benefits More than Adults in Real Life but Have Poorer Outcomes

One seemingly paradoxical finding in the risk taking literature is that adolescents trade off risks and benefit more than adults in real life (see Reyna et al., 2011; Reyna & Farley, 2006), but have poorer outcomes, for example, they are prone to unhealthy risk taking such as participation in crime, reckless driving, and unprotected sex (Figner &

Weber, 2011; Reyna et al., 2012). Traditional dual-process theories cannot explain this, as these theories suggest that a risks and benefits analysis (Type 2 thinking) should have a protective effect against unhealthy risk taking by promoting careful consideration and accurate analysis of risks (Evans & Stanovich, 2013; Steinberg, 2008).

Fuzzy-trace theory explains this effect, because although gist processing can lead to predictable violations of coherence criteria of rationality (though this effect is mitigated when expected values actually differ), it is also predicted to have a protective effect against unhealthy risk taking in the real world. This is because in the real world, many unhealthy risks are taken when the risks are low and the benefits are high, and so a direct trade-off of risk and reward leads to risk taking. For example, the risks of getting HIV from unprotected sex are low, and the benefits may be seen as high, and the risks of getting caught for committing a crime are often low, but the benefits can be high. In these cases, direct trading-off of risk and reward (verbatim processing) is predicted to increase unhealthy risk taking. In contrast, someone relying on simpler, meaning-based categorical distinctions would see the decision as one between no risk of a bad outcome and a benefit with some risk of a bad outcome. When this bad outcome was particularly serious (such as HIV or a criminal record), a person relying on this gist would be likely to pick no risk of the bad outcome rather than some risk of the bad outcome, despite potential benefits (Reyna & Mills, 2014).

Therefore, fuzzy-trace theory predicts greater levels of unhealthy risk taking in individuals relying on verbatim processing, and less unhealthy risk taking in individuals relying on gist processing. Research has confirmed this prediction by showing that reliance on simpler levels of gist (simpler, more categorical distinctions, as opposed to fine-grained distinctions) increasingly has a protective effect against risk taking (this means that cognitively we would expect children to take the most risks absent other confounding factors, which is what is seen in laboratory experiments; see Defoe et al., 2015; Mills et al., 2008). One study gave adolescents alternative measures of risk perception that differed in cue specificity and response format. Measures that emphasized verbatim retrieval and cued fine-grained verbatim processing produced positive correlations between perceived risk and risky behavior (higher risk perceptions were associated with more risk taking). In contrast, measures that assessed gist-based judgments of risk and cued gist processing produced a negative correlation between risk and risky behavior (higher risk perceptions were associated with less risk taking). Endorsement of simple gist values and principles (such as "no risk is better than some risk") provided the greatest protection against risk taking (Mills et al., 2008). In addition, the simpler a gist principle was, the greater its protective effect against risk taking—when looking at one type of unhealthy risk taking in adolescents, initiation of sex (a risky behavior in adolescents due to the risks of negative outcomes such as sexually transmitted infections or unintended pregnancy), adolescents who endorsed an ordinal principle ("less risk is better than more risk") were more than twice as likely to take risks than those who endorsed a categorical principle ("no risk is better than some risk") (Mills et al., 2008).

This reliance on either gist or verbatim processing has been shown to have a discrete influence on risky decision making and has an effect even when controlling for inhibition and motivational or affective factors such as reward sensitivity. For example, Reyna et al. (2011) showed that verbatim- and gist-based processing when making decisions about risk predicted risk taking beyond what was predicted by traits commonly associated with risk taking (or risk avoidance) such as sensation seeking (seeking sensory pleasure and excitement) and behavioral activation (moving toward something that is desired), representing affective factors, and inhibition. Importantly, gist or verbatim processing was the most consistent predictor of real-life risk taking—intentions to have sex, sexual behavior, and number of partners decreased when gist-based reasoning was triggered by retrieval cues in questions about perceived risk, and intentions to have sex and numbers of partners increased when verbatim-based reasoning was triggered by different retrieval cues in questions about perceived risk (Reyna et al., 2011).

The protective effect of gist processing has also been shown in the context of juvenile crime. One study looked at delinquent 18-year-olds and compared them to nondelinquent 18-year-olds and an older nondelinquent sample. Framing tasks were used to assess participants' reliance on gist or verbatim representations. Consistent with the predictions of fuzzy-trace theory, there was a developmental trend from delinquent 18-year-olds (who had broken the law and were involved in an alternative to incarceration program) who showed the least standard framing effects, to nondelinquent 18-year-olds who showed an intermediate level of standard framing effects, to older nondelinquents who showed the strongest standard framing effects (indicating the most reliance on gist; Helm, Reyna, Corbin, Wilhelms, & Weldon, 2014). These results support the prediction that reliance on gist-based representations is associated with a mature, healthy approach to risk taking.

Finally, the relationship between gist processing and risk can be seen in the effect that endorsing certain gist representations has on risk taking. It has been shown that teaching and emphasizing gist representations can reduce unhealthy risk taking. For example, this teaching has been used to successfully reduce sexual risk taking by delivering interventions giving simple gist facts (e.g., unintended pregnancy is virtually certain to occur if unprotected sex is engaged in repeatedly over time), in addition to more complex verbatim information (e.g., 90% risk of pregnancy after a year of unprotected sex), producing sustained effects on behavioral outcomes and psychosocial mediators of adolescent risk taking (Reyna & Mills, 2014).

Finding 4: Errors that Go Beyond Representations: Other Processing and Retrieval "Errors" When Making Risky Decisions

As noted above, traditional dual-process theories associate biases in risk preference with Type 1 processing (Evans & Stanovich, 2013). Fuzzy-trace theory provides a different explanation of biases in risk preference. According to fuzzy-trace theory, framing effects occur due to cognitive representations of sure and risky options (as described above). This is one explanation of why adults have seemingly "irrational" risk preferences, but this is not the only reason. Biases in risk preference and decision making can occur at other stages of the decision making process—for example, the processing of information. Errors in reasoning about risk can arise as a result of processing interference resulting in base rate neglect. For example, overlapping classes involved in a decision can cause processing interference which can lead to biases in risk preference. For example, when people are asked to make a judgment about the likelihood of a patient having a disease given a positive test result, e.g., when 80% of people with a positive test result have the disease, 80% of people with a negative test result do not have the disease, and 10% of people in the entire population have the disease. Here, there are overlapping classes (e.g., people with the disease and people with a positive test result). Reasoners focus on target members of a class and lose track of the larger universe of possibilities. This applies to judgments of risk that involve a target class of events (e.g., patients who have a disease) and a larger class of events including both targets and nontargets (e.g., the patients with a positive test result). Here, people compare target and nontarget events (e.g., people who had a disease and people who did not have a disease) and automatically extract the gist of which class of events is "bigger." As noted earlier, people pay less attention to the more inclusive class, which is the denominator in the calculation of risk (e.g., the rate of the disease in the entire population). This phenomenon is a type of denominator neglect (ignoring the base rate and focusing on the numerator). This type of confusion is illustrated through the widespread misunderstanding of genetic risks. For example, people often confuse the probability of a woman developing breast cancer if she has BRCA1 or BRCA2 gene mutations[1] (which is a high probability) with the probability of a woman with breast cancer having BRCA1 or BRCA2 mutations (which is a low probability as a relatively large number of women have breast cancer and these women rarely have one of these gene mutations). Denominator neglect and simultaneous focus on the relative gist of numerators lead people to think that the latter probability is higher than it is (Reyna, Lloyd, & Whalen, 2001; Wolfe & Reyna, 2010; see Wolfe et al., 2015 for a fuzzy-trace theory-based intervention that eliminates denominator neglect using icons).

Similar processing errors also occur when evaluating other risks. For example, if people are told that in a given year children had 20 accidents playing on slides and 5 on swings, many of them will conclude that slides are riskier than swings, ignoring the fact that more children may play on slides (Brainerd & Reyna, 2005). The probability that children were on certain equipment given that they had an accident is confused with the probability that they had an accident given that they were on certain equipment. In fact, the frequency of accidents on a certain type of equipment could be higher because children played on that equipment more often. Research has shown that these processing errors are made even late in development and can

---

[1] BRCA stands for *br*east *ca*ncer susceptibility gene. People who have BRCA1 or BRCA 2 gene mutations have a greatly increased risk of breast cancer and (for women) ovarian cancer.

be easily remedied by keeping classes of events clearly distinct, for example, by using visual aids that clearly show the numbers in each class (Reyna, 2004; Reyna et al., 2001; Wolfe & Reyna, 2010).

Neuroscience of Risk

As discussed above, recognizing an influence of mental representation (specifically gist or verbatim) on decisions regarding risk predicts and explains many findings in the literature on risk. Mental representation of information has an effect on risk taking, independent of concepts traditionally associated with risk such as affective motivational factors (including sensitivity to reward) and inhibition. Research has begun to identify neural substrates of each of these constructs, helping us to understand risk taking in the brain. This research provides support for the hypothesis that cognitive representation of information has an influence separate from that of affect and inhibition, since different areas of the brain have been associated with each construct.

Reward Sensitivity

The most important affective/motivational factor when considering risky decisions is sensitivity to reward. The reward circuit of the brain consists of the midbrain dopamine areas (the ventral tegmental area and substantia nigra) and the basal ganglia structures they project to (the ventral striatum, the dorsal striatum, and the ventromedial prefrontal cortex (vmPFC)). Dopaminergic activity in these areas has been linked to current and anticipated rewards. Specifically, increased dopamine in the striatum is associated with anticipation of a reward (Glimcher, Camerer, Fehr, & Poldrack, 2009).

Studies have shown that reward sensitivity is somewhat generalizable across stimuli, so, for example, an individual who is sensitive to monetary rewards is likely to also be sensitive to social rewards or food rewards (Delgado, Nystrom, Fissell, Noll, & Fiez, 2000; Levy & Glimcher, 2011). This "common currency" can also be seen in the brain, where common areas of neural activation (vmPFC and the dorsal striatim) have been shown to vary with reward valuations across domains (Levy & Glimcher, 2011). However, research suggests there are also discrete neural networks that respond to particular rewards. For example, the dorsal hypothalamic region has been shown to respond mainly to food rewards, whereas the posterior cingulate cortex has been shown to respond mainly to monetary rewards (Levy & Glimcher, 2011) (for a more detailed review of the literature regarding neural correlates of sensitivity to reward, see Reyna & Huettel, 2014).

Inhibitory Mechanisms

Activity in the dorsolateral prefrontal cortex (dlPFC) and anterior cingulate cortex (ACC) has been shown to activate with self-control and healthy behaviors, suggesting that they are involved when an individual avoids unhealthy risk taking (Casey et al., 2011; Hare, Camerer, & Rangel, 2009). This activity can be manifested as response inhibition, cognitive distraction (distancing), or reappraisal of the meaning of a stimulus (Ochsner & Gross, 2008; Venkatramen & Huettel, 2012). The dlPFC modulates the value signal encoded in the ventromedial PFC (vmPFC) (and other reward areas described below), and dlPFC activity is correlated with successful self-control (e.g., in go/no-go tasks (Casey et al., 2011) or when choosing healthy foods (Hare et al., 2009)). A recent electroencephalogram (EEG) study showed that people with higher dlPFC activity during resting state took fewer risks during a gambling task, suggesting that the dlPFC is involved in exercising self-control and avoidance of risk (Gianotti et al., 2009).

Mental Representations and Gist Processing

Memory studies and studies of decision making have provided insight into the neural substrates of gist and verbatim processing. These studies have provided insight into the brain regions associated with gist and verbatim processing and have also identified differences in functional connectivity depending on whether an individual is relying on gist or verbatim processing (see Reyna & Huettel, 2014).

One way to distinguish between gist and verbatim processing in the brain is to use tasks in which gist and verbatim strategies lead to different choices and measure activation in the brain while participants make these choices. For example, Venkatraman, Payne, Bettman, Luce, and Huettel (2009) explored the use of verbatim strategies (trading off risk and reward) versus gist strategies (categorical some/none thinking) using a risky-choice gambling task. They presented subjects with a series of five outcome gambles containing gain and loss outcomes (probabilities are shown in parentheses), such as $80 (0.2), $40 (0.25), $0 (0.2), −$25 (0.15), and -$70(0.2). Subjects could improve the gambles, for example, by adding $15 to either the $0 outcome (so it became $15) or the -$70 outcome (so it became -$55). Venkatramen and colleagues assessed three strategies: increasing the magnitude of the highest gain (Gmax), decreasing the magnitude of the worst loss (Lmin), or improving the probability of winning something by adding to the $0 outcome (Pmax). The only strategy that created a simple categorical difference between the options was the Pmax strategy (this strategy increased the chance of winning something versus winning nothing). The other two strategies (Gmax and Lmin) did not focus on the probability of winning something versus winning nothing, but instead focused on maximizing the magnitudes of potential gains or minimizing losses. Gmax (i.e., maximizing expected value or utility) and Lmin changed fine-grained distinctions but not categorical distinctions and therefore represent more verbatim processing. Therefore, this task made it possible to diagnose cognitive representations relied on by analyzing the choices subjects made—subjects who used the Gmax or Lmin (adding to the maximum possible win or the maximum possible loss) strategies were likely to be relying on verbatim processing, and subjects who used the Pmax strategy (adding to the middle value and therefore maximizing the probability of winning *something*) were likely to be relying on gist processing.

In this study, Venkatraman et al. (2009) found that activation in the posterior parietal cortex and dlPFC predicted gist-based simplifying choices, whereas activation in the vmPFC and anterior insula predicted verbatim, analytical choices. Functional connectivity analysis showed positive correlation between the dorsomedial PFC (dmPFC) and the dlPFC for gist-based choices (simplifying strategies) and between the dmPFC and insula for verbatim-based choices (compensatory strategies). Areas associated with conflict (the ACC and dmPFC) showed increased activation when participants made choices that conflicted with their dominant strategy (e.g., when a participant who generally preferred a gist-based simplifying option made a compensatory choice). Further research should be carried out to confirm the relationship between these areas and different mental representations, in order to confirm and further explore these relationships.

Conclusions

Research into the cognitive aspects of risk can provide insight into how people make decisions regarding risks. Early work showed that risk preference did not just depend on expected utility for an individual by showing that superficial changes in the wording of questions regarding risk influenced people's decisions. Prospect theory provided a psychophysical explanation of inconsistent risk preferences, and traditional dual-process theories explored the types of cognitive processes involved in decisions relating to risk. Theories such as construal level theory and fuzzy-trace theory added to these traditional theories by identifying additional factors that are important in decisions to take risks—notably, how options are mentally represented. Recognition of mental representation as an important construct in risk taking helps to explain seemingly counterintuitive findings in the developmental literature, including findings suggesting that adolescents are more rational (in the sense of trading-off of rewards and risks), but are also more prone to unhealthy risk taking.

Some traditional dual-process accounts of risk taking focus on the relationship between impulsivity and inhibition/controlled deliberation. Other dual-process accounts emphasize distinctions between Type 1 processes which are generally automatic, fast, and intuitive and Type 2 processes which are generally slow, logical, and sequential (Casey & Caudle, 2013; Epstein, 1994; Evans & Stanovich, 2013; Kahneman, 2011; Steinberg, 2008). Fuzzy-trace theory goes beyond traditional dual-process accounts, incorporating the influences of affective/motivational factors (such as emotion and reward sensitivity) and inhibition, but predicting that risk taking is about more than the distinction between Type 1 and Type 2 thinking. While traditional dual-process theories suggest that reasoning is primarily Type 2 thinking, fuzzy-trace theory suggests that there is another type of reasoning—intuitive reasoning using gist representations. This intuitive reasoning is not associated with impulsivity. It is sophisticated and developmentally advanced. Specifically, this reasoning increases from childhood to adulthood and generally supports healthy decision making and is the natural tendency of most adults. Based on this important additional component, fuzzy-trace theory recognizes three constructs that are important in risk taking—hot motivational/affective factors such as reward sensitivity and emotion (similar to Type 1), cold metacognitive factors such as reflection and inhibition (similar to Type 2), and gist versus verbatim mental representations.

These three components work together when individuals make decisions about risk. The recognition of more impulsive vs. more deliberative thinking, but also an independent role of mental representations, means that fuzzy-trace theory recognizes two routes to risk taking. One route is the route recognized by traditional dual-process theories. It is reactive and characterized by impulsivity or a failure to inhibit behavior, succumbing to emotion or temptation (similar to Type 1 or socioemotional as in imbalance theory, but separating intuition as a distinct kind of thinking) (see Reyna et al., 2011; Reyna & Mills, 2014; Rivers et al., 2008; Steinberg, 2007). The other is a reasoned route characterized by more verbatim-based analysis (relying on surface-level information rather than bottom-line meaning), taking account of the degree of risk and amount of reward and doing so roughly multiplicatively (Reyna et al., 2011). Research suggests that the second route, based on the type of mental representation relied on (precise, surface-level verbatim, or simple meaningful gist), is a major source of adolescent risk taking (Reyna et al., 2011; Reyna & Farley, 2006). The important role of mental representations is also supported by work on construal level theory, which shows a direct influence of the way information is represented on decisions to take or avoid risks.

The recognition of the importance of mental representations allows fuzzy-trace theory to explain counterintuitive findings and trends in the risk taking literature. Specifically, through the distinction between gist and verbatim processing, fuzzy-trace theory predicts findings showing that reliance on precise representations decreases from adolescence to adulthood while risk taking also decreases, that consistency in gain/loss risk preference decreases from adolescence to adulthood while risk taking also decreases, and that reliance on gist can have a protective effect against risk taking.

These important distinctions can advance our understanding of how risk is represented in the brain. Research has suggested the neural underpinnings of reward sensitivity lie in the dopaminergic circuitry of the brain as well as the prefrontal cortex, and the neural underpinnings of inhibition are mainly in the dorsolateral prefrontal cortex and the anterior cingulate cortex. Research is now also providing insight into the areas of the brain that may be involved in capturing gist, suggesting that the posterior parietal cortex and prefrontal cortex may be important areas (Reyna & Huettel, 2014).

Overall, emerging research into the cognitive and neurobiological aspects of risk, including work on fuzzy-trace theory and construal level theory, suggests an important role of a representational component in risk preference and risk taking. This approach builds on prospect theory and traditional dual-process theories, but explains and predicts findings in the literature that cannot be explained through these traditional theories. This understanding of the cognitive aspects of risk can help promote healthy attitudes to risk through encouraging reliance on bottom-line meaning, rather than surface-level information.

Acknowledgement Preparation of this manuscript was supported in part by a grant from the National Institutes of Health (National Institute of Nursing Research award RO1NR014368-01) to Valerie F. Reyna.

References

Adam, M. B., & Reyna, V. F. (2005). Coherence and correspondence criteria for rationality: Experts' estimation of risks of sexually transmitted infections. *Journal of Behavioral Decision Making, 18*(3), 169–186. https://doi.org/10.1002/bdm.493

Boily, M. C., Baggaley, R. F., Wang, L., Masse, B., White, R. G., Hayes, R. J., & Alary, M. (2009). Heterosexual risk of HIV-1 infection per sexual act: systematic review and meta-analysis of observational studies. *The Lancet Infectious Diseases, 9*(2), 118–129. https://doi.org/10.1016/S1473-3099(09)70021-0

Bonner, C., & Newell, B. R. (2008). How to make risk seem riskier: The ratio bias versus construal level theory. *Judgment and Decision making, 3*(5), 411–416.

Brainerd, C. J., & Reyna, V. F. (2005). The Science of False Memory. Oxford, UK: Oxford University Press.

Brainerd, C. J., Reyna, V. F., & Ceci, S. J. (2008). Developmental reversals in false memory: A review of data and theory. *Psychological Bulletin, 134*(3), 343–382. https://doi.org/10.1037/0033-2909.134.3.343

Casey, B. J., & Caudle, K. (2013). The teenage brain: Self-control. *Current Directions in Psychological Science, 22*(2), 82–87. https://doi.org/10.1177/0963721413480170

Casey, B. J., Jones, R. M., & Hare, T. A. (2008). The adolescent brain. *Annals of the New York Academy of Sciences, 1124*(1), 111–126. https://doi.org/10.1196/annals.1440.010

Casey, B. J., Somerville, L. H., Gotlib, I. H., Ayduk, O., Franklin, N. T., Askren, M. K., & Shoda, Y. (2011). Behavioral and neural correlates of delay of gratification 40 years later. *Proceedings of the National Academy of Sciences, 108*(36), 14998–15003. https://doi.org/10.1073/pnas.1108561108

Chandron, S., & Menon, G. (2004). When a day means more than a year: Effects of temporal framing on judgments of health risk. *Journal of Consumer Research, 31*, 375–389. https://doi.org/10.1086/422116

Dahl, R. E. (2004). Adolescent brain development: A period of vulnerabilities and opportunities. Keynote aggress. *Annals of the New York Academy of Sciences, 1021*(1), 1–22. https://doi.org/10.1016/j.pragma.2004.05.004

De Martino, B., Kumaran, D., Seymour, B., & Dolan, R. J. (2006). Frames, biases, and rational decision making in the human brain. *Science, 313*(5787), 684–687. https://doi.org/10.1126/science.1128356

Defoe, I. N., Dubas, J. S., Figner, B., & Van Aken, M. A. (2015). A meta-analysis on age differences in risky decision making: Adolescents versus children and adults. *Psychological Bulletin, 141*(1), 48–84. https://doi.org/10.1037/a0038088

Delgado, M. R., Nystrom, L. E., Fissell, C., Noll, D. C., & Fiez, J. A. (2000). Tracking the hemodynamic responses to reward and punishment in the striatum. *Journal of Neurophysiology, 84*(6), 3072–3077.

Epstein, S. (1994). Integration of the cognitive and the psychodynamic unconscious. *American Psychologist, 49*(8), 709–724. https://doi.org/10.1037/0003-066X.49.8.709

Evans, J. S. B., & Stanovich, K. E. (2013). Dual-process theories of higher cognition, advancing the debate. *Perspectives on Psychological Science, 8*(3), 223–241. https://doi.org/10.1177/1745691612460685

Figner, B., & Weber, E. U. (2011). Who takes risks when and why? Determinants of risk taking. *Current Directions in Psychological Science, 20*(4), 211–216. https://doi.org/10.1177/0963721411415790

Fox, C. R., & Tannenbaum, D. (2011). The elusive search for stable risk preferences. *Frontiers in Psychology, 2*(298), 1–4. https://doi.org/10.3389/fpsyg.2011.00298

Fujita, K., Henderson, M. D., Eng, J., Trope, Y., & Liberman, N. (2006). Spatial distance and mental construal of social events. *Psychological Science, 17*(4), 278–282. https://doi.org/10.1111/j.1467-9280.2006.01698.x

Fukukura, J., Ferguson, M. J., & Fujita, K. (2013). Psychological distance can improve decision making under information overload via gist memory. *Journal of Experimental Psychology: General, 142*(3), 658–665. https://doi.org/10.1037/a0030730

Gianotti, L. R., Knoch, D., Faber, P. L., Lehmann, D., Pascual-Marqui, R. D., Diezi, C., … Fehr, E. (2009). Tonic activity level in the right prefrontal cortex predicts individuals risk taking. *Psychological Science, 20*(1), 33–38. https://doi.org/10.1111/j.1467-9280.2008.02260.x

Gladwin, T. E., Figner, B., Crone, E. A., & Wiers, R. W. (2011). Addiction, adolescence, and the integration of control and motivation. *Developmental Cognitive Neuroscience, 1*(4), 364–376. https://doi.org/10.1016/j.dcn.2011.06.008

Glimcher, P. W., Camerer, C. F., Fehr, E., & Poldrack, R. A. (Eds.). (2009). *Neuroeconomics: Decision making and the brain*. New York, NY: Academic Press.

Hare, T. A., Camerer, C. F., & Rangel, A. (2009). Self-control in decision making involves modulation of the vmPFC valuation system. *Science, 324*, 646–648. https://doi.org/10.1126/science1168450

Helm, R. K., & Reyna, V. F. (2017). Logical but incompetent plea decisions: A new approach to plea bargaining grounded in cognitive theory. *Psychology, Public Policy, and Law, 23*(3), 367–380. https://doi.org/10.1037/law0000125

Helm, R. K., Reyna, V. F., Corbin, J. C., Wilhelms, E. A., & Weldon, R. B. (2014, November). *Verbatim reasoning distinguishes risky decision making in juvenile delinquents: A fuzzy trace theory approach*. Poster presented at the 35th Annual Meeting of the Society for Judgment and Decision Making, Long Beach, CA.

Kahneman, D. (2003). A perspective on judgment and choice: Mapping bounded rationality. *American Psychologist, 58*(9), 697–720. https://doi.org/10.1037/0003-066X.58.9.697

Kahneman, D. (2011). *Thinking fast and slow*. London: Penguin.

Kahneman, D., & Frederick, S. (2007). Frames and brains: Elicitation and control of response tendencies. *Trends in Cognitive Sciences, 11*(2), 45–46. https://doi.org/10.1016/j.tics.2006.11.007

Kühberger, A., & Tanner, C. (2010). Risky choice framing: Task versions and a comparison of prospect theory and fuzzy-trace theory. *Journal of Behavioral Decision Making, 23*(3), 314–329. https://doi.org/10.1002/bdm.656

Kwack, Y., Payne, J. W., Cohen, A. L., & Huettel, S. A. (2015). The rational adolescent: Strategic information processing during decision making revealed by eye tracking. *Cognitive Development, 36*, 20–30. https://doi.org/10.1016/j.cogdev.2015.08.001

Kahneman, D., & Frederick, S. (2002). Representativeness revisited: Attribute substitution in intuitive judgment. In T. Gilovich, D. Griffin, & D. Kahneman (Eds.), Heuristics and biases (pp. 49–81). New York: Cambridge University Press.

Lermer, E., Streicher, B., Sachs, R., Raue, M., & Frey, D. (2015). The effect of construal level on risk taking. *European Journal of Social Psychology, 45*(1), 99–109. https://doi.org/10.1002/ejsp.2067

Lermer, E., Streicher, B., Sachs, R., Raue, M., & Frey, D. (2016). Thinking concretely increases the perceived likelihood of risks: The effect of construal level on risk estimation. *Risk Analysis, 36*, 623–637. https://doi.org/10.1111/risa.12445

Levy, D. J., & Glimcher, P. W. (2011). Comparing apples and oranges: Using reward-specific and reward-general subjective value representation in the brain. *The Journal of Neuroscience, 31*(41), 14693–14707. https://doi.org/10.1523/JNEUROSCI.2218-11.2011

Loewenstein, G. F., Weber, E. U., Hsee, C. K., & Welch, N. (2001). Risk as feelings. *Psychological Bulletin, 127*(2), 267–286. https://doi.org/10.1037/0033-2909.127.2.267

Machina, M. J. (1982). "Expected utility" analysis without the independence axiom. *Econometrica: Journal of the Econometric Society, 50*(2), 277–323. https://doi.org/10.2307/1912631

Mills, B., Reyna, V. F., & Estrada, S. (2008). Explaining contradictory relations between risk perception and risk taking. *Psychological Science, 19*(5), 429–433. https://doi.org/10.1111/j.1467-9280.2008.02104.x

Ochsner, K. N., & Gross, J. J. (2008). Cognitive emotion regulation: Insights from social cognitive and affective neuroscience. *Current Directions in Psychological Science, 17*(2), 153–158. https://doi.org/10.1111/j.1467-8721.2008.00566.x

Raue, M., Streicher, B., Lermer, E., & Frey, D. (2014). How far does it feel? Construal level and decisions under risk. *Journal of Applied Research in Memory and Cognition, 4*, 256–264. https://doi.org/10.1016/j.jarmac.2014.09.005

Reyna, V. F. (1996). Conceptions of memory development with implications for reasoning and decision making. *Annals of Child Development, 12*, 87–118.

Reyna, V. F. (2004). How people make decisions that involve risk. A dual-process approach. *Current Directions in Psychological Science, 13*(2), 60–66. https://doi.org/10.1111/j.0963-7214.2004.00275.x

Reyna, V. F. (2008). A theory of medical decision making and health: fuzzy trace theory. *Medical Decision Making, 28*(6), 850–865.

Reyna, V. F. (2012). A new intuitionism: Meaning, memory, and development in fuzzy-trace theory. *Judgment and Decision making, 7*(3), 332–359.

Reyna, V. F., & Brainerd, C. J. (1994). The origins of probability judgment: A review of data and theories. In G. Wright & P. Ayton (Eds.), *Subjective probability* (pp. 239–272). New York, NY: Wiley.

Reyna, V. F., & Brainerd, C. J. (1995). Fuzzy-trace theory: An interim synthesis. *Leaning and Individual Differences, 7*(1), 1–75. https://doi.org/10.1016/1041-6080(95)90031-4

Reyna, V. F., & Brainerd, C. J. (2008). Numeracy, ratio bias, and denominator neglect in judgments of risk and probability. *Learning and Individual Differences, 18*(1), 89–107. https://doi.org/10.1016/j.lindif.2007.03.011

Reyna, V. F., & Brainerd, C. J. (2011). Dual processes in decision making and developmental neuroscience: A fuzzy-trace model. *Developmental Review, 31*(2–3), 180–206. https://doi.org/10.1016/j.dr.2011.07.004.

Reyna, V. F., & Casillas, W. (2009). Development and Dual Processes in Moral Reasoning: A Fuzzy-trace Theory Approach. *Psychology of Learning and Motivation, 50*, 207–236. https://doi.org/10.1016/S0079-7421(08)00407-6.

Reyna, V. F., & Ellis, S. C. (1994). Fuzzy-trace theory and framing effects in children's risky decision making. *Psychological Science, 5*(5), 275–279. https://doi.org/10.1111/j.1467-9280.1994.tb00625.x

Reyna, V. F., & Farley, F. (2006). Risk and rationality in adolescent decision making: Implications for theory, practice, and public policy. *Psychological Science in the Public Interest, 7*(1), 1–44. https://doi.org/10.1111/j.1529-1006.2006.00026.x

Reyna, V. F., & Huettel, S. A. (2014). Reward, representation, and impulsivity: A theoretical framework for the neuroscience of risky decision making. In V. F. Reyna & V. Zayas (Eds.), *The neuroscience of risky decision making* (pp. 11–42). Washington, DC: American Psychological Association.

Reyna, V. F., & Lloyd, F. J. (2006). Physician decision making and cardiac risk: Effects of knowledge, risk perception, risk tolerance, and fuzzy processing. *Journal of Experimental Psychology: Applied, 12*(3), 179–195. https://doi.org/10.1037/1076-898X.12.3.179

Reyna, V. F., & Mills, B. A. (2014). Theoretically motivated interventions for reducing sexual risk taking in adolescence: A randomized controlled experiment applying fuzzy-trace theory. *Journal of Experimental Psychology: General, 143*(4), 1627–1648. https://doi.org/10.1037/a0036717

Reyna, V. F., Lloyd, F. J., & Whalen, P. (2001). Genetic testing and medical decision making. *Archives of Internal Medicine, 161*(20), 2406–2408. https://doi.org/10.1001/archinte.161.20.2406

Reyna, V. F., Estrada, S. M., DeMarinis, J. A., Myers, R. M., Stanisz, J. M., & Mills, B. A. (2011). Neurobiological and memory models of risky decision making in adolescents versus young adults. *Journal of Experimental Psychology: Learning, Memory, and Cognition, 37*(5), 1125–1142. https://doi.org/10.1037/a0023943

Reyna, V. F., Chapman, S. B., Dougherty, M. R., & Confrey, J. E. (Eds.). (2012). *The adolescent brain: Learning, reasoning, and decision making*. Washington, DC: American Psychological Association.

Reyna, V. F., Chick, C. F., Corbin, J. C., & Hsia, A. N. (2014). Developmental reversals in risky decision making, intelligence agents show larger decision biases than college students. *Psychological Science, 25*(1), 76–84. https://doi.org/10.1177/0956797613497022

Reyna, V. F., Wilhelms, E. A., McCormick, M. J., & Weldon, R. B. (2015). Development of risky decision making: Fuzzy-trace theory and neurobiological perspectives. *Child Development Perspectives, 9*(2), 122–127. https://doi.org/10.1111/cdep.12117

Rivers, S. E., Reyna, V. F., & Mills, B. (2008). Risk taking under the influence: A fuzzy-trace theory of emotion in adolescence. *Developmental Review, 28*(1), 107–144. https://doi.org/10.1016/j.dr.2007.11.002.

Sagristano, M. D., Trope, Y., & Liberman, N. (2002). Time-dependent gambling: Odds now, money later. *Journal of Experimental Psychology: General, 131*(3), 364–376. https://doi.org/10.1037//0096-3445.131.3.364

Slovic, P. (2001). Cigarette smokers: Rational actors or rational fools? In P. Slovic (Ed.), *Smoking: Risk, perception and policy* (pp. 97–124). Thousand Oaks, CA: SAGE.

Slovic, P., Finucane, M. L., Peters, E., & Macgregor, D. (2006). Risk as analysis and risk as feelings: Some thoughts about affect, reason, risk, and rationality. *Risk Analysis, 24*(2), 311–322.

Somerville, L. H., & Casey, B. J. (2010). Developmental neurobiology of cognitive control and motivational systems. *Current Opinion in Neurobiology, 20*(2), 236–241. https://doi.org/10.1016/j.conb.2010.01.006

Somerville, L. H., Hare, T., & Casey, B. J. (2011). Frontostriatal maturation predicts cognitive control failure to appetitive cues in adolescents. *Journal of Cognitive Neuroscience, 23*(9), 2123–2134. https://doi.org/10.1162/jocn.2010.21572

Stanovich, K. E., & West, R. F. (2008). On the relative independence of thinking biases and cognitive ability. *Journal of Personality and Social Psychology, 94*(4), 672–695. https://doi.org/10.1037/0022-3514.94.4.672

Steinberg, L. (2007). Risk taking in adolescence: New perspectives from brain and behavioral science. *Current Directions in Psychological Science, 16*(2), 55–59. https://doi.org/10.1111/j.1467-8721.2007.00475.x

Steinberg, L. (2008). A social neuroscience perspective on adolescent risk taking. *Developmental Review, 28*(1), 78–106. https://doi.org/10.1111/j.1467-8721.2007.00475.x

Trope, Y., & Liberman, N. (2000). Temporal construal and time-dependent changes in preference. *Journal of Personality and Social Psychology, 79*(6), 876–889. https://doi.org/10.1037/0022-3514.79.6.876

Trope, Y., & Liberman, N. (2003). Temporal construal. *Psychological Review, 110*(3), 403–421. https://doi.org/10.1037/0033-295X.110.3.403

Trope, Y., & Liberman, N. (2010). Construal-level theory of psychological distance. *Psychological Review, 117*(2), 440–463. https://doi.org/10.1037/a0018963

Tversky, A., & Kahneman, D. (1981). The framing of decisions and the psychology of choice. *Science, 211*(4481), 453–458. https://doi.org/10.1126/science.7455683.

Tversky, A., & Kahneman, D. (1986). Rational choice and the framing of decisions. *Journal of Business, 59*(4), S251–S278.

Usher, M., Russo, Z., Weyers, M., Brauner, R., & Zakay, D. (2011). The impact of the mode of thought in complex decisions: Intuitive decisions are better. *Frontiers in Psychology, 2*, 37. https://doi.org/10.3389/fpsyg.2011.00037

von Neumann, J., & Mortgenstern, O. (1944). *Theory of games and economic behavior*. Princeton, NJ: Princeton University Press.

Venkatraman, V., Payne, J. W., Bettman, J. R., Luce, M. F., & Huettel, S. A. (2009). Separate neural mechanisms underlie choices and strategic preferences in risky decision making. *Neuron, 62*(4), 593–602. https://doi.org/10.1016/j.neuron.2009.04.007

Venkatramen, V. F., & Huettel, S. A. (2012). Strategic control in decision making under uncertainty. *European Journal of Neuroscience, 35*(7), 1075–1082. https://doi.org/10.1111/j.1460-9568.2012.08009.x

Wakslak, C. J., Trope, Y., Liberman, N., & Alnoy, R. (2006). Seeing the forest when entry is unlikely: Probability and the mental representation of events. *Journal of Experimental Psychology: General, 135*(4), 641–653. https://doi.org/10.1037/0096-3445.135.4.641

Weber, E. U., & Johnson, E. J. (2009). Mindful judgment and decision making. *Annual Review of Psychology, 60*, 53–85. https://doi.org/10.1146/annurev.psych.60.110707.163633

Wilhelms, E. A., Corbin, J. C., & Reyna, V. F. (2015). Gist memory in reasoning and decision making. In A. Feeney & V. Thompson (Eds.), *Reasoning as memory* (pp. 93–109). New York, NY: Psychology Press.

Wilhelms, E. A., Helm, R. K., Setton, R. A., & Reyna, V. F. (2014). Fuzzy trace theory explains paradoxical dissociations in affective forecasting. In E. A. Wilhelms & V. F. Reyna (Eds.), *Neuroeconomics, judgment, and decision making* (pp. 49–73). New York, NY: Psychology Press.

Wolfe, C. R., & Reyna, V. F. (2010). Semantic coherence and fallacies in estimating joint probabilities. *Journal of Behavioral Decision Making, 23*(2), 203–223. https://doi.org/10.1002/bdm.650

Wolfe, C. R., Reyna, V. F., Widmer, C. L., Cedillos, E. M., Fisher, C. R., Brust-Renck, P. G., & Weil, A. M. (2015). Efficacy of a web-based intelligent tutoring system for communicating genetic risk of breast cancer. A fuzzy-trace theory approach. *Medical Decision Making, 35*(1), 46–59. https://doi.org/10.1177/0272989X14535983

Chapter 5
Emotional Aspects of Risk Perceptions

Mary Kate Tompkins, Pär Bjälkebring, and Ellen Peters

Abstract Understanding the public's perceptions of risk is of great importance to governments, businesses, and scientists worldwide because the public influences what policies are enacted. As a result, how people perceive (and misperceive) the risks of various hazards and activities has been of interest to academic and other researchers for many years. Researchers in the field of judgment and decision making have examined and understood risk perceptions in two primary ways: risk as feelings and risk as analysis. Risk as analysis assumes people judge risk by assessing the desirability and likelihood of possible outcomes and integrating this information in a logical fashion. In contrast, risk as feelings suggests that people make risk judgments based at least in part on their feelings about possible hazards and activities. Risk as feelings calls attention to the vital role that affect and emotions play in the process of judging risk. Affect and emotions are beneficial in that they allow us to navigate efficiently through our risky and uncertain world. The primary aim of this chapter is to provide an overview of research that highlights the role of affect and emotions in risk perceptions. We focus on two related lines of work that have been fundamental to our understanding of risk as feelings: the affect heuristic and the appraisal-tendency framework.

Introduction

Understanding the public's perceptions of risk is of great importance to governments, businesses, and scientists worldwide because the public's views determine, in part, what policies are enacted, how industries are managed, and what products

M. K. Tompkins (✉) · E. Peters
Department of Psychology, The Ohio State University, Columbus, OH, USA
e-mail: Tompkins.61@osu.edu

P. Bjälkebring
Department of Psychology, University of Gothenburg, Gothenburg, Sweden

Department of Psychology, The Ohio State University, Columbus, OH, USA

M. Raue et al. (eds.), *Psychological Perspectives on Risk and Risk Analysis*,
https://doi.org/10.1007/978-3-319-92478-6_5

are deemed acceptable (Slovic, 1987). As a result, how and why people perceive and misperceive the risks of various hazards and activities has been of interest to academic and other researchers for many years (Slovic, 1999). Researchers in the field of judgment and decision making, in particular, have examined and understood risk perceptions as emerging from two processes, one that is feeling based and another that is based on analysis (Loewenstein, Weber, Hsee, & Welch, 2001; Slovic, Finucane, Peters, & MacGregor, 2002). The present chapter focuses on the importance of risk as feelings in understanding individuals' reactions to risk.

Risk as feelings and risk as analysis refer to two qualitatively different modes of information processing when judging risk. The notion of two different modes of information processing has its roots in dual-process theories of thinking and deciding. The analytic/deliberative mode (called System 2 by some researchers; Kahneman, 2003; Stanovich & West, 2000) is characterized by logical, reason-based, and deliberative processing. The affective/experiential mode (called System 1) is characterized by intuitive, automatic, and affective processing (Epstein, 1994; Loewenstein et al., 2001). The analytic mode is thought to be rule based and relatively controlled, whereas the affective/experiential mode is thought to be associative and rapid, producing thoughts and feelings in a relatively effortless manner. The central defining feature of this mode of processing is thought to be its affective basis (Slovic et al., 2002).

Until the 1990s, research in decision making focused on the rational, deliberative, and reason-based "cold" processes used when making decisions (Shafir, Simonson, & Tversky, 1993). Affect and emotions were not seen as an integral part of decision making other than as anticipated outcomes (e.g., a person may anticipate feeling disappointed about obtaining a different outcome and those thoughts about possible future feelings may influence choice; Loewenstein et al., 2001) or as a potential goal (e.g., the goal to be happy). In fact, one of the authors of the present chapter was told by a professor in her graduate school department that "you can't study emotions in decision making." Instead, affect's role in decision making was viewed as in opposition to reason, with decision making based on "hot processes" considered to be irrational and biased (Peters, Västfjäll, Gärling, & Slovic, 2006). Today, these interrelated modes of affective and deliberative processing are thought to influence each other and to guide judgments and decisions. For example, our first impressions of an individual are often based in affect and can have a long-lasting influence on how one thinks about that person's competence. However, this first impression can be overcome by thinking harder about the person (e.g., "In the beginning I did not like him, but now he has proven to be a great resource"). Both modes of information processing are important to making good decisions about risks because people have the need for rapid, but also controlled, risk assessments depending on their current situation (Damasio, 1994; Loewenstein et al., 2001; Loewenstein & Lerner, 2003; Peters, Hess, Västfjäll, & Auman, 2007). Although risk as analysis is perhaps still viewed as the essence of good decision making in our society, the risk-as-feelings framework calls attention to the vital role that affect and emotion play in the process of judging risk.

The primary aim of this chapter is to provide an overview of relevant research focused on the role of affect and emotion in understanding people's risk perceptions. In particular, we focus on two related lines of work that have been fundamental to our understanding of risk as feelings: the affect heuristic and the appraisal-tendency framework. These research streams differ in their focus on valenced affect (i.e., good and bad feelings in the affect heuristic) vs. discrete emotions (e.g., anger and sadness in the appraisal-tendency framework). Relative to affect, discrete emotions tend to be richer and more intense than subtle feelings of goodness or badness and are characterized by a number of cognitive-appraisal dimensions in addition to valence (Lerner & Keltner, 2000; Smith & Ellsworth, 1985). For example, fear is characterized as being negative and low on the cognitive-appraisal dimension of certainty; thus, fear is associated with viewing future events as unpredictable and incomprehensible (Lerner, Li, Valdesolo, & Kassam, 2015).

The affect heuristic and the appraisal-tendency framework can also be differentiated by their focus on integral vs. incidental affect and emotions. Integral affect and integral emotions are experienced as one considers a stimulus. These feelings are part of one's learned or constructed representation of a stimulus. For example, the positive feelings you experience when considering black raspberry chip ice cream is an example of integral affect. In comparison, incidental affect and incidental emotions are feelings that are unrelated to the stimulus, but can be misattributed to the stimulus or can influence decision processes in other ways (Peters, 2006; Peters et al., 2007). An example of incidental emotions includes feeling angry about missing a bus; these incidental emotions may then carry over to an evaluation of a job candidate (see Table 5.1 for additional examples). Research related to the appraisal-tendency framework focuses primarily on the role of incidental emotions in judgment and decision processes, whereas integral affect is the primary focus of the affect heuristic. These concepts will be further elaborated on in subsequent sections.

The organization of this chapter is as follows: First, we describe the affect heuristic and the research testing this framework in the domain of risk perceptions. Next, we review related evidence concerning how affect is important to the construction of judgments when numeric information is involved, and we discuss differences in the results based on numeracy (i.e., numeric ability). Third, we summarize the appraisal-tendency framework and highlight studies testing its emotion-specific view of risk. Lastly, we conclude with a discussion of future avenues of research.

Table 5.1 Examples of integral vs. incidental affect and emotion

	Affect	Emotion
Integral	Positive feelings about black raspberry chip ice cream may lead you to purchase it	Angry feelings about drunk drivers may cause you to vote for harsh punishments for them
Incidental	A negative mood from a rainy, cold day may carry over onto and increase perceptions of the risks of climate change	Happy feelings about getting a gift may carry over onto an evaluation of a job candidate and make that person appear more qualified

Affect and Risk Perceptions: The Affect Heuristic

Affect is more specifically defined as a feeling of goodness or badness that is part of one's internal representation of an object that is experienced as a feeling state (with or without conscious thought) when considering that object (Slovic et al., 2002; Slovic, Finucane, Peters, & MacGregor, 2004). The extent to which it influences judgments and decisions is thought to vary along a continuum. Affect is theorized to influence judgments and decisions most often in complex, unfamiliar, or unanticipated situations (Forgas, 1995). When resources are limited or the judgment is complex, relying on affect can be quicker, more efficient, and easier than weighing the pros and cons of various reasons when making judgments. For example, early work by Zajonc (1980) first demonstrated that people's affective reactions to stimuli are typically more rapid than cognitive evaluations. In one such study, participants viewed polygons for one millisecond each. Following exposure, participants indicated how much they liked each of the polygons and whether they had seen each polygon before. Participants judged their affect toward the polygons faster than they indicated whether they recognized them. Additionally, the majority of participants showed better discrimination between objectively old and objectively new stimuli in their affective judgments than in their recognition responses. Relying on affect was quicker and also more accurate than making cognitive judgments in Zajonc's studies.

This reliance on affect as information in the process of making judgments and decisions is characterized as the affect heuristic (Finucane, Alhakami, Slovic, & Johnson, 2000; Slovic et al., 2002; Slovic et al., 2004; Slovic & Peters, 2006; Slovic, Peters, Finucane, & MacGregor, 2005). Initial support for the affect heuristic in judgments of risk, in particular, came from research examining the relation between people's risk and benefit perceptions across diverse hazards. Objectively, risks and benefits tend to be positively correlated across hazards (e.g., stocks with high risk will also tend to offer high returns in financial markets; if highly risky stocks do not offer high returns, they will not be purchased and will disappear from the market). However, the opposite is true when it comes to people's subjective judgments of the same objects, activities, and hazards (Fischhoff, Slovic, Lichtenstein, Read, & Combs, 1978; Slovic, 1987). Researchers have studied a wide variety of hazards in many domains (e.g., technologies, products, activities) and found that the greater benefit people perceived, the less risk they perceived for these hazards (and vice versa). For example, antibiotics and railroads were judged as low in risk and high in benefit, whereas pesticides and nuclear power were seen as high in risk and low in benefit (Fischhoff et al., 1978; Slovic, Peters, Grana, Berger, & Dieck, 2007). Alhakami and Slovic (1994) provided initial evidence that people's overall affective evaluation of a hazard could account for this inverse relationship between risk and benefit perceptions (see Fig. 5.1). Specifically, they found that perceived risks and perceived benefits of hazards were linked to the strength of an individual's positive or negative affective evaluation of the hazard. If the individuals felt good about the activity, they tended to judge the risk as low and the benefit as high; the opposite

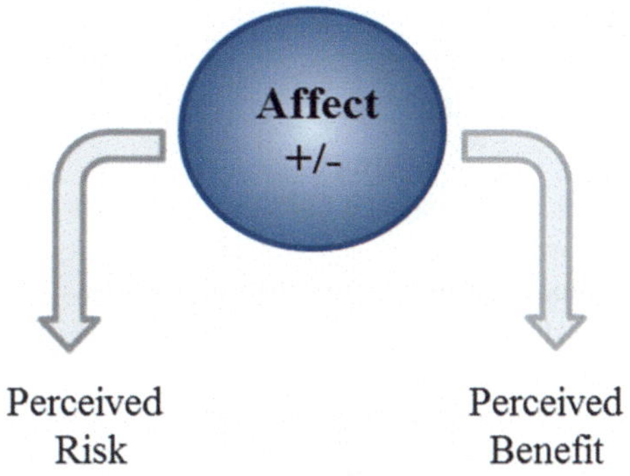

Fig. 5.1 This affect heuristic model illustrates affect's confounding link between the inverse association of risk and benefits, as found by Alhakami and Slovic (1994). Image adapted from Finucane et al. (2000)

was true if they felt bad about the activity (i.e., they perceived high risk and low benefit). These results suggest that individuals make risk judgments based not only on their cognitions but also on their feelings.

If people rely on affect when making risk and benefit judgments, then providing additional information related to the benefits of an activity should alter risk perceptions toward that activity, just as providing information about the risks should alter benefit perceptions. This idea was tested and supported in an experiment by Finucane et al. (2000; see Fig. 5.2). Consistent with the affect heuristic model, providing information that the benefit of a technology was high decreased risk perceptions (presumably because individuals' overall affective evaluation became more positive and they used it to make their risk judgments, see Fig. 5.2a). Similarly, information that the benefit was low increased risk perceptions (Fig. 5.2c).

In a second study, Finucane and colleagues tested whether reliance on affect increased when the opportunity to deliberate was reduced through time pressure (participants were allowed only limited time to indicate their responses). As mentioned before, Zajonc (1980) first demonstrated that affective reactions to stimuli are typically more rapid than cognitive evaluations. In Finucane and colleague's study, participants reported perceived risk and benefit judgments toward various activities and products (e.g., air travel, food preservatives) under time pressure or not. In the time-pressure condition, a countdown clock notified participants they had a limited amount of time to respond to each item. In the no-time-pressure condition, participants were free to complete the items at their own pace. Finucane and colleagues predicted that the inverse relation between perceived risk and benefit would be stronger in the time-pressure condition than the no-time-pressure condition because individuals would have less opportunity to deliberate and would therefore rely more on their affective feelings toward the activity or product to make their judgments. Consistent with predictions, researchers found that the negative correlation between individuals' perceived risk and benefit judgments across items was *stronger* for those in the time-pressure condition than those in the no-time-pressure condition. These results support the idea that an affect heuristic is used when judging risks and benefits and its use increases with less opportunity to deliberate.

In addition to studying the affect heuristic in the domains of natural and technological hazards, support for the affect heuristic has also been found in the financial

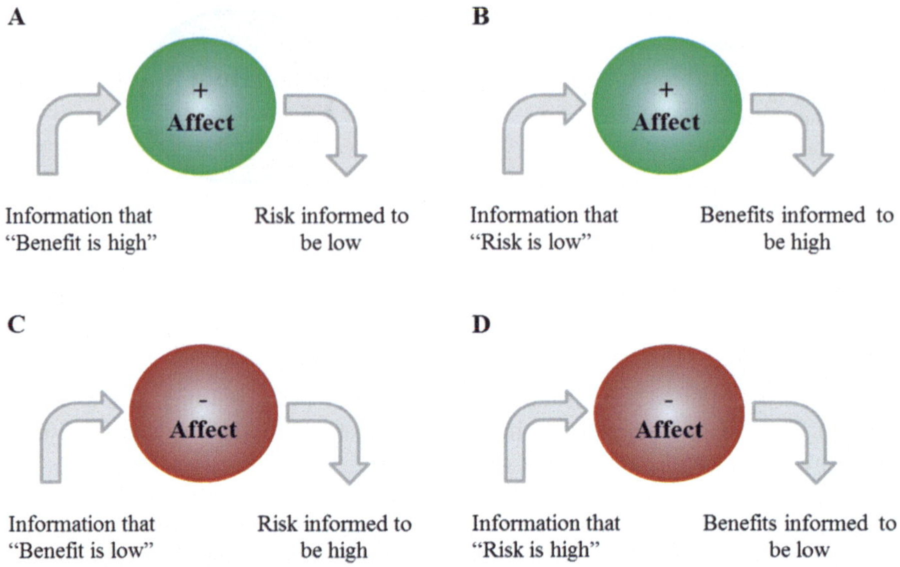

Fig. 5.2 This model illustrates how information about benefits (**a**) or risks (**b**) increases the overall affective view of a hazard and leads to risk and benefit judgments that are affectively congruent with the provided information. Furthermore, information about benefits and risks can lead to a more negative overall evaluation of a hazard (**c**, **d**), resulting in risk and benefit judgments opposite of those in (**a**, **b**). Image adapted from Finucane et al. (2000)

domain. Across several studies, Ganzach (2000) asked finance students (with extensive educational training) to judge the likely risks and returns of investing in familiar or unfamiliar stocks. When stocks were familiar to participants, the authors of this study predicted that participants would bring their expertise to bear and their judgments would reflect the relation between risk and return as it exists in the financial market (i.e., a positive relation). However, when stocks were unfamiliar, the authors predicted participants would use global affective evaluations of the stock to judge risk and return. Consistent with the affect heuristic framework, students perceived a negative relation between risk and return for unfamiliar assets (e.g., they judged high risk with low return). For familiar assets, however, judgments of risk and return were positively rather than negatively correlated (e.g., they judged high risk with high return). This study suggests that reliance on the affect heuristic in risk judgments may depend on the familiarity level of the target risk item (although see Alhakami & Slovic, 1994[1]). The importance of familiarity needs to be further explored in this and other domains, but these findings are consistent with prior theorizing by Forgas (1995) that affect influences judgments and decisions most often in complex, unfamiliar, or unanticipated situations. Overall, Ganzach's findings sup-

[1] Prior research by Alhakami and Slovic (1994) did not find evidence that familiarity was predictive of this inverse relationship between risk and benefits; however, these researchers did not test specifically for the interaction of affect and familiarity in their model.

port the notion that reliance on affect in financial judgments is likely at least in circumstances when the target risk is unfamiliar and difficult to judge.

More recent theorizing has argued that affect has four primary functions in the construction of judgments and decisions (for reviews, see Peters, 2006; Peters, Lipkus, & Diefenbach, 2006; Peters, Västfjäll, Gärling, & Slovic, 2006). First, affect can act as *information* to guide judgment and decision processes (Schwarz & Clore, 1983); this function characterizes the affect heuristic at work. These feelings provide information concerning what to choose, what not to choose, and how to judge target objects or attributes. Second, affect can act as a *spotlight* that directs individuals' attention or focus to different information. The information in the spotlight then guides the judgments or choices that follow. Third, it can act as a *motivator* of behavior, such as eliciting approach or avoidance tendencies. Fourth, affect serves a *common currency* across judgments and decisions. It allows individuals to make simple comparisons of good and bad feelings instead of complex trade-offs among conflicting analytical arguments or reasons. These functions of affect may be particularly important in the construction of risk judgments and decisions as indicated below.

The independent effects of three of these functions of affect were tested and supported recently in an experimental study of graphic warnings on cigarette packaging (Evans et al., 2015); graphic health warnings include text plus a pictorial warning that is marked by a lifelike or realistic description that is vividly or plainly shown. Graphic warnings on cigarette packs are thought to increase perceptions of smoking's health risks and to reduce smoking rates, but current evidence is based primarily on observational research conducted outside the United States. Evans et al. (2015) randomly assigned smokers to receive cigarettes with warnings featuring basic text, graphic images, or graphic images and elaborated text for 4 weeks. Their results provided support for three functions of affect in risk perceptions and intentions to smoke. First, affect functioned as information; exposure to graphic images (vs. text-only warnings) elicited greater negative affect to smoking, which increased risk perceptions. Second, this negative affect also acted as a motivator of behavioral intentions in that greater negative affect independently also led directly to greater quit intentions. Third, the function of affect as a spotlight was also supported; negative affect elicited by the images promoted greater scrutiny of risk information, which increased perceived credibility of the warning labels and ultimately led to increased risk perceptions and quit intentions. Overall, negative affect elicited by graphic (vs. text-only) warnings increased risk perceptions and quit intentions in three different ways, by serving as information, as a motivator, and as a spotlight that led people to think more about smoking's risks.

Taken together, the correlational and experimental studies previously discussed demonstrate that affect has marked influences on people's risk assessments. Individuals make risk judgments based not only on their cognitions but also on their integral feelings. Work by Alhakami and Slovic (1994), Finucane et al. (2000), and others demonstrates that if people feel good about a hazard, they tend to judge the risk as low and the benefit as high; the opposite is true if people feel bad about the hazard (i.e., they perceive high risk and low benefit). Additionally, various studies illustrate that people rely more on affective processes when less opportunity exists to deliberate or when the judgment is complex or unfamiliar (e.g., Finucane et al., 2000; Ganzach, 2000). Relying on affect can be particularly beneficial in these circumstances because it provides a more efficient mode of processing. We turn next to the important role of affect in the construction of risk perceptions when numeric information is involved.

Risk Perceptions and Numeracy

Risk likelihoods are often provided to people in a numeric format. Although numbers are generally considered dry and abstract, how they are presented can sway individuals' risk judgments by eliciting various levels of affect. For example, in a study by Slovic, Monahan, and MacGregor (2000), experienced psychologists and psychiatrists assessed the likelihood that a mental patient would commit an act of violence after being discharged from the hospital. The likelihood of the adverse event was presented in either a frequency format ("20 out of every 100" similar patients are estimated to commit an act of violence) or an equivalent probabilistic format (20% chance). Interestingly, Slovic and colleagues found that clinicians who received the risk information in a frequency format were more likely to refuse to discharge the patient than those who received the risk information in a probabilistic format. Additional follow-up studies found that representations of risk in a frequency format ("20 out of every 100") led to frightening images of violent patients (e.g., "Some guy going crazy and killing someone"), whereas the equivalent probabilistic format (20% chance) elicited comments about the number itself being small and abstract (Slovic & Peters, 2006). Presumably, these images of violent patients evoked negative affect, which, in turn, increased risk perceptions among those who received the information in a frequency format (see also Hoffrage & Garcia-Retamero, Chap. 12).

However, individuals differ in their susceptibility to this effect based on their objective numeracy skills (defined as the ability to process and use basic probability and mathematical concepts; Peters et al., 2006). Peters and colleagues ran a version of the previously described format effect experiment and found that individuals who were higher in objective numeracy were less susceptible to the presentation format effect (Peters, Västfjäll, Slovic, et al., 2006). Specifically, individuals higher in objective numeracy rated the risk of the adverse event approximately the same across formats, whereas individuals lower in objective numeracy perceived more risk when the likelihood of the adverse event was presented in the frequency format (10 of 100) vs. the probabilistic format (10% of 100). Peters and colleagues speculated that individuals higher in objective numeracy may be more likely or able to transform the numeric risk information from one format to the other (i.e., 10% = 10 out of 100) so that they have both formats available. Those lower in objective numeracy, on the other hand, were thought less likely or able to do the same transformation, leaving them with information only in the format they were provided.

Thus, when given the frequency format, they would be influenced by its affective imagery, but, when given the probability format, they would simply perceive a small abstract number.

Additional findings from Peters and colleagues' work demonstrated that individuals higher in objective numeracy derive greater integral affective meaning from numeric information and number comparisons, such as probabilities, compared to those lower in objective numeracy (Peters, Västfjäll, Slovic, et al., 2006). In one study, Peters and colleagues asked participants to imagine they had a chance to win a $5 prize by drawing a colored jelly bean from one of two bowls containing white and colored beans. The smaller bowl had a smaller number, but larger proportion (1 in 10, 10%), of colored jellybeans than the larger bowl (9 in 100, 9%) and thus offered a better chance of winning. However, prior research has demonstrated that individuals often choose the larger bowl because the greater number of colored beans is more inviting (Denes-Raj & Epstein, 1994). Peters and colleagues predicted that individuals lower in objective numeracy would be the ones who found the absolute number of colored beans more inviting and who chose the larger bowl because they derived less affective meaning from the presented proportions. Individuals higher in objective numeracy would instead rely on integral affective meaning derived from the objective probabilities (the 9% vs. the 10%) to guide their decision in this task. Consistent with predictions, individuals lower in objective numeracy were more likely than the highly numerate to choose the larger bowl with the *lower* likelihood of winning, the suboptimal choice. The reason for this difference appeared to be that individuals with lower in objective numeracy derived less precise affective feelings about the larger bowl's 9% chance of winning. Specifically, experimenters asked participants, "how clear a feeling do you have about the goodness or badness of [the larger bowl's] 9% chance of winning?" and found that individuals lower in objective numeracy had less precise feelings about the 9% chance of winning than did the highly numerate. In a sample of Ghanaian adults, the association between lower objective numeracy and poorer performance on this task has also replicated using a health-risk scenario that involved selecting a village that had a greater likelihood of meeting someone with HIV (Peters, Baker, Dieckmann, Leon, & Collins, 2010).

Reliance on affect, while generally helpful, can sometimes mislead people when the potential consequences of an event evoke particularly strong positive or negative affect. Several studies by Rottenstreich and Hsee (2001) found that individuals were mostly insensitive to large differences in the likelihood of an event occurring (i.e., probability neglect) if the event was rich in affect. For example, Rottenstreich and Hsee asked participants how much they would be willing to pay to avoid a 1% (or 99%) chance of receiving a short, painful electric shock (affect-rich stimulus) or to avoid a $20 cash penalty (affect-poor stimulus). They found that the median price participants paid to avoid receiving the electric shock was similar across the probability conditions, 1% vs. 99%, despite the large difference in the likelihood of occurrence. The variation in probability of the shock appeared to have little to no weight on people's responses. The opposite was true for people's payments to avoid the cash penalty (affect-poor stimulus), such that people were sensitive to variation in its probability of occurrence. Additional studies by Rottenstreich and Hsee replicated this result with positive outcomes (e.g., kissing a movie star vs. receiving cash). As discussed by Loewenstein et al. (2001), people seem to be sensitive to the possibility instead of the probability of affect-rich outcomes in decisions under uncertainty. More recent research has replicated this probability neglect finding and found that the difference remains even after accounting for differences in evaluations between monetary and non-monetary outcomes (e.g., McGraw, Shafir, & Todorov, 2010).

Summary: The Affect Heuristic

In many of these examples, use of the affect heuristic led participants astray. However, in general, it is thought to be an efficient mechanism that helps us process risk information in ways that allow us to navigate our complex world effectively. Without these integral affective reactions, severe impairments in risky decision making can occur (see Bechara, Damasio, Damasio, & Anderson, 1994; Bechara, Damasio, Tranel, & Damasio, 1997; Bechara, Tranel, Damasio, & Damasio, 1996; Damasio, 1994). In particular, decision-makers can get lost in thought, unable to choose and act (Peters et al., 2009). These affective reactions depend on characteristics of the individual, such as objective numeracy, but also depend greatly on contextual factors (e.g., the presence of a small loss) that help to determine affect and, thus, preference for risks (Bateman, Dent, Peters, Slovic, & Starmer, 2007). We turn next to research on discrete emotions, such as sadness and anger, which are more complex than simple feelings of goodness or badness.

Emotions and Risk Perceptions: The Appraisal-Tendency Framework (ATF)

Emotions are defined as multifaceted, simultaneous reactions that have experiential, cognitive, behavioral, and expressive components (Lerner et al., 2015). Like affect, emotions can be experienced with or without conscious awareness. Differences in emotions are not only characterized by experienced feelings (e.g., physiological reactions) but also by the way in which people differentially appraise or assess their environment along a number of cognitive dimensions. Researchers have proposed a variety of discrete cognitive-appraisal dimensions to characterize different emotion states. These dimensions include, but are not limited to, *pleasantness*, *certainty*, *attentional activity*, *anticipated effort*, *control*, and *responsibility* (e.g., Lerner & Keltner, 2000, 2001; Smith & Ellsworth, 1985). For example, surprise is proposed to be characterized by high pleasantness (the extent to which one feels pleasure), low certainty (the extent to which future events seem predictable and comprehensible), low anticipated effort (the degree to which physical or mental exertion seems to be needed), and high responsibility (the extent to which someone or something other than oneself is responsible; Lerner et al., 2015). The pleasantness dimension, in particular, can be thought of as the valenced affect from the affect heuristic (Peters, Burraston, & Mertz, 2004).

Instead of making predictions based only on an emotion's valence, Lerner and Keltner (2000, 2001) proposed an emotion-specific model for understanding the influences of emotions on judgments and decisions, known as the appraisal-tendency framework (ATF). An important distinguishing factor of the ATF from the affect heuristic and other theories is that emotions of the same valence (negative to positive, or unpleasant to pleasant) can have different influences on risk judgments due to the unique cognitive-appraisal dimensions associated with specific emotions (Lerner et al., 2015; Lerner & Keltner, 2000; Lerner & Keltner, 2001). For example, sadness and anger are both negative in valence, but researchers have found that they can have different effects on judgments of likelihood. Specifically, sad individuals judged saddening events as being more likely to occur than angering events, whereas angry individuals judged angering events as being more likely to occur than saddening events (De Steno, Petty, Wegener, & Rucker, 2000). Furthermore, the ATF posits that two emotions of different valences (like happiness and anger) can have similar influences on judgments and decisions if they are similar along another appraisal, such as certainty. Experiencing greater levels of happiness or anger, for example, was found to be associated with greater optimism of future life events, whereas greater fear was associated with less optimism (Lerner & Keltner, 2001). Instead of making predictions based only on an emotion's valence, the ATF proposes an emotion-specific model for understanding risk perceptions.

Most ATF research has examined differential effects of incidental fear and anger (both negative emotions) on risk judgments because of their differences in appraisals of certainty (the extent to which future events seem predictable and understandable) and control (the extent to which events seem caused by an individual or situational factors; Lerner & Tiedens, 2006). According to the ATF, fear arises from appraisals of low certainty and low individual control, whereas anger arises from appraisals of high certainty and high individual control (see Table 5.2). Thus, the appraisal-tendency hypothesis predicts that making people fearful should decrease feelings of certainty about what is going to happen and decrease feelings of individual control, whereas making people angry should increase feelings of certainty and individual control. Lerner and Keltner (2000, 2001) were interested in certainty and control dimensions, in particular, because they conceptually map closely onto "unknown risk" and "dread risk" factors that were previously found to be central determinants of risk perceptions (Fischhoff et al., 1978; Slovic, 1987). "Dread risk" is defined at the high end by perceived lack of control, dread, and catastrophic potential (similar to the ATF's control dimension), whereas "unknown risk" is defined at the high end by hazards judged to be unknown, unobservable, and delayed in their harm (similar to the ATF's certainty dimension; Slovic, 1987).

Table 5.2 Cognitive-appraisal dimensions for fear and anger based on the appraisal-tendency framework

Negatively valenced emotion		
	Fear	Anger
Pleasantness	Low	Low
Certainty	Low	High
Attentional activity	Medium	Medium
Anticipated effort	High	Medium
Control	Low	High
Responsibility	Medium	High
Appraisal tendency	Perceive negative events as unpredictable and under situational control	Perceive negative events as predictable, under human control, and brought about by others
Influence on risk perception	*Perceive high risk*	*Perceive low risk*

Table modified from Lerner and Keltner (2000), Taylor & Francis Ltd, www.tandfonline.com

Across a series of correlational and experimental studies, Lerner and colleagues predicted and found that incidental anger and fear had opposite effects on individuals' risk perceptions and risky choices (Fischhoff, Gonzalez, Lerner, & Small, 2005; Lerner, Gonzalez, Small, & Fischhoff, 2003; Lerner & Keltner, 2001). Specifically, incidental fear evoked greater risk perceptions than did incidental anger (Lerner & Keltner, 2000, 2001). In the first correlational study, Lerner and Keltner (2000) examined the relations of naturally occurring fear and anger with individuals' risk perceptions. Participants completed measures of dispositional fear and anger and estimated the number of US deaths per year caused by a variety of events (e.g., strokes, floods). Consistent with predictions, Lerner and Keltner found that greater fear was associated with higher risk perceptions (i.e., higher death estimates across the events), whereas anger was negatively associated with risk perceptions (i.e., more anger related to lower death estimates across the events). In a second correlational study, Lerner and Keltner (2001) examined the influence of dispositional fear and anger on risky choices and found that more fearful individuals made more risk-averse choices and angrier individuals made more risk-seeking choices. These correlational studies highlight that emotions of the same valence can have opposite associations with risk perceptions and preferences.

Lerner and colleagues also conducted experimental manipulations of fear and anger to demonstrate their causal impact on risk perceptions (Fischhoff et al., 2005; Lerner et al., 2003; Lerner & Keltner, 2001). In one experimental study, Lerner and Keltner (2001) induced incidental fear or anger with a writing exercise. Participants were asked to describe three to five things that made them most fearful or angry and to elaborate on one situation that made them most afraid or angry. Participants then estimated the likelihood that an assortment of events would happen to them in the future (e.g., having a heart attack before age 50). Results from this study indicated that fearful participants reported less optimistic risk estimates of future events than angry participants. Furthermore, the effect of emotion condition on participants' risk estimates was explained by self-reported appraisals of control. In other words, reduced feelings of control from participants in the fearful state compared to the angry state seemed to cause fearful participants to perceive greater risks to future events. These findings provide additional support for the appraisal-tendency hypothesis.

In a second experimental study, Lerner et al. (2003) tested whether the divergent effects of anger and fear generalized to risks of terrorism and policy preferences during the aftermath of the September 11th terrorist attacks in a nationally representative sample. In this study, participants completed a writing exercise similar to the exercise described above, but they wrote specifically about the terrorist attacks and watched news clips related to terrorism. Lerner and colleagues predicted and found that individuals who felt more fearful (naturally occurring or experimentally induced) about the terrorist attacks perceived greater risks of future acts of terrorism (e.g., greater perceived likelihood that another major terrorist attack will occur within the next 12 months) than individuals who felt angry. Furthermore, because anger evokes appraisals of certainty and individual control, whereas fear evokes appraisals of situational control, angry individuals endorsed different terrorism policies than fearful individuals. Specifically, angry individuals supported vengeful policies (e.g., deporting foreigners in the United States who lack valid visas) more than fearful individuals, whereas fearful individuals preferred more conciliatory policies (e.g., strengthen ties with countries in the Moslem world) than angry individuals. These study findings are valuable in that they illustrate the unique impact of emotions on the public's perceptions of terrorist risks, an issue of intense interest, and they provide implications for public policy. Additionally, the stimuli used as part of the fear and anger manipulations came from national news media and demonstrate how media in the real world can impact the public's risk perceptions. Somewhat less clear from this study was whether the results were due to integral affect about past or possible future terrorist attacks or whether they were due to the incidental affect elicited by the films in the moment (with testing conducted immediately afterwards).

Relatively few studies have examined the influence of mixed emotions on risk judgments. Instead, most emotion studies tend to manipulate one incidental emotion at a time. However, experiencing mixed emotions is common, especially if we consider feelings about technologies and hazards. For example, people may feel high levels of anger and fear regarding nuclear energy. When people experience mixed emotions, cognitive appraisals presumably are also mixed. In one study, Peters et al. (2004) examined the influence of mixed emotions on risk perceptions of stigmatized technologies. The authors measured individuals' fear and anger toward radiation sources, as well as several cognitive-appraisal dimensions integral to the radiation sources (measured as valenced affect, causation, coping, and importance). As expected, participants experienced both angry and fearful feelings. To compute a mixed-emotion variable, the experimenters averaged participants' fear and anger ratings toward radiation sources. Results from this study indicated that the discrete cognitive-appraisal dimensions (previously described) independently predicted this mixed-emotion variable and the presence of greater mixed emotions predicted higher risk perceptions toward radiation. For example, individuals who perceived nuclear power plants as more important (a cognitive-appraisal dimension related to increased attention) reported greater angry and fearful feelings, and individuals with greater mixed angry and fearful feelings perceived more risk toward nuclear power plants. Interestingly, this study also found that valenced affect toward radiation sources independently predicted risk perceptions over and above the mixed-emotion variable. In other words, simple negative feelings (valence) predicted risk perceptions toward nuclear power plants directly as well as indirectly through individuals' mixed emotions. Peters and colleagues speculated that affect toward radiation sources may have been more consistent (i.e., mostly good or bad) than the other cognitive-appraisal dimensions when mixed emotions were present. This consistency may make affect more important for predicting responses to hazards when people experience a mixture of emotions. Results from this study are unique in that they provide evidence for both the affect heuristic model and a cognitive-appraisal model of risk perceptions when people experience multiple emotions simultaneously toward a hazard such as radiation.

More recent research on mixed emotions has investigated how risk perceptions and negative emotions change over time in the midst of a crisis. During the economic crisis from September 2008 to October 2009, Burns, Peters, and Slovic (2012) examined changes in the public's risk perceptions toward the financial crisis. Consistent with predictions, they found that in general, individuals experienced mixed negative emotions and individuals who experienced greater negative emotion (comprised of sadness, anxiety, fear, anger, worry, stress) toward the financial crisis perceived greater risk emanating from the crisis. Modeling each discrete negative emotion separately did not alter conclusions, providing support for the affect heuristic model. In regard to change over time, trajectory plots from this study illustrated that people's risk perceptions and negative emotions toward the financial crisis moved together; both declined quickly in the beginning and then tapered off over time. A key finding from this study was that negative emotions to the crisis almost entirely accounted for the initial downward trend in risk perceptions. These results highlight the large role emotions play in the public's risk perceptions toward a crisis and in changes in those risk perceptions over time. Furthermore, these results support the notion that individuals' overall summary of feelings toward a hazardous event or activity may be more predictive of risk perceptions than specific emotions when mixed emotions are present.

Summary: Emotions and Risk Perceptions

Overall, these findings are valuable to our understanding of how emotions influence the public's response to risk in the world. In support of the risk-as-feelings framework, a variety of studies illustrate that emotions can have causal impacts on risk perceptions. This effect appears to be driven by cognitive-appraisal dimensions, including simple valenced affect (Johnson & Tversky, 1983). Additionally, these findings highlight that emotions of the same valence can have opposite influences on risk perceptions and preferences in some cases (Lerner & Keltner, 2001). In the real world, controversial topics that are relevant to public policy (e.g., global warming, welfare, national healthcare, war on terror, abortion, immigration) are complex issues and likely elicit a mix of emotions and cognitive appraisals. In these cases, affect may be more important than specific emotions in predicting people's risk judgments and choices (Peters et al., 2004). Further research is needed to better understand the impact of mixed emotions and mixed cognitive appraisals on the public's risk perceptions, preferences, and endorsement of policies.

Future Research Directions

In addition to the questions already raised, a variety of interesting avenues exist for future risk research. Below, we discuss three topics that would expand our understanding of how affective and deliberative processes interact to form and influence risk judgments. Specifically, we discuss the potential role of emotions in the cultural cognition theory of risk, the influence of arousal on risk perceptions over time, and emotion regulation.

Cultural Cognition Theory of Risk

Despite a large accumulation of scientific evidence, the American public tends to disagree on many risk issues, such as climate change, nuclear power, and vaccines (Kahan et al., 2012; Kahan, Jenkins-Smith, & Braman, 2011). Experts have questioned (and even despaired over) why the public fails to form beliefs consistent with scientific evidence on climate change and other issues of risk. One potential explanation is that members of the public are less informed or know too little science to understand the evidence (referred to hereafter as the science comprehension theory). Another potential explanation is that individuals tend to form perceptions of societal risks that are in line with values that are characteristic of the groups with which they identify (referred to as the cultural cognition theory of risk or worldviews) in ways that produce emotional reactions to risks (Peters et al., 2004). In the United States, people tend to subscribe to hierarchical, individualistic worldviews (these individuals tend to be more right leaning) or to egalitarian, communitarian worldviews (these individuals tend to be more left leaning). Those individuals who hold egalitarian, communitarian worldviews, for example, tend to be morally suspicious of commerce and industry and tend to have greater negative emotional reactions to environmental risks and to perceive great risks from them; those who hold hierarchical, individualistic worldviews tend to be more supportive of commerce and industry while having less negative reactions to and being skeptical of environmental risks.

Although science illiteracy is rampant, recent research suggests that this cannot be the only explanation for why the public fails to form beliefs consistent with scientific evidence. Instead, there is evidence to support the cultural cognition theory of risk. The science comprehension theory of risk predicts that individuals higher in science literacy and numeracy should perceive greater climate change risk, consistent with scientific evidence on climate change. However, a recent study on climate change risk perceptions revealed that members of the public with the highest levels of science literacy and numeracy were *not* the most concerned about climate change (Kahan et al., 2012). Instead, those highest in science literacy and numeracy were the most polarized on the issues, based on differences in the endorsement of cultural cognitions. Specifically, individuals who supported hierarchical and individualistic views of the world perceived less climate change risk, whereas those who supported egalitarian and communitarian views of the world perceived greater environmental risk. In contrast, individuals lower in science literacy and numeracy were not as polarized in their risk perceptions based on these cultural cognitions.

These results support the notion that individuals perceive risks according to their cultural worldviews (see also Chauvin, Chap. 2; Bostrom et al., Chap. 11; and Renn, Chap. 16). Based on the cultural cognition theory of risk, individuals form risk perceptions that are consistent with values of groups with which they identify, and those with higher ability (measured as science literacy and numeracy) may be better at recognizing and attaining the goal of belonging (Kahan et al., 2011; Kahan et al., 2012; Kahan, Peters, Dawson, & Slovic, 2013). Kahan and colleagues suggest that people may be motivated to fit interpretations of scientific evidence to their cultural worldviews because of the potential negative consequences of going against their peers (e.g., being shunned by their group; Kahan et al., 2012). This explanation suggests that emotional factors, such as fear of social rejection, may be driving people to perceive risk in line with their groups' values and those with greater ability are simply better able to recognize and/or act on this social risk. However, this emotional account has not yet been empirically tested. Additional research is needed to test whether emotional reactions related to social belongingness or perceived ostracism are key components in explaining the polarizing impact of cultural cognitions on environmental risk perceptions.

Arousal

Relatively few studies have examined the influence of arousal on risk perceptions and behavior. Arousal is a neurophysiological state that is considered to be a dimension of affect, ranging on a continuum from deactivation (sleepy and drowsiness) to activation (alertness and frenetic excitement; Russell, 2003). Affect that is high in arousal is experienced as feeling excited (positive) or tense (negative), whereas affect that is low in arousal results in feeling calm (positive) or lethargic (negative). Consistent with prior studies on affect (e.g., Johnson & Tversky, 1983), the experience of incidental arousal also can carry over to people's judgments and behaviors. Researchers have found, for example, that sexual arousal (elicited by self-stimulation and/or watching sexually arousing stimuli) increased rated willingness to engage in sexually unsafe behaviors (Ariely & Loewenstein, 2006; Ditto, Pizarro, Epstein, Jacobson, & MacDonald, 2006). Other research has found that negative arousal caused by anger can also lead to riskier decisions (e.g., choosing a riskier course of action to treat a disease in a hypothetical scenario; Rydell et al., 2008). For a more comprehensive understanding of the role of arousal and valence on risk perceptions, future research is needed to test the impact of positive vs. negative affect as well as discrete emotions on risk perceptions at both high and low levels of arousal.

Additionally, many judgments and decisions are made over time (e.g., investments, home purchases), but most judgment and decision making research is conducted at onetime point. Very little is known about how affective and deliberative modes of processing interact over time. Prior research suggests that higher levels of arousal can motivate greater information processing, as it has been found to increase encoding and memory for associated information (Cahill, Babinsky, Markowitsch, & McGaugh, 1995; Kensinger, 2009; Laney, Campbell, Heuer, & Reisberg, 2004; Mather & Sutherland, 2011). These findings suggest that higher levels of affective arousal will increase the deliberative processing of risk information and memory for that information over time, even after the initial experienced feelings diminish. The previously reviewed research on graphic cigarette warning labels (that include text about the health risks of smoking plus a pictorial warning marked by a lifelike or realistic description that is vividly or plainly shown) supports this notion (Evans et al., 2015). Prior research on graphic cigarette warning labels has found that more graphic images (e.g., a picture of advanced mouth cancer) are higher in arousal relative to less graphic images (e.g., a picture of stained teeth caused by nicotine) and text-only warnings (Kees, Burton, Andrews, & Kozup, 2010). In a clinical trial, Evans et al. (2015) found that the presence of graphic images (compared to text-only warnings) predicted greater processing of risk information (i.e., greater scrutiny of the warning information), and this result was mediated by negative affect toward smoking, thus providing support for affect acting as a spotlight on congruent information. Additionally, Evans and colleagues found that graphic images vs. text-only warnings increased memory for label content early in the study and that increased memory led to greater smoking-risk knowledge at the end of the study, as well as 1 month later. These results support the idea that arousal can enhance processing of risk information, as well as long-term understanding and memory of risk information.

More research is needed to better understand how affective arousal can motivate greater cognitive processing over time, even after the feelings fade. This research could provide a richer theoretical framework for the dual-process approach to judgment and decision making.

Emotion Regulation

Research suggests that people can actively control many aspects of their emotional reactions by using different processes and strategies (Gross, 2003). These processes and strategies by which people manage their own emotions are commonly referred to as emotion regulation (Koole, 2009). Some emotion regulation strategies such as positive reframing (reappraisal), acceptance, and humor have been shown to be successful strategies to cope with daily failures in real-life settings (Stoeber & Janssen, 2011). For example, a person who was rejected from an Ivy League university could think, "I would not have fit there anyway and now I can study at a college closer to my family. In the long run, my state university will be better for me." However, not all emotion regulation strategies are functional, and some emotion regulation strategies can lead the person to be worse off rather than better (e.g., extensive alcohol and drug use; Gross, 2003).

A missing link in the literature is whether these strategies can be applied to risk perceptions and behaviors. An exception is a study by Magar, Phillips, and Hosie (2008) that examined the association between emotion regulation strategies and risky behaviors. Results from this study indicated that the use of suppression (i.e., efforts to redirect one's attention from negative thoughts) as an emotion regulation strategy was related to starting smoking at a younger age. On the other hand, people who used reappraisal (i.e., changing the way one views a situation in order to modify its emotional impact) as an emotion regulation strategy participated in fewer real-life risky behaviors (e.g., cigarette smoking); they also had fewer alcohol-induced problem behaviors such as fighting and arguing, even after controlling for social desirability. Magar and colleagues speculated that consistent use of reappraisal may reduce the need for instant gratification. This research linked emotion regulation strategies to real-life risky behaviors, but more research is needed about the processes underlying this association. For example, emotion regulation may influence the affective evaluations underlying risk perceptions, which then influence risky behaviors in turn.

Understanding how people use analytic strategies to influence their emotions would create another level of understanding for the theories in this chapter. Ample research now exists suggesting that deliberative and affective processing influence each other greatly. Further understanding their dynamic relations will provide additional insights into people's risk perceptions.

Conclusions

In this chapter, we provided an overview of research that supports a risk-as-feelings framework for understanding the public's perceptions of risk. In particular, we focused on two related lines of work that have been fundamental to our understanding of risk as feelings: the affect heuristic and the appraisal-tendency framework.

Taken together, numerous correlational and experimental studies across a variety of domains (e.g., technological, environmental, economic, political) demonstrate that affect and emotions have marked influences on people's risk assessments. Although these feelings can sometimes mislead and lead to worse decisions, affect and emotions allow us to navigate effectively and efficiently through our complex and uncertain world. Without these affective and emotional reactions, severe impairments in risky decision making can occur and decision-makers can get lost in thought, unable to choose and act. Future studies examining research questions related to mixed emotions, group belonging, arousal and emotion regulation, and the balance between feelings and deliberation would further enhance the risk-as-feelings framework.

Acknowledgement Support for this chapter was provided by the National Science Foundation (SES-1155924 and -1558230).

References

Alhakami, A., & Slovic, P. (1994). A psychological study of the inverse relationship between perceived risk and perceived benefit. *Risk Analysis, 14*(6), 1085–1096.

Ariely, D., & Loewenstein, G. (2006). The heat of the moment: The effect of sexual arousal on sexual decision making. *Journal of Behavioral Decision Making, 19*(2), 87–98.

Bateman, I., Dent, S., Peters, E., Slovic, P., & Starmer, C. (2007). The affect heuristic and the attractiveness of simple gambles. *Journal of Behavioral Decision Making, 20*, 365–380.

Bechara, A., Damasio, A. R., Damasio, H., & Anderson, S. W. (1994). Insensitivity to future consequences following damage to human prefrontal cortex. *Cognition, 50*, 7–15.

Bechara, A., Damasio, H., Tranel, D., & Damasio, A. R. (1997). Deciding advantageously before knowing the advantageous strategy. *Science, 275*, 1293–1294.

Bechara, A., Tranel, D., Damasio, H., & Damasio, A. R. (1996). Failure to respond autonomically to anticipated future outcomes following damage to prefrontal cortex. *Cerebral Cortex, 6*, 215–225.

Burns, W. J., Peters, E., & Slovic, P. (2012). Risk perception and the economic crisis: A longitudinal study of the trajectory of perceived risk. *Risk Analysis, 32*(4), 659–677.

Cahill, L., Babinsky, R., Markowitsch, H. J., & McGaugh, J. L. (1995). The amygdala and emotional memory. *Nature, 377*, 295–296.

Damasio, A. R. (1994). *Descartes' error: Emotion, reason, and the human brain*. New York, NY: G. P. Putnam's Sons.

De Steno, D., Petty, R. E., Wegener, D. T., & Rucker, D. D. (2000). Beyond valence in the perception of likelihood: The role of emotion specificity. *Journal of Personality & Social Psychology, 78*(3), 397–416.

Denes-Raj, V., & Epstein, S. (1994). Conflict between intuitive and rational processing: When people behave against their better judgment. *Journal of Personality and Social Psychology, 66*, 819–829.

Ditto, P. H., Pizarro, D. A., Epstein, E. B., Jacobson, J. A., & MacDonald, T. K. (2006). Visceral influences on risk taking behavior. *Journal of Behavioral Decision Making, 19*(2), 99–113.

Epstein, S. (1994). Integration of the cognitive and the psychodynamic unconscious. *American Psychologist, 49*, 709–724.

Evans, A. T., Peters, E., Strasser, A. A., Emery, L. F., Sheerin, K. M., & Romer, D. (2015). Graphic warning labels elicit affective and thoughtful responses from smokers: Results of a randomized clinical trial. *PLoS One, 10*(12), e0142879. https://doi.org/10.1371/journal.pone.0142879

Finucane, M. L., Alhakami, A., Slovic, P., & Johnson, S. M. (2000). The affect heuristic in judgments of risk and benefits. *Journal of Behavioral Decision Making, 13*, 1–17.
Fischhoff, B., Gonzalez, R. M., Lerner, J. S., & Small, D. A. (2005). Evolving judgments of terror risks: Foresight, hindsight, and emotion. *Journal of Experimental Psychology: Applied, 11*, 124–139.
Fischhoff, B., Slovic, P., Lichtenstein, S., Read, S., & Combs, B. (1978). How safe is safe enough? A psychometric study of attitudes towards technological risks and benefits. *Policy Sciences, 9*, 127–152.
Forgas, J. P. (1995). Mood and judgment: The affect infusion model (AIM). *Psychological Bulletin, 117*, 39–66.
Ganzach, Y. (2000). Judging risk and return of financial assets. *Organizational Behavior and Human Decision Processes, 83*, 353–370.
Gross, J. J. (2003). Emotion regulation: Affective, cognitive, and social consequences. *Psychophysiology, 39*(3), 281–291.
Johnson, E. J., & Tversky, A. (1983). Affect, generalization, and the perception of risk. *Journal of Personality & Social Psychology, 45*, 20–31.
Kahan, D., Jenkins-Smith, H., & Braman, D. (2011). Cultural cognition of scientific consensus. *Journal of Risk Research, 14*, 147–174.
Kahan, D., Peters, E., Wittlin, M., Slovic, P., Ouellette, L. L., Braman, D., & Mandel, G. (2012). The polarizing impact of science literacy and numeracy on perceived climate change risks. *Nature Climate Change, 2*, 732–745.
Kahan, D. M., Peters, E., Dawson, E. C., & Slovic, P. (2013). *Motivated numeracy and enlightened self-government* (Working Paper No. 307). Public Law, Yale Law School. Retrieved from http://ssrn.com/abstract=2319992
Kahneman, D. (2003). A perspective on judgment and choice: Mapping bounded rationality. *American Psychologist, 58*, 697–720.
Kees, J., Burton, S., Andrews, J. C., & Kozup, J. (2010). Understanding how graphic pictorial warnings work on cigarette packaging. *Journal of Public Policy & Marketing, 29*(2), 265–276.
Kensinger, E. A. (2009). Remembering the details: Effects of emotion. *Emotion Review, 1*(2), 99–113.
Koole, S. L. (2009). The psychology of emotion regulation: An integrative review. *Cognition and Emotion, 23*(1), 4–41.
Laney, C., Campbell, C. V., Heuer, F., & Reisberg, D. (2004). Memory for thematically arousing events. *Memory & Cognition, 32*, 1149–1159.
Lerner, J. S., Gonzalez, R. M., Small, D. A., & Fischhoff, B. (2003). Effects of fear and anger on perceived risks of terrorism: A national field experiment. *Psychological Science, 14*(2), 144–150.
Lerner, J. S., & Keltner, D. (2000). Beyond valence: Toward a model of emotion-specific influences on judgment and choice. *Cognition & Emotion, 14*(4), 473–493.
Lerner, J. S., & Keltner, D. (2001). Fear, anger, and risk. *Journal of Personality & Social Psychology, 81*(1), 146–159.
Lerner, J. S., Li, Y., Valdesolo, P., & Kassam, K. S. (2015). Emotion and decision making. *Annual Review of Psychology, 66*, 799–823.
Lerner, J. S., & Tiedens, L. Z. (2006). Portrait of the angry decision maker: How appraisal tendencies shape anger's influence on cognition. *Journal of Behavioral Decision Making, 19*, 115–137.
Loewenstein, G., & Lerner, J. S. (2003). The role of affect in decision making. In R. Davidson, K. Scherer, & H. Goldsmith (Eds.), *Handbook of affective science* (pp. 619–642). Oxford: Oxford University Press.
Loewenstein, G. F., Weber, E. U., Hsee, C. K., & Welch, E. S. (2001). Risk as feelings. *Psychological Bulletin, 127*(2), 267–286.
Magar, E. C. E., Phillips, L. H., & Hosie, J. A. (2008). Self-regulation and risk-taking. *Personality and Individual Differences, 45*(2), 153–159.

Mather, M., & Sutherland, M. R. (2011). Arousal-biased competition in perception and memory. *Perspectives on Psychological Science, 6*, 114–133.

McGraw, P., Shafir, E., & Todorov, A. (2010). Valuing money and things: Why a $20 item can be worth more and less than $20. *Management Science, 56*, 816–830.

Peters, E. (2006). The functions of affect in the construction of preferences. In S. Lichtenstein & P. Slovic (Eds.), *The construction of preference* (pp. 454–463). New York, NY: Cambridge University Press.

Peters, E., Baker, D. P., Dieckmann, N. F., Leon, J., & Collins, J. (2010). Explaining the effect of education on health: A field study in Ghana. *Psychological Science, 21*(10), 1369–1376.

Peters, E., Dieckmann, N. F., Västfjäll, D., Mertz, C. K., Slovic, P., & Hibbard, J. H. (2009). Bringing meaning to numbers: The impact of evaluative categories on decisions. *Journal of Experimental Psychology: Applied, 15*(3), 213–227.

Peters, E., Hess, T. M., Västfjäll, D., & Auman, C. (2007). Adult age differences in dual information processes: Implications for the role of affective and deliberative processes in older adults' decision making. *Perspectives on Psychological Science, 2*(1), 1–23.

Peters, E., Lipkus, I. M., & Diefenbach, M. A. (2006). The functions of affect in health communications and in the construction of health preferences. *Journal of Communication, 56*, S140–S162.

Peters, E., Västfjäll, D., Gärling, T., & Slovic, P. (2006). Affect and decision making: A "hot" topic. *Journal of Behavioral Decision Making, 19*(2), 79–85.

Peters, E., Västfjäll, D., Slovic, P., Mertz, C. K., Mazzocco, K., & Dickert, S. (2006). Numeracy and decision making. *Psychological Science, 17*, 407–413.

Peters, E. M., Burraston, B., & Mertz, C. K. (2004). An emotion-based model of risk perception and stigma susceptibility: Cognitive appraisals, affective reactivity, worldviews, and risk perceptions in the generation of technological stigma. *Risk Analysis, 24*(5), 1349–1367.

Rottenstreich, Y., & Hsee, C. K. (2001). Money, kisses, and electric shocks: On the affective psychology of risk. *Psychological Science, 12*(3), 185–190.

Russell, J. A. (2003). Core affect and the psychological construct of emotion. *Psychological Review, 110*, 145–172.

Rydell, R. J., Mackie, D. M., Maitner, A. T., Claypool, H. M., Ryan, M. J., & Smith, E. R. (2008). Arousal, processing, and risk taking: Consequences of intergroup anger. *Personality and Social Psychology Bulletin, 34*(8), 1141–1152.

Schwarz, N., & Clore, G. L. (1983). Mood, misattribution, and judgments of Well-being: Informative and directive functions of affective states. *Journal of Personality and Social Psychology, 45*, 513–523.

Shafir, E., Simonson, I., & Tversky, A. (1993). Reason-based choice. *Cognition, 49*, 11–36.

Slovic, P. (1987). Perception of risk. *Science, 236*, 280–285.

Slovic, P. (1999). Trust, emotion, sex, politics, and science: Surveying the risk-assessment battlefield. *Risk Analysis, 19*(4), 689–701.

Slovic, P., Finucane, M. L., Peters, E., & MacGregor, D. G. (2002). The affect heuristic. In T. Gilovich, D. Griffin, & D. Kahneman (Eds.), *Heuristics and biases: The psychology of intuitive judgment* (pp. 397–420). New York, NY: Cambridge University Press.

Slovic, P., Finucane, M. L., Peters, E., & MacGregor, D. G. (2004). Risk as analysis and risk as feelings: Some thoughts about affect, reason, risk, and rationality. *Risk Analysis, 24*, 311–322.

Slovic, P., Monahan, J., & MacGregor, D. M. (2000). Violence risk assessment and risk communication: The effects of using actual cases, providing instructions, and employing probability vs. frequency formats. *Law and Human Behavior, 24*, 271–296.

Slovic, P., & Peters, E. (2006). Risk perception and affect. *Current Directions in Psychological Science, 15*(6), 322–325.

Slovic, P., Peters, E., Finucane, M. L., & MacGregor, D. G. (2005). Affect, risk, and decision making. *Health Psychology, 24*, S35–S40.

Slovic, P., Peters, E., Grana, J., Berger, S., & Dieck, G. S. (2007). Risk perception of prescription drugs: Results of a national survey. *Drug Information Journal, 41*, 81–100.

Smith, C. A., & Ellsworth, P. C. (1985). Patterns of cognitive appraisal in emotion. *Journal of Personality & Social Psychology, 48*(4), 813–838.
Stanovich, K. E., & West, R. F. (2000). Individual differences in reasoning: Implications for the rationality debate? *Behavioral and Brain Sciences, 23*, 645–726.
Stoeber, J., & Janssen, D. P. (2011). Perfectionism and coping with daily failures: Positive reframing helps achieve satisfaction at the end of the day. *Anxiety, Stress, and Coping, 24*(5), 477–497.
Zajonc, R. B. (1980). Feeling and thinking: Preferences need no inferences. *American Psychologist, 35*, 151–175.

Chapter 6
The Group Effect: Social Influences on Risk Identification, Analysis, and Decision Making

Eric Eller and Dieter Frey

Abstract Both laypeople and professionals are embedded in social contexts when faced with risk-related questions and make risk judgments and decisions in groups rather than alone. There is a rich body of knowledge from psychological research on how social factors in general and group dynamics specifically influence human judgment formation and decision making. This chapter provides an overview of some of the most important insights from group psychology applied to real-world situations in which people seek appropriate risk identification, analysis, judgments, and decisions. We discuss how groups tend to (1) impede individuals from thinking freely on what risks could occur (risk identification), (2) limit themselves to information commonly known by all group members instead of considering all the relevant information available to the group (risk analysis), and (3) agree on relatively extreme risk judgments after discussing risks in a group setting (risk judgments and decisions). We close the chapter with recommendations on how a group's risk identification, judgment formation, and decision making can be improved both by individual group members as well as from an organizational perspective.

Introduction

Should I get vaccinated? What sort of insurance do I need? Is it safe to go swimming today? Should we use condoms? Should I buy that car? What should I invest my money in? Should I go see a doctor? Can I allow my daughter to attend that festival? These questions are samples of the countless risk-related decisions one faces in everyday life. Almost any important decision comes with possible negative consequences and thereby entails risk. Often neither the quality nor likelihood of these possible negative consequences can be known; thus, one must overcome inevitable uncertainty in deciding whether one gets vaccinated, purchases insurance or goes swimming on a particular day.

D. Frey · E. Eller (✉)
Department of Psychology, Ludwig-Maximilian University Munich, Munich, Germany
e-mail: eric.eller@psy.lmu.de

M. Raue et al. (eds.), *Psychological Perspectives on Risk and Risk Analysis*,
https://doi.org/10.1007/978-3-319-92478-6_6

Companies and other organizations face comparable risk questions concerning the organization's success: *What could harm our reputation? How can our ongoing production or services be interrupted? What if a key supplier doesn't respect our agreements? How are we exposed to technological change? What new laws could be introduced and how would these affect us? How could a natural catastrophe affect our company? How could we become a victim of acts of fraud such as cyber-attacks or information theft?* Identifying the most important risks at an early stage, gaining an accurate understanding of the risks identified, and responding to potential threats effectively is not only at the core of every professional risk management system but also more generally a very basic precondition for assuring an organization's performance and long-term success.

At the latest since Lewin's (1936) *field theory*, psychologists consider judgments and decisions as determined not only by the decision maker herself but also by her surroundings—especially her social surroundings. People often make important risk decisions embedded in a social context and thereby not alone but rather in groups (De Dreu, Nijstad, & van Knippenberg, 2008; Gardner & Steinberg, 2005; Kerr, MacCoun, & Kramer, 1996). This is true for risk decisions both in one's private and professional life. A reason for the high popularity of having important judgments and decisions made in groups is the high trust people place in group judgments and decisions (Brandstätter, 1997). Psychological research has developed a rich store of knowledge on the social factors of human judgment formation and decision making in the last few decades. In numerous investigations, psychologists have examined the influence of groups on how humans perceive, judge and respond to risks (e.g., see Frey & Greif, 1997; Frey & Irle, 2008 for an overview). We summarize the most important findings that we believe are especially relevant for both private and professional risk judgment formations and decision making. We thereby discuss (1) why humans consider other peoples' behavior and seek exchange with others for their risk evaluations and decisions, (2) what groups struggle with in their identification and analysis of risks, and (3) how a group's judgments and decisions can be biased. Based on a reflection of such psychological knowledge applied to real-world risk problems, we make suggestions on how group risk judgments and decisions can be improved both from the perspective of an individual group member and from an organizational perspective. This chapter can serve as a starting point for improving risk decision making both in a private and a corporate context.

Group Effects: What Happens When One Is Part of a Group

This book is a great illustration of the vulnerability of human risk judgment formation and decision making. It reflects the extensive research on risk psychology, the high complexity of risk perception, judgment formation and decision making, and how difficult it is for laypersons and professionals to come up with adequate risk judgments and decisions. Given the high difficulty of dealing with risk, the question

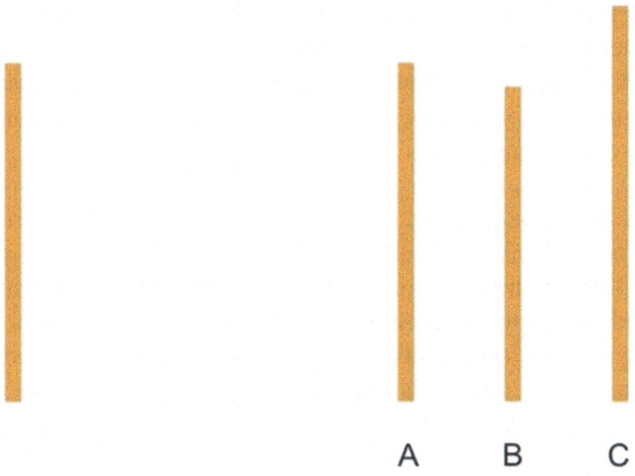

Fig. 6.1 Asch's (1951) test measures for demonstrating the effect of group conformity

arises as to what strategies people use to nevertheless make important risk judgments and decisions.

Numerous psychological theories provide grounds for assuming that individuals seek social reassurance for their risk judgments. Festinger's (1954) *social comparison theory* suggests that individuals compare their assumptions to those of others as a strategy to validate their judgments. Humans constantly test their hypotheses on their surroundings (Bruner & Postman, 1948) and therefore verify or disprove existing assumptions by consulting the behavior of others (Lilli & Frey, 1993). For example, an individual might have certain assumptions on whether it is safe to go hiking on a certain day. By consulting the behaviors of others (e.g., whether or not others are hiking), the person verifies or disproves these assumptions. The psychological concept of *social proof* describes that people often assume the behavior of others reflect reality and consider the behavior of others to determine appropriate behavior for themselves. Thus, individuals often adopt behaviors of others simply because they assume what others do must be the right behavior (Cialdini, Wosinska, Barrett, Butner, & Gornik-Durose, 1999). For risk judgments, this means that people consider how others evaluate and deal with the risk and adapt their risk judgments accordingly. As an example, showing people that their friends on Facebook use specific security features has been demonstrated to be a particularly effective strategy for raising awareness of security behavior (Das, Kramer, Dabbish, & Hong, 2014).

To demonstrate how fundamentally our everyday judgments and decisions are based on what others do and say, we want to ask you for a very easy judgment. Please take a look at Fig. 6.1: Which of the three lines on the right is the same length as the line on the left? The answer is very clear: no doubt the correct answer is B. Everybody can see that the line on the left has the same length as line B.

You now find yourself in a very similar situation as the participants of a classic psychological experiment conducted by Asch (1951). For the experiment, participants in groups of nine persons were asked one after another to give answers to easy tasks such as the one illustrated above. Whereas the correct answer (which is, admittedly, A in the task illustrated above) was very clear for the participants, all of the other eight group members (which were in fact not participants but actors) consistently stated a wrong answer such as B in our example. When all other group members consistently stated a wrong answer, a third of Asch's participants indicated obviously wrong judgments in 50% or more of the tasks. Across all participants in that experimental condition, these social pressures led to obviously wrong judgments for 32% of the questions. A large number of Asch's participants thus adapted their judgments to the obviously wrong judgments of their peers and stated the same wrong result as everybody else. They either assumed that what everybody else perceived must be right, or that not being different than everybody else in the group was more important than making a valid judgment. When participants were asked to make their judgments in written form (and there was therefore no more social pressure), there were almost no wrong judgments made (Prose, 1997).

Asch's experiment is one of many psychological experiments demonstrating the phenomenon of group conformity (Erb, Bohner, Rank, & Einwiller, 2002). People are generally willing to behave in a way that is consistent with the behavior of others and thereby adapt to group norms. Asch found that a majority's influence on one's judgment (i.e., the willingness to adapt to obviously wrong judgments) is higher the less clearly the task is defined (Asch, 1951). In a similar study, participants showed a higher tendency to adapt their judgments to the wrong judgments of their peers when participants were uncertain about the correctness of their judgment (Deutsch & Gerard, 1995). We claim that correct risk judgments are in most cases not easy to come up with or to recognize and, therefore it is likely that adapting one's judgment to a majority's handling of risk is a particularly widespread strategy when it comes to dealing with risk.

How does social proof and group conformity affect real-life risk decisions? Let's say you decide to start skiing this winter and visit a skiing resort for the first time. We assume that it is very likely that you would decide to wear a helmet. The reason for our assumption is that you would see almost everybody else wearing one: as per the National Ski Areas Association (NSAA, 2014), 73% of all skiers and snowboarders wore a helmet in US ski areas in the 2013/2014 season. In Switzerland, 87% of all skiers and snowboarders wore a helmet in the 2012/2013 season (Beratungsstelle für Unfallverhütung, 2013). As you observe that the broad majority of skiers wear a helmet, you may consider it *normal* and thus *right* to do so as well. The fact that almost every skier wears a helmet may be used as proxy that one ought to wear a helmet. Furthermore, this social proof can lead to the perception that skiing without a helmet is risky. However, your reasoning might have been exactly the opposite only a decade and a half ago: in 2002, only 25% of skiers wore a helmet in the USA (NSAA, 2014) and only 16% in Switzerland (Beratungsstelle für Unfallverhütung, 2013). If you had started skiing in that time, you would very likely not have worn a helmet, simply because it was normal not to do so. The fact that almost no one wore a helmet would probably have been interpreted as a social proof for a lower risk. What has changed in the meantime is the majority's behavior and thereby what is

Fig. 6.2 A person's social identity is based on perceived membership of social groups

seen as appropriate risk behavior within the group of skiers. Research has indicated an effect of social influences on helmet usage in various domains. For example, Wise and Scott (2012) explain the increasing use of helmets in the National Hockey League (NHL) in the 1960s by the process of emerging norms in a social group. As per the authors, player usage decisions were partly influenced by their immediate social network. Comparably, social influence has been demonstrated to be a critical factor predicting the use of protective gear among in-line skaters (De Nooijer, De Wit, & Steenhuis, 2004).

People tend to conform to groups by behaving according to the group's norms and expectations because they want to be (seen as) a valuable part of the group. Tajfel and Turner's (1979) *social identity theory*, people identify themselves not only as individuals but also as group members. A person's social identity is his or her self-concept based on perceived membership of social groups. For example, your social identity might be based on which town you are from, which university you went to, which company and department you work for, which sports team you are a fan of, which political party or religion you belong to or feel close to, or whether you are a skier or not (Ellemers & Haslam, 2012; see Fig. 6.2).

Humans are very sensitive to what is desired and expected within a group and willing to behave accordingly. As one feels part of a group, characteristics of the group become characteristics of the individual. Thus, what is considered *normal behavior* or *typical views* within the group becomes what an individual considers *normal behavior* or *typical views* of herself. Because the other group members are perceived as similar to oneself, an individual tends to believe that she *ought* to have similar views as the other group members and *ought* to behave in a similar way. In groups, one feels a certain pressure to conform to the group's norms and thereby to what is perceived as normal behavior in that particular group (Turner & Reynolds, 2011). Going back to our skiing example, when starting skiing you would very likely adapt to the existing norms on whether to wear a helmet simply because you want to feel and also be perceived as a normal member of the group of skiers. While the general group of skiers did not perceive wearing a helmet as necessary a decade and a half ago, a subgroup composed of "free riders" had already adopted the norm of helmet use. Those who wanted to be perceived as a part of such a particular subgroup might have felt compelled to wear helmets at that time.

Groups Are Less Creative than Individuals in Their Risk Identification

Before a risk can be analyzed and evaluated, it is first necessary to have the risk identified and thereby be aware of the risk. In a corporate context, this is often conducted very explicitly: companies try to gain a holistic picture of their risk situation by systematically identifying as many potential risks as possible in a first step. Only after this can the identified risks be analyzed. Risk identification is therefore a necessary condition for accurate risk judgments and adequate risk management (Lermer, Streicher, Eller, & Sachs, 2014).

Since many persons can contribute more perspectives and have more knowledge available than a single person, it might appear obvious to involve as many persons as possible in the identification of risks and therefore brainstorm about potential risks in groups. It is a common approach in organizations that a number of colleagues or experts sit together and gather what risks might be relevant and worth having a closer look at, for example when setting up a new project. Such brainstorming is a popular method of idea generation that was originated by Alex F. Osborn in 1939 (as cited in Taylor, Berry, Block, & Block, 1958). Following the principle of *quantity generates quality*, the aim of brainstorming is to collect as many ideas as possible. Individuals are encouraged to express any idea that comes to mind and to avoid any form of judgment or criticism regarding both one's own ideas and the ideas of others. Every idea that comes to mind shall be captured, regardless of how wild it may be (Diehl & Stroebe, 1987). Whereas brainstorming was introduced and is mostly used as a method for general idea generation, it is indeed often specifically used for the generation of risk ideas and thus risk identification.

The introduction and widespread adoption of brainstorming suggests that individuals are generally more productive in their idea generation when collecting ideas in a group rather than alone (Osborn, 1957, as cited in Mullen, Johnson, & Salas, 1991). Indeed, individuals often believe that they are more creative and thus able to generate more ideas in groups (Pauhus, Dzindolet, Poletes, & Camach, 1993). The question of whether groups enhance or rather inhibit creativity has been investigated by numerous psychological experiments (for reviews, see Lamm & Trommsdorff,

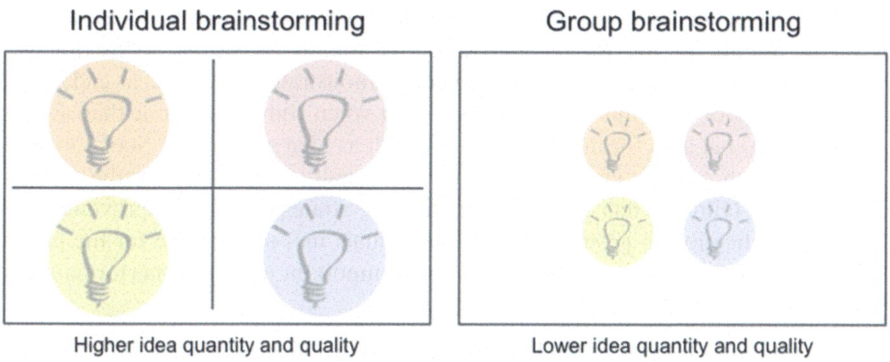

Fig. 6.3 Individual brainstorming is more effective than group brainstorming

1973; Mullen et al., 1991). Thereby it has been indicated that brainstorming in groups is generally less productive, both in quality and quantity, than when the same set of individuals work independently without interaction (see Fig. 6.3). People likely generate more and better ideas for potential risks when working independently than when working in a group. The loss of productivity increases with the size of the group (i.e., the larger the group, the worse the individual performance) and when an authoritative person is present (Diehl & Stroebe, 1987; Mullen et al., 1991).

How can the loss of productivity be explained? There are generally three main reasons discussed for the phenomenon of groups impeding their members' creativity (cf. Diehl & Stroebe, 1987; Mullen et al., 1991):

1. The group setting blocks the productivity of the individual since only one idea can be expressed at a time. This can prohibit individual group members from expressing their ideas while listening to other group members, until they finally forget the idea or suppress it because it seems no longer relevant.
2. The presence of others creates a certain social inhibition. Being in a group with other persons increases an individuals' self-consciousness and excitement level. In a sense, being in a group distracts the individual members from the actual task at hand. Individuals anticipate the other group members' reactions before expressing an idea (*Does the idea make me appear clever? Will someone laugh about my idea?*). Such thoughts demand cognitive resources that are no longer available for the task of risk identification. Also, individuals might consciously come to the conclusion of not expressing an idea because they fear negative evaluation by their peers. The inhibiting effect on idea generation is especially high when other group members are perceived as experts on the particular issue. Additionally, team members will hesitate to express ideas that are expected not to be in the interest of a present manager or other authority.
3. Individuals give less effort in groups than when they work on their own. It is a well-known psychological effect that individuals tend to decrease their level of performance when being part of a group and performance of the whole group is

measured rather than individual performance. The phenomenon is described as *social loafing* or the *Ringelmann effect* (Karau & Williams, 1993; Latané, Williams, & Harkins, 1979) and has been demonstrated for physical endeavors such as tugs-of-war (individuals pull stronger when competing alone than as part of a group) but also for intellectual tasks such as idea generation. Social loafing is high when group members do not feel personally responsible for the group's success or failure. Thus, it can be an effective strategy for the improvement of risk identification in groups to make individuals feel responsible for the group risk identification process and to stress how important individual performance is for the group result.

When groups impede individuals in generating ideas for potential risks, one might ask how one can still benefit from the large amount of information and the many perspectives that several rather than only one person can contribute to risk identification. A straightforward solution is to simply ask several persons for their ideas individually. Accordingly, a method that can reduce the negative effects of groups on individuals' idea generation is *brainwriting*: every person writes down as many ideas as possible, usually without any direct interaction (Heslin, 2009; Paulus & Yang, 2000). When you set up your next project at work and want your colleagues to come up with ideas for potential risks, asking your friends or colleagues individually will probably give you more and better ideas than asking them to brainstorm in a group setting. If already in a group setting, it helps to make everybody *brainwrite* individually first and then discuss the ideas in a second step (and then again think about it individually and so forth). Generally, such combinations of collecting and working on ideas both individually and in a group can help to combine the best of both worlds: using the efficiency of individual brainwriting without missing the inspiration, fun, motivation, and legitimation and acceptance one can get from groups.

Groups Have More Information but Fail at Using It

Risks are often not easy to understand and evaluate. One often feels that she has insufficient information to understand or judge a particular risk. A reason why it is very popular to discuss risks in groups is the widely shared notion that groups simply know more than individuals and therefore must be able to make better risk judgments than a single person. Indeed, groups would be predestined to make good judgments and decisions if they were able to exchange the large amount of information that is distributed among the group members, each with different knowledge, perspectives, experiences, and opinions, and then base their judgments and decisions on the entirety of knowledge available. For groups making high-quality judgments and decisions, it is a crucial precondition that they share information and thus inform each other about information they did not have before (Valacich, Sarker, Pratt, & Groomer, 2009; Wittenbaum, Hollingshead, & Botero, 2004).

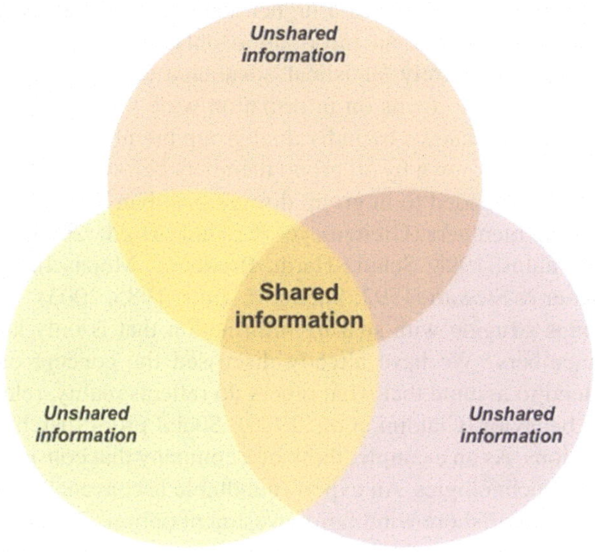

Fig. 6.4 Groups generally fail at exchanging unshared information and mainly discuss shared information in group discussions

Unfortunately, research has consistently indicated that groups fail at sharing information that is known only by individual group members. How individuals share information within groups can be measured with the so-called *hidden profile paradigm* (Stasser & Titus, 1985, 2003). The paradigm is characterized by an asymmetrical distribution of information among all group members: some of the available information is shared and thereby known to all group members before the discussion, whereas other information is unshared and thereby known only by one group member and unknown by the rest of the group (see Fig. 6.4). Hidden profile tasks require the exchange of unshared information to allow the group to make an appropriate judgment or decision. If the group is not able to exchange unique information, the resulting judgment or decision is poor. Imagine you are in a group deciding between two options A and B: if the arguments for the better solution A are unshared (i.e., individual group members have unique knowledge about one or several arguments) but the arguments for the worse solution B are shared (i.e., all group members know all of the arguments), the group will only recognize the superiority of solution A if able to exchange the unshared information (Greitemeyer & Schulz-Hardt, 2003; Mennecke, Hoffer, & Valacich, 1995). The hidden profile paradigm thereby reflects the challenge for groups to talk about what only single-group members know. Only if groups are able to exchange such information can they benefit from the advantage of having more information available than a single person.

The consistent finding of hidden profile experiments is that groups generally fail at uncovering hidden profiles: groups mostly discuss what everybody already knew before the discussion. Considering all information available to a group, information known by many group members has a higher statistical likelihood of being mentioned in a group discussion than information only known by individual group members. However, this purely statistical advantage cannot entirely explain the findings that groups tend to focus on information widely known in the group and neglect information only known by individual group members. Additionally, information that was already known by all group members before the discussion is more often repeated and responded to in group discussions than information that is new to most of the group members (Greitemeyer & Schulz-Hardt, 2003; Lightle, Kagel, & Arkes, 2009; Paulus, 1998; Schulz-Hardt, Brodbeck, Mojzisch, Kerschreiter, & Frey, 2006; Stasser & Stewart, 1992; Stasser & Titus, 1985, 2003).

Why do groups struggle with sharing information that is only known by individual group members? We have already discussed the concept of social proof above: people tend to assume that what others do reflects reality, relevance or simply appropriate behavior (Cialdini et al., 1999). Social proof thereby has an effect on group discussions. As an example, think of a company that considers investing in alternative energy technologies. An expert roundtable is convened to discuss potential risks related to an offshore wind farm investment option. The individual experts would probably be uncertain which facts and arguments should be shared with the group. And this is where they might start watching out for a social proof: as soon as another person in the group expresses an argument or fact that a particular expert also had in mind, this can be taken as evidence (i.e., social proof) that this piece of information must be a relevant one. As a result, this particular expert would probably express agreement, and the discussion would continue on this particular piece of information, increasing its perceived relevance within the group as a whole. The piece of information might then be repeated throughout the discussion and, thus, have a disproportionately high impact on the group judgment or decision. On the other hand, it is quite unlikely that an individual would express a thought that is exclusively known by that person, simply because there would be no social evidence that this thought is relevant to the group discussion (Greitemeyer & Schulz-Hardt, 2003).

A second explanation for a group's tendency to mostly talk about what everybody already knew before the discussion relates to the concept of *impression management*. Being part of the roundtable discussion on alternative energy technologies, it would certainly be important for you to make a valid judgment in the best interest of the group or company. However, you would probably also have other more personal concerns, such as whether the group would perceive you as a valuable (e.g., competent, knowledgeable, interesting, likeable, etc.) group member. Group members evaluate one another more positively when expressing shared rather than unshared information (Wittenbaum, Hubbell, & Zuckerman, 1999). Thus, a group member is perceived as a more valuable member by her peers when expressing what others already knew than when expressing new and thereby potentially irritating information. Experiencing such social consequences of expressing shared as opposed to unshared information can cause group members not to express unshared information, simply to enhance their impression on other group members.

Both social proof and impression management lead to the same result: groups failing to share information that is only known by individual group members. Considering the prevalence of group discussions for risk analysis and risk decision making, that finding is particularly problematic. A main reason for the implementation of think tanks, roundtables, and other discussion groups for risk analysis is that the evaluation of risks often requires a broad range of information. Teaming a number of experts with different backgrounds, perspectives, and information is a popular strategy to satisfy the described need for diverse information. However, research around the hidden profile paradigm suggests that these experts tend not to make judgments and decisions based on all available information but rather simply on their common knowledge. In the worst case, this means that the individual experts' expertise is excluded from the judgment formation or decision making process. Interestingly, the tendency to talk about shared information rather than information only known by individual group members is particularly high when the group believes it does not have sufficient information to solve the problem anyway (Stasser & Stewart, 1992): groups struggle with sharing information, especially when the task is to make an estimation or judgment rather than to solve a problem. Since it is in the very nature of risk analysis that one does not have all the information, risk issues are judged rather than "solved." Therefore, groups discussing risk are particularly prone to the tendency to discuss shared rather than unshared information.

What can be done? First, research has indicated that not agreeing before the discussion (i.e., group dissent) increases the group's ability to exchange unshared information. In an experiment by Schulz-Hardt et al. (2006), different groups of three persons had the task of selecting one out of four fictional job applicants. While one of the four candidates was clearly the best choice based on the total available information, the information was distributed to participants in different ways (i.e., creating a hidden profile or not):

1. *Full information.* Groups in which all participants had all information always chose the best candidate and solved the task (100%). There was no hidden profile in this condition.
2. *No dissent.* Groups in which all group members had information speaking for the same wrong option hardly ever solved the task (7%).
3. *Dissent without best choice.* Groups in which all participants had information speaking for different but wrong options solved the task significantly more often than in the no dissent condition (25%).
4. *Dissent with best choice.* Groups in which all participants had information speaking for different options including one person with information speaking for the best candidate solved the task even more often (59%).

These results indicate that the more different the views are before a group discussion, the more likely it is that groups use their advantage of having lots of information. Thus, the more group members disagree before a discussion, the higher the group's potential of making an accurate risk judgment. Making groups aware of the expertise of each group member helps groups to unveil unshared information (Stasser, Steward, & Wittenbaum, 1995; Stasser, Vaughan, & Stewart, 2000). Thus, making the individual group members' backgrounds and professional emphases as visible and clear as possible can help groups to make judgments on the totality of all relevant information that is available to the group. From this perspective, surface-level group diversity (e.g., with regard to personality, race, or gender) can also be seen as beneficial for a group's judgments and decisions, for instance, by fostering the expectancy of information differences (Phillips & Loyd, 2006; Phillips, Northcraft, & Neale, 2006). Finally, a straightforward approach to help groups exchange information is to simply take the particular step of information collection and information sharing out of the group setting. One can ask all group members individually about their knowledge and views on the risk before the group comes together to discuss it. The group discussion can then start with a presentation of all the collected information (Lermer et al., 2014).

Groups Make Extreme Risk Judgments

As we have discussed, it is generally important for people to be accepted and liked by their peers. People are therefore particularly sensitive to what is expected behavior within groups: *How do they usually deal with risk? Who has a say in this group and what is her position? What are the group's values?* People are willing to adapt to these expectations to gain acceptance. In groups, people adopt behaviors and opinions of others because they assume that what others do or say must be right (social proof). Also, people behave in a way that conforms to a group's norms in order to feel and be perceived as a valuable group member and thereby build a positive social identity. In group discussions, group conformity can have the effect that group members share information and state arguments that conform with the group's overall attitude and point of view.

Stoner (1968) asked participants in a study to estimate different kinds of risks individually, then had them discuss and evaluate the risks in groups, and finally asked his participants again individually to reestimate the risks after the discussion. What Stoner found was the first evidence for the phenomenon of *group polarization*: discussing the risks in groups seemed to make his participants more extreme in their risk evaluation. Both the group judgment and the average of all individual judgments after the discussion were riskier than the individual judgments before the discussion. Further experiments demonstrated that the effect works both in the direction of riskier decisions through group discussions but also in the direction of more cautious decisions. In other words, groups are more extreme in their risk judgment than individuals, and this extremity can be manifested both in riskier judgments and decisions (*risky shift*) and in more cautious judgments and decisions (*cautious shift*; Sunstein, 1999). As discovered by Moscovici and Zavalloni (1969), the initial risk judgment among all group members before the group discussion determines whether the group experiences a risky shift or a cautious shift: a risky shift usually happens if the initial tendency is rather risky, whereas a cautious shift usually happens if the initial tendency is rather cautious. Accordingly, the effect of

Fig. 6.5 Illustration of group polarization

group polarization is especially high when the group members already have similar views before the group discussion.

An example for a risky shift could be a group of avid kite surfers talking about their sport: as the overall attitude on kite surfing is very positive in this group, it is likely that most statements would highlight its desirability and advantages while devaluing the risks of the sport. Each member of the group would come up with arguments supporting the sport underpinned with various information and personal experiences all casting a positive light on kite surfing. By presenting all these information, views, and arguments supporting the group's overall position, the group convinces itself of a more extreme version of its initial position (see Fig. 6.5). In order to appear as an active group member, it is also an effective strategy to express statements that are similar to those of the other group members, but somewhat more extreme. This results in more extreme group judgments. If there was any doubt about the high desirability of kite surfing in the beginning of the discussion, the group would now, after the discussion, be more certain than ever before: kite surfing is great and the risk is low. On the contrary, a conversation among the worried mothers of these kite surfers would probably develop a totally different dynamic. Generally considering kite surfing to be a very dangerous pastime, each mother would express her concerns about the sport—all casting a damning light on kite surfing. Thus, the mothers group would convince itself of a more and more negative view on kite surfing and agree more than before their conversation that kite surfing is bad and very dangerous. The latter is an example for a cautious shift.

An important conclusion of what is known about group polarization is that initial tendencies play an important role for the outcome of group discussions (which is in many cases simply a more extreme version of the initial tendency; for an overview, see Sunstein, 1999). In our view, this bears the potential for manipulating a group's judgment or decision by influencing the initial tendency of group discussions. As an example, when an authority or thought leader expresses her position right in the beginning of the discussion, it is quite likely that the group will adopt that position, many group members will express further information and arguments speaking for that position, and the group will in the end come to a conclusion that is similar but somehow more extreme than initially suggested by the authority. Accordingly, a team leader of executives who wants his team to come up with an accurate risk judgment (and not simply to confirm his opinion), would not express his view in the beginning of a group discussion.

Minority Influence Can Improve Group Risk Decisions

In the beginning of this chapter, we discussed Salomon Asch's findings on group conformity from one of his classical group experiments: participants were asked to judge the length of different lines in small groups one after another. Apart from one participant per group, all other group members were actors and consistently expressed wrong judgments. Asch (1951) found that his participants adopted and stated the obviously wrong judgments of their peers for 32% of the questions. However, what would have happened if at least one other group member had stated the correct result? Would a person expressing statements in opposition to those of the majority possibly have encouraged participants to express what they knew was correct? Asch's (1951) experiment indeed contained such a condition in which, for some groups, all the "actor" participants consistently gave wrong answers *except for one*. In that condition, the percentage of the "subject" participants' incorrect answers decreased dramatically to 10%. The availability of only one group member that behaved inconsistent to the rest of the group encouraged a considerable proportion of participants to state what they knew was right instead of conforming with the group's majority.

Moscovici's (1980) research on minority influence indicates that not only majorities but also minorities can have significant influence on other group members and thereby even have an impact on a group's majority. Minorities can be especially successful in influencing others when (1) there is high consistency within the minority and (2) the minority expresses its opinion with certainty and conviction. Minorities can thereby stimulate others to question the status quo and to consider alternative options for their judgment formation (Nemeth, 2011; Wood, Lundgren, Ouellette, Busceme, & Blackstone, 1994). In 1969, Moscovici and his colleagues conducted one of the best-known experiments demonstrating the influence that highly consistent minorities have on groups (Moscovici, Lage, & Naffrechoux, 1969) which has many similarities to Asch's (1951) conformity experiment described above: a series of blue slides was presented to groups of six persons, respectively, who were asked one after another to indicate the color of each slide. In the control condition, there were no actors among the group members and the group members repeatedly identified all slides correctly as blue. In the experimental condition, however, there were two actors among the members of each group who consistently identified the color of the presented slides (wrongly) as green. As a result, participants adopted the minority judgment in 8% of their answers (i.e., designating a slide as green). Almost a third (32%) of all participants adopted the minority judgment at least once. It is important to note that such minority influence existed only when the minority consistently indicated that the slides were green in all trials. In another condition, in which the actors designated most but not all slides as green (and were thus inconsistent in their behavior), there was almost no effect on the majority.

Moscovici's research indicates that majority influence (as demonstrated by Asch's experiment) indeed leads to public adaptation in many cases but mostly does not affect individual's private conviction. Thus, people superficially adapt to what is expected by a group's majority but do not change their personal attitude or belief. In contrast, individuals influenced by minorities really change their personal convictions. Minorities thereby influence fewer individuals than majorities but are generally more effective in influencing private convictions rather than only public behavior (Brandstätter, 1997; Erb et al., 2002; Maass, 1997; Moscovici & Lage, 1976; Nemeth, 2011; Nemeth & Wachtler, 1974; Wood et al., 1994).

In group discussions, minority dissent (i.e., having at least one group member questioning or disagreeing with the majority's point of view) can positively impact many of the general problems that occur in group discussions that we have discussed in this chapter: in groups, people tend to (1) be less creative, (2) base their judgments on only relatively scarce information (i.e., what every group member already knew before the discussion), and (3) make extreme risk judgments. Several studies have indicated that minority dissent can increase the level of creativity within groups as well as the amount of information considered for a group's judgment formation and can thus improve a group's problem-solving capability (e.g., Nemeth, 2011; Nemeth & Kwan, 1987; Nemeth & Rogers, 1996; Nemeth & Wachtler, 1974). Having a member in a group discussion who questions the status quo and therefore questions the majority's point of view can effectively reduce the effect of group conformity (Janis, 1971). For this purpose, it can be fruitful to intentionally create dissent in group discussions by introducing the role of a *devil's advocate* who has the explicit task to disagree. Whereas the effectiveness of the devil's advocate technique is controversially discussed (for an overview, see Nemeth, 2011), authentic dissent based on the existence of divergent opinions can be considered as generally more effective (i.e., leading to more divergent thinking) than such techniques (Nemeth, Connell, Rogers, & Brown, 2001).

Conclusion and Recommendations

Knowing how and why social factors can influence our everyday and professional risk judgments and decisions is an important step toward a conscious and effective handling of risk. Our aim was to provide a comprehensive overview of the most important findings from social psychology on how social contexts (i.e., groups) influence risk perception, judgment formation and decision making:

1. Group conformity makes people adapt to how majorities perceive and handle risk, which can be explained by the concept of social proof (*everybody says that; therefore it is right*) and social identity theory (*what is right for my group must be right for me*).
2. Groups are less creative in their risk identification both in terms of quality and quantity of the identified risks than if the same persons work individually.
3. In discussions, groups often fail to exchange unshared information and thereby mainly discuss information that was already known by every group member before the discussion.
4. Groups often make relatively extreme risk judgments because they tend to persuade themselves of a more extreme (i.e., riskier or more cautious) version of the group's initial risk judgment or decision in group discussions.

We believe that being aware of how human risk perception, judgment formation, and decision making works—and how they can be biased—is crucial for improving how we deal with risk. However, the value of such theoretical knowledge is limited as long as there are no practical improvement opportunities linked to the theoretical findings. In the previous sections of the present chapter we tried to stress that every group member has an influence on how the group comes to its judgments and decisions. We discussed that by challenging the status quo, everyone can prevent the groups that surround him or her from making poor judgments and decisions. In addition, it matters how risk-related questions are addressed. A group's effectiveness in its judgment formation and decision making seems to depend on whether the group structure matches the task. Organizations can improve risk judgments and decisions by thoughtfully structuring their risk judgment procedures.

In this manner, we suggest that establishing suitable risk judgment processes based on a combination of individual and group performance is an effective approach toward answering complex risk-related questions. There are a number of relatively well-established standard methods based on exactly this principle: the advantages of groups (i.e., wealth of information, perspectives and opinions as well as high legitimation and acceptance of group decisions) shall be maintained by having the social threats related to groups minimized as much as possible. By following such an approach, experts are usually first surveyed individually and the aggregated results are then discussed in a group setting. Examples for such methods are the *Delphi method* and the *nominal group technique* (see Van de Ven & Delbecq, 1974).

We make the following practical recommendations for structured organizational risk judgment procedures based on insights from psychological research:

1. For identifying risks, asking a number of persons individually rather than in a group context is generally more promising. The method of *brainwriting* is therefore recommended over the more conventional brainstorming techniques done in a group setting. It may be constructive to have the identified potential risks discussed and developed in a group setting subsequently (and thus use combinations of individual and group performances). It is thereby crucial to make sure ideas are discussed without consideration of who had the idea, for example by preserving the anonymity of the risk identification step or by having the identified risks evaluated by a different group. Otherwise, knowing that the risk will eventually be evaluated (in step 2) can inhibit individuals in their risk identification (in step 1).
2. For risk analysis, it can be helpful to have selected process steps isolated from group contexts. We have seen that groups fail at exchanging unshared information. Besides making teams aware of the different levels of expertise existent among their peers, a straightforward approach is to exclude the process of information exchange from the group context. Thus, group members can be asked about facts, information, perspectives and opinions they consider important for the risk analysis before the group comes together. The group analysis can then start with a comprehensive summary of all information collected from all group members.
3. When risk judgments and decisions are made in groups, they often tend to be more extreme than when the same persons judge and decide on the risk on their own. Having risks evaluated by a number of persons individually and then aggregate these evaluations in a second step is therefore in most cases more promising than asking the same persons to meet and come to a decision as a group.

We believe that building adequate methods and processes is an important precondition for gaining accurate and reliable risk judgments and decisions. Decision makers need to be aware not only of what organizations deal with but also of how to approach particular topics and questions. We believe taking into account psychological determinants of risk perception and judgment formation is a crucial characteristic of effective corporate risk management systems.

References

Asch, S. E. (1951). Effects of group pressure upon the modification and distortion of judgments. In H. Guetzkow (Ed.), *Groups, leadership, and men: Research in human relations* (pp. 222–236). Oxford: Carnegie Press.

Beratungsstelle für Unfallverhütung. (2013). *Tragquoten von Schutzartikeln beim Ski- und Snowboardfahren*. Bern. Retrieved from http://www.bfu.ch/de/Documents/05_Die_bfu/07_Medien/2013-03-11_bfu_Erhebung_PSA_Schneesport_d.pdf

Brandstätter, H. (1997). Gruppenleistung und Gruppenentscheidung. In D. Frey & S. Greif (Eds.), *Sozialpsycholigie. Ein Handbuch in Schlüsselbegriffen*. Munich: Beltz.

Bruner, J., & Postman, L. (1948). An approach to social perception. In W. Dennis (Ed.), *Current trends in social psychology*. Oxford: U. Pittsburgh Press.

Cialdini, R. B., Wosinska, W., Barrett, D. W., Butner, J., & Gornik-Durose, M. (1999). Compliance with a request in two cultures: The differential influence of social proof and commitment/consistency on collectivists and individualists. *Personality and Social Psychology Bulletin, 25*, 1242–1253.

Das, S., Kramer, A. D. I., Dabbish, L. A., & Hong, J. I. (2014). Increasing security sensitivity with social proof. In *Proceedings of the 2014 ACM SIGSAC conference on computer and communications security—CCS'14* (pp. 739–749).

De Dreu, C. K., Nijstad, B. A., & van Knippenberg, D. (2008). Motivated information processing in group judgment and decision making. *Personality and Social Psychology Review, 12*, 22–49.

De Nooijer, J., De Wit, M., & Steenhuis, I. (2004). Why young Dutch in-line skaters do (not) use protection equipment. *The European Journal of Public Health, 14*, 178–181.

Deutsch, M., & Gerard, H. B. (1995). A study of normative and informational social influences upon individual judgment. *The Journal of Abnormal and Social Psychology, 51*, 629–626.

Diehl, M., & Stroebe, W. (1987). Productivity loss in brainstorming groups: Toward the solution of a riddle. *Journal of Personality and Social Psychology, 53*, 497–509.

Ellemers, N., & Haslam, A. (2012). Social identity theory. In P. A. M. Van Lange, A. W. Kruglanski, & E. T. Higgins (Eds.), *Handbook of theories of social psychology* (pp. 379–398). Thousand Oaks, CA: SAGE.

Erb, H.-P., Bohner, G., Rank, S., & Einwiller, S. (2002). Processing minority and majority communications: The role of conflict with prior attitudes. *Personality and Social Psychology Bulletin, 28*, 1172–1182.

Festinger, L. (1954). A theory of social comparison processes. *Human Relations, 7*, 117–140.

Frey, D., & Greif, S. (1997). *Sozialpsychologie: Ein Handbuch in Schlüsselbegriffen*. Munich: Beltz.

Frey, D., & Irle, M. (2008). *Theorien der Sozialpsychologie, Bd.2, Soziales Lernen, Interaktion und Gruppenprozesse*. Bern: Huber.

Gardner, M., & Steinberg, L. (2005). Peer influence on risk taking, risk preference, and risky decision making in adolescence and adulthood: An experimental study. *Developmental Psychology, 41*, 625–635.

Greitemeyer, T., & Schulz-Hardt, S. (2003). Preference-consistent evaluation of information in the hidden profile paradigm: Beyond group-level explanations for the dominance of shared information in group decisions. *Journal of Personality and Social Psychology, 84*, 322–339.

Heslin, P. A. (2009). Better than brainstorming? Potential contextual boundary conditions to brainwriting for idea generation in organizations. *Journal of Occupational and Organizational Psychology, 82*, 129–145.

Janis, I. (1971). Groupthink. *Psychology Today, 5*, 43–46.

Karau, S. J., & Williams, K. D. (1993). Social loafing: A meta-analytic review and theoretical integration. *Interpersonal Relations and Group Processes, 65*, 681–706.

Kerr, N. L., MacCoun, R. J., & Kramer, G. P. (1996). Bias in judgment: Comparing individuals and groups. *Psychological Review, 103*, 687–719.

Lamm, H., & Trommsdorff, G. (1973). Group versus individual performance on tasks requiring ideational proficiency (brainstorming): A review. *European Journal of Social Psychology, 3*, 361–388.

Latané, B., Williams, K., & Harkins, S. (1979). Many hands make light the work: The causes and consequences of social loafing. *Journal of Personality and Social Psychology, 37*, 822–832.

Lermer, E., Streicher, B., Eller, E., & Sachs, R. (2014). *Psychological influences II: Risk assessment in groups* (Munich Re Emerging Risk Discussion Papers). Retrieved from: https://www.munichre.com/site/corporate/get/documents_E1286451571/mr/assetpool.shared/Documents/0_Corporate%20Website/1_The%20Group/Focus/Emerging%20Risks/Emerging-Risk-Discussion-Paper-2014-10-en.pdf

Lewin, K. (1936). *Principles of topological psychology*. New York: McGraw-Hill.

Lightle, J. P., Kagel, J. H., & Arkes, H. R. (2009). Information exchange in group decision making: The hidden profile problem reconsidered. *Management Science, 55*, 568–581.

Lilli, W., & Frey, D. (1993). Die Hypothesentheorie der sozialen Wahrnehmung. In D. Frey & M. Irle (Eds.), *Theorien der Sozialpsychologie, Band 1: Kognitive Theorien* (pp. 49–78). Bern: Verlag Hans Huber.

Maass, A. (1997). Minoritäten. In D. Frey & S. Greif (Eds.), *Sozialpsycholigie. Ein Handbuch in Schlüsselbegriffen* (pp. 245–249). Munich: Beltz.

Mennecke, B. E., Hoffer, J. A., & Valacich, J. S. (1995). An experimental examination of group history and group support system use on information sharing performance and user perceptions. In *Proceedings of the Hawaii international conference on system sciences*.

Moscovici, S. (1980). Toward a theory of conversion behavior. *Advances in Experimental Social Psychology, 13*, 209–239.

Moscovici, S., & Lage, E. (1976). Studies in social influence III: Majority versus minority influence in a group. *European Journal of Social Psychology, 6*, 149–174.

Moscovici, S., Lage, E., & Naffrechoux, M. (1969). Influence of a consistent minority on the responses of a majority in a color perception task. *Sociometry, 32*, 365–380.

Moscovici, S., & Zavalloni, M. (1969). The group as a polarizer of attitudes. *Journal of Personality and Social, 12*, 125–135.

Mullen, B., Johnson, C., & Salas, E. (1991). Productivity loss in brainstorming groups: A meta-analytic integration. *Basic and Applied Social Psychology, 12*, 3–23.

Nemeth, C., & Rogers, J. (1996). Dissent and the search for information. *British Journal of Social Psychology, 31*, 67–76.

Nemeth, C., & Wachtler, J. (1974). Creating the perceptions of consistency and confidence: A necessary condition for minority influence. *Sociometry, 37*, 529–540.

Nemeth, C. J. (2011). Minority influence theory. In P. A. M. Van Lange, A. W. Kruglanski, & E. T. Higgins (Eds.), *Handbook of theories of social psychology* (pp. 362–379). London: SAGE.

Nemeth, C. J., Connell, J. B., Rogers, J. D., & Brown, K. S. (2001). Improving decision making by means of dissent. *Journal of Applied Social Psychology, 31*, 48–58.

Nemeth, C. J., & Kwan, J. L. (1987). Minority influence, divergent thinking and detection of correct solutions. *Journal of Applied Social Psychology, 17*, 788–799.

NSAA. (2014). Helmet usage and safety fact sheet. *Lakewood*. Retrieved from: https://www.nsaa.org/media/209466/HelmetFactSheet_10_1_2014.pdf

Pauhus, P. B., Dzindolet, M. T., Poletes, G., & Camach, L. M. (1993). Perception of performance in group brainstorming: The illusion of group productivity. *Personality and Social Psychology Bulletin, 19*, 78–89.

Paulus, P. B. (1998). Developing consensus about groupthink after all these years. *Organizational Behavior and Human Decision Processes, 73*, 362–374.

Paulus, P. B., & Yang, H. C. (2000). Idea generation in groups: A basis for creativity in organizations. *Organizational Behavior and Human Decision Processes, 82*, 76–87.

Phillips, K. W., & Loyd, D. L. (2006). When surface and deep-level diversity collide: The effects on dissenting group members. *Organizational Behavior and Human Decision Processes, 99*, 143–160.

Phillips, K. W., Northcraft, G. B., & Neale, M. A. (2006). Surface-level diversity and decision-making in groups: When does deep-level similarity help? *Group Processes & Intergroup Relations, 9*, 467–482.

Prose, F. (1997). Gruppeneinfluß auf Wahrnehmungsurteile. Die Experimente von Sherif und Asch. In D. Frey & S. Greif (Eds.), *Sozialpsychologie. Ein Handbuch in Schlüsselbegriffen*. Munich: Beltz.

Schulz-Hardt, S., Brodbeck, F. C., Mojzisch, A., Kerschreiter, R., & Frey, D. (2006). Group decision making in hidden profile situations: Dissent as a facilitator for decision quality. *Journal of Personality and Social Psychology, 91*, 1080–1093.

Stasser, G., Steward, D., & Wittenbaum, G. M. (1995). Expert roles and information exchange during discussion: The importance of knowing who knows what. *Journal of Experimental Social Psychology, 31*, 244–265.

Stasser, G., & Stewart, D. (1992). Discovery of hidden profiles by decision-making groups: Solving a problem versus making a judgment. *Journal of Personality and Social Psychology, 63*, 426–434.

Stasser, G., & Titus, W. (1985). Pooling of unshared information in group decision making: Biased information sampling during discussion. *Journal of Personality and Social Psychology, 48*, 1467–1478.

Stasser, G., & Titus, W. (2003). Hidden profiles: A brief history. *Psychological Inquiry, 14*, 304–313.

Stasser, G., Vaughan, S. I., & Stewart, D. D. (2000). Pooling unshared information: The benefits of knowing how access to information is distributed among group members. *Organizational Behavior and Human Decision Processes, 82*, 102–116.

Stoner, J. (1968). Risky and cautious shifts in group decisions: The influence of widely held values. *Journal of Experimental Social Psychology, 4*, 442–459.

Sunstein, C. R. (1999). *The law of group polarization*. John M. Olin Program in Law and Economics Working Paper (Vol. 91).

Tajfel, H., & Turner, J. (1979). An integrative theory of intergroup conflict. *The Social Psychology of Intergroup Relations, 33*, 33–47.

Taylor, D. W., Berry, P. C., Block, C. H., & Block, C. H. (1958). Does group participation when or using inhibit brainstorming facilitate creative thinking ? *Administrative Science Quarterly, 3*, 23–47.

Turner, J. C., & Reynolds, K. J. (2011). Self-categorization theory. In P. Van Lange, A. Kruglanski, & E. T. Higgins (Eds.), *Handbook of theories of social psychology* (Vol. 46, pp. 399–417). London: SAGE.

Valacich, J. S., Sarker, S., Pratt, J., & Groomer, M. (2009). Understanding risk-taking behavior of groups: A "decision analysis" perspective. *Decision Support Systems, 46*, 902–912.

Van de Ven, A. H., & Delbecq, A. L. (1974). The efectiveness of nominal, delphi, and interacting group decision making processes. *Academy of Management Journal, 17*, 605–621.

Wise, S., & Scott, S. (2012). *The puck stops here: Evolving social norms of helmet usage in the national hockey league*. Retrieved from: https://computationalsocialscience.org/wp-content/uploads/2012/09/WiseAndScott2012.pdf

Wittenbaum, G. M., Hubbell, A. P., & Zuckerman, C. (1999). Mutual enhancement: Toward an understanding of the collective preference for shared information. *Journal of Personality and Social Psychology, 77*(5), 967–978.

Wittenbaum, G. M., Hollingshead, A. B., & Botero, I. C. (2004). From cooperative to motivated information sharing in groups: Moving beyond the hidden profile paradigm. *Communication Monographs, 71*, 286–310.

Wood, W., Lundgren, S., Ouellette, J. A., Busceme, S., & Blackstone, T. (1994). Minority influence: A meta-analytic review of social influence processes. *Psychological Bulletin, 115*(3), 323–345.

Part III
Modeling Decision Making under Risk

Chapter 7
The Use of Heuristics in Decision Making Under Risk and Uncertainty

Martina Raue and Sabine G. Scholl

Abstract When making decisions under risk and uncertainty, people often rely on heuristics. A heuristic is a simple decision rule that allows one to make judgments without integrating all the information available. Especially in complex situations and under time pressure, simplification supports humans in coping with their limited capacity to process information. In this chapter, we introduce two main approaches: the *heuristics and biases program* (including the availability, representativeness, affect, as well as anchoring and adjustment heuristics) and the *fast and frugal heuristics*. Sometimes, the use of heuristics can lead people astray and result in errors, which is the focus of the heuristics and biases program. But in many other instances, heuristics support effective decision making in complex situations and lead to sufficient outcomes, which is the focus of the fast and frugal heuristics approach. We discuss the underlying processes, criticisms, and limitations of both approaches. We also consider practical implications of heuristics using the perception of climate change as an example and introduce applications in the form of nudges and decision trees.

Imagine you are out in nature in an area where you may encounter wildlife. Do you know how much distance you are supposed to keep from a wild animal? The general recommendation is to keep a distance of 100 yards (91 meters) from bears and wolves and at least 25 yards (23 meters) from other wildlife (United States National Park Service, 2017). Now, imagine you actually see a bear or a wolf. Would you be able to judge whether you are 50 or 100 meters away from it? This might be challenging, especially while experiencing some level of anxiety in the presence of danger that can make accurate judgments more difficult. To make this judgment easier, especially for children, the organization Leave No Trace suggests to use a *rule of*

M. Raue (✉)
AgeLab, Massachusetts Institute of Technology, Cambridge, MA, USA
e-mail: maraue@mit.edu

S. G. Scholl
School of Social Sciences, University of Mannheim, Mannheim, Germany

M. Raue et al. (eds.), *Psychological Perspectives on Risk and Risk Analysis*,
https://doi.org/10.1007/978-3-319-92478-6_7

thumb: "make a thumbs up, extend your arm all the way, close one eye, and see if you can hide the animal with your thumb. If you can't hide the entire animal with your thumb take a few steps back and try again. When you can hide the whole animal, this means you are a safe distance from wildlife" (Leave No Trace, 2016). The rule of thumb has become synonymous with making complex decisions a little easier. Another term that is used in the scientific literature is *heuristic*.

Decisions under risk and uncertainty can be very complex, because often one must consider many significant threads of information that could be relevant for the decision. For example, if one is considering a medical treatment regimen, she must weigh the severity and likelihood of side effects as opposed to the effectiveness of the treatment, the cost of the treatment, the available alternatives, and so on. When buying a house, one must not only consider the down payment and mortgage but also interest rates, inflation, and changes in the housing market as well as personal circumstances, which may change over time. Similarly, complex public matters containing elements of risk, such as environmental policy or public health, can be overwhelming for individuals who want to ponder all the information available. Also, when making quick decisions under time pressure, such as while driving in heavy traffic or engaging in risky sports, one cannot possibly include all available information in the decision making process.

Humans can consciously process only a limited amount of information at a time, which is known as *bounded rationality* (Simon, 1955). The combination of bounded rationality, complexity of a task, and time pressure has important consequences for the way judgments and decisions are made. Constrained by these boundary conditions, people need to simplify their decision processes while at the same time maintaining a sufficient level of accuracy. In order to make a decision despite uncertainty, people often use heuristics. A heuristic is a simple decision rule that allows one to make a judgment without integrating all the information available. Heuristics have the advantage of reducing time and effort while still producing good judgments and decisions most of the time (Kahneman & Tversky, 1972).

According to some researchers, judgments based on heuristics may correspond to or even outperform judgments based on careful analysis (Hart, 2005). In many cases, a good enough or satisfying outcome is sufficient and an optimal outcome not feasible (Simon, 1955). Others argue that using heuristics may result in errors and biases (Tversky & Kahneman, 1974). A decision is biased, for example, when some piece of information is given more weight than it should receive, for instance, when someone overestimates the risk of an airplane crash due to exposure to recent extensive media coverage (Kasperson et al., 1988). When sufficient information is not available or too complex to process, people are more susceptible to biasing factors (e.g., warning labels on cigarette packages or extensive media coverage; Slovic, Peters, Finucane, & MacGregor, 2005). However, critics have argued that the term *bias* may not always be appropriate in such situations. Rather, people adapt to the context at hand using the best judgment tools they have in the given situation (e.g., Neth & Gigerenzer, 2015). Many heuristics can be used in a wide variety of circumstances but usually work best for a particular set of situations. Errors may occur, for example, when a heuristic that works well for one problem, environment, or context is used in a decision problem for which it does not fit well (Reimer & Rieskamp, 2007).

In this chapter, we introduce different heuristics for decision making under risk and uncertainty. We focus on two main approaches, the *heuristics and biases program* (Tversky & Kahneman, 1974) and the *fast and frugal heuristics* (Gigerenzer, Todd, & The ABC Research Group, 1999). While the heuristics and biases program focuses on the biases produced by heuristics, the fast and frugal heuristics approach focuses on the advantages of heuristics. The heuristics and biases program originally included the availability heuristic, the representativeness heuristic, and the anchoring and adjustment heuristic. However, more recent research (Kahneman & Frederick, 2002) argues that within the heuristics and biases program, the anchoring and adjustment heuristic should be replaced with the affect heuristic, to complete a set of heuristics that is based on *attribute substitution* (i.e., substituting one question with another), which we consider in the following.

In the literature on the heuristics and biases program, the terms risk and uncertainty are often used interchangeably. More accurately, the term risk refers to a known distribution of negative outcomes, while this is not true in the case of uncertainty (Edwards, 1954; Knight, 1921; Luce & Raiffa, 1957). Accordingly, researchers of fast and frugal heuristics point out that one must differentiate between situations of risk—where probabilities are known and an optimal solution could be calculated—and situations of uncertainty, where probabilities are unknown and one must find a satisfying solution (e.g., Gigerenzer et al., 1999).

The Heuristics and Biases Program

Heuristics were first studied systematically by Tversky and Kahneman (1974) in their heuristics and biases program. Kahneman and Tversky started their research program based on the question of how people come up quickly with intuitive answers to complex questions (Kahneman, 2016). In one early experiment, they asked mathematical psychologists to make judgments on the replicability and the robustness of statistical results. Despite the fact that these participants had statistical expertise, they were overly confident in the results of studies based on small sample sizes (Tversky & Kahneman, 1971). Tversky and Kahneman came up with several similar tasks that demonstrated people's belief in small numbers, which is a mental shortcut or heuristic that does not require deliberate analysis, but may lead to errors. The observation of these types of errors (also known as *biases*) resulted in their research program of heuristics and biases. The heuristics and biases program focuses on understanding cognitive processes that underlie human judgment and bases its research on the observation of biases and errors, which then leads to the diagnosis of the use of heuristics (Kahneman & Frederick, 2002).

The Availability Heuristic

Heuristics are especially useful in complex situations when there is insufficient time or mental capacity for deliberate analysis. The availability heuristic allows the reduction of complexity when making judgments about frequencies or probabilities (Tversky & Kahneman, 1973). In such decision situations, the question about probability or frequency is substituted by the question about availability. In a classic study, Tversky and Kahneman (1973) gave participants one of two lists of 30 male and female names, respectively. List A consisted of 10 women and 20 men, where the women were very famous and the men were less famous. List B, on the other hand, consisted of 20 less famous women and 10 very famous men. In other words, both lists differed in the gender proportion and in terms of celebrity of either women or men. Next, participants were asked to estimate if there were more women or more men on their list. Over 80% of participants believed wrongly that list A had more female names and list B had more male names. This finding was explained by the reliance on the availability heuristic, namely, that participants could more easily remember famous names and therefore overestimated the corresponding category. In a similar experiment, participants in the United States were asked whether there are more English words that start with a letter k or words with the letter k in the third position. For most people, it is easier to think of words that start with a k than words that have a k in the third position. Therefore, it was not surprising that most participants wrongly concluded that there are more words that start with a k, even though there are in fact more words with k in the third position (Tversky & Kahneman, 1973).

The availability heuristic can also explain why people fear highly unlikely events such as terrorist attacks or airplane crashes. These events are easily available if they have recently been covered extensively in the media. Fear of terrorism was the second biggest fear among Americans in 2016 (Chapman University, 2016), despite it being a very unlikely cause of death in the United States. Exposure to excessive media coverage with emotional images makes those fears come to mind very easily. On the other hand, most people are not that often presented with images of people dying from heart attacks or cancer, which are far likelier causes of death (Kahan et al., 2012; Lerner, Gonzalez, Small, & Fischhoff, 2003; Slovic & Peters, 2006; Västfjäll, Peters, & Slovic, 2008). Personal experience can be another prompt that makes events easily available and has been shown to increase risk perception, for example, spurring the purchase of insurance coverage against floods or earthquakes after the occurrence of such an event (Keller, Siegrist, & Gutscher, 2006; Slovic, Monahan, & MacGregor, 2000).

Schwarz, Bless, and colleagues (1991) addressed the underlying cognitive processes of the availability heuristic to disentangle whether judgments are based on the ease of retrieval or on the content of the information retrieved. They developed an experimental method that made it possible to manipulate both the ease of retrieval and the content of information. Participants were asked to recall 6 or 12 situations in which they felt self-confident. A pre-study revealed that most people find it easy to recall 6 situations in which they felt self-confident but find it difficult to recall 12 of those situations. Subsequently, participants rated their self-confidence. If people make judgments based on retrieved content, the memory of 12 examples for self-confident behavior should result in a higher rating of self-confidence than the memory of 6 examples. If people make judgments based on the ease of retrieval, the contrary should be true—the relative ease of coming up with 6 examples of self-confidence as opposed to 12 should increase self-confidence. Indeed, participants who were asked to remember fewer examples for self-confident behavior rated themselves as more self-confident than participants who were asked to remember more examples, supporting the ease-of-retrieval explanation. These results and numerous follow-up studies consistently supported the assumption that the ease of retrieval is the underlying process of the availability heuristic (for an overview, see Schwarz, Bless, et al., 1991; Wänke, 2013).

These findings have implications, for example, in consumer psychology. Consumers who can easily retrieve arguments in favor of a product are more likely to buy the product, but if they have difficulties retrieving arguments, the contrary outcome may result (Wänke, Bohner, & Jurkowitsch, 1997). For instance, Volkswagen advertised its Golf compact car with the slogan "I like Golf, because...," which encouraged the consumer to come up with arguments for the Golf. At the same time, the company made sure that these arguments could be easily retrieved by showing TV commercials that promoted positive characteristics of the Golf (e.g., efficiency, roominess, safety).

The availability heuristic is also relevant in many other situations, such as daily decision making. For instance, in group decision making, people tend to overestimate their own contribution and underestimate the contributions of others, because their own contribution can be recalled more easily (Ross & Sicoly, 1979). This helps explain some of the conflicts couples have over who takes out the trash or cleans the dishes.

A vast amount of scientific work on the availability heuristic reinforces that it is a robust phenomenon but also that its use is more or less likely based on certain constraints (Greifeneder, Bless, & Pham, 2010). For instance, people do not use the availability heuristic if the ease of retrieval is perceived as irrelevant for the judgment at hand. In one study, participants were told that the background music played during their participation in a study would facilitate the recall of information (i.e., ease of retrieval). Under these circumstances, participants did not make their judgements based on the ease of retrieval but on the content retrieved (Schwarz, Bless, et al., 1991). Various follow-up studies confirmed these effects of the attribution of perceived ease of retrieval (for an overview, see Greifeneder et al., 2010). Further research suggests that ease of retrieval is used in cases where processing intensity is limited or in situations with low personal relevance. However, when the judgment task is of high personal relevance, people are motivated to use a more systematic processing strategy (Rothman & Schwarz, 1998).

The Representativeness Heuristic

In some decision situations, an event or object may appear representative for a wider group of events or objects, prompting the use of the representativeness heuristic. One may use the representativeness heuristic to judge probabilities of occurrence or affiliations. Within this approach, it is assumed that the representativeness of an event or a person for a superordinate category (e.g., a group) is the base for judgments (Tversky & Kahneman, 1974). Here, the question about probability is substituted by the question about representativeness. The more representative an element is perceived for a certain superordinate category (e.g., an effect for a cause or a sample for a population), the larger one estimates the probability that the element, the effect, or the sample is part of the corresponding superordinate category, cause, or population. For example, a lung cancer patient may seem more representative for the group of smokers than for the group of non-smokers, which may lead to accurate judgments in this case.

The representative heuristic is useful in many situations and often leads to adequate judgments, if people can easily and correctly judge the representativeness of an event. Nonetheless, systematic errors may occur because probability and representativeness correlate more in some situations than in others and because people do not always have a correct idea of what is representative for a category, a cause, or a population. Some of the errors that come with the representativeness heuristic (and are even made by experts trained in statistics) are discussed in the following.

Conjunction Fallacy

Imagine the following scenario: "Linda is 31 years old, single, outspoken, and very bright. She majored in philosophy. As a student, she was deeply concerned with issues of discrimination and social justice, and also participated in anti-nuclear demonstrations" (Kahneman & Tversky, 1982, p. 126). Participants were presented with eight options that may represent Linda, two of which were (1) Linda is a bank teller and (2) Linda is a bank teller and active in the feminist movement. Participants were asked to rank the probabilities of these options. Most participants (86%) perceived the events occurring in conjunction, Linda as bank teller and active feminist, as more likely than the single event, Linda as bank teller. From a statistical standpoint, these participants were in error, because the probability of a conjunction of events (bank teller and feminist) is a special case of a more general case (bank teller), and because of this the likelihood of occurrence cannot be more likely (a bias called extension neglect).

Base-Rate Neglect

The base rate is the underlying distribution of specific features such as the number of bank tellers in a certain population. For example, imagine the following scenario: "Steve is very shy and withdrawn, invariably helpful but with little interest in people or in the world of reality. A meek and tidy soul, he has a need for order and a passion for detail" (Tversky & Kahneman, 1974, p.1124). In which occupation is Steve most likely engaged? Is he most likely (1) a physician, (2) a salesman, or (3) a librarian? In several problems similar to this, Kahneman and Tversky (1973) demonstrated that participants base their judgments on the representativeness of a person for a certain occupation. Since the description of Steve is very similar to the stereotype of a librarian, it may seem likely that Steve is a librarian. In many cases, the use of the representativeness heuristic results in good judgments because representativeness and the probability of group membership often correlate. However, systematic errors occur when the underlying base rate is neglected. In the above example, one needs to consider that there are generally less librarians in the population than salesmen. Even when participants were informed about base rates in these types of problems, they generally did not consider them in their judgments.

Insensitivity to Sample Size

People often wrongly conclude that small samples represent the larger population and therefore expect that small samples will have the same characteristics as the underlying population. For example, participants were asked to imagine that someone (player A) would compete in a squash game against the more advanced player B. Player A can decide if he wants to play for 9 or 15 points. Most participants did not think that this would make a difference. From a statistical viewpoint, however, the game of 9 points represents a smaller sample and will be less representative for a series of games than the game of 15 points; therefore, the probability of winning will be higher for the more advanced player in the 15-point game than in the 9-point game, because an atypical outcome is less likely to occur in the larger sample (Kahneman & Tversky, 1982).

Misconceptions of Chance

Similar to the expectation that small samples are representative for a larger population, people expect that the characteristics of an infinite sequence of random events will also be found in a shorter version of that sequence (Kahneman & Tversky, 1972). For example, when people are asked about the likelihood of the coin toss sequences head-head-head-tail-tail-tail and head-tail-tail-head-tail-head, most people judge the latter sequence as more representative of a random event and therefore more likely. In this case, randomness is determined by evaluating the characteristics of the outcome sequences. Most people expect that sequence to conform to statistical definitions of randomness, such as relative frequencies of heads and tails or number of alternations between head and tail. However, randomness may also be evaluated by focusing on the generating process of the coin toss. In this case, tossing an unbiased coin results in the two sequences that have the exact same probability of occurrence ($1/2^n = 1/2^6 = 1/64$), because a preceding event does not influence the probability of the subsequent event (Scholl & Greifeneder, 2011).

Critics and De-Biasing Efforts

These biases that were described in relation to the representativeness heuristic were critically evaluated in subsequent studies. Critics questioned whether participants in the studies mentioned above had a different understanding of the tasks than the investigators. They argued that information was not presented according to common conversational norms. For example, the norm of relevance states that only relevant information should be communicated (Grice, 1975). Therefore, participants would have assumed that the information that was presented would be relevant for the judgment that was expected from them. Critics also argued that the detailed description of cases and the rather scarce presentation of base rates led participants to assume that the former was more important than the latter (Schwarz, Strack, Hilton, & Naderer, 1991). Presenting the task as a "psychological task" may also have the consequence that psychological information (case descriptions) will be considered as more relevant than statistical information (base rate). Schwarz, Strack, and colleagues (1991) demonstrated that the insensitivity to base rates is reduced when the task is labeled as a "statistical task." In line with these findings is the observation that base rates are more considered when they are especially salient (Gigerenzer, Hell, & Blank, 1988; Schwarz, 1996). Also, when relevant rules were made more accessible and logical problems were practiced beforehand by participants, the conjunction fallacy could be reduced or eliminated (Agnoli, 1991; Agnoli & Krantz, 1989). In more transparent versions of these tasks, it was shown that more intelligent and statistically sophisticated people were more likely to apply logical rules and overcome erroneous intuitions when sufficient information was available (Kahneman, 2000; Kahneman & Frederick, 2002).

Gigerenzer and colleagues (e.g., Gigerenzer & Murray, 2015) more generally criticize the content-blind application of statistical norms in psychological research by arguing that statistical norms cannot always be easily applied to real-world judgments, because failing to apply statistics does not necessarily lead to poor performance in the real world. Fiedler and von Sydow (2015) also question statistical norms as a general standard of comparison for human performance, drawing on an analogy from psychophysics, in which deviations of subjective experiences of physical stimuli (e.g., sound) from objective measures of the stimuli are not regarded as human failure. While Vranas (2000) points out that research in psychology needs appropriate norms to study judgments under uncertainty, he also stresses that such norms may differ for each individual in the real world; in certain cases statistical norms may be appropriate, while in others conversational norms may seem more useful. In this line, Zaval and Cornwell (2016) state, "when individuals have a choice between statistical, conceptual experience and vivid, personal experience, [...], they will tend to rely on the latter" (p. 6). Similarly, Scholl and Bless (2016) argue that one must differentiate between the use of heuristics in experimental studies versus in natural settings where available information is often also relevant.

Other studies have shown that presenting information in a frequency format (e.g., 1 in 10), which is suggested to be more natural, can reduce or eliminate the errors of the conjunction fallacy and base-rate neglect (Cosmides, 1996; Gigerenzer & Hoffrage, 1995; Tversky & Kahneman, 1983). People are simply not good at judging probabilities (0.10) or percentages (10%), and most people make less errors when statistical information is presented in frequencies (1 in 10) rather than probabilities. However, Kahneman and Frederick (2002) point out that changing the format does not undermine the role of representativeness but rather makes logical conclusions easier to be applied. In line with that, research has shown that the error of conjunction fallacy can be reduced among statistically sophisticated participants when they were asked to compare the two critical options directly. But in the absence of this prompt, the statistical experts based their judgments on representativeness, just like everyone else. As Gould (1992) points out, most people *feel* that Linda cannot just be a bank teller but must be a feminist bank teller (in Kahneman & Frederick, 2002). Kahneman and Frederick (2002) argue that some of the criticism around the representativeness heuristic stemmed from very illustrative examples being used to demonstrate the effects. The Linda problem may have been a good illustration of conjunction fallacy, but it was a less obvious example of the general human tendency of dominance violation (i.e., a general case is always more likely than a subordinate, more specific case). In spite of the critics, the representativeness heuristic is a robust phenomenon. This heuristic has been shown to affect clinical psychologists (Bruchmüller, Margraf, & Schneider, 2012), patients (McDowell, Occhipinti, & Chambers, 2013), gamblers (Holtgraves & Skeel, 1992), as well as brokers (Chen, Kim, Nofsinger, & Rui, 2007).

The Affect Heuristic

The affect heuristic (Finucane, Alhakami, Slovic, & Johnson, 2000), the risk-as-feelings hypothesis (Loewenstein, Weber, Hsee, & Welch, 2001), and the feelings-as-information theory (Schwarz, 1990) propose that people use feelings as a cue for decision making. As with the availability and representativeness heuristics, the affect heuristic is based on attribute substitution. Affect is used as a simple attribute for the more complex evaluation of a decision problem. Whereas feelings elicited by the target of judgment may provide valid information, feelings that are due to an unrelated influence often result in biased judgments. Whether one feels positive about new technologies or negative about climate change affects perceptions of risks and benefits as well as decisions and actions around these complex issues (For an overview, see Slovic, 2010). For example, studies on the risk perception of nuclear energy have demonstrated that judgments of risk are high when perceived benefits are low and vice versa. However, in the real world, these aspects are often positively correlated: technologies that are highly risky are often also highly beneficial; otherwise they would not be worth the risk. It was found that affect was the reason for this inverse relationship between perceived risk and benefit among individuals (see also Tompkins, Bjälkebring, & Peters, Chap. 5). Positive feelings about a new technology led people to judge its risks as low and benefits as high, while negative feelings led to high risk and low benefit perceptions (Slovic, Finucane, Peters, & MacGregor, 2004).

Negative affect also serves as an explanation for people's concern about human-made hazards as opposed to natural hazards (Siegrist & Sütterlin, 2014). Furthermore, the increase of risk perception by using frequency formats (e.g., a disease will kill 50 out of 1000 people) instead of probabilities (5%) to present risk is explained by more realistic imaginations of the threat (e.g., 50 people dying from the disease) causing an emotional reaction. Similarly, cigarette warning labels use vivid images of people suffering from smoking-related medical conditions. Eventually, affect may underlie some of the original findings attributed to the availability heuristic, because affective images are easier to recall. For example, risks that are more affectively charged are also more present in the media (Lichtenstein, Slovic, Fischhoff, Layman, & Combs, 1978; see also Pachur, Hertwig, & Steinmann, 2012 for a comparison of the availability and the affect heuristics; Slovic et al., 2004). In addition to affect that is experienced in relation to a stimulus (integral affect), research has also demonstrated the influence of feelings that are unrelated to a stimulus (e.g., mood) but can be misattributed to it (incidental affect). For example, Hirshleifer and Shumway (2003) reported that the weather influenced stock market returns in 26 countries from 1982 to 1997. Specifically, sunshine in the city that hosted the country's major stock exchange increased the likelihood that the market went up. Presumably, sunshine improved investors' moods, which rendered them more optimistic about the future of the economy.

Do individuals always rely on their affect when making judgments and decisions? Research in the realm of feelings as information goes one step further and addresses the boundary conditions under which individuals rely on affect in their judgments as well as the underlying cognitive processes (for an overview, see Schwarz, 1990). The idea is that individuals often attend to their feelings as a source of information—but that the use of a given feeling depends on the perceived informational value of that feeling for the current judgment. When the informational value of a feeling is called into question, individuals use other sources of information. Participants in a famous study by Schwarz and Clore (1983) reported higher life satisfaction (and a more positive mood) when they were called on sunny days as opposed to rainy days. However, the negative influence of bad weather was eliminated when the interviewer first asked participants about the current weather conditions in their town—which made it salient to participants that their current weather-related mood was an unrelated source for their judgment of life satisfaction. Several follow-up studies showed that individuals do not rely on their feelings when they become aware that their feelings may be due to an unrelated source.

Schwarz and Clore used the term *discounting effect* to describe situations in which individuals do not use their negative feelings as information because they have become aware that these may be due to an unrelated source (e.g., bad weather, writing about sad life events). However, when in a good mood, subjects did not show a discounting effect when the source of their mood was made salient (it was assumed that people seek information for unpleasant mood states because they deviate from the regular pleasant mood state). Other studies have also found that reliance on feelings decreases when participants perceive their feelings as irrelevant for the judgment at hand (e.g., Pham, 1998) or when more alternative informational sources are accessible (e.g., Sedikides, 1995). Affect's influence also decreases relative to the participants' level of processing capacity (e.g., Greifeneder & Bless, 2007) and level of certainty (Faraji-Rad & Pham, 2016).

The Anchoring and Adjustment Heuristic

While originally part of the heuristics and biases program (Tversky & Kahneman, 1974), the anchoring and adjustment heuristic does not fit the definition of attribute substitution (i.e., substituting one question with another).[1] Rather, the anchoring and adjustment heuristic increases the plausibility of a value based on a particular anchor given in the situation. For example, imagine one decides to sell an antique chair and has seen a similar chair on a flea market for a low price (low anchor) or at an auction for a high price (high anchor). The perceived value of the chair and the ultimate price may be very different depending on the anchor that the seller encountered at either the flea market or the auction (Chapman & Johnson, 2002).

When people have very little or no information, they often use an anchor as a basis for their judgment, which may be recalled from their memory (self-generated anchor) or provided in the situation (situationally provided anchor). While relevant anchors can offer a good basis for adequate judgments, irrelevant anchors can bias judgments. In a classic study on irrelevant anchors, participants were asked to judge the percentage of African states in the United Nations (UN). Before the participants made their judgments, a manipulated fortune wheel was spun that showed either the number 10 or the number 65. Then the participants were asked to judge whether the number of African states in the UN was larger or smaller than this number (the anchor 10 vs. 65). Subsequently, they stated their estimates of the percentage of African states in the UN. While participants with the low anchor (10) judged the percentage on average as 25%, participants with the high anchor (65) judged the percentage on average as 45%. The irrelevant anchors provided by the wheel of fortune influenced people's judgments (Tversky & Kahneman, 1974).

In most studies on the anchoring and adjustment heuristic, the classic paradigm is to ask participants to make a comparative judgment ("is the number smaller or

[1] Kahneman and Frederick (2002) suggested that the anchoring heuristic needs to be replaced by the affect heuristic in the list of "major general-purpose heuristics" (p. 6).

larger than the anchor?") before making an absolute judgment ("estimate the number!"). Anchors can be made salient in various other ways such as questions about checking a control number on the questionnaire or asking participants for their phone number (Wilson, Houston, Etling, & Brekke, 1996). Irrelevant anchors provided in a situation often result in biased judgments, but anchors that are technically relevant for the current situation can also lead to incorrect judgments. For example, the sequence of numbers in a math task can serve as an anchor. Participants indicated lower estimates when asked to guess the result of 1*2*3*4*5*6*7*8 than when asked for the result of 8*7*6*5*4*3*2*1. The median estimate was 512 for the former and 2250 for the latter. This was explained with the observation that people often make an estimate based on the first couple of numbers they encounter instead of making a complete calculation (Tversky & Kahneman, 1974).

Anchor effects have been found in various domains: Even experienced judges were misguided by anchors such as questions from journalists or demands from prosecutors (Englich, Mussweiler, & Strack, 2006). For example, in one study judges were presented with the description of a case and asked to make a decision on an appropriate punishment. In one condition, the prosecution demanded 34 months of jail while in another condition 12 months. The sentences of the judges in both conditions differed by 8 months, which was explained by anchoring and adjustment based on the prosecution's suggestion (Englich & Mussweiler, 2001). In general, judges have been shown to impose higher punishments when the prosecutor—as done in the German law system—requests the penalty before the plea (Englich, Mussweiler, & Strack, 2005). Anchor effects were also shown to influence physician's judgments (Brewer, Chapman, Schwartz, & Bergus, 2007), purchase decisions (Wansink, Kent, & Hoch, 1998), as well as salary and price negotiations (Galinsky & Mussweiler, 2001).

While the anchoring and adjustment effect was described as early as 1974, its underlying processes were not systematically investigated until the 1990s. Self-generated anchors (e.g., based on knowledge or memory) often offer a good starting point for judgments. People generally adjust their judgments dynamically away from the anchor and stop searching once their estimate seems plausible. For example, when asked when George Washington was elected president of the United States, people might use the date of the Declaration of Independence in 1776 as an anchor, because they know that this is close to the true answer (1798; Epley & Gilovich, 2006). There is usually a range of plausible estimates, which is larger when the person has less knowledge, but in general low anchors cause lower estimates than high anchors. Because most people terminate their search once a plausible value is reached, self-generated anchors often lead to insufficient adjustments (Epley & Gilovich, 2006; Strack & Mussweiler, 1997). Underlying cognitive processes for self-generated and situationally provided anchors differ. Despite the name "anchoring and adjustment heuristic," the process of *adjustment* has been suggested to only occur in self-generated anchors, not in situationally provided anchors. The process of adjustment is effortful, but incentives for accuracy can improve adjustments from self-generated anchors. However, such incentives do not affect responses to situationally provided anchors, and therefore adjustment does not seem to be a plausible explanation in the latter case (Epley & Gilovich, 2006).

Rather, *numerical priming* (Critcher & Gilovich, 2008; Wilson et al., 1996) and *selective accessibility* (Mussweiler & Strack, 1999) serve as explanations for anchor effects, with the latter being the most widely accepted explanation. Numerical priming means that the relative judgment or other factors prime numerical values, which make them available for subsequent judgments and influence numerical estimates. This approach assumes that the numerical value exclusively predicts the size of the anchoring effect (independent of the context of the target element of judgment). However, this strict numerical explanation is criticized because it cannot explain why the anchoring effect is reduced when comparative and absolute judgments are incompatible. For example, when the comparative judgment referred to the width of a building but the absolute judgment referred to its height, anchoring effects were weaker than in cases where both judgments referred to the same judgmental dimension (Strack & Mussweiler, 1997).

In the selective accessibility model, Mussweiler and Strack (1999; see also Strack & Mussweiler, 2003) argue that anchoring effects are not produced by insufficient adjustment but rather by the enhanced accessibility of information that is consistent with the situationally provided anchor. Based on an anchor value, people search for selective information that is compatible with or proves this value. In contrast to self-generated anchors, where people know that the anchor is most likely not the true value, situationally provided anchors need to be evaluated as potential answers (Epley & Gilovich, 2006). The selective testing of information (*selective hypothesis testing*) increases the accessibility of anchor-consistent memories. Because subsequent judgments are based on accessible information, the anchor biases the judgment. This assumption is supported by studies showing that participants who were presented with a lower anchor (e.g., "Is the average temperature in Antarctica higher or lower than −43 °C?") also wrote down more thoughts that were consistent with the lower anchor (e.g., "Antarctica has the lowest temperature on earth"), while participants who were presented with a higher anchor ("Is the average temperature in Antarctica higher or lower than -17°C?") wrote down more thoughts that were consistent with the higher anchor (Mussweiler & Strack, 1999). Interestingly, the selective accessibility model implies stronger anchoring effects when people think intensively about the anchor (because this activates more anchor-consistent information), which was also shown empirically (Mussweiler & Strack, 2000). Anchoring effects decrease or even disappear when people make more intuitive judgments, which are based on experiential knowledge (e.g., judgments on the average temperature in someone's home town). People focus less on the provided anchor when making more deliberative judgments, which focus on the anchor and not on experiential knowledge (Plessner & Czenna, 2008).

Anchoring effects have been demonstrated with numerical (comparison with given numbers) as well as semantical (comparison between objects or events regarding a given entity such as height) anchors and turn out to be a very robust phenomenon when anchors are situationally provided. They even occur when situational constraints should oppose anchor effects, when the anchor is extreme and therefore not plausible (e.g., "Was Gandhi older or younger than 140 years?"; Strack & Mussweiler, 1997), when participants were explicitly told about the biasing effect of the anchor (Wilson et al., 1996), or when they were rewarded for correct judgments (Tversky & Kahneman, 1974). Expertise can reduce anchoring effects (Smith, Windschitl, & Bruchmann, 2013), but they were also demonstrated with experts (Englich et al., 2005; Northcraft & Neale, 1987). A reduction of the anchoring effect was shown with the consider-the-opposite strategy. Participants were asked to think about reasons for higher (or lower) values of the anchor and to choose a value that is lower (higher) than the anchor (Mussweiler, Strack, & Pfeiffer, 2000). Anchoring effects can affect judgments in various situations and may result in errors and biases when the anchor is arbitrary or random.

The heuristics from Tversky and Kahneman's heuristics and biases program have become quite famous in the last decades and have been widely covered in the scientific and popular press. The fast and frugal heuristics are less known outside of science, but along with the heuristics and biases, they have led to practical improvements in decision making that have recently been more widely adopted, for instance, in the form of decision trees.

Fast and Frugal Heuristics

The fast and frugal heuristics approach emphasizes the advantages of using heuristics in situations of uncertainty and is based on the mathematical modeling of decision situations. The main goal of the fast and frugal heuristics approach is to highlight that heuristics can be simple without necessarily sacrificing accuracy (Hafenbrädl, Waeger, & Marewski, 2016). On the one hand, the approach is descriptive by focusing on how people make decisions under uncertainty. The result of this line of research is the *adaptive toolbox*, a repertoire of heuristics that is available to individuals. On the other hand, the approach is prescriptive by focusing on the environmental structures in which heuristics will lead to a better outcome than competing strategies (Gigerenzer, 2016). Gigerenzer and colleagues (1999) point out that fast and frugal heuristics that match cognition and environment are *ecologically rational*. In other words, in a given environment, heuristics reduce effort and increase accuracy by matching the structure of the task environment with the computational capabilities of the actor. Fast and frugal heuristics are simple rules that can even outperform complex algorithms in real-world situations. For example, when one catches a flying frisbee, it is impossible to analyze all factors that affect its trajectory such as spin and wind. Therefore, humans—and also dogs—rely on the gaze heuristic: they gaze at the object and adjust their running speed to keep the optimal angle constant, which actually is a very effective way to catch it (Mousavi & Gigerenzer, 2014; Todd & Gigerenzer, 2012). In conclusion, Gigerenzer and colleagues stress that research should consider how people are *able* to make decisions when studying how people *should* make decisions.

This research is based on three methodological principles, which are (1) algorithmic models, (2) tests of prediction, and (3) competitive testing (Gigerenzer, 2016). Each heuristic is thereby based on three theoretical principles. First, rules for searching, stopping, and decision making are specified. These rules include where to search, when to stop searching (without computing an optimal stopping point), and how to make a decision after the search has stopped. The specific rules will be outlined for each heuristic in the following sections. Second, fast and frugal heuristics are formulated in a highly transparent way, which should make it easy to understand how they function in making decisions. Third, fast and frugal heuristics are ecologically rational, in that they are strategies that are adapted to the environment to make accurate inferences (Goldstein & Gigerenzer, 2002). In any given decision situation, one can choose among a large set of heuristics, and the mechanisms underlying this choice depend on cognitive capacities and their interplay with the environment. The use of heuristics may develop through personal experience, training (e.g., medical diagnostics), or direct learning (e.g., how to catch a flying object) or over the course of evolution (Mousavi & Gigerenzer, 2014). Studies have shown that people also learn which heuristic is successful in which environment (Rieskamp & Otto, 2011). The heuristics of the adaptive toolbox are often classified along nonexclusive categories such as information processing (e.g., sequential order), applicability in a certain domain, compensation of unknown factors (e.g., medical diagnosis or weather forecasts), or mainly based on memory (Marewski & Gigerenzer, 2012).

The first heuristic that was systematically studied by Gigerenzer and colleagues was the take-the-best heuristic, which helps to decide between two alternatives (Gigerenzer & Goldstein, 1996). The take-the-best heuristic belongs to the class of lexicographic heuristics, which takes the value of predictors into account. This heuristic structures the natural environment by ignoring all but the most important predictor and is therefore characterized by one-reason decision making. Specifically, the rules of the take-the-best heuristic state: search two objects (e.g., cities) regarding their value on predictors ranging from the most valid to the least valid one (e.g., having an airport, a soccer team, a library), stop searching when you find the first predictor where the value of the two objects differ (e.g., one has an airport, the other one does not), and choose the object with the higher value on this predictor. The decision rule is to predict that the alternative with the higher predictor value (e.g., having an airport) has the higher value on the criterion (i.e., city size). In contrast, the class of tallying heuristics treats predictor variables equally (e.g., having an airport is as important as having a soccer team) and adds predictors instead of weighing them (i.e., choosing the option which has both an airport *and* a soccer team).

The recognition heuristic (another lexicographic heuristic) is one of the most-researched heuristics. The formal rule of the heuristic states that in the case of a definite number of alternatives, rank all recognized alternatives higher on the criterion than the unrecognized ones (Goldstein & Gigerenzer, 2002). Specifically, search an object that you recognize, stop searching when an object is recognized and another is not, and choose the recognized object. The success of the recognition heuristic is based on less knowledge (i.e., recognition only) rather than more knowledge. It can serve as a useful heuristic when deciding between alternatives in situations in which individuals recognize one of two objects and is informed by familiarity. In a classic experiment that demonstrates the recognition heuristic, German participants were asked to compare the relative size of two American cities,

San Diego and San Antonio, and the majority correctly concluded that San Diego is larger. This is explained by the observation that the majority of Germans recognized San Diego as an American city, but not San Antonio. In a series of additional experiments, Americans outperformed Germans in relative judgments of German cities and vice versa if they recognized one city in the foreign country but not the other (Gigerenzer & Goldstein, 1996).

Kahneman and Frederick (2002) point out that the recognition heuristic may also be susceptible to errors, because recognition may be influenced by unrelated factors such as media coverage. Reimer and Rieskamp (2007) argue that there are situations where the heuristic is useful (e.g., when comparing city sizes) and situations where it is not useful (e.g., when comparing the altitudes of cities above sea level). Others pointed out that the heuristic may be powerful, but is much less used than the authors originally proposed, because people often include instead of ignore further information (Pohl, 2017) and that the recognition heuristic is used more often when participants are asked to form deliberative (instead of intuitive) judgments (Hilbig, Scholl, & Pohl, 2010). The tendency of humans to rely on heuristics can also be used to influence them. For example, marketers employ the recognition heuristic by familiarizing their customers with brand names through commercials, with the aim of encouraging purchase when they have to make a choice between the familiar and the unfamiliar brand (Marewski & Pohl, 2010).

Another useful heuristic in allocation decisions is the 1/N heuristic (a tallying heuristic). For example, the complex decision of allocating money to stock options may be solved by simply dividing the money by the amount of stock options in question, which follows the general wisdom of not putting all one's eggs in the same basket. In one study, the 1/N heuristic was compared to 14 alternative optimization models, which were based on 10 years of stock data (DeMiguel, Garlappi, & Uppal, 2009). Although Benartzi and Thaler (2001) have argued that applying the 1/N heuristic is suboptimal, it turned out that despite its lower turnover, none of the optimization models consistently outperformed the heuristic.

Fast and frugal heuristics have been widely studied, with a focus on *when and why* they perform well and *whether and when* people use them. Systematic comparisons with statistical models demonstrated that the effectiveness of fast and frugal heuristics depends on the environment. Fast and frugal heuristics can perform quite well in uncertain environments or in situations that have not been encountered before. Participants were found to be sensitive to whether recognition is a valid cue for a given domain or not (e.g., the judgment of city sizes), but do not seem to adjust their decision strategy to the specific recognition validity (high vs. low) of the current set of items they are faced with in the recognition task at hand (Pohl, Michalkiewicz, Erdfelder, & Hilbig, 2017). It has also been demonstrated that fast and frugal heuristics are especially used under time pressure, when information is costly to search for or has to be retrieved from memory (e.g., Reimer & Rieskamp, 2007). However, critics of the fast and frugal approach have argued that there is no sufficient experimental proof that people rely on those heuristics or that they represent cognitive reality (e.g., Glöckner, 2008; Hilbig et al., 2010; Pohl, 2011).

However, researchers of the fast and frugal approach have quite successfully applied their insights to improve decision making processes in the real world.

Practical Applications

Heuristics can be very useful for both experts and laypeople. Despite the extensive knowledge that guides their decision making, doctors, pilots, or managers can still benefit from heuristics, because they cannot know all the alternatives or foresee all future outcomes. The heuristics and biases approach is already widely known, and many policymakers, legal scholars, or managers are especially aware of their biasing effects, but practitioners are often less familiar with the fast and frugal approach and the advantages of heuristics (e.g., Kelman, 2011). The fast and frugal heuristics program has been quite successful, for example, in creating decision aids (e.g., decision trees), especially in medicine, to support fast and frugal decision making. Practical applications from the heuristics and biases program are often based on highlighting biases and finding interventions to correct them (e.g., see next section on climate change), but the approach has also served as a basis for "nudges."

Climate Change

Protecting the environment is a task for the government and the people. In order to engage people in pro-environmental behavior, successful interventions need to consider human decision making in situations of uncertainty. Heuristics and biases have been discussed in the judgment of risks from climate change. Evaluating climate change is a very complex issue, and people's beliefs are often malleable and may be easily shaped by irrelevant information in the decision context at hand (Zaval & Cornwell, 2016). Research has shown that concerns about climate change peak during hot and dry summers, which has become known as the *local warming effect*. The availability heuristic was suggested as one explanation for this effect, because the current weather is easily accessible and replaces the more complex issue of climate change (Li, Johnson, & Zaval, 2011; Zaval, Keenan, Johnson, & Weber, 2014). In one study, participants who perceived the current day's temperature as higher than usual overestimated the number of warm days throughout the year, which increased their awareness of climate change (Zaval et al., 2014). However, a simple prompt that reminded participants of how the weather felt over the past year (rather than today) eliminated the local warming effect (Druckman, 2015). Also, the anchor heuristic may come into play when making judgments about climate change, if the current day's unusually high temperature serves as an anchor for the judgment of the average temperature. Thus, judgments on climate change may be based on heuristics, which has major implications for public policy, but can also influence polling results. Zaval and Cornwell (2016) summarize several solutions on how to translate heuristics into opportunities in order to improve public understanding of climate change and motivate action. These solutions include green defaults (e.g., automatic enrollment in green energy programs; Pichert & Katsikopoulos, 2008), re-framing information (e.g., focus on social benefits rather than personal sacrifice; Gifford & Comeau, 2011), conveying to social norms (e.g., by providing information on one's neighbors energy consumption in comparison with oneself; Ayres, Raseman, & Shih, 2012), or effective labeling (e.g., eco-labels as a heuristic that simplify pro-environmental decisions; Young, Hwang, McDonald, & Oates, 2010). Simple interventions like these have also been introduced under the umbrella of *nudging* and have been adopted by governments worldwide (Thaler & Sunstein, 2008).

Similarly, researchers of the fast and frugal approach suggest that simple heuristics that rely on *less* rather than more information might be useful to encourage pro-environmental behavior. They argue that too much information on climate change may confuse people more than help to encourage pro-environmental behavior (Artinger, Bortoleto, & Katsikopoulos, 2016). This has also been called *environmental numbness*, which results from being overwhelmed by information on environmental dangers that seem distant and not causing immediate effects (e.g., Gifford, 2011).

Nudges

Mainly based on the heuristics and biases program and subsequent research that demonstrates how human judgment can be biased, Thaler and Sunstein (2008) introduced *nudges* to improve decision making. Especially in areas such as health, wealth, and welfare that often involve decision making under risk and uncertainty, humans tend to make decisions that are not in their best interest. They do not save enough, they do not eat healthy enough, they do not exercise enough, and so on. This behavior may be attributed to certain biases and the complexity of decision situations. Nudges respond to behavioral biases or a lack of knowledge and have become quite popular in public policy research. Thaler and Sunstein describe policymakers as *choice architects*, who inevitably structure the choices people make (e.g., be it simply through the design of a legal form or by providing a "default option" for a decision). Structuring choices in a way that makes it easier for people to make better decisions is a nudge. A nudge ideally gives people a little push toward a good choice but always offers the option to deliberately decide otherwise. For example, healthy eating can be nudged by placing healthy food in the beginning of the line and at eye level in a cafeteria.

Default options which offer the possibility to opt out are nudges and a useful policy instrument to change people's behavior. Setting the default to being an organ donor (Johnson & Goldstein, 2003) or to enrolling in a retirement plan (Benartzi & Thaler, 2013) has been very successful interventions to promote the default behavior (i.e., being an organ donor, saving for retirement), because people can follow a simple heuristic set by policymakers or employers (e.g., "If the government sets a rule, I will follow it"). A comparison of nudges and traditional policy tools (e.g., incentives, mandates, bans) has demonstrated the effectiveness of various nudges across domains such as finance, health, and education, but the authors still acknowledge the importance of traditional policies (Benartzi et al., 2017).

Critics argue that defaults are not a one-size-fits-all instrument, because the default heuristic might not be useful for everyone and may depend highly on individual situations. Another main criticism of nudges concerns the underlying idea of *libertarian paternalism*, which does offer choice, but at the same time aims at achieving the choice architects' goals and presumes that one is not able to make a decision in his or her best interest (e.g., Gigerenzer, 2015; Schlag, 2010; Wilkinson, 2013). However, even critics have appreciated structuring the environment in a way that makes better options more salient.

Fast and frugal researchers also call for an "intuitive design of environments, which enhance performance by triggering successful heuristic strategies" (Mousavi & Gigerenzer, 2014, p. 9). However, they suggest environments that support informed decision making and educate the decision maker without pushing him or her in a certain direction (e.g., Gigerenzer, 2015). As an alternative to nudges, Grüne-Yanoff and Hertwig (Grüne-Yanoff & Hertwig, 2015; Hertwig & Grüne-Yanoff, 2017) introduced *boosts*, which are based on fastw and frugal heuristics and aim at expanding (boosting) people's decision making competences by supporting them to apply their existing skills and tools more effectively. For example, boosting statistical understanding to make informed medical decisions may include the presentation of statistical information in frequencies rather than probabilities (see also Hoffrage & Garcia-Retamero, Chap. 12). Another example of boosts are decision trees, which are introduced in the following. A lack of motivation among the target audience to be cognitively engaged may hinder the effectiveness of boosts (Grüne-Yanoff & Hertwig, 2015) and put nudges at an advantage in decisions that people care less about.

Decision Aids

Decision aids are rule-based tools that rely on real data and support people in making good decisions without having to process an overwhelming amount of information. Fast and frugal heuristics have been applied systematically to guide decision making. They have especially been implemented in the creation of simple decision trees for complex tasks in which individuals must make decisions under risk or uncertainty. Decision trees make information more accessible and intuitively understandable. For example, a fast and frugal tree was successfully implemented in the diagnosis of depression (Jenny, Pachur, Williams, Becker, & Margraf, 2013) or ischemic heart disease (Green & Mehr, 1997). In these trees, few questions have to be answered sequentially with either "yes" or "no." While answering "no" leads to an immediate decision (e.g., if one answers "no" to the question, "have you cried more than usual within the last week?" the tree leads to "no clinically depressed mood"), answering "yes" results in either additional questions or in a diagnosis (e.g., "clinically depressed mood"). Gigerenzer (2016) points out that, especially in the United States, patients are often overdiagnosed to avoid potential lawsuits and managers tend to make justifiable decisions instead of deciding what they believe is best (simply because they cannot deliberately argue well for the latter). He suggests that decision trees take costs of all stakeholders into account and help to overcome defensive decision making.

Another practical example of a decision aid is checklists or tools to judge the avalanche risk when hiking or skiing in the backcountry (Haegeli, Haider, Longland, & Beardmore, 2009; McCammon & Haegeli, 2006; Uttl, Mitchell, White, & McDouall, 2012). These tools have been compared to a tallying heuristic, which means that criterion variables (e.g., steepness, temperature) are detected, counted, and compared to a threshold (e.g., avalanche risk on a given day). The resulting heuristic could then be stated as follows: "Avoid a slope when more predictors are present than the threshold allows" (Hafenbrädl et al., 2016). Hafenbrädl and colleagues (2016) point out that this strategy is not only simple and accurate but also helps to overcome group biases such as failing to share information (see also Eller & Frey, Chap. 6, for an overview of group influences). An evaluation of five decision aids to judge avalanche risks suggests that up to 92% of historical avalanche accidents in the United States could have been prevented if a decision aid had been used. Training, type of activity, or type of avalanche did not influence these findings (McCammon & Hägeli, 2007). In addition, it was found that simpler methods of judging avalanche risks were superior to more complex methods (McCammon & Hägeli, 2004).

Summary and Conclusion

Heuristics play a central role in human judgment and decision making processes, especially in situations of risk and uncertainty. Research has shown that heuristics can be very useful in complex situations that involve risk or uncertainty, because they reduce processing time and effort (e.g., humans can safely cross a street without making complex calculations on how fast cars are approaching). While in other situations, they may lead the decision maker astray (e.g., over- or underestimation of risk due to an anchor or easily available information). In this chapter, we introduced two main approaches that have intensively researched heuristics from different perspectives. The heuristics and biases program has shown how heuristics simplify decisions through attribute substitution, in terms of replacing a complex question with a simpler one (e.g., how easily available is an answer, how representative is an example for a category, or how do I feel about it?). In its original version, the program also included the anchoring and adjustment heuristic, which was later separated because its underlying mechanism is based on an anchor rather than on attribute substitution. The heuristics and biases program has become famous for its demonstrations of human errors and biases in decision making. At the same time, the financial crisis of 2008 has taught us that even complex algorithms may fail in situations of uncertainty while creating an illusion of certainty

(Mousavi & Gigerenzer, 2014; Shefrin, 2013). Errors and biases introduced in this chapter have especially been demonstrated in experimental settings, and critics have pointed out that decision making in the real world may be less flawed. Besides this criticism, the heuristics and biases program sets the stage for decades of research on heuristics and has inspired researchers in psychology and economics alike (Fiedler & von Sydow, 2015). In contrast to the heuristics and biases program, the fast and frugal heuristics approach is based on computational models and suggests that people can choose from an adaptive toolbox of simple heuristics that can outperform more complex strategies in many situations. Human errors may still result when applying a heuristic in a context that is not ecologically rational.

Most decisions we make in our daily lives have many components of uncertainty and risk—simply because we cannot foresee the future. We have introduced some of the many heuristics we may rely on and useful tools that have been developed based on this research, which offer guidance in the daily jungle of unknowns. While some researchers consider the introduced approaches to be conflicting (e.g., Gigerenzer, 1991), not all share this view, and blending insights from both schools is suggested to be most promising for further improving decision making (e.g., Dana & Davis-Stober, 2016; Kelman, 2011). Thus, future research should focus more on the development of tools that combine insights from both approaches. In some situations of risk or uncertainty, one might be motivated to engage in informed decision making and appreciate the use of decision trees or boosts; in other situations a nudge may be more useful. In yet other situations, existing tools could be lifesaving (e.g., the use of a heuristic to judge avalanche risks), and research efforts should especially focus on enhancing the motivation and willingness to use decision aids in these kinds of situations. It is also unclear how people deal with heuristic conflicts, which may occur when intuitive heuristics (e.g., follow the behavior of others) and more systematic heuristic tools (e.g., an avalanche decision aid) are present at the same time.

Furthermore, beyond ready-to-use boosts, nudges, and decision trees, a guidance for do-it-yourself heuristics could support people in individual situations they face (e.g., How to nudge yourself? How to create a decision tree? How to reframe a decision?) and increase motivation to use them. Finally, a big challenge for the use of intuitive heuristics, but also for tools that are based on heuristics, remains dynamically changing environments in a world of uncertainty, where a useful heuristic or tool suddenly may not fit anymore because something has changed.

References

Agnoli, F. (1991). Development of judgmental heuristics and logical reasoning: Training counteracts the representativeness heuristic. *Cognitive Development, 6*(2), 195–217.

Agnoli, F., & Krantz, D. H. (1989). Suppressing natural heuristics by formal instruction: The case of the conjunction fallacy. *Cognitive Psychology, 21*(4), 515–550.

Artinger, F. M., Bortoleto, A. P., & Katsikopoulos, K. V. (2016). Environmental behavior and fast and frugal heuristics. In F. Beckenbach & W. Kahlenborn (Eds.), *New perspectives for environmental policies through behavioral economics* (pp. 195–211). Heidelberg: Springer. https://doi.org/10.1007/978-3-319-16793-0_8

Ayres, I., Raseman, S., & Shih, A. (2012). Evidence from two large field experiments that peer comparison feedback can reduce residential energy usage. *Journal of Law, Economics, and Organization, 29*(5), 992–1022. https://doi.org/10.1093/jleo/ews020

Benartzi, S., Beshears, J., Milkman, K. L., Sunstein, C. R., Thaler, R. H., Shankar, M., et al. (2017). Should governments invest more in nudging? *Psychological Science, 28*(8), 1041–1055. https://doi.org/10.1177/0956797617702501

Benartzi, S., & Thaler, R. H. (2001). Naive diversification strategies in defined contribution saving plans. *The American Economic Review, 91*(1), 79–98. https://doi.org/10.2307/2677899

Benartzi, S., & Thaler, R. H. (2013). Behavioral economics and the retirement savings crisis. *Science, 339*, 1152–1153.

Brewer, N. T., Chapman, G. B., Schwartz, J. A., & Bergus, G. R. (2007). The influence of irrelevant anchors on the judgments and choices of doctors and patients. *Medical Decision Making, 27*(2), 203–211. https://doi.org/10.1177/0272989X06298595

Bruchmüller, K., Margraf, J., & Schneider, S. (2012). Is ADHD diagnosed in accord with diagnostic criteria? Overdiagnosis and influence of client gender on diagnosis. *Journal of Consulting and Clinical Psychology, 80*(1), 128–138. https://doi.org/10.1037/a0026582

Chapman, G. B., & Johnson, E. J. (2002). Incorporating the irrelevant: Anchors in judgments of belief and value. In T. Gilovich, D. W. Griffin, & D. Kahneman (Eds.), *Heuristics and biases: The psychology of intuitive judgment* (pp. 120–138). New York, NY: Cambridge University Press.

Chapman University. (2016). *America's top fears 2016*. Retrieved August 3, 2017, from https://blogs.chapman.edu/wilkinson/2016/10/11/americas-top-fears-2016/

Chen, G., Kim, K. A., Nofsinger, J. R., & Rui, O. M. (2007). Trading performance, disposition effect, overconfidence, representativeness bias, and experience of emerging market investors. *Journal of Behavioral Decision Making, 20*(4), 425–451. https://doi.org/10.1002/bdm.561

Cosmides, L. (1996). Are humans good intuitive statisticians after all? Rethinking some conclusions from the literature on judgment under uncertainty. *Cognition, 58*(1), 1–73. https://doi.org/10.1016/0010-0277(95)00664-8

Critcher, C. R., & Gilovich, T. (2008). Incidental environmental anchors. *Journal of Behavioral Decision Making, 21*(3), 241–251.

Dana, J., & Davis-Stober, C. P. (2016). Rational foundations of fast and frugal heuristics: The ecological rationality of strategy selection via improper linear models. *Minds and Machines, 26*(1–2), 61–86. https://doi.org/10.1007/s11023-015-9372-z

DeMiguel, V., Garlappi, L., & Uppal, R. (2009). Optimal versus naive diversification: How inefficient is the 1/N portfolio strategy? *The Review of Financial Studies, 22*(5), 1915–1953. https://doi.org/10.1093/rfs/hhm075

Druckman, J. N. (2015). Eliminating the local warming effect. *Nature Climate Change, 5*(3), 176–177. https://doi.org/10.1038/nclimate2536

Edwards, W. (1954). The theory of decision making. *Psychological Bulletin, 51*(4), 380–417. https://doi.org/10.1037/h0053870

Englich, B., & Mussweiler, T. (2001). Sentencing under uncertainty: Anchoring effects in the courtroom. *Journal of Applied Social Psychology, 31*(7), 1535–1551. https://doi.org/10.1111/j.1559-1816.2001.tb02687.x

Englich, B., Mussweiler, T., & Strack, F. (2005). The last word in court—A hidden disadvantage for the defense. *Law and Human Behavior, 29*(6), 705–722. https://doi.org/10.1007/s10979-005-8380-7

Englich, B., Mussweiler, T., & Strack, F. (2006). Playing dice with criminal sentences: The influence of irrelevant anchors on experts' judicial decision making. *Personality and Social Psychology Bulletin, 32*, 188–200.

Epley, N., & Gilovich, T. (2006). The anchoring-and-adjustment heuristic: Why the adjustments are insufficient. *Psychological Science, 17*(4), 311–318.

Faraji-Rad, A., & Pham, M. T. (2016). Uncertainty increases the reliance on affect in decisions. *Journal of Consumer Research., 44*(1), 1–21. https://doi.org/10.2139/ssrn.2715333

Fiedler, K., & von Sydow, M. (2015). Heuristics and biases: Beyond Tversky and Kahneman's (1974) judgment under uncertainty. In M. W. Eysenck & D. Groome (Eds.), *Cognitive psychology revisiting the classic studies* (pp. 146–161). London: SAGE.

Finucane, M. L., Alhakami, A., Slovic, P., & Johnson, S. M. (2000). The affect heuristic in judgments of risks and benefits. *Journal of Behavioral Decision Making, 13*, 1–17.

Galinsky, A. D., & Mussweiler, T. (2001). First offers as anchors: The role of perspective-taking and negotiator focus. *Journal of Personality and Social Psychology, 81*(4), 657–669. https://doi.org/10.1037/0022-3514.81.4.657

Gifford, R. (2011). The dragons of inaction: Psychological barriers that limit climate change mitigation and adaptation. *American Psychologist, 66*(4), 290–302. https://doi.org/10.1037/a0023566

Gifford, R., & Comeau, L. A. (2011). Message framing influences perceived climate change competence, engagement, and behavioral intentions. *Global Environmental Change, 21*(4), 1301–1307.

Gigerenzer, G. (1991). How to make cognitive illusions disappear: Beyond "heuristics and biases". *European Review of Social Psychology, 2*(1), 83–115.

Gigerenzer, G. (2015). On the supposed evidence for libertarian paternalism. *Review of Philosophy and Psychology, 6*(3), 361–383. https://doi.org/10.1007/s13164-015-0248-1

Gigerenzer, G. (2016). Introduction: Taking heuristics seriously. In A. Samson (Ed.), *The behavioral economics guide* (pp. V–XI). London: Behavioral Science Solutions.

Gigerenzer, G., & Goldstein, D. G. (1996). Reasoning the fast and frugal way: Models of bounded rationality. *Psychological Review, 103*(4), 650–669. https://doi.org/10.1037/0033-295X.103.4.650

Gigerenzer, G., Hell, W., & Blank, H. (1988). Presentation and content: The use of base rates as a continuous variable. *Journal of Experimental Psychology: Human Perception and Performance, 14*(3), 513–525. https://doi.org/10.1037/0096-1523.14.3.513

Gigerenzer, G., & Hoffrage, U. (1995). How to improve Bayesian reasoning without instruction: Frequency formats. *Psychological Review, 102*(4), 684.

Gigerenzer, G., & Murray, D. J. (2015). *Cognition as intuitive statistics*. New York, NY: Psychology Press.

Gigerenzer, G., Todd, P. M., & The ABC Research Group. (1999). *Simple heuristics that make us smart*. New York, NY: Oxford University Press.

Glöckner, A. (2008). Does intuition beat fast and frugal heuristics? In H. Plessner, C. Betsch, & T. Betsch (Eds.), *Intuition in judgment and decision making* (pp. 309–326). New York, NY: Taylor & Francis.

Goldstein, D. G., & Gigerenzer, G. (2002). Models of ecological rationality: The recognition heuristic. *Psychological Review, 109*(1), 75–90. https://doi.org/10.1037/0033-295X.109.1.75

Gould, S. J. (1992). *Bully for brontosaurus: Reflections in natural history*. New York, NY: Norton.

Green, L., & Mehr, D. R. (1997). What alters physicians' decisions to admit to the coronary care unit? *Journal of Family Practice, 45*(3), 219–226.

Greifeneder, R., & Bless, H. (2007). Relying on accessible content versus accessibility experiences: The case of processing capacity. *Social Cognition, 25*(6), 853–881. https://doi.org/10.1521/soco.2007.25.6.853

Greifeneder, R., Bless, H., & Pham, M. T. (2010). When do people rely on affective and cognitive feelings in judgment? A review. *Personality and Social Psychology Review, 15*(2), 107–141. https://doi.org/10.1177/1088868310367640

Grice, H. P. (1975). Logic and conversation. In P. Cole, & J. L. Morgan (Eds.) Syntax and semantics, (3), 41–58. New York, NY: Academic Press.

Grüne-Yanoff, T., & Hertwig, R. (2015). Nudge versus boost: How coherent are policy and theory? *Minds and Machines, 26*(1–2), 149–183. https://doi.org/10.1007/s11023-015-9367-9

Haegeli, P., Haider, W., Longland, M., & Beardmore, B. (2009). Amateur decision-making in avalanche terrain with and without a decision aid: A stated choice survey. *Natural Hazards, 52*(1), 185–209. https://doi.org/10.1007/s11069-009-9365-4

Hafenbrädl, S., Waeger, D., & Marewski, J. N. (2016). Applied decision making with fast-and-frugal heuristics. *Journal of Applied Research in Memory and Cognition, 5*(2), 215–231.
Hart, S. (2005). Adaptive heuristics. *Econometrica, 73*(5), 1401–1430.
Hertwig, R., & Grüne-Yanoff, T. (2017). Nudging and boosting: Steering or empowering good decisions. *Perspectives on Psychological Science, 5*, 1–14. https://doi.org/10.1177/1745691617702496
Hilbig, B. E., Scholl, S. G., & Pohl, R. F. (2010). Think or blink—Is the recognition heuristic an "intuitive" strategy? *Judgment and Decision making, 5*(4), 300–309.
Hirshleifer, D., & Shumway, T. (2003). Good day sunshine: Stock returns and the weather. *The Journal of Finance, 58*(3), 1009–1032. https://doi.org/10.1111/1540-6261.00556
Holtgraves, T., & Skeel, J. (1992). Cognitive biases in playing the lottery: Estimating the odds and choosing the numbers. *Journal of Applied Social Psychology, 22*(12), 934–952. https://doi.org/10.1111/j.1559-1816.1992.tb00935.x
Jenny, M. A., Pachur, T., Williams, S. L., Becker, E., & Margraf, J. (2013). Simple rules for detecting depression. *Journal of Applied Research in Memory and Cognition, 2*(3), 149–157.
Johnson, E. J., & Goldstein, D. (2003). Do defaults save lives? *Science, 302*(5649), 1338–1339. https://doi.org/10.1126/science.1091721
Kahan, D. M., Peters, E., Wittlin, M., Slovic, P., Ouellette, L. L., Braman, D., & Mandel, G. (2012). The polarizing impact of science literacy and numeracy on perceived climate change risks. *Nature Climate Change, 2*(10), 732–735. https://doi.org/10.1038/nclimate1547
Kahneman, D. (2000). A psychological point of view: Violations of rational rules as a diagnostic of mental processes. *Behavioral and Brain Sciences, 23*(5), 681–683.
Kahneman, D. (2016). Heuristics and biases. In R. J. Sternberg, S. T. Fiske, & D. J. Foss (Eds.), *Scientists making a difference* (pp. 171–174). Cambridge: Cambridge University Press. https://doi.org/10.1017/CBO9781316422250
Kahneman, D., & Frederick, S. (2002). Representativeness revisited: Attribute substitution in intuitive judgment. In T. Gilovich, D. W. Griffin, & D. Kahneman (Eds.), *Heuristics and biases: The psychology of intuitive judgment* (pp. 49–81). New York, NY: Cambridge University Press.
Kahneman, D., & Tversky, A. (1972). Subjective probability: A judgment of representativeness. *Cognitive Psychology, 3*(3), 430–454. https://doi.org/10.1016/0010-0285(72)90016-3
Kahneman, D., & Tversky, A. (1973). On the psychology of prediction. *Psychological Review, 80*(4), 237–251. https://doi.org/10.1037/h0034747
Kahneman, D., & Tversky, A. (1982). On the study of statistical intuitions. *Cognition, 11*(2), 123–141.
Kasperson, R. E., Renn, O., Slovic, P., Brown, H. S., Emel, J., Goble, R., et al. (1988). The social amplification of risk: A conceptual framework. *Risk Analysis, 8*(2), 177–187.
Keller, C., Siegrist, M., & Gutscher, H. (2006). The role of the affect and availability heuristics in risk communication. *Risk Analysis, 26*(3), 631–639. https://doi.org/10.1111/j.1539-6924.2006.00773.x/full
Kelman, M. (2011). *The heuristics debate*. New York, NY: Oxford University Press.
Knight, F. H. (1921). *Risk, uncertainty and profit*. New York, NY: Hart.
Leave No Trace. (2016). *Using the thumb trick: Keep a safe distance from wildlife*. Retrieved August 17, 2017, from https://lnt.org/blog/using-thumb-trick-keep-safe-distance-wildlife
Lerner, J. S., Gonzalez, R. M., Small, D. A., & Fischhoff, B. (2003). Effects of fear and anger on perceived risks of terrorism: A national field experiment. *Psychological Science, 14*, 144–150. https://doi.org/10.1111/1467-9280.01433
Li, Y., Johnson, E. J., & Zaval, L. (2011). Local warming: Daily temperature change influences belief in global warming. *Psychological Science, 22*(4), 454–459. https://doi.org/10.1177/0956797611400913
Lichtenstein, S., Slovic, P., Fischhoff, B., Layman, M., & Combs, B. (1978). Judged frequency of lethal events. *Journal of Experimental Psychology: Human Learning and Memory, 4*(6), 551–578.
Loewenstein, G. F., Weber, E. U., Hsee, C. K., & Welch, N. (2001). Risk as feelings. *Psychological Bulletin, 127*(2), 267–286. https://doi.org/10.1037/0033-2909.127.2.267
Luce, R. D., & Raiffa, H. (1957). *Games and decisions*. New York, NY: Wiley.

Marewski, J. N., & Gigerenzer, G. (2012). Heuristic decision making in medicine. *Dialogues in Clinical Research, 14*(1), 77–89.

Marewski, J. N., & Pohl, R. F. (2010). Recognition-based judgments and decisions: Introduction to the special issue (Vol. 1). *Judgment and Decision Making, 5*(4), 207–215.

McCammon, I., & Haegeli, P. (2006). Evaluation of a rule-based decision aid for recreational travelers in avalanche terrain. In *Proceedings of the international snow science workshop*, Telluride, CO.

McCammon, I., & Hägeli, P. (2004). Comparing avalanche decision frameworks using accident data from the United States. In *Proceedings of the international snow science workshop*, Jackson, WY.

McCammon, I., & Hägeli, P. (2007). An evaluation of rule-based decision tools for travel in avalanche terrain. *Cold Regions Science and Technology, 47*(1–2), 193–206. https://doi.org/10.1016/j.coldregions.2006.08.007

McDowell, M. E., Occhipinti, S., & Chambers, S. K. (2013). The influence of family history on cognitive heuristics, risk perceptions, and prostate cancer screening behavior. *Health Psychology, 32*(11), 1158–1169. https://doi.org/10.1037/a0031622

Mousavi, S., & Gigerenzer, G. (2014). Risk, uncertainty, and heuristics. *Journal of Business Research, 67*(8), 1671–1678. https://doi.org/10.1016/j.jbusres.2014.02.013

Mussweiler, T., & Strack, F. (1999). Hypothesis-consistent testing and semantic priming in the anchoring paradigm: A selective accessibility model. *Journal of Experimental Social Psychology, 35*(2), 136–164. https://doi.org/10.1006/jesp.1998.1364

Mussweiler, T., & Strack, F. (2000). The use of category and exemplar knowledge in the solution of anchoring tasks. *Journal of Personality and Social Psychology, 78*(6), 1038–1052. https://doi.org/10.1037/0022-3514.78.6.1038

Mussweiler, T., Strack, F., & Pfeiffer, T. (2000). Overcoming the inevitable anchoring effect: Considering the opposite compensates for selective accessibility. *Personality and Social Psychology Bulletin, 26*(9), 1142–1150. https://doi.org/10.1177/01461672002611010

Neth, H., & Gigerenzer, G. (2015). Heuristics: Tools for an uncertain world. In R. A. Scott & S. M. Kosslyn (Eds.), *Emerging trends in the social and behavioral sciences an interdisciplinary, searchable, and linkable resource* (pp. 1–18). Hoboken, NJ: Wiley. https://doi.org/10.1002/9781118900772.etrds0394

Northcraft, G. B., & Neale, M. A. (1987). Experts, amateurs, and real estate: An anchoring-and-adjustment perspective on property pricing decisions. *Organizational Behavior and Human Decision Processes, 39*(1), 84–97.

Pachur, T., Hertwig, R., & Steinmann, F. (2012). How do people judge risks: Availability heuristic, affect heuristic, or both? *Journal of Experimental Psychology: Applied, 18*(3), 314–330. https://doi.org/10.1037/a0028279

Pham, M. T. (1998). Representativeness, relevance, and the use of feelings in decision making. *Journal of Consumer Research, 25*(2), 144–159. https://doi.org/10.1086/209532

Pichert, D., & Katsikopoulos, K. V. (2008). Green defaults: Information presentation and pro-environmental behaviour. *Journal of Environmental Psychology, 28*(1), 63–73. https://doi.org/10.1016/j.jenvp.2007.09.004

Plessner, H., & Czenna, S. (2008). The benefits of intuition. In H. Plessner, C. Betsch, & T. Betsch (Eds.), *Intuition in judgment and decision making* (pp. 251–265). New York, NY: Taylor & Francis.

Pohl, R. F. (2011). On the use of recognition in inferential decision making: An overview of the debate. *Judgment and Decision Making, 6*(5), 423–438.

Pohl, R. F. (2017). Cognitive illusions. In R. F. Pohl (Ed.), *Cognitive illusions intriguing phenomena in judgement, thinking and memory* (2nd ed., pp. 3–21). New York, NY: Routledge.

Pohl, R. F., Michalkiewicz, M., Erdfelder, E., & Hilbig, B. E. (2017). Use of the recognition heuristic depends on the domain's recognition validity, not on the recognition validity of selected sets of objects. *Memory & Cognition, 45*(5), 776–791. https://doi.org/10.3758/s13421-017-0689-0

Reimer, T., & Rieskamp, J. (2007). Fast and frugal heuristics. In R. Baumeister & K. D. Voss (Eds.), *Encyclopedia of social psychology* (pp. 347–349). Thousand Oaks, CA: SAGE.

Rieskamp, J., & Otto, P. E. (2011). SSL: A theory of how people learn to select strategies. In G. Gigerenzer, R. Hertwig, & T. Pachur (Eds.), *Heuristics: The foundations of adaptive behavior* (pp. 244–266). New York, NY: Oxford University Press.

Ross, M., & Sicoly, F. (1979). Egocentric biases in availability and attribution. *Journal of Personality and Social Psychology, 37*(3), 322–336.

Rothman, A. J., & Schwarz, N. (1998). Constructing perceptions of vulnerability: Personal relevance and the use of experiential information in health judgments. *Personality and Social Psychology Bulletin, 24*(10), 1053–1064. https://doi.org/10.1177/01461672982410003

Schlag, P. (2010). Nudge, choice architecture, and libertarian paternalism. *Michigan Law Review, 108*(6), 913–924.

Scholl, S. G., & Greifeneder, R. (2011). Disentangling the effects of alternation rate and maximum run length on judgments of randomness. *Judgment and Decision Making, 6*(6), 531–541.

Scholl, S. G. & Bless, H. (2016). Urteilsheuristiken. In D. Frey & H.-W. Bierhoff, (Eds.). Enzyklopädie der Psychologie: Selbst und Soziale Kognition - Sozialpsychologie, Band 1 (pp. 387–408). Göttingen: Hogrefe.

Schwarz, N. (1990). Feelings as information: Informational and motivational functions of affective states. In E. T. Higgins & R. M. Sorrentino (Eds.), *Handbook of motivation and cognition foundations of social behavior* (Vol. 2, pp. 527–561). New York, NY: Guilford Press.

Schwarz, N. (1996). *Cognition and communication: Judgmental biases, research methods, and the logic of conversation*. Mahwah, NJ: Lawrence Erlbaum Associates.

Schwarz, N., Bless, H., Strack, F., Klumpp, G., Rittenauer-Schatka, H., & Simons, A. (1991). Ease of retrieval as information: Another look at the availability heuristic. *Journal of Personality and Social Psychology, 61*(2), 195–202. https://doi.org/10.1037/0022-3514.61.2.195

Schwarz, N., & Clore, G. L. (1983). Mood, misattribution, and judgments of Well-being: Informative and directive functions of affective states. *Journal of Personality and Social Psychology, 45*(3), 513–523.

Schwarz, N., Strack, F., Hilton, D., & Naderer, G. (1991). Base rates, representativeness, and the logic of conversation: The contextual relevance of "irrelevant" information. *Social Cognition, 9*(1), 67–84. https://doi.org/10.1521/soco.1991.9.1.67

Sedikides, C. (1995). Central and peripheral self-conceptions are differentially influenced by mood: Tests of the differential sensitivity hypothesis. *Journal of Personality and Social Psychology, 69*(4), 759–777. https://doi.org/10.1037/0022-3514.69.4.759

Shefrin, H. (2013, September 1). *Assessing the contribution of hyman minsky's perspective to our understanding of economic instability*. https://doi.org/10.2139/ssrn.2311045

Siegrist, M., & Sütterlin, B. (2014). Human and nature-caused hazards: The affect heuristic causes biased decisions. *Risk Analysis, 34*(8), 1482–1494. https://doi.org/10.1111/risa.12179

Simon, H. A. (1955). A behavioral model of rational choice. *The Quarterly Journal of Economics, 69*, 99–118.

Slovic, P. (2010). *The feeling of risk*. New York, NY: Routledge.

Slovic, P., Finucane, M. L., Peters, E., & MacGregor, D. G. (2004). Risk as analysis and risk as feelings: Some thoughts about affect, reason, risk, and rationality. *Risk Analysis, 24*(2), 311–322.

Slovic, P., Monahan, J., & MacGregor, D. G. (2000). Violence risk assessment and risk communication: The effects of using actual cases, providing instruction, and employing probability versus frequency formats. *Law and Human Behavior, 24*(3), 271.

Slovic, P., & Peters, E. (2006). Risk perception and affect. *Current Directions in Psychological Science, 15*(6), 322–325. https://doi.org/10.1111/j.1467-8721.2006.00461.x

Slovic, P., Peters, E., Finucane, M. L., & MacGregor, D. G. (2005). Affect, risk, and decision making. *Health Psychology, 24*(4S), S35.

Smith, A. R., Windschitl, P. D., & Bruchmann, K. (2013). Knowledge matters: Anchoring effects are moderated by knowledge level. *European Journal of Social Psychology, 43*(1), 97–108.

Strack, F., & Mussweiler, T. (1997). Explaining the enigmatic anchoring effect: Mechanisms of selective accessibility. *Journal of Personality and Social Psychology, 73*(3), 437–446. https://doi.org/10.1037/0022-3514.73.3.437

Strack, F., & Mussweiler, T. (2003). Heuristic strategies for estimation under uncertainty: The enigmatic case of anchoring. In G. V. Bodenhausen & A. J. Lambert (Eds.), *Foundations of social cognition: A festschrift in honor of Robert S. Wyer, Jr* (pp. 79–95). Mahwah, NJ: Lawrence Erlbaum Associates.

Thaler, R. H., & Sunstein, C. R. (2008). *Nudge: Improving Decisions about Health, Wealth and Happiness*. Yale University Press.

Todd, P. M., & Gigerenzer, G. (2012). Environments that make us smart: Ecological rationality. *Current Directions in Psychological Science, 16*(3), 167–171.

Tversky, A., & Kahneman, D. (1971). Belief in the law of small numbers. *Psychological Bulletin, 76*(2), 105–110. https://doi.org/10.1037/h0031322

Tversky, A., & Kahneman, D. (1973). Availability: A heuristic for judging frequency and probability. *Cognitive Psychology, 5*, 207–232.

Tversky, A., & Kahneman, D. (1974). Judgment under uncertainty: Heuristics and biases. *Science, 185*, 1124–1131.

Tversky, A., & Kahneman, D. (1983). Extensional versus intuitive reasoning: The conjunction fallacy in probability judgment. *Psychological Review, 90*(4), 293–315.

United States National Park Service. (2017). *Wildlife viewing—Yellowstone national park*. Retrieved August 17, 2017, from https://www.nps.gov/yell/planyourvisit/viewanim.htm

Uttl, B., Mitchell, C., White, C. A., & McDouall, J. (2012). Avalanche accident risk reduction tools in a North American context. In *Proceedings of the International Snow Science Workshop*, Anchorage, AK, pp. 834–839.

Västfjäll, D., Peters, E., & Slovic, P. (2008). Affect, risk perception and future optimism after the tsunami disaster. *Judgment and Decision Making, 3*(1), 64–72.

Vranas, P. B. (2000). Gigerenzer's normative critique of Kahneman and Tversky. *Cognition, 76*(3), 179–193.

Wänke, M. (2013). Almost everything you always wanted to know about ease-of-retrieval effects. In C. Unkelbach & R. Greifeneder (Eds.), *The experience of thinking how the fluency of mental processes influences cognition and behaviour* (pp. 151–169). London: Psychology Press.

Wänke, M., Bohner, G., & Jurkowitsch, A. (1997). There are many reasons to drive a BMW: Does imagined ease of argument generation influence attitudes? *Journal of Consumer Research, 24*(2), 170–177. https://doi.org/10.1086/209502

Wansink, B., Kent, R. J., & Hoch, S. J. (1998). An anchoring and adjustment model of purchase quantity decisions. *Journal of Marketing Research, 35*(1), 71.

Wilkinson, T. M. (2013). Nudging and manipulation. *Political Studies, 61*(2), 341–355. https://doi.org/10.1111/j.1467-9248.2012.00974.x

Wilson, T. D., Houston, C. E., Etling, K. M., & Brekke, N. (1996). A new look at anchoring effects: Basic anchoring and its antecedents. *Journal of Experimental Psychology: General, 125*(4), 387–402. https://doi.org/10.1037/0096-3445.125.4.387

Young, W., Hwang, K., McDonald, S., & Oates, C. J. (2010). Sustainable consumption: Green consumer behaviour when purchasing products. *Sustainable Development, 18*(1), 20–31.

Zaval, L., & Cornwell, J. F. M. (2016). Cognitive biases, non-rational judgments, and public perceptions of climate change. In M. C. Nisbet, M. Schafer, E. Markowitz, S. Ho, S. O'Neill, & J. Thaker (Eds.), *Oxford research encyclopedia of climate science* (Vol. 1). Oxford: Oxford University Press. https://doi.org/10.1093/acrefore/9780190228620.013.304

Zaval, L., Keenan, E. A., Johnson, E. J., & Weber, E. U. (2014). How warm days increase belief in global warming. *Nature Climate Change, 4*(2), 143–147. https://doi.org/10.1038/nclimate2093

Chapter 8
Behavioral Models of Decision Making Under Risk

Michael H. Birnbaum

Abstract This chapter reviews experiments testing theories of how people make choices between risky prospects, gambles in which the consequences and their probabilities are specified. When people prefer a small amount of cash to the expected value of a gamble, they are said to be risk averse. The St. Petersburg paradox is an extreme case of risk aversion in which people prefer a small cash payment rather than one chance to play a gamble of infinite expected value. Expected utility theory was proposed to explain this paradox by allowing that the utility of money is not a linear function of its cash value but instead shows diminishing marginal returns. Allais proposed two paradoxes that contradicted expected utility theory, and a number of modern theories have been proposed to explain the Allais paradoxes. Among these are original and cumulative prospect theory, configural weighting theory, the priority heuristic, and others. The chapter notes that some decisions are based on experience, where consequences and their probabilities are learned. The chapter also considers models of the variability in decision behavior. New critical tests and their results are reviewed that conclude that neither version of prospect theory can be retained as accurate descriptions of choice behavior and that tests of the heuristic models have yielded data that systematically violate the predictions of those models. The configural weight models remain the best description of the evidence so far accumulated.

Some decisions are based on vague ideas or beliefs of the exact consequences of one's actions given imprecise, uncertain, or ambiguous information concerning the probabilities of consequences contingent on one's alternative courses of actions. For whom should I vote? What job should I take? Should I marry this person? Should I undergo the medical operation my doctor recommended? Such decisions are made in the face of *uncertainty*. The term, *decision making under risk*, in contrast, refers to situations in which a decision-maker has valid information concerning the exact consequences and the probabilities of consequences of the alternative courses of action. For example, should I buy a lottery

M. H. Birnbaum (✉)
Decision Research Center, California State University, Fullerton, CA, USA
e-mail: m@fullerton.edu

M. Raue et al. (eds.), *Psychological Perspectives on Risk and Risk Analysis*,
https://doi.org/10.1007/978-3-319-92478-6_8

ticket for $1 that has one chance in a million of paying $1 million dollars? Researchers studying decisions under risk are attracted to such questions because gambles defined on events with known probabilities (such as tosses of fair coins or rolls of dice) allow one to manipulate important ingredients in the decision process itself, separated from the mechanisms by which beliefs about probability are formed.

Behavioral models of risky decision making are theories that attempt to give empirically accurate descriptions of what people do when confronted with risky decision making problems. Whereas a normative model specifies what a person ought to do to stay consistent with certain principles of rationality, a behavioral model seeks to explain the empirical choices that people actually make, whether these actual choices are deemed rational or not.

In the simplest paradigm for study of decision making, researchers ask participants to make decisions among gambles stated in terms of probabilities to receive monetary consequences. For example, would you rather have $45 for sure, or would you prefer instead to play a risky gamble in which you have a 50–50 chance to win $100 or $0, based on the toss of a fair coin? Because the coin has a probability of ½ to be called correctly, you have a probability of ½ to win $100 and a probability of ½ to win $0. Most people prefer $45 for sure to the risky gamble, even though the gamble would pay $50 on average. This systematic preference for the sure thing contradicts a rule called *expected value*, which was once thought to be a rational principle a person should follow.

Expected Value

The expected value (EV) of a gamble is the mean value of the consequences of a gamble, weighted by their probabilities. Suppose a random process has n possible mutually exclusive and exhaustive outcomes, and let gamble $G = (x_1, p_1; x_2, p_2; x_3, p_3; \ldots; x_i, p_i; \ldots; x_n, p_n)$ represent a gamble with probability p_i to receive consequence x_i, where x_i is the monetary consequence if outcome i occurs. Because the outcomes are mutually exclusive and exhaustive, $\sum p_i = 1$. We can define the EV of gamble G as follows:

$$\mathrm{EV}(G) = \Sigma\, p_i\, x_i$$

The gamble based on a coin flip is denoted G = ($100, ½; $0, ½), and G has an EV of $50 = (0.5)($100) + (0.5)($0). So, on average, a person who could play G infinitely many times would expect to win $50 per play, but on any single play of the gamble, the person would win either $0 or $100.

Risk Aversion and St. Petersburg Paradox

EV seemed a reasonable objective measure to many scholars in the eighteenth century, so they considered it paradoxical that when given a choice, people did not always prefer the option with the higher EV. For example, many people prefer $45 for sure to G = ($100, ½; $0, ½), even though the sure thing has a lower EV ($45) than the gamble ($50). When people prefer a sure thing to a gamble with the same or higher EV, they are said to be "risk averse."

Risk aversion seemed puzzling, especially when scholars realized that one could construct gambles with infinite value, and people preferred quite small amounts of cash to such gambles. For example, suppose we toss a coin, and if it is heads, you win $2, but if it is tails, we toss again. On the next toss, if it is heads, the payoff is $4, and if tails, we toss again. Each time that tails occurs, the prize for heads on the next toss doubles. The expected value of this gamble is as follows:

$$\text{EV} = \$2(1/2) + \$4(1/4) + \$8(1/8) + \$16(1/16) + \ldots = \infty$$

If a person conformed to EV, she should prefer this gamble to any finite amount of money one might offer; indeed, a person should prefer playing this gamble once to all of the money in the world. Yet, most people say they would choose $20 for sure to one chance to play this gamble, even though the gamble has infinite expected value.

This preference for the sure thing over such gambles (with infinite EV) is now called the *St. Petersburg paradox*, which was discussed in a classic paper by Bernoulli (1738/1954), who presented his paper in St. Petersburg. Bernoulli said it was not necessarily rational to follow EV, but instead to choose the option with the best expected utility.

Expected Utility

Bernoulli (1738/1954) provided a theory of risk aversion that addressed the original versions of the St. Petersburg paradox. This theory proposed that the utility of money is not necessarily equal to its objective value, but might, instead, be a nonlinear function of money. Let $u(x)$ represent the utility (subjective value) of a certain amount of wealth, x. Define expected utility (EU) as follows:

$$\text{EU}(G) = \Sigma p_i u(x_i) \tag{8.1}$$

where $u(x_i)$ is the utility of objective value x_i.

Bernoulli theorized that utility of money might be a logarithmic function of wealth, but he acknowledged that other functions, such as the square root function, might also work. Both of these functions are negatively accelerated; that is, there is

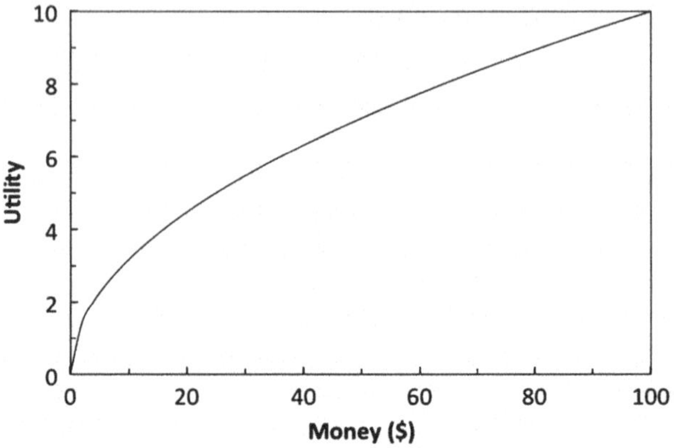

Fig. 8.1 Negatively accelerated utility function. In this example, the value of x whose utility is halfway between \$0 and \$100 is \$25, because $u(x) = x^{0.5}$

a diminishing marginal increment in utility of each additional dollar to the overall utility of wealth; that is, $u(W + x) - u(W)$ decreases as W (wealth) increases for a given increment in wealth, x. For example, if a person had a total wealth of $W =$ \$50, an increase of $x =$ \$100 in wealth would have a much greater impact than if the person had a total wealth of \$1 million. Figure 8.1 illustrates a hypothetical utility function: $u(x) = x^{0.5}$ (a power function with exponent of 0.5 is also known as the square root function). In this negatively accelerated function (Fig. 8.1), the subjective increase in utility from \$0 to \$25 is the same as the subjective increase in utility from \$25 to \$100. Thus, it takes a bigger increase of money as one moves up the wealth scale to produce the same increase in utility.

Expected utility theory is the theory that people prefer A over B if and only if $\text{EU}(A) > \text{EU}(B)$; that is, A will be preferred to B whenever the expected utility of option A exceeds that of B. EU theory could explain not only risk aversion and the original St. Petersburg paradox, but it could also explain why a pauper who was given a lottery ticket should be happy to sell it for less than EV and why a rich person should be happy to buy it at the same price.

For example, imagine a pauper whose total wealth is just \$50 and who is given a choice between $S =$ \$45 for sure and $G =$ 50–50 gamble to win \$100 or \$0. Suppose $u(x) = x^{0.5}$, as in Fig. 8.1. EU theory then implies that the utility of choosing the sure thing, S, is $u(\$50 + \$45) = u(\$95) = 9.75$. In contrast, the EU of choosing gamble G is $u(\$50 + \$100)(0.5) + u(\$50) = 9.66$. Because $\text{EU}(S) > \text{EU}(G)$, the theory says the pauper would prefer \$45 for sure over gamble G. Thus, the pauper who was given a lottery ticket (a chance to play gamble G) would be happy to sell it for \$45.

Now consider a richer person whose total wealth is \$1000, who is deciding whether to buy gamble G from the pauper. The utility of Q, the status quo (to not buy) is $u(\$1000) = 31.62$, assuming again that $u(x) = x^{0.5}$. The utility of B, the option to buy the gamble for \$45 from the pauper, has expected utility of $u(\$1000 + \$100 - \$45)(0.5) + u(\$1000 - \$45)(0.5) = 31.69$. Because $\text{EU}(B) > \text{EU}(Q)$, this person should prefer to buy the gamble for \$45. This example shows that even if both people have the same utility function (but different levels of wealth), they can both improve their individual utilities by trading.

It is also reasonable that some people have different utility functions from others, reflecting different attitudes toward risk. For example, if a venturesome person had $u(x) = x^2$, then that person would prefer the risky gamble to a sure thing with the same EV and would be called "risk-seeking." Such a risk-seeking person would even be willing to buy this gamble at a price exceeding \$50 and would outbid the wealthy but risk averse person to buy gamble *G*.

Von Neumann and Morgenstern (1947) showed that expected utility theory could be deduced from four basic axioms of preference and proved that if these axioms are assumed, utility could in principle be measured on an interval scale. The four axioms are *completeness* (for any two lotteries, *A* and *B*, a person either prefers *A* to *B*, *B* to *A*, or is indifferent), *transitivity* [for any three lotteries, *A*, *B*, and *C*, if a person prefers *A* to *B* and *B* to *C*, then the person prefers *A* to *C*], *independence* [for any three lotteries *A*, *B*, and *C*, where *A* is preferred to *B*, and for any probability between 0 and 1, $pA + (1 - p)C$ is preferred to $pB + (1 - p)C$], and *continuity* [for any three lotteries, such that *A* preferred to *B* preferred to *C*, there exists a probability *p* such that *B* is indifferent to $pA + (1 - p)C$]. This axiomatic theory was accepted by many as the definition of what a rational person should do when confronted with decisions under risk.

Much of economic theory had been deduced from the assumptions that people are rational but may differ in their utilities or tastes and that EU theory was rational. For a time, it was also believed that people behave according to this rational theory; therefore, it was thought that classic economic theory not only prescribed what a rational economic actor should do but was also descriptive of actual behavior of individuals. However, both the assumption of rationality of EU and the assumption that people are rational came into question when Allais proposed his paradoxes.

Allais Paradoxes

Allais (1953) criticized EU theory from both descriptive and normative perspectives. He developed paradoxes that have generated continued discussion in the scientific literature that continue to this day, because they revealed contradictions between what seemingly rational people did and what EU theory requires. For example, consider the following two choice problems:

Problem 1: *A*: (\$1 million, 0.11; \$0, 0.89)

B: (\$2 million, 0.10; \$0, 0.90)

Problem 2: *C:* (\$1 million, with certainty)

D: (\$2 million, 0.10; \$1 million, 0.89; \$0, 0.01)

According to EU theory, a person should prefer *C* over *D* if and only if she prefers *A* over *B*; however, many people prefer *C* over *D* and *B* over *A*, contrary to the theory. This paradox is known as the "constant consequence" paradox because 0.89 probability to win \$0 is common to both *A* and *B*, whereas this common consequence of \$0 was changed to a common value of \$1 million in *C* and *D* (in *B*, the common consequence of 0.89 to win \$0 is included in the branch of 0.90 to win \$0). To understand why these preferences violate EU, note that EU(*C*) preferred to EU(*D*) means $u(1\text{ M}) > 0.10u(2\text{ M}) + 0.89u(1\text{ M}) + 0.01u(0)$, which is the same as $0.11u(1\text{ M}) > 0.10u(2\text{ M}) + 0.01u(0)$. However, if EU(*B*) is preferred to EU(*A*), it means $0.11u(1\text{ M}) + 0.89u(0) < 0.10u(2\text{ M}) + 0.90u(0)$, which leads to the contradiction that $0.11u(1\text{ M}) < 0.10u(2\text{ M}) + 0.01u(0)$. If a theory leads to contradiction, it cannot be true.

A "constant ratio" paradox was also developed, which can be illustrated by the following choices:

Problem 3: *E*: \$3000 for sure

F: (\$4000, 0.8; \$0, 0.2)

Problem 4: *G*: (\$3000, 0.25; \$0, 0.75)

H: (\$4000, 0.20; \$0, 0.80)

According to EU theory, a person should prefer *E* to *F* if and only if she prefers *G* to *H*; however, many people prefer *E* to *F* and prefer *H* to *G*. The "constant ratio" refers to the fact that the probabilities to win in *G* and *H* of Problem 4 are a constant ratio (one fourth) of those in *E* and *F* of Problem 3. These paradoxes refuted EU as a descriptive model of how people choose between risky gambles. In the views of Allais (1979), these paradoxes reflected shortcomings of EU as a rational model as well.

Subjectively Weighted Utility and Prospect Theory

Edwards (1954) used a subjectively weighted utility model to account for the Allais paradoxes. According to the model of Edwards, the value of a gamble is given by the following:

$$\mathrm{PV}(G) = \sum w(p_i)u(x_i) \tag{8.2}$$

where PV(*G*) is the prospect value of a gamble and $w(p_i)$ is the weight of the probability. Whereas EU theory allowed a nonlinear transformation between objective wealth and utility, this new theory theorized in addition to a nonlinear transformation between objective probability and the (subjective) decision weight assigned to that probability. An example of an inverse S-shaped probability weighting function is shown in Fig. 8.2. In such a function, the weight given to small probabilities is

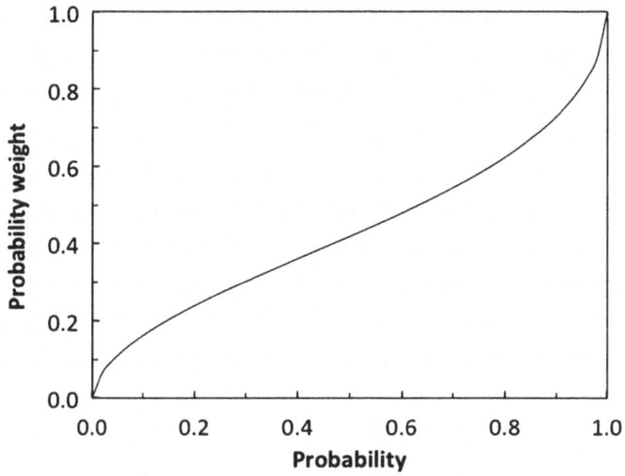

Fig. 8.2 An inverse S-shaped probability weighting function. Note that small probabilities receive weights greater than their probabilities

relatively greater than the objective probability value, and the weight given to large probabilities is lower than the objective probability.

If people placed greater relative weight on small probabilities, as in Fig. 8.2, it could explain why a person who is otherwise risk averse (e.g., for 50–50 gambles) might be willing to buy a lottery ticket that provides only a tiny chance to win a large prize. Edwards also incorporated another revision of EU theory that had been proposed by Markowitz (1952). The utility function in Eq. (8.2) was defined in terms of changes from a reference level rather than absolute wealth. With this revision, x might be either a gain or a loss relative to the status quo, and Edwards (1962) further theorized that different functions might be required for gambles composed strictly of gains, strictly of losses, or combinations of gains and losses.

Tversky, a former student of Edwards, and Kahneman published a variant of this model in *Econometrica* under the name "prospect theory" (Kahneman & Tversky, 1979). As Kahneman (2003) later noted, there was not much new in this paper compared to the literature in psychology, but the paper had a tremendous impact in the field of economics, where it helped inspire the field of behavioral economics, the study of how people actually behave in experiments on economics.

Although "prospect theory" could account for the Allais paradoxes, it made some strange predictions that seemed unrealistic. For example, it predicts that people should prefer gamble I = ($100, 0.01; $99, 0.01; $98, 0.098) to J = ($102; 0.5; $101, 0.5), even though every outcome of J is better than any outcome of I. If the weighting function is nonlinear, and if small probabilities get greater weight, then splitting a certain amount of probability into smaller pieces could increase weight enough to make worse gambles seem better. Because it seemed unlikely that people would violate stochastic dominance (e.g., choose I) in such cases, Kahneman and Tversky (1979) postulated "editing rules" that people supposedly used to avoid such implications of this model, and they postulated other restrictions and exceptions to

Eq. (8.2). Edwards (1954) model (Eq. 8.2) is now sometimes called "stripped" prospect theory, when it is applied without the restrictions and editing rules that were added to prospect theory by Kahneman and Tversky (1979).

Rank-dependent weighting was proposed (Quiggin, 1985, 1993) as a way to account for the Allais paradoxes without violating stochastic dominance. Luce and Fishburn (1991, 1995) developed a generalized version called rank- and sign-dependent utility (RSDU) that allowed different rank-dependent weighting functions for gains and losses (Luce, 2000). Tversky and Kahneman (1992) adopted a version of this model and called it cumulative prospect theory (CPT). According to RSDU or CPT, the value of a gamble on strictly nonnegative consequences is given by the following:

$$\mathrm{CPV}(G) = \Sigma\left[W(P_i) - W(Q_i)\right]u(x_i) \tag{8.3}$$

where W is a strictly monotonic function from $W(0) = 0$ to $W(1) = 1$ that assigns decumulative weight to decumulative probability, P_i is the decumulative probability to win x_i or more, and Q_i is the probability to win strictly more than x_i.

This CPT model (Eq. 8.3) always satisfies stochastic dominance, and it also satisfies other principles that had required editing rules in original prospect theory. CPT could account for the Allais paradoxes by means of an inverse S-shaped decumulative weighting function, like that in Fig. 8.2 (except that the x-axis now represents decumulative probability). This function assigns more weight to branches leading to smallest and largest consequences of a gamble than to branches leading to intermediate ones.

For a time, CPT appeared a better description than EU theory, but it had not been tested against an earlier approach called "configural weighting" that had been proposed in the 1970s that shared some features of rank-dependent weighting but which differed in important ways.

Configural Weighting Models

Birnbaum (1974; Birnbaum & Stegner, 1979) proposed configural weight models in which the rank of a stimulus affects its weight. Those aspects of a stimulus that are more unfavorable often seem to receive greater weight—a person who is described as "phony and understanding" or "sincere and mean" is not rated as neutral in likeableness, but instead is given a low rating, closer in value to the lower-evaluated information than to the higher. Similarly, a 50–50 gamble to receive either \$0 or \$100 is evaluated closer in value to \$0 than to \$100, as if \$0 gets a greater weight than \$100. Although these rank-affected, configural weight models had much in common with the models later developed independently as "rank-dependent utility," the configural weight models can be distinguished from rank-dependent ones because they make different predictions in certain cases; for example, they do not always imply stochastic dominance.

Configural weighting provides a different interpretation of risk aversion than found in EU theory: according to EU theory, risk aversion is produced by curvature of the utility function (Fig. 8.1); according to configural weighting theory, however, risk aversion or risk-seeking is mainly produced by over- or under-weighting of the lower-valued consequences or aspects of a gamble or stimulus. For example, suppose the utility function is linear, $u(x) = x$, and people give twice as much weight to the lower consequence in a 50–50 gamble as to the higher one. Then the value of a 50–50 gamble to win \$100 or \$0 is \$33. The intuition is that people give extra attention to lower-valued consequences, leaving less weight for higher-valued consequences. A configural weight model that captures this intuition is the transfer of attention exchange (TAX) model, which postulates that attention is diverted ("taxed") from higher-valued outcomes and transferred to lower-valued consequences.

Consider the simple case of a 50–50 gamble to win either x or y, where $x > y \geq 0$. The TAX model for this gamble can be written as follows:

$$\text{TAX}(G) = (0.5 + \omega)u(x) + (0.5 - \omega)u(y)$$

where ω is the configural weight transferred from the lower-valued to the higher-valued consequence or aspect of the gamble or stimulus ($-0.5 \leq \omega \leq 0.5$). If $\omega = 0$, TAX reduces to EU; if $\omega = 0.5$, it becomes a maximum model, and with $\omega = -0.5$, it becomes a minimum model. For gambles on small amounts of cash ($x <$ \$150), with college students, one can approximate $u(x) = x$, and $\omega = -1/6$, so the lowest consequence would get a weight of 2/3 and the highest a weight of 1/3. If a person had these parameters, that person would prefer \$45 for sure to the 50–50 gamble to win \$100, would prefer the gamble to \$20, and would be indifferent between the gamble and \$33 for sure.

For gambles with two possible consequences of the form, $G = (x, p; y)$, $x > y \geq 0$, the TAX model can be written as follows:

$$\text{TAX}(G) = \left[au(x) + bu(y)\right] / (a + b)$$

where a and b are the weights of the higher and lower consequences, which have utilities of $u(x)$ and $u(y)$, respectively. For a risk-averse person, weights in a Special Case TAX model are given as follows:

$$a = t(p) - \delta t(p) / 3$$

$$b = t(1 - p) + \delta t(p) / 3$$

where $t(p)$ is a function of p, usually approximated as a power function, and $\delta > 0$ is a constant reflecting the transfer of weight (attention) from the higher-valued consequence to the lower-valued consequence. When the transfer goes the other direction, $\delta < 0$, one replaces $t(p)$ with $t(1 - p)$ in the above equations.[1]

With three-branch gambles of the form, $G = (x, p; y, q; z, 1 - p - q)$, $x > y > z \geq 0$, the model is again a weighted average, $\text{TAX}(G) = [Au(x) + Bu(y) + Cu(z)]/(A + B + C)$, where the weights (for branches with highest, middle, and lowest consequences) are as follows (in the Special TAX model) for a person who places greater weight on lower-valued consequences:

$$A = t(p) - 2\delta t(p)/4$$

$$B = t(q) + \delta t(p)/4 - \delta t(q)/4$$

$$C = t(1 - p - q) + \delta t(p)/4 + \delta t(q)/4$$

Previous research has shown that modal choices by undergraduates for gambles involving small positive values can be roughly approximated by $t(p) = p^{0.7}$, $u(x) = x$, and $\delta = 1$. Although these "prior" parameters (which were not "best-fit" but were roughly based on previous data) have done fairly well in predicting new group data for the last 20 years, data fitting also shows that the estimated utility function should be negatively accelerated, especially when consequences cover a large range of values.

There are two aspects of the weights that deserve emphasis: First, the transfer of weights has the implication that risk aversion or risk-seeking can be explained by greater or reduced weight on the lower-valued consequence.

Second, the weighting of branches need not satisfy the property of coalescing, which is the assumption that splitting a branch of a gamble would not affect its utility. For example, coalescing implies that A = (\$96, 0.85; \$96, 0.05; \$12, 0.10) should have the same utility as B = (\$98, 0.90; \$12, 0.10). Note that A and B are (objectively) the same; B is called the *coalesced* form of the gamble, and A is one of many possible *split* forms of the same gamble. Instead, splitting a branch in this model increases the weight given to the consequences of the split branch. This implication follows from the fact that $t(p)$ is negatively accelerated, like many other psychophysical functions. In this averaging model, splitting the branch leading to the highest consequences tends to make a gamble A better than B (subjectively). Splitting the branch leading to the lowest consequence would tend to make a gamble seem worse.

Differences in the properties and predictions between the configural weight models and RSDU models including CPT were identified and tested by Birnbaum

[1]As noted in Birnbaum (2008b, p. 471), the convention for ranking consequences was changed from lowest to highest, used in early papers on configural weighting, to highest to lowest, to agree with the conventions used in CPT; therefore, $\delta < 0$ in Birnbaum & Navarrete (1998) corresponds to $\delta > 0$ here and in papers after 2008.

in a series of experiments that refuted this class of models as descriptive of decision making (Birnbaum, 2004a, 2004b, 2006; Marley & Luce, 2005). The configural weight models, based on previous data, correctly predicted where to find new violations, which Birnbaum (2008b) called "new paradoxes" because these critical properties refuted CPT in the same way that Allais paradoxes refuted EU; that is, they lead to contradictions in the model that cannot be explained by revising parameters or functions in the model. More than a dozen critical tests have been devised that reveal that CPT is systematically violated (reviewed in Birnbaum, 2008b, 2008c). Two of these critical tests among these models are reviewed in the next sections.

Violations of Stochastic Dominance

If the probability to win a prize of *x* or greater in gamble *F* is always at least as high and sometimes higher than the corresponding probability in gamble *G*, we say that gamble *F* dominates gamble *G* by first-order stochastic dominance. According to rank- and sign-dependent utility theories, including CPT and EU, first-order stochastic dominance must be satisfied. The configural weight models, however, imply that special choice problems can be constructed in which people will violate stochastic dominance.

Birnbaum and Navarrete (1998) tested choice problems such as the following that were predicted by configural weight models (such as TAX) to violate stochastic dominance:

Problem 5: *K*: ($96; 0.90; $14, 0.05; $12, 0.05)

L: ($96, 0.85; $90, 0.05; $12, 0.10)

Birnbaum and Navarrete (1998) found that about 70% of undergraduates choose *L* over *K*, even though *K* dominates *L*. Note that the probability to win $96 is higher in *K* than *L*, the probability to win $90 or more is the same, the probability to win $14 or more is higher in *K* than *L*, and the probability to win $12 or more is the same. There have now been dozens of studies reporting similar, substantial violations of stochastic dominance in choice problems of this type, using different types of participants, different types of monetary incentives, different types of probability mechanisms, different formats for presenting choice problems, and different types of event framing (Birnbaum, 2004a, 2004b, 2006, 2007, 2008b; Birnbaum & Bahra, 2012a). These robust violations indicate that no form of rank- and sign-dependent utility function, including CPT, can be considered as a descriptive model of risky decision making, but they were predicted by the configural weight models that were used to design the experiment.

Dissection of the Allais Paradox

Birnbaum (2004a) noted that constant consequence paradigm of Allais can be decomposed into three simpler properties: transitivity, coalescing, and restricted branch independence. *Transitivity* is the assumption that if one prefers A to B and prefers B to C, then one should prefer A to C. *Coalescing* is the assumption that if two branches of a gamble lead to the same consequence, they can be combined by adding their probabilities, without changing utility. For example, in Problem 1, coalescing implies that the gamble, A = ($1 million, 0.11; $0, 0.89), is identical in utility to A_s = ($1 million, 0.10; $1 million, 0.01; $0, 0.89), because A_s is one of the "split" forms of A, which is the "coalesced" form of A_s.

Restricted branch independence is the assumption that if two gambles with the same number of branches and same probability distribution over those branches have a common consequence on a branch, the common consequence can be changed to another value without altering the preference. For example, A_s = ($1 million, 0.10; $1 million, 0.01; $0, 0.89) is preferred to B_s = ($2 million, 0.10; $0, 0.01; $0, 0.89) if and only if C_s = ($1 million, 0.10; $1 million, 0.01; $1 million, 0.89) is preferred to D_s = ($2 million, 0.10; $0, 0.01; $1 million, 0.89), where the common branch of 0.89 to win $0 in the first choice has been changed to a common branch of 0.89 to win $1 million in the second.

If a person satisfied transitivity, coalescing, and restricted branch independence (all implied by EU), that person would not display the constant consequence paradox of Allais (Birnbaum, 2004a).

Consider the choice problems in Table 8.1. According to EU theory, the preference should be the same in all six choice problems, in the sense that A preferred to B if and only if (iff) A_s preferred to B_s, iff C_s preferred to D_s, iff C preferred to D, iff E_s preferred to F_s, and iff E preferred to F.

Original prospect theory (OPT), CPT, TAX, and EU all make different predictions for such a dissection of this Allais paradox, so one can compare all four theories by testing this "dissection" of the Allais paradox (Birnbaum, 2004a, 2007). Implications of the theories are shown in Table 8.2. As shown in Table 8.2, in EU theory, both restricted branch independence (columns in Table 8.2) and coalescing (rows in Table 8.2) are satisfied. OPT implies restricted branch independence and violates coalescing, to account for the Allais paradox. That is, OPT implies A_s is preferred to B_s, iff C_s is preferred to D_s and iff E_s is preferred to F_s. To explain an Allais paradox such as a reversal between the choice between A and B and between E and F, there must be a reversal either between choices of A versus B and A_s versus B_s or between the choices of E_s versus F_s and E versus F. OPT also had editing rules of combination and cancellation that imply coalescing and restricted branch independence, respectively, so OPT could mimic EU by invoking these editing rules, in which case the model does not predict Allais paradoxes.

Table 8.2 shows that, in contrast, CPT assumes coalescing and attributes the Allais paradox to violations of restricted branch independence; thus, A is preferred to B iff A_s is preferred to B_s, and E_s is preferred to F_s, iff E is preferred to F. If cancel-

Table 8.1 Six choice problems dissecting Allais paradox into tests of coalescing and restricted branch independence

No.	"Safe"	"Risky"
1	*A*: ($1 M, 0.11; $0, 0.89)	*B*: ($2 M, 0.10; $0, 0.90)
1s	A_s: ($1 M, 0.10; $1 M, 0.01; $0, 0.89)	B_s: ($2 M, 0.10; $0, 0.01; $0, 0.89)
2s	C_s: ($1 M, 0.10; $1 M, 0.01; $1 M, 0.89)	D_s: ($2 M, 0.10; $0, 0.01; $1 M, 0.89)
2	*C*: $1 M for sure	*D*: ($2 M, 0.10; $1 M, 0.89; $0, 0.01)
3s	E_s: ($1 M, 0.10; $1 M, 0.01; $2 M, 0.89)	F_s: ($2 M, 0.10; $0, 0.01; $2 M, 0.89)
3	*E*: ($2 M, 0.89; $1 M, 0.11)	*F*: ($2 M, 0.99; $0, 0.01)

According to coalescing, Choices No. 1 and 1s, 2 and 2s, and 3 and 3s are equivalent choice problems. According to restricted branch independence, Choices No. 1s, 2s, and 3s should all be either "safe" or they should all be "risky," but one should not switch systematically

Table 8.2 Comparison of decision theories

Restricted branch independence		
Coalescing	Satisfied	Violated
Satisfied	EUT	CPT
Violated	OPT	CWT

Notes: *EUT*expected utility theory, *CPT* cumulative prospect theory, *OPT* original prospect theory, *CWT* configural weight theory (TAX). The editing rules of combination and cancellation produce satisfaction of coalescing and restricted branch independence, respectively

lation was invoked, CPT could also mimic EU and would not predict Allais paradoxes.

Configural weight models such as TAX violate coalescing and with typical parameters, they often imply opposite violations of restricted branch independence from those required by CPT to account for the Allais paradoxes. According to this model, it should be possible to construct choice problems in which the Allais paradox would be reversed when the choices are presented in canonical split form. Canonical split form means that probabilities on ranked branches are equal, and the number of branches is minimal, as in choices A_s versus B_s and in E_s versus F_s.

Empirically, there are strong violations of both coalescing and of restricted branch independence, and the violations of restricted branch independence are indeed opposite the direction required by CPT to account for the Allais paradox (Birnbaum, 2004a, 2007, 2008b). Thus, EU and both versions of prospect theory can be rejected because they both cannot account for violations of both coalescing and restricted branch independence in the dissection of the Allais paradox.

A number of studies have now been completed testing between configural weight models and CPT investigating these and other critical behavioral properties that can be used to distinguish between these models. The results strongly refute both versions of prospect theory in favor of the predictions made by the configural models (Birnbaum, 2004a, 2004b, 2006, 2008b; Birnbaum & Bahra, 2012a).

Another criticism of CPT was developed, based on the idea that other process assumptions could be made to emulate its predictions for certain cases where the model had some success; the priority heuristic was constructed to fit previously published data.

Priority Heuristic and Relative Arguments

Brandstätter, Gigerenzer, and Hertwig (2006) based their priority heuristic model on the lexicographic semiorder that had been used by Tversky (1969) to describe intransitive preferences that Tversky believed he found in a small number of selected individuals.

According to the priority heuristic (PH), a person first compares lowest consequences of a gamble and chooses the gamble with the higher lowest consequence if they differ by more than 10% of the largest consequence in either gamble, rounded to the nearest prominent number. When the lowest consequences are not sufficiently different, the person chooses the gamble with the smaller probability to get the lowest consequence, if these differ by 0.1 or more. If the probabilities of the lowest consequences differed by less than 0.1, the person is theorized to next compare the highest prizes and choose by that criterion, if they differ sufficiently. When there are more than two branches and the first three comparisons yield no decision, the person next compares the probabilities to win the highest prize and decides on that basis alone, if there is any difference. And if all four criteria yield no decision, the person chooses randomly, without examining anything else. At each stage, the decision is based on only one reason, which is a contrast on one dimension. For example, comparing A = ($5.00, 0.29; $0, 0.71) versus C = ($4.50, 0.38; $0, 0.62), a person first compares the lowest outcomes, and since they are $0 in both alternatives; next, she examines the probability to receive the lowest outcome, but since the difference is less than 0.10, she compares the highest consequences and decides that A is better than C.

A claim was made that the PH fit certain published choice data as well or better than EU, CPT, or TAX, but this claim was challenged and shown to hold only with selected data and only when certain assumptions are forced onto theories that do not make those assumptions (Birnbaum, 2008a); when other data sets were analyzed, the model performed very poorly, and when best-fit parameters are estimated from the data for all models, the PH with its best-fit parameters did not outperform CPT or TAX with their best-fit parameters.

The PH model had been constructed to account for the Allais paradoxes in original form, but it could not account for new examples such as the dissection of the Allais paradoxes (Birnbaum, 2004a), nor for violations of stochastic dominance (Birnbaum, 1999), nor for violations of restricted branch independence (Birnbaum & Navarrete, 1998). Although these phenomena had been published in the literature, they had not been included in the contest of fit that claimed high accuracy for the PH.

The PH implies systematic violations of transitivity that do not appear empirically. For example, with gambles *A* = ($5.00, 0.29; $0, 0.71), *C* = ($4.50, 0.38; $0, 0.62), and *E* = ($4.00, 0.46; $0, 0.54), the PH predicts that the majority should prefer *A* to *C*, and prefer *C* to *E*, and yet prefer *E* to *A*. But new studies by Birnbaum and Gutierrez (2007), Regenwetter, Dana, and Davis-Stober (2011), and Birnbaum and Bahra (2012b), among others, designed to test the predictions of the PH found that majority preferences did not show the predicted patterns of PH. In fact, the PH predicted only 30% of the modal choices correctly in Birnbaum and Gutierrez (a random coin toss would have correctly predicted 50%). PH model also does significantly worse than chance in predicting violations of restricted branch independence, because it predicts the opposite pattern of violations from what is observed in both group data and the majority of individuals analyzed separately (Birnbaum & Bahra, 2012a).

The PH implies that attributes or dimensions of a stimulus do not combine, nor do they interact, but experimental tests of combination and interaction showed evidence that people integrate information between dimensions and that the dimensions interact. For example, consider the following two choice problems:

Problem 6: *X* = ($100, 0.9; $5, 0.1)

Y = ($50, 0.9; $20, 0.1)

Problem 7: *X'* = ($100, 0.1; $5, 0.9)

Y' = ($50, 0.1; $20, 0.9)

According to the PH, a person should choose *Y* and *Y'* because the probabilities are the same and the lowest consequences are better by the same amount in both gambles. According to another lexicographic semiorder, a person might choose *X* and *X'*, if they examined the highest consequences first. Because the probabilities are the same in both gambles within each choice, probability should not make any difference in these models. However, most people choose *X* over *Y* in Problem 6 and choose *Y'* over *X'* in Problem 7, contrary to any lexicographic semiorder model. These violations also contradict other similarity models that decide by comparing contrasts between components but do not postulate that components interact (Birnbaum, 2008c, 2010).

The perceived relative arguments model (Loomes, 2010), like the priority heuristic and regret theory (Loomes, Starmer, & Sugden, 1991; Loomes & Sugden, 1982), can also violate transitivity. The Loomes (2010) model assumes that people make choices by combining contrasts between the components, so it differs from the PH. However, empirical studies of predicted intransitivity by regret theory and perceived relative arguments model have not confirmed its predictions, and this model also fails to account for violations of restricted branch independence (Birnbaum & Diecidue, 2015).

In principle, violations of transitivity, if substantial and systematic, would rule out a large class of models that includes EV, EU, CPT, and TAX. Therefore, it would be extremely important to know if stimuli can be found that produce predictable, systematic violations of transitivity. But Birnbaum and Diecidue (2015) noted that specific tests for intransitivity have not shown convincing evidence favoring either the PH, regret theory, or similarity models over the family of transitive models.

Decisions from Description and from Experience

Much of the research and theory presented to this point has been based on cases where a decision-maker makes a decision based on descriptions of the consequences and their likelihoods. This paradigm matches many real-life situations where people make decisions without previous experience. However, in some cases, people make repeated decisions and can use their experience to revise beliefs about the likelihoods and utilities of the consequences.

Hertwig, Barron, Weber, and Erev (2004) contrast two paradigms for decision making research. The first method asks people to make a single decision based on descriptions of the relevant chances and consequences, and the second method involves learning of probabilities based on experience with a sequence of events representing some unknown stochastic process. A sick person deciding which of two medical treatments to choose seems to match the first method, whereas an experienced person deciding what to order from a frequently visited restaurant seems to illustrate the second. With description, many people say they prefer a small chance at a large prize to a sure thing with the same expected value. For example, many people prefer M = ($100, 0.01; $0, 0.99) over N = $1 for sure, based on a description.

Such risk-seeking behavior for small probabilities to win positive consequences is consistent with OPT, CPT, and TAX, given typical parameters. However, when people are asked to sample from the two options, and then asked to make a choice, they often choose the safe option over the risky gamble. Hertwig et al. (2004) argued that perhaps different theories of decision making might be required for these two types of situation. They note that learning and perception of probabilities might be overly influenced by the particular sequence of events.

However, Fox and Hadar (2006) noted that from the perspective of experience, some people who drew small samples might experience M as "$0 always occurs" (since the unlikely event of $100 might never occur in a small sample); in contrast, they experience N as "always pays $1"; they never experience the population, so subjectively, the choice was between always $0 and always $1. In many studies done in this field, sampling is left to the participant and to chance, so the experience has not been constrained to match the description.

Glöckner, Hilbig, Henninger, and Fiedler (2016) present a current review of the literature on description versus experience, a reanalysis of earlier studies, and new experiments designed to disentangle different interpretations. They conclude that sampling and regression effects are important components of the previous studies, but they argue that other factors (such as uncertainty) play roles as well. For example, how does one learn from a brief experience that something is a "sure thing?"

When one hears the description, "you win \$50 no matter what color you draw from the urn," it denotes a sure thing. This case is different from the situation of 15 trials that yield only \$50 prizes. There is still the chance that other prizes might occur that have not yet been experienced. One factor that has not yet been addressed in this literature on experience versus description that has been considered by some in the description literature is the role of error or variability of response to producing choice behavior.

Models of Error or Variability

When a person is presented the same choice problem on two occasions, the same person will often make a different choice responses on the two trials. For example, consider the next two choice problems:

Problem 8: *R* = (\$98, 0.10; \$2, 0.90)

S = (\$40, 0.20; \$2, 0.80)

Problem 9: *R'* = (\$98, 0.90; \$2, 0.10)

S' = (\$98, 0.80; \$40, 0.20)

Problems 8 and 9 were included, separated by a number of intervening trials, among a list of 31 choice problems. Following a brief intervening task of about 10 min, the same people were asked to respond to the same choice problems a second time. It was found that the same people made different responses 20% of the time on Problem 9, and 31% reversed preferences on two presentations of Problem 8. According to EU, a person should prefer *R* over *S* if and only if she prefers *R'* over *S'*. But if the same person can change responses when Problem 8 is presented twice, should we be surprised if that same person made different responses on Problems 8 and 9?

In the past, researchers argued that if significantly more people chose *R* in Problem 8 and *S'* in Problem 9 than the number who made the opposite pattern of reversal (*S* and *R'*), then the "significant" difference meant one should reject EU. However, it has recently been shown that if different choice problems have different rates of error, then such asymmetry of reversals could occur even if EU held true. The idea that inherent variability or errors in choice might produce some or all of the apparent violations in tests of the Allais paradoxes (or of other behavioral properties such as transitivity) has been an important focus of recent research (Birnbaum, 2013; Birnbaum & Bahra, 2012a; Carbone & Hey, 2000; Loomes, 2005; Regenwetter et al., 2011; Wilcox, 2008).

A family of models known as "true and error" models has been developed, based on the idea that one can estimate the error component from preference reversals by the same person to the same choice problems within a brief session. These models allow that a person's "true" preferences may have variability between sessions (blocks of trials), due to such factors as changing parameters or changing models, and they allow separation of such variability due to a mixture of models from variability produced by "error" that produces reversals within a session. They allow each choice problem to have a different rate of error, and they allow different people to have differing amounts of noise or unreliability in their responses.

When these models have been applied to repeated judgments, it has been found that the violations of EU, as in the Allais paradoxes; violations of CPT, as in the "new paradoxes"; and violations of the priority heuristic, as in the tests of interactive independence, cannot be attributed to this type of error (Birnbaum, 2008b, 2008c, 2010). On the other hand, violations of transitivity have been found to be of low frequency when the inherent variability of the data is fit by the true and error model.

Concluding Comments

The field of risky decision making is one of the oldest topics in behavioral science and has influenced both psychology and economics. Over the years, new models have been developed, and new evidence has accumulated to refute some theories in favor of others. When new evidence violates a currently popular model, the findings are often called "paradoxes" or "anomalies." Data have shown that EV, EU, SWU, OPT, and CPT can be rejected based on violations of critical properties. Intransitive models such as regret theory, lexicographic semiorders, and the priority heuristic have not yet been able to show where to find the predicted intransitive preference cycles nor have they been successful in predicting results of new experiments designed to test them. Configural weight models, such as TAX, remain the best account of the major phenomena, but as new research is conducted, it seems likely that more accurate and elegant models can be developed. As new theories are developed, new tests are designed, and new information is gained about how people deal with risk in making decisions.

References

Allais, M. (1953). Fondements d'une Théorie Positive des Choix Comportant un Risque et Critique des Postulats et Axiomes de l'Ecole Américaine. *Econometrica, 21*, 503–546.

Allais, M. (1979). The foundations of a positive theory of choice involving risk and a criticism of the postulates and axioms of the American school (1952). In M. Allais & O. Hagen (Eds.), *Expected utility hypotheses and the Allais Paradox* (pp. 27–145). Dordrecht: Reidel/Springer.

Bernoulli, D. (1954). Exposition of a new theory on the measurement of risk. *Econometrica, 22*, 23–36 (English translation of 1738 paper).

Birnbaum, M. H. (1974). The nonadditivity of personality impressions. *Journal of Experimental Psychology Monograph, 102*, 543–561.

Birnbaum, M. H. (2004a). Causes of Allais common consequence paradoxes: An experimental dissection. *Journal of Mathematical Psychology, 48*, 87–106.

Birnbaum, M. H. (2004b). Tests of rank-dependent utility and cumulative prospect theory in gambles represented by natural frequencies: Effects of format, event framing, and branch splitting. *Organizational Behavior and Human Decision Processes, 95*, 40–65.

Birnbaum, M. H. (2006). Evidence against prospect theories in gambles with positive, negative, and mixed consequences. *Journal of Economic Psychology, 27*, 737–761.

Birnbaum, M. H. (2007). Tests of branch splitting and branch-splitting independence in Allais paradoxes with positive and mixed consequences. *Organizational Behavior and Human Decision Processes, 102*, 154–173.

Birnbaum, M. H. (2008a). Evaluation of the priority heuristic as a descriptive model of risky decision making: Comment on Brandstätter, Gigerenzer, and Hertwig (2006). *Psychological Review, 115*, 253–260.

Birnbaum, M. H. (2008b). New paradoxes of risky decision making. *Psychological Review, 115*, 463–501.

Birnbaum, M. H. (2008c). New tests of cumulative prospect theory and the priority heuristic: Probability-outcome tradeoff with branch splitting. *Judgment and Decision making, 3*, 304–316.

Birnbaum, M. H. (2010). Testing lexicographic semiorders as models of decision making: Priority dominance, integration, interaction, and transitivity. *Journal of Mathematical Psychology, 54*, 363–386.

Birnbaum, M. H. (2013). True-and-error models violate independence and yet they are testable. *Judgment and Decision making, 8*, 717–737.

Birnbaum, M. H., & Bahra, J. P. (2012a). Separating response variability from structural inconsistency to test models of risky decision making. *Judgment and Decision making, 7*, 402–426.

Birnbaum, M. H., & Bahra, J. P. (2012b). Testing transitivity of preferences in individuals using linked designs. *Judgment and Decision making, 7*, 524–567.

Birnbaum, M. H., & Diecidue, E. (2015). Testing a class of models that includes majority rule and regret theories: Transitivity, recycling, and restricted branch independence. *Decision, 2*, 145–190.

Birnbaum, M. H., & Gutierrez, R. J. (2007). Testing for intransitivity of preferences predicted by a lexicographic semiorder. *Organizational Behavior and Human Decision Processes, 104*, 97–112.

Birnbaum, M. H., & Navarrete, J. (1998). Testing descriptive utility theories: Violations of stochastic dominance and cumulative independence. *Journal of Risk and Uncertainty, 17*, 49–78.

Birnbaum, M. H., & Stegner, S. E. (1979). Source credibility in social judgment: Bias, expertise, and the judge's point of view. *Journal of Personality and Social Psychology, 37*, 48–74.

Brandstätter, E., Gigerenzer, G., & Hertwig, R. (2006). The priority heuristic: Choices without tradeoffs. *Psychological Review, 113*, 409–432.

Birnbaum, M. H. (1999). Paradoxes of Allais, stochastic dominance, and decision weights. In J. Shanteau, B. A. Mellers, & D. A. Schum (Eds.), *Decision science and technology: Reflections on the contributions of Ward Edwards* (pp. 27-52). Norwell, MA: Kluwer Academic Publishers.

Carbone, E., & Hey, J. D. (2000). Which error story is best? *Journal of Risk and Uncertainty, 20*, 161–176.

Edwards, W. (1954). The theory of decision making. *Psychological Bulletin, 51*, 380–417.

Edwards, W. (1962). Subjective probabilities inferred from decisions. *Psychological Review, 69*, 109–135.

Fox, C. R., & Hadar, L. (2006). "Decisions from experience" = sampling error + prospect theory: Reconsidering Hertwig, Barron, Weber & Erev (2004). *Judgment and Decision making, 1*, 159–161.

Glöckner, A., Hilbig, B., Henninger, F., & Fiedler, S. (2016). The reversed description-experience gap: Disentangling sources of presentation format effects in risky choice. *Journal of Experimental Psychology: General, 145*, 486–508.

Hertwig, R., Barron, G., Weber, E. U., & Erev, I. (2004). Decisions from experience and the effect of rare events in risky choice. *Psychological Science, 15*, 534–539.

Kahneman, D. (2003). Experiences of collaborative research. *American Psychologist, 58*, 723–730.
Kahneman, D., & Tversky, A. (1979). Prospect theory: An analysis of decision under risk. *Econometrica, 47*, 263–291.
Loomes, G. (2005). Modeling the stochastic component of behavior in experiments: Some issues for interpretation of data. *Experimental Economics, 8*, 301–323.
Loomes, G. (2010). Modeling choice and valuation in decision experiments. *Psychological Review, 117*, 902–924.
Loomes, G., Starmer, C., & Sugden, R. (1991). Observing violations of transitivity by experimental methods. *Econometrica, 59*, 425–440.
Loomes, G., & Sugden, R. (1982). Regret theory: An alternative theory of rational choice under uncertainty. *The Economic Journal, 92*, 805–824.
Luce, R. D. (2000). *Utility of gains and losses: Measurement-theoretical and experimental approaches*. Mahwah, NJ: Lawrence Erlbaum Associates.
Luce, R. D., & Fishburn, P. C. (1991). Rank- and sign-dependent linear utility models for finite first order gambles. *Journal of Risk and Uncertainty, 4*, 29–59.
Luce, R. D., & Fishburn, P. C. (1995). A note on deriving rank-dependent utility using additive joint receipts. *Journal of Risk and Uncertainty, 11*, 5–16.
Markowitz, H. (1952). The utility of wealth. *Journal of Political Economy, 60*, 151–158.
Marley, A. A. J., & Luce, R. D. (2005). Independence properties vis-à-vis several utility representations. *Theory and Decision, 58*, 77–143.
Quiggin, J. (1985). Subjective utility, anticipated utility, and the Allais paradox. *Organizational Behavior and Human Decision Processes, 35*, 94–101.
Quiggin, J. (1993). *Generalized expected utility theory: The rank dependent model*. Boston: Kluwer.
Regenwetter, M., Dana, J., & Davis-Stober, C. P. (2011). Transitivity of preferences. *Psychological Review, 118*, 42–56.
Tversky, A., & Kahneman, D. (1992). Advances in prospect theory: Cumulative representation of uncertainty. *Journal of Risk and Uncertainty, 5*, 297–323.
Tversky, A. (1969). Intransitivity of preferences. *Psychological Review,* 76, 31–48.
Von Neumann, J., & Morgenstern, O. (1947). *Theory of games and economic behavior* (2nd ed.). Princeton: Princeton University Press https://archive.org/details/theoryofgamesand030098mbp
Wilcox, N. (2008). Stochastic models for binary discrete choice under risk: A critical primer and econometric comparison. In J. C. Cox & G. W. Harrison (Eds.), *Research in experimental economics vol. 12: Risk aversion in experiments* (pp. 197–292). Bingley: Emerald.

Chapter 9
Cognitive Architectures as Scaffolding for Risky Choice Models

Cvetomir M. Dimov and Julian N. Marewski

Abstract Debates in decision making, such as the debate about the empirical validity of the priority heuristic, a model of risky choice, are sometimes difficult to resolve, because hypotheses about decision processes are either formulated qualitatively or not precisely enough. This lack of precision often leaves empirical tests with response times and other detailed behavioral data inconclusive. One way to increase the precision of decision models is to implement them in broad cognitive frameworks such as the cognitive architecture ACT-R. ACT-R can be used to construct detailed process models of how people make, for example, risky choices, and to derive process predictions about, among others, eye movements, absolute response times, or brain activation. These precise process models make explicit their underlying assumptions, which facilitate direct model comparisons and make the models amenable to strict empirical tests. We demonstrate the level of detail that ACT-R provides with an ACT-R implementation of the inferential heuristic take-the-best. We end by addressing the question of why cognitive architectures are still not widespread in judgment and decision making.

> Psychologists treat other peoples' theories like toothbrushes — no self-respecting person wants to use anyone else's. It's amusing, but it also points to a conflict that we may be nurturing within our profession to the detriment of our science.
> Walter Mischel, 2008, on Theory Integration in Psychology

C. M. Dimov (✉)
Department of Organizational Behavior, Faculty of Business and Economics, University of Lausanne, Lausanne, Switzerland

Department of Psychology, Carnegie Mellon University, Pittsburgh, PA, USA
e-mail: cvetomir.dimov@unil.ch

J. N. Marewski
Department of Organizational Behavior, Faculty of Business and Economics, University of Lausanne, Lausanne, Switzerland
e-mail: cvetomir.dimov@unil.ch

M. Raue et al. (eds.), *Psychological Perspectives on Risk and Risk Analysis*,
https://doi.org/10.1007/978-3-319-92478-6_9

The Toothbrush Problem

In a beautiful essay, published in the *American Psychological Association's Observer*, Mischel (2008) once tellingly remarked that many psychologists treat their theories like toothbrushes: No self-respecting person would ever be willing to use that of somebody else (see epigram above). Indeed, it does not take a systematic survey to realize how correct Mischel is. Much work in the psychological sciences coexists in parallel, without much cross-talk across frameworks, subfields, or disciplines. Research in judgment and decision making is no exception.

In this chapter, we argue that this does not have to be so and point to one avenue for theory integration. In doing so, we borrow from a branch of cognitive psychology that has been characterized, for over 40 years, by steady, systematic, successful efforts to integrate empirical research into a single overarching, cumulative theory. This branch of cognitive psychology—research on cognitive architectures—can provide a common scaffolding for risk taking models and thus allow us to directly compare those models' assumptions and to rigorously test their empirical validity.

Specialized Scientific Worker = Isolated Areas of the Mind

Psychology as a discipline is characterized by a division of labor: Much like workers in a factory, most scientists focus on areas of their specialty; personality psychologists worry about personality, memory researchers study memory, and decision making scientists look at decisions. Within those fields, in turn, the scientific workers specialize further, namely, on paradigms, methods, and theoretical frameworks. And steadily publishing on personality, memory, and decision making helps those workers earn a name and reputation in their respective niches—and, possibly, other objects of desire, including grants, tenured jobs, or promotions.

Yet, contrary to psychological scientists, the cognitive system's different components do not work in full isolation. Rather, emotions shape decision making, decision making almost always requires memory, and memory can exploit seeing, reading, or hearing. Theory integration implies pulling together areas that highly specialized scientists have separated. But how can theory integration be achieved?

Cognitive Architectures

> Even if the mind has parts, modules, components, or whatever, they all mesh together to produce behavior. (...) If a theory covers only one part or component, it flirts with trouble from the start. Newell (1990, p. 17)

One means to systematically integrate existing theories and empirical findings is *cognitive architectures*. Cognitive architectures are broad, quantitative theories of cognition that cover diverse task domains, components of cognition, and behavior, ranging from emotions to the emergence of norms (see Box 9.1).

Among the architectures developed to date (e.g., *EPIC*, Meyer & Kieras, 1997; *Soar*, Newell, 1992, see also Laird, 2012, for a more recent version), the *ACT-R architecture* (Anderson et al., 2004) is, perhaps, the most detailed and encompassing one. ACT-R integrates theories of memory, perception, action, and other aspects of cognition into one *formal* framework built out of computer code and mathematical equations. Those different cognitive functions are cast into separate *modules* in

Box 9.1 Emotions, Norms, and Cognitive Architectures
Appraisal theory (Scherer, 2001), a process theory of emotion, has on several occasions been integrated into a cognitive architecture (see, e.g., Marinier, Laird, & Lewis, 2009). In addition, there have been recent attempts to integrate ACT-R with the physiological simulation *HumMod* (Hester et al., 2011) in order to account for effects of physiology on cognition (Dancy, Ritter, Berry, & Klein, 2015). In the area of social phenomena, the cognitive architecture EMIL (Conte, Andrighetto, & Campennl, 2013) attempts to explain how cognitive and social processes interact to produce norms, and how norms can influence cognition.

ACT-R: A *declarative* module models how information is stored in and retrieved from memory; there are *visual* and *aural* modules, which model vision and hearing, respectively; there are also *vocal* and *manual* modules to capture speech and, say, typing on a keyboard; there is an *intentional* module that keeps track of goals; and there is a module that holds task-relevant information, the *imaginal module*. Within each of the modules, information is processed serially, but the modules themselves can operate in parallel (Byrne & Anderson, 2001). The modules' operations are coordinated by a central *production system*. That system consists of if-then rules (so-called production rules) whose conditions (their "if" parts) are pitted against the modules' respective current states. When a rule's conditions are met, then it can direct other modules to change their state. In doing so, the rules do not directly access the modules' content but operate through dedicated communication channels (labeled *buffers*). Those channels act as bottlenecks in information transfer (Salvucci & Taatgen, 2008).

The information-processing bottlenecks, modules, and if-then rules are designed such that, ideally, the architecture will learn and forget information like a human might do or such that, in driving a car or solving mathematical problems, the architecture will react as quickly as an actual driver and commit similar mistakes as a human problem-solver. Indeed, in pulling together different aspects of cognition into an integrative theory, ACT-R has been successfully applied to a vast array of domains, ranging from associative recognition (e.g., Schneider & Anderson, 2012), time perception (Taatgen, Van Rijn, & Anderson, 2007), and inferential decision making (e.g., Marewski & Mehlhorn, 2011) to driving (Salvucci, 2006), learning in school (Koedinger, Anderson,

Box 9.2 Intuition and ACT-R
How does ACT-R capture intuitive processes? Various proposals have been made. For instance, in line with the idea that intuition builds up through extensive experience on a task, it has been recently argued that *instance-based learning theory*, a theory also implemented in ACT-R, conforms to the criteria for intuitive decision making (Thomson, Lebiere, Anderson, & Staszewski, 2015). Marewski and Mehlhorn (2011), in turn, suggested to model implicit processes with ACT-R's subsymbolic system (see below).

Hadley, & Mark, 1997), and intuition (see Box 9.2). In short, ACT-R can be best thought of as a computer program with built-in human constraints.

Working with that computer program, in turn, allows ACT-R modelers to act both as specialists and generalists. Much like specialists in mainstream psychological research, they can use ACT-R to explore, for example, decision making behavior under risk. Yet, in modeling such specific behavior, those specialists automatically also use the other computerized aspects of the architecture, such as declarative memory, goal-keeping, and perception. The advantage is that all of those aspects might not fall into the specialists' own expertise but might come to bear when the architectural computer code is initialized. That is, by implementing their own risky choice model in ACT-R, researchers are virtually forced to work from the assumptions and theories developed by other specialists about various aspects of cognition. For example, if one models how a participant chooses between two lotteries presented on a computer screen, one cannot escape the constraint put forth by the visual module when modeling how the participant acquires information about those lotteries from the screen. Also, when the model requires storing information in a temporary storage, it cannot avoid the time costs and capacity restrictions of the imaginal module and so on. Since those assumptions and theories are cast as computer code and mathematical equations into the architecture, those working on risky choice start from well-specified grounds, instead of from vague or fully unspecified auxiliary assumptions about other processes that can play a role when choosing between two lotteries (e.g., computing expected values in one's head, resolving cognitive conflicts between outputs of distinct systems, remembering past experiences in risky choice, acting upon one's desire to make short-term profit, or pressing a key in a computer-based psychological experiment in order to indicate one's decision).

In short, ACT-R is not only an overarching theory that formally integrates cognitive theories, but working with it also forces specialized researchers to make their own theory (e.g., about risk taking) consistent with those of others (e.g., about memory). As a matter of fact, ACT-R is a genuinely cumulative theory: Since the 1970s, the architecture's equations and computer code have been constantly updated and amended—be it to integrate new theories or in order for the architecture to be able to account for new empirical findings. This way, ACT has been replaced by ACT* and ACT* by ACT-R, with, for example, the "R" added to "ACT" standing for novel insights about how the human memory system exploits the statistical structure of human task environments (Anderson & Schooler, 1991). The architecture's current version is called ACT-R 7.

Heuristics-And-Biases Vs. Fast-And-Frugal Heuristics: An Alien's Perspective

While within the ACT-R community much research can be characterized with the terms "cumulative" and "integrative," this seems to be less true for judgment and decision making research. Instead, segregation—including controversies among the proponents of competing theoretical frameworks—shapes the field. Take the *heuristics-and-biases* (Tversky & Kahneman, 1974) and *fast-and-frugal heuristics* (Gigerenzer, Todd,, & the ABC Research Group, 1999) frameworks (see also Raue & Scholl, Chap. 7). These two approaches to understand and describe decision making are often compared with and pitted against each other (e.g., Gigerenzer, 1996; Mellers, Hertwig, & Kahneman, 2001; Samuels, Stich, & Bishop, 2002).

Integrative cognitive architectures can help recognizing and bridging eventual differences between competing theories. They can also aid understanding where differences are more a matter of rhetoric than a matter of substance. To illustrate how, we invite you to witness a dialogue between an alien and a researcher coming from the fast-and-frugal heuristics tradition.

If one adopts the perspective of an alien looking at the differences between both frameworks from a distance, the following picture might emerge: While both approaches to decision making recognize that simple rules of thumb or *heuristics* sometimes work well and sometimes not, one approach focuses on examining those situations in which people suffer from serious fallacies, biases, and reasoning errors. According to this approach, conditions under which people exhibit biases and fallacies unveil the innards of our decision making system in the same way that visual illusions unveil the innards of our visual system. Consequently, by uncovering the biases that we exhibit when making decisions, we will learn something about the underlying decision processes. This focus on the biases and fallacies that heuristic decision mechanisms produce leaves the impression that they are subpar mechanisms for decision making.

In contrast, the competing fast-and-frugal framework focuses on the upside of heuristics: It stresses how people can make smart decisions by relying on simple rules and that many so-called biases, fallacies, or reasoning errors are artifacts of sorts—originating, for example, in researchers' methods or in poorly specified theories (e.g., Marewski, Schooler, & Gigerenzer, 2010). Yet, overall, from the perspective of an alien, those two theoretical approaches seem hard to distinguish—eventual differences seem more a matter of shades, rather than of colors.

Of course, researchers working with those frameworks might disagree with the alien (and object that he or she lacks the human ability to see colors). The fast-and-frugal heuristics framework, so the counter-arguments might go—and we have made those arguments in the past ourselves (Marewski, Gaissmaier, & Gigerenzer, 2010a, 2010b)—differs from the heuristics-and-biases framework on several grounds. First, the fast-and-frugal heuristics framework is built around precise models of heuristics that are cast into algorithmic rules and that can be implemented, for instance, in computer simulations. In contrast, with notable exceptions (e.g., *elimination-by-aspects*, Tversky, 1972), many of the heuristics put forward in the heuristics-and-biases literature represent vague verbal notions (Gigerenzer, 1996).

Second, in developing precise models of heuristics, the fast-and-frugal heuristics framework places emphasis on describing decision making *processes*, such as how information is searched for, when information search will stop, and how the acquired information will be used to make decisions. On the other hand, many of the notions proposed in the heuristics-and-biases framework remain relatively vague about underlying processes of information acquisition and information evaluation.

Third, fast-and-frugal heuristics operate on the statistical structure of task environments. When a heuristic is well-adapted to an environment, using that heuristic can help a person make smart decisions, while if there is a mismatch between the environment and a heuristic, the decisional outcome can be bad (Todd & Gigerenzer, 2007).

To illustrate these three points, let us consider the *fluency heuristic* (Schooler & Hertwig, 2005). This heuristic can be seen as a computational instantiation of Tversky and Kahneman's (1973) classic notion of *availability*. The fluency heuristic uses a sense of *retrieval fluency*, modeled in terms of the time it takes to retrieve a piece of information from memory. When inferring, for instance, which of two companies will be more successful in the future, it assesses the retrieval time for each of the two companies and then picks the company, whose name is perceived as having been more quickly retrieved. The fluency heuristic exploits existing correlations between the criterion of interest and retrieval speed: If, in a task environment, criterion values (e.g., future success of a company) are correlated with occurrence frequency (e.g., how often that company is mentioned in the media) and therefore with speed of retrieval, using the fluency heuristic will lead to good inferences. If, however, criterion values are not correlated with occurrence frequency, using this heuristic will not be adaptive.

Compare this with the availability heuristic, defined as "the ease with which instances or associates can be brought to mind" (Tversky & Kahneman, 1973, p. 164). This heuristic does not specify, for example, what the ease of bringing something to mind is and how it is evaluated. In addition, within research on heuristics-and-biases, environmental context is typically not considered at all. Instead, content-blind normative yardsticks are applied to judge performance, including the rules of logic or Bayes' theorem.

These distinctions however seem to not convince our alien. Exasperated, it might reply that, if one wants to appreciate eventual differences between the frameworks, one has to first translate them into the same theoretical language. Languages that allow for comparison, so the alien might add, can be found in architectural approaches to cognition—the alien is actually not from distant Mars, but an ACT-R modeler.

Integration Through Architectural Specification

When implementing models of decision making from the fast-and-frugal and heuristics-and-biases frameworks in a detailed quantitative theory like ACT-R, one quickly realizes how much precision both frameworks lack. Notably, even the seemingly precise search, stopping, and decision rules of the fast-and-frugal heuristics framework can turn out to be fairly vague when compared to the demands for model specification imposed by a detailed cognitive theory. For instance, in implementing the fast-and-frugal *recognition heuristic* (Goldstein & Gigerenzer, 2002) into ACT-R, we had to specify, among others, what information is stored in working memory, whether forgetting takes place or not, and whether attribute information is retrieved or not. Overall, we came up with 39 ACT-R implementations of the recognition heuristic (Marewski & Mehlhorn, 2011) and we suspect that there might be several more out there we did not (yet) come up with. When trying to implement vague verbal notions into ACT-R, such as the *availability* heuristic, matters get even worse.

Yet, even if there are multiple implementations of different heuristics, all of those implementations afford making precise quantitative predictions about behavior. For example, in a two-alternative choice task, an ACT-R model would be able to predict how different pieces of information will be acquired and processed to derive a decision, precisely specifying at what point in time what cognitive processes occur in parallel and when they do not. Since ACT-R's different modules are mapped onto brain regions, model predictions would not only include the temporal and spatial dynamics of eye movements or hand movements but also the associated patterns of activity in the brain, as measured in functional magnetic resonance imaging (fMRI) or electroencephalography (EEG) studies. Such detailed predictions, in turn, afford strong model tests and, along the way, further theory refinement. Needless to say, comparing the ACT-R implementations of several heuristics actually makes it possible to precisely carve out where those heuristics might differ and where their assumptions might overlap.

Likewise, in implementing fast-and-frugal heuristics and their counterparts from the heuristics-and-biases literature into ACT-R, both frameworks can be placed on equal footing with respect to how heuristic and other reasoning processes interact with task environments. This is because ACT-R makes precise assumptions about how the different modules' activities are shaped by the environment.

Finally, with ACT-R it is also possible to evaluate and improve human performance, for instance, by first modeling what mistakes humans typically make when tackling a given task, and by subsequently modeling how (a) changes in the task structure (e.g., changes in the instructions) can help humans make better decisions or how (b) teaching humans different problem-solving strategies can do the same job.

Cognitive Architectures Are Rarely Used in Judgment and Decision Making Research, and Less So in Risk Taking

With some exceptions (e.g., Dougherty, Gettys, & Ogden, 1999; Fechner et al., 2016; Marewski & Schooler, 2011; Nellen, 2003; Schooler & Hertwig, 2005; Thomas, Dougherty, Sprenger, & Harbison, 2008; Thomson et al., 2015), architectural frameworks are rarely used in judgment and decision making research. Yet, especially when it comes to understanding risky choice, cognitive architectures might help to both integrate existing theories and to resolve ongoing controversies.

Take, for example, the recent exchange between Brandstätter, Gigerenzer, and Hertwig (2008) on the one hand, and Johnson, Schulte-Mecklenbeck, and Willemsen (2008) on the other. The former authors had proposed a simple algorithmic model of risky choice, called the *priority heuristic* (Brandstätter, Gigerenzer, & Hertwig, 2006; see also Birnbaum, Chap. 8). To illustrate how this heuristic works, imagine that you are faced with two gambles. Gamble A pays \$150 with a probability of 0.75 and \$200 with a probability of 0.25. With gamble B on the other hand, you can earn \$250 with a probability of 0.20 and \$140 with a probability of 0.80. Which one would you choose?

The priority heuristic describes the process that people follow when they make choices between such gambles. It is a lexicographic heuristic, because it postulates that people consider *sequentially* the reasons to choose one gamble over another. Specifically, it considers reasons in the following order: the minimum gain of the gambles, the probability of the minimum gain, and the maximum gain. Upon considering each reason, this heuristic can stop and choose a gamble and ignore all further information, if a reason, such as the minimum gain, sufficiently favors one gamble over the other. To illustrate this process, let us consider the gamble just mentioned. In making a choice on this gamble, the heuristic will first compare the minimum gains: \$150 for gamble A and \$140 for gamble B. Because their difference (\$150 – \$140 = \$10) is less than the psychological threshold postulated by this heuristic (0.1 × higher minimum gain of \$150 = \$15), the priority heuristic will move to the next reason and compare the probability of the minimum gain. The difference between the probabilities of the minimum gains (0.25 – 0.20 = 0.05) is smaller than the postulated threshold of 0.1, which compels the priority heuristic to compare the maximum gains (\$200 vs. \$250). It then chooses gamble B, because it has the higher maximum gain.

Johnson et al. (2008) set out to test experimentally how far the priority heuristic's predictions about decision processes were in line with actual human behavior. To test such process predictions, one needs to acquire data about the decision steps with a *process tracing* tool. To this end, they used a web browser implementation of a well-known process tracing tool, *MouselabWEB* (Willemsen & Johnson, 2016). MouselabWEB tracks the mouse cursor during a psychological experiment to infer the sequence of information acquisition steps. In the corresponding experiment, they showed subjects 16 different gambles. At the beginning of each trial, all information about the gambles was hidden. In order to uncover each gamble's payoffs and payoff probabilities, participants needed to click on boxes, which contained that information. Each trial consisted of multiple such clicks, through which participants acquired information about the gambles while making their mind up about which one they should choose. For all trials, the gambles chosen as well as acquisition times and search patterns were recorded. Two quantities were used to specify the search patterns: the amount of attention paid to various pieces of information and the probability to shift attention from one piece of information to another, called *transition probability*. In the aforementioned example, a naïve interpretation of the priority heuristic will predict equal attention to all three pieces of information considered and a transition between minimum gains and probabilities of minimum gain, followed by a transition between probabilities of minimum gain and maximum gains.

In testing whether those behavioral data are in line with the predictions made by the priority heuristic, Johnson et al. (2008) did not consider, for example, working and long-term memory limitations and theories of visual attention shift. Their results demonstrated that people would sometimes acquire information not required by the priority heuristic, which resulted in a more even distribution of attention and transition probabilities across payoff and probabilities than predicted by the heuristic. As a result, they concluded that participants' information acquisition patterns did not match well the priority heuristic's predictions.

Unsurprisingly, Brandstätter et al. (2008) replied that predicting the exact value of the probability of transitioning from attending one piece of information (e.g., payoff value) to attending another piece of information (e.g., payoff probability) is very sensitive to various information acquisition assumptions that one makes. For example, one can assume that a subject reads all information once prior to initiating the decision process, which would lead to different transition probabilities than if one assumes that the decision process is immediately initiated, or that some pieces of information are read multiple times prior to deciding. One can eliminate such auxiliary assumptions, or at least reduce them in number, by implementing the model in a cognitive architecture. If both groups of authors had implemented the priority heuristic into an architectural theory such as ACT-R, it would have been possible to derive precise quantitative predictions about information search patterns and reading times as influenced by working memory limitations and visual and memory dynamics, this way aiding to more conclusively evaluate the priority heuristic's ability to account for human behavior.

An Example of an ACT-R Model of Decision Making

The priority heuristic deals with gambles, in which information about payoffs and payoff probabilities are fully specified and known or knowable. That is, the priority heuristic deals with *decisions under risk*. There is, however, a broader set of problems, for which due to its dynamic nature, complexity, or lack of information, not all details about the problem at hand are fully specified (e.g., the outcome probabilities are not known or knowable; the outcomes are difficult or impossible to express with a single value). Such situations are labeled *decisions under uncertainty* (Hafenbrädl, Waeger, Marewski, & Gigerenzer, 2016). We will use a model of decision under uncertainty to provide a concrete example of how decision models are rendered more precisely with ACT-R. Consider the *take-the-best heuristic* (Gigerenzer & Goldstein, 1996) from the fast-and-frugal heuristic approach—a model that stands in the tradition of Tversky's (1972) elimination-by-aspects and that assumes, like the priority heuristic, simple lexicographic decision processes. Take-the-best describes the process of inferring which of two alternatives (e.g., two pesticides) scores higher on a criterion (e.g., health risk) based on those alternatives' attributes (e.g., the pesticides' chemical composition, the way the pesticides have to be applied, the minimum duration of treatment, the pesticides' potential of interaction with other chemicals, etc.). Take-the-best uses those attributes as *cues* and considers them sequentially in order of their predictive value (i.e., the cues' *validity*) for inferring the criterion. The heuristic makes a decision as soon as the two alternatives have different values on a cue (e.g., one pesticide requires fewer applications than another).

Figure 9.1 demonstrates how different cognitive capacities, as modeled with ACT-R, interact to produce a complete model of the various cognitive processes that

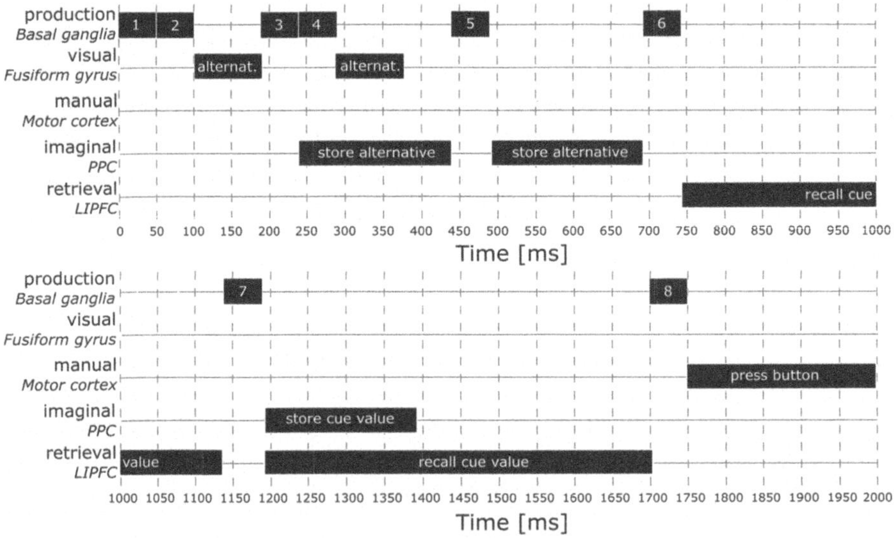

Fig. 9.1 A process trace of an ACT-R model of take-the-best for a trial, on which take-the-best makes a decision on the first cue. This model provides an example of how complex a simple heuristic, like take-the-best, can be if one considers all cognitive processes that underlie its execution (for ACT-R implementations of take-the-best, see Dimov, Marewski, & Schooler, 2013; Nellen, 2003). Moreover, it hints at the large number of potential interactions between the various cognitive processes, which could lead to predictions, which are unexpected if one only considers the process of interest in isolation. Note that ACT-R operates stochastically. This figure offers one possible outcome, among many, of a single run of the model. Furthermore, note that across different trials (e.g., involving more cues), the same model can make different predictions about the temporal dynamics of cognitive processes. *LIPFC* lateral inferior prefrontal cortex, *PPC* posterior parietal cortex

might come with relying on this heuristic. Specifically, the ACT-R model mimics the sequence of processes that a participant using take-the-best would follow in a two-alternative choice experiment. In the experiment the participant is seated in front of a computer display, presented with two alternatives on the screen and required to respond by pressing a key on the keyboard. The entire decision process on this simulated decision trial lasts for 2 s (the time, in milliseconds, is presented on the x-axis). The decision process is decomposed into cognitive components relevant for this task, including what area of the brain might be active (y-axis). In this specific model, five modules coordinate to produce behavior: The visual and manual modules interact with the world, the imaginal module holds task-relevant information, such as the current attribute under consideration, while the retrieval module retrieves information from long-term memory. The procedural module coordinates the operation of the other modules.

The model starts by looking at the screen and encoding the alternatives. Specifically, production 1 sends a command to the visual system to shift attention to an alternative on the screen, while production 2 tells the visual system to encode (i.e., read) that alternative. Once the alternative's name has been read, it is stored in the imaginal buffer by production 3, which also shifts attention to the second alternative. Production 4 then commands the visual system to encode the second alternative. In the meantime, the imaginal buffer is storing the first alternative's name. The process continues with sequential recall of cue values of the two alternatives for the cue currently considered and completes when production 8 commits to a choice by sending a command to the manual module to press the key on the keyboard, which chooses an alternative.

Take-the-best is just one model of how people make decisions. Yet, also many other decisional processes have been modeled with ACT-R. For example, ACT-R models incorporating *instance-based learning mechanisms* (Gonzalez, Lerch, & Lebiere, 2003) have successfully explained learning behavior in binary choice tasks (Lejarraga, Dutt, & Gonzalez, 2012). Moreover, some have used ACT-R to model behavior in strategic games, such as in a version of the *Prisoner's Dilemma* (Juvina, Lebiere, Martin, & Gonzalez, 2011; Juvina, Lebiere, & Gonzalez, 2015), while others have modeled subjects' beliefs in repeated games (Spiliopoulos, 2013). Implementing models, like the priority heuristic, the *most-likely heuristic* (Brandstätter et al., 2006, p. 417) and others will be beneficial when testing the empirical validity of and comparing the theoretical assumptions behind models of risky choice.

Principled Approaches to Model Development and Testing

Why are cognitive architectures still relatively rarely used in judgment and decision making research? Part of the problem might be that working with ACT-R and similarly complex computational theories comes with important entry-level barriers, requiring end users to understand the workings of the architecture, to possess advanced programming skills, and to become familiar with the theoretical language (and jargon) that comes with ACT-R. Another part of the problem is that ACT-R and similar architectures are sometimes thought of as being overly complex and able to account for all kinds of data (see e.g., Pohl, 2011). Yet, this view might be misguided—for at least two reasons.

First, working with ACT-R forces researchers to clearly spell out their assumptions as well as to work with existing ones. At the same time, in implementing models in ACT-R, researchers are, ideally, not free to change the basic architectural structure. Instead they have to work with and from what is already there—else their model might actually not run at all. This helps to reduce arbitrariness in model specification.

Second, careful ACT-R research comes with a series of principles for model development and testing. These include the stratagem of *nested*, *competitive*, *predictive*, and *distributional modeling* (see, e.g., Marewski & Mehlhorn, 2011).

Nested modeling (see Grainger & Jacobs, 1996; Jacobs & Grainger, 1994) refers to the principle that new models ought to be related to their respective precursors, for instance, by including them as a special case. New models ought to also be tested for their ability to account for the same data those older models were already able to account for (Grainger & Jacobs, 1996; Jacobs & Grainger, 1994).

Competitive modeling refers to the principle that models ought to be tested comparatively, against each other, rather than in isolation (e.g., Fum, Del Missier, & Stocco, 2007; Gigerenzer & Brighton, 2009). In comparative model tests, a model's ability to account for human data is evaluated against that of other models, enabling researchers to gauge model performance.

The principle of constrained modeling has been advocated by various architectural theorists (e.g., Anderson, 2007). Newell (1990), for instance, argued that models ought to be developed on different experiments and different experimental tasks. To illustrate the point, eventual "reading components" in the priority heuristic might be calibrated to data from one experiment and those parameters then carried over into attempts to model human choices in a different task in a new experiment. This way, different aspects of a model are, literally, constrained by separate data sets.

In the cognitive sciences, many have argued that a model's ability to *predict* new data (rather than to *fit* existing data) is one important standard by which models ought to be evaluated (e.g., Marewski & Olsson, 2009; Pitt, Myung, & Zhang, 2002; Roberts & Pashler, 2000). That is, models should be evaluated on new samples of data, with all components of the model, including its free parameters, previously having been fixed on (i.e., *calibrated* to) other samples. This way, the model parameters and structures cannot adjust to the data set on which the model is actually tested, and well-known methodological problems (e.g., overfitting) can be addressed. Cross-validation is one canon of methods to test a model's ability to predict new data; others include, for example, the *generalization criterion method* (Busemeyer & Wang, 2000).

The principle of distributional modeling, in turn, prescribes testing a model's ability to actually predict distributional data, rather than mere measures of central tendency. For instance, rather than merely testing how well a model predicts medians of reaction times as behavioral measure, one ought to test in how far the model is capable of accounting for the underlying response time distribution (e.g., Ratcliff & Smith, 2004).

In short, when used in conjunction, those and related methodological principles can help to design strong tests of architectural—and any other model for that matter—implementations of theories. Strong tests, in turn, can help resolve existing controversies, and, in doing so, aid theory integration.

Conclusion

People change their toothbrushes (hopefully) every few weeks. But what leads scientists to adopt new theories? Obviously, getting—in the first place—exposure to those novel ideas is important. Moreover, those new ideas must be understandable—ideas that are packed into jargon and/or that are too distant from one's own specialty are harder to appreciate. We hope that those paragraphs, written in plain and general terms, will be of use to those readers whose specialty is one or the other facet of "risk" and who have not yet been exposed to architectural approaches to human behavior and cognition.

Acknowledgments This chapter is embedded into Swiss National Science Foundation grant 100014_146702, on which also part of the chapter's write-up is based. We would like to thank Piotr Patrzyk for many helpful comments.

References

Anderson, J. R. (2007). *How can the human mind occur in the physical universe?* New York: Oxford University Press.

Anderson, J. R., Bothell, D., Byrne, M. D., Douglass, S., Lebiere, C., & Qin, Y. (2004). An integrated theory of the mind. *Psychological Review, 111*, 1036–1060.

Anderson, J. R., & Schooler, L. J. (1991). Reflections of the environment in memory. *Psychological Science, 2*, 396–408.

Brandstätter, E., Gigerenzer, G., & Hertwig, R. (2006). The priority heuristic: Making choices without trade-offs. *Psychological Review, 113*, 409–432.

Brandstätter, E., Gigerenzer, G., & Hertwig, R. (2008). Risky choice with heuristics: Reply to Birnbaum (2008), Johnson, Schulte-Mecklenbeck, and Willemsen (2008), and Rieger and Wang (2008). *Psychological Review, 115*, 281–289.

Busemeyer, J. R., & Wang, Y. M. (2000). Model comparisons and model selections based on generalization criterion methodology. *Journal of Mathematical Psychology, 44*, 171–189.

Conte, R., Andrighetto, G., & Campennl, M. (Eds.). (2013). *Minding norms: Mechanisms and dynamics of social order in agent societies*. Oxford: Oxford University Press.

Dancy, C. L., Ritter, F. E., Berry, K. A., & Klein, L. C. (2015). Using a cognitive architecture with a physiological substrate to represent effects of a psychological stressor on cognition. *Computational and Mathematical Organization Theory, 21*, 90–114.

Dimov, C. M., Marewski, J. N., & Schooler, L. J. (2013). Constraining ACT-R models of decision strategies: An experimental paradigm. In M. Knauff, M. Pauen, N. Sebanz, & I. Wachsmuth

(Eds.), *Proceedings of the 35th annual conference of the Cognitive Science Society* (pp. 2201–2206). Austin, TX: Cognitive Science Society.

Dougherty, M. R., Gettys, C. F., & Ogden, E. E. (1999). MINERVA-DM: A memory processes model for judgments of likelihood. *Psychological Review, 106*, 180–209.

Fechner, H. B., Pachur, T., Schooler, L. J., Mehlhorn, K., Battal, C., Volz, K. G., & Borst, J. P. (2016). Strategies for memory-based decision making: Modeling behavioral and neural signatures within a cognitive architecture. *Cognition, 157*, 77–99.

Fum, D., Del Missier, F., & Stocco, A. (2007). The cognitive modeling of human behavior: Why a model is (sometimes) better than 10,000 words. *Cognitive Systems Research, 8*, 135–142.

Gigerenzer, G. (1996). On narrow norms and vague heuristics: A reply to Kahneman and Tversky. *Psychological Review, 103*, 592–596.

Gigerenzer, G., & Brighton, H. (2009). Homo heuristicus: Why biased minds make better inferences. *Topics in Cognitive Science, 1*, 107–143.

Gigerenzer, G., & Goldstein, D. G. (1996). Reasoning the fast and frugal way: Models of bounded rationality. *Psychological Review, 103*, 650–669.

Gigerenzer, G., Todd, P. M., & The ABC Research Group. (1999). *Simple heuristics that make us smart*. New York: Oxford University Press.

Goldstein, D. G., & Gigerenzer, G. (2002). Models of ecological rationality: The recognition heuristic. *Psychological Review, 109*, 75–90.

Grainger, J., & Jacobs, A. M. (1996). Orthographic processing in visual word recognition: A multiple read-out model. *Psychological Review, 103*, 518–565.

Hafenbrädl, S., Waeger, D., Marewski, J. N., & Gigerenzer, G. (2016). Applied decision making with fast-and-frugal heuristics. *Journal of Applied Research in Memory and Cognition, 5*, 215–231.

Hester, R. L., Brown, A. J., Husband, L., Iliescu, R., Pruett, D., Summers, R., et al. (2011). HumMod: A modeling environment for the simulation of integrative human physiology. *Frontiers in Physiology, 2*, 1–12.

Jacobs, A. M., & Grainger, J. (1994). Models of visual word recognition: Sampling the state of the art. *Journal of Experimental Psychology: Human Perception and Performance, 20*, 1311–1334.

Johnson, E. J., Schulte-Mecklenbeck, M., & Willemsen, M. C. (2008). Process models deserve process data: Comment on Brandstätter, Gigerenzer, and Hertwig (2006). *Psychological Review, 115*, 263–272.

Juvina, I., Lebiere, C., Martin, J. M., & Gonzalez, C. (2011). Intergroup prisoner's dilemma with intragroup power dynamics. *Games, 2*, 21–51.

Juvina, I., Lebiere, C., & Gonzalez, C. (2015). Modeling trust dynamics in strategic interaction. *Journal of Applied Research in Memory and Cognition, 4*, 197–211.

Koedinger, K. R., Anderson, J. R., Hadley, W. H., & Mark, M. (1997). Intelligent tutoring goes to school in the big city. *International Journal of Artificial Intelligence in Education, 8*, 30–43.

Laird, J. E. (2012). *The soar cognitive architecture*. Cambridge, MA: MIT Press.

Lejarraga, T., Dutt, V., & Gonzalez, C. (2012). Instance-based learning: A general model of repeated binary choice. *Journal of Behavioral Decision Making, 25*, 143–153.

Marewski, J. N., Gaissmaier, W., & Gigerenzer, G. (2010a). Good judgments do not require complex cognition. *Cognitive Processing, 11*, 103–121.

Marewski, J. N., Gaissmaier, W., & Gigerenzer, G. (2010b). We favor formal models of heuristics rather than lists of loose dichotomies: A reply to Evans and Over. *Cognitive Processing, 11*, 177–179.

Marewski, J. N., & Mehlhorn, K. (2011). Using the ACT-R architecture to specify 39 quantitative process models of decision making. *Judgment and Decision making, 6*, 439–519.

Marewski, J. N., & Olsson, H. (2009). Beyond the null ritual: Formal modeling of psychological processes. *Zeitschrift für Psychologie/Journal of Psychology, 217*, 49–60.

Marewski, J. N., & Schooler, L. J. (2011). Cognitive niches: An ecological model of strategy selection. *Psychological Review, 118*, 393–437.

Marewski, J. N., Schooler, L. J., & Gigerenzer, G. (2010). Five principles for studying people's use of heuristics. *Acta Psychologica Sinica, 42*, 72–87.

Marinier, R. P., Laird, J. E., & Lewis, R. L. (2009). A computational unification of cognitive behavior and emotion. *Cognitive Systems Research, 10*, 48–69.

Mellers, B., Hertwig, R., & Kahneman, D. (2001). Do frequency representations eliminate conjunction effects? An exercise in adversarial collaboration. *Psychological Science, 12*, 269–275.

Meyer, D. E., & Kieras, D. E. (1997). A computational theory of executive cognitive processes and multiple-task performance: Part I. Basic mechanisms. *Psychological Review, 104*, 3–65.

Mischel, W. (2008). The toothbrush problem. *Observer*. Retrieved December 09, 2016, from http://www.psychologicalscience.org/observer/the-toothbrush-problem

Nellen, S. (2003). The use of the "take-the-best" heuristic under different conditions, modeled with ACT-R. In F. Detje, D. Dörner, & H. Schaub (Eds.), *Proceedings of the fifth international conference on cognitive modeling* (pp. 171–176). Bamberg: Universitätsverlag Bamberg.

Newell, A. (1990). *Unified theories of cognition*. Harvard University Press.

Newell, A. (1992). Soar as a unified theory of cognition: Issues and explanations. *Behavioral and Brain Sciences, 15*, 464–492.

Pitt, M. A., Myung, I. J., & Zhang, S. (2002). Toward a method of selecting among computational models of cognition. *Psychological Review, 109*, 472–491.

Pohl, R. F. (2011). On the use of recognition in inferential decision making: An overview of the debate. *Judgment and Decision making, 6*, 423–438.

Ratcliff, R., & Smith, P. L. (2004). A comparison of sequential sampling models for two-choice reaction time. *Psychological Review, 111*, 333–367.

Roberts, S., & Pashler, H. (2000). How persuasive is a good fit? A comment on theory testing. *Psychological Review, 107*, 358–367.

Salvucci, D. D. (2006). Modeling driver behavior in a cognitive architecture. *Human Factors, 48*, 362–380.

Salvucci, D. D., & Taatgen, N. A. (2008). Threaded cognition: An integrated theory of concurrent multitasking. *Psychological Review, 115*, 101–130.

Samuels, R., Stich, S., & Bishop, M. (2002). Ending the rationality wars: How to make disputes about human rationality disappear. In R. Elio (Ed.), *Common sense, reasoning and rationality* (pp. 236–268). New York, NY: Oxford University Press.

Scherer, K. R. (2001). Appraisal considered as a process of multilevel sequential checking. In K. R. Scherer, A. Schorr, & T. Johnstone (Eds.), *Appraisal processes in emotion: Theory, methods, research* (pp. 92–120). New York and Oxford: Oxford University Press.

Schneider, D. W., & Anderson, J. R. (2012). Modeling fan effects on the time course of associative recognition. *Cognitive Psychology, 64*, 127–160.

Schooler, L. J., & Hertwig, R. (2005). How forgetting aids heuristic inference. *Psychological Review, 112*, 610–628.

Spiliopoulos, L. (2013). Beyond fictitious play beliefs: Incorporating pattern recognition and similarity matching. *Games and Economic Behavior, 81*, 69–85.

Taatgen, N. A., Van Rijn, H., & Anderson, J. (2007). An integrated theory of prospective time interval estimation: The role of cognition, attention, and learning. *Psychological Review, 114*, 577–598.

Thomas, R. P., Dougherty, M. R., Sprenger, A. M., & Harbison, J. (2008). Diagnostic hypothesis generation and human judgment. *Psychological Review, 115*, 155–185.

Thomson, R., Lebiere, C., Anderson, J. R., & Staszewski, J. (2015). A general instance-based learning framework for studying intuitive decision making in a cognitive architecture. *Journal of Applied Research in Memory and Cognition, 4*, 180–190.

Todd, P. M., & Gigerenzer, G. (2007). Environments that make us smart: Ecological rationality. *Current Directions in Psychological Science, 16*, 167–171.

Tversky, A. (1972). Elimination by aspects: A theory of choice. *Psychological Review, 79*, 281–299.

Tversky, A., & Kahneman, D. (1973). Availability: A heuristic for judging frequency and probability. *Cognitive Psychology, 5*, 207–232.

Tversky, A., & Kahneman, D. (1974). Judgment under uncertainty: Heuristics and biases. *Science, 185*, 1124–1131.

Willemsen, M. C., & Johnson, E. J. (2016). *MouselabWEB: Monitoring information acquisition processes on the Web*. Retrieved December 7th, 2016, from http://www.mouselabweb.org/

Byrne, M. D., & Anderson, J. R. (2001). Serial modules in parallel: The psychological refractory period and perfect time-sharing. Psychological Review, 108, 847-869.

Gonzalez, C., Lerch, J. F., & Lebiere, C. (2003). Instance-based learning in dynamic decision making. Cognitive Science, 27, 591-635.

Chapter 10
Risk Culture: An Alternative Approach to Handling Risks

Bernhard Streicher, Eric Eller, and Sonja Zimmermann

Abstract This chapter consists of two parts: the first part describes existing approaches to handling risk and uncertainty and points out their limitations, whereas the second part introduces a model for risk culture, which aims to overcome these limitations and integrates different lines of research. In more detail, the first part starts with a description of risk management, which is built on the ideas of the Age of Enlightenment, and centers rationality as the main principle of decision making. This description is followed by fast-and-frugal decision trees, which aim to reduce the complexity of dealing with risks to simple guidelines and, thereby, enable fast decision making in resource-restricted situations. Finally, as a third existing approach to handling risk, we discuss intuition, which builds on the competence of experts. Whereas all three approaches have their practical usefulness, they also have limitations. None of these approaches are capable of handling every kind of risk ranging from daily situations to calculable and predictable risk and emerging uncertainty. Therefore, we argue in favor of a more holistic view in the second part of the chapter: risk culture can be understood as the way people handle risks in a specific social context. It is essential to understand the relevant factors of risk culture and their interactions in order to enhance risk competence. We introduce a model of risk culture that contains different levels of accessibility ranging from formal structures, like documented risk management procedures, over trusted rules of thumb for decision making, to basic assumptions like implicit beliefs or shared experiences in handling risks. Furthermore, the model considers relevant factors for the dimensions of individuals, social interactions, and organizational structures. We demonstrate how the model can be used as an integrative framework for existing risk research and sketch an avenue for future research, in particular, for the development of a measurement, and for the practical application of risk culture.

B. Streicher (✉) · S. Zimmermann
Institute of Psychology, UMIT - Private University for Health Sciences, Medical Informatics and Technology, Hall in Tyrol, Austria
e-mail: bernhard.streicher@umit.at

E. Eller
Department of Psychology, Ludwig-Maximilian University Munich, Munich, Germany

M. Raue et al. (eds.), *Psychological Perspectives on Risk and Risk Analysis*,
https://doi.org/10.1007/978-3-319-92478-6_10

Introduction

People and organizations have to continuously make decisions. On one hand, many of these decisions are easy because they have no negative outcomes, their outcomes are predictable, or the decisions are reversible. Deciding which bread to buy for breakfast or whether to take rain protection on a short stroll on a cloudy day accounts for easy decisions. On the other hand, some decisions are difficult: important information is sketchy or lacking, outcomes are unpredictable, situations are highly complex, interactions between relevant factors are unknown or incalculable, decisions are irreversible, or negative outcomes are likely or are potentially severe. One example of such a decision is arranging the equipment and supply for a long expedition in an extremely remote area like a polar region. This decision describes a situation where agents face risk or uncertainty. The term risk refers to a known distribution of negative outcomes, although this is not true in the case of uncertainty (Knight, 1921). Accordingly, research has linked risk with well-known, accessible, or objective probabilities and uncertainty with unknown, unobtainable, or subjective probabilities (Gigerenzer, 2002; Knight, 1921; Leroy & Singell, 1987). There is often a continuous transition between risk and uncertainty (Gigerenzer, 2002) depending on knowledge, information, time, or level of perspective (Tannert, Elvers, & Jandrig, 2007). For example, whether a new virus has a pandemic potential is highly uncertain as long as information is sketchy. During the course of the spread of infections, the virus' means of transmission and its harm are better understood, and, accordingly, the risks become more predictable. The same is true for many economic dynamics like trends in markets, development and impact of new technologies, or changes in regulations and market conditions. To give a final example, from a general perspective, the risk of getting injured or dying in a traffic accident within 1 year is very well known, e.g., it was 1 out of 200 for German citizens in 2016 (Destatis, 2017). However, the risk of such an event for a specific individual is uncertain and depends on a complex interaction of individual behavior, behavior of other road users, weather and road conditions, and the like. Overall, individuals and organizations use different strategies in order to cope with risk and uncertainty. The general principles of these strategies can be applied to both risk and uncertainty (Wu & Gonzalez, 1999; Wu, Zhang, & Gonzalez, 2007). Therefore, we use the term risk when referring to both risky and uncertain situations.

Prominent strategies for dealing with risk include (1) rational risk management approaches, (2) simplified decision making strategies that are based on very few indicators (labeled fast-and-frugal decision trees), and (3) intuition. All of these approaches have their benefits but also their limitations. One important limitation stems from so-called human factors, i.e., people sometimes astray from rational decision making for different reasons. For example, human factors played a major role in the catastrophic nuclear power plant accident in Chernobyl in 1986. After having a close look at the causes of the accident, experts revealed severe negligence at every level of the risk management process (Van der Pligt & Midden, 1990). Human failure was identified as one of the most important factors. In particular, the combination of closed-mindedness, biased information search, and time pressure, in addition to a strict hierarchical structure of chain of command within the team in charge, resulted in having less qualified (but hierarchically high-ranking) persons making fatal decisions. The example of the Chernobyl disaster, the aftermath of which is still causing serious health-related, societal, environmental, and economic problems, highlights the potential for tremendously negative outcomes from poor decision making, as well as the necessity for reliable and applicable models for understanding human decision making under risk, the limitations of rational risk management procedures in highly complex and uncertain situations, the sometimes misleading influences of formal and informal structures (e.g., hierarchy), and human factors (e.g., biased information search).

In order to handle risks reasonably, it is desirable to fully understand the respective preconditions and outcomes. However, as illustrated by the Chernobyl example, it is very often impossible to gain full knowledge, to receive all relevant information, or to take a lot of time before making a decision. Furthermore, the options of actions decrease as time elapses, and, in turn, the occurrence of a potentially negative event becomes more likely. The Chernobyl disaster could have been prevented, but options decreased as the start of a nuclear meltdown approached. With the onset of the meltdown, it was no longer possible to take preventive actions. At this point, the occurrence of the event was unavoidable and, therefore, became a certainty. In general, in the face of uncertainty, it is essential to make high-quality decisions without perfect knowledge or predictability. On the long run, the success of people, organizations, and social and political systems depends on making good decisions in the face of risk and uncertainty.

This chapter consists of two parts: the first part starts with an overview of three prominent approaches on handling risk and uncertainty including risk management, fast-and-frugal decision trees, and intuition. We analyze these approaches, point out their limitations, and discuss both the theoretical and practical need for an alternative approach to handling risk. In the second part of the chapter, we make a suggestion for an integrative and more holistic approach: we introduce a new model for risk culture.

In principle, risk culture refers to how people handle risks in a specific social context such as an organization. Risk culture is shaped by, for example, formal structures including shared expectations, experiences, beliefs, and values, as well as individual states and assumptions. At the same time, the risk culture of a specific social category (i.e., group, organization, society) influences how members of this social group perceive, assess, and handle risk. Accordingly, we argue that risk culture determines how people and organizations respond to risks, and, therefore, it is essential to understand the relevant factors of risk culture and their interactions, in order to enhance risk competence. Our model of risk culture aims to overcome the limitations of existing approaches to handling risk as described in the first part of the chapter. Furthermore, we demonstrate how our model of risk culture is capable of integrating existing research on risk perception, assessment, and decision making. Finally, building on risk culture, we sketch an avenue for future research to support people and organizations in improving the quality of their judgments and decision making in risky and uncertain situations.

Existing Approaches for Handling Risks (Part 1)

Reasoning and Risk Management

During the Age of Enlightenment, thinkers like Francis Bacon, René Descartes, David Hume, Adam Smith, or Immanuel Kant established reason and reasoning as the prime source of information, knowledge, legitimacy, and, therefore, decision making (Berlin, 1984). These ideas include the assumptions that reasons exist beyond mythologies or religions that form and predict the natural world and its phenomena and social constructions; the underlying mechanism and principles can be explored, understood, and formally described; every person is capable of a free and reasonable mind; and, therefore, every person "can dare to know" and has the legitimacy to question the world. Rethinking humans' epistemological potential led to an ongoing explosion of knowledge, invention, innovation, growth, and welfare. In the past, negative events were handled with good faith, sacrifices, or the resignation to a fate. Now potentially negative events could be approached with reasoning and understanding. In many fields, the recognition of underlying principles reduces uncertainty, and risk becomes calculable and manageable. For instance, as long as the underlying kinematics of the planetary system remained unknown, the occurrence of a solar eclipse was uncertain. However, the state of current knowledge allows predictions of its occurrence and calculations of its potential risks (e.g., sudden widespread loss of photovoltaic power and potential collapse of the power grid system). By searching for underlying principles and by replacing belief with reasoning, humans have created a tool to unravel the mystery of the unpredictability of negative events.

With regard to organizations, the ideas of the Age of Enlightenment found their way into the so-called scientific management and idea of rationalization (Taylor, 1911). This concept assumes that organizations and "tasks are designable and controllable in a top-down fashion and that organizational control should therefore be used to identify and eliminate [...] risks" (Weichbrodt, 2015, p. 221). Following this line of thinking, one widespread approach to gain competence in risk is to apply management strategies and tools to risky situations. For example, insurance companies define their risk appetite (i.e., the level of risk that they assess as acceptable) for different kinds of risk scenarios (e.g., a lasting low-interest phase or a US hurricane) and align their business activities (e.g., underwriting, reserving, investments, reinsurance) accordingly. This approach has been widely labeled as *risk management*, which reflects the assumption that risks are measurable, determinable, calculable, and, therefore, manageable in a rational fashion. This does not mean that risks can generally be avoided or prevented (Hope & Sparks, 2000). The goal of risk management is to identify the probability and amount of potential harm and to develop and enforce strategies, which prevent or reduce the harm to an acceptable level. Different models exist that describe the continuous process of risk management (e.g., Ehrengren, 2006; Ehrengren & Hörnsten, 2011; VanVactor, 2007). Most models are circular and comprise consecutive and repeatable steps or stages as displayed in Fig. 10.1.

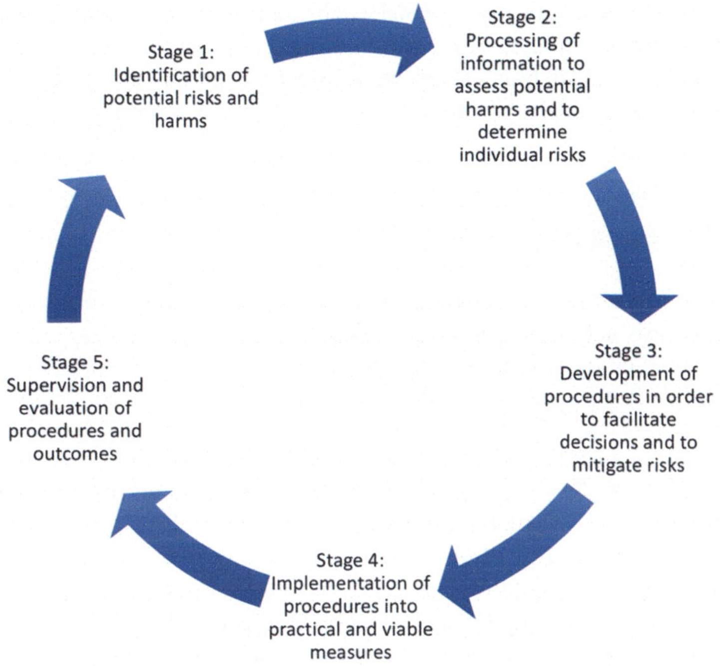

Fig. 10.1 Prototypical sequence of a risk management process

Stage 1: Identification of Risks

A basic element of these models is that potential risks initially need to be identified by compiling relevant information (stage 1). Gathering information on potential risk can be daunting and misleading. For example, one-sided or frequently repeated information spread by social networks or the media tend to skew risk perceptions (Lu, Xie, & Liu, 2015; Moussaïd, Brighton, & Gaissmaier, 2015). Therefore, valid and reliable sources of information are a basic requirement for successful risk assessment. However, uncertainty regarding the quality of information is one of the main problems that may occur during the information gathering process. This can be caused by conflicting information due to different sources, equivocal data, lack of data or valid models, or simply too much information. The collection of ill-defined data may prevent a thorough understanding of the facts and, consequently, hamper decision making (Ruan, Liu, & Carchon, 2003). Therefore, care has to be taken to collect valid and reliable information and to develop models accordingly that contribute to a better understanding of a particular hazard, risk, or situation.

For example, nowadays the use of electronic equipment is paramount, and huge parts of our daily lives, economy, and society depend upon it. Solar winds, which are a stream of high-energy charged particles ejected from the sun, are suspected of causing malfunction of electronic equipment on earth (Odenwald, 2017). In order to calculate the potential risk and harm of solar winds on one's own equipment or on business in general, all relevant information on the issue should be compiled, and latest developments in forecasting solar winds and shielded technology should be monitored. However, reliable information on precisely forecasting the damage of solar winds is not available. Therefore, considering the quality of information is crucial in order to avoid ill-defined models and to avoid the under- or overestimation of risks.

Stage 2: Processing Information

The second step aims at processing the compiled information in order to assess potential hazards and to determine specific risks (stage 2). Negative outcomes are typically classified by likelihood (e.g., *highly unlikely* to *very likely*; *0%* to *100%*; *1:1* to *1:100.000.000*) within a certain time or number of events and by the severity of consequences (e.g., *slight harm* to *possible fatality*, *limited malfunction* to *total system failure*; approximated costs; biasing effects at different scales cf., Lermer, Streicher, Sachs, & Frey, 2013). Accordingly, in the example of solar winds, the next step is to use the available information to calculate the probability of occurrence of specific events (e.g., from partial failure to complete breakdown) and their costs (e.g., from short shutdown of single desktop computers to insolvency). For example, based on past experiences and existing data, one could categorize solar winds by their potential to severely damage and calculate the probability of occurrence for each category. Unfortunately, a severe problem of information processing and risk assessment is the proneness to the biasing influences of human factors. Since this problem is paramount and can cause flawed decision making, the underlying psychological mechanisms and effects are described in more detail below, following the description of the risk management process.

Stages 3 and 4: Development and Implementation of Procedures

After understanding and reviewing risks and their inherent consequences, the third and fourth steps involve development and implementation of effective measures to either eliminate risks or to mitigate the damage potential to an accepted level (stages 3 and 4). The level of acceptance is shaped by individual or organizational resources and strategies, behavior of relevant others like business competitors, legal restrictions, operational standards, societal and cultural understanding, and, last but not least, the general understanding by the involved persons of how risk should be handled. This general understanding of how to deal with risk is shaped by factors such as formal decision making procedures as well as implicit learning experiences and beliefs. Later on in the chapter, we argue that this general understanding is best described by the concept of risk culture, which enables the integration of different approaches to dealing with risks.

One measure for handling risks is the elimination of risks, for example, the extinction of poliomyelitis in central Europe and the United States after the invention of a vaccine. Poliomyelitis was a severe and epidemic disease among children caused by the polio virus. Other measures are prevention (e.g., vaccination), monitoring and controlling (e.g., spread of influenza infections), and the development of standard operating procedures (SOP; e.g., consistent hand disinfection in hospitals) or personal protective equipment (e.g., wearing a surgical mask). In particular, SOPs aim to facilitate decision making in stressful and time-limited situations as well as to avoid pitfalls of routines. One significant pitfall is learned carelessness, which can cause defiance from risk-savvy, good decision making. People tend to develop carelessness when continuously making risky decisions without experiencing negative consequences (Frey, Ullrich, Streicher, Schneider, & Lermer, 2016). SOPs help people maintain good decision making, regardless of their current feelings or mind-sets about the situation, by following an evaluated routine.

In general, risk management includes continuous reevaluation of all measures, specifically their effectiveness, costs, acceptance, and practicability. Applying stages 3 and 4 to the example of hazards of solar storms on electronic equipment could result in the disentanglement of systems, construction of independent subsystems and/or back-up systems, installation of shielded technology, and implementation of a monitoring process for the effectiveness of these measures.

Stage 5: Evaluation of Procedures

Finally, not only should the measures be constantly evaluated but the whole process itself (stage 5). This supervision and evaluation addresses the usefulness of the formal elements (e.g., decision making process, involved persons, monitoring tools, data basis and selection, models), the communication and knowledge of the formal process among members, the appropriate application of these elements, the monitoring of relevant fields (e.g., costs and benefits of new technologies, changing environments, changes in regulations), the effective identification and assessment of risks, as well as the suitability of decision, intervention strategies, and actions. The aim is to optimize the process of risk management and to detect emerging risks, but not necessarily to avoid or to eliminate any risk (Hope & Sparks, 2000). Furthermore, evaluating the process helps to enhance the resilience of the organization by learning from good and poor practice. Overall, practices of risk management ought to be considered in the preparation and execution of any risk-relevant task, in order to make decisions according to the accepted risk level (VanVactor, 2007). In the solar storm example, the evaluation might result in replication of outdated equipment, improvement of protective measures like early warnings, a shift of focus from technology to people, and training their behavior in critical situations.

Standards of Risk Management

The outlined stages of a risk management environment are formalized in norms, in order to both empower organizations to make good decisions in risky environments and set comparable standards for different organizations and businesses. One of the most widely used, and globally accepted, standard is *ISO 31000*, which was first introduced in 2009. Several hundred risk management professionals were involved in finalizing the first version. ISO 31000 contains four main objectives covering the use of vocabulary; a set of performance criteria; one common overarching process for identifying, analyzing, evaluating, and treating risks; and lastly guidance on how that process should be integrated into the decision making processes of any organization (Purdy, 2010). This process is due for review every 5 years. The draft of the latest revised version was circulated for comments before the end of 2017. Accordingly, the new version should be introduced in 2018 (Tranchard, 2017). Another standard, which initially emerged in 2003, is the enterprise risk management (*ERM*), which uses a more holistic approach to the methods and processes in identifying and minimizing risks. ERM is aimed at all companies and businesses regardless of their background (Bromiley, McShane, Nair, & Rustambekov, 2015; Sax & Torp, 2015). As with ISO 31000, the ERM is frequently reviewed and updated according to the latest developments.

Human Factors as Limitations of Risk Management

Although ISO 31000 and ERM are widely used as standard tools to ensure the quality of risk management, the basic ideas of classic risk management face limitations. Handling risks on the basis of reasoning works fine as long as the risks and outcomes are well understood, measurable, and predictable and as long as the decision making processes are either robust or shielded against biasing influences like personal preferences or lack of experience. However, the constraints of this approach stem from human factors as well as from the complexity of some risks.

Human factors comprise psychological aspects of cognitive, emotional, affective, and physical states on a personal and social level (for more details on human factors and biases see also Helm & Reyna, Chap. 4; Tompkins, Bjälkebring & Peters, Chap. 5; Eller & Frey, Chap. 6; and Raue & Scholl, Chap. 7). For example, negative versus positive moods can lead to differences in the perception and assessment of the same risk (Loewenstein, Weber, Hsee, & Welch, 2001), and groups tend to adjust decisions to the opinion of the group member with a higher social status or perceived group norm, even if this decision is irrational and ignores obvious risks (Janis, 1972).

Even if clearly defined rules for decision making exist, people are prone to be influenced by unrelated factors, which leads to biased judgment and decision making. Such biases can stem from various sources such as the influence of emotions and affective reactions in the judgments of risks (Loewenstein, Weber, Hsee, & Welch, 2001; Slovic, Finucane, Peters, & MacGregor, 2004; Slovic & Peters, 2006); bodily states like physical arousal (cf. embodiment; Meier, Schnall, Schwarz, & Bargh, 2012; Raue, Streicher, Lermer, & Frey, 2017); social influences and group dynamics (e.g., Janis, 1982); the negation of base rates and statistical illiteracy (Gigerenzer, 2002); the overestimation of unlikely events and the underestimation of likely events (Kahneman & Tversky, 1972, 1973); framing effects (i.e., loss or gain frames; Kahneman & Tversky, 1972, 1973); self-serving biases (e.g., overconfidence bias: Epley & Gilovich, 2001; Fellner & Krügel, 2012; Tversky & Kahneman, 1983); levels of cognitive representation (Lermer, Streicher, Sachs, Raue, & Frey, 2015; Raue, Streicher, Lermer, & Frey, 2015); affected parties (e.g., self vs. other; Lermer, Streicher, Sachs, & Frey, 2013); or potentially misleading rule of thumbs, which people use to make quick decisions. All these influences contribute to the regular observation that people sometimes remarkably deviate from the economic rational agent model (e.g., Edwards, 1954), especially with regard to risk perception and decision making in complex and risky situations.

Some of the misleading influences are based on poor knowledge. One example of poor statistical knowledge is when people erroneously judge a conjunction of two events as being more likely than one of the events, labeled conjunction fallacy (Tversky & Kahneman, 1982, 1983; see also Raue & Scholl, Chap. 7). In general, the probability of one event is, at least, equal to, or higher than, the probability of this event in combination with another event, regardless of how likely or coherent the combination of the two events seems to be. The effects of conjunction fallacy can be observed in a range of areas including estimations of word frequencies, prognoses in medicine, judgments of personality, or political prognoses (Agnoli & Krantz, 1989; Tversky & Kahneman, 1983). For example, in the 1980s, political experts rated the probability of the single event that the United States would break diplomatic relations with the Soviet Union in the following year as 1%. In contrast, another group of experts rated the combined probability of the Soviet Union invading Poland, and the United States breaking diplomatic relations, as having a 4% probability of occurrence (Tversky & Kahneman, 1983). The latter experts wrongly judged the probability of the occurrence of the two events higher as the probability of just one event. Accordingly, probabilities and outcomes should be assessed separately and not in combination. Applying a short cognitive-orientated training helps people to overcome conjunction fallacy (Streicher, Lermer, Sachs, Schneider, & Frey, 2015).

People are unaware of the influence of the vast majority of misleading heuristics and situational factors. For example, one of the best-known and most replicated biasing heuristic is anchoring (Tversky & Kahneman, 1974). An anchoring bias is defined as the adjustment of an estimate toward an initial value, which usually proves to be unsatisfactory (Englich, 2008). For example, even the intended sentences of experienced legal professionals were influenced by obviously random and irrelevant anchor values such as numbers produced by dices (Englich, Mussweiler, & Strack, 2006). In numerous replications, participants' absolute estimates were influenced in the direction of the primary comparison value (cf. Epley & Gilovich, 2004). Anchoring effects have far reaching impacts, no matter if it concerns general knowledge (Epley & Gilovich, 2001; McElroy & Dowd, 2007; Mussweiler & Englich, 2005; Mussweiler & Strack, 2001a, 2001b), estimates of probability (e.g., Chapman & Johnson, 1999), or court decisions (Englich, Mussweiler, & Strack, 2006). One practical recommendation to avoid anchoring effects on estimations is to avoid the presentation of numbers, such as the outcome of computer models before or during the estimation processes of experts.

Unfortunately, the influences of anchoring and other unconscious judgmental biases are remarkably robust and are difficult to overcome (e.g., Fischhoff, 1982; LeBoeuf & Shafir, 2009; Wilson, Houston, Etling, & Brekke, 1996). Even expertise, motivation, and cognitive capacity do not seem to diminish the effects significantly (Furnham & Boo, 2011; Mussweiler, Strack, & Pfeiffer, 2000). Considering the misleading potential and its possibly destructive effects of the mentioned biasing factors, the question on how to establish high-quality risk assessments becomes even more important.

The impact of psychological effects on risk management can be tremendous. As pointed out, the Chernobyl disaster is one such example. Another example is the wrong decision of RWE, one of the biggest energy suppliers in Germany, to build new gas and coal power plants in 2007. At the time of the decision, the energy market in Germany underwent a radical transformation from conventional electricity generation to using renewable energy sources, which resulted in a declining demand or market for new conventional power plants. Overall, this wrong decision summed up to a ten billion Euro loss. Any investment in an open market contains the risk of a false investment. Therefore, all relevant information and potential chances of success for the investment are to be considered before making a commitment. In the case of RWE, at the time the decision for investment was made, all the relevant information regarding the transformation of the energy market had been freely available and widespread for some years. However, the risk perception of the RWE management was strongly biased in favor of a market remaining stable and business as usual. Apparently, lack of experience, overconfidence in one's abilities, and closed-mindedness caused by a homogenous, non-diverse board of management paved the way to poor risk management (Obmann, 2017).

These examples highlight some of the main limitations of classic risk management with regard to human factors, as well as the importance of recognizing and considering psychological aspects within decision making under risk. Furthermore, the high complexity of many risk situations poses further challenges for risk management.

Fast-and-Frugal Decision Trees

The Problem of Complexity

The complexity of a risk and, accordingly, its inherent uncertainty increase with the number of relevant factors, the number of involved stakeholders, changing or undetermined environments (e.g., new threats, technologies, or market regulations), the amount of relevant data, or the amount of ill-defined or lacking information. One prominent reaction to the complexity of risks within the paradigm of reasoning, such as classic risk management, is to address complexity with complexity: in order to predict risks and make reasonable decisions, the complexity of reality has to be understood and measured. This thinking results in an increasing complexity of models and more extensive risk management standards with a more complex reality. One example of an inflationary increase in complexity of risk management standards is banking supervision and regulation. The first regulations of Basel I (1988–1992) tried to catch the complexity of the financial sector in a manageable 30 pages (main official documents without additional papers; Basel Committee on Banking Supervision, 1988). Fueled by the finance crisis, starting in 2007, the real global complexity of the financial sector became salient. The current Basel III regulation tries to cover and handle this complexity with some 1428 pages of the main official documents and a maze of consultative papers, accompanying documents, and working papers. However, it is highly questionable whether these increases in codes of conducts and regulations from Basel I to Basel III results in a similar increase in the quality and effectiveness of risk management in the financial sector. In this example, it seems like the complexity of risks cannot be addressed satisfactorily by increasing the complexity of models and risk management standards (cf. Aikman et al., 2014).

Models are often used to understand and handle the complexity of the real world. These models simulate and, by doing so, aim to predict reality (e.g., models for extreme weather events, for the predicting interest rates or other market developments like real estate prices). One particular problem when increasing the complexity of models is the so-called overfitting of models (Babyak, 2004). In order to simulate and predict reality, a model needs to have a good fit to reality. However, the amount of explained variance (i.e., how many real outcomes in the past can be predicted with the model) and, accordingly, the fit of a model increase with the number of variables that contribute to the model, regardless of whether the variables are of any real-world relevance or not. Existing data, which represent events in the past, is used for the construction of models for risk prediction. For example, in order to predict the future development of the real estate market in a specific region and, therefore, the risk of a failed investment, it might be reasonable to incorporate existing data such as past interest rates, market developments, degrees of liquidity, employment rates, attractiveness of the area, infrastructure, crime rates, and the like in the model. The more complex the risk, the more variables are incorporated in the model. Furthermore, such complex models usually do not predict past events on first construction, but their *descriptive power* (i.e., how good the model describes past events) is continuously adjusted by different methods (e.g., repeated simulations with varied values and/or different selections of data sets). Such adjustments can force a model to fit existing data and past events. However, a good model fit and a good description of the past do not imply that the model contains all the relevant variables or that irrelevant variables were ignored, nor that the system itself and the mechanisms causing a specific risk are understood, nor that the model has a reasonable good *predictive power* (i.e., how good the model predicts future events). In the worst case, such a so-called overfitted model perfectly explains past events by using irrelevant variables and data. For example, in the ancient world, the prediction of important future events and political decisions were based on the shapes, looks, and arrangements of bones and intestines of sacrificial animals. Unfortunately, in this case, the predictive power of such a model (i.e., sacrificial animals) and, therefore, its quality and usefulness to handle risks would be zero. But, even if the utmost care is taken to select relevant variables and data in order to construct and adjust complex models, the predictive validity remains unknown until the first negative event occurs. Overall, predicting the complexity of the real world and its events by using complex models is limited, which sets, in addition to human factors, another boundary to classic risk management.

Reducing Complexity with Decision Trees

One prominent approach to overcome the confusing complexity of risky situations is to develop and apply simple but successful guidelines for specific actions under specific conditions. This approach can be either used intentionally or unconsciously. The resulting guidelines are called rules of thumbs or heuristics (Gigerenzer & Gaissmaier, 2011). Heuristics can describe *how* a decision is made (i.e., a decision making strategy) or *what* decision to make under specific conditions (i.e., a recommended action) or a combination of both. For example, a heuristic for backcountry skiers, in order to reduce the risk of being caught by an avalanche, combines a strategy (i.e., check the current regional avalanche bulletin) and a recommended action (i.e., only enter slopes of a certain degree depending on the alert level of the bulletin). Without a simple heuristic, predicting avalanches requires the knowledge of the extremely complex interactions of weather impact (snowfall, wind, radiation, etc.), transformation of snow crystals, inhomogeneous stability of snow, steepness of the slopes, exposition of the slope, and more variables. It is impossible for backcountry skiers to accurately measure all of these variables on the spot for a single hillside and make a precise and correct prediction. However, on the basis of avalanche statistics, it is possible to predict the likelihood of avalanches in a specific terrain (i.e., steepness and exposure) under specific conditions. Different alert levels of the avalanche bulletin represent different conditions. This makes it possible for a single person to reduce her/his risk of being caught by an avalanche to an acceptable risk level. The heuristic used in this example is to compare the steepness of a slope before entering it with the alert level of the bulletin. This heuristic produces valid and reliable recommendations for action without the necessity of understanding, measuring, or knowing any of the other relevant variables. Accordingly, heuristics seem to be a promising approach to enhancing the quality of decisions in complex risky situations.

One simple and effective structure of a heuristic follows a binary decision tree, known as fast-and-frugal decision tree (FFT; Martignon, Katsikopoulos, & Woike, 2008; Martignon, Vitouch, Takezawa, & Forster, 2003; for more details see: Raue & Scholl, Chap. 7). Applying the idea of FFT to the example of the avalanche heuristic above, on a first level, one would evaluate whether the steepness of the hillside is within the recommended steepness covered by the current alert level of the avalanche bulletin (see Fig. 10.2 for decision tree). If the evaluation is positive, then on a second level, one would check for any disadvantageous indicators (e.g., poor range of vision, higher snowfall or snowdrift than predicted by the avalanche bulletin). If the second evaluation is positive as well (i.e., no disadvantageous indica-

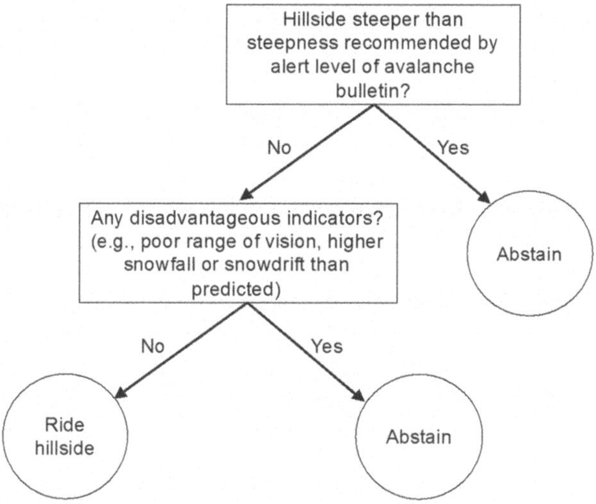

Fig. 10.2 Possible fast-and-frugal tree for the decision to ride a hillside in avalanche terrain

tors exist), one could enter the terrain and ride the hillside. If the evaluation, either at level 1 or level 2, is negative, one should abstain. As the example illustrates, a variable is evaluated on every level using a binary answer format (e.g., *yes* vs. *no*, *negative* vs. *positive*, *true* vs. *false*, *high-risk* vs. *low-risk*). Furthermore, an FFT has at least one exit option at every level. In other words, a final decision can be made at every level of the tree. In order to keep the tree simple and decision making fast, two levels are recommended (Phillips, Neth, Woike, & Gaissmaier, 2017). However, maintaining the binary decision at each level, an FFT can have more than two levels, if more core variables have to be considered.

In everyday life, people often use decision making strategies in risk situations that follow an FFT structure without even being aware of it. For example, if customers buy a product of some value (e.g., a car) or sign a contract with long-term obligations (e.g., life insurance), they often rely on the credibility and competence of a salesperson. However, if a salesperson is unfamiliar to a customer, and if no long-term history of social interactions and satisfying exchanges exist, a customer can't be sure whether she/he will be exploited by the salesperson or benefit from the deal. In order to solve this social dilemma, customers aim to know whether they can trust the salesperson (Streicher, Frey, & Osswald, 2011). In order to judge the trustworthiness of an unfamiliar salesperson, customers might first evaluate whether she/he is friendly or sympathetic (level 1). If the outcome of this evaluation is negative, they might not trust the person and consider refraining from the deal. If they think the salesperson is friendly and sympathetic, they then might evaluate the competence of the salesperson (level 2). If the outcome of the second evaluation is positive as well, customers might judge a salesperson as trustworthy and consider signing a contract. This outlined FFT is a common decision making strategy among laypersons. As a side note, professional salespersons around the globe are unfortunately well aware that customers use this FFT and try to take advantage of it by generating a friendly, sympathetic, and competent impression of themselves.

FFTs are effectively used in many areas of life, such as medicine, law, consumer choice, investments, or social interactions, as either implicit guidelines or explicit rules (e.g., Aikman et al., 2014; Dhami, 2003; Dhami & Ayton, 2001; Gigerenzer & Gaissmaier, 2011; Jenny, Pachur, Williams, Becker, & Margraf, 2013; Luan & Reb, 2017). FFTs are, in particular, successful in highly complex, time-restricted, information-limited, and/or stressful situations, because they focus on very few key variables. Compared to other models, which try to integrate as much information as possible, FFTs ignore potentially available information (Phillips, Neth, Woike, & Gaissmaier, 2017). For example, an FFT for a medical emergency first-aider is to check the pulse and breathing of a casualty. If both evaluations are negative, reanimation measures have to be executed without further examination. This procedure ignores a huge amount of potentially available medical information, and builds on poor diagnoses (e.g., "I'm stressed, my fingers are cold, and I can't feel a pulse right now. So maybe she/he has no heartbeat."), but works perfectly well to save lives in an emergency.

In order to create the underlying algorithm for a new FFT, the core variables for predicting a particular risk have to be identified. Core variables represent essential aspects of a system (e.g., human body, climate, snow, or financial market) and associated risk (e.g., cardiac or circulatory troubles, storms or flooding, avalanches, changes in interest rates, or financial crises). For example, pulse is a core variable for heartbeat and blood circulation; having no pulse indicates the risk of serious cardiac problems. Core variables should be accessible and easy to measure. The identification of core variables requires both a fundamental understanding of the system and a system that is stable. In this context, a system is stable if outcomes are caused by a set of variables and/or by the interaction of the same variables and if the underlying principles remain the same. For example, the blood circulation is propelled by the heartbeat. Without a heartbeat, blood stops circulating. The principles of the human blood circulatory system are stable. Ideally, core variables like pulse can be measured easily. If a core variable is difficult to measure, a work-around is to identify accessible variable(s) that reflects the core variable(s) and that can be used as a substitute. For example, the variables, which predict when the stable structure of a snowfield breaks loose and turns into an avalanche, are very difficult to measure. However, winter sport-related avalanches only occur within a certain spectrum of hillside steepness. Therefore, steepness is one excellent substitute core variable for avalanche risk.

On the one hand, the success of an FFT depends on the understanding of the risk; the better the knowledge, the easier the deduction of an FFT and the more successful is its application. As pointed out above, during the course of avalanche research, it was possible to develop a simple FFT for the individual winter tourist. On the other hand, success of heuristics, in general, depends on the stability of the relevant system. As long as the variables, which determine a system, and their interactions remain stable (e.g., because they are based on the law of physics like in the avalanche forecast example above), simple heuristics can help to solve highly complex situations. If no core variables can be singled out, but many variables predict the risk with similar weight (i.e., these variables are similarly important), other models will make better predictions (e.g., machine learning based on logistic regression models; for a detailed description and discussion, see Phillips, Neth, Woike, & Gaissmaier, 2017). For example, climate and, as a result, extreme weather events are the outcomes of many variables with similar importance and their highly complex interactions. Regarding the climate system, single core variables, which could be used for prediction and FFTs, do not exist. Moreover, FFTs are not helpful in detecting early signals of an unknown, but upcoming, risk, or if the underlying principles and, therefore, the core variables change, or in predicting or preventing rare events. For example, the crash of the US real estate market and the following global financial crisis were, for a long time, an unknown risk. However, early signals of the crisis, like unfunded speculations or unclear transfer of risks from one market segment to another market segment (e.g., shifting and hiding risks from the real estate market to unrelated financial products), indicated the possibility of an upcoming crisis. In this case, an example of a significant change in underlying principles and core variables would be a change in legal regulations from a ban of transfer of risks to the allowance of such transfers. Overall, a shift of relevance of variables, the occurrence of unknown variables, an unknown or ill-defined interaction of variables, or a significant shift in complexity can all jeopardize the success of an FFT.

Risky situations with shifting variables are typically based on changing environments like the predictions of markets, the prediction of the life-cycle of products, or the vulnerability of supply chains and grids. For the RWE case discussed above, it can be assumed that the RWE management used some kind of heuristic, which worked very well in the past, but had a bad fit for the changes in the energy market. This comes with some speculation, but the heuristic might have assumed that the major players in the energy market in Germany would remain the same and that the increasing demands on energy are best addressed by building new big, conventional power plants. Even if an elaborated FFT fits well, good decision making is not a given. For example, every winter, dozens of backcountry tourists are trapped by avalanches despite the fact that they knew how to apply the above described FFT were aware of the alert level of the bulletin and knew how to measure the steepness of a slope, but—again—human factors seem to hinder people applying the FFT and following its recommendation (e.g., Arbeitsgemeinschaft österreichischer Lawinenwarndienste, 2015). Both examples highlight again the potentially biasing influence of human factors. Therefore, it can be concluded that FFTs can be useful, but that their successful application is limited due to features of the risk itself and/or human factors. Therefore, the question as to how to ensure good decision making in risky, complex, and changing situations remains unanswered.

Intuition

One further solution to the problem of good decision making in risky situations is to rely on the judgment of experts. In complex risky situations, experts typically build their judgment on intuition. Intuition refers to a fast and automatic process of thinking and is based on prior knowledge and experience in the field of interest (Kahneman, 2011; Plessner, Betsch, & Betsch, 2008). The process of intuitive decision making comprises an automatic, unaware perception and processing of relevant information. Contrary to heuristics, the intuitive decision making process can include but is not limited to the consideration of a reduced amount of information (e.g., just two core variables) or to a decision making rule (e.g., FFT). Generally speaking, compared to heuristics intuition is a more holistic and spontaneous process that leads to some sort of affective state—so-called gut feelings. Intuitive judgments and decisions are based on this affective state. For example, experienced drivers intuitively identify risky traffic situations. If traffic on a highway is dense and it starts to rain, experienced drivers feel awkward, and they adjust their driving accordingly by lowering speed and keeping their distance, without the need to intentionally search for relevant information and consciously assess the riskiness of the situation. The validity and reliability of an expert's intuition depend on her/his expertise. People acquire expertise when they experience a learning history in the field of interest with feedback on their (mis)judgments. During the learning history, the process of recognizing the specific features of a situation, and assessing relevant factors, becomes automatic. This implies that experts are only experts if relevant information is accessible or transferable from similar fields of interest, if the field of interest has some degree of statistical regularity and predictability, and outcomes are not random. Thus, the two basic preconditions of valid intuitive judgments are high context stability and high learning experience in the regularities of the respective context. For example, experts can have remarkably valid intuitions in stable (learning) environments such as in playing chess. Since every chess game follows the same rules, the learning history of master chess players is highly valid for the identification of promising moves in future chess games. However, in changing environments, or in the context of new risks, the learning history of experts can lack relevance and validity and thus lead to biased judgments and decisions (Kahneman & Klein, 2009).

On the upside, experts can enhance the quality of decision making in complex risky situations. On the downside, experts are—again—also prone to biasing influences, which can lead to biased decision making. Whether a specific expert's intuitions are valid for a specific problem requires a detailed analysis of both the expert's learning experience and of the decision context and is often only reliably determinable in hindsight. In particular, the self-evaluation of potential experts and non-experts does not seem to be a reliable predictor for good intuitions. Therefore, the questions remain as to how to reduce the unwanted influences of human factors, how to enhance the quality of decisions in complex risky situations, and how to make people and organizations risk savvy.

Risk Culture (Part 2)

In the aftermath of the 2008 financial crisis, an increasing demand for improved models, other than classic risk management, for successfully dealing with uncertainty and complex risks emerged. Nowadays, this demand not only stems from the finance and insurance industry but from society in general, as well as organizations operating in a complex and uncertain context. Accordingly, organizations recognized the contribution of social psychological insights on risk perception, risk judgment, risk behavior, and potential pitfalls. However, transferring academic results on the issue into effective and reliable practice is far from being trivial. For example, countless studies demonstrated an anchoring bias, but there is no reliable measure on how to prevent or avoid this effect in daily life. In our opinion, one major obstacle in this endeavor is the lack of an integrative model of psychological risk research (see also Dimov & Marewski, Chap. 9). Such a model should (a) be capable of integrating different theories and relevant empirical results (*integrative*); (b) specify relevant factors and levels (*measureable*); (c) be useful in the understanding, description, and initiation of change in behavior of different groups or organizations (*applicable*); and (d) generate new research questions or approaches (*productive*).

Our idea of such a model argues along the line that the perceptions, thoughts, and behavior of people are, besides biological factors and personality traits (see Lauriola & Weller, Chap. 1), significantly shaped, influenced, and determined by the cultural context in which people grow up and live (Church, 2017; Lonner, 2015). While there are different definitions of culture, one concurrent description is that culture comprises the shared implicit and explicit assumptions, attitudes, values, and beliefs that create sense and meaning and are expressed as specific behavior, rules, rituals, norms, and so on (Schein, 2010; Schneider, Ehrhart, & Macey, 2013). Accordingly, culture teaches people, among other things, that the standards of what is important and what is irrelevant, what feelings and thoughts are appropriate and which are not, what should be done and how it should it be done, and what should be avoided (Deal & Kennedy, 1982). People are exposed to the culture of their wider society but also to the more specific subcultures of their social groups. One line of research on subcultures addresses the question of how the specific culture of an organization affects employees' attitudes and behavior and the performance of the organization. Research on organizational culture, for example, demonstrated a positive link between different aspects of organizational culture, like adaptability, values toward change, action orientation or market orientation, and performance and long-term success (Costanza, Blacksmith, Coats, Severt, & DeCostanza, 2016; Hartnell, Ou, & Kinicki, 2011). We argue that the way people perceive and assess risk, and how they handle risks and uncertainty, is shaped by their *risk culture*. Risk culture refers to the shared understanding of what is perceived as a risk, how risks are assessed and valued, how to address risks, and what risks are acceptable (Gottschalk-Mazouz, 2008). The concept of risk culture aims to describe, understand, measure, and change risk perception and behavior of individuals as members of social groups and organizations.

Road traffic is one example of how societal risk culture affects human perception and behavior. Some decades ago in Germany, the widespread risk culture of driving a car without a seatbelt was accepted. For example, before introducing fines for driving unbuckled in 1984, the rate of belted backseat passengers within city limits was below 20% (Bundesanstalt für Straßenwesen, 2016). With ever-increasing traffic and faster cars, accident rates have increased. Society learned that with more and more vehicles on the road, the death rate would tremendously increase if this risk culture and the according risk behavior remained unchanged. As a result of this shared learning experience, intoxicated and unbuckled driving is nowadays commonly frowned upon. These days, the percentage of belted passengers is close to 100%. Accordingly, and because of other factors like electronic safety features, the yearly death rate in Germany dropped from 11.300 in 1991 to 3.206 in 2016, while the number of vehicles increased by 20 million from about 35–55 million (Kraftfahrtbundesamt, 2017). Unfortunately, during the last few years, driving using a smartphone has become an acceptable risk for many social groups despite the significantly higher chance of causing an accident (Lipovac, Đerić, Tešić, Andrić, & Marić, 2017). However, the change in percentages of belted passengers reflects how changes in risk cultures lead to corresponding changes in behavior. Risk culture also shapes the acceptance of certain risks. Although, in particular, the risk of dying in a traffic accident has continuously decreased over the past decades, the societal accepted risk of traffic accidents is fairly high compared to the societal acceptance of other risks. For example, whereas the risk of getting injured or dying in a traffic accident (with a likelihood of about 1:200 per year; Destatis, 2017) is widely accepted, a similar likelihood of getting injured or dying would be perceived as totally unacceptable when considering food safety, workplace safety, pharmaceutical products, or factory fumes. However, different social groups accept different levels of risk associated with the same issue: a start-up might be willing to risk a greater investment compared to an established company; ambitious semiprofessional soccer players will accept greater risks of injuries compared to a leisure soccer team of seniors; smokers are—at least implicitly—willing to accept the risks of smoking-related diseases, whereas non-smokers avoid these risks.

Basic Assumptions of Risk Culture

The previous examples show the following: first, risk culture is stable yet changeable. For example, the societal risk culture regarding traffic risks is stable for a medium period of time, but changeable over a longer period of time. Second, risk culture includes shared learning experiences. For example, German society has learned that driving unbuckled results in an unacceptable death rate, and, therefore, taking these specific risks should be avoided. Third, risk perceptions, assessment, and behavior of people, either as individuals or as members of a social group or organization, are modeled by risk culture. Accordingly, risk culture is a major force for explaining differences in risk perception and behavior between individuals, groups, and organizations. Fourth, risk taking by individuals and groups can be influenced by risk culture without the individuals being aware of this influence. For example, strong non-smoking campaigns, like in Australia, can lead to a societal change in the risk culture associated with smoking (Chapman & Wakefield, 2001; Pierce, Macaskill, & Hill, 1990). It is not necessary for an individual to be aware of this shift in risk culture to adapt her/his behavior and to restrain from smoking. Fifth, one risk culture does not imply one level of acceptability. Within one risk culture, the acceptability of taking a certain risk, like using a mobile phone while driving, can be high, whereas—at the same time—the willingness to take another risk, like drunk or unbuckled driving, is low. The same is true for risks from different domains (cf. Blais & Weber, 2006). Sixth, different risk cultures can lead to different perceptions, assessments, and handling of risks (cf. Gottschalk-Mazouz, 2008). For example, the risk culture of young, social media accustomed drivers might include a high acceptance of smartphone use while driving, whereas the risk culture of elderly drivers might include a low acceptance of this behavior. Seventh, risk culture and its implied levels of acceptance of risks are not correlated per se with a rational, reasonable, or adequate handling of risks. For example, an organization or a social group, like young adults, could simultaneously have different rationales for dealing with risks from different domains: an irrational, high-risk behavior for smartphone use while driving, a reasonable level of risk taking in outdoor sports, and a restrictive, low risk taking approach to financial decisions. Eighth, an appropriate risk culture does not mean avoiding risks or aiming for a zero-risk safety culture. Appropriateness in this context is having a good fit between risk culture, accepted risks, existing risks, and risk taking. For example, a family-owned enterprise has a bad fit, and, accordingly, its risk culture is not appropriate if it aims to avoid business risks, but operates in a changing global market without monitoring of latest development and is prone to biased decision making by an old patriarch. In this case, a good fit and, accordingly, an appropriate risk culture would include monitoring market developments and a structured decision making process, which aims to reduce biasing and also includes external experts and experienced employees.

Levels and Dimensions of Risk Culture

As with most other concepts of culture, our model of risk culture comprises different *levels* of visibility and obviousness ranging from visible, explicit, and accessible behavior to unobvious, implicit, and hidden assumptions. Following the concept of Schein (2010), three levels can by identified:

1. *Artifacts* comprise all visible, explicit, and accessible behaviors, structures, norms, processes, outcomes, and the like. Members are aware of artifacts and artifacts are obvious to outsiders. Accordingly, artifacts are easy to observe and to measure. Using road traffic as an example, artifacts include traffic regulations,

driver behavior in traffic, observable violations of traffic regulations, and formal driver education.

2. *Espoused beliefs and values* reflect the strategies, agendas, goals, philosophies, and principles associated with risks. Members are aware of them, yet they are not necessarily observable from the outside. In the example of road traffic, this level comprises such beliefs and values as the belief that drivers of sports cars don't have to obey all the rules, the conviction that it is fine to park in a disabled parking space for a quick shopping stop, or the belief that it is okay to drive faster than the speed limit.
3. *Basic assumptions* include feelings, affects, un- or subconscious influences of personality and temperament, cognitive states and representations, thoughts, implicit group norms, hidden agendas, and shared implicit learning experiences. Using road traffic a shared experience, the group norm, implicit belief, or feeling could be as follows: nothing can happen when driving fast in rainy conditions and not keeping a safe distance; the perception that everyone uses their smartphones while driving and, therefore, the use is justified; the perception that one's own driving is superior to others, which leads to the common belief that accidents only happen to other drivers; or the false perception of continuous control over the vehicle. Basic assumptions are the main drivers of a risk culture and can be in contradiction to the norms and regulations, which are defined in artifacts. Therefore, when exploring risk culture, it is essential to dig deeply beneath the surface of artifacts into the in-depth understanding of basic assumptions. Unfortunately, from a methodological point of view, basic assumptions are sometimes subconscious to members of a risk culture and not obvious to outsiders.

In addition to these three levels (i.e., artifacts, espoused beliefs and values, basic assumptions), our model identifies three *dimensions* of risk culture (see Table 10.1). The dimensions are not independent or unrelated, but follow the established distinction between person, social relations, and structures of the environment and the context (cf. Gerrig & Zimbardo, 2001). This trichotomy allows for an easier integration of different psychological approaches and theories into the model and gives guidance for the development of measurements and interventions. All three dimensions comprise factors, which span from the level of artifacts to the level of basic assumptions (see Table 10.1 for examples).

1. *Person* includes all risk-relevant factors related to an individual person such as motivation, affects, feelings, mind-sets, thoughts, beliefs, values, cognitive representations, interoception, experiences, competencies, expectations, decision making, behavior, and the like.
2. *Social* comprises all risk-relevant factors related to social perceptions and social interactions such as group experiences in decision making and consequences of behavior; group structure, norms, and rituals; relationship between leader and members including leadership style; identification with group norms and goals; formal and informal decision making processes; and diversity in groups and group size.

Table 10.1 Model of risk culture and examples of how a risk culture is formed by risk-relevant psychological factors and organizational procedures

	Dimension of risk culture		
Level of risk culture	Person	Social	Structure
Artifacts	• Risk judgment • Risk behavior • Social demographics • Individual performance	• Diversity of groups • Formal group norms • Leader behavior • Group performance	• Organizational structure and hierarchy • Formalized decision making process • Risk management • Risk and safety rules • Implemented FFTs
Espoused beliefs and values	• Personal motives, values, and beliefs • Professional identity • Accepted rule violations • Routines	• Informal group norms and identity • Perceived hierarchy and social status • Leader expectations • Ownership of rules and tolerated violations	• Organizational identity • Actual decision making process and error handling • Goals and values • Organizational (lack of) control
Basic assumptions	• Loss and gain perceptions • Negative and positive feelings • Cognitive biases • Gut feelings • Intuition	• Shared experiences • Perceived expectations of others • Group rituals • Group biases	• Implicit organizational rules • Organizational narratives • Organizational rituals • Defensive decision making

3. *Structure* relates to all formal and informal structures of the system and context such as decision making processes, responsibilities and accountabilities, norms and regulations, demands, organizational goals and values, risk management processes, and organizational self-concept.

These three dimensions are particularly helpful in organizational research, since they reflect the typical elements of an organization, but they can be easily applied to non-organizational settings as well. Furthermore, they are helpful in integrating existing theories and empirical research and in identifying relevant factors in order to develop measurements. However, we see this structure as a starting point for further research. Another structure would be to focus on the dynamics between internal and external risks on the one hand and the elements of the social system on the other hand. Accordingly, one can think of using different dimensions like *me* (i.e., phenomena related to an individual person), *us* (i.e., phenomena related to a social construct), and *risk* (i.e., phenomena related to internal and external risks and uncertainty). Such a structure might be more helpful in exploring the dynamics and interrelations of a risk culture.

Combining the three levels (i.e., artifacts, espoused beliefs and values, basic assumptions) with the three dimensions (i.e., person, social, structure) produces a 3×3 matrix (see Table 10.1). This matrix works as a framework, which enables integration of existing research on risk. For example, the concepts of risk management, heuristic, fast-and-frugal decision trees, intuition, biases, and human factors, which were outlined in the first part of the chapter, can be located in this matrix. Risk management and implemented decision trees as formal decision making structures are located on the level *artifacts* and the dimension *structure*. Heuristics, intuition and cognitive biases refer to *basic assumptions* of a *person*. Individual human factors are located on all levels of the dimension *person*, whereas the dimension *social* contains all human factors related to social dynamics (see also Eller & Frey, Chap. 6).

Integration of Existing Research

For those familiar with psychological research and theories, we provide a glimpse of the integrative power of the model and outline some examples of how risk-related psychological theories and approaches can be linked to the model of risk culture. The following list is far from exhaustive, and some theories and approaches are included only once but can be linked to more than one segment of the 3 × 3 matrix of our risk culture model:

- *Person x artifacts*: Risk perception and behavior (e.g., Jessor, 1991; Sjöberg, 2000); sensation seeking (Zuckerman, 1979); and domain-specific risk taking (e.g., Blais & Weber, 2006; Nicholson, Soane, Fenton-O'Creevy, & Willman, 2005)
- *Person x espoused beliefs and values*: Self-efficacy (Bandura, 1977, 1982); action identification theory (Vallacher & Wegner, 1985, 1987; Wegner & Vallacher, 1986); theory of planned behavior (Ajzen, 1985, 1991); and regulatory focus theory (Higgins, 2004, 2006)
- *Person x basic assumptions*: Intuitive decision making, theory of somatic marker and interoception (e.g., Bechara & Naqvi, 2004; Damasio, 1996; Damasio, Tranel, & Damasio, 1991); heuristics and biases (e.g., Gigerenzer, Todd, and the ABC Research Group, 1999; Tversky & Kahneman, 1974); selective exposure to information and information search (e.g., Frey, 1986; Hart et al., 2009); prospect theory (Kahneman & Tversky, 1979; Tversky & Kahneman, 1981); psychological distance, mental representation and construal level theory (e.g., Lermer, Streicher, Sachs, Raue, & Frey, 2015; Raue, Streicher, Lermer, & Frey, 2015; Trope & Liberman, 2010); embodiment (e.g., Meier, Schnall, Schwarz, & Bargh, 2012; Raue, Streicher, Lermer, & Frey, 2017; Wilson & Golonka, 2013); and feelings as information and risks as feelings (e.g., Loewenstein, Weber, Hsee, & Welch, 2001; Schwarz, 1990; Slovic, Finucane, Peters, & MacGregor, 2004)
- *Social x artifacts*: Idea generation, brainstorming (e.g., Diehl & Stroebe, 1987, 1991); information search and decision making (e.g., Schulz-Hardt, Brodbeck, Mojzisch, Kerschreiter, & Frey, 2006; Stasser & Titus, 2003); leadership styles (e.g., Wehman, Goldstein, & Williams, 1977); group norms (e.g., Patil, Tetlock, & Mellers, 2017); team size (e.g., Aubé, Rousseau, & Tremblay, 2011); and team diversity (e.g., Balkundi, Kilduff, Barsness, & Michael, 2007)

- *Social x espoused beliefs and values*: Social learning theory, social cognitive theory (Bandura, 1986); risky and cautious shifts (Stoner, 1968); groupthink theory (Janis, 1972); group polarization (e.g., Moscovici & Zavalloni, 1969); leader-member exchange (e.g., Gerstner & Day, 1997; Rockstuhl, Dulebohn, Ang, & Shore, 2012); social identity theory (Tajfel & Turner, 1979); and social norms (e.g., Warner, 2017; Zamboanga, Audley, Iwamoto, Martin, & Tomaso, 2017)
- *Social x basic assumptions*: Rituals (e.g., Brooks et al., 2016; Hobson, Gino, Norton, & Inzlicht, 2017; Streicher, Zorn, & Lermer, 2016); social comparison theory (Festinger, 1954); group conformity (e.g., Asch, 1951; Erb, Bohner, Rank, & Einwiller, 2002); shared learning (e.g., Bunderson & Reagans, 2011); and learned carelessness (Frey & Schulz-Hardt, 1996; Frey, Ullrich, Streicher, Schneider, & Lermer, 2016)
- *Structure x artifacts*: Risk management (e.g., Ehrengren, 2006; Ehrengren & Hörnsten, 2011; VanVactor, 2007); hierarchy and organizational structure (e.g., Hale & Borys, 2013a, 2013b; Weichbrodt, 2015); fast-and-frugal trees (e.g., Martignon, Katsikopoulos, & Woike, 2008; Martignon, Vitouch, Takezawa, & Forster, 2003); and organizational climate (e.g., Schein, 2010)
- *Structure x espoused beliefs and values*: Organizational and entrepreneurship identity (e.g., Hytti, 2005; Stein, 2015); error management culture (e.g., Fruhen & Keith, 2014); and goal setting (Locke & Latham, 1990)
- *Structure x basic assumptions*: Organizational narratives (e.g., Vaara, Sonenshein, & Boje, 2016); implicit organizational rules (e.g., March, 1991; Reason, Parker, & Lawton, 1998); and organizational rituals (e.g., Hobson, Schroeder, Risen, Xygalatas, & Inzlicht, 2017)

Application and Future Research

We argue that our model of risk culture is not only capable of integrating existing research but is also applicable to solving existing practical problems. However, in our understanding, since its application should be evidence-based, the potential of applicability is accompanied by some speculation because a valid and reliable measure is first needed. Despite the increasing amount of publications addressing the importance of risk culture in global newspapers, practitioner literature and from finance regulation authorities after the financial crisis (Ashby, Palermo, & Power, 2012), to the best of our knowledge only one validated measure on risk culture currently exists (Sheedy, Griffin, & Barbour, 2017). In fact, the authors of this measure refer to risk climate (rather than risk culture), which they define as "the shared perceptions among employees of the relative priority given to risk management" (Sheedy, Griffin, & Barbour, 2017, p. 103). The 16-item scale assesses risk climate on 4 factors (i.e., *avoidance*, *value*, *proactivity*, and *manager*). Since this measure is restricted to financial institutions and contains only four factors, more research is urgently required to develop valid and reliable instruments that measure risk culture in its full scope and that are applicable to different contexts and social systems.

As a first step, future research should identify the most influential variables in the 3 × 3 matrix of our model of risk culture for each level and dimension that are associated with risk perception, assessment, and behavior. Then these variables should be measured in organizations with accessible risk behavior and performance. Ideally, these organizations should stem from a broad variety of contexts. Data analyses could follow different goals: first, to identify significant predictors for risk perception, assessment, and behavior on each level and dimension; second, to identify different clusters of risk cultures such as intentional risk seeking, unintentional risk taking, unintentional risk avoiding, and intentional risk-avoiding organizations; third, to differentiate between organizations with a questionable risk culture and/or poor performance and those that are more successful; fourth, to understand the interaction between different variables and, more generally speaking, the dynamics of risk culture; and fifth, to validate a measure.

Once a validated measure exists, the risk culture of a specific organization or social group can be evaluated. In our opinion, organizations would, as a first step, benefit the most if the appropriateness of their existing risk culture is evaluated (that means whether the risk culture and, therefore, the way the organization understands and handles risks comply with the real existing risk) and the second if problematic variables are identified in order to conduct specific interventions and, as a result, establish an appropriate risk culture for that organization. For example, a problematic risk culture might reveal the factor of implicit shared learning experience as the main central factor for risk-relevant decisions. That means that other factors, like formal decision making processes, external experts, or data, have only a marginal influence on decisions. Such a risk culture might be appropriate for small, experience-based businesses in stable environments like craft enterprises. However, such a risk culture can jeopardize an organization in a changing, complex high-risk market, as outlined above in the case of RWE. Therefore, the risk culture of an organization has to be measured to allow for evidence-based interventions (e.g., by means of training, re-structuring, role-modeling, etc.).

In summary, risk culture is a promising approach to integrating different avenues of research and adequately understanding risk perception, assessment, and behavior. Risk culture is not a "one size fits all" in the sense that there is no single perfect risk culture for all social groups and organizations to achieve. Different groups and organizations do have different acceptable levels of risks, different risk competences, and are confronted with different risks. Therefore, a risk culture, which is appropriate for one organization or social group, may be inappropriate for another. Conducting activities that can result in severe injuries like base jumping might be an acceptable risk for highly trained and experienced sport professionals, but not for amateurs. Investing money in start-ups or new technologies might be an appropriate risk for specialized, financially strong enterprises but can put a small family business on the edge. Therefore, we have to aim at understanding, measuring, and, if appropriate, changing the risk culture of social groups and organizations at all levels and dimensions in order to make them risk savvy.

References

Agnoli, F., & Krantz, D. H. (1989). Suppressing natural heuristics by formal instruction: The case of the conjunction fallacy. *Cognitive Psychology, 21*(4), 515–550. https://doi.org/10.1016/0010-0285(89)90017-0

Aikman, D., Galesic, M., Gigerenzer, G., Kapadia, S., Katsikopoulos, K. V., Kothiyal, A., Murphy, E., … Neumann, T. (2014). *Taking uncertainty seriously: Simplicity versus complexity in financial regulation* (Financial Stability Paper No. 28). London: Bank of England.

Ajzen, I. (1985). From intentions to actions: A theory of planned behavior. In J. Kuhl & J. Beckman (Eds.), *Action-control* (pp. 11–39). Heidelberg: Springer.

Ajzen, I. (1991). The theory of planned behavior. *Organizational Behavior and Human Decision Processes, 50*(2), 179–211.

Arbeitsgemeinschaft österreichischer Lawinenwarndienste. (2015). *Saisonbericht der österreichischen Lawinenwarndienste 2014/2015* [Saisonal report of the Austrian avalanche warning services]. Retrieved from https://lawine.tirol.gv.at/fileadmin/lawine.tirol.gv.at/downloads/jahresberichte/OeBericht_2014_2015_Download_Version.pdf

Asch, S. E. (1951). Effects of group pressure upon the modification and distortion of judgments. In H. Guetzkow (Ed.), *Groups, leadership and men; research in human relations* (pp. 177–190). Oxford: Carnegie Press.

Ashby, S., Palermo, T., & Power, M. (2012). *Risk culture in financial organisations: An interim report*. Retrieved from http://www.lse.ac.uk/accounting/CARR/pdf/risk-culture-interim-report.pdf

Aubé, C., Rousseau, V., & Tremblay, S. (2011). Team size and quality of group experience: The more the merrier? *Group Dynamics: Theory, Research, and Practice, 15*(4), 357–375. https://doi.org/10.1037/a0025400

Babyak, M. A. (2004). What you see may not be what you get: A brief, nontechnical introduction to overfitting in regression-type models. *Psychosomatic Medicine, 66*(3), 411–421. https://doi.org/10.1097/01.psy.0000127692.23278.a9

Balkundi, P., Kilduff, M., Barsness, Z. I., & Michael, J. H. (2007). Demographic antecedents and performance consequences of structural holes in work teams. *Journal of Organizational Behavior, 28*(2), 241–260. https://doi.org/10.1002/job.428

Bandura, A. (1977). Self-efficacy: Toward a unifying theory of behavioral change. *Psychological Review, 84*(2), 191.

Bandura, A. (1982). Self-efficacy mechanism in human agency. *American Psychologist, 37*(2), 122.

Bandura, A. (1986). *Social foundations of thought and action: A social cognitive theory*. Englewood Cliffs, NJ: Prentice-Hall.

Basel Committee on Banking Supervision. (1988). *International convergence of capital measurement and capitel standards*. Retrieved from https://www.bis.org/publ/bcbs04a.pdf

Bechara, A., & Naqvi, N. (2004). Listening to your heart: Interoceptive awareness as a gateway to feeling. *Nature Neuroscience, 7*(2), 102–103. https://doi.org/10.1038/nn0204-102

Berlin, I. (1984). *The age of enlightenment: The eighteenth-century philosophers*. New York, NY: Plume.

Blais, A.-R., & Weber, E. U. (2006). A Domain-Specific Risk Taking (DOSPERT) scale for adult populations. *Judgment and Decision making, 1*, 33–47.

Bromiley, P., McShane, M., Nair, A., & Rustambekov, E. (2015). Enterprise risk management: Review, critique, and research directions. *Long Range Planning: International Journal of Strategic Management, 48*(4), 265–276. https://doi.org/10.1016/j.lrp.2014.07.005

Brooks, A. W., Schroeder, J., Risen, J. L., Gino, F., Galinsky, A. D., Norton, M. I., & Schweitzer, M. E. (2016). Don't stop believing: Rituals improve performance by decreasing anxiety. *Organizational Behavior and Human Decision Processes, 137*, 71–85.

Bunderson, J. S., & Reagans, R. E. (2011). Power, status, and learning in organizations. *Organization Science, 22*(5), 1182–1194. https://doi.org/10.1287/orsc.1100.0590

Bundesanstalt für Straßenwesen. (2016). *Gurte, Kindersitze, Helme und Schutzkleidung - 2015* [Seat belts, child seats, helmets, and protective clothing - 2015]. Retrieved from http://www.bast.de/DE/Publikationen/Foko/Downloads/2016-15.pdf?__blob=publicationFile&v=2

Chapman, G. B., & Johnson, E. J. (1999). Anchoring, activation, and the construction of values. *Organizational Behavior and Human Decision Processes, 79*, 1–39. https://doi.org/10.1006/obhd.1999.2841

Chapman, S., & Wakefield, M. (2001). Tobacco control advocacy in Australia: Reflections on 30 years of progress. *Health Education and Behavior, 28*(3), 274–289. https://doi.org/10.1177/109019810102800303

Church, A. T. (2017). *The Praeger handbook of personality across cultures: Evolutionary, ecological, and cultural contexts of personality* (Vol. 3). Santa Barbara, CA: Praeger.

Costanza, D. P., Blacksmith, N., Coats, M. R., Severt, J. B., & DeCostanza, A. H. (2016). The effect of adaptive organizational culture on long-term survival. *Journal of Business and Psychology, 31*(3), 361–381. https://doi.org/10.1007/s10869-015-9420-y

Damasio, A. R. (1996). The somatic marker hypothesis and the possible functions of the prefrontal cortex. *Philosophical Transactions of the Royal Society of London Series B, Biological Sciences, 351*(1346), 1413–1420. https://doi.org/10.1098/rstb.1996.0125

Damasio, A. R., Tranel, D., & Damasio, H. C. (1991). Somatic markers and the guidance of behavior: Theory and preliminary testing. In H. S. Levin (Ed.), *Frontal lobe function and dysfunction* (3rd ed., pp. 217–229). New York: Oxford University Press.

Deal, T., & Kennedy, A. A. (1982). *Corporate cultures*. Reading, MA: Addison-Wesley.

Destatis. (2017). *Destatis - Statistisches Bundesamt* [Destatis - Federal Office of Statistics]. Retrieved from https://www-genesis.destatis.de/genesis/online

Dhami, M. K. (2003). Psychological models of professional decision making. *Psychological Science, 14*(2), 175–180.

Dhami, M. K., & Ayton, P. (2001). Bailing and jailing the fast and frugal way. *Journal of Behavioral Decision Making, 14*(2), 141–168.

Diehl, M., & Stroebe, W. (1987). Productivity loss in brainstorming groups: Toward the solution of a riddle. *Journal of Personality and Social Psychology, 53*(3), 497–509. https://doi.org/10.1037/0022-3514.53.3.497

Diehl, M., & Stroebe, W. (1991). Productivity loss in idea-generating groups: Tracking down the blocking effect. *Journal of Personality and Social Psychology, 61*(3), 392–403. https://doi.org/10.1037/0022-3514.61.3.392

Edwards, W. (1954). The theory of decision making. *Psychological Bulletin, 51*(4), 380–417. https://doi.org/10.1037/h0053870

Ehrengren, L. (2006). Risk-related global production flexibility. *International Journal of Business Environment, 1*(3), 301–319. https://doi.org/10.1504/IJBE.2006.010926

Ehrengren, L., & Hörnsten, B. (2011). Performance and risk management in strategic cooperation: A comparative study of business and military sectors. *International Journal of Productivity and Performance Management, 60*(4), 387–403. https://doi.org/10.1108/17410401111123553

Englich, B. (2008). When knowledge matters: Differential effects of available knowledge in standard and basic anchoring. *European Journal of Social Psychology, 38*(5), 896–904. https://doi.org/10.1002/ejsp.479

Englich, B., Mussweiler, T., & Strack, F. (2006). Playing dice with criminal sentences: The influence of irrelevant anchors on experts' judicial decision making. *Personality and Social Psychology Bulletin, 32*(2), 188–200. https://doi.org/10.1177/0146167205282152

Epley, N., & Gilovich, T. (2001). Putting adjustment back into the anchoring and adjustment heuristic: Differential processing of self-generated and experimenter-provided anchors. *Psychological Science, 12*, 391–396. https://doi.org/10.1111/1467-9280.00372

Epley, N., & Gilovich, T. (2004). Are adjustments insufficient? *Personality and Social Psychology Bulletin, 30*(4), 447–460.

Erb, H.-P., Bohner, G., Rank, S., & Einwiller, S. (2002). Processing minority and majority communications: The role of conflict with prior attitudes. *Personality and Social Psychology Bulletin, 28*, 1172–1182. https://doi.org/10.1177/01461672022812003

Fellner, G., & Krügel, S. (2012). Judgmental overconfidence: Three measures, one bias? *Journal of Economic Psychology, 33*(1), 142–154. https://doi.org/10.1016/j.joep.2011.07.008

Festinger, L. (1954). A theory of social comparison processes. *Human Relations, 7*(2), 117–140.

Fischhoff, B. (1982). Debiasing. In D. Kahneman, P. Slovic, & A. Tversky (Hrsg.), Judgment under uncertainty: Heuristics and biases (pp. 422–444). Cambridge, MA: Cambridge University Press. doi: https://doi.org/10.1017/cbo9780511809477.032

Frey, D. (1986). Recent research on selective exposure to information. In L. Berkowitz (Ed.), Advances in experimental social psychology (Vol. 19, pp. 41–80). Academic Press.

Frey, D., & Schulz-Hardt, S. (1996). Eine Theorie der gelernten Sorglosigkeit. [A theory of learned carelessness]. In H. Mandel (Ed.), *Bericht über den 40. Kongress der Deutschen Gesellschaft für Psychologie* (pp. 604–611). Göttingen: Hogrefe.

Frey, D., Ullrich, B., Streicher, B., Schneider, E., & Lermer, E. (2016). Theorie der gelernten Sorglosigkeit [Theory of learned carelessness]. In H.-W. Bierhoff & D. Frey (Eds.), *Enzyklopädie der Psychologie. Sozialpsychologie Band 1: Selbst und soziale Kognition* (pp. 429–469). Göttingen: Hogrefe.

Fruhen, L. S., & Keith, N. (2014). Team cohesion and error culture in risky work environments. *Safety Science, 65*, 20–27. https://doi.org/10.1016/j.ssci.2013.12.011

Furnham, A., & Boo, H. C. (2011). A literature review of the anchoring effect. *The Journal of Socio-Economics, 40*(1), 35–42. https://doi.org/10.1016/j.socec.2010.10.008

Gerrig, R. J., & Zimbardo, P. G. (2001). *Psychology and life*. Boston, MA: Allyn and Bacon.

Gerstner, C. R., & Day, D. V. (1997). Meta-analytic review of leader-member exchange theory: Correlates and construct issues. *Journal of Applied Psychology, 82*(6), 827–844.

Gigerenzer, G. (2002). *Calculated risks: How to know when numbers deceive you*. New York, NY: Simon & Schuster.

Gigerenzer, G., & Gaissmaier, W. (2011). Heuristic decision making. *Annual Review of Psychology, 62*, 451–482. https://doi.org/10.1146/annurev-psych-120709-145346

Gigerenzer, G., Todd, P. M., & the ABC Research Group. (1999). Simple heuristics that make us smart. New York, NY: Oxford University Press.

Gottschalk-Mazouz, N. (2008). Risikokulturen [Risk cultures]. In J. Köngeter (Ed.), *Sicherheit und Risiko wasserbaulicher Anlagen. 37. IWASA Internationales Wasserbau-Symposium Aachen* [Safetey and risk of hydraulic facilities. 37th IWASA International Symposium of Hydraulic Engineering Aachen] (pp. 1–22). Aachen: Shaker.

Hale, A., & Borys, D. (2013a). Working to rule, or working safely? Part 1: A state of the art review. *Safety Science, 55*, 207–221.

Hale, A., & Borys, D. (2013b). Working to rule or working safely? Part 2: The management of safety rules and procedures. *Safety Science, 55*, 222–231.

Hart, W., Albarracin, D., Eagly, A. H., Brechan, I., Lindberg, M. J., & Merrill, L. (2009). Feeling validated versus being correct: A meta-analysis of selective exposure to information. *Psychological Bulletin, 135*(4), 555–588. https://doi.org/10.1037/a0015701

Hartnell, C. A., Ou, A. Y., & Kinicki, A. (2011). Organizational culture and organizational effectiveness: A meta-analytic investigation of the competing values framework's theoretical suppositions. *Journal of Applied Psychology, 96*, 677–694. https://doi.org/10.1037/a0021987

Higgins, E. T. (2004). Making a theory useful: Lessons handed down. *Personality and Social Psychology Review, 8*(2), 138–145.

Higgins, E. T. (2006). Theory development as a family affair. *Journal of Experimental Social Psychology, 42*(2), 129–132.

Hobson, N. M., Gino, F., Norton, M. I., & Inzlicht, M. (2017). When novel rituals lead to intergroup bias: Evidence from economic games and neurophysiology. *Psychological Science, 28*(6), 733–750. https://doi.org/10.1177/0956797617695099

Hobson, N. M., Schroeder, J., Risen, J., Xygalatas, D., & Inzlicht, M. (2017). The psychology of rituals: An integrative review and process-based framework. *Personality and Social Psychology Review*. Advance online publication. https://doi.org/10.1177/1088868317734944

Hope, T., & Sparks, R. (2000). *Crime, risk and insecurity*. London: Routledge.

Hytti, U. (2005). New meanings for entrepreneurs: From risk taking heroes to safe-seeking professionals. *Journal of Organizational Change Management, 18*(6), 594–611. https://doi.org/10.1108/09534810510628521

Janis, I. (1972). *Victims of groupthink: A psychological study of foreign-policy decisions and fiascoes*. Boston, MA: Houghton Mifflin.

Janis, I. (1982). *Groupthink. Psychological studies of policy decisions and fiascoes* (2nd ed.). Boston, MA: Houghton Mifflin.

Jenny, M. A., Pachur, T., Williams, S. L., Becker, E., & Margraf, J. (2013). Simple rules for detecting depression. *Journal of Applied Research in Memory and Cognition, 2*(3), 149–157.

Jessor, R. (1991). Risk behavior in adolescence: A psychosocial framework for understanding and action. *Journal of Adolescent Health, 12*(8), 597–605.

Kahneman, D. (2011). *Thinking, fast and slow*. New York, NY: Farrar, Straus and Giroux.

Kahneman, D., & Klein, G. (2009). Conditions for intuitive expertise: A failure to disagree. *American Psychologist, 64*(6), 515.

Kahneman, D., & Tversky, A. (1972). Subjective probability: A judgment of representativeness. *Cognitive Psychology, 3*, 430–454.

Kahneman, D., & Tversky, A. (1973). On the psychology of prediction. *Psychological Review, 80*, 237–251.

Kahneman, D., & Tversky, A. (1979). Prospect theory: An analysis of decision under risk. *Econometrica, 47*, 263–291. https://doi.org/10.2307/1914185

Knight, F. H. (1921). *Risk, uncertainty, and profit, Hart, Schaffner and Marx Prize Essays, 31*. Boston, MA, & New York, NY: Houghton Mifflin Company.

Kraftfahrtbundesamt. (2017). *Bestand in den Jahren 1960 bis 2017 nach Fahrzeugklassen* [Inventory of motor vehicles from 1960 to 2017]. Retrieved from https://www.kba.de/DE/Statistik/Fahrzeuge/Bestand/FahrzeugklassenAufbauarten/b_fzkl_zeitreihe.html

LeBoeuf, R. A., & Shafir, E. (2009). Anchoring on the "here" and "now" in time and distance judgments. *Journal of Experimental Psychology, 35*, 81–93. https://doi.org/10.1037/a0013665

Lermer, E., Streicher, B., Sachs, R., & Frey, D. (2013). How risky? The impact of target person and answer format on risk assessment. *Journal of Risk Research, 16*(7), 903–919. https://doi.org/10.1080/13669877.2012.761267

Lermer, E., Streicher, B., Sachs, R., Raue, M., & Frey, D. (2015). The effect of construal level on risk taking. *European Journal of Social Psychology, 45*(1), 99–109. https://doi.org/10.1002/ejsp.2067

Leroy, S. F., & Singell, L. D., Jr. (1987). Knight on risk and uncertainty. *Journal of Political Economy, 95*(2), 394.

Lipovac, K., Đerić, M., Tešić, M., Andrić, Z., & Marić, B. (2017). Mobile phone use while driving-literary review. *Transportation Research Part F: Traffic Psychology and Behaviour, 47*, 132–142. https://doi.org/10.1016/j.trf.2017.04.015

Locke, E. A., & Latham, G. P. (1990). *A theory of goal setting and task performance*. Englewood Cliffs, NJ: Prentice Hall.

Loewenstein, G. F., Weber, E. U., Hsee, C. K., & Welch, N. (2001). Risk as feelings. *Psychological Bulletin, 127*(2), 267–286. https://doi.org/10.1037/0033-2909.127.2.267

Lonner, W. J. (2015). Half a century of cross-cultural psychology: A grateful coda. *American Psychologist, 70*(8), 804–814. https://doi.org/10.1037/a0039454

Lu, X., Xie, X., & Liu, L. (2015). Inverted U-shaped model: How frequent repetition affects perceived risk. *Judgment and Decision making, 10*(3), 219–224.

Luan, S., & Reb, J. (2017). Fast-and-frugal trees as noncompensatory models of performance-based personnel decisions. *Organizational Behavior and Human Decision Processes, 141*, 29–42.

March, J. G. (1991). How decisions happen in organizations. *Human-Computer Interaction, 6*(2), 95–117. https://doi.org/10.1207/s15327051hci0602_1
Martignon, L., Katsikopoulos, K. V., & Woike, J. K. (2008). Categorization with limited resources: A family of simple heuristics. *Journal of Mathematical Psychology, 52*(6), 352–361.
Martignon, L., Vitouch, O., Takezawa, M., & Forster, M. R. (2003). Naive and yet enlightened: From natural frequencies to fast and frugal decision trees. In L. M. D. Hardman (Ed.), *Thinking: Psychological perspectives on reasoning, judgment, and decision making* (pp. 189–211). Chichester: Wiley.
McElroy, T., & Dowd, K. (2007). Susceptibility to anchoring effects: How openness-to-experience influences responses to anchoring cues. *Judgment and Decision making, 2*(1), 48–53.
Meier, B. P., Schnall, S., Schwarz, N., & Bargh, J. A. (2012). Embodiment in social psychology. *Topics in Cognitive Science, 4*(4), 705–716. https://doi.org/10.1111/j.1756-8765.2012.01212.x
Moscovici, S., & Zavalloni, M. (1969). The group as a polarizer of attitudes. *Journal of Personality and Social, 12*(2), 125–135.
Moussaïd, M., Brighton, H., & Gaissmaier, W. (2015). The amplification of risk in experimental diffusion chains. *Proceedings of the National Academy of Sciences of the United States of America, 112*(18), 5631–5636. https://doi.org/10.1073/pnas.1421883112
Mussweiler, T., & Englich, B. (2005). Subliminal anchoring: Judgmental consequences and underlying mechanisms. *Organizational Behavior and Human Decision Processes, 98*, 133–143. https://doi.org/10.1016/j.obhdp.2004.12.002
Mussweiler, T., & Strack, F. (2001a). Considering the impossible: Explaining the effects of implausible anchors. *Social Cognition, 19*, 145–160. https://doi.org/10.1521/soco.19.2.145.20705
Mussweiler, T., & Strack, F. (2001b). The semantics of anchoring. *Organizational Behavior and Human Decision Processes, 86*, 234–255. https://doi.org/10.1006/obhd.2001.2954
Mussweiler, T., Strack, F., & Pfeiffer, T. (2000). Overcoming the inevitable anchoring effect: Considering the opposite compensates for selective accessibility. *Personality and Social Psychology Bulletin, 26*, 1142–1150. https://doi.org/10.1177/01461672002611010
Nicholson, N., Soane, E., Fenton-O'Creevy, M., & Willman, P. (2005). Personality and domain-specific risk taking. *Journal of Risk Research, 8*(2), 157–176. https://doi.org/10.1080/1366987032000123856
Obmann, C. (2017, Juli 14). Richtungsweisende Entscheidung [Trend-setting decision]. *Handelsblatt*, pp. 58–59.
Odenwald, S. (2017). *National Aeronautics and Space Administration (NASA). Imager for magnetopause-to-aurora global exploration (IMAGE)*. Ask the space scientist. Retrieved from https://image.gsfc.nasa.gov/poetry/ask/askmag.html
Patil, S. V., Tetlock, P. E., & Mellers, B. A. (2017). Accountability systems and group norms: Balancing the risks of mindless conformity and reckless deviation. *Journal of Behavioral Decision Making, 30*(2), 282–303. https://doi.org/10.1002/bdm.1933
Phillips, N. D., Neth, H., Woike, J. K., & Gaissmaier, W. (2017). FFTrees: A toolbox to create, visualize, and evaluate fast-and-frugal decision trees. *Judgment and Decision making, 12*(4), 344.
Pierce, J. P., Macaskill, P., & Hill, D. (1990). Long-term effectiveness of mass media led antismoking campaigns in Australia. *American Journal of Public Health, 80*(5), 565–569. https://doi.org/10.2105/AJPH.80.5.565
Plessner, H., Betsch, C., & Betsch, T. (Eds.). (2008). *Intuition in judgment and decision making*. Mahwah, NJ: Lawrence Erlbaum.
Purdy, G. (2010). ISO 31000:2009—Setting a new standard for risk management. *Risk Analysis, 30*(6), 881–886. https://doi.org/10.1111/j.1539-6924.2010.01442.x
Raue, M., Streicher, B., Lermer, E., & Frey, D. (2015). How far does it feel?: Construal level and decisions under risk. *Journal of Applied Research in Memory and Cognition, 4*(3), 256–264. https://doi.org/10.1016/j.jarmac.2014.09.005

Raue, M., Streicher, B., Lermer, E., & Frey, D. (2017). Being active when judging risks: Bodily states interfere with accurate risk analysis. *Journal of Risk Research, 20*(4), 445–462. https://doi.org/10.1080/13669877.2015.1057206

Reason, J., Parker, D., & Lawton, R. (1998). Organizational controls and safety: The varieties of rule-related behaviour. *Journal of Occupational and Organizational Psychology, 71*(4), 289–304. https://doi.org/10.1111/j.2044-8325.1998.tb00678.x

Rockstuhl, T., Dulebohn, J. H., Ang, S., & Shore, L. M. (2012). Leader-member exchange (LMX) and culture: A meta-analysis of correlates of LMX across 23 countries. *Journal of Applied Psychology, 97*(6), 1097–1130. https://doi.org/10.1037/a0029978

Ruan, D., Liu, J., & Carchon, R. (2003). Linguistic assessment approach for managing nuclear safeguards indicator information. *Logistics Information Management, 16*(6), 401–419. https://doi.org/10.1108/09576050310503385

Sax, J., & Torp, S. S. (2015). Speak up! Enhancing risk performance with enterprise risk management, leadership style and employee voice. *Management Decision, 53*(7), 1452–1468. https://doi.org/10.1108/md-10-2014-0625

Schein, E. H. (2010). *Organizational culture and leadership* (4th ed.). San Francisco, CA: Jossey-Bass.

Schneider, B., Ehrhart, M. G., & Macey, W. H. (2013). Organizational climate and culture. *Annual Review of Psychology, 64*, 361–388. https://doi.org/10.1146/annurev-psych-113011-143809

Schulz-Hardt, S., Brodbeck, F. C., Mojzisch, A., Kerschreiter, R., & Frey, D. (2006). Group decision making in hidden profile situations: Dissent as a facilitator for decision quality. *Journal of Personality and Social Psychology, 91*(6), 1080–1093.

Schwarz, N. (1990). Feelings as information: Informational and motivational functions of affective states. In E. T. Higgins & R. M. Sorrentino (Eds.), *Handbook of motivation and cognition foundations of social behavior* (Vol. 2, pp. 527–561). New York, NY: Guilford Press.

Sheedy, E. A., Griffin, B., & Barbour, J. P. (2017). A framework and measure for examining risk climate in financial institutions. *Journal of Business and Psychology, 32*, 101–116.

Sjöberg, L. (2000). Factors in risk perception. *Risk Analysis, 20*(1), 1–12.

Slovic, P., Finucane, M. L., Peters, E., & MacGregor, D. G. (2004). Risk as analysis and risk as feelings: Some thoughts about affect, reason, risk, and rationality. *Risk Analysis, 24*(2), 311–322.

Slovic, P., & Peters, E. (2006). Risk perception and affect. *Current Directions in Psychological Science, 15*(6), 322–325. https://doi.org/10.1111/j.1467-8721.2006.00461.x

Stasser, G., & Titus, W. (2003). Hidden profiles: A brief history. *Psychological Inquiry, 14*(3), 304–313.

Stein, M. (2015). Double trouble: Sibling rivalry and twin organizations in the 2008 credit crisis. *British Journal of Management, 26*(2), 182–196. https://doi.org/10.1111/1467-8551.12072

Stoner, J. (1968). Risky and cautious shifts in group decisions: The influence of widely held values. *Journal of Experimental Social Psychology, 4*(4), 442–459.

Streicher, B., Frey, D., & Osswald, S. (2011). Forming fairness judgments: Why people favor unfair information. In E. Kahls & J. Maes (Eds.), *Justice and conflict: Theoretical and empirical contributions* (pp. 185–196). New York, NY: Springer.

Streicher, B., Lermer, E., Sachs, R., Schneider, E., & Frey, D. (2015). *How to be bias-savvy: Training reduces overconfidence and conjunction fallacy*. Paper presented at the 24th Conference of the Society for Risk Analysis Europe (SRA-E), Maastricht.

Streicher, B., Zorn, I., & Lermer, E. (2016). *The dark side of rituals: Lower risk estimation and riskier behavior*. Paper presented at the 25th Conference of the Society for Risk Analysis Europe (SRA-E), Bath.

Tajfel, H., & Turner, J. (1979). An integrative theory of intergroup conflict. *The Social Psychology of Intergroup Relations, 33*(47), 33–47.

Tannert, C., Elvers, H.-D., & Jandrig, B. (2007). The ethics of uncertainty. In the light of possible dangers, research becomes a moral duty. *EMBO Reports, 8*(10), 892–896. https://doi.org/10.1038/sj.embor.7401072

Taylor, F. W. (1911). *The principles of scientific management*. New York, NY: Harper & Brothers.

Tranchard, S. (2017). *ISO 31000 revision moves towards a clearer and more concise text*. Retrieved from https://www.iso.org/news/2017/02/Ref2165.html

Trope, Y., & Liberman, N. (2010). Construal-level theory of psychological distance. *Psychological Review, 117*, 440–463. https://doi.org/10.1037/a0018963

Tversky, A., & Kahneman, D. (1974). Judgment under uncertainty: Heuristics and biases. *Science, 185*(4157), 1124–1131.

Tversky, A., & Kahneman, D. (1981). The framing of decisions and the psychology of choice. *Science, 211*(4481), 453–458.

Tversky, A., & Kahneman, D. (1982). Judgments of and by representativeness. In D. Kahneman, P. Slovic, & A. Tversky (Eds.), *Judgment under uncertainty: Heuristics and biases*. Cambridge: Cambridge University Press.

Tversky, A., & Kahneman, D. (1983). Extensional versus intuitive reasoning: The conjunction fallacy in probability judgment. *Psychological Review, 90*(4), 293–315. https://doi.org/10.1037/0033-295X.90.4.293

Vaara, E., Sonenshein, S., & Boje, D. (2016). Narratives as sources of stability and change in organizations: Approaches and directions for future research. *The Academy of Management Annals, 10*(1), 495–560. https://doi.org/10.1080/19416520.2016.1120963

Vallacher, R. R., & Wegner, D. M. (1985). *A theory of action identification*. Hillsdale, NJ: Erlbaum.

Vallacher, R. R., & Wegner, D. M. (1987). What do people think they're doing? Action identification and human behavior. *Psychological Review, 94*(1), 3.

Van der Pligt, J., & Midden, C. J. (1990). Chernobyl: Four years later: Attitudes, risk management and communication. *Journal of Environmental Psychology, 10*(2), 91–99. https://doi.org/10.1016/s0272-4944(05)80120-3

VanVactor, J. D. (2007). Risk mitigation through a composite risk management process: The U.S. Army risk assessment. *Organization Development Journal, 25*(2), 133–138.

Warner, T. D. (2017). Adolescent sexual risk taking: The distribution of youth behaviors and perceived peer attitudes across neighborhood contexts. *Journal of Adolescent Health*. https://doi.org/10.1016/j.jadohealth.2017.09.007

Wegner, D. M., & Vallacher, R. R. (1986). Action identification. In R. M. Sorrentino & E. T. Higgins (Eds.), *Handbook of motivation and cognition* (Vol. 1, pp. 550–582). New York, NY: Guilford.

Wehman, P., Goldstein, M. A., & Williams, J. R. (1977). Effects of different leadership styles on individual risk taking in groups. *Human Relations, 30*(3), 249–259. https://doi.org/10.1177/001872677703000303

Weichbrodt, J. (2015). Safety rules as instruments for organizational control, coordination and knowledge: Implications for rules management. *Safety Science, 80*, 221–232. https://doi.org/10.1016/j.ssci.2015.07.031

Wilson, A. D., & Golonka, S. (2013). Embodied cognition is not what you think it is. *Frontiers in Psychology, 4*, 1–13. https://doi.org/10.3389/fpsyg.2013.00058

Wilson, T. D., Houston, C., Etling, K. M., & Brekke, N. (1996). A new look at anchoring effects: Basic anchoring and its antecedents. *Journal of Experimental Psychology: General, 4*, 387–402. https://doi.org/10.3724/sp.j.1041.2008.00160

Wu, G., & Gonzalez, R. (1999). Nonlinear decision weights in choice under uncertainty. *Management Science, 45*(1), 74–85.

Wu, G., Zhang, J., & Gonzalez, R. (2007). Decision under risk. In D. J. Koehler & N. Harvey (Eds.), *Blackwell handbook of judgment and decision making*. Oxford: Blackwell.

Zamboanga, B. L., Audley, S., Iwamoto, D. K., Martin, J. L., & Tomaso, C. C. (2017). The risks of being 'manly': Masculine norms and drinking game motives, behaviors, and related consequences among men. *Psychology of Men and Masculinity, 18*(4), 280–292. https://doi.org/10.1037/men0000064

Zuckerman, M. (1979). *Sensation seeking: Beyond the optimal level of arousal*. Hillsbaum, NJ: Lawrence Erlbaum.

Part IV
Communicating Risks to the Public

Chapter 11
Communicating Risks: Principles and Challenges

Ann Bostrom, Gisela Böhm, and Robert E. O'Connor

Abstract Risk communication is about exchanging risk information and opinions, and influences how people perceive and act on risks. This chapter first describes how risk communicators attract people's attention and present information. Then the chapter explores what influences understanding and acceptance or rejection of messages, with a focus on uncertainty and mental models. Next, the chapter describes how people evaluate and use risk messages and how risk messaging relates to behavioral tendencies and behavioral responses, with an emphasis on choice architecture and habits. Finally, the chapter concludes with a discussion of the importance of matching risk communication goals and methods to audience attributes.

Introduction

Risk communication is "an interactive process of exchange of information and opinion between individuals, groups and institutions" (NRC, 1989, p. 2). Risk communication includes a wide range of potential participants—risk communicators and audiences—from scientists to journalists, educators, nurses and doctors, pharmacists, insurance agents, and other professional intermediaries and even to neighbors, family, and friends. Everybody communicates risk. Journalists communicate risk in mass media, often through stories (e.g., McComas & Shanahan, 1999), not

---

A. Bostrom (✉)
Daniel J. Evans School of Public Policy & Governance, University of Washington, Seattle, WA, USA
e-mail: abostrom@uw.edu

G. Böhm
Department of Psychosocial Science, Faculty of Psychology, University of Bergen, Bergen, Norway

Department of Psychology, Inland Norway University of Applied Sciences, Lillehammer, Norway

R. E. O'Connor
Social, Behavioral and Economic Sciences Directorate, National Science Foundation, Alexandria, VA, USA

M. Raue et al. (eds.), *Psychological Perspectives on Risk and Risk Analysis*,
https://doi.org/10.1007/978-3-319-92478-6_11

always through probabilities (e.g., Jennings & Hulme, 2010). Government agencies communicate risk through warnings, pamphlets, websites, and so forth and by tasking intermediaries to communicate risk, as well as through dedicated channels such as the US National Oceanic and Atmospheric Administration's weather radio. Family and friends are important sources of information about risks (e.g., IOM & NRC, 2010).

The goals for risk communication vary accordingly, across an impressive range, from "rais[ing] the level of understanding of relevant issues or actions for those involved and satisf[ying] them that they are adequately informed within the limits of available knowledge" (NRC, 1989, p. 2) to changing people's minds and behaviors and even policies and institutions. Among these goals, advocacy, for example, of health or environmental behaviors, is arguably the most controversial, especially in the absence of analytic and deliberative, democratic processes to determine the aims advocated. When evident, persuasive intent can also provoke boomerang effects (i.e., a reaction opposite to that desired or expected, also called reactance; see, e.g., Quick et al., 2013).

Rather than attempting to surveil this vast domain, in this chapter we focus on select elements of the psychology of risk communications that are common across many goals and situations, and which continue to challenge those involved in risk communication.

Risk communication as a field spans disparate and sometimes disconnected areas of research and practice, from crisis informatics (e.g., Starbird et al., 2015; Sutton, Palen, & Shklovski, 2008; Vieweg, Hughes, Starbird, & Palen, 2010) to structured decision making in communities (Gregory et al., 2012), with much of the available research focusing on risk communication that advocates or attempts to persuade people to take specific health behaviors (e.g., Reynolds & Seeger, 2014). This complexity manifests itself in the heterogeneity of theories applied to risk communication. Pertinent theories tackle risk communication on multiple levels, from what might be called the microlevel or physiology and psychology of individual risk perception and risk information appraisal (e.g., Keller et al., 2012), to the meso-level of interpersonal and one-to-many risk information sharing (e.g., Siegrist, Earle, & Gutscher, 2003), and the macro-level of how risk information spreads and evolves in society (Pidgeon, Kasperson, & Slovic, 2003).

When is risk communication effective? Achieving risk awareness, understanding, or even informed consent with regard to risky decisions poses challenges that at least superficially differ from the potential risk communication goals of changing attitudes and/or behaviors. Further, enduring social change is likely to require institutions and incentives that align with risk communication efforts, as in the cases of leaded gasoline and smoking (Oreskes & Conway, 2010). Repeated exposure, false and missed alarms, risk tradeoffs, and competing risks can all influence the effects of risk communications.

Health and environmental psychologists and other behavioral researchers have investigated risk perceptions, communication, and decision making for many decades (see, e.g., Fischhoff, 2012; Slovic, 2001). Early theories of risk perception focused primarily on identifying factors that might explain which risks people would deem acceptable or unacceptable (Fischhoff, Slovic, Lichtenstein, Read, & Combs, 1978), including and in addition to the magnitude and probability of harm. Research on individual risk perception and interpretation of risk information is still nascent, however (Keller et al., 2012). Only recently have technologies—such as easier-to-use eye trackers—and research approaches advanced to allow researchers to track how people process visual and text information in microscopic detail (e.g., Keller, Kreuzmair, Leins-Hess, & Siegrist, 2014). An example from eye tracking is Munafò, Roberts, Bauld, and Leonards (2011), which shows that the greater number of eye movements of non-smokers are directed at health warnings on plain packages than on branded packages, while this does not hold for daily smokers.

The many sciences of risk communication paint the task of how to communicate risks as one that requires an informed sensitivity to the nuances of culture, psychology, and politics, as well as domain-specific expertise, and analytical sophistication to characterize specific risks and vulnerabilities, and how they are created, vary, and can be changed. Understanding the underlying causal hazardous processes as well as the overarching social and psychological contexts are thus an important, if not essential, starting point for risk communicators.

In the following, we use stages of change as a general framework to introduce specific topics in four areas: exposure and attention, understanding and acceptance, evaluative reactions and behavioral tendencies, and behavioral response. We conclude with reflections on the role of psychological research in risk communication.

Elements of Risk Communication

At a minimum, risk communication is about influencing how humans perceive risks. Sometimes the intention is to affirm the perceptions that people already hold. For example, warnings about the dangers from smoking aimed at non-smokers are not intended to change their views or behavior, but instead to confirm their understanding that smoking is unhealthy and to encourage them to continue their abstinence. Sometimes the intention is to inform with no obvious persuasive element. For example, the purpose of messages about the risks from hip replacement surgery may be to help potential patients make more informed decisions, decisions that align with their preferences and not necessarily their surgeon's. Generally, the intention is to raise awareness, change attitudes, or change behaviors. For example, the goal of some climate change communications is to alert citizens to the societal threat it poses by raising awareness of the seriousness of its potential consequences.

Risk communication also occurs in many different settings. It can involve individuals or groups that communicate via diverse media in one-to-one, one-to-many, or other modes, assume various roles (e.g., journalists, physicians, educators, lobbyists, politicians), and pursue manifold goals. Given this book's focus on psychological aspects, we concentrate on interindividual processes and start out with a general framework that is based on the traditional *Shannon-Weaver model of communication* (Shannon & Weaver, 1963 and, e.g., Pierce, 1980), according to which a sender

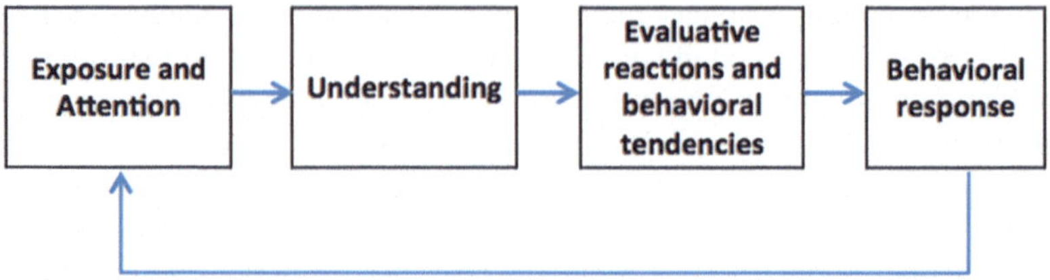

Fig. 11.1 Key components of risk information processing

sends a message to a receiver. Risk communications involve the content of the message and the sender's intention.

Complex and diverse factors influence the communication process so that the message may not be understood by the receiver as intended or, if understood, may still fail to have the intended effect. These components of the processing of risk communications are distinguished in traditional models of persuasive communication such as the *Yale attitude change approach.* In his pioneering model, McGuire (1985) distinguished the following stages: presentation (exposure), attention, comprehension, yielding (acceptance), retention, and behavior, which are reflected in the stages of risk information processing we discuss in this chapter (Fig. 11.1).

While risk communication and persuasive communication are not the same, they have substantial overlap. Persuasive communication attempts to influence a person's intentions, attitudes, beliefs, or behaviors. This can, in many instances, be said about risk communication, only that risk communication messages have, because they convey risk information, a more specific content, whereas persuasive messages may focus on other topics. Building on these stages of processing, we structure this section on four key components of risk communication:

A. Exposure and attention:

   1. Exposure: What do risk communicators express and how do they communicate? That is, which types of risks and which dissemination pathways prevail in risk communications?
   2. Attention: How do messages attract people's attention? Important aspects are design and format features of risk messages.

B. Understanding and acceptance:

   1. Information processing: What governs understanding (e.g., expression of uncertainty, mental models)?
   2. Acceptance of the message: Which messages are believed to be true? An influential factor is, for example, trust in sender.

C. Evaluative reactions and behavioral tendencies:

   1. Evaluative reactions to the message: Cognitive (e.g., perceived risk) and emotional (e.g., fear) responses.

2. Behavioral preferences: Which behavioral options are taken into account? What influences behavioral tendencies (e.g., perceived efficacy, culture, identity protection)?

D. Behavioral response:

1. Behavior: Which contextual factors influence behavior (e.g., nudging, incentives)?
2. Habit: Which factors foster retention and maintenance of behavior? Which factors foster change?

Exposure and Attention

Exposure to risk information can be accidental or intentional. Further, selective attention and confirmatory processing can act in a spiral of reinforcement (e.g., Zhao, 2009), in which people preferentially attend to and remember information that reinforces their prior beliefs about a risk, such as climate change. People selectively seek out risk information sources that align with their priors, and those sources reinforce their priors (e.g., Feldman, Myers, Hmielowski, & Leiserowitz, 2014; Zhao, Rolfe-Redding, & Kotcher, 2016), potentially creating polarization, for example, in which those who oppose climate change mitigation become more strongly opposed and those who support climate change mitigation become more supportive. As information sharing has gone online, macro-level research on the social, temporal, and spatial spread and reach of communications has begun to surface, enabling large-scale examination of risk information exposure patterns and mechanisms; to date these appear to validate psychological studies (e.g., Jasny, Waggle, & Fisher, 2015). Reinforcing spirals of selective attention and confirmatory processing (i.e., paying attention to and remembering only information that agrees with one's prior beliefs) appear to apply to personal experience as a source of risk information as well (Taylor, de Bruin, & Dessai, 2014). This means that interpretations of experiences (e.g., extreme weather events) tend to align with and reinforce prior beliefs (e.g., global warming is causing more extreme weather events). Thus reliance on sources for risk communication varies by interest, attitudes, and beliefs. For example, in a Dutch study of food risk communication sources, most respondents relied selectively on scientific institutions (government and scientific sources) or personal sources (family and friends), while a minority with strong interests in the issues relied on a broader swath of all available sources, and the remaining respondents who held little interest in the issues relied primarily on food labels (Kornelis, De Jonge, Frewer, & Dagevos, 2007).

Dissemination strategies for risk communications vary by goal and context, but many have as a goal to reach people who may not be aware of or attending to potential risks. Current warning processes in the USA for risks such as tornados or flash-floods may include reverse 9-1-1 (in which warning systems autodial cellphones with warnings), social media posts, radio spots, TV banners, or sirens (e.g., Morss,

Demuth, Bostrom, Lazo, & Lazrus, 2015), which are designed to capture attention and evoke an immediate response.

Design elements (e.g., visual, textual, graphical, numerical) can help people discern, understand, and remember what to do. Visual features that capture attention are color, motion, orientation, and size (Wolfe & Horowitz, 2004). Visual design elements can help capture and focus attention (e.g., Wogalter, 2006). For example, text features such as headers and subheadings can greatly facilitate text comprehension (Schriver, 1997). A case in point is this chapter, in which the section headings can help readers identify specific content. Pictographs (i.e., dot plots or other icons in arrays) can help people understand probabilities of harms (Zikmund-Fisher et al., 2014). Some strategies, however, can differentially disadvantage potential message recipients. As discussed further in the next section, people with low numeracy have difficulty understanding or using numbers and may be more susceptible to framing effects (Peters & Levin, 2008). Framing refers here to how a given piece of information is presented (or framed) in communications (Scheufele & Iyengar, 2012; although framing can refer to other related phenomena, Cacciatore, Scheufele, & Iyengar, 2016). For example, a 70% chance of contracting influenza and getting sick can also be presented as a 30% chance of remaining healthy and not contracting influenza. Numeracy influences attention to and interpretation of numbers and pictographs in risk messages; low numerates focus initially on the pictographs more than do high numerates (Keller et al., 2014), but anthropomorphic pictographs improve risk perception and recall more for high numerates (Zikmund-Fisher et al., 2014).

Understanding and Acceptance: Uncertainty and Mental Models

Expressing Uncertainty in Risk Communications

One essential component of virtually all risk communication is to provide an understanding of the risk phenomenon at hand (Rakow, Heard, & Newell, 2015), for example, of the processes that may lead to exposure to a risk and what the potential consequences are. Such information is usually based on scientific evidence, so that risk communication commonly includes information about scientific facts. An inherent feature of all scientific explanations and predictions is uncertainty. Hence, communicating risks inevitably entails communicating uncertainty, for example, in the form of probabilities of events or ranges of predictions.

Uncertainty can have many meanings. Risk is traditionally defined as an uncertain negative outcome (Aven & Renn, 2009) so that in the literature on risk perception and communication the prevailing concept of uncertainty refers to the probability with which the uncertain outcome may occur. Yates and Stone (1992) argued more than 20 years ago that the uncertainty component of the risk construct is more diverse and includes other aspects of uncertainty in addition to the probability of the outcome, for example, uncertainty with respect to which outcomes might possibly occur or uncertainty with respect to the reliability of probability estimates. With the emergence of global risks, and in the recent debate about climate change in particular, the inherently uncertain and preliminary nature of all scientific knowledge has become a focal point in the public discussion, in the media and in politics. Such scientific uncertainty arises, for example, from insufficient data, contradictory results, divergent interpretations of results, and lack of knowledge concerning causal relations, model components, and parameters (Dumanoski, Farland, & Krimsky, 1999; Van der Sluijs, 2008; Zehr, 2000). It is this scientific uncertainty that has been used as an argument in strategic SCAM messages (see below) to foster climate skeptical views in public opinion (Oreskes & Conway, 2010). In contrast, consensus among scientists has been identified as the element of scientific uncertainty that plays a particularly crucial role in risk communications in that perceived scientific consensus has been shown to determine belief in the reality of climate change as well as climate change risk perceptions and support for climate policy (Lewandowsky, Gignac, & Vaughan, 2013; Van der Linden, Leiserowitz, Feinberg, & Maibach, 2015).

Bassarak, Pfister, and Böhm (2017) show that controversial societal risks such as climate change are characterized by a psychological quality that they called *disputed risk* and which reflects not only epistemic uncertainty about what is correct but also evaluative uncertainty about how to form an opinion about the risk issue. Pfister, Jungermann, and Fischer (2017) summarize the list of things to which uncertainty in decision situations can refer as follows: (a) the probability of events or states, (b) the truth of facts and information, (c) the strength of arguments and reasons, (d) the personal endorsement of or commitment to goals and values, and, finally, (e) uncertainty itself (e.g., if a decision-maker is uncertain about the probability of an event).

The uncertain and preliminary nature of science is difficult to understand for many lay people and poses a major challenge for effectively communicating scientific information to the general public (Rabinovich & Morton, 2012). One reason for this difficulty is that stochastic uncertainty and in particular the language of probability theory is incomprehensible or misleading to lay people (Borgida & Nisbett, 1977; Pidgeon & Fischhoff, 2011; Roten, 2006; Utts, 2003). Another reason is that lay people seek and prefer certain and unambiguous information that can guide them in their everyday decisions (Rabinovich & Morton, 2012). The very features of the scientific discourse that scientists use to assure quality, such as explicitly expressing uncertainties or limiting conditions, may be viewed as confusing, untrustworthy, and disqualifying by the public (Frewer et al., 2003; Johnson & Slovic, 1998). Indeed, the existence of uncertainty has been used successfully as an argument in strategic communications that aim to discredit science, as exemplified by attempts to manufacture doubt in climate research (Oreskes & Conway, 2010). The use of appeals to uncertainty as argumentative strategy to forestall mitigative actions is so pervasive in scientific or technological controversies that it has been assigned a name in scholarly analyses: *Scientific Certainty Argumentation Methods* or SCAMs for short (Freudenburg, Gramling, & Davidson, 2008). One possible mechanism by which uncertainty may undermine willingness to act, as suggested by SCAMs, may be a tendency of uncertainty to trigger wishful thinking, for example, by reducing the perceived severity or probability of the predicted outcome (Markowitz & Shariff, 2012).

On the other hand, results from one of the most prevalent paradigms in the study of risk perception—psychometric studies (which measure the psychological dimensions of risk perceptions, e.g., Fischhoff et al., 1978; Slovic, Fischhoff, & Lichtenstein, 1984)—suggest that uncertainty in the sense of lack of knowledge (i.e., epistemic uncertainty) may be unrelated to perceived risk and to the willingness to support mitigative or preventive action. These studies have repeatedly found that the extent to which a risk is unknown (e.g., new, unobservable, having delayed impacts) is independent of the extent to which a risk is dreaded (e.g., ascribed catastrophic potential and fatal consequences) and of the desire to enforce strict risk reducing regulations (Slovic, 1987). Some personal background variables have been identified that moderate how a recipient reacts to uncertainty expressed in risk communication messages. One such variable is epistemic beliefs. For example, Rabinovich and Morton (2012) showed that messages that convey high uncertainty in the prediction of climate change impacts are more persuasive for people who endorse a Kuhnian model of science as debate, than for people who hold a classical view of science as a search for truth, whereas the reverse was true for low uncertainty messages.[1] Please check if the change is fine in this occurrence and modify the subsequent occurrences, if necessary. Another influential variable is numeracy, with the less numerate showing considerable difficulty in understanding and using numerical probability information (Peters et al., 2006).

Probability is arguably the aspect of uncertainty that is most commonly conveyed in risk communications (for an introduction and summary, see Teigen, 2012). For the sake of brevity, we will only briefly discuss different ways of communicating probability. Probabilities are often expressed either numerically or verbally. How numerical probability information is processed and understood depends highly on the recipient's numeracy (Rakow et al., 2015). A common phenomenon is that numerical expressions that are mathematically equivalent (e.g., probabilities, percentages, relative frequencies, odds) are not perceived as such and evoke different judgments (see also Hoffrage & Garcia-Retamero, Chap. 12). For example, a seminal study by Slovic, Monahan, and MacGregor (2000) demonstrated that forensic psychologists and psychiatrists judged a mental patient more harshly when he was described as having a 20% chance of committing a violent offense than when this chance was expressed as 20 in 100. Even the same format, say, a relative frequency, has a different impact depending on the specific numbers that are used. For example, a 1 in 100 chance of an adverse event sounds less risky than 10,000 in a million (Teigen, 2012). Efforts to reduce the volatility of risk perceptions have included the

[1] Kuhn (1962) interprets the history of science as showing that scientific disciplines experience paradigm shifts in which traditions are shattered through very human processes. An alternative view is that science progresses incrementally as scientists make new discoveries and accumulate facts.

development of standardized scales (e.g., Lermer, Streicher, Sachs, & Frey, 2013; Woloshin, Schwartz, Byram, Fischhoff, & Welch, 2000).

Risk communicators frequently express probabilities verbally rather than numerically. For example, the Intergovernmental Panel on Climate Change (IPCC) has developed careful guidelines for translating probabilities to verbal phrases (e.g., virtually certain, likely, very unlikely) in their assessment reports. Such verbal probabilities are commonly not understood by the audience as intended, though (Budescu, Por, Broomell, & Smithson, 2014). Verbal probability expressions are ambiguous as to which numerical probability they express. Some expressions are more ambiguous and cover a rather broad probability range (e.g., possible); others are narrower (e.g., improbably) (Budescu & Wallsten, 1995). Both individual and situational factors contribute to variations in the interpretation of verbal probability phrases. Two such factors are the perceived base rate (perceptions of how common an outcome is) and severity of an outcome (Weber & Hilton, 1990). Thus, probability words such as *likely* or *possible* are interpreted differently depending on how common versus rare and how mundane versus serious the target event is perceived to be, for example, *it's possible it will rain today in Seattle*, as compared to *it's possible an asteroid will hit London in our lifetimes*. Tests of the effects of including numerical uncertainties adjacent to verbal probabilities suggest that this more effectively conveys intended probabilities, despite the increased cognitive burden (e.g., Budescu, Por, & Broomell, 2012).

Verbal probability expressions possess directionality in that some phrases focus on the occurrence (positive directionality, e.g., *perhaps*) whereas other phrases focus on the nonoccurrence of the event (negative directionality, e.g., *unlikely*), which influences subsequent judgments and decisions (Teigen & Brun, 1999). Generally positive phrases describe higher probabilities than negative phrases, but some positive and negative expressions cover similar probability ranges. For example, the expressions *possible* and *somewhat uncertain* both refer to a probability of about 40% (Teigen, 2012). Positive and negative phrases differ in their argumentative direction; they convey optimism and encouragement (e.g., think of a medical treatment that is possible to be successful) versus pessimism and discouragement (e.g., a treatment that is somewhat uncertain to help). The important lesson to be learned is that risk messages convey not only information about facts (the probability of an outcome) but also pragmatic information about conversational implications such as encouragement or discouragement.

Deciding how best to communicate uncertain risks quantitatively is not simple, as there are few generally accepted rules of thumb. Rakow et al. (2015) note appropriately that effective quantified risk messaging requires attention to the potential ambiguity of such messages, the evaluability of the quantitative information with respect to the severity of the implied risks, and the audiences' levels of numeracy.

Mental Models

People interpret risk messages and hazardous events through their existing mental model(s) (Morgan, Fischhoff, Bostrom, Lave, & Atman, 1992; Morgan, Fischhoff, Bostrom, & Atman, 2002). For this reason eliciting and analyzing mental models of hazardous processes can be a useful starting place for developing effective risk communications (Bostrom, Fischhoff, & Morgan, 1992; Böhm & Pfister, 2001; Bruine de Bruin & Bostrom, 2013; Eggers, Ackerlund, Thorne, & Butte, 2010; Löfstedt, 1991; Morgan et al., 1992; Niewöhner, Cox, Gerrard, & Pidgeon, 2004; Wood, Kovacs, Bostrom, Bridges, & Linkov, 2012).

Mental models are knowledge structures that an individual "runs" or simulates to make inferences and to solve problems. Mental models encompass causal beliefs, but can be piecemeal and incomplete (Johnson-Laird, 2004; Norman, 1983), and developed in context as a function of one's goals or the problem at hand, rather than stored in long- term memory (Kahneman & Tversky, 1982; Tversky, 1993). Mental models are recognized as essential building blocks for user-focused design, computer science and interface development (e.g., Narayanan & Hegarty, 1998; Norman, 1988), and science education (e.g., Mishra & Brewer, 2003) and have gained widespread recognition as a fundamental determinant of human decisions and behavior (e.g., in the 2015 World Development report by the World Bank). The elicitation of mental models of physical processes, such as how electricity works, has for several decades been a focus of studies in science education, cognitive anthropology, and cognitive psychology (e.g., Gentner & Stevens, 1983; Kempton, 1986; Mishra & Brewer, 2003; Nersessian, 1992), as well as health (Jungermann, Schütz, & Thürung, 1988; Meyer, Leventhal, & Gutmann, 1985). Mental models research for risk communication builds on these studies (e.g., Bostrom et al., 1992), by examining mental models of hazardous processes and assessing what information the message recipient would need to mitigate the risk induced by those hazards (Bruine de Bruin & Bostrom, 2013; Morgan et al., 2002).

Like other mental models, mental models of hazardous processes vary according to level of expertise (e.g., Morss et al., 2015). Experts have more structured and coherent mental models in general and are less likely to infer parts of hazardous processes from analogous risks, or to exhibit large gaps in their knowledge, for example, with regard to exposure processes (e.g., Bostrom et al., 1992; Lazrus, Morss, Demuth, Lazo, & Bostrom, 2016). They are also more likely to understand specifics that enable them to distinguish one hazardous process from another. For example, mental models studies have found that laypeople may confuse or conflate risks that share common properties, such as stratospheric ozone depletion and global warming (both of which involve anthropogenic emissions of gases) (Reynolds, Bostrom, Read, & Morgan, 2010).

Until one has determined the mental models of the recipients of risk messages, and subjected draft communication materials to empirical evaluation, it is generally not possible to reliably choose the content of effective risk communication messages or predict how messages will be interpreted. Determining mental models requires analyzing decision making and behaviors, or using ethnographic or cognitive research approaches designed for this purpose (for examples and specifics, see Böhm & Pfister, 2001; Bruine de Bruin & Bostrom, 2013; Gentner, 2002; Gentner & Stevens, 1983).

Evaluative Reactions and Behavioral Tendencies

Evaluative Reactions

How people use and evaluate risk messages has been a topic of many studies, including, for example, studies of whether official warnings promote hurricane evacuation (they do, Huang, Lindell, & Prater, 2016). As one might anticipate given the findings on selective attention and confirmatory processing discussed above, prior trust in the message sender/source is an important determinant of message processing (e.g., White, Cohrs, & Göritz, 2011; for further discussion of trust in risk communication and management, see Löfstedt, 2005; Siegrist, Earle, & Gutscher, 2010). As noted above, another major determinant of an individual's evaluation of risk messages and of responses to risk events is their mental models. Mental models determine not only which risks are perceived and how they are evaluated but also emotional reactions and behavioral responses (Böhm, 2003; Böhm & Pfister, 2000, 2005, 2017). An important proximate cause of behavior is the emotions that an individual experiences vis-à-vis a risk event. Behavioral tendencies result from the emotional responses to a few dimensions of the message or situation, including agency, outcome desirability, fairness, certainty, and coping potential (Ellsworth & Scherer, 2003; Keller et al., 2012; Scherer, 1999), which are assessed based on an individual's mental model of the situation. These appraisal dimensions differentiate different specific emotions such as fear, anger, sadness, or disappointment. It is important to distinguish such specific emotions as it has been shown that different specific emotions can have different effects on risk evaluations and behaviors, even if they share the same valence. For example, fear amplifies perceived risk, whereas anger reduces perceived risk, even though both emotions have a negative valence (Lerner & Keltner, 2000, 2001; see also Tompkins et al., Chap. 5).

A specific emotion that deserves particular attention when considering risk communication is fear, as a considerable amount of risk communication practice and research has been concerned with fear appeals. Inducing fear has long been seen as a viable way to reduce people's risk taking. Recent meta-analyses conclude that threat appeals (fear) and efficacy—the perceived ability to achieve something or attain a given goal—do drive attitudes and behavior (Peters, Ruiter, & Kok, 2013; Ruiter, Abraham, & Kok, 2001; Ruiter, Kessels, Peters, & Kok, 2014; Tannenbaum et al., 2015). Theories such as the extended parallel process model (EPPM) suggest that excessive fear might be counterproductive, for example, by producing denial (Maloney, Lapinski, & Witte 2011), but the preponderance of evidence finds that fear effectively motivates action, though more so in combination with efficacy (Tannenbaum et al., 2015).

Although it has been theorized that fear appeals can backfire if they are too strong, there is little evidence of this, but also little evidence regarding how much fear appeals actually evoke (Tannenbaum et al., 2015). Further, efficacy and actionable information motivate risk reduction action more than does fear (Ruiter et al., 2014).

Behavioral Tendencies

As mentioned in the preceding section, the literature on fear appeals demonstrates clearly that the effect of such appeals depends crucially on whether behavioral options exist and are communicated that are easy to perform and effective in reducing the risk (e.g., Ruiter et al., 2014). Similarly, knowledge about available behaviors and their effectiveness is the most important type of knowledge for predicting behavior, for example, in the realm of ecological behaviors (Kaiser & Fuhrer, 2003). For politically relevant behaviors, perceived effectiveness of policy options was shown to be the strongest predictor of policy preferences in an international survey on climate change risk perception and policy support (Bostrom et al., 2012). Taken together, these results suggest that the mental representation of behavioral options—most notably, knowledge about them and judgments concerning their effectiveness and the ease with which they can be performed—plays a pivotal role in shaping risk behaviors and should therefore have an important place in risk communications.

One of the most widely used concepts is perceived efficacy, that is, a person's perceived ability to produce certain attainments. Many authors draw on Bandura's (1997) seminal work, which distinguished self-efficacy from outcome expectancies. Self-efficacy refers to people's belief in their capability to execute certain behaviors, whereas outcome expectations are judgments about the outcomes that are likely to result from these behaviors (Bandura, 2006). Both are important determinants of behavioral responses (Bandura, 1997). The distinction between the behavior and its consequences is sometimes not as clearly drawn as by Bandura, and the concept of efficacy is used more loosely. Self-efficacy and outcome expectancy may be conflated, as exemplified by the following example item: "There are simple things I can do that reduce the negative consequences of the climate crisis" (see Brody, Zahran, Vedlitz, & Grover, 2008; Brody, Grover, & Vedlitz, 2012; Heath & Gifford, 2006; Kellstedt, Zahran, & Vedlitz, 2008; Mead et al., 2012; Milfont, 2012; Morton, Rabinovich, Marshall, & Bretschneider, 2011; Spence, Poortinga, Butler, & Pidgeon, 2011; Van Zomeren, Spears, & Leach, 2010). Also, different terms are used (e.g., personal efficacy rather than self-efficacy; e.g., Kellstedt et al., 2008). And several very similar concepts exist (e.g., perceived behavioral control in the theory of planned behavior). Some papers that claim to measure efficacy actually measure other, related constructs (e.g., ascription of responsibility) (see Kellstedt et al., 2008; Milfont, 2012) or some combination of efficacy and other constructs (see Brody et al., 2008; Brody et al., 2012; Mead et al., 2012).[2] Notwithstanding this

[2] See also Aitken, Chapman, and McClure's (2011) measures of powerlessness, Gifford and

sometimes blurry conceptualization, a rich research tradition exists that documents that self-efficacy exerts a strong influence on behavior and on successful goal attainment in the realm of health as well as environmental risks. A 2014 meta-analysis that examined the effects of experimental manipulation of risk appraisal on behavior and attention across health and environmental domains found that these manipulations were most successful when coping appraisals (including self- and response efficacy) were also heightened (Sheeran, Harris, & Epton, 2014).

Environmental risks, and particularly global risks such as climate change, have an important collective dimension so that forms of efficacy become pertinent that relate to social or collective action. Bandura (2001) distinguishes two forms of social agency: proxy agency that relies on others to act on one's behalf to secure desired outcomes and collective agency that is exercised through socially coordinative and interdependent effort. Proxy agency is partly reflected in efficacy approaches that look at political action, for example, in Lubell's (2002) concept of government efficacy, that is, beliefs in the responsiveness of governments to citizen demands. Collective agency is reflected in concepts of collective efficacy. According to Bandura (2000), collective efficacy is an emergent group quality and refers to people's shared beliefs in their collective power to produce desired results. Again, other authors have used other terms for this concept (e.g., group efficacy, Van Zomeren et al., 2010). In addition, other efficacy variants have been introduced to address the social and collective nature of environmental action. For example, van Zomeren et al.'s (2010) concept of participative efficacy, which focuses on the perceived ability to make a personal contribution to achieving a group goal. Hanss and Böhm (2013) identified a component of efficacy that reflects the perceived ability to indirectly contributing to sustainability by motivating others.

Interestingly, Bandura's original conception of collective efficacy does not draw the distinction between efficacy and outcome expectancy that he made on the level of self-efficacy. This lack of distinction persists among some authors (see Lubell, Zahran, & Vedlitz, 2007; Roser-Renouf, Maibach, Leiserowitz, & Zhao, 2014; Thaker, 2012; Van Zomeren et al., 2010; for distinction between these see Koletsou & Mancy, 2011). The relationships between self-efficacy, collective efficacy, and outcome expectancy are complex and yet to be fully explored. Disparate findings in climate change research indicate that outcome expectancy is a function of (or is influenced by) collective efficacy (Roser-Renouf et al., 2014), that collective efficacy is predicted by individual self-efficacy (Truelove, 2009), and that self-efficacy is distinct from collective efficacy (Van Zomeren et al., 2010). Several studies suggest that in the environmental domain collective efficacy may be a more important

Comeau's (2011) measures of perceived competence, climate change engagement, and moral engagement; Lin's (2013) measures of perceived behavioral control, Lorenzoni et al.'s (2007) barriers to personal engagement with climate change, Lubell et al.'s (2007) measures of perceived personal influence, Ortega-Egea, García-de-Frutos and Antolín-López's (2014) measures of attitudes and knowledge, Tobler, Visschers, and Siegrist's (2012) behavioral costs, feeling of powerlessness, and climate benefit, Truelove and Parks' (2012) measures of effectiveness knowledge and effectiveness beliefs, and Whitmarsh's (2009) measures of intent oriented action vs. impact oriented action.

predictor of behavior than self-efficacy, given that collective action is crucial (Homburg & Stolberg, 2006; Van Zomeren et al., 2010).

Similar to other environmental perception research, much of the above research on efficacy with regard to climate change mitigation is survey research, including surveys with experimental manipulations (Bolsen, Leeper, & Shapiro, 2014; Gifford & Comeau, 2011; Greenhalgh, 2011; Morton et al., 2011; Van Zomeren et al., 2010); use of mixed methods, which employ several different methods, such as interviews and surveys (Lorenzoni, Nicholson-Cole, & Whitmarsh, 2007); and use of multiple wave panel data, in which the same people answer questions at intervals over a period of time (Milfont, 2012). Greater use of experimental and mixed methods approaches could strengthen the findings. The few intervention studies that exist in environmental psychology on the role of efficacy beliefs do not provide an unequivocal picture as to whether behavioral change was actually brought about by strengthened efficacy beliefs (Hanss & Böhm, 2013). For health risks, messages conveying efficacy tend to increase health behaviors such as vaccination (e.g., O'Keefe, 2013; Peters et al., 2013), in both self-report and observational studies.

Culture Theory, Identity Protection, and Risk Communication

Risk communication takes place within a context that includes both the nature of the risk to be communicated and the cultural cognitions of the audience for the risk messages. It seems obvious that risk communications on hygiene practices, for example, would differ if designed for undergraduates at a Norwegian college, upland villagers in Angola, or residents of a Southside Chicago nursing home. Less obvious to risk communicators is how different cultural assumptions in demographically similar groups can influence the receptivity of risk communications (e.g., Barnes & Dove, 2015).

One effort to understand different receptivity to health and environmental messages is the culture theory developed by anthropologist Mary Douglas, political scientist Aaron Wildavsky, and social psychologist Karl Dake (Dake, 1991, 1992; Douglas & Wildavsky, 1982; Wildavsky, 1987; Dake and Wildavsky, 1990, 1991). This culture theory posits four dimensions: egalitarianism, fatalism, hierarchy, and individualism. In the US context, egalitarians believe that the country suffers from powerful, huge organizations that exploit nature and the work force, stultifying creativity and cooperation. People who score highly on the egalitarian scale are less likely to trust a risk message from a pharmaceutical company than one from an environmental group. People who score highly on the fatalism scale have low expectations about their ability to influence the world around them, so are typically unlikely to take behavioral steps in response to risk warnings (Ellis, 1993). People who score highly on the hierarchy scale trust those in power, including official experts who comment on health and environmental risks. They respect pronouncements from scientific societies and other leaders. Finally, people who score highly on the individualism scale have confidence in their ability to manage threats, including health and environmental ones. They prize competition among individuals and have little respect for government environmental and health programs. Although the dimensions of culture theory correlate somewhat with measures of political ideology, the correlations are not so strong as to create multicollinearity problems, that is, to make it impossible to determine which dimension is driving which (Riplinger, Song, Nowlin, Jones, & Jenkins-Smith, 2012). Jones (2011) argues that cultural theory may provide advantages over political ideology in that a more nuanced understanding of the origins of risk perceptions may provide insights that can help identify policy compromises for difficult issues such as climate change.

In risk communication research, some researchers have operationalized culture theory on two scales (individualism to communitarianism, egalitarianism to hierarchicalism) each composed of a few items (Kahan, 2012; see also Chauvin, Chap. 2 and Renn, Chap. 16). These scales have proved useful in understanding risk perceptions in different realms including public health (e.g., Kahan, Braman, Cohen, Gastil, & Slovic, 2010) and regulatory policy (Lodge, Wegrich, & McElroy, 2010). An exception to the general utility of the cultural variables is the paucity of studies examining fatalists (Mamadouh, 1999), perhaps because of their general cluelessness. One extension of culture theory is the identity-protective cognition theory popularized by Kahan (e.g., Kahan, Braman, Gastil, Slovic, & Mertz, 2007). Kahan posits that people hold identities that are shaped by their cultural worldviews (e.g., egalitarianism, fatalism, hierarchy, individualism) and that "as a means of identity self-defense, individuals appraise information in a manner that buttresses beliefs association with belonging to particular groups (p. 470)." For example, for individuals who (1) identify strongly with a conservative Christian sect in the USA and (2) understand that the sect rejects the theory of evolution, rejecting the validity of evolution is necessary to protect their identity as conservative Christians. One environmental application of identity-protective cognition theory is McCright and Dunlap's (2011) use of the theory to explain climate change denialism among conservative white males in the USA.

In theory, culture theories should help risk communicators target specific groups, and tailor risk communications to those groups to improve the effectiveness of health and environmental communications (e.g., Kahan, Jenkins-Smith, Tarantola, Silva, & Braman, 2015; McKenzie-Mohr, Lee, Schultz, & Kotler, 2012). While there is considerable evidence for the effectiveness of targeting and tailoring health and environmental risk communications in general, evidence is variable and thin for specific risk topics, such as global warming (Bostrom, Böhm, & O'Connor, 2013; but see Hine et al., 2016; Myers, Nisbet, Maibach, & Leiserowitz, 2012), although attitudes and beliefs in many recent studies polarize based on cultural cognition or political orientation (e.g., Kahan et al., 2015).

Behavioral Response

As highlighted in the previous section and Box11.1, risk communications that stress effective action and efficacy promote protective behaviors, as do fear appeals (Tannenbaum et al., 2015). Risk perceptions, broadly construed, tend to predict risk-related behaviors (e.g., Brewer et al., 2007), but not always (Van der Pligt, 1996).

Much behavior is susceptible to context effects. A relevant example of this is that the default in a decision context has a significant influence on choice (Johnson & Goldstein, 2003). If the default is that home insurance policies include flood insurance unless one opts out, more people will have flood insurance than if they have to opt in to purchase it. This type of choice architecture, or nudging, can be used to influence risk decision making (Thaler and Sunstein, 2008).

Box 11.1 Lessons from Hazard Warnings

Lessons in hazards warning research conducted by both sociologists and psychologists align well with findings from other research on designing risk messages, with some variations in specifics. This is evident from summaries of hazards warning research from 1989 to the present by Sorensen and others:

> Sufficient research has been conducted to discern a poor message from a good one and even a good one from one that reflects state-of-the-art practices. [...].
>
> Five specific topics that are important to include in assembling the actual content of a public warning message are the nature, location, guidance, time, and source of the hazard or risk. The style aspects that are important to include are message specificity, consistency, accuracy, certainty, and clarity (Sorensen, 2000, p. 121).

Effective warning messages contain five essential elements:

1. The source of the warning (so that recipients can assess the expertise and trustworthiness of the source).
2. Identification of the hazard, including its certainty, severity, immediacy, and the duration of dangerous conditions.
3. The specific areas at risk (and safe areas, if not obvious), described in a way people can identify and understand.
4. What to do (i.e., a protective action people see as effective and feasible), when and how to do it, and what it will accomplish.
5. Where to go for further information and assistance.

(Lindell & Brooks, 2012, *p. 14, paraphrased, numbering added; see also* Mileti & Sorensen, 2015)

Nudges and Habits

The purpose of much risk communication is to inform individuals or organizations about the risks they face in the hope that they will make wiser decisions regarding those risks. Despite extensive risk communication campaigns, there are countless examples of unhealthy behavior and environmentally destructive acts.

Much environmentally destructive and unhealthy behavior arises not from choices involving deliberative thinking regarding options, but from the power of defaults and habits (Kahneman, 2011). Research by psychologists and behavioral economists suggests approaches that, although not substituting for good risk communication, may lead to healthier and environmentally friendlier behavior. The "nudge" literature (Thaler and Sunstein, 2008, is the seminal work) argues that defaults are both inevitable and are powerful in influencing behavior. Food items placed at an eye level in a school cafeteria will benefit from that placement in that more students will choose those items than if the same items are placed in less accessible locations. The nudge advocates suggest that placing healthy items at eye level and less healthy items elsewhere makes sense as, after all, some items inevitably must have an advantageous placement. The students who crave the three-cheese pizza can still find it. The idea is that a choice architecture is inevitable, so policymakers should use insights from psychology and behavioral economics to nudge people and organizations toward wiser choices. The idea is libertarian paternalism (see also Raue & Scholl, Chap. 7).

A different, but related literature, looks to the power of habits to understand why people and organizations so often continue to act in unhealthy and environmentally dangerous ways. Then, the literature looks to ways of breaking destructive habits (Duhigg, 2012, summarizes much of the literature). In light of the cognitive limitations of the human brain, we all behave habitually to simplify our lives. If every morning we needed to deliberate the virtues of teeth brushing and similar activities, getting out of the house would take most of the morning. Alcoholics know that excessive drinking is unhealthy, but get drunk anyway. There are cues that stimulate a drinking routine. Practitioners of habit reversal therapy try to reprogram the brain to respond to cues (and the rewards from responding to the cues) by creating new routines to respond to cues. For example, a smoker whose cue for smoking is a chemical craving and whose reward is a good feeling through satisfaction of the craving might be encouraged to develop a new habit of chewing a piece of Nicorette in response to the cue. The idea is that, over time with repetition, the person (now a non-smoker) will unthinkingly reach for a piece of Nicorette rather than a cigarette when feeling a nicotine craving.

Neither the nudge scholars nor the searchers for habit-breaking mechanisms argue that risk communication is irrelevant. The argument is instead that much of our behavior does not flow entirely from a deliberative process of decision making. Understanding the psychological processes behind the power of defaults and habits can contribute to healthier behavior for people and the environment.

Matching Risk Communication Goals with Audience Attributes

As is evident from the above, meeting communication goals requires going beyond good intentions. Risk messages go through a number of processing stages—from exposure and attention via understanding and evaluation to, in some cases, behavioral intentions and action. How a communication influences depends on its effects at each of these stages: Risk communications and specific features of communications may or may not attract attention; risk communications may be interpretable and facilitate correct inferences or lead to erroneous inferences; risk communications may or may not be seen as trustworthy or perceived as coming from a credible source; and whether a risk communication supports and informs effective risk decision making and action depends on all of the above, which are each contingent on audience attributes.

Although recent risk communication handbooks and how-to documents emphasize actionable information, they also address strategic framing and the politics of engagement (e.g., Fischhoff, Brewer, & Downs, 2011; Heath & O'Hair, 2010; Ropeik & Gray, 2002). Engaging stakeholders in deliberations about risk, informing democratic debates about risk acceptability, and supporting decision making about risks can also be the goals of risk communications (Gregory et al., 2012; National Research Council, 1989). Among the most popular risk communication papers of the last two decades is Fischhoff's "risk perception and communication unplugged" article (Fischhoff, 1995), with its developmental stages of risk management, and the proposition that risk management starts with the numbers—probabilities and magnitudes—and advances to include explanations, behavioral context, values, and engagement. A key point in this article is that sharpened conflict may be the outcome of successful communications. Unlike the view of the power of communications implicitly expressed in the classic film "Cool Hand Luke" ("What we've got here is failure to communicate."), successful risk communications may bring adversaries to understand the depth of their differences in ways that exacerbate conflict.

Identifying the goals of a particular risk communication or risk communication campaign is essential for success and also for assessing success. Risk communications range from telling a child to step back from the curb until the traffic light changes, to international collaborations, debates, and even cyber battles to distort or sabotage communications addressing climate change. We know a great deal about how openness to risk messages varies by the particular goals of the communication, the characteristics of messages (e.g., numeric, visual), and the nature of the audience (e.g., cultural beliefs, mental models, demographic group). Studies to date show that strategies that would seem logically to produce effective results can have unexpected negative consequences or, perhaps more frequently, are effective with some segments of the population, have no effect with other groups, and are actually counterproductive with some people. A good message for college students may be ineffective among older populations. The challenge in designing risk communication messages is to align the goals of the communication with the audience's background in such a way that the message can be processed by the recipient effectively. As this chapter notes, emerging research on microprocessing of risk messages promises to afford new insights into the psychology of risk message processing. Despite the bloom of meta-analyses on risk communication in recent years, we know less about how these factors interact to influence what is heard, understood, and acted upon. There is a continued need for integrative multivariate research that examines the psychology of risk communication across the message-to-mass-movement continuum in order to better understand how risk interpretation relates to action. Risk interpretation and action can mitigate risks, but also coproduce risk in the short and longer terms (Eiser et al., 2012; Tierney, 2014). A more systemic view on risk communication acknowledges the intricate ways in which the components of the communication process interact.

Acknowledgments We gratefully acknowledge the assistance of Kate Crosman with the review of the efficacy literature, support for Bostrom's contributions through NSF1463492, and the many helpful suggestions from reviewers and editors.

References

Aitken, C., Chapman, R., & McClure, J. (2011). Climate change, powerlessness and the commons dilemma: Assessing New Zealanders' preparedness to act. *Global Environmental Change, 21*(2), 752–760.

Aven, T., & Renn, O. (2009). On risk defined as an event where the outcome is uncertain. *Journal of Risk Research, 12*(1), 1–11.

Bandura, A. (1997). Self-efficacy: The exercise of control. New York: Freeman.

Bandura, A. (2000). Exercise of human agency through collective efficacy. *Current Directions in Psychological Science, 9*(3), 75–78.

Bandura, A. (2001). Social cognitive theory: An agentic perspective. *Annual Review of Psychology, 52*, 1–26.

Bandura, A. (2006). Guide for constructing self-efficacy scales. In F. Pajares & T. Urdan (Eds.), *Adolescence and education. Volume 5: Self-efficacy beliefs of adolescents* (pp. 307–337). Greenwich, CT: Information Age Publishing.

Barnes, J., & Dove, M. R. (Eds.). (2015). *Climate cultures: Anthropological perspectives on climate change*. New Haven, CT: Yale University Press.

Bassarak, C., Pfister, H.-R., & Böhm, G. (2017). Dispute and morality in the perception of societal risks: Extending the psychometric model. *Journal of Risk Research, 20*(3), 299–325.

Böhm, G. (2003). Emotional reactions to environmental risks: Consequentialist versus ethical evaluation. *Journal of Environmental Psychology, 23*(2), 199–212.

Böhm, G., & Pfister, H.-R. (2000). Action tendencies and characteristics of environmental risks. *Acta Psychologica, 104*(3), 317–337.

Böhm, G., & Pfister, H.-R. (2001). Mental representation of global environmental risks. *Research in Social Problems and Public Policy, 9*, 1–30.

Böhm, G., & Pfister, H.-R. (2005). Consequences, morality, and time in environmental risk evaluation. *Journal of Risk Research, 8*(6), 461–479.

Böhm, G., & Pfister, H.-R. (2017). The perceiver's social role and a risk's causal structure as determinants of environmental risk evaluation. *Journal of Risk Research, 20*(6), 732–759.

Bolsen, T., Leeper, T. J., & Shapiro, M. A. (2014). Doing what others do: Norms, science, and collective action on global warming. *American Politics Research, 42*(1), 65–89.
Borgida, E., & Nisbett, R. E. (1977). The differential impact of abstract vs. concrete information on decisions. *Journal of Applied Social Psychology, 7*, 258–271.
Bostrom, A., Böhm, G., & O'Connor, R. E. (2013). Targeting and tailoring climate change communications. *Wiley Interdisciplinary Reviews: Climate Change*. https://doi.org/10.1002/wcc.234
Bostrom, A., Fischhoff, B., & Morgan, M. G. (1992). Characterizing mental models of hazardous processes: A methodology and an application to radon. *Journal of Social Issues, 48*(4), 85–100.
Bostrom, A., O'Connor, R. E., Böhm, G., Hanss, D., Bodi, O., … Sælensminde, I. (2012). Causal thinking and support for climate change policies: International survey findings. *Global and Environmental Change: Human and Policy Dimensions, 22*(1), 210–222.
Brewer, N. T., Chapman, G. B., Gibbons, F. X., Gerrard, M., McCaul, K. D., & Weinstein, N. D. (2007). Meta-analysis of the relationship between risk perception and health behavior: The example of vaccination. *Health Psychology, 26*(2), 136–145.
Brody, S., Grover, H., & Vedlitz, A. (2012). Examining the willingness of Americans to alter behaviour to mitigate climate change. *Climate Policy, 12*(1), 1–22.
Brody, S. D., Zahran, S., Vedlitz, A., & Grover, H. (2008). Examining the relationship between physical vulnerability and public perceptions of global climate change in the United States. *Environment and Behavior, 40*(1), 72–95.
Bruine de Bruin, W. B., & Bostrom, A. (2013). Assessing what to address in science communication. *Proceedings of the National Academy of Sciences, 110*(3), 14062–14068.
Budescu, D. V., Por, H.-H., & Broomell, S. B. (2012). Effective communication of uncertainty in the IPCC reports. *Climatic Change, 113*(2), 181–200.
Budescu, D. V., Por, H.-H., Broomell, S. B., & Smithson, M. (2014). The interpretation of IPCC probabilistic statements around the world. *Nature Climate Change, 4*(6), 508–512.
Budescu, D. V., & Wallsten, T. S. (1995). Processing linguistic probabilities: General principles and empirical evidence. *The Psychology of Learning and Motivation, 32*, 275–318.
Cacciatore, M. A., Scheufele, D. A., & Iyengar, S. (2016). The end of framing as we know it… and the Future of Media Effects. *Mass Communication and Society, 19*(1), 7–23.
Dake, K. (1991). Orienting dispositions in the perception of risk: an analysis of contemporary world-views and cultural biases. *Journal of Cross-Cultural Psychology, 22*(1), 61–82.
Dake, K. (1992). Myths of nature: Culture and the social construction or risk. *Journal of Social Issues, 48*(4), 21–37.
Dake, K., Wildavsky, A. (1990). Theories of risk perception: who fears what and why? *Daedalus 119*, 41–60.
Dake, K., Wildavsky, A. (1991). Individual differences in risk perception and risktaking preferences. In: Garrick, B.J., Geckler, W.C. (Eds.), The Analysis, Communication, and Perception of Risk. Plenum, New York.
Douglas, M., & Wildavsky, A. (1982). *Risk and culture: An essay on the selection of technological and environmental dangers*. Berkeley, CA: University of California Press.
Duhigg, C. (2012). *The power of habit: Why we do what we do in life and business*. New York, NY: Random House.
Dumanoski, D., Farland, W., & Krimsky, S. (1999). Science in the public arena: A panel discussion. In S. M. Friedman, S. Dunwoody, & C. L. Rogers (Eds.), *Communicating uncertainty, media coverage of new and controversial science* (pp. 167–178). Mahwah, NJ: Erlbaum Associates.
Eggers, S., Ackerlund, S., Thorne, S., & Butte, G. (2010). *Growers' understanding and implementation of FDA's GAPs Guidance: Mental models research report*. Prepared for FDA, Linda Verrill, Ph.D., Project Officer by Decision Partners. June 2010. Task Order No. 5, Contract Number: HHSF223200510007I. Retrieved from http://www.fda.gov/Food/FoodborneIllnessContaminants/BuyStoreServeSafeFood/ucm218562.htm
Eiser, J. R., Bostrom, A., Burton, I., Johnston, D. M., McClure, J., Paton, D., … White, M. P. (2012). Risk interpretation and action: A conceptual framework for responses to natural hazards. *International Journal of Disaster Risk Reduction. Review Article, 1*, 5–16.

Ellis, R. (1993). *American political cultures*. Oxford: Oxford University Press.

Ellsworth, P. C., & Scherer, K. R. (2003). Appraisal processes in emotion. In R. J. Davidson, H. Goldsmith, & K. R. Scherer (Eds.), *Handbook of the affective sciences* (pp. 572–595). New York, NY: Oxford University Press.

Feldman, L., Myers, T. A., Hmielowski, J. D., & Leiserowitz, A. (2014). The mutual reinforcement of media selectivity and effects: Testing the reinforcing spirals framework in the context of global warming. *Journal of Communication, 64*(4), 590–611.

Fischhoff, B. (1995). Risk perception and communication unplugged: Twenty years of process. *Risk Analysis, 15*(2), 137–145.

Fischhoff, B. (2012). *Risk analysis and human behavior*. New York, NY: Earthscan.

Fischhoff, B., Brewer, N., & Downs, J. (2011). *Communicating risks and benefits: An evidence based user's guide*. Washington, DC: Government Printing Office.

Fischhoff, B., Slovic, P., Lichtenstein, S., Read, S., & Combs, B. (1978). How safe is safe enough? A psychometric study of attitudes towards technological risks and benefits. *Policy Sciences, 9*(2), 127–152.

Freudenburg, W. R., Gramling, R., & Davidson, D. J. (2008). Scientific certainty argumentation methods (SCAMs): Science and the politics of doubt. *Sociological Inquiry, 78*, 2–38.

Frewer, L., Hunt, S., Brennan, M., Kuznesof, S., Ness, M., & Ritson, C. (2003). The views of scientific experts on how the public conceptualize uncertainty. *Journal of Risk Research, 6*, 75–85.

Gentner, D. (2002). Psychology of mental models. In N. J. Smelser & P. B. Bates (Eds.), *International encyclopedia of the social and behavioral sciences* (pp. 9683–9687). Amsterdam: Elsevier.

Gentner, D., & Stevens, A. (Eds.). (1983). *Mental models*. Hillsdale, NJ: Erlbaum.

Gifford, R., & Comeau, L. A. (2011). Message framing influences perceived climate change competence, engagement, and behavioral intentions. *Global Environmental Change, 21*(4), 1301–1307.

Greenhalgh, T. (2011). *Assessing a combined theories approach to climate change communication* (Unpublished doctoral dissertation). University of Nevada, Las Vegas.

Gregory, R., Failing, L., Harstone, M., Long, G., McDaniels, T., & Ohlson, D. (2012). *Structured decision making: A practical guide to environmental management choices*. New York, NY: Wiley.

Hanss, D., & Böhm, G. (2013). Promoting purchases of sustainable groceries: An intervention study. *Journal of Environmental Psychology, 33*, 53–67.

Heath, R. L., & O'Hair, H. D. (Eds.). (2010). *Handbook of risk and crisis communication*. London: Routledge.

Heath, Y., & Gifford, R. (2006). Free-market ideology and environmental degradation: The case of belief in global climate change. *Environment and Behavior, 38*(1), 48–71.

Hine, D. W., Phillips, W. J., Cooksey, R., Reser, J. P., Nunn, P., Marks, A. D., … Watt, S. E. (2016). Preaching to different choirs: How to motivate dismissive, uncommitted, and alarmed audiences to adapt to climate change? *Global Environmental Change, 36*, 1–11.

Homburg, A., & Stolberg, A. (2006). Explaining pro-environmental behavior with a cognitive theory of stress. *Journal of Environmental Psychology, 26*, 1–14.

Huang, S. K., Lindell, M. K., & Prater, C. S. (2016). Who leaves and who stays? A review and statistical meta-analysis of hurricane evacuation studies. *Environment and Behavior, 48*(8), 991–1029.

Institute of Medicine (IOM), & National Research Council (NRC). (2010). *Enhancing food safety: The role of the food and drug administration*. Washington, DC: The National Academies Press. https://doi.org/10.17226/12892

Jasny, L., Waggle, J., & Fisher, D. R. (2015). An empirical examination of echo chambers in US climate policy networks. *Nature Climate Change, 5*, 782–786.

Jennings, N., & Hulme, M. (2010). UK newspaper (mis) representations of the potential for a collapse of the Thermohaline Circulation. *Area, 42*(4), 444–456.

Johnson, B. B., & Slovic, P. (1998). Lay views on uncertainty in environmental health risk assessment. *Journal of Risk Research, 1*, 261–279.
Johnson, E. J., & Goldstein, D. G. (2003). Do defaults save lives? *Science, 302*, 1338–1339.
Johnson-Laird, P. N. (2004). The history of mental models. In K. Manktelow & M. C. Chung (Eds.), *Psychology of reasoning: Theoretical and historical perspectives* (pp. 179–212). New York, NY: Psychology Press.
Jones, M. D. (2011). Leading the way to compromise? Cultural theory and climate change opinion. *PS: Political Science & Politics, 44*(4), 720–725.
Jungermann, H., Schütz, H., & Thürung, M. (1988). Mental models in risk assessment: Informing people about drugs. *Risk Analysis, 8*(1), 147–155.
Kahan, D. M. (2012). Cultural cognition as a conception of the cultural theory of risk. In R. Hillerbrand, P. Sandin, S. Roeser, & M. Peterson (Eds.), *Handbook of risk theory: Epistemology, decision theory, ethics and social implications of risk* (pp. 725–759). London: Springer.
Kahan, D. M., Braman, D., Cohen, G. L., Gastil, J., & Slovic, P. (2010). Who fears the HPV vaccine, who doesn't, and why? An experimental study of the mechanisms of cultural cognition. *Law and Human Behavior, 34*, 501–516.
Kahan, D. M., Braman, D., Gastil, J., Slovic, P., & Mertz, C. K. (2007). Culture and identity-protective cognition: Explaining the white-male effect in risk perception. *Journal of Empirical Legal Studies, 4*, 465–505.
Kahan, D. M., Jenkins-Smith, H., Tarantola, T., Silva, C. L., & Braman, D. (2015). Geoengineering and climate change polarization: Testing a two-channel model of science communication. *The Annals of the American Academy of Political and Social Science, 658*(1), 192–222.
Kahneman, D. (2011). *Thinking fast and slow*. New York: Farrar, Straus and Giroux.
Kahneman, D., & Tversky, A. (1982). The simulation heuristic. In D. Kahneman, P. Slovic, & A. Tversky (Eds.), *Judgment under uncertainty: Heuristics and biases* (pp. 201–208). New York, NY: Cambridge University Press.
Kaiser, F. G., & Fuhrer, U. (2003). Ecological behavior's dependency on different forms of knowledge. *Applied Psychology, 52*(4), 598–613.
Keller, C., Bostrom, A., Kuttschreuter, M., Savadori, L., Spence, A., & White, M. (2012). Bringing appraisal theory to environmental risk perception: A review of conceptual approaches of the past 40 years and suggestions for future research. *Journal of Risk Research, 15*(3), 237–256.
Keller, C., Kreuzmair, C., Leins-Hess, R., & Siegrist, M. (2014). Numeric and graphic risk information processing of high and low numerates in the intuitive and deliberative decision modes: An eye-tracker study. *Judgment and Decision making, 9*(5), 420–432.
Kellstedt, P. M., Zahran, S., & Vedlitz, A. (2008). Personal efficacy, the information environment, and attitudes toward global warming and climate change in the United States. *Risk Analysis, 28*(1), 113–126.
Kempton, W. (1986). Two theories of home heat control. *Cognitive Science, 10*(1), 75–90.
Koletsou, A., & Mancy, R. (2011). Which efficacy constructs for large-scale social dilemma problems? Individual and collective forms of efficacy and outcome expectancies in the context of climate change mitigation. *Risk Management, 13*(4), 184–208.
Kornelis, M., De Jonge, J., Frewer, L., & Dagevos, H. (2007). Consumer selection of food- safety information sources. *Risk Analysis, 27*, 327–335.
Kuhn, T. (1962). The Structure of Scientific Revolutions. Chicago: University of Chicago Press.
Lazrus, H., Morss, R. E., Demuth, J. L., Lazo, J. K., & Bostrom, A. (2016). Know what to do if you encounter a flash flood: Mental models analysis for improving flash flood risk communication and public decision making. *Risk Analysis, 36*, 411–427.
Lermer, E., Streicher, B., Sachs, R., & Frey, D. (2013). How risky? The impact of target person and answer format on risk assessment. *Journal of Risk Research, 16*(7), 903–919.
Lerner, J. S., & Keltner, D. (2000). Beyond valence: Toward a model of emotion-specific influences on judgement and choice. *Cognition and Emotion, 14*(4), 473–493.

Lerner, J. S., & Keltner, D. (2001). Fear, anger, and risk. *Journal of Personality and Social Psychology, 81*(1), 146–159.
Lewandowsky, S., Gignac, G. E., & Vaughan, S. (2013). The pivotal role of perceived scientific consensus in acceptance of science. *Nature Climate Change, 3*(4), 399–404.
Lin, S. P. (2013). The gap between global issues and personal behaviors: Pro-environmental behaviors of citizens toward climate change in Kaohsiung, Taiwan. *Mitigation and Adaptation Strategies for Global Change, 18*(6), 773–783.
Lindell, M. K., & Brooks, H. (Eds.). (2012, April 24–26). *Workshop on weather ready nation: Science imperatives for severe thunderstorm research*, Birmingham AL. Final Report. Sponsored by National Oceanic and Atmospheric Administration and National Science Foundation. Hazard Reduction & Recovery Center, Texas A&M University, College station TX 77843-3137, 17 September 2012.
Lodge, M., Wegrich, K., & McElroy, G. (2010). Dodgy kebabs everywhere? Varieties of worldviews and regulatory change. *Public Administration, 88*(1), 247–266.
Löfstedt, R. E. (1991). Climate change perceptions and energy use decisions in northern Sweden. *Global Environmental Change, 4*, 321–324.
Löfstedt, R. E. (2005). *Risk management in post-trust societies*. New York, NY: Palgrave Macmillan.
Lorenzoni, I., Nicholson-Cole, S., & Whitmarsh, L. (2007). Barriers perceived to engaging with climate change among the UK public and their policy implications. *Global Environmental Change, 17*(3), 445–459.
Lubell, M. (2002). Environmental activism as collective action. *Environment and Behavior, 34*, 431–454.
Lubell, M., Zahran, S., & Vedlitz, A. (2007). Collective action and citizen responses to global warming. *Political Behavior, 29*(3), 391–413.
Mamadouh, V. (1999). Grid-group cultural theory: An introduction. *GeoJournal, 47*(3), 395–409.
Markowitz, E. M., & Shariff, A. F. (2012). Climate change and moral judgement. *Nature Climate Change, 2*, 243–247.
McComas, K., & Shanahan, J. (1999). Telling stories about global climate change measuring the impact of narratives on issue cycles. *Communication Research, 26*(1), 30–57.
McCright, A. M., & Dunlap, R. E. (2011). Cool dudes: The denial of climate change among conservative white males in the United States. *Global Environmental Change, 21*(4), 1163–1172.
McGuire, W. J. (1985). Attitudes and attitude change. In G. Lindzey & E. Aronson (Eds.), *Handbook of social psychology* (Vol. 2, pp. 233–346). New York, NY: Random House.
McKenzie-Mohr, D., Lee, N. R., Schultz, P. W., & Kotler, P. (2012). *Social marketing to protect the environment: What works*. Irvine, CA: SAGE.
Mead, E., Roser-Renouf, C., Rimal, R. N., Flora, J. A., Maibach, E. W., & Leiserowitz, A. (2012). Information seeking about global climate change among adolescents: The role of risk perceptions, efficacy beliefs, and parental influences. *Atlantic Journal of Communication, 20*(1), 31–52.
Meyer, D., Leventhal, H., & Gutmann, M. (1985). Common-sense models of illness: The example of hypertension. *Health Psychology, 4*, 115–135.
Mileti, D. S. & Sorensen, J. H. (2015). *A Guide to public alerts and warnings for dam and levee emergencies*. U.S. Army Corps of Engineers.
Milfont, T. L. (2012). The interplay between knowledge, perceived efficacy, and concern about global warming and climate change: A one-year longitudinal study. *Risk Analysis, 32*(6), 1003–1020.
Mishra, P., & Brewer, W. F. (2003). Theories as a form of mental representation and their role in the recall of text information. *Contemporary Educational Psychology, 28*(3), 277–303.
Morgan, M. G., Fischhoff, B., Bostrom, A., & Atman, C. J. (2002). *Risk communication: A mental models approach*. Cambridge: Cambridge University Press.
Morgan, M. G., Fischhoff, B., Bostrom, A., Lave, L., & Atman, C. J. (1992). Communicating risk to the public. *Environmental Science and Technology, 26*(11), 2048–2056.

Morss, R. E., Demuth, J. L., Bostrom, A., Lazo, J. K., & Lazrus, H. (2015). Flash flood risks and warning decisions: A mental models study of forecasters, public officials, and media broadcasters in boulder, Colorado. *Risk Analysis, 35*(11), 2009–2028.

Morton, T. A., Rabinovich, A., Marshall, D., & Bretschneider, P. (2011). The future that may (or may not) come: How framing changes responses to uncertainty in climate change communications. *Global Environmental Change, 21*(1), 103–109.

Munafò, M., Roberts, N., Bauld, L., & Leonards, U. (2011). Plain packaging increases visual attention to health warnings on cigarette packs in non-smokers and weekly smokers but not daily smokers. *Addiction, 106*(8), 1505–1510.

Myers, T. A., Nisbet, M. C., Maibach, E. W., & Leiserowitz, A. A. (2012). A public health frame arouses hopeful emotions about climate change: A letter. *Climatic Change, 113*(3–4), 1105–1112.

Maloney, E. K., Lapinski, M. K., & Witte, K. (2011). Fear appeals and persuasion: A review and update of the extended parallel process model. Social and Personality Psychology Compass, 5(4), 206-219. DOI: 10.1111/j.1751-9004.2011.00341.

Narayanan, N. H., & Hegarty, M. (1998). On designing comprehensible interactive hypermedia manuals. *International Journal of Human-Computer Studies, 48*, 267–301.

National Research Council (NRC), Committee on Risk Perception and Communication. (1989). *Improving risk communication*. Washington, DC: National Academy Press.

Nersessian, N. J. (1992). How do scientists think? Capturing the dynamics of conceptual change in science. In R. N. Giere (Ed.), *Cognitive models of science* (pp. 3–45). Minneapolis, MN: University of Minnesota Press.

Niewöhner, J., Cox, P., Gerrard, S., & Pidgeon, N. (2004). Evaluating the efficacy of a mental models approach for improving occupational chemical risk protection. *Risk Analysis, 24*(2), 349–361.

Norman, D. A. (1983). Some observations on mental models. In D. Gentner & A. L. Stevens (Eds.), *Mental models* (pp. 7–14). Hillsdale, NJ: Lawrence Erlbaum Associates.

Norman, D. A. (1988). *The psychology of everyday things*. New York, NY: Basic Books.

O'Keefe, D. J. (2013). The relative persuasiveness of different message types does not vary as a function of the persuasive outcome assessed: Evidence from 29 meta-analyses of 2,062 effect sizes for 13 message variations. *Annals of the International Communication Association, 37*(1), 221–249.

Oreskes, N., & Conway, E. M. (2010). *Merchants of doubt: How a handful of scientists obscured the truth on issues from tobacco smoke to global warming*. New York, NY: Bloomsbury.

Ortega-Egea, J. M., García-de-Frutos, N., & Antolín-López, R. (2014). Why do some people do "more" to mitigate climate change than others? Exploring heterogeneity in psycho-social associations. *PLoS One, 9*(9), e106645.

Peters, E., & Levin, I. P. (2008). Dissecting the risky-choice framing effect: Numeracy as an individual-difference factor in weighting risky and riskless options. *Judgment and Decision making, 3*(6), 435–448.

Peters, E., Västfjäll, D., Slovic, P., Mertz, C. K., Mazzocco, K., & Dickert, S. (2006). Numeracy and decision making. *Psychological Science, 17*(5), 407–413.

Peters, G. J. Y., Ruiter, R. A., & Kok, G. (2013). Threatening communication: A critical re-analysis and a revised meta-analytic test of fear appeal theory. *Health Psychology Review, 7*(1), 8–31.

Pfister, H.-R., Jungermann, H., & Fischer, K. (2017). *Psychologie der Entscheidung*. Berlin: Springer.

Pidgeon, N., & Fischhoff, B. (2011). The role of social and decision sciences in communicating uncertain climate risks. *Nature Climate Change, 1*, 35–41.

Pidgeon, N., Kasperson, R. E., & Slovic, P. (2003). *The social amplification of risk*. Cambridge: Cambridge University Press.

Pierce, J. R. (1980). *An introduction to information theory: Symbols, signals and noise* (2nd ed.). New York, NY: Dover Publications.

Quick, B. L., Shen, L., & Dillard, J. P. (2013). Reactance theory and persuasion. Chapter 11 in Dillard and Shen (Eds), The SAGE handbook of persuasion: Developments in theory and practice, 167–183.

Rabinovich, A., & Morton, T. A. (2012). Unquestioned answers or unanswered questions: Beliefs about science guide responses to uncertainty in climate change risk communication. *Risk Analysis, 32*(6), 992–1002.

Rakow, T., Heard, C. L., & Newell, B. R. (2015). Meeting three challenges in risk communication phenomena, numbers, and emotions. *Policy Insights from the Behavioral and Brain Sciences, 2*(1), 147–156.

Reynolds, B., & Seeger, M. (2014). *Crisis and emergency risk communication*. Atlanta, GA: Centers for Disease Control and Prevention.

Reynolds, T. W., Bostrom, A., Read, D., & Morgan, M. G. (2010). Now what do people know about global climate change? Survey studies of educated laypeople. *Risk Analysis, 30*, 1520–1538.

Ripberger, J. T., Song, G., Nowlin, M. C., Jones, M. D., & Jenkins-Smith, H. C. (2012). Reconsidering the relationship between cultural theory, political ideology, and political knowledge. *Social Science Quarterly, 93*(3), 713–731.

Ropeik, D., & Gray, G. M. (2002). *Risk: A practical guide for deciding what's really safe and what's dangerous in the world around you*. Boston, MA: Houghton Mifflin.

Roser-Renouf, C., Maibach, E. W., Leiserowitz, A., & Zhao, X. (2014). The genesis of climate change activism: From key beliefs to political action. *Climatic Change, 125*(2), 163–178.

Roten, F. C. v. (2006). Do we need a public understanding of statistics? *Public Understanding of Science, 15*, 243–249.

Ruiter, R. A., Abraham, C., & Kok, G. (2001). Scary warnings and rational precautions: A review of the psychology of fear appeals. *Psychology and Health, 16*(6), 613–630.

Ruiter, R. A., Kessels, L. T., Peters, G. J. Y., & Kok, G. (2014). Sixty years of fear appeal research: Current state of the evidence. *International Journal of Psychology, 49*(2), 63–70.

Scherer, K. R. (1999). Appraisal theory. In T. Dalgleish & M. Power (Eds.), *Handbook of cognition and emotion* (pp. 637–663). New York, NY: Wiley.

Scheufele, D. A., & Iyengar, S. (2012). The state of framing research: A call for new directions. In K. Kenski & K. H. Jamieson (Eds.), *The Oxford handbook of political communication theories* (pp. 1–26). Oxford: Oxford University Press.

Schriver, K. A. (1997). *Dynamics in document design: Creating text for readers*. New York, NY: Wiley.

Shannon, C. E., & Weaver, W. (1963). *The mathematical theory of communication*. Urbana, IL: University of Illinois Press.

Sheeran, P., Harris, P. R., & Epton, T. (2014). Does heightening risk appraisals change people's intentions and behavior? A meta-analysis of experimental studies. *Psychological Bulletin, 140*(2), 511–543.

Siegrist, M., Earle, T. C., & Gutscher, H. (2003). Test of a trust and confidence model in the applied context of electromagnetic field (EMF) risks. *Risk Analysis, 23*(4), 705–716.

Siegrist, M., Earle, T. C., & Gutscher, H. (2010). *Trust in risk management: Uncertainty and scepticism in the public mind*. London: Earthscan.

Slovic, P. (Ed.). (2001). *The perception of risk*. London: Earthscan.

Slovic, P. (1987). Perception of risk. *Science, 236*, 280–285.

Slovic, P., Fischhoff, B., & Lichtenstein, S. (1984). Behavioral decision theory perspectives on risk and safety. *Acta Psychologica, 56*(1), 183–203.

Slovic, P., Monahan, J., & MacGregor, D. G. (2000). Violence risk assessment and risk communication: The effects of using actual cases, providing instruction, and employing probability versus frequency formats. *Law and Human Behavior, 24*(3), 271–296.

Sorensen, J. H. (2000). Hazard warning systems: Review of 20 years of progress. *Natural Hazards Review, 1*(2), 119–125.

Spence, A., Poortinga, W., Butler, C., & Pidgeon, N. F. (2011). Perceptions of climate change and willingness to save energy related to flood experience. *Nature Climate Change, 1*(1), 46–49.

Starbird, K., Dailey, D., Walker, A. H., Leschine, T. M., Pavia, R., & Bostrom, A. (2015). Social media, public participation, and the 2010 BP Deepwater horizon oil spill. *Human and Ecological Risk Assessment: An International Journal, 21*(3), 605–630.

Sutton, J., Palen, L., & Shklovski, I. (2008, May). *Backchannels on the front lines: Emergent uses of social media in the 2007 southern California wildfires.* Paper proceeded at the Fifth International ISCRAM Conference, Washington, DC. Retrieved from http://jeannettesutton.com/uploads/BackchannelsISCRAM08.pdf

Tannenbaum, M. B., Hepler, J., Zimmerman, R. S., Saul, L., Jacobs, S., Wilson, K., & Albarracín, D. (2015). Appealing to fear: A meta-analysis of fear appeal effectiveness and theories. *Psychological Bulletin, 141*(6), 1178–1204.

Taylor, A., de Bruin, W. B., & Dessai, S. (2014). Climate change beliefs and perceptions of weather-related changes in the United Kingdom. *Risk Analysis, 34*, 1995–2004.

Teigen, K. H. (2012). Risk communication in words and numbers. In K. P. Knutsen, S. Kvam, P. Langemeyer, A. Parianou, & K. Solfjeld (Eds.), *Narratives of risk: Interdisciplinary studies* (pp. 240–254). Münster: Waxmann Verlag.

Teigen, K. H., & Brun, W. (1999). The directionality of verbal probability expressions: Effects on decisions, predictions, and probabilistic reasoning. *Organizational Behavior and Human Decision Processes, 80*, 155–190.

Thaker, J. (2012). *Climate change in the Indian mind: Role of collective efficacy in climate change adaptation* (Doctoral dissertation). Retrieved from http://digilib.gmu.edu/jspui/bitstream/handle/1920/7882/Thaker_dissertation_2012.pdf?sequence=1&isAllowed=y

Tierney, K. (2014). *The social roots of risk: Producing disasters, promoting resilience.* Stanford, CA: Stanford University Press.

Tobler, C., Visschers, V. H., & Siegrist, M. (2012). Addressing climate change: Determinants of consumers' willingness to act and to support policy measures. *Journal of Environmental Psychology, 32*(3), 197–207.

Truelove, H. B. (2009). *An investigation of the psychology of global warming: Perceptions, predictors of behavior, and the persuasiveness of ecological footprint calculators.* (Doctoral dissertation). Retrieved from http://www.dissertations.wsu.edu/dissertations/summer2009/h_truelove_082209.pdf

Truelove, H. B., & Parks, C. (2012). Perceptions of behaviors that cause and mitigate global warming and intentions to perform these behaviors. *Journal of Environmental Psychology, 32*(3), 246–259.

Tversky, B. (1993). Cognitive maps, cognitive collages, and spatial mental models. In A. U. Frank & I. Campari (Eds.), *Spatial information theory: A theoretical basis for GIS* (pp. 14–24). Berlin: Springer.

Thaler, R. H., & Sunstein, C. R. (2008). Nudge: Improving decisions about health, wealth, and happiness. New Haven, CT: Yale University Press.

Utts, J. (2003). What educated citizens should know about statistics and probability. *The American Statistician, 57*, 74–79.

Van der Linden, S., Leiserowitz, A. A., Feinberg, G. D., & Maibach, E. W. (2015). The scientific consensus on climate change as a gateway belief: Experimental evidence. *PLoS One, 10*(2), e0118489.

Van der Pligt, J. (1996). Risk perception and self-protective behavior. *European Psychologist, 1*(1), 34–43.

Van der Sluijs, J. P. (2008, September). *Complexity and Uncertainty: The need for new ways of interfacing climate science and climate policy.* Essay presented at the Workshop Science Policy Interface and Climate Change, Netherlands. Retrieved from http://www.nusap.org/kqa/Modesl_of_Science_and_Policy_essay_0.pdf

Van Zomeren, M., Spears, R., & Leach, C. W. (2010). Experimental evidence for a dual pathway model analysis of coping with the climate crisis. *Journal of Environmental Psychology, 30*(4), 339–346.

Vieweg, S., Hughes, A. L., Starbird, K., & Palen, L. (2010, April). *Microblogging during two natural hazards events: What Twitter may contribute to situational awareness.* Paper proceeded at the SIGCHI conference on human factors in computing systems, Atlanta, GA. Retrieved from http://dl.acm.org/citation.cfm?id=1753486

Weber, E. U., & Hilton, D. J. (1990). Contextual effects in the interpretations of probability words: Perceived base rate and severity of events. *Journal of Experimental Psychology: Human Perception and Performance, 16*(4), 781.

White, M. P., Cohrs, J. C., & Göritz, A. S. (2011). Dynamics of trust in medical decision making: An experimental investigation into underlying processes. *Medical Decision Making, 31*, 710–720.

Whitmarsh, L. (2009). Behavioural responses to climate change: Asymmetry of intentions and impacts. *Journal of Environmental Psychology, 29*(1), 13–23.

Wildavsky, A. (1987). Choosing preferences by constructing institutions: A cultural theory of preference formation. *American Political Science Review, 81*, 3–21.

Wogalter, M. S. (2006). *Handbook of warnings*. Mahwah, NJ: Lawrence Erlbaum.

Wolfe, J. M., & Horowitz, T. S. (2004). What attributes guide the deployment of visual attention and how do they do it? *Nature Reviews Neuroscience, 5*(6), 495–501.

Woloshin, S., Schwartz, L. M., Byram, S., Fischhoff, B., & Welch, H. G. (2000). A new scale for assessing perceptions of chance: a validation study. *Medical Decision Making, 20*(3), 298–307.

Wood, M., Kovacs, D., Bostrom, A., Bridges, T., & Linkov, I. (2012). Flood risk management: US Army Corps of Engineers and layperson perceptions. *Risk Analysis, 32*(8), 1349–1368.

World Bank Group. (2015). *Mind, society, and behavior* (World Development Report 2015). World Bank, Washington, DC. Retrieved from http://www.investiniran.ir/OIETA_content/media/image/2015/03/4406_orig.pdf.

Yates, J. F., & Stone, E. R. (1992). The risk construct. In J. F. Yates (Ed.), *Risk-taking behavior* (pp. 1–25). New York, NY: Wiley.

Zehr, S. C. (2000). Public representations of scientific uncertainty about global climate change. *Public Understanding of Science, 9*(2), 85–103.

Zhao, X. (2009). Media use and global warming perceptions a snapshot of the reinforcing spirals. *Communication Research, 36*(5), 698–723.

Zhao, X., Rolfe-Redding, J., & Kotcher, J. E. (2016). Partisan differences in the relationship between newspaper coverage and concern over global warming. *Public Understanding of Science, 25*(5), 543–559.

Zikmund-Fisher, B. J., Witteman, H. O., Dickson, M., Fuhrel-Forbis, A., Kahn, V. C., Exe, N. L., … Fagerlin, A. (2014). Blocks, ovals, or people? Icon type affects risk perceptions and recall of pictographs. *Medical Decision Making, 34*(4), 443–453.

Chapter 12
Improving Understanding of Health-Relevant Numerical Information

Ulrich Hoffrage and Rocio Garcia-Retamero

Abstract In this chapter, we discuss why risks are often not communicated in a transparent and understandable way and why this is problematic. At the core of the chapter are four examples that illustrate how risk communication can be improved. These examples are (a) the use of natural frequencies in the context of diagnostic reasoning, (b) the use of visual aids to support the beneficial effect of natural frequency representations, (c) the use of natural frequencies to clarify the distinction between relative and absolute risk reduction, and (d) a clarification of the meaning and pitfalls of survival rates that are often used to quantify the benefit of screening programs. In each of these topics, we describe original empirical studies illuminating a specific problem as well as how these problems can be overcome, and we discuss practical implications of the results and the proposed solutions. Subsequently, we illustrate, using an example from mammography screening, what transparent risk communication could look like. The chapter concludes with a discussion of training programs designed to enhance health-related, high-stakes decision making.

Even though patients and physicians differ in many respects, they still have much in common. First and foremost, they need each other. Patients need the knowledge and help provided by medical experts. There is no doubt that the advancement in medicine and health care contributed tremendously to the increase of life expectancy during the course of civilization. Conversely, the different players within the health-care system need patients: they are not only there for the patients but also because of them. Bluntly speaking, without patients, they would not have anything to do, and their professions would not even exist. Furthermore, each side wants to trust the other side: distressed patients place their trust in physicians before the treatment,

U. Hoffrage (✉)
Department of Organizational Behavior, Faculty of Business and Economics, University of Lausanne, Lausanne, Switzerland
e-mail: ulrich.hoffrage@unil.ch

R. Garcia-Retamero
Department of Experimental Psychology, University of Granada, Granada, Spain

M. Raue et al. (eds.), *Psychological Perspectives on Risk and Risk Analysis*,
https://doi.org/10.1007/978-3-319-92478-6_12

particularly because physicians usually provide the expected help and physicians may rely on the gratefulness of their cured patients.

Although patients do not always get better after treatment, the commonalities continue even then. Sometimes, physicians make mistakes or do not exclusively act in the best interest of the patient because of constraints or conflicts of interest. Because many patients are aware of this problem, the trust they associate with physicians is sometimes mixed with a pinch of mistrust that is often intensified by the respective communication: regarding risks and side effects when interacting with physicians, patients often ask other patients. But also patients make mistakes, for example, by ignoring instructions or advice and by unfairly holding the physician responsible for the deterioration of their condition, which occasionally may even lead to legal disputes. For this reason, also physicians have reason to report on risks and side effects when dealing with patients. This chapter focuses on risks and side effects of risk communication. We will discuss why risk communication is often not transparent, what problems this lack of transparency may cause, and how transparency can be increased.

Why Is Risk Communication Often Not Transparent?

The commonality between physicians and patients, and in particular the possibility to help or hurt each other, can also be observed in risk communication. Laypeople are often unable to assess how dangerous various activities, substances, and technologies are. They also often do not know what certain symptoms mean, how critical their individual condition is, and what could be done about it. In fact, the world is full of risks, and people experience lots of uncertainty (Ahmed, Naik, Willoughby, & Edwards, 2012). As Benjamin Franklin put it in a letter to Jean-Baptiste Leroy on Nov 13, 1789, "in this world nothing can be said to be certain, except death and taxes!" (Franklin, 1817, p. 266). Experts are, ideally, able to provide helpful and relevant information. This is the great chance of risk communication. However, Franklin's statement can also be turned against those who communicate risks and uncertainties: Information provided by experts may be plainly wrong. And even if it is not plainly wrong, it may sometimes be just incomplete or ambiguous, and it is not always clear whether the physician or the patient is to be held responsible for the misunderstanding. Mistakes and possible misunderstandings, such as these, are the risks of risk communication.

Why is health-relevant risk information so often presented in an ambiguous, non-transparent, and sometimes even misleading way? There are five reasons that we want to mention and discuss here—and this list is certainly not complete.

First, physicians want to help patients, and those physicians who convey simple messages and who appear to be confident may help patients to build trust. One may even argue that such confidence—and in the extreme form, even overconfidence—has the potential to function like a placebo effect (Hoffrage, 2016). In contrast, transparent communication that discloses the often modest effects of most treatments and the uncertainties that are often involved when it comes to measuring such effects is not as persuasive as simple messages are (Gigerenzer & Muir Gray, 2011). Many physicians may have learned that transparent information that reveals the full, and often complex, picture is not what many patients want—or have hoped—to hear. As a result, these physicians may believe that transparent risk communication does not necessarily support the therapeutic process in an optimal way. In a nutshell, many doctors believe that maintaining an illusion of certainty will increase patients' compliance, reduce their anxiety, and decrease confusion (Gigerenzer, 2002).

Second, and related to the first, many people prefer simply to trust their doctors rather than to attempt to understand information about medical screenings and treatments (Mechanic & Meyer, 2000). "Trust your doctor" is a simple heuristic followed even by highly educated patients (Wegwarth & Gigerenzer, 2013). The relationship between patients and physicians has been referred to as the "sacred trust" in classic literature (Starr, 1949).

Third, there is a lack of awareness that the same information can be presented in different ways, leading to different conclusions. The general public lacks basic risk literacy, i.e., the ability to accurately interpret information about risk (Fagerlin, Ubel, Smith, & Zikmund-Fisher, 2007; Peters et al., 2006; see also www.riskliteracy.org). That is, many people do not understand the relationship between the different ways in which probabilistic information can be expressed. For instance, they cannot transform percentages into frequencies and vice versa. In addition, many people do not have much experience with graphical displays and have problems reading even the most basic visual formats, such as simple bar charts (Garcia-Retamero & Cokely, 2013). This is not just a problem for the general population; medical professionals also have trouble recognizing deceptive information formats: Problematic numerical and visual presentations appear even in high-ranking medical journals (Skolbekken, 1998).

Fourth, risk communication is not free of disruptive interests (Gigerenzer & Muir Gray, 2011). Medical care can only be provided when costs are covered. Presentation formats that make benefits seem larger and drawbacks smaller promote higher use of treatments and screenings. In fact, this is a key component of pharmaceutical marketing practices, which are designed to cover the enormous costs of developing new drugs (Michaels, 2006).

Fifth, it is legitimate and fully understandable if physicians and caregivers as well as authorities or hospital managements want to protect themselves against legal disputes. From the doctors' perspective, it may be more acceptable to over-screen and overtreat patients rather than risk losing them and being accused of malpractice if an ailment goes undetected or is insufficiently treated (Studdert et al., 2005; Wegwarth & Gigerenzer, 2013).

Why Is Nontransparent Risk Communication Problematic?

The lack of transparency and understanding of health-related information is not a new phenomenon. Doctors' incentives to provide an illusion of certainty and patients' desire to believe in the possibility of a cure have been present since the dawn of medicine. Today, however, lack of transparency has become even more problematic than before, for three reasons. First, doctors have been increasingly encouraged to involve patients in decision making rather than pursuing a paternalistic model in which they make the decisions for their patients (Hanson, 2008). To participate in decisions about their health, patients need to be able to understand the complex risks and benefits of different medical treatments and screenings, and doctors need to be able to accurately and transparently communicate these risks and benefits (Schwartz & Woloshin, 2007).

Second, the Internet and other media provide an unprecedented amount of information about health and medicine (Murray, Stevenson, Kerr, & Burns, 2010). Today, many people first consult the Internet about their ailment and then—if at all—their doctor. Numerous websites, forums, and blogs provide information on all sorts of medical problems and medical treatments ranging from cold remedies to plastic surgery. However, this information is often incomplete or presented in formats that could bias the reader toward certain options (Kurzenhäuser & Hoffrage, 2012). Patients who lack risk literacy may not understand the many ways in which the same information can be communicated and how these different information formats can bias their judgments and decisions.

Finally, in today's globalized world, health risks are often communicated to highly diverse audiences in different countries. Modern social media and communication networks enable remarkably fast dissemination of new health information. A promotional message or a press release designed for and sent to citizens in one particular country can quickly circle the globe. Numerous retellings and translations can easily distort the message's meaning, particularly if it was not transparent to begin with.

How to Improve Risk Communication

Is there a way to achieve transparent communication? In the following, we will present four different examples of how certain figures and statistics that are commonly used in health-relevant risk communication can be misunderstood and show how the risk of such misunderstandings could be reduced by using transparent information formats. Specifically, we will focus on the meaning of test results, the usage of visual aids, and the meaning of risk reduction and survival rates.

The Meaning of Test Results

A 52-year-old woman accepted an invitation to undergo mammography screening. Despite the absence of relevant symptoms, the woman received a suspicious finding—requiring further examinations to clarify if the suspicious lump was indeed breast cancer. In 2014, about 5.3 million women aged between 50 and 69 years

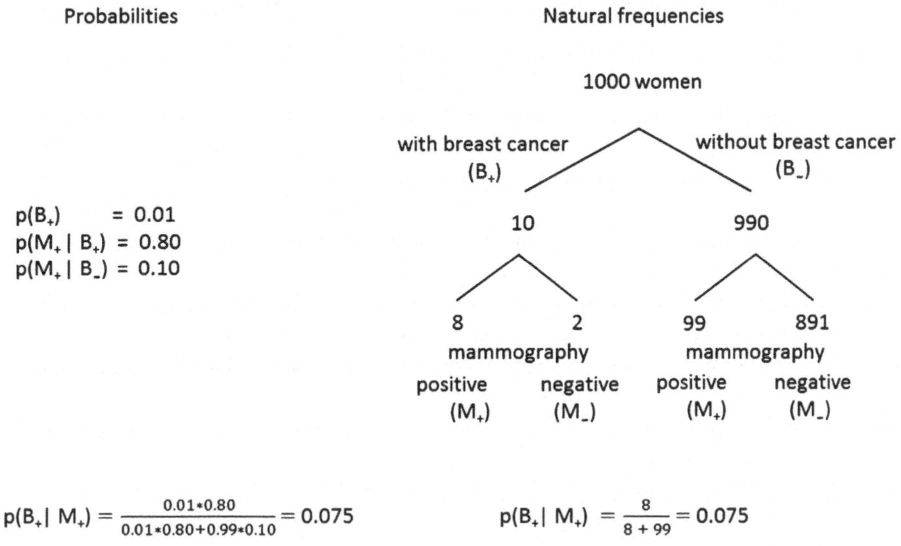

Fig. 12.1 Representation of the same information in terms of probabilities and natural frequencies (adapted from Hoffrage, Kurzenhäuser, & Gigerenzer, 2000)

received an invitation to undergo mammography screening in Germany. Of the 2.9 million women accepting this invitation, about 124,000 (4.3%) were asked to present for further examination (Malek & Kääb-Sanyal, 2016).

However, what is the exact meaning of such a reinvitation? The most frequent reason is a positive finding at the first mammography screening. How high is the probability that it is really breast cancer? This probability, the so-called positive predictive value (PPV), depends on three different parameters. In a survey conducted in the United States, the participating physicians received the following information in this context (Eddy, 1982; age information added and numbers rounded here):

(a) Prevalence: The probability that a symptom-free woman aged 52 years has breast cancer (B+) is 1%.
(b) Sensitivity: If a symptom-free woman aged 52 years has breast cancer, the probability that she will receive a positive mammogram (M+) result is 80%.
(c) Specificity: However, if a symptom-free woman aged 52 years does not have breast cancer (B-), the probability that she will still receive a positive mammogram result is 10%.

Based on this information, 95 of the 100 physicians sampled by Eddy (1982) estimated the woman's probability of having breast cancer—after a positive screening result—to be about 75%. However, inserting the three given values into Bayes' theorem (see left side of Fig. 12.1) reveals that the PPV is 7.5%! The difficulty of calculating the correct PPVs by means of the given information has been shown in several studies that included physicians (Hoffrage & Gigerenzer, 1998), medical students (Hoffrage, Lindsey, Hertwig, & Gigerenzer, 2000), and laypeople (Gigerenzer & Hoffrage, 1995); for an overview see Ghosh and Ghosh (2005).

In individual cases, misjudgments may lead to serious errors in decision making regarding further diagnostics and therapy. Such misjudgments may be avoided if natural frequencies instead of probabilities are used to communicate relevant information. Natural frequencies are the number of different cases occurring in a representative random sample (Gigerenzer & Hoffrage, 1995; Hoffrage, Gigerenzer, Krauss, & Martignon, 2002). Usually, the conditional probabilities presented within textbooks have been derived from natural frequencies. Conversely, probabilities can be easily (re-)translated into natural frequencies. In a first step, prevalence is related to a fictitious number of people (in the following, the number of 1000 is used) to calculate the number of people affected by the disease in the random sample (1% of 1000 equals 10; Fig. 12.1, right-hand side). In a second step, the number of affected patients receiving a positive result is determined by means of the sensitivity of the test (80% of 10 equals 8). Finally, the number of positive results in the group of healthy people is identified by means of the specificity of the test in a third step (the false-alarm rate of 10% in relation to the Fig. 990 equals 99). Thus, 107 in 1000 women receive a positive result (8 + 99), but only 8 of these 107 women actually have breast cancer. The quotient 8/107 is 7.5%, and thus the PPV already mentioned above is a result of Bayes' theorem. Strictly speaking, natural frequencies can also be viewed as applying this rule to a fictitious basic population.

A number of studies (for overviews, see Ghosh & Ghosh, 2005, and Gigerenzer, Gaissmaier, Kurz-Milcke, Schwartz, & Woloshin, 2007) on communicating relevant information have shown that the application of natural frequencies instead of probabilities results in an about threefold increase (from maybe 15% or 20% to approximately 50%) in the percentage of correct diagnostic inferences (inferences consistent with Bayes' theorem). A teaching unit in which medical students were instructed on how to translate probabilities into natural frequencies and subsequently how to extract the correct solution from there led to much better performance when students were later tested on probability problems—compared to the traditional method according to which students were introduced to Bayes' theorem and instructed how to insert the respective probabilities (Kurzenhäuser & Hoffrage, 2002).

Many women accept their invitation to mammography screening because they hope for a negative result and thus for "peace of mind." Are such expectations justified? Figure 12.1 shows that 893 negative results are to be expected in our fictitious random sample. Here, two types of negative results need to be distinguished: First, breast cancer is overlooked in 2 of 10 women affected by this type of cancer (B+), and, secondly, 891 of the 990 healthy women (B−) receive a correct negative result (which yields a total of 2 + 891 = 893 negative results). Thus, for a woman who could be 99% sure to be not affected by breast cancer without undergoing mammography screening (1—prevalence), this probability increased by 0.78 percentage points to 99.78% (=891/893) after the receipt of a negative result. Representation by means of natural frequencies thus helps people understand that even a negative result cannot be equated with security (99.78% does not equal 100%) and that the gain is only marginal (here, 0.78 percentage points).

Improving Risk Understanding and Decision Making by Using Visual Aids

As we mentioned above, doctors and their patients often have difficulties making diagnostic inferences about medical tests from information about the prevalence of a disease and the sensitivity and specificity of medical tests (e.g., mammography). In the previous section, we showed how to improve the accuracy of diagnostic inferences by providing information about medical tests in natural frequencies (as compared to probabilities), which improves these inferences from about 10% to nearly 50%. Even though the effect of numerical format (natural frequencies vs. probabilities) is substantial, a recent study conducted by Garcia-Retamero and Hoffrage (2013) indicates that transparent visual aids can increase understanding above and beyond the beneficial effect of natural frequencies.

Transparent visual aids are simple graphical representations of numerical expressions of probability and include icon arrays and bar and line charts, among others (Garcia-Retamero & Cokely, 2013). These visual aids can confer benefits when communicating risk information about health because they accurately and clearly represent the relevant risk information by making part-to-whole relationships in the data visually available (Lipkus, 2007; Spiegelhalter, Pearson, & Short, 2011).

Participants in the study by Garcia-Retamero and Hoffrage (2013) were a large sample of doctors and patients in Spain who made diagnostic inferences about three medical tests on the basis of information about disease prevalence and the sensitivity and specificity of the tests. Half of the doctors and patients in the study received the information in numbers without a visual aid, while the other half received numbers along with a visual aid representing the numerical information. In particular, they received a grid such as the one depicted in Fig. 12.2. The authors measured accuracy of diagnostic inferences controlling for individual differences in numeracy—the ability to accurately interpret and make good decisions based on numerical information about risk (Anderson & Schulkin, 2014; Cokely, Galesic, Schulz, Ghazal, & Garcia-Retamero, 2012).

The study yielded three important findings:

1. In line with results of Hoffrage and Gigerenzer (1998) and Hoffrage, Lindsey, et al. (2000), doctors and patients made more accurate inferences when information was communicated in natural frequencies as compared to probabilities (see Fig. 12.3).
2. Visual aids boosted accuracy even when compared to a control condition in which the information was provided in terms of natural frequencies.
3. Doctors were more accurate in their diagnostic inferences than patients, though differences in accuracy disappeared when differences in numerical skills were

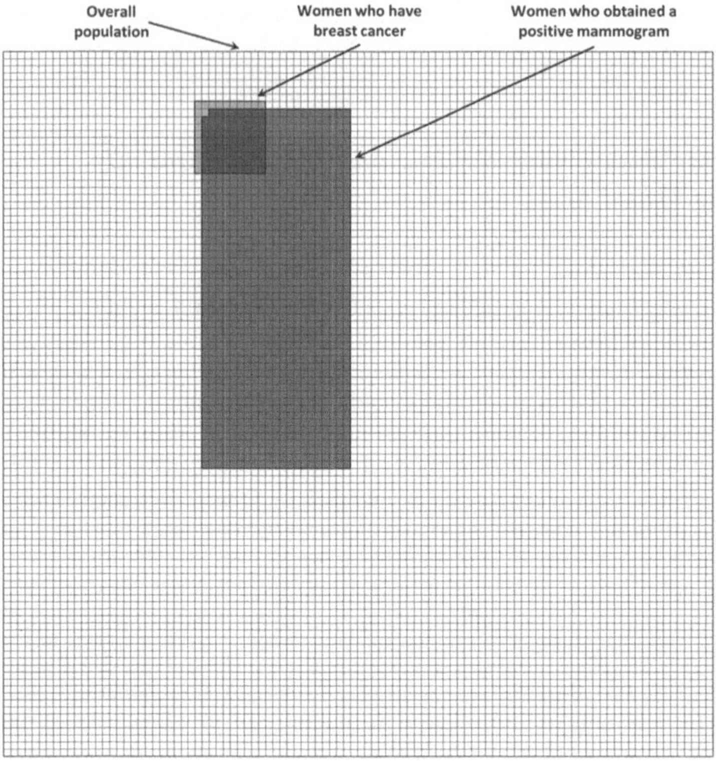

Fig. 12.2 Visual aid representing the overall number of women at risk, the number of women who have breast cancer, and the number of women who obtained a positive mammogram. Reprinted from Garcia-Retamero and Hoffrage (2013) with permission of Elsevier

controlled for. That is, it is not simply that doctors had more medical training. Rather, the difference in accuracy was fully mediated by differences in numeracy.

These findings can have important implications for medical practice as they suggest suitable ways to communicate quantitative medical data.

A follow-up study conducted by Garcia-Retamero, Cokely, and Hoffrage (2015) sheds light on the mechanisms that enable visual aids to improve accuracy of risk understanding. Participants in this follow-up study were a large sample of patients in Spain. As in the study conducted by Garcia-Retamero and Hoffrage (2013), patients in this study made diagnostic inferences about three medical tests on the basis of information about disease prevalence and the sensitivity and specificity of the tests. Similarly, half of the patients in this study received the information in numbers without a visual aid, while the other half received numbers along with a visual aid representing the numerical information (see Fig. 12.2). The authors also controlled for differences in numeracy, and investigated whether visual aids improve patients' accuracy of diagnostic inferences, and patients' ability to judge their own

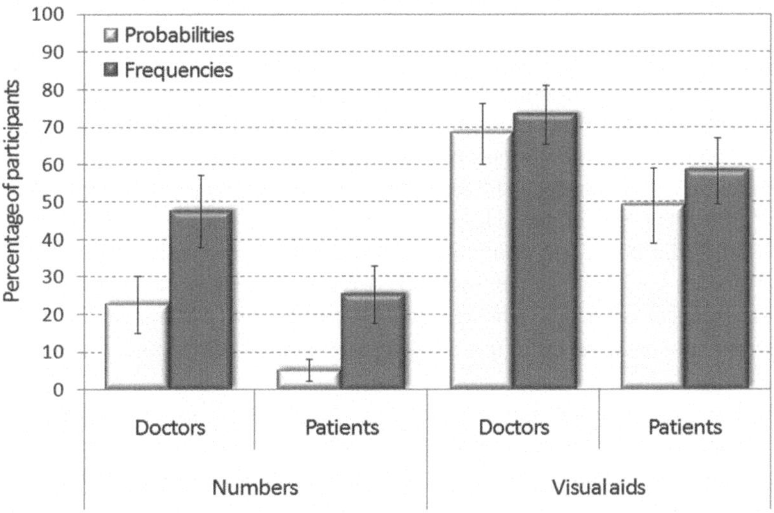

Fig. 12.3 Percentage of participants who made accurate diagnostic inferences, by visual aids condition, numerical format, and type of participant. Error bars represent one standard error. Reprinted from Garcia-Retamero and Hoffrage (2013) with permission of Elsevier

understanding (i.e., metacognitive judgment calibration as related to overconfidence bias).

When information about the medical tests was presented via numerical information without the visual aid, results showed that highly numerate patients made more accurate inferences and had a much better sense of how accurate their diagnostic inferences were as compared to patients with low numeracy. That is, patients with high numeracy more accurately assessed accuracy of their diagnostic inferences, which in part explained why these inferences were more accurate (e.g., they were less overconfident, and so they did not stop deliberating until they actually understood the diagnostic information). However, when they received a visual aid representing the numerical information, most patients avoided overconfidence, including those with low levels of numeracy. That is, in the visual condition, both patients with high and low numeracy were often well calibrated, and they made more accurate diagnostic inferences as a result. Visual aids helped patients evaluate the diagnostic information and their own understanding of the information, promoting more accurate and better-calibrated judgments.

These results are consistent with previous research, which shows that transparent visual aids can improve risk comprehension associated with different medical treatments and lifestyles (Tait, Voepel-Lewis, Zikmund-Fisher, & Fagerlin, 2010). Moreover, transparent visual aids can promote consideration of beneficial treatments despite side effects (Waters, Weinstein, Colditz, & Emmons, 2007), they can also reduce errors and biases (Fagerlin, Wang, & Ubel, 2005), they can promote healthy behavior (Garcia-Retamero & Cokely, 2011), and they can improve recall of health-relevant information (Gaissmaier et al., 2012).

Risk Reduction

Natural frequencies are not only helpful for interpreting positive test results but also for deciding on the implementation of a certain type of diagnostics or therapy. Should women accept the invitation to mammography screening? Should men have their prostate-specific antigen (PSA) level determined for early detection of prostate cancer? Should people undergo bypass interventions to reduce the risk of heart failure? What is the benefit in comparison to the risks and disadvantages? The main benefit of such medical interventions is risk reduction, for instance, to die of breast or prostate cancer or to have a heart attack. The question is: What are the risks without a diagnostic or therapeutic intervention compared to the risks if the intervention was taken?

Let's have a look at the figures for mammography screening. Without screening, 4 in 200 healthy women aged between 50 and 69 years who have not been diagnosed with breast cancer will die of this disease within this period of 20 years (Weymayr, 2010). If all women would undergo mammography screening, one less woman would die of breast cancer in this period. The most common ways to communicate the reduction in risk are as follows:

a. Relative risk reduction (RRR) amounts to 25%: In 1 of 4 women (=25%), death by breast cancer can be prevented.
b. Absolute risk reduction (ARR) amounts to 0.5%: Only 3 in 200 women instead of 4 in 200 women die from breast cancer; 1 in 200 (= 0.5%) women can be saved.
c. Number-needed-to-screen (NNS) amounts to 200: A total of 200 women have to undergo mammography screening to find the one women benefitting in terms of surviving the next 10 years. Not only the effectiveness of screening methods but also that of therapeutic interventions may be evaluated this way. For therapeutic interventions, this measure has been coined number-needed-to-treat (NNT) and is determined as follows: ARR equals 1/NNT (corresponding to 1/NNS for screening methods).

Note the large difference between the communicated values (25%, 0.5%, and 200). Further note that these values are based on the same data, which often leads to considerable confusion (Gigerenzer et al., 2007). Which of the three values is relevant for a woman who has received an invitation to mammography screening? She is 1 in 200, so that undergoing the screening procedure only reduces her individual risk by 0.5% – which of course, also applies to the other 199 women who have received the same invitation. The figure of 25% exclusively refers to the 4 women who would die of breast cancer without screening—and nobody knows at this point in time who the 4 women are. If they were known, the screening procedure would not be necessary. RRR values are commonly used for communicating diagnostic, therapeutic, or preventive measures (Kurzenhäuser, 2003; Kurzenhäuser & Hoffrage, 2012). Whereas ARR values tend to be low as a rule, RRR values are usually high. The use of RRR values in expert literature, the general press, and patient information suggests relatively high benefits, but this measure is irrelevant in individual cases. Most people do not understand this value correctly (Gigerenzer et al., 2007), and its application is particularly questionable when the diagnostic, therapeutic, or preventive measures also involve risks (Woloshin & Schwartz, 2009). In such cases, the people seeking advice may have decided not for but against the implementation of the measure if risk reduction had been communicated in a more transparent way. A study with focus groups conducted in Switzerland (Matter-Walstra & Hoffrage, 2001) showed that most women highly overestimated the benefit of mammography screening and were hardly aware of the risks (false-positive results and overtreatment, which means treatment of patients who have a type of cancer that will be correctly diagnosed but that would never be detected clinically and hence should better not be treated). After the women had been informed in a clear and transparent manner on RRR and ARR as well as on the relation of these two values, the spontaneous readiness to participate in mammography screening in this study dropped from 68% to 11%.

Survival Rates, Lead-Time Bias, and Overdiagnosis

Another measure which is often used to quantify the benefit of screening programs is survival rate, mostly the 5-year survival rate. Related to this, Rudy Giuliani, the former Mayor of New York, hit the headlines in 2007. During his electoral campaign and in the context of his candidacy for the office as the President of the United States, Giuliani compared the benefits of the American healthcare system with those of the British healthcare system: "I had prostate cancer five, six years ago. My chance of surviving prostate cancer — and, thank God, I was cured of it — in the United States? 82%. My chance of surviving prostate cancer in England? Only 44% under socialized medicine" (cited according to Wegwarth & Gigerenzer, 2011). After the comparison of the two figures, Giuliani drew a superficially plausible but nevertheless incorrect conclusion. On closer examination, the difference between the two 5-year survival rates had nothing to do with the nationalization of the health system but with the fact that a screening program for prostate cancer was available in the United States but not in Britain.

But the conclusion that the availability of a screening program would reduce the mortality rate would also be wrong. Screening programs enable early detection of many cancer diseases, but early diagnosis does by no means imply that death can be postponed. Let's take, as a fictitious example, triplets who simultaneously develop clinically apparent prostate cancer at the age of 83 years and die of the disease at the age of 86 years. The first of the triplets does not participate in any screening program and dies 3 years after the spontaneous diagnosis of the disease. The second of the triplets undergoes a PSA test at the age of 80 years, followed by a biopsy and the diagnosis of prostate cancer. The third of the triplets has the luck to meet a unique person at the age of 20 years who is able to tell him on the basis of the form of his earlobes that he will have prostate cancer. The disease will not break out for another

63 years but he will die from it after 66 years. What is the triplet's contribution to study results regarding the 5-year survival rate? The first of the triplets will not survive the spontaneous diagnosis by 5 years, and the second is still alive 5 years after the diagnosis was made by means of the PSA test. The case of the third triplet would enhance the reputation of earlobe diagnostics, not only with regard to the 5-year survival rate but also with regard to the 50-year survival rate—a measure unknown in clinical practice. The lead-time bias affects the three diagnostic methods with their different survival rates differentially: In our fictitious example, such statistics make spontaneous diagnosis look like the worst method and earlobe diagnosis appear to be the best method. But the fact that the respective survival rates do not allow for any statements on mortality is often overlooked. Regardless of when and why the triplets learn about the diagnosis of cancer, each of them dies the same year.

Lead-time bias is further enhanced by overdiagnosis bias. Screening programs not only bring forward the time of diagnosis but also further the detection of slowly growing types of cancer, which may never metastasize or manifest clinically. The autopsy prevalence of prostate cancer among US men aged 61–70 is around 65%, and for men aged 71–80, it is even above 80% (Haas, Delongchamps, Brawley, Wang, & de la Roza, 2008). Most men do not know about their condition and die of other reasons. What would happen with 5-year survival statistics if such comparatively harmless types of cancer could be detected by means of a highly sensitive test? Such overdiagnoses (correct but rather irrelevant and superfluous diagnoses without any life-extending effects) would push up 5-year survival rates and make the method of diagnosis look rather successful, even if the diagnosis does not at all influence the time of death.

Survival statistics are a good measurement tool for comparing effects of cancer therapies in randomized studies. However, such statistics are useless for comparing groups of patients whose disease was diagnosed by different means (early diagnosis vs. symptom-based discovery). "5-year survival rates are artificially inflated by bringing forward the time of diagnosis and by including tumors with a favorable prognosis. In reality, however, this inflation does not necessarily reduce mortality rates. For this reasons, 5-year survival rates are unsuitable for estimating the effect of early diagnoses" (Wegwarth & Gigerenzer, 2011, p. 4). Most physicians are unaware of these relations. In one of the respective studies, the percentage of physicians who were able to correctly explain lead-time bias and overdiagnosis bias was less than 10% (Wegwarth, Gaissmaier, & Gigerenzer, 2011).

Sound knowledge of these distortions seems to be indispensable for estimating the benefits of screening programs. For a woman diagnosed with breast cancer by means of early detection mammography, Welch and Frankl calculated a probability rate of 13% that death by breast cancer will be avoided because of early diagnosis (this calculation is based on an assumed relative reduction in mortality of 20%). In view of such a low probability rate, the authors concluded that "Most women with screen-detected breast cancer have not had their life saved by screening. They are instead either diagnosed early (with no effect on their mortality) or overdiagnosed" (Welch & Frankel, 2011, p. 2043). Jørgensen, Gøtzsche, Kalager, and Zahl (2017) estimate that between 25% and 33% of breast tumors diagnosed in women who were offered screening mammography were overdiagnosed, that is, these tumors would never have caused a noticeable health problem or led to death.

Lead-time bias and overdiagnosis must also be considered when evaluating the success of cancer screening programs for men. Based on the initial results of the European Randomized Study of Screening for Prostate Cancer (ERSPC), with a total of 162,243 men (randomly assigned to screening versus no screening) from 7 countries, the authors estimated a model according to which "there would be nine fewer prostate-cancer deaths and 73 life-years gained over the lifetime of 1000 men who underwent annual screening between the ages of 55 and 69 years" (Heijnsdijk et al., 2012, p. 601). These numbers, which quantify the benefits of the program, correspond to an absolute risk reduction of 0.9% and an increase of life expectancy of 27 days per man. However, the authors continue that the "harms caused by the introduction of such screening would be the overdiagnosis and overtreatment of 45 cases and the loss of 1134 life-years free of prostate cancer (i.e., lead-time years). After adjustment of the number of life-years gained from screening by consideration of quality-of-life effects, 56 QALYs would be gained, which is a 23% reduction from the predicted number of life-years gained." In other words, while screening 1000 men will save the life of 9, it will lead to overdiagnosing 45. While every man will, on average, live 26 days longer (compared to his peers who do not undergo screening), he will know about the diagnosis (again, on average, and compared to those peers) 414 days earlier. Quality of life is presumably lower with the diagnosis than without, which is also reflected in the fact that the authors' estimate of the 56 extra quality-adjusted life-years (QALYs) is *below* the number of (unadjusted) 73 life-years gained. However, there is probably variance with respect to how people tradeoff lifetime with quality of life. Some may prefer to live longer, even if this means to also live longer with the diagnosis and the resulting worries and therapies with their often adverse side effects. Others may prefer not to know, not to worry, and not to undergo therapy, even if this means to die earlier. Embracing the idea of informed decision making, we think that people who have to decide whether they want to participate in a screening program or not should be informed about the benefits, the harms, and the respective chances in these two lotteries in a transparent and understandable way.

Successful Risk Communication

The abovementioned prevalence of breast cancer and test parameters for mammography screening were taken from a US publication of 1982 (Eddy, 1982). We would like to explicitly state that both sensitivity and specificity of mammography screening largely depend on the framework conditions under which programs are carried out. Significantly less diagnoses of breast cancer will be overlooked, and considerably less false-positive findings will occur in quality-assured, systematically conducted screening programs in which analyses are carried out by specially trained and experienced radiologists rather than in small gynecological practices.

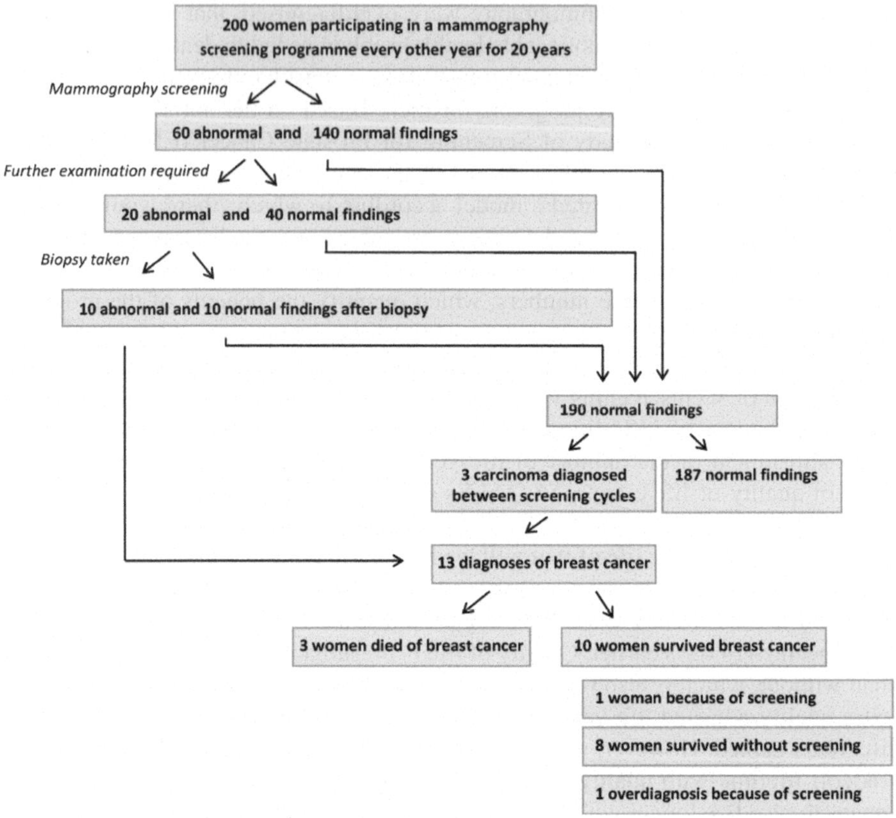

Fig. 12.4 Benefits of mammography screening (adapted from Weymayr, 2010, p. 22)

Improvements can be observed not only with regard to the figures themselves but also with regard to the manner of their communication. We would like to conclude our article by showing such a positive example. Unfortunately, the number of good examples is rather low (the overview of information material on mammography screening presented in Kurzenhäuser, 2003; Kurzenhäuser & Hoffrage, 2012, is rather sobering), but some change is on the way.

The presentations designed by the Mammography Cooperative (Kooperationsgemeinschaft Mammographie) in collaboration with the German Cancer Research Center (Deutsches Krebsforschungszentrum) can be viewed as exemplary, and they are adopted by many physicians and journalists. In these presentations, figures are presented as natural frequencies throughout: the diagnostic properties of the screening (PPV and cases of cancer overlooked) and its benefit (risk reduction) and risks (false alarms and overdiagnoses) relate to one and the same fictitious basic population and are thus directly comparable (see Fig. 12.4). We would like to add that the authors of these presentations are very familiar with the results of studies such as the one mentioned above.

The author put the overview shown in Fig. 12.4 into the following words (Weymayr, 2010, p. 23), which have been published in an information brochure for the general public (Das Mammographie Screening-Programm, n.d., p. 10):

The following figures, which are based on experiences made in other countries and on scientific investigations, shall give you a clear idea of how the benefits and risks are roughly distributed within the entire program:

- Of 200 women participating in a mammography screening program every other year for 20 years, 140 do not receive a suspicious finding. The remaining 60 women require further examination.
- Forty of these 60 women receive a normal finding when further examined, but the remaining 20 women are advised to have a biopsy taken.
- For 10 of these 20 women, the suspicion was not confirmed, and the other 10 women receive the diagnosis breast cancer within the screening program. Over the 20-year period, 3 of the remaining 190 women also receive the diagnosis of breast cancer but between two screening circles.
- Three of the overall 13 women with the diagnosis of breast cancer die of the disease, and 10 women do not.
- One of these 10 women would not have learned about her diagnosis of breast cancer without the mammography screening program; 8 women would have been successfully treated, even without participating in the screening program but some of them would have required a more arduous course of treatment. One in 200 women is saved from death by breast cancer because of her regular participation in the mammography screening program.

This overview meets all criteria of the catalogue compiled by the specialist team for patient information of the German Network for Evidence-based Medicine (DNEbM), which was developed to support physicians in counseling patients on early cancer diagnosis (Griebenow, 2008; Koch & Mühlhauser, 2008). The overview also corresponds with the demands for better risk communication in the context of screening programs (Jørgensen, Brodersen, Hartling, Nielsen, & Gøtzsche, 2009). The overview is transparent, and the manner of communication of the most important figures allows for a direct comparison of benefits and risks. This way, every woman is able to decide, either by herself or after consultation with her physician, if she would like to participate in the lottery (also termed screening). For further commendable presentations, see Albert et al. (2010) and Gøtzsche, Hartling, Nielsen, and Brodersen (2012). We would like to encourage physicians, expert societies, patient organizations, health insurances, and authorities to take up this example and compile further transparent overviews on the diagnosis and treatment of diseases. The Harding Center for Risk Literacy at the Max Planck Institute for Human Development in Berlin refers to even more condensed overviews that allow one to easily compare benefits and harms with the term "fact boxes" (see also McDowell, Rebitschek, Gigerenzer, & Wegwarth, 2016; Schwartz, Woloshin, & Welch, 2007, 2009) and has already produced a number of these boxes (Harding Center for Risk Literacy, 2018).

Conclusions

Risks are unavoidable. They have always been and will always be around—but poor risk communication and misunderstanding are really unnecessary. The starting point of this chapter was the observation that risks are often not communicated in a transparent and understandable way. We have discussed various reasons for this and have argued why it is particularly problematic. The core of the chapter was then four examples that illustrated how risk communication could be improved. These examples were (a) the use of natural frequencies in the context of diagnostic reasoning, (b) the use of visual aids to support the beneficial effect of natural frequency representations, (c) the use of natural frequencies to clarify the distinction between relative and absolute risk reduction, and (d) a clarification of the meaning and pitfalls of survival rates that are often used to quantify the benefit of screening programs. In each of these topics, we described original empirical studies illuminating a specific problem, and we discussed practical implications of the results.

From a theoretical point of view, this research provides additional converging evidence on the usefulness of the ecological approach to communicating risks, which has already led to important theoretical and practical applications in medicine, law, and education (see Gigerenzer & Muir Gray, 2011). Critically, the ecological approach suggests that problems in understanding relevant health information often do not reside in people's mind, but in the representation of the task. That is, problems with numerical concepts do not result simply because cognitive biases and lack of numeracy prevent risk understanding and good decision making. Rather, errors occur because ineffective information formats complicate and mislead adaptive decision-makers.

The ecological approach of risk communication emphasizes the importance of considering the fit between people, their cognitive processes, and task environments when designing interventions (Gigerenzer & Edwards, 2003). With results supporting the ecological approach, the research reviewed in this chapter converged to demonstrate that information formats that exploit people's inherent capacity to recognize relationships in naturally occurring problems (so-called transparent information formats) can dramatically enhance risk comprehension and communication and recall and foster better decisions.

It is interesting how many current debates there are in mainstream cognitive and educational psychology about the weak and often mixed evidence concerning whether or not general intelligence and cognitive ability training programs work (e.g., "brain training"; Cokely, Ghazal, & Garcia-Retamero, 2014; Cokely et al., 2018). In the meantime, however, for people who are genuinely interested in general skill training programs that are likely to promote valued life outcomes (e.g., better high-stakes decision making), there is no doubt that acquired numeracy skills can be improved as long as people rely on the right kinds of guidance, motivation, and deliberate practice (Arkes, 1991; Butterworth, 2006; Fong, Krantz, & Nisbett, 1986; Larrick, 2004; Morewedge et al., 2015; Soll, Milkman, & Payne, 2015; Torgerson, Porthouse, & Brooks, 2005; Xin & Jitendra, 1999). Experimental protocols are currently underway to evaluate and refine our existing training systems into large-scale online adaptive tutoring systems for use by diverse members of the public and professionals alike. This same information technology that we use for in-depth training is also designed to provide a platform for ongoing customized and adaptive decision support and targeted risk communication applications (Cokely et al., 2014, 2018). Risk communication is a challenge—with the risk of misunderstandings lurking everywhere—but it is a challenge that can be mastered.

Acknowledgments The authors thank the editors of this book for helpful comments on an earlier version and the Swiss National Science Foundation (100014–140503/1) and the Ministerio de Economía y Competitividad (Spain) (PSI2011-22954 and PSI2014-51842-R) for financial support. Parts of this chapter are adopted from Hoffrage and Koller (2015).

References

Ahmed, H., Naik, G., Willoughby, H., & Edwards, A. G. (2012). Communicating risk. *British Medical Journal, 344*, e3996.

Albert, U., Alt, D., Kreienberg, R., Naβ-Griegoleit, I., Schulte, H., & Wöckel, A. (2010). Früherkennung von Brustkrebs—Eine Entscheidungshilfe für Frauen. In *Leitlinienprogramm Onkologie. der Arbeitsgemeinschaft der Wissenschaftlichen Medizinischen Fachgesellschaften e.V., der Deutschen Krebsgesellschaft e.V. und der Deutschen Krebshilfe e.V.* (Hrsg.). Retrieved June 19, 2018, from https://www.leitlinienprogramm-onkologie.de/fileadmin/user_upload/Downloads/Patientenleitlinien/Patientenleitlinie_Brustkrebs_Frueherkennung.pdf

Anderson, B. L., & Schulkin, J. (2014). *Numerical reasoning in judgments and decision making about health*. Cambridge: Cambridge University Press.

Arkes, H. R. (1991). Costs and benefits of judgment errors: Implications for debiasing. *Psychological Bulletin, 110*(3), 486–498. https://doi.org/10.1037//0033-2909.110.3.486

Butterworth, B. (2006). Mathematical expertise. In K. A. Ericsson, N. Charness, P. J. Feltovich, & R. R. Hoffman (Eds.), *The Cambridge handbook of expertise and expert performance* (pp. 553–568). New York, NY: Cambridge University Press.

Cokely, E. T., Feltz, A., Ghazal, S., Allan, J. N., Petrova, D., & Garcia-Retamero, R. (2018). Decision making skill: From intelligence to numeracy and expertise. In K. A. Ericsson, R. R. Hoffman, A. Kozbelt, & A. M. Williams (Eds.), Cambridge handbook of expertise and expert performance (2nd Ed.) (pp. 476–505). New York, NY: Cambridge University Press.

Cokely, E. T., Galesic, M., Schulz, E., Ghazal, S., & Garcia-Retamero, R. (2012). Measuring risk literacy: The Berlin Numeracy Test. *Judgment and Decision Making, 7*(1), 25–47.

Cokely, E. T., Ghazal, S., & Garcia-Retamero, R. (2014). Measuring numeracy. In B. L. Anderson & J. Schulkin (Eds.), *Numerical reasoning in judgments and decision making about health* (pp. 11–38). Cambridge: Cambridge University Press.

Eddy, D. M. (1982). Probabilistic reasoning in clinical medicine: Problems and opportunities. In D. Kahneman, P. Slovic, & A. Tversky (Eds.), *Judgment under uncertainty: Heuristics and biases* (pp. 249–267). Cambridge: Cambridge University Press.

Fagerlin, A., Ubel, P. A., Smith, D. M., & Zikmund-Fisher, B. J. (2007). Making numbers matter: Present and future research in risk communication. *American Journal of Health Behavior, 31*, 47–56.

Fagerlin, A., Wang, C., & Ubel, P. A. (2005). Reducing the influence of anecdotal reasoning on people's health care decisions: Is a picture worth a thousand statistics? *Medical Decision Making, 25*(4), 398–405.

Fong, G. T., Krantz, D. H., & Nisbett, R. E. (1986). The effects of statistical training on thinking about everyday problems. *Cognitive Psychology, 18*(3), 253–292. https://doi.org/10.1016/0010-0285(86)90001-0

Franklin, W. T. (1817). *The private correspondence of Benjamin Franklin* (Vol. 1, 2nd ed.). London: Henry Colborn.

Gaissmaier, W., Wegwarth, O., Skopec, D., Müller, A., Broschinski, S., & Politi, M. C. (2012). Numbers can be worth a thousand pictures: Individual differences in understanding graphical and numerical representations of health-related information. *Health Psychology, 31*, 286–296.

Garcia-Retamero, R., Cokely, E., & Hoffrage, U. (2015). Visual aids improve diagnostic inferences and metacognitive judgment calibration. *Frontiers in Psychology, 6*, 932 https://doi.org/10.3389/fpsyg.2015.00932

Garcia-Retamero, R., & Cokely, E. T. (2011). Effective communication of risks to young adults: Using message framing and visual aids to increase condom use and STD screening. *Journal of Experimental Psychology: Applied, 17*(3), 270–287.

Garcia-Retamero, R., & Cokely, E. T. (2013). Communicating health risks with visual aids. *Current Directions in Psychological Science, 22*(5), 392–399.

Garcia-Retamero, R., & Hoffrage, U. (2013). Visual representation of statistical information improves diagnostic inferences in doctors and their patients. *Social Science & Medicine, 83*, 27–33.

Ghosh, A. K., & Ghosh, K. (2005). Translating evidence-based information into effective risk communication: Current challenges and opportunities. *Journal of Laboratory and Clinical Medicine, 145*(4), 171–180.

Gigerenzer, G. (2002). *Calculated risks: How to know when numbers deceive you*. New York, NY: Simon & Schuster.

Gigerenzer, G., & Edwards, A. (2003). Simple tools for understanding risks: From innumeracy to insight. *British Medical Journal, 327*, 741–744.

Gigerenzer, G., Gaissmaier, W., Kurz-Milcke, E., Schwartz, L. M., & Woloshin, S. (2007). Helping doctors and patients make sense of health statistics. *Psychological Science in the Public Interest, 8*(2), 53–96.

Gigerenzer, G., & Hoffrage, U. (1995). How to improve Bayesian reasoning without instruction: Frequency formats. *Psychological Review, 102*(4), 684–704.

Gigerenzer, G., & Muir Gray, J. A. (Eds.). (2011). *Better doctors, better patients, better decisions: Envisioning health care 2020*. Cambridge, MA: MIT Press.

Gøtzsche P. C., Hartling O. J., Nielsen M., & Brodersen J. (2012). *Screening for breast cancer with mammography*. The Nordic Cochrane Centre. Retrieved June 19, 2018, from http://nordic.cochrane.org/screening-breast-cancer-mammography

Griebenow, B. (2008). Beratung zur Krebsfrüherkennung: Vor- und Nachteile darstellen. *Deutsches Ärzteblatt, 105*(33), A-1724/B-1488/C-1456.

Haas, G. P., Delongchamps, N., Brawley, O. W., Wang, C. Y., & de la Roza, G. (2008). The worldwide epidemiology of prostate cancer: Perspectives from autopsy studies. *The Canadian Journal of Urology, 15*(1), 3866–3871.

Hanson, J. L. (2008). Shared decision making: Have we missed the obvious? *Archives of Internal Medicine, 168*, 1368–1370.

Harding Center for Risk Literacy. (2018). Retrieved June 19, 2018, from https://www.harding-center.mpg.de/en/fact-boxes

Heijnsdijk, E. A., Wever, E. M., Auvinen, A., Hugosson, J., Ciatto, S., Nelen, V., … Zappa, M. (2012). Quality-of-life effects of prostate-specific antigen screening. *New England Journal of Medicine, 367*(7), 595–605.

Hoffrage, U. (2016). Overconfidence. In R. F. Pohl (Ed.), *Cognitive illusions: Intriguing phenomena in thinking, judgement, and memory* (2nd ed., pp. 291–314). Hove: Psychology Press.

Hoffrage, U., & Gigerenzer, G. (1998). Using natural frequencies to improve diagnostic inferences. *Academic Medicine, 73*(5), 538–540.

Hoffrage, U., Gigerenzer, G., Krauss, S., & Martignon, L. (2002). Representation facilitates reasoning: What natural frequencies are and what they are not. *Cognition, 84*(3), 343–352.

Hoffrage, U., & Koller, M. (2015). Chances und risks in medical risk communication. *German Medical Science, 13*, Doc07 (pp. 1–7). https://doi.org/10.3205/000211

Hoffrage, U., Kurzenhäuser, S., & Gigerenzer, G. (2000). Wie kann man die Bedeutung medizinischer Testbefunde besser verstehen und kommunizieren? [How to improve the communication and understanding of medical test results?]. *Zeitschrift für Ärztliche Fortbildung und Qualitätssicherung, 94*, 713–719.

Hoffrage, U., Lindsey, S., Hertwig, R., & Gigerenzer, G. (2000). Communicating statistical information. *Science, 290*, 2261–2262.

Jørgensen, K. J., Brodersen, J., Hartling, O. J., Nielsen, M., & Gøtzsche, P. C. (2009). Informed choice requires information about both benefits and harms. *Journal of Medical Ethics, 35*(4), 268–269.

Jørgensen, K. J., Gøtzsche, P. C., Kalager, M., & Zahl, P. (2017). Screening in Denmark: A cohort study of tumor size and overdiagnosis. *Annals of Internal Medicine, 166*(5), 313–323. https://doi.org/10.7326/M16-0270 (see also the summary for patients. Retrieved June19, 2018, from, http://annals.org/aim/article/2597576/breast-cancer-tumor-size-overdiagnosis).

Koch, K., & Mühlhauser, I. (2008). *Kriterien zur Erstellung von Patienteninformationen zu Krebsfrüherkennungsuntersuchungen: Stellungnahme des Fachbereichs Patienteninformation des Deutschen Netzwerkes für Evidenzbasierte Medizin (DNEbM)*. Retrieved June 19, 2018, from http://www.ebm-netzwerk.de/pdf/stellungnahmen/dnebm-080630.pdf

Kurzenhäuser, S. (2003). Welche Informationen vermitteln deutsche Gesundheitsbroschüren über die Screening-Mammographie? [What information is provided in German health information pamphlets on mammography screening?]. In *Zeitschrift für ärztliche Fortbildung und Qualitätssicherung* (Vol. 97, pp. 53–57).

Kurzenhäuser, S., & Hoffrage, U. (2002). Teaching Bayesian reasoning: An evaluation of a classroom tutorial for medical students. *Medical Teacher, 24*(5), 516–521.

Kurzenhäuser, S., & Hoffrage, U. (2012). Designing risk communication in health. In P. M. Todd, G. Gigerenzer, & the ABC Research Group (Eds.), *Ecological rationality: Intelligence in the world* (pp. 428–453). New York, NY: Oxford University Press.

Larrick, R. P. (2004). Debiasing. In D. Koehler & N. Harvey (Eds.), *The Wiley Blackwell handbook of judgment and decision making* (pp. 316–338). Malden, MA: Blackwell Publishing Ltd. https://doi.org/10.1002/9780470752937.ch16

Lipkus, I. M. (2007). Numeric, verbal, and visual formats of conveying health risks: Suggested best practices and future recommendations. *Medical Decision Making, 27*, 696–713. https://doi.org/10.1177/0272989X07307271

Malek, D., & Kääb-Sanyal, V. (2016). Jahresbericht Evaluation 2014. Deutsches Mammographie-Screening-Programm. In: *Kooperationsgemeinschaft Mammographie*, Berlin. (Hrsg.) Retrieved June 19, 2018, from http://newsroom.mammo-programm.de/download/fachpublikation/KOOPMAMMO_Jahresbericht_EVAL2014_20161206_klein.pdf

Matter-Walstra, K., & Hoffrage, U. (2001). Individuelle Entscheidungsfindung am Beispiel der Brustkrebs-Früherkennung: Erfahrungen aus Fokusgruppen in der Schweiz [Individual decision making concerning breast cancer screening: Observations with focus groups in Switzerland]. *Schweizer Zeitschrift für Managed Care und Care Management, 3*(5), 26–29.

McDowell, M., Rebitschek, F. G., Gigerenzer, G., & Wegwarth, O. (2016). A simple tool for communicating the benefits and harms of health interventions: A guide for creating a fact box. *Medical Decision Making Policy & Practise, 1*, 1–10.

Mechanic, D., & Meyer, S. (2000). Concepts of trust among patients with serious illness. *Social Science and Medicine, 51*, 657–668.

Michaels, D. (2006). Regarding "Phenylpropanolamine and hemorrhagic stroke in the hemorrhagic stroke project": Mercenary epidemiology—Data reanalysis and reinterpretation for sponsors with financial interest in the outcome. *Annals of Epidemiology, 16*, 49–52.

Morewedge, C. K., Yoon, H., Scopelliti, I., Symborski, C. W., Korris, J. H., & Kassam, K. S. (2015). Debiasing decisions: Improved decision making with a single training intervention. *Policy Insights from the Behavioral and Brain Sciences, 2*(1), 129–140. https://doi.org/10.1177/2372732215600886

Murray, A. S., Stevenson, E., Kerr, F., & Burns, C. (2010). "A heartbeat moment:" Qualitative study of GP views of patients bringing health information from the internet to a consultation. *British Journal of General Practice, 60*, 88–94.

Peters, E., Västfjäll, D., Slovic, P., Mertz, C. K., Mazzocco, K., & Dickert, S. (2006). Numeracy and decision making. *Psychological Science, 17*, 407–413.

Schwartz, L. M., & Woloshin, S. (2007). Participation in mammography screening: Women should be encouraged to decide what is right for them, rather than being told what to do. *British Medical Journal, 335*, 731–732.

Schwartz, L. M., Woloshin, S., & Welch, H. G. (2007). The drug facts box: Providing consumers with simple tabular data on drug benefit and harm. *Medical Decision Making, 27*, 655–662.

Schwartz, L. M., Woloshin, S., & Welch, H. G. (2009). Using a drug facts box to communicate drug benefits and harms: Two randomized trials. *Annals of Internal Medicine, 150*(8), 516–527.

Skolbekken, J. A. (1998). Communicating the risk reduction achieved by cholesterol reducing drugs. *British Medical Journal, 316*, 1956–1958.

Soll, J. B., Milkman, K. L., & Payne, J. W. (2015). A user's guide to debiasing. In G. Keren & G. Wu (Eds.), *The Wiley Blackwell handbook of judgment and decision making* (pp. 924–951). Chichester: Wiley. https://doi.org/10.1002/9781118468333.ch33

Spiegelhalter, D., Pearson, M., & Short, I. (2011). Visualizing uncertainty about the future. *Science, 333*(6048), 1393–1400.

Starr, P. (1949). *The social transformation of American medicine*. New York, NY: Basic Books.

Studdert, D. M., Mello, M. M., Sage, W. M., DesRoches, C. M., Peugh, J., Zapert, K., et al. (2005). Defensive medicine among high-risk specialist physicians in a volatile malpractice environment. *Journal of the American Medical Association, 293*, 2660–2662.

Tait, A. R., Voepel-Lewis, T., Zikmund-Fisher, B. J., & Fagerlin, A. (2010). The effect of format on parents' understanding of the risks and benefits of clinical research: A comparison between text, tables, and graphics. *Journal of Health Communication, 15*(5), 487–501.

Torgerson, C., Porthouse, J., & Brooks, G. (2005). A systematic review of controlled trials evaluating interventions in adult literacy and numeracy. *Journal of Research in Reading, 28*(2), 87–107.

Waters, E. A., Weinstein, N. D., Colditz, G. A., & Emmons, K. M. (2007). Reducing aversion to side effects in preventive medical treatment decisions. *Journal of Experimental Psychology: Applied, 13*(1), 11–21.

Wegwarth, O., Gaissmaier, W., & Gigerenzer, G. (2011). Deceiving numbers: Survival rates and their impact on doctors' risk communication. *Medical Decision Making, 31*(3), 386–394. https://doi.org/10.1177/0272989X10391469

Wegwarth, O., & Gigerenzer, G. (2011). Risikokommunikation: Risiken und Unsicherheiten richtig verstehen lernen. *Deutsches Ärzteblatt, 108*(9), A448–A451.

Wegwarth, O., & Gigerenzer, G. (2013). Overdiagnosis and overtreatment: Evaluation of what physicians tell their patients about screening harms. *JAMA Internal Medicine, 173*(22), 2086–2087.

Welch, H. G., & Frankel, B. A. (2011). Likelihood that a woman with screen-detected breast cancer has had her "life saved" by that screening. *Archives of Internal Medicine, 171*(22), 2043–2046.

Weymayr, C. (2010). *Kennzahlen Mammographie-Screening*. Dokumentation 2010, im Auftrag der Kooperationsgemeinschaft Mammographie, Version 1.2. Retrieved June 19, 2018, from http://fachservice.mammo-programm.de/download/Kennzahlen_Mammographie-Screening_in_Deutschland_2010.pdf

Woloshin, S., & Schwartz, L. M. (2009). Numbers needed to decide. *Journal of the National Cancer Institute., 101*(17), 1163–1165.

Xin, Y. P., & Jitendra, A. K. (1999). The effects of instruction in solving mathematical word problems for students with learning problems: A meta-analysis. *The Journal of Special Education, 32*(4), 207–225.

Chapter 13
Developing Health Risk Communications: Four Lessons Learned

Tamar Krishnamurti and Wändi Bruine de Bruin

Abstract In this chapter, we summarize our research on the development of health risk communications and focus on four lessons we have learned from doing so: (1) Effective communications must be accessible and actionable to the intended audience; (2) effective communications must use an appropriate delivery method; (3) effective communications must be pretested and evaluated prior to wide-scale roll-out; and (4) effective communication design and evaluation requires interdisciplinary teams. While the examples provided in this chapter focus on the health domain, we believe that the four lessons outlined here will be helpful to those who wish to implement effective risk communications to a wide range of target audiences on a broad set of applied topics.

Even the most critical risk communications can fail if they are not designed with consumers' understanding, motivations, and decision making capabilities in mind. If a risk communication does not resonate with the target audience's mental model of the world they live in, they may not notice, understand, or accept it—let alone act upon it. One striking example of this is the failure of abstinence-only sex education programs in the USA, which strictly emphasized abstinence as a strategy for protecting against unwanted pregnancy and sexually transmitted infections. This communication strategy was partially predicated on educators' idealization that abstinence from sex, when implemented correctly, should be 100% effective in terms of avoiding unwanted pregnancy and sexually transmitted infections (Santelli et al., 2006). Moreover, based on educators' intuitions that discussing condoms would encourage teens to have sex, abstinence-only programs either omitted or

T. Krishnamurti (✉)
Division of General Internal Medicine, University of Pittsburgh School of Medicine, Pittsburgh, PA, USA

Department of Engineering and Public Policy, Carnegie Mellon University, Pittsburgh, PA, USA
e-mail: tamark@pitt.edu

W. Bruine de Bruin
Centre for Decision Research, Leeds University Business School, University of Leeds, Leeds, UK

Department of Engineering and Public Policy, Carnegie Mellon University, Pittsburgh, PA, USA

M. Raue et al. (eds.), *Psychological Perspectives on Risk and Risk Analysis*,
https://doi.org/10.1007/978-3-319-92478-6_13

misrepresented information about condom effectiveness (Santelli et al., 2006). However, a review conducted by Mathematica Policy Research (2007) for the US Department of Health and Human Services found that, after 25 years of national investment, abstinence-only approaches have been ineffective for promoting abstinence.

Part of the problem with abstinence-only programs has been that some adolescents interpret "abstinence" as including oral and anal sex, which are behaviors that could put them at risk for sexually transmitted infections (Schuster, Bell, Berry, & Kanouse, 1998). Educators often leave these misunderstandings unaddressed, because they feel uncomfortable covering taboo behaviors (Halperin, 1999).

Moreover, contrary to educators' intuitions, omitting accurate information about condoms actually undermined the effectiveness of "abstinence-only" programs, as programs that do address condom use have tended to be more effective for reducing pregnancy risk (Kohler, Manhart, & Lafferty, 2008). As compared to "abstinence-only" program recipients, recipients of comprehensive programs are more likely to use condoms when they do have sex (Kirby, 2008). Indeed, teens who eventually break a "virginity pledge" are less likely than sexually active teens to use contraception at first intercourse (Bearman & Brueckner, 2001) and to acquire a sexually transmitted infection (Brückner & Bearman, 2005; Underhill, Montgomery, & Operario, 2007).

To effectively help people to reduce the risks that they face, educators must understand audience members' actual wants and needs and gather evidence on communication strategies that work, rather than design communications based on their own intuitions. In this chapter, we discuss four lessons learned from our research on designing and implementing health risk communications: (1) Effective communications must be accessible and actionable to the intended audience; (2) effective communications must use an appropriate delivery method; (3) effective communications must be pretested and evaluated prior to wide-scale rollout; and (4) effective communication design and evaluation requires interdisciplinary teams.

Lesson 1: Effective Communications Must Be Accesible and Actionable to the Intended Audience

To facilitate recipients' understanding, health risk communications should use plain explanations and simple wording (McGaw & Sturmey, 1989; Neuhauser & Paul, 2011; Overland, Hoskins, McGill, & Yue, 1993). Even recipients with high reading comprehension levels benefit from materials that are easy to read (Davis et al., 2006; Smith, Trevena, Nutbeam, Barratt, & McCaffery, 2008). Yet, many risk communication materials are written at the university level (Daraz, Macdermid, Wilkins, Gibson, & Shaw, 2011; Davis et al., 1996; Neuhauser & Paul, 2011; Paashe-Orlow, Taylor, & Brancati, 2003).

Experts may fail to use clear explanations or understandable language, because they no longer think like non-experts in their domain (Ericsson, Krampe, & Tesch-Römer, 1993). As noted above, sex educators may use the term "abstinence" without debunking some teens' beliefs that it includes oral and anal sex (Schuster et al., 1998). Even seemingly simple wording like "boil your tap water" or "wash your hands" may fail, if experts do not realize that their recipients do not see the need, miss important details about the recommended length and procedure, or ignore recommendations when they are busy (Angulo et al., 1997; Pittet, 2001).

As another example of misunderstood wording, the US Food and Drug Administration (2012) has been using the term "breakthrough" therapy to designate drugs that "treat a serious or life threatening condition" and "may demonstrate a substantial improvement…over available therapies" even when the evidence is only preliminary. We found that adding the "breakthrough" label to factual evidence increased consumers' beliefs about the strength of the supporting evidence for the drug and the drug's effectiveness (Krishnamurti, Woloshin, Schwartz, & Fischhoff, 2015). These results even held for physicians who were randomized to the same conditions (Kesselheim et al., 2016).

Additionally, experts may provide statistical information that is confusing, especially for recipients with lower numeracy. Relative risk information, which presents how risks change between different behaviors, can be especially misleading. For example, eating bacon can increase the *relative* risk of bowel cancer by 20% as compared to avoiding bacon—which sounds large in the absence of knowledge that the *absolute* risk is only 6% for bacon eaters and 5% for bacon avoiders (example taken from Spiegelhalter & Pearson, 2009). Yet, absolute numbers, such as a 6% chance cancer risk, may be hard to interpret without a reference point against which to judge whether that risk is high or low (Barrio, Goldstein, & Hofman, 2016; Fagerlin, Zikmund-Fisher, & Ubel, 2007).

Experts may also emphasize the risk of onetime exposure without recognizing that people take many risks more than once and that risks accumulate with repeated exposure. For example, the probability of pregnancy given a single act of unprotected intercourse is only 5%, but the *cumulative risk* increases to 90% after a year of regular unprotected sexual intercourse. Couples may engage in unprotected sex because they underestimate that cumulative risk of pregnancy (Biggs & Foster, 2013). A focus on short-term probabilities may also make different birth control methods seem more similar in their effectiveness. For example, when considering only 1 year of use, hormonal birth control methods such as the pill tend to be 99% effective, whereas non-hormonal birth control methods such as condoms tend to be less than 90% effective. That difference is much more pronounced when considering that sexual activity may continue for 5 years (95% vs. 59%) or 15 years (86% vs. 21%) (Shaklee & Fischhoff, 1990).

In a well-intentioned attempt to include all the information they themselves deem pertinent about a topic, experts may also inadvertently lose the attention of the very audience they are hoping to inform. In addition to being written at the university level (Paashe-Orlow et al., 2003), the standard informed consent documents that are provided to patients who are considering enrollment into clinical trials tend to provide overwhelming lists of all possible risk and benefit information. In a randomized study, a concise consent form, designed with information that pilot-test participants had highlighted in a traditional consent form as being most critical to their decision making, was better at engaging patients than the traditional much lengthier document, without affecting comprehension or judgments of risk and benefit (Krishnamurti & Argo, 2016). In fact, the concise consent form was 30% the length of the original document yet still an almost perfect fit with existing requirements for the information that needs to be covered in informed consent forms, such as risks and benefits to the participants (US Food and Drug Administration, 1996).

The mental models methodology offers a systematic procedure for developing effective risk communication content. This approach involves the following steps, which aim to identify what people want or need to make more informed decisions. First, it starts with developing an expert model, which aims to summarize the existing literature on the risk under consideration, and how it can be reduced. Second, it uses in-depth interviews and follow-up surveys with members of the intended audience, so as to identify how they view the risk and attempt to reduce it, as well as what they want to know about it. Third, intervention content is designed to focus on what intended recipients want (as disclosed in step 2) and need (as identified by any gaps between step 1 and step 2). The language is adapted from the interviews, so that intervention content is natural to the target audience and respectfully incorporates their values. Hence, the resulting communication is driven by both experts and intended recipients, rather than on experts' preferences or (often unfounded) intuitions alone.

As an example, one notable mental models intervention (entitled "What Could You Do?") helped sexually active adolescents to reduce their risk of sexually transmitted infections by modeling how to negotiate abstinence and condom use with sexual partners, because adolescents indicated that they struggled to do so (Downs et al., 2004). Previous comprehensive sex education programs had recommended risk reduction strategies such as abstinence and condom use, but not focused on how to talk about them and navigate relationships. Perhaps as a result, the What Could You Do intervention was one of only four sex education programs from the previous 20 years that was deemed effective, in a review conducted by Mathematica Policy Research (2010). The mental models approach has been successfully applied in numerous health contexts including emergency contraception use (Krishnamurti, Eggers, & Fischhoff, 2008), sexually transmitted infections (Bruine de Bruin, Downs, & Fischhoff, 2007; Downs et al., 2004), vaccines (Downs, Bruine de Bruin, & Fischhoff, 2008), avian flu (Bruine de Bruin, Fischhoff, Brilliant, & Caruso, 2006; Fischhoff, Bruine de Bruin, Güvenç, Brilliant, & Caruso, 2006), and many other domains (see extensive use of the approach in climate change communication research; Morgan, Fischhoff, Bostrom, & Atman, 2002).

Lesson 2: Effective Commmunications Must Use an Appropriate Delivery Method

Risk communications can be delivered in many formats, from drug labels to social media posts. With advances in technology, the presentation and delivery of risk information have the potential to be increasingly interactive and personalized. Advances in technology also allow for access to a much wider audience. For example, even in the lowest income bracket, more than 72% of US adults own a smartphone, with no differences in ownership across racial or ethnic groups (Pew Research Center, 2015a, 2015b), making mobile platforms a potentially highly effective approach for delivery of health communications and interventions.

The "What Could You Do" sex education program, which was introduced above, used an interactive DVD format that was critical to its success (Bruine de Bruin et al., 2007; Downs et al., 2004). Viewers could self-navigate between different scenarios relevant to adolescents, including one in which a character met someone at a party and one with a long-term sexual partner. Viewers could choose the character's actions and were then asked to engage in *cognitive rehearsal* or "practice in their heads" how they would implement those actions in situations that they might face. Indeed, thinking beforehand about what one might do in a difficult situation tends to improve *self-efficacy* or confidence about being able to execute the action, and the likelihood of actually implementing it (Bandura, 2000). Overall, the DVD format was more effective than a paper format, in promoting risk reduction behaviors (Downs et al., 2004).

In choosing a delivery format, especially one that is technology-based, one must be mindful not only of the penetration of that technology in the target audience but also of how audience members interact with that technology. A DVD format, for example, may not be as effective for patients who are on the go. Social media and smartphone apps are becoming an increasingly popular means of targeting groups that would otherwise be hard to reach. For example, in a smartphone app designed for both communicating and assessing individual patient pregnancy risk information (*MyHealthyPregnancy*), the app was successful at communicating medical risk information to those patients who frequently missed routine medical care because of remote access to personalized care information (Krishnamurti et al., 2017).

Well-designed smartphone apps are a promising means for two-way communications and for collecting the kinds of real-time data that can allow for timely modifications of messaging. A *user-centered design approach* (Gould & Lewis, 1985; Kujala, 2003) is key to creating content and a layout that resonates with members of the target audience.

Classic paper communications should not automatically be discarded in favor of newer approaches, however. For example, mobile health apps that have been carefully designed and tested may fail to work for populations such as older adults, who are less tech-savvy even when they have smartphones at their disposal (Isaković, Sedlar, Volk, & Bešter, 2016). Even when an audience is tech-savvy, it has been suggested that interactive features (such as graphs that appear one feature at a time) may look appealing but can actually distract consumers from attending to the presented risk information (Zikmund-Fisher et al., 2012).

Lesson 3: Effective Communications Must Be Pretested and Evaluated Prior to Wide-Scale Implementation

User-testing is a key component of any risk communication development and involves systematic evaluation of people's ability to use the communication materials. Even when formative research with members of the target audience has informed communication development, user-testing should be done on all materials to ensure that they are understood well and effectively communicate any actionable items. Such user-testing may involve *think-aloud interviews* with intended users, in which they are asked to read the communication out loud and think out loud while processing the presented information (Ericsson & Fox, 2011). Afterward, they may also be asked to provide more detailed feedback about the communication. Such think-aloud interviews tend to reveal elements of the communication that are misinterpreted, cause potential confusion, and are still in need of improvement.

Once a communication has been through an iterative process of user-testing and updating, the final version should be evaluated for effectiveness before rolling it out more broadly (Davis, Krishnamurti, Fischhoff, & Bruine de Bruin, 2013). Large-scale implementation of an untested risk communication can be both costly and have perverse and long-lasting effects. A case in point is the Healthgrades regulation enacted in both Pennsylvania and New York in the early 1990s. These states mandated that cardiac physicians receive public performance grades based on their patients' mortality rates. The intent of this communication was to motivate physicians to improve performance, allowing consumers to select those physicians that would provide them with the best care. A study of national data on Medicare patients, however, found that the presence of cardiac surgery report cards actually resulted in physicians selectively treating healthier patients, presumably to maintain a higher health grade, and producing worse outcomes in those patients with the greatest need for care (Dranove, Kessler, McClellan, & Satterthwaite, 2002). Such a failed implementation can also undermine consumers' trust, which is difficult to restore once lost (Cvetkovich & Lofstedt, 2013).

It is also imperative that evaluation studies have a rigorous design. Methodological problems often undermine the conclusions drawn about a communication effectiveness. Common methodological problems include *volunteer bias*, which can occur when volunteers sign up for an intervention that is being tested, because volunteers are more likely to respond well to a communication (Davis et al., 2013). Another common methodological problem is *sequence generation bias*, in which the participants receiving the communication are determined using a nonrandom process, with, for example, all the people in a certain geographic region receiving an alert (Davis et al., 2013).

Randomized controlled trials are the gold standard of evaluations. Ideally, such trials would use a randomizer tool to select participants from the entire population of target consumers and then use randomization, again, to assign them to the risk communication or a no-communication control group. When possible, consumers should remain unaware that they are participating in a study of the communication, since mere knowledge of being observed can induce behavior change (Schwartz, Fischhoff, Krishnamurti, & Sowell, 2013). It can, however, be unethical to provide information to one group and not another, especially when that information may help consumers to avoid risks. In those situations, it may be acceptable to promise the control group that they will receive the information that was provided to other groups, after the study has been completed. In rare cases, it may truly be unfeasible or unethical to randomly assign members of the population to a risk communication intervention, for example, because that communication could inadvertently increase risks to the recipients (such as with abovementioned "abstinence-only" sex education). If so, a solution would be to allow for volunteers in an evaluation but employ statistical corrections to help adjust for estimated differences between volunteers and non-volunteers (Davis & Krishnamurti, 2013). Although the details of the statistical approach are beyond the scope of this chapter, we wish to highlight that validated procedures, such as this, are available to help estimate what the result of an evaluation might have been if non-volunteers had been recruited.

Lastly, evaluation work does not end once a risk communication has been rolled out. Target audience knowledge, understanding, and needs may change over time. Risks and risk reduction methods may also evolve. Therefore, messages that were once effective may become redundant or outdated. A sustainable approach to routine evaluation of any risk communication should be part of the initial design plan.

Lesson 4: Effective Communication Design and Evaluation Require Interdisciplinary Teams

Developing and implementing risk communications require expertise from across several domains. For any given topic, technical experts are crucial for providing accurate information regarding the absolute risks and benefits. Social scientists are necessary for providing evidence about the level of understanding and the drivers of consumer behavior, as well as to help design methodologically rigorous evaluations. Statistical experts can provide the know-how to organize and analyze large datasets of consumer behavior.

Yet many risk communication teams are dominated by technical experts. Such communications are often written by experts who have decades of domain knowledge. However, as noted, they may no longer think like non-experts (Ericsson et al., 1993) and have inaccurate intuitions about what interventions people want or need. As a result, communications may reflect their beliefs about what will be effective rather than be based on the social science evidence of how to inform the target audience. Appropriate evaluation of communications may also be lacking when there is an absence of methodological or statistical proficiency on the team.

Forming interdisciplinary teams can be a challenge, because experts often remain isolated in their academic silos. As a result, they have developed their own specialist terminologies, theories, methodologies, and professional networks. Moreover, organizations may view external perspectives as threatening (LaPalombara, 2001).

Our own most successful interdisciplinary teams have included individuals who were motivated by changing a host of real-world situations, from financial crashes to preterm births. Because of the severity of these situations, each team member recognized that their own expertise—while necessary—was not sufficient to achieve the desired change.

In our experience, even when a cohesive interdisciplinary team has formed, the members face the challenge of promoting a shared understanding and vocabulary. Effective teams can be facilitated by defining clear risk communication goals and by drawing on the most recent scientific information from each expert's discipline to inform the achievement of those goals (Wong-Parodi & Strauss, 2014).

Conclusion

In this chapter, we discussed four key lessons for providing effective applied risk communications:

1. Effective communications must be written in an accessible and actionable way. If recipients view a risk communication but cannot understand what it means or do not know what to do with the presented content, the risk communication will fail.
2. Effective communications must have an appropriate delivery method. Communications can take numerous formats from booklet to virtual reality. Selecting the appropriate format requires careful consideration of time and cost but also accessibility for and engagement of the target audience.
3. Effective communications must be designed iteratively and evaluated prior to wide-scale rollout. Ideally all design takes a user-centered approach, in which the target group's input is incorporated at each step. At a minimum, pre-testing and evaluation will allow us to understand whether the risk communication is having the intended effect.
4. Effective communication design and evaluation usually require the collaboration of an interdisciplinary team. Defining risk requires technical expertise, and communicating it requires behavioral expertise. The most effective risk communication approaches will marry the skill sets of several disciplines to determine the most pertinent information, the best framing for that information, and the optimal delivery method.

The nature and delivery of risk communications are evolving at an unprecedented rate, as work in areas like precision medicine, epidemiology, machine learning, human-computer interaction, and behavioral and social sciences come together. The four lessons detailed here can and should be applied to the creation of any risk communication from a physician-patient consultation to a Facebook-based public awareness campaign. More detailed information on the specifics of effective communication design is available in other chapters in this book, as well as in "how-to" guides (Fischhoff, Brewer, & Downs, 2012; Morgan et al., 2002). While the examples of applied risk communication provided in this chapter focus on the health domain, we believe that the four lessons outlined here will be helpful to those who wish to implement effective risk communications to a wide range of target audiences on a broad set of applied topics.

References

Angulo, F. J., Tippen, S., Sharp, D. J., Payne, B. J., Collier, C., Hill, J. E., … Swerdlow, D. L. (1997). A community waterborne outbreak of salmonellosis and the effectiveness of a boil water order. *American Journal of Public Health, 87*, 580–584.

Bandura, A. (2000). Self-efficacy: The foundation of agency. In W. J. Perrig & A. Grob (Eds.), *Control of human behavior, mental processes, and consciousness. Essays in the honor of the 60th birthday of August Flammer* (pp. 17–33). Mahwah NJ: Lawrence Erlbaum Associates.

Barrio, P. J., Goldstein, D. G., & Hofman, J. M. (2016, May 7–12). Improving comprehension of numbers in the news. In *Association for computing machinery conference on human factors in computing systems*, San Jose, CA.

Bearman, P. S., & Brueckner, H. (2001). Virginity pledges and first intercourse. *American Journal of Sociology, 106*, 859–912.

Biggs, M. A., & Foster, D. G. (2013). Misunderstanding the risk of conception from unprotected and protected sex. *Womens Health Issues, 23*(1), e47–e53.

Brückner, H., & Bearman, P. (2005). After the promise: The STD consequences of adolescent virginity pledges. *Journal of Adolescent Health, 36*(4), 271–278.

Bruine de Bruin, W., Downs, J. S., & Fischhoff, B. (2007). Adolescents' thinking about the risks and benefits of sexual behavior. In M. C. Lovett & P. Shah (Eds.), *Thinking with data* (pp. 421–439). Mahwah, NJ: Erlbaum.

Bruine de Bruin, W., Fischhoff, B., Brilliant, L., & Caruso, D. (2006). Expert judgments of pandemic influenza risks. *Global Public Health, 1*(2), 179–194.

Cvetkovich, G., & Lofstedt, R. E. (2013). *Social trust and the management of risk.* London: Routledge.

Daraz, L., Macdermid, J. C., Wilkins, S., Gibson, J., & Shaw, L. (2011). The quality of websites addressing fibromyalgia: An assessment of quality and readability using standardized tools. *British Medical Journal – Open, 1*, 1–10.

Davis, A. L., & Krishnamurti, T. (2013). The problems and solutions of predicting participation in energy efficiency programs. *Applied Energy, 111*, 277–287.

Davis, A. L., Krishnamurti, T., Fischhoff, B., & Bruine de Bruin, W. (2013). Setting a standard for electricity pilot studies. *Energy Policy, 62*, 401–409.

Davis, T. C., Bocchini, J. A., Jr., Fredrickson, D., Arnold, C., Mayeaux, E. J., Murphy, P. W., … Patterson, M. (1996). Parent comprehension of polio vaccine information pamphlets. *Pediatrics, 97*, 804–810.

Davis, T. C., Wolf, M. S., Bass, P. F., Middlebrooks, M., Kennen, E., Baker, D. W., & Parker, R. M. (2006). Low literacy impairs comprehension of prescription drug warning labels. *Journal of General Internal Medicine, 21*, 847–851.

Downs, J. S., Bruine de Bruin, W., & Fischhoff, B. (2008). Parents' vaccination comprehension and decisions. *Vaccine, 26*, 1595–1607.

Downs, J. S., Murray, P. J., Bruine de Bruin, W., White, J. P., Palmgren, C., & Fischhoff, B. (2004). An interactive video program to reduce adolescent females' STD risk: A randomized controlled trial. *Social Science and Medicine, 59*, 1561–1572.

Dranove, D., Kessler, D., McClellan, M., & Satterthwaite, M. (2002). *Is more information better? The effects of report cards' on health care providers* (No. w8697). National Bureau of Economic Research.

Ericsson, K. A., & Fox, M. C. (2011). Thinking aloud is not a form of introspection but a qualitatively different methodology: Reply to Schooler (2011). *Psychological Bulletin, 137*, 351–354.

Ericsson, K. A., Krampe, R. T., & Tesch-Römer, C. (1993). The role of deliberate practice in the acquisition of expert performance. *Psychological Review, 100*, 363–406.

Fagerlin, A., Zikmund-Fisher, B. J., & Ubel, P. A. (2007). "If I'm better than average, then I'm ok?": Comparative information influences beliefs about risk and benefits. *Patient Education and Counseling, 69*, 140–144.

Fischhoff, B., Brewer, N., & Downs, J. S. (2012). *Communicating risks and benefits: An evidence based user's guide*. Silver Spring, MD: Food and Drug Administration.

Fischhoff, B., Bruine de Bruin, W., Güvenç, U., Brilliant, L., & Caruso, D. (2006). Analyzing disaster risks and plans: An Avian Flu Example. *Journal of Risk and Uncertainty, 33*, 131–149.

Gould, J. D., & Lewis, C. (1985). Designing for usability: Key principles and what designers think. *Communications of the ACM, 28*(3), 300–311.

Halperin, D. T. (1999). Heterosexual anal intercourse: Prevalence, cultural factors, and HIV infection and other health risks part 1. *AIDS Patient Care and STDs, 13*, 717–730.

Isaković, M., Sedlar, U., Volk, M., & Bešter, J. (2016). Usability pitfalls of diabetes mHealth apps for the elderly. *Journal of Diabetes Research*. vol. 2016, 1604609.

Kesselheim, A. S., Woloshin, S., Eddings, W., Franklin, J. M., Ross, K. M., & Schwartz, L. M. (2016). Physicians' knowledge about FDA approval standards and perceptions of the "breakthrough therapy" designation. *JAMA, 315*, 1516–1518.

Kirby, D. B. (2008). The impact of abstinence and comprehensive sex and STD/HIV education programs on adolescent sexual behavior. *Sexuality Research & Social Policy, 5*, 18–27.

Kohler, P. K., Manhart, L. E., & Lafferty, W. E. (2008). Abstinence-only and comprehensive sex education and the initiation of sexual activity and teen pregnancy. *Journal of Adolescent Health, 42*, 344–351.

Krishnamurti, T., & Argo, N. (2016). A patient-centered approach to informed consent results from a survey and randomized trial. *Medical Decision Making, 36*(6), 726–740.

Krishnamurti, T., Davis, A., Wong-Parodi, G., Fischhoff, B., Sadovsky, Y., & Simhan, Y. (2017). MyHealthyPregnancy: A feasibility pilot of a behavioral decision research-based tool for assessing and communicating pregnancy risk. JMIR Mhealth and Uhealth. 5(4): e42.

Krishnamurti, T., Eggers, S. L., & Fischhoff, B. (2008). The impact of over-the-counter availability of, "Plan B" on teens' contraceptive decision making. *Social Science & Medicine, 67*(4), 618–627.

Krishnamurti, T., Woloshin, S., Schwartz, L. M., & Fischhoff, B. (2015). A randomized trial testing US Food and Drug Administration "breakthrough" language. *JAMA Internal Medicine, 175*(11), 1856–1858.

Kujala, S. (2003). User involvement: A review of the benefits and challenges. *Behaviour & Information Technology, 22*, 1–16.

LaPalombara, J. (2001). Power and politics in organizations: Public and private sector comparisons. In M. Dierkes, A. B. Antal, J. Child, & I. Nonaka (Eds.), *Handbook of organizational learning and knowledge*. Oxford: Oxford University Press.

Mathematica Policy Research. (2007). *Impacts of four title V, Section 510 abstinence education programs*. http://files.eric.ed.gov/fulltext/ED496286.pdf

Mathematica Policy Research. (2010). *Identifying programs that impact teen pregnancy, sexually transmitted infections, and associated sexual risk behaviors*. https://www.hhs.gov/ash/oah/oah-initiatives/webinars/evreviewweb2011.pdf

McGaw, S., & Sturmey, P. (1989). The effects of text readability and summary exercises on parental knowledge of behaviour therapy: The portage parent readings. *Educational Psychology, 9*(2), 127–132.

Morgan, M. G., Fischhoff, B., Bostrom, A., & Atman, C. J. (2002). *Risk communication: A mental models approach*. New York, NY: Cambridge University Press.

Neuhauser, L., & Paul, K. (2011). Readability, comprehension, and usability. In B. Fischhoff, N. T. Brewert, & J. S. Downs (Eds.), *Communicating risks and benefits: An evidence-based user's guide* (pp. 129–148). Silver Spring, MD: U. S. Department of Health and Human Services.

Overland, J. E., Hoskins, P. L., McGill, M. J., & Yue, D. K. (1993). Low literacy: A problem in diabetes education. *Diabetic Medicine, 10*(9), 847–850.

Paashe-Orlow, M. K., Taylor, H. A., & Brancati, F. L. (2003). Readability standards for informed-consent forms as compared with actual readability. *New England Journal of Medicine, 348*, 721–726.

Pew Research Center. (2015a). *Spring 2015 global attitudes survey*. Retrieved from Pew Research Center http://www.pewglobal.org/2015/06/23/spring-2015-survey/

Pew Research Center. (2015b). *The smartphone difference*. Washington, DC: Pew Research Center.

Pittet, D. (2001). Compliance with hand disinfection and its impact on hospital-acquired infections. *Journal of Hospital Infections, 48*, S40–S46.

Santelli, J., Ott, M. A., Lyon, M., Rogers, J., Summers, D., & Schleifer, J. D. (2006). Abstinence and abstinence-only education: A review of US policies and programs. *Journal of Adolescent Health, 38*, 72–81.

Schuster, M. A., Bell, R. M., Berry, S. H., & Kanouse, D. E. (1998). Impact of a high school condom availability program on sexual attitudes and behaviors. *Family Planning Perspectives, 30*, 67–72.

Schwartz, D., Fischhoff, B., Krishnamurti, T., & Sowell, F. (2013). The Hawthorne effect and energy awareness. *Proceedings of the National Academy of Sciences, 110*, 15242–15246.

Shaklee, H., & Fischhoff, B. (1990). The psychology of contraceptive surprises: Cumulative risk and contraceptive effectiveness. *Journal of Applied Social Psychology, 20*(5), 385–403.

Smith, S. K., Trevena, L., Nutbeam, D., Barratt, A., & McCaffery, K. J. (2008). Information needs and preferences of low and high literacy consumers for decisions about colorectal cancer screening: Utilizing a linguistic model. *Health Expectations, 11*, 123–136.

Spiegelhalter, D., & Pearson, M. (2009). *Understanding uncertainty: 2845 ways of spinning risk*. Retrieved January 13, 2017, from https://plus.maths.org/content/understanding-uncertainty-2845-ways-spinning-risk-0

Underhill, K., Montgomery, P., & Operario, D. (2007). Sexual abstinence only programmes to prevent HIV infection in high income countries: Systematic review. *BMJ, 335*(7613), 248.

US Food and Drug Administration. (1996). *Guidance for industry E6 good clinical practice: consolidated guidance*. http://www.fda.gov/downloads/Drugs/Guidances/ucm073122.pdf

US Food and Drug Administration. (2012). Safety and Innovation Act, 21 USC 356 § 3187.

Wong-Parodi, G., & Strauss, B. H. (2014). Team science for science communication. *Proceedings of the National Academy of Sciences, 111*, 13658–13663.

Zikmund-Fisher, B. J., Witteman, H. O., Fuhrel-Forbis, M. A., Exe, N. L., Kahn, V. C., & Dickson, M. (2012). Animated graphics for comparing two risks: A cautionary tale. *Journal of Medical Internet Research, 14*, e106..

Part V
Practical Implications for Industry, Policy and Research

Chapter 14
Measuring Subjective Risk Estimates

Eva Lermer, Bernhard Streicher, and Martina Raue

Abstract Insights from the growing risk literature unearth a range of challenges that have to be addressed in order to receive valid risk estimates and to interpret them realistically. The present chapter highlights some often-neglected influences and their consequences. These include a clear goal definition of the measurement and a thoughtful consideration of the chosen risk perspective and answer format. At the same time, the chapter aims at contributing to an integrative perspective in the field of measuring risk estimates. As a suggestion for a starting point for the development of an integrative framework, a model, the risk assessment matrix (RAM), is presented. The risk assessment matrix combines evidence-based theoretical approaches of probabilistic reasoning (singular vs. distributional) and thinking style (intuitive vs. deliberative). The chapter closes with a summary of the presented influences and some practical recommendations for researchers and practitioners.

The question of how people perceive and estimate risks is of increasing importance in today's world—which has become more complex due to globalization, technological progress, and increasing interrelations and interdependencies. This growing complexity makes it more and more difficult to predict consequences of actions and events. As reflected by the quantity of research literature devoted to this matter, risk estimates per se are a complex issue, not least because they are influenced by many different factors (e.g., mood, personality, context and framing, etc.). However, benchmarked against the amount of research performed, little real-world clarity exists on how to scientifically measure subjective risk estimates. A current example

E. Lermer (✉)
Department of Experimental Psychology, University of Regensburg, Regensburg, Germany

FOM University of Applied Sciences for Economics and Management, Munich, Germany
e-mail: eva.lermer@ur.de

B. Streicher
Institute of Psychology, UMIT - Private University for Health Sciences, Medical Informatics and Technology, Hall in Tyrol, Austria
e-mail: bernhard.streicher@umit.at

M. Raue
AgeLab, Massachusetts Institute of Technology, Cambridge, MA, USA
e-mail: maraue@mit.edu

M. Raue et al. (eds.), *Psychological Perspectives on Risk and Risk Analysis*,
https://doi.org/10.1007/978-3-319-92478-6_14

of this dearth can be found in the banking sector. In the context of investment decisions, regulators around the globe see the assessment of a client's risk tolerance as an essential component of product recommendations. But there is no consensus about what the construct "risk tolerance" really is and how it should be measured (Kitces, 2016), especially since it is not clear how laypeople perceive and estimate investment risks.

One reason for the arbitrary understanding and measurement of clients' risk tolerance might stem from the way risk has been studied in the scientific area. Many studies investigate how people perceive and handle risks, but comparatively few studies focus on the *methodology of risk assessment.* Studies focusing on the latter topic reveal that apparently trivial features such as the answer format or the degree of abstraction of the target person (e.g., abstract stereotype *average peer* vs. unique individual *friend*) can have a substantial impact on how people perceive risks and make decisions and on the quality of their judgments (Reeves & Lockhart, 1993). This impact opens the door for substantial biasing and questions the validity of various reported research findings. Furthermore, this could be an explanation for (presumed) contradictory findings and the lack of a framework in which results from different approaches could be integrated in order to increase the general understanding of how people handle risks—which in turn would foster practical implications.

The present chapter provides an overview of different influences (e.g., scales), their effects on subjective risk estimates (driven by, e.g., risk literacy vs. intuitive representation), and how these findings can be applied in order to be useful for a better understanding of risk assessment. First, we address the influence of different answer formats (e.g., ranking scale, numerical scale); second, we explain how the focus on the target (e.g., oneself vs. some person) affects risk assessments; third, we point out the differences between spontaneous and deliberative answers; fourth, we reflect on different ways of thinking about risks; and finally, we sketch an integrative framework for the measurement of risk perceptions.

Different Answer Formats Lead to Different Estimates

Surprisingly, as Windschitl and Wells (1996) point out, only a few researchers seem to be aware of the problem of biased results caused by different answer formats:

> "... in much psychological research, there seems to be an implicit assumption that the consequences of measuring uncertainty one way versus another are generally not significant. Rarely do authors mention their rationale for choosing a Likert-type scale ranging from 1 = *very unlikely* to 7 = *very likely* or a percentage scale ranging from 0% to 100% [...]. Researchers commonly ask people to estimate the probability that a given event has happened, the chance that a given statement is true, or the odds that an event will occur. Regardless of whether the requested response format is a probability estimate (e.g., "Give a number between 0 and 1.0") or a frequency estimate (e.g., "Out of 100 times, how many times would this event occur?"), the assumption is that people's numeric answers are accurate reflections of underlying feelings of uncertainty." (pp. 343–344)

The amount of research on how people make probability judgments is huge (for an overview, see Kahneman, 2012) and reveals two key findings relevant for assessing risk estimates: First, people are not good at dealing with probabilities, and second, people are not good at quantifying their estimates. This becomes especially clear when people are asked to express their feelings in a quantitative way (e.g., as percentages)—which in general does not match their intuitive, everyday thinking. But for researchers (and of course practitioners), it is often much more comfortable to operate with numerical, quantitative data (e.g., participants' answer: *75%*) than with verbal, qualitative information (e.g., participants' answer: *frequently*). Qualitative data in some cases can hardly be compared on an interpersonal or intrapersonal level. This becomes obvious when the same expression (e.g., *frequently*) is used for different events but actually represents different frequencies:

> "Thus, "frequently" suffering from headaches reflects higher absolute frequencies than "frequently" suffering from heart attacks. Moreover, different respondents use the same term to denote different objective frequencies of the same behavior. For example, suffering from headaches "occasionally" denotes a higher frequency for respondents with a medical history of migraines than for respondents without that history." (Schwarz, 1999, p. 99)

Schwarz (1999) argues that vague quantifiers (i.e. verbal measures) such as "frequently" or "sometimes" reflect the participants' estimated frequency oriented toward the participants' subjective standard. Therefore, he concludes that the use of vague quantifiers is the worst possible choice (see Pepper, 1981; Moxey & Sanford, 1992, for reviews). On the other side, Windschitl and Wells (1996) argue that verbal measures (with verbal expressions such as *likely*) are advantageous because they can provide more information regarding the participants' actual or intuitive way of thinking (this aspect will be considered in the fourth section of the chapter). Furthermore, many people have difficulty thinking about probabilities in a numerical way. Research has shown that even highly educated people have difficulty with simple numeracy questions (Lipkus, Samsa, & Rimer, 2001). Moreover, some findings indicate that low numeracy (ability to use mathematics in everyday life) increases susceptibility to influences of mood or the information format (percentages vs. frequencies) and to biases in decision making (e.g., framing; Reyna, Nelson, Han, & Dieckmann, 2009). The question about how to assess probabilities is accordingly multidimensional.

Fortunately, the search for an ideal answer format is not new and has been a popular research topic for decades. With today's knowledge, one has to conclude that every aspect of an answer format has an impact, for instance, verbal vs. numeric format (e.g., rating scale from *not at all* to *very likely* vs. open percentages; Lermer, Streicher, Sachs, & Frey, 2013; Windschitl & Wells, 1996), linear vs. logarithmic format (e.g., 11-step from *0% to 100%* vs. *1 = 1:1 to 9 = 1:100.000.000*; Lermer et al., 2013; Woloshin, Schwartz, Byram, Fischhoff, & Welch, 2000), midpoint of the scale (e.g., *−5 to 5* vs. *0 to 10*; Harris & Hahn, 2011), range and labeling of the response categories (e.g., *no more likely* to *50 times as likely* vs. *no more likely* to *10 or more times as likely*; e.g., Slovic, 2001), or number of response categories (e.g., 4-step vs. 7-step scales; Preston & Colman, 2000; Weijters, Cabooter, & Schillewaert,

Verbal and numerical qualitative linear scales

no chance	very unlikely	Unlikely	moderate chance	likely	very likely	certain to happen

no chance		1	2	3	4	5	6	7	certain to happen	
-5	-4	-3	-2	-1	0	1	2	3	4	5

Closed 11-step percentage scale

[ ]	[ ]	[ ]	[ ]	[ ]	[ ]	[ ]	[ ]	[ ]	[ ]	[ ]
0%	10%	20%	30%	40%	50%	60%	70%	80%	90%	100%

Open percentage scale: ___ %

Closed (logarithmic) frequency scale

1	2	3	4	5	6	7	8	9
1:1	1:10	1:100	1:1.000	1:10.000	1:100.000	1:1.000.000	1:10.000.000	1:100.000.000

Semi open frequency scale: **1 out of *n***

Open frequency scale: ***X* out of *Y***

Visual analog scale (qualitative)

No chance —————————— Certain

Visual analog scale (quantitative)

0 % —————————— 100 %

Fig. 14.1 Commonly used answer formats for measuring risk estimates (adapted from Lermer, Raue, & Frey, 2016)

2010). Figure 14.1 shows a selection of commonly used answer formats for measuring risk estimates. Examples like these abound in today's psychological literature. Unfortunately, that does not make things any easier. In view of the significant body of studies on scales, one would presume to find some standards for the risk context. But there is no standard measure for subjective probability estimates (Haase, Renkewitz, & Betsch, 2013).

A major reason for this lack of standards may be that studies comparing the impact of different scales fail at delivering consistent results (Haase et al., 2013). However, several studies investigating the influences of different answer formats on risk estimates provide important insights regarding different aspects (e.g., Diefenbach, Weinstein, & O'Reilly, 1993; Haase et al., 2013; Lermer et al., 2013; Weinstein et al., 2007; Woloshin et al., 2000). For example, some scales are advisable in terms of *usability*, but are outperformed by other scales on dimensions such as *sensitivity to changes of the objective probability* of an event. Diefenbach et al. (1993) point out that rating scales (e.g., 7-step verbal labeled linear scale ranging from *no chance* to *certain to happen*) outperform other answer formats in regard to *usability*. This format is intuitive and easy to handle, especially when compared with answer formats like *open percentages* (for valid criticism concerning the use of percentages, see Gigerenzer, 2002; Gigerenzer, Hertwig, Van den Broek, Fasolo, & Katsikopoulos, 2005). Diefenbach et al.' (1993) finding that rating scales are advantageous is in line with the findings of Weinstein et al. (2007). The latter report that a 7-step verbal scale was the best predictor of vaccination *behavior* (compared to a 2-step and 6-step verbal scale and a percentage scale with 13 increments).

On the other side, Haase et al. (2013) showed that the 7-step verbal scale was outperformed by numeric scales (i.e., *open percentages* and *open frequency* format) in terms of *sensitivity to mirror changes of the objective probability* and *accuracy*. The authors assume the superior performance of the numeric formats is because they have a higher resolution in terms of possible categories. Another advantage of numeric formats is that for many research questions, exact numerical values are needed (for instance, to make comparisons with actual statistics; e.g., Lermer, Streicher, Sachs, Raue, & Frey, 2016).

In sum, it seems as if insights from previous research cannot be simply brought together in order to create generally valid recommendations, because none of the formats are consistently superior (Haase et al., 2013).

Kind of Target: Unrealistic Optimism or Equal Vulnerability

When risk estimates are assessed, it is of enormous importance to consider the risk perspective, that is, the question of "who will be affected?." Plentiful research shows that estimating personal risks leads to different estimates than estimating the same risks for someone else (e.g., an "average person"; Lermer et al., 2013). Much of this literature is dedicated to the bias called *unrealistic optimism* (or *optimism bias*) displaying the assumption that others are more at risk of experiencing negative events compared to oneself (e.g., Weinstein, 1980, 1984, 1989). Many studies suggest *downward comparisons* as an explanation for these "it won't happen to me" assumptions. Generally, a person will feel aversion toward being confronted with potentially negative outcomes (e.g., risks). People are motivated to end aversive feelings and to reestablish subjective well-being. One way to do this is to compare oneself with a less fortunate other. The comparison target can be real (i.e., an existing person) or imagined (i.e., an imagined other who is worse off). This process is known as downward comparison (Lermer, 2013; Perloff & Fetzer, 1986; Wills, 1981). In most studies on downward comparisons, participants are asked to estimate their perceived subjective risk (e.g., car accident) and the risk of another person, commonly an abstract person (e.g. average driver; McKenna, 1993). The interesting point here is that in most studies the description of the "other person" has not been questioned or chosen deliberately. There is hardly any explanation or discussion of how to select or describe the "other person" (e.g., as anyone; someone of the same age, gender, or nation; someone with similar personality, education, or world view as oneself; a specific other, etc.). There are good reasons to argue that the description of the other person has an impact on the process of the comparison.

Some of the first researchers who investigated the influence of the kind of other person on participants' judgments and consequently on downward comparisons were Perloff and Fetzer (1986). In particular, they examined the impact of the degree of abstraction of the "other person" (e.g., vague target: average student vs. specific target: best friend). Their study results showed that abstract targets facilitate downward comparisons. That means that participants tend to perceive themselves as less vulnerable than abstract targets, leading to lower risk estimates for oneself than for the other person. Specific targets lead to no differences in vulnerability estimates, meaning equal risk estimates are provided for oneself and for one's best friend. Lermer et al. (2013) replicated and extended this finding by showing that the optimism bias (i.e., higher risk estimates for the other person than for oneself) disappears as soon as the target is perceived as specific, which can be accomplished simply by giving the other person a name such as Anton or Petra. Therefore, when assessing risk estimates, it is very important to consider the choice of the risk perspective (and degree of abstraction of the target), in particular when personal risk estimates are to be compared with risk estimates for other persons.

Kind of Probabilistic Reasoning: Singular or Distributional Approach

Another interesting explanation for the finding that risk estimates for "another person" can lead to different judgments comes from research focusing on probabilistic reasoning (i.e., the way people arrive at judgements of probability). This research shows how the description of the target person can lead to different ways of information processing. A potential difference lies in the perception of a person as a single entity (e.g., Anton) or as an instance of a class (e.g., one person of all married persons). Reeves and Lockhart (1993) were among the first researchers who explored this approach in the context of probabilistic reasoning. Here is an example (adapted from Klar, Medding, & Sarel, 1996) with two versions of a problem which (at first glance) are very similar but lead to different kinds of information processing, resulting in different outcomes:

Version I When the question is "What do you think: How likely is it that a *person* will get divorced?" people might use the following strategy:

A. Do I have any information about the "person"? If the answer is *no* I have to search for other cues, such as:

B. Do I have some information about the base rate (information about the frequency of an event within a class) of this event (e.g., number of divorces in a population)? If the answer is *no* the judgment will be very likely a random guess. But if the answer is *yes* (even if this is only based on an intuitive feeling, e.g., "I think I read somewhere that every third marriage ends up in divorce") the judgment will be guided by this impression.

In this case it is very likely that the answer to the question "How likely do you think is it that a *person* will get divorced" will be "I think the probability is about 33%."

Here the judgment is driven by representing the target as an instance of a class: the *person* as one entity of the class "married persons." Reeves and Lockhart (1993) call this strategy of probabilistic reasoning *distributional approach*. By using the distributional approach, one derives probability estimates from the assumed relative frequency of the occurrence of an event within a class.

The strategy of problem-solving can be totally different when seemingly trivial features change, such as providing the person a name:

Version II When the question is "What do you think: How likely is it that *Anton* will get divorced?" people might use the following strategy:

A. Do I have any information about Anton? If the answer is *no,* I have to search for other cues such as:
B. Can I deduce some information about Anton? If the answer is also *no* the answer will most likely be a random guess, too (as in version I). However, the crux of the matter here is that the target is perceived as having a unique identity (and not as an instance of class as in version I). This triggers another information-search process for cues to answer the question. It is likely that when thinking about a named person people have associations coming to mind, such as: "Well, I never met an Anton. I think this is an older forename. Perhaps Anton is from a former generation. In the past, marriages lasted longer. Therefore, it is not very likely that Anton will get divorced. Maybe the probability is 5%."

The latter judgment is based on assumptions about the specific target. Reeves and Lockhart (1993) call this strategy of probabilistic reasoning the *singular approach*. By using the singular approach, probability estimates are derived from dispositions attributed to the unique identity. Research on probabilistic reasoning show that when assessing risk estimates, it is crucial to consider the approach people may use (Lermer, 2013), because different approaches lead to different results. For instance, Lermer et al. (2013) have shown that risk estimates are higher when driven by a distributional approach of probabilistic reasoning compared to a singular approach. Considering the two different approaches can contribute to a valid measurement and interpretation of collected data.

Simple but Important: What Kind of Risk Perception Is Supposed to Be Measured?

Another important question that has to be answered before making a measurement is *what is supposed to be measured*? Results of a subjective risk measurement depend very much on how the questions are framed and which thinking style is activated as a result of this framing. For example, people can be either asked to give emotion-based answers which might stem from spontaneous associations, or people can be asked to provide fact-based and rational answers derived from a more thoughtful cognitive process. A different focus of questions can result in different answers. Moreover, if questions do not contain a specific focus (e.g., "Please estimate the risk of …"), it will remain unclear which approach people used for answering the question and what approach is measured. Furthermore, different people may use different approaches (e.g., spontaneous association vs. effortful and thoughtful cognitive process) while answering the same question, which can cause unwanted variance in the answers provided. Therefore, it is important to consider potential differentiations between measuring subjective risk representations (e.g., based on spontaneous associations) and risk literacy (e.g., based on a thoughtful cognitive process).

One example on how the focus of the question impacts risk estimations is the West African Ebola virus epidemic from 2013 to 2016. At the time, the news in Germany was full of reports about the spread of the virus in Africa along with detailed information about individual cases of infection in countries like the United States, Spain, and the United Kingdom. The mainly affected countries, though, were Guinea, Liberia, and Sierra Leone. In the affected countries about 28,000 people were infected and about 11,000 people died (Robert Koch Institute, 2016). Germany was not affected by the epidemic. There were no reported cases of Ebola fever in Germany, and none of the German aid workers involved in combating the epidemic in West Africa were infected. Three patients (who had been infected with Ebola fever in West Africa) were flown to Germany and brought to special treatment centers (in Hamburg, Frankfurt, and Leipzig). Two of them were cured and one died. Although the number of infected persons in West African countries and in comparatively unaffected countries differed widely, citizens in safe countries began having irrational fears of infection (for an explanation of this so-called freakout, see Slovic, 2014). When we asked students in our seminars at this time about their risk perceptions and their fear of being infected with Ebola, we received different answers depending on how the question was raised. Asking the question in a casual way (e.g., from *not at all* to *very concerned*) led to answers with a wide variance. But asking the question and simultaneously emphasizing rationality (i.e., please consider your answer consciously) reduced the variance and led to responses which were more realistic (i.e., that an infection in Europe is extremely unlikely). This indicates the relevant differentiation between asking people to describe how they intuitively feel about a risk and testing their risk literacy (i.e., how skilled are people at estimating their actual risk).

Slovic, Finucane, Peters, and MacGregor (2004) describe these two ways in which people comprehend risk as *risk as feelings* and *risk as analysis*. This differentiation is based on the dual-process idea of two modes of thinking and information processing, which Epstein (1994) called the *experimental system* and *rational system*. Other researchers label them as *system 1* and *system 2* (e.g., Kahneman, 2003; Kahneman & Frederick, 2002; Stanovich & West, 2000). Answers from both thinking styles are correct from the perspective of the respective individual, but reflect different aspects of the mind's workings. System 1 reflects the output of a spontaneous, automatic, and, at least in part, unconscious process (applied to the Ebola example: true emotional response). System 2 stems from a reflective, effortful, and, in most parts, conscious process. Not having that in mind before measuring subjective risk estimates can lead to wrong conclusions, such as false assumptions in respect to behavioral intentions (e.g., purchase of insurances or risk avoidance behavior).

Answer Format and Thinking Style: Intuitive vs. Deliberative

People can think about probabilities in two ways: intuitively and deliberatively. Windschitl and Wells (1996), for instance, demonstrated that numeric measures (e.g., percentages) trigger a more deliberative kind of reasoning. There is good reason to assume that numeric answer formats make mathematical concepts more salient and by this lead to more rule-based thinking (Haase et al., 2013). This may result in higher accuracy of the estimates, partly because of a subjectively perceived demand to give a correct answer, or at least an answer one could explain (Lermer et al., 2013). In contrast, a verbal probability estimate such as *very likely* is much easier to justify than a numeric answer. Moreover, both rule-based reasoning and a perceived need to give an accurate answer may lead to responses that do not reflect how the respondent actually thinks about the probabilities (see Ebola example above). This is an important aspect because the way people think most of the time is more intuitive than deliberative (see Kahneman, 2012), at least as long as they are not confronted with problems that obviously require more cognitive effort. For example, when asked whether a train will be delayed, most people would answer that it is likely rather than stating that there is a 95% chance (Windschitl & Wells, 1996).

Verbal measures allow for more intuitive thinking and "to be somewhat immune to accuracy checks" (Windschitl & Wells, 1996, p. 346). This goes hand in hand with an increased susceptibility to various influences and biases, which may be seen as a disadvantage (see also Raue & Scholl, Chap. 7). But intuitive scales also have their advantages. Windschitl and Wells (1996), for instance, report that verbal measures involving response categories such as *very likely* (compared to numeric measures with response categories such as *80% chance*) show more sensitivity to psychological uncertainty and are better in predicting individual preferences and behavior intentions (see also Weinstein et al., 2007). Therefore, it can be assumed that intuitive scales are better in reflecting psychological effects. Lermer et al. (2013) demonstrated that scales leaving more space for intuitive answers (i.e., *qualitative scale*) showed unrealistic optimism effects (whereas numeric scales such as *open percentages* did not). Their results showed generally that risk estimates on these scales are more prone to context influences (i.e., influence of the risk perspective).

This concept of scales triggering either more intuitive or deliberative thinking once again highlights the importance of determining consciously the issue that is of interest (e.g., intuitive perception of a risk vs. measuring accuracy skills) before making a measurement. The influences on risk estimates presented in this chapter are not the whole story. Measuring risk estimates is a complex challenge, but it is also a very popular research topic. Accordingly, there are several further relevant insights to be found in literature (e.g., influence of affect, arousal, experience, context, framing). A major problem, however, is that there is no integrative framework that links different findings or at least a common baseline where research findings can be integrated—because presently it seems as if there can be no simple answer to the question of which scale is appropriate.

Risk Assessment Matrix: A Suggestion for an Integrative Model

The discrepancy between the number of studies on risk estimates (comprising numerous important insights) and the scarcity of concrete recommendations (not least for practitioners) today demonstrates that something is going wrong here. The current state of research proves that the issue (measuring subjective risk estimates) is multifaceted.

At least three key issues need to be addressed:

1. Even in academic research, the reasoning behind the choice of the answer format for measuring risk estimates appears not to be reflected thoroughly in most cases. Therefore, it can be assumed that at least some findings are questionable. Examples for research findings supporting this view are:
   (a) Scales can lead to statistical artifacts (finding due to the used method; Harris & Hahn, 2011).
   (b) Scales differ in their sensitivity to displaying psychological effects and in their robustness against context influences (Lermer et al., 2013).
   (c) Scales influence accuracy (Haase et al., 2013).
2. There are many important risk research findings, but they are not connected to each (relevant) other. However, many of these findings support the assumption that a more differentiated perspective would be appropriate – analogous to Figner and Weber's (2011) statement: "… different *whos* react differently to different *whens*" (p. 211).

Table 14.1 Risk Assessment Matrix

		Probabilistic reasoning	
	Thinking	Distributional approach	Singular approach
Answer format	Intuitive	I Abstract target (e.g., a person) Intuitive answer format (e.g., rating scale)	II Specific target (e.g., oneself, named person) Intuitive answer format (e.g., rating scale)
	Deliberative	III Abstract target (e.g., a person) Deliberative answer format (e.g., open percentages)	IV Specific target (e.g., oneself, named person) Deliberative answer format (e.g., open percentages)

As a first step toward a systematic measurement of subjective risk estimates, Lermer et al. (2013) developed the risk assessment matrix (RAM; see Table 14.1). The RAM combines two relevant dimensions in the context of measuring risk estimates: probabilistic reasoning (distributional vs. singular approach) and thinking triggered by the answer format (intuitive vs. deliberative). This model may serve as a starting point for orientation and for the development of an elaborated integrated framework.

Several benefits emerge from the RAM. In the first place, the RAM aims at reminding researchers as well as practitioners to choose the answer format thoughtfully by considering the influences of the scale and the risk perspective. As described in the previous section, research has shown that numeric formats (e.g., percentages) tend to trigger more ruled-based, deliberative thinking, whereas verbal measures (e.g., verbal rating scales) allow for more intuitive thinking. The two ways of information processing can lead to different responses by reflecting different associations. This aspect is displayed by the rows of the RAM (different answer formats can trigger different thinking: intuitive vs. deliberative). A further benefit of the RAM is that it reminds one to consider the risk perspective. The way information about *a person* is processed by a respondent may differ basically from the thought process triggered by an estimate for a specific target (e.g., *oneself, named person*). As described above, there is some evidence that estimates for an abstract target (e.g., *a person*) lead to a distributional approach of probability reasoning (Lermer et al., 2013). Here probabilities are equated with the relative frequency (base rate) the respondent has in mind. For estimates concerning a specific target (e.g., named person), a singular approach of reasoning is very likely. These probabilities are oriented to dispositions attributed to the unique identity (Lermer et al., 2013; Reeves & Lockhart, 1993). This aspect is displayed by the columns of the RAM (probabilistic reasoning: distributional vs. singular approach). Since the RAM is only a starting point, an evidence-based theoretical framework is necessary for the development of useful practical implications. There are a wealth of models for how people estimate risk. However, to the best of our knowledge, only the RAM considers the basic influences described in this chapter.

Moreover, looking at practice leads to the conclusion that there is a problem of transferring relevant insights. One reason for this may lie in the fact that many valuable research findings (especially from the field of social cognition) are so complex and difficult to understand (even for other researchers) that they do not manage to cross the divide from the ivory tower of science to the main street of practice. Another reason may be found in the socialization of psychologists: From their first lecture onward, they are taught that there are no simple answers in psychology, that effects can be caused by many factors, that human behavior is better explained in terms of probabilities than in simple models, and that complexity is the norm in general. What is good practice in science turns into bad communication: generally speaking, psychologists are poor sellers of their wide and profound knowledge. However, over the last decade, a thirst for psychological insight emerged from business areas like global manufacturing, banking, and insurance. For different reasons these industries realized the limits of their classical risk management approaches and turned to psychology to predict customer behavior, optimize decision making processes, maintain unbiased qualitative risk assessment, or improve their organizational risk culture in general. For example, when assessing a client's risk tolerance, a bank customer consultant evaluates the client's relevant knowledge and her well-considered commitment to a specific risk level than her/his spontaneous estimation of the general popularity of a specific product. Following the insights presented here, the consultant is advised—following the RAM—to ask questions which follow a singular approach (i.e., framed in relation to the client her/himself) and evoke a deliberative thinking style (e.g., by asking to carefully think about the question and by using percentage or frequency scales).

Conclusion

The present chapter aims at contributing to a better understanding of measuring subjective risk estimates—a topic that is important for various scientific (e.g., psychology, medicine) and economic contexts (e.g., insurances or banks). However, despite a wealth of research on this issue, there still is no clear recommendation as to which instrument is suitable in which contexts. It has to be assumed that in most cases the choice of instrument is not reflected consciously and that the resulting consequences are not considered. This chapter outlines some basic aspects that should be taken into account when measuring risk estimates. In a nutshell, these are the thoughtful reflection of what is supposed to be measured and the numeracy skills of the respondents, the influence of the risk perspective, and the impact of the answer format. Several practical implications can be derived from these insights. These include some questions that should be raised before measuring subjective risk estimates:

A. What is supposed to be measured? Is it the intuitive feeling someone has about a risk or is it the respondent's risk literacy? People are able to think about risks in different ways (e.g., intuitive vs. deliberative), which can result in different responses.

B. Who is the target and how is he or she described? The chosen risk perspective can have different influences of varying strengths: First, personal risk estimates are a class of their own and can be biased due to several reasons (e.g., optimism, experience, affect). Risk estimates for another target can also be influenced by different aspects. One important influence arises out of the strategy of probabilistic reasoning triggered by the perceived degree of abstraction of the target. Generally, it can be assumed that risk estimates for an abstract target (e.g., a person) tend to lead to a distributional approach. Here the target is perceived as an instance of a class, and the estimate is very likely based on the perceived relative frequency of the event. If, however, the target is perceived as a unique identity (e.g., self, named person), it is very likely that a singular approach will be used. In this case the estimate derives from the dispositions attributed to the unique identity.

C. What kind of answer format should be used? Almost every aspect of an answer format (e.g., format: verbal vs. numeric; range; labeling and number of the categories) has an impact on the estimate. One of the most important aspects that should be considered is that different answer formats can trigger either a more intuitive or deliberative kind of thinking. Broadly speaking, verbal scales leave more space for intuitive estimates, whereas numerical scales tend to trigger a more deliberative, rule-based kind of thinking.

There are far more questions that should be considered when measuring subjective risk estimates. For instance, an interesting approach on how people reason about risk is described by the fuzzy-trace theory (Reyna, 2004; see also Helm & Reyna, Chap. 4). Moreover, worthwhile recommendations can be found in the literature on risk perception and risk communication (e.g., Fischhoff, 1995; Keller & Siegrist, 2009; Hess, Visschers, & Siegrist, 2011; Hoffrage, Lindsey, Hertwig, & Gigerenzer, 2000; Keller, Siegrist, & Gutscher, 2006; Visschers, Meertens, Passchier, & De Vries, 2009). The list presented in this chapter displays a selection of some basic aspects that have not been taken sufficiently into account.

References

Diefenbach, M. A., Weinstein, N. D., & O'Reilly, J. (1993). Scales for assessing perceptions of health hazard susceptibility. *Health Education Research, 8*(2), 181–192.

Epstein, S. (1994). Integration of the cognitive and the psychodynamic unconscious. *American Psychologist, 49*, 709–724.

Figner, B., & Weber, E. U. (2011). Who takes risks when and why? Determinants of risk taking. *Current Directions in Psychological Science, 20*(4), 211–216.

Fischhoff, B. (1995). Risk perception and communication unplugged: Twenty years of process. *Risk Analysis, 15*(2), 137–145.

Gigerenzer, G. (2002). *Das Einmaleins der Skepsis: Über den richtigen Umgang mit Zahlen und Risiken* [Calculated risks: How to know when numbers deceive you] (3rd ed.). Berlin: Berlin Verlag.

Gigerenzer, G., Hertwig, R., Van Den Broek, E., Fasolo, B., & Katsikopoulos, K. V. (2005). "A 30% chance of rain tomorrow": How does the public understand probabilistic weather forecasts? *Risk Analysis, 25*(3), 623–629.

Haase, N., Renkewitz, F., & Betsch, C. (2013). The measurement of subjective probability: Evaluating the sensitivity and accuracy of various scales. *Risk Analysis, 33*(10), 1812–1828.

Harris, A. J., & Hahn, U. (2011). Unrealistic optimism about future life events: A cautionary note. *Psychological Review, 11*, 135–154.

Hess, R., Visschers, V. H., & Siegrist, M. (2011). Risk communication with pictographs: The role of numeracy and graph processing. *Judgment and Decision making, 6*(3), 263.

Hoffrage, U., Lindsey, S., Hertwig, R., & Gigerenzer, G. (2000). Communicating statistical information. *Science, 290*(5500), 2261–2262.

Kahneman, D. (2003). A perspective on judgment and choice. *American Psychologist, 58*, 697–720.

Kahneman, D. (2012). *Thinking fast and slow*. London: Allen Lane.

Kahneman, D., & Frederick, S. (2002). Representativeness revisited: Attribute substitution in intuitive judgment. In T. Gilovich, D. Griffin, & D. Kahneman (Eds.), *Heuristics and biases: The psychology of intuitive judgment* (pp. 49–81). New York, NY: Cambridge University Press.

Keller, C., & Siegrist, M. (2009). Effect of risk communication formats on risk perception depending on numeracy. *Medical Decision Making, 29*(4), 483–490.

Keller, C., Siegrist, M., & Gutscher, H. (2006). The role of the affect and availability heuristics in risk communication. *Risk Analysis, 26*(3), 631–639.

Kitces, M. (2016). *The sorry state of risk tolerance questionnaire for financial advisors*. Retrieved from https://www.kitces.com/blog/risk-tolerance-questionnaire-and-risk-profiling-problems-for-financial-advisors-planplus-study/

Klar, Y., Medding, A., & Sarel, D. (1996). Nonunique invulnerability: Singular versus distributional probabilities and unrealistic optimism in comparative risk judgments. *Organizational Behavior and Human Decision Processes, 67*(2), 229–245.

Lermer, E. (2013). *The impact of answer format and construal level on risk assessment and behavior* (Doctoral thesis). Ludwig Maximilian University, Munich, Germany.

Lermer, E., Raue, M., & Frey, D. (2016). Risikowahrnehmung und Risikoverhalten [risk perception and risk behavior]. In D. Frey & H.-W. Bierhoff (Hrsg.) *Enzyklopädie der Psychologie. Sozialpsychologie 2: Soziale Motive und soziale Einstellungen* [Enzyclopedia of Psychology. Social psychology 2: Social motives and social attitudes] (pp. 535–580). Göttingen: Hogrefe.

Lermer, E., Streicher, B., Sachs, R., & Frey, D. (2013). How risky? The impact of target person and answer format on risk assessment. *Journal of Risk Research, 16*, 903–919.

Lermer, E., Streicher, B., Sachs, R., Raue, M., & Frey, D. (2016). Thinking concretely increases the perceived likelihood of risks: The effect of construal level on risk estimation. *Risk Analysis, 36*, 623–637.

Lipkus, I. M., Samsa, G., & Rimer, B. K. (2001). General performance on a numeracy scale among highly educated samples. *Medical Decision Making, 21*(1), 37–44.

McKenna, F. P. (1993). It won't happen to me: Unrealistic optimism or illusion of control? *British Journal of Psychology, 84*, 39–50.

Moxey, L. M., & Sanford, A. J. (1992). Context effects and the communicative functions of quantifiers: Implications for their use in attitude research. In N. Schwarz & S. Sudman (Eds.), *Context effects in social and psychological research* (pp. 279–296). New York, NY: Springer.

Pepper, S. C. (1981). Problems in the quantification of frequency expressions. In D. W. Fiske (Ed.), *Problems with language imprecision: New directions for methodology of social and behavior science* (Vol. 9, pp. 25–41). San Francisco, CA: Jossey-Bass.

Perloff, L. S., & Fetzer, B. (1986). Self-other judgments and perceived vulnerability to victimization. *Journal of Personality and Social Psychology, 50*, 302–310.

Preston, C. C., & Colman, A. M. (2000). Optimal number of response categories in rating scales: Reliability, validity, discriminating power, and respondent preferences. *Acta Psychologica, 104*, 1–15.

Reeves, T., & Lockhart, R. S. (1993). Distributional versus singular approaches to probability and errors in probabilistic reasoning. *Journal of Experimental Psychology: General, 122*(2), 207.

Reyna, V. F. (2004). How people make decisions that involve risk a dual-processes approach. *Current Directions in Psychological Science, 13*(2), 60–66.

Reyna, V. F., Nelson, W. L., Han, P. K., & Dieckmann, N. F. (2009). How numeracy influences risk comprehension and medical decision making. *Psychological Bulletin, 135*(6), 943–973.

Robert Koch Institute. (2016). *Informationen zum Ebolafieber-Ausbruch in Westafrika 2014/2015*. Retrieved May 21, 2017, from http://www.rki.de/DE/Content/InfAZ/E/Ebola/Kurzinformation_Ebola_in_Westafrika.html

Schwarz, N. (1999). Self-reports: How the questions shape the answers. *American Psychologist, 54*(2), 93–105.

Slovic, P. (2001). Cigarette smokers: Rational actors or rational fools? In P. Slovic (Ed.), Smoking, risk perception, and policy (pp. 97–124). Thousand Oaks, CA: Sage.

Slovic, P. (2014). *Yes, our Ebola freakout is irrational. But there is still a good reason to have the jitters*. Retrieved from https://www.washingtonpost.com/posteverything/wp/2014/10/27/yes-our-ebola-freakout-is-irrational-but-theres-still-a-good-reason-to-have-the-jitters/?utm_term=.5fd75d289d0b

Slovic, P., Finucane, M. L., Peters, E., & MacGregor, D. G. (2004). Risk as analysis and risk as feelings: Some thoughts about affect, reason, risk, and rationality. *Risk Analysis, 24*(2), 311–322.

Stanovich, K. E., & West, R. F. (2000). Individual differences in reasoning: Implications for the rationality debate. *Behavioral and Brain Sciences, 23*, 645–665.

Visschers, V. H., Meertens, R. M., Passchier, W. W., & De Vries, N. N. (2009). Probability information in risk communication: A review of the research literature. *Risk Analysis, 29*(2), 267–287.

Weijters, B., Cabooter, E., & Schillewaert, N. (2010). The effect of rating scale format on response styles: The number of response categories and response category labels. *International Journal of Research in Marketing, 27*(3), 236–247.

Weinstein, N. D. (1980). Unrealistic optimism about future life events. *Journal of Personality and Social Psychology, 39*, 806–820.

Weinstein, N. D. (1984). Why it won't happen to me: Perceptions of risk factors and susceptibility. *Health Psychology, 3*, 431–457.

Weinstein, N. D. (1989). Optimistic biases about personal risks. *Science, 246*, 1232–1233.

Weinstein, N. D., Kwitel, A., McCaul, K. D., Magnan, R. E., Gerrard, M., & Gibbons, F. X. (2007). Risk perceptions: Assessment and relationship to influenza vaccination. *Health Psychology, 26*, 146–151.

Wills, T. A. (1981). Downward comparison principles in social psychology. *Psychological Bulletin, 90*, 245–271.

Windschitl, P. D., & Wells, G. L. (1996). Measuring psychological uncertainty: Verbal versus numeric methods. *Journal of Experimental Psychology: Applied, 2*(4), 343–364.

Woloshin, S., Schwartz, L. M., Byram, S., Fischhoff, B., & Welch, H. G. (2000). A new scale for assessing perceptions of chance: A validation study. *Medical Decision Making, 20*(3), 298–307.

Chapter 15
Risk and Uncertainty in the Insurance Industry

Rainer Sachs

Abstract Understanding risk is the foundation of the insurance industry. The industry has developed practices and methods for risk transfer and risk management. The development process started with rather intuitive, experience-based methods. Over time more and more risks could also be quantified, and highly sophisticated mathematical models were developed. After several decades of successful applications, the industry starts to realize the limitation of these models. Looking for new business opportunities and being confronted with an increasingly interconnected risk landscape, the industry sees the need for complementary methods to assess both risk and uncertainty. Using emerging risks and complex risks as examples for non-quantifiable risks, the challenges and possible solutions are explained.

Introduction

The world is in large parts not deterministic and foreseeable.

This does not mean that predictions are not possible. They are in most circumstances restricted to limited time horizons, e.g., weather forecasts, or are governed by fundamental laws of nature, e.g., sunrise or chemical reactions. The discovery of these fundamental laws of nature made natural sciences a very successful undertaking. In the mathematical sciences, the development of statistical time series models helped tremendously to understand and model relationships between different variables and enabled us to predict future outcomes (e.g., Box, Jenkins, & Reinsel, 2008; Harvey, 1989). The degree of sophistica-

This article expresses solely the opinion of the author. The article shall not constitute or be deemed to constitute a representation of the views of Munich Re.

R. Sachs (✉)
Munich Reinsurance Company, Integrated Risk Management, Munich, Germany
e-mail: rsachs@munichre.com

M. Raue et al. (eds.), *Psychological Perspectives on Risk and Risk Analysis*,
https://doi.org/10.1007/978-3-319-92478-6_15

tion and popularity varied across disciplines and points in time. For example, deterministic nonlinear models and complex systems theory have been used in a wide range of applications since the 1990s (Casdagli & Eubank, 1992; Kantz & Schreiber, 1997).

Even if the underlying system is not deterministic but of random nature, the mathematical science can offer tools to peek into the future. Stochastic models can be applied to random processes, as they are observed in nature, for example, heat transfer (Gardiner, 2002; van Kampen, 1992), and economics. Even if we are not able to predict the exact outcome in detail, these models allow us to forecast statistical results like mean values and confidence intervals. Deterministic and stochastic time series analyses are possibilities to address risk and uncertainty.

For most practical purposes of our daily lives, both on individual as well as organizational level, resorting to the fundamental laws of nature or mathematical models will not be possible or feasible. Too many unknown influence factors will render strictly deterministic and even stochastic models useless. A particularly important influence factor is human behavior and human decision making. For example, the question whether or not to start a particular career or engage in a relationship cannot be answered using mathematical models. For an insurance company, the decision to offer risk transfer products for emerging technologies at adequate prices is equally difficult.

We have to accept the fact that even with the best models and accurate data, we will not be able to predict the exact outcomes of our decisions and the consequences of events. There will always remain the possibility of unexpected outcomes and surprises. Even though we may be able to forecast many developments, much remains uncertain. Hence we are normally confronted with unexpected events and surprising consequences of our decisions.

The tools and methods of risk management have been developed to deal with the unexpected. This article provides an overview of risk management approaches from a practitioner's point of view.

Section "Enterprise Risk Management" contains a brief summary of enterprise risk management, based on an example from the insurance industry. There is a fundamental difference between risk and uncertainty, which is explained in Section "Risk and Uncertainty". In insurance we are quite often faced with emerging risks, which can be assessed only qualitatively due to lack of statistical data. Section "Uncertainty Management and Emerging Risks" focuses on emerging risk management practices and their challenges. A specific challenge is the understanding of the global risk landscape and its interdependencies. Section "Complex Risk Management" contains a specific example of how to deal with complex risks and their inherent uncertainty. Strategies of uncertainty governance are outlined in Section "Governance of Uncertainty".

Enterprise Risk Management

The professional management of risks is at the very heart of the insurance industry. Hence the industry developed more and more refined tools to identify risks, to model and evaluate them, and finally to manage and steer risks. In that sense the existence of risks is the foundation of the insurance industry. If there were no risks, there would be no need for insurance.

An insurance contract is a particular type of risk transfer from the insured to the insurance company or from the insurance company to the reinsurance company. It is obvious that not all risks can be insured.

Insurability is based on a number of principles, for example, that potential losses must be fortuitous and independent, that the number of comparable events must be large, and, above all, that potential losses must be measurable. How much or how little we know about the events to be insured determines their measurability. And measurability is what ultimately makes it possible to transfer risk from an insured to an insurer.

Risks are in general not accepted without any reward. The reward in the financial industry is called return. In a psychological context, reward is usually some kind of positive sensation. There is no return without risk. This relationship is commonly expressed as "there is no free lunch." In addition, there is a positive correlation between risk and return. Higher returns come with higher risk. In order to improve our decisions and behavior in the risk-return space, we need risk management. The goal of a risk management strategy could be to minimize risk given a particular return expectation. Another reasonable strategy could be return maximization under certain risk restrictions. The second approach is typical for risk appetite strategies in the insurance industry.

Risk strategies are an essential part of enterprise risk management (ERM) frameworks in the insurance industry. These frameworks are holistic approaches to deal with all risks in the entire organization and simultaneously balance the expectations of the different stakeholders. Stakeholders for an insurance company are the insured or policyholder, the shareholders and the regulator, or financial supervisory authority. Each stakeholder has a different preference in the risk-return space. The policyholder, for instance, prefers low risk, that is, high security, over return. The shareholder on the other side has higher return expectations and is ready to accept a certain amount of risk. With ERM the company strives for transparency of its risk situation and a balance between the different stakeholders' expectations.

There are a number of principles, which are deduced from regulatory requirements and give guidance for the design of risk management structure and tools. The following list contains a list of principles used at Munich Re Group:

- *Management Accountability:* The management team is ultimately responsible for the active management of the respective risk exposures and achievement of a sufficient return for the risks taken.
- *Independent Oversight:* Risk oversight occurs at the level of business units, board oversight, and supervisory board oversight.

- *Embedding:* Risk management functions are embedded in the operation at all levels. The risk management functions act as risk supervisors while respecting the responsibilities of the business units.
- *Fit and Proper:* All staff in charge of risk management needs to be appropriately trained and experienced in risk management techniques. They also need to have relevant business knowledge and understand the needs of the business units.
- *Proportionality:* The principle of proportionality implies that risk management should focus on significant risks, that is, risks with a potential to have a sustained negative impact on the company.
- *Risk Transparency:* Risk transparency is essential so that risks are well understood by senior management and can be balanced against business goals which are recorded in the business plans.
- *Risk Management Convergence:* The purpose of risk management convergence is to avoid overlaps and inconsistencies by harmonizing and standardizing the risk management procedures.
- *Risk Awareness:* All employees need to be aware of the risks they face when performing their functions. This awareness implies an openness to regularly monitor and if necessary challenge existing concepts, procedures, and rules.

Risk and Uncertainty

As has been already mentioned, the measurability of risks is a necessary condition for insurability. Measurable risks are also the main focus of ERM systems, as they can be modeled, evaluated, and steered.

Measurability and in particular quantification of risks depend on the level of knowledge, the availability of models, and data. Financial markets, for instance, provide huge amount of data, and many mathematical models are extensively researched and applied for risk management purposes (for an overview, see McNeil, Frey, & Embrechts, 2005). Similar tools are applied to natural catastrophes like windstorms and earthquakes and also to biometric risks like morbidity and mortality rates. Actuarial models provide the basis for quantitative risk management in the insurance industry. With these models the insurance company is able to infer expected outcomes and a quantified description of the unexpected. Risk is typically measured at some maximal occurrence probability, for example, the 1-in-200 year (99.5% quantile) or the 1-in-1000 year (99.9% quantile) event. Naturally these worst case estimates depend on the quality of the models and data and are invalidated occasionally. The Tohoku earthquake in Japan in 2011, for instance, was stronger than the models had anticipated. With experience and ongoing refinements of models, these surprises should in principle become less frequent.

There remains a large source of surprises, however, and it turns out that this source is by far the larger part of the unexpected. When we characterize the unexpected by the level of knowledge and understanding, we can in very simple terms distinguish between three categories (see Fig. 15.1) (Sachs & Wadé, 2013). Risk is

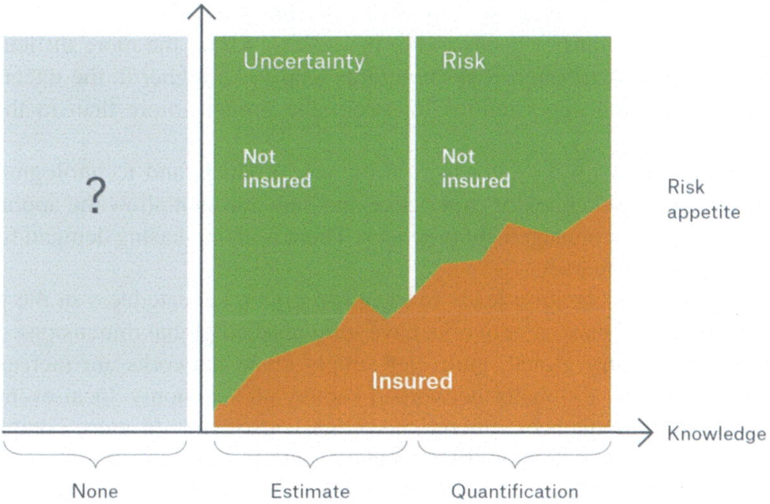

Fig. 15.1 Risk and uncertainty are two faces of the unexpected. Risk appetite and insurability increase with knowledge. Standard examples for risks are natural catastrophes or mortality risks, where statistical data is easily available. Unexpected consequences from new technologies, for example, artificial intelligence or genetic engineering, are examples for uncertainty

the part of the unexpected which can be quantified. This means in particular that there is sufficient amount of data and models available. Data in this context means experience that can be processed numerically. We do not know what the outcome of a potential individual occurrence may be, but we can determine probabilities and sample spaces using statistical methods. This is where the insurance industry's actual risk management and risk transfer take place. The capacity to insure risk, also called the risk appetite, is substantial in this domain.

The leftmost part in Fig. 15.1 is the domain of the unknown. There are no reasonable approaches to deal with the unknown, in particular in the insurance industry. This domain is not of any real relevance for the transfer of risk. Neither excessive data collection nor sophisticated methods of utilizing expertise are of any use here. Since there is no knowledge to be had here, we are clearly outside the remit of the insurance industry. There is no risk appetite for the unknown (for a more granular and entertaining description of levels of decreasing knowledge, see Lo & Mueller, 2010).

The middle domain in Fig. 15.1 is termed uncertainty, where we have some knowledge but are not able to quantify this knowledge due to lack of data and/or lack of mathematical models. Risk appetite in the uncertainty domain is lower than in the risk domain. Nevertheless, the motivation to embark into uncertainty for the insurance industry is based on the following arguments:

- Competition is fierce in standard risk business. When everyone has comparable tools to quantify risk, the only way to remain competitive in the market is to become more cost efficient.

- How little we know about the risk also determines how high the price or risk premium for the transfer needs to be: the less we know, the more difficult and expensive the risk transfer. Risk premiums tend to be higher in the uncertainty domain. There are opportunities for profitable growth, more than in the risk domain.
- Progress comes with the introduction of new products and technologies with their own new risks. Lack of experience and data does not allow the application of established risk management practices. There is an increasing demand for risk transfer from the market.
- The ongoing globalization leads to increasing interconnectedness in the global risk landscape. Financial networks have long reached global dimensions. In the production industry global, multi-tier supply chain networks are increasingly common. In such a globally networked society and economy, local events can have global consequences. Interconnectedness also leads to more complexity, where surprises become more likely and give rise to more uncertainty.

These arguments support the demand to research, develop, and implement concepts and methods to deal with uncertainty successfully. There are currently boundaries to the transfer of risk that cut across uncertainty. These boundaries separate the insurable from the non-insurable. By consciously working these boundaries of insurability, for example, by developing new methods or generating knowledge, rather than focusing only on risks that we know and understand well, we can gradually push back these boundaries and tap into new business opportunities. The non-insurable may become insurable. At Munich Re, we are engaged in a number of areas in pushing back these boundaries and extending the insurability of risk.

Uncertainty Management and Emerging Risks

As has been explained in the previous section, the proven risk management methods are not readily available in the context of uncertainty. Even if the title of this section implies that uncertainty is something that can be managed, it should be emphasized that this need not be the case. The title simply serves to express its proximity to the term risk management. Uncertainty is far less able to be managed, but rather be approached differently (Weick & Sutcliffe, 2007). The general principles of ERM frameworks can be applied, however. The main differences to risk are the lack of data and lack of (mathematical) models in the context of uncertainty. Hence we need to search for solutions in these two directions—data and models.

Let us suppose, data is in principle available, but scarce. This means that all we have to do is gather enough data or wait long enough and we will be in a position to describe these uncertain events using risk management methods. Quite often in reality, we usually do not have the time or possibility to gather enough data. Cross-company cooperation—for instance, as part of industry initiatives—helps improve the available data, but is often restricted by competition and legal requirements.

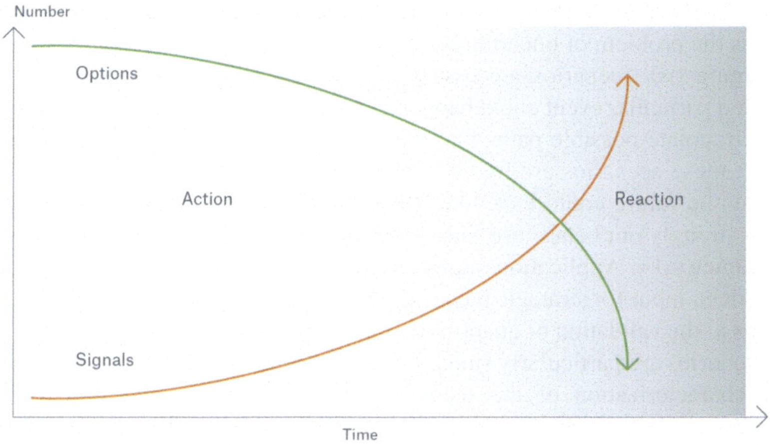

Fig. 15.2 The dynamics of emerging risks: typical course of signals and options for action with emerging risks

New technologies and their associated risks for example can evolve over time horizons of several decades. Rarely any profit-oriented organization, and undoubtedly no insurance company, can simply wait for such a long time to gather data and knowledge for a comfortable and statistically valid risk assessment. Any risk transfer solution with such a long development phase would be too late for the market. The market would have long forgotten about insurance and would have developed other ways to manage the risk. The insurance industry would have put itself out of the competition.

Rather than simply waiting for and collecting more data, we need to develop the uncertainty management toolbox. The models we have to implement are less of mathematical but of organizational and procedural nature (Weick & Sutcliffe, 2007). Insights from organizational and social sciences offer promising paths forward.

At Munich Re, we therefore approach uncertainty due to lack of data with scenarios that describe potential and conceivable major loss events and with emerging risk processes. The classical retrospective approach is thus supplemented by a prospective one.

Emerging risks can be either developing trends or shock events. The occurrence probability and loss potential of emerging risks are highly uncertain. Yet there are strong reasons to believe that if they materialized the consequences would be significant for the organization.

Emerging risk management is based on the idea that trends or indications for shock risks develop over a long period as depicted in Fig. 15.2 (Sachs & Wadé, 2013). Though only weak signals are perceptible in the early stages of their development, there are many possibilities for managing the risks. The longer we wait for the signals indicating a new risk to become clearer, the more limited is the action we can take. Early identification of weak signals, combined with active management, addresses the problem of uncertainty.

Emerging risk scenarios are essentially stories, how a particular trend could evolve or a particular event could happen. By using no or only few observations, we try to extrapolate possible paths into the future. In contrast to time series analysis methods, these scenarios are by no means predictions but offer plausible alternatives how the future could look like. Depending how important these alternatives and how strongly our beliefs are, such scenarios can be used in a number of ways in ERM frameworks. Applications range from creating risk awareness for staff and stakeholders, input for strategic business planning, background for tactical business decisions to the validation of quantitative enterprise risk models. For validation purposes scenarios are particularly suited if we were able to arrive at a minimum quantitative characterization of the scenario. Essentially we would need only two parameters: the occurrence probability and the corresponding loss amount. What we aim to achieve is the translation of an emerging risk from the uncertainty domain into the risk domain of Fig. 15.1.

The translation effectively occurs by making systematic use of expert judgment and intuition. Data and quantitative tools are replaced by experience and qualitative assessment. There is an important link between experience, learning, decision making, and error culture within an organization. This link can briefly be summarized as follows: "Good decisions come from experience. Experience comes from bad decisions" (Tremper, 2008; Manser, 2008).

In large organizations like insurance companies, there is typically a large, heterogeneous, and multidisciplinary staff. This forms an excellent starting point for an emerging risk process. At Munich Re the central platform to identify, analyze, and evaluate emerging risks is the emerging risk think tank. Its staff consists of experienced specialists with both deep knowledge in their own field and the ability to connect and communicate with other disciplines. An ideal think tank member is a specialist and generalist at the same time.

The result of the emerging risk process should be a plausible and quantifiable scenario. The quantification will be based on subjective risk estimates. Thus it is extremely important that the analysis is not systematically biased. If we systematically underestimated the risk, we would offer risk transfer solutions at inadequate prices, that is, too cheap. We would make a loss in the long run as premium income would not be sufficiently high for the loss experienced. If, on the other hand, we systematically overestimated the risk, we would put ourselves out of the market, because the insurance premium we charge would be too high.

Therefore, we aim at an unbiased view which is as closely to an objective assessment as possible, bearing in mind that this will never be strictly possible in reality. Lack of data and models will almost never lead to objective and statistically unbiased results. However, we are confident that we can do a lot better than in the past by rigorously questioning and improving our risk management processes. The emerging risk process, if designed appropriately, can be regarded as a method to manage uncertainty.

Expert judgment is the basic input into the emerging risk management process. Therefore, it is important to understand how experts arrive at their conclusions, in particular how experts judge risks. Psychological research can offer theories to explain human risk judgment and its pitfalls. As has been researched for decades, humans tend to overestimate the impact of losses over gains. Not only that humans are loss averse in general—in economic terms having more is typically better than having less—but also changes in outcome are perceived differently in loss situations versus gain situations. This may even lead to risk-seeking behavior as an attempt to recover from a loss situation, as can be observed in casinos and the stock market. These ideas were the basis for prospect theory (Kahneman & Tversky, 1979; see also Helm & Reyna, Chap. 4; and Birnbaum, Chap. 8). There are numerous other effects that influence human decision making under uncertainty. However, people perform quite well in this difficult task, often by using simple rules of thumb. Social proof is one example: if my peers are engaged in a certain activity, I should do so as well. These decision making rules are often described as heuristics (see also Raue & Scholl, Chap. 7). They support decision making under difficult conditions, for example, lack of data and high complexity. Heuristics have been researched extensively for comprehensive and accessible overviews (see Gigerenzer, 2007; Kahnemann, 2011). Well-known heuristics are the recognition heuristic, the anchor heuristic, or the availability heuristic. All of these can have significant impact on experts' risk estimates. As these effects happen subconsciously, experts are not aware of them and may still think their estimates are unbiased.

At Munich Re we have been looking into these topics for several years. Together with social psychologists, we improved our own understanding of heuristics and their impact on subjective risk estimates significantly. In an article by Eller, Lermer, Streicher, and Sachs (2013), we provided an overview of psychological influence factors on individual level and how these can be coped with in risk management.

Psychological effects on subjective risk estimates do not happen on individual level only. There are also important effects in groups. In an organizational context, it is equally important to consider group effects, as many risk assessment processes involve groups. By using a large set of expert knowledge, this helps to avoid idiosyncratic biases, but group effects remain. As has been mentioned earlier, at Munich Re, the emerging risk think tank is the central platform in the process. Group think, that is, the tendency to arrive at suboptimal decisions in homogeneous groups, can be reduced by staffing the group appropriately. However, social loafing, information sharing, and polarization are not as easily eliminated (see also Eller & Frey, Chap. 6). We collected and described a selection of psychological effects relevant for risk estimates in groups (Lermer, Streicher, Eller, & Sachs, 2014). We also suggested specific settings for different steps in the emerging risk process. While some steps are better performed on individual level (e.g., collection of information), others work better in a group setting (e.g., evaluation).

For Munich Re it is important to understand the different influence factors and their impact on risk estimates. In the beginning we started to search for some sort of "fudge factor," which would transform subjective into objective risk estimates. Such a factor would be driven by a range of psychological, sociological, and individual parameters. Coming from quantitative risk management, such an outcome would clearly be desirable and could easily be integrated into our systems. This turned out to be neither possible nor feasible.

We realized however, while we cannot simply correct subjective risk estimates directly, we can change the way how we arrive at those estimates. After thorough process analysis, we were in the position to redesign and improve our emerging risk process. The improved process takes potential biases and distortions into account and aims to reduce their influence. By learning from disciplines outside classical (i.e., mathematical) risk management, we could develop a better model for uncertainty management.

Complex Risk Management

Emerging risks in the section above are characterized by their high uncertainty regarding occurrence probability and loss severity. Yet we are able to identify specific trends or events and map their consequences. Hence we can construct scenarios for each emerging risk and be fairly sure about its accuracy, if an emerging risk materialized.

Emerging risks can and will arise from virtually any part of the global risk landscape. A common structure for this landscape is the STEEP framework, where STEEP is short for sociology, technology, economic, environment, and politics. The Munich Re Emerging Risk Radar, a graphical tool to structure and monitor emerging risks, is designed accordingly. The challenge in any emerging risk process is to cover the entire spectrum of potential emerging risks and provide sound and detailed knowledge from every discipline to the process. There is limited room for surprises, such as we will see consequences we would not have anticipated at all.

This approach is limited, however. Looking ahead, there are developments that will probably render an emerging risk scenario process useless. Unlike in the past, there is no amount of waiting or data collection that would prove helpful here. It is an area that comprises events of substantial complexity. And complex is more than just complicated. Complex events take place in interconnected, strongly interdependent structures and are characterized by a low degree of predictability. Complex risks are governed not only by their individual trigger events and foreseeable consequences, but by their internal dependency structure. There can be feedback features, which can give rise to self-enforcing dynamics. Globalized trade flows and financial markets are examples of such structures. Falling stock markets lead to even more sales lead to even lower prices and so on. This effect also works in the other direction and can lead to bubbles. In Fig. 15.3 we attempt to capture the most relevant drivers (outer boxes) and consequences (inner boxes) of higher complexity in the global risk landscape.

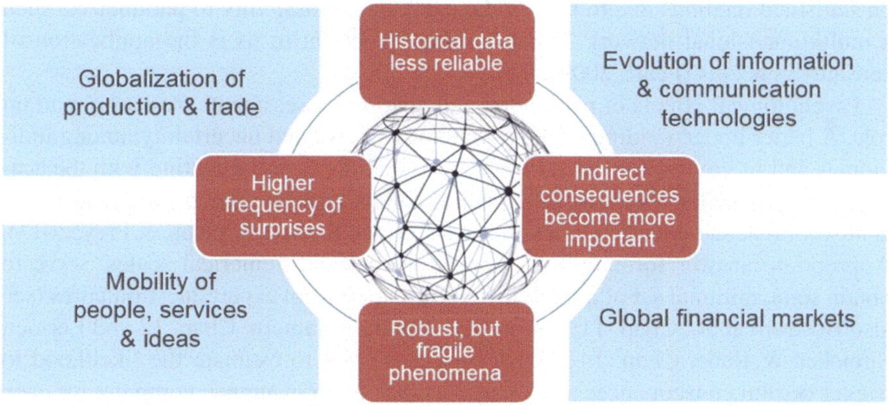

Fig. 15.3 Interdependency in the global risk landscape increases complexity. Possible consequences are lower predictability and higher relevance of systemic risk

Higher complexity in the global risk landscape has two major consequences, which are particularly important for an insurance company (Sachs & Wadé, 2013):

1. Even local events can have global consequences. Examples in the recent past are the subprime crisis in 2007 in the USA, which led to a global economic crisis, or the Thailand floods in 2012, which impacted key hardware suppliers and hence the IT industry on a global scale. Diversification, that is, spreading the risk and hence balancing the portfolio, in a tightly interconnected risk landscape is difficult. There is even a dark side of diversification: more diversification in connected networks can actually increase the risk for systemic events, that is, the default of a single node can cause the collapse of the entire network (for an example, see: Battison, Gatti, & Gallegati, 2008).
2. There are thousands of conceivable events which could trigger a large loss via direct and indirect consequences, feedback mechanisms, and so on. It is neither very promising nor economically feasible to single out a few events, try to develop scenarios, and prepare for those. Almost certainly these events will not materialize in reality, but some other will instead.

At Munich Re, we endeavor to map the global risk landscape and its mutual dependencies in a database in order to make complex events transparent that result from the ever-increasing global interconnectedness.

With the Complex Accumulation Risk Explorer (CARE), we want to establish a framework for the systematic collection and connection of knowledge from different disciplines. Our approach is forward looking and focuses on thinkable yet plausible consequences of significant events. Using this knowledge we are able to construct a network of connected events that span the entire risk landscape from environmental, political and technological to economic risks.

We depend increasingly on the assessments and views of experts and amateurs to identify and characterize such events and their connections. We put less emphasis on statistical methods due to lack of data and the impossibility to parametrize such a multidimensional network. What is more important to us is the application of causality concepts (Pearl, 2009).

Psychological effects of perception and distorted assessments play an important role. A better understanding of the psychology of risk and uncertainty among individuals and in groups is an area in which Munich Re is collaborating with the academia. In particular, we have developed methods to make expert judgment in the context of risk and uncertainty less biased (Lermer, Streicher, Sachs, & Frey, 2013). Appropriate answer formats, for example, verbal and numerical scales, serve to obtain some minimal set of quantitative information from expert questionnaires (see also Bostrom et al., Chap. 11; Hoffrage & Garcia-Retamero, Chap. 12 and Lermer, Streicher, & Raue, Chap. 14). For instance, we aim to estimate the likelihood to trigger certain consequences and their relevance to an insurance company for each event in the database.

There are essentially two different applications for such a system. First, we are able to extract event trees, both forward and backward in time. Thus we could qualitatively assess the drivers and implications of individual events. This would form the basis for any detailed follow-up study and already contains the condensed knowledge of a heterogeneous expert group. All collected knowledge could be reused easily. Second, we could analyze the global risk landscape as a whole and rank all events according to measures like loss relevance, for example.

Figure 15.4 contains a snapshot of the database, where we arranged all events in the database according to their loss relevance (vertical axis) and the breadth of their consequences (horizontal axis). The latter is measured by a Gini coefficient, which is based on a classification of our insurance portfolio. We are mostly interested in

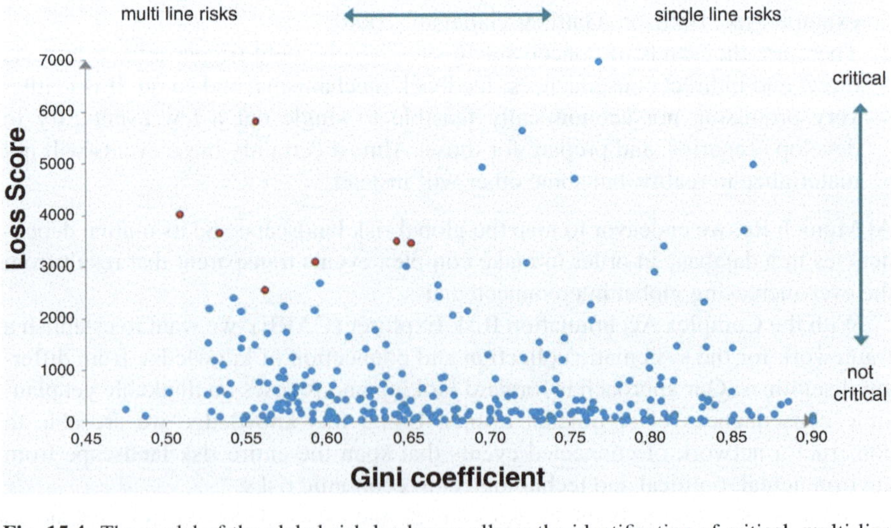

Fig. 15.4 The model of the global risk landscape allows the identification of critical, multi-line risks (top left area)

events with high loss relevance and potential implications on many different parts of our portfolio. These multi-line risks can have potential impact on different parts of our portfolio, for example, a combination of property insurance, life insurance, and asset management. These risks are typically overlooked in segmented organizations, where each business unit assesses risks by itself and tends to neglect impacts on other units.

We will continue to enhance the CARE system and work with experts from both the insurance industry as well as outside to improve coverage and stability of the database. As the global risk landscape is continuously changing, we will also see an evolution of the CARE system. While it will never be a world model of risks, CARE can complement the existing and well-established quantitative risk management tools.

Governance of Uncertainty

In the previous sections, we have demonstrated that risk management in the insurance industry has its limits when we do not have adequate data and models for proper quantification. These limits will become more important going forward. Technological and economic progress are the main drivers for increasing complexity in the global risk landscape. Uncertainty will be more significant than risk in the future.

With these changes arises the need to develop established enterprise risk management practices further. This holds true for the risk industry in particular and for the economy and society in general, too. There are two obvious strategies at hand:

1. *Same, same …*: Stricter and more comprehensive application of existing approaches will be the solution. The underlying assumption is that the risk landscape has not changed fundamentally, but only evolved to be more complicated.
2. *… but different*: An equally valid assumption could be that there is a regime shift in the risk landscape. In times of rising complexity, forecasting and control are an illusion and existing risk management practices will not be useful. We need to develop a different toolbox to cope with uncertainty.

These two strategies should not be regarded as mutually exclusive. We do not suggest to follow either one or the other. They should be pursued simultaneously, as both have their individual merits.

Emerging risk management is an example for the first strategy. It is based on detection of early warning signals, so we would expect useful results from current Big Data initiatives. Big Data tries to find answers by analyzing huge, unstructured data sets. More information is not useful by itself. The search for the needle in a haystack is not improved by adding more hay. But in a combination with smart algorithms and clever framing of questions, this will provide an added value.

Another example is the systematic development of worst case scenarios. Such a scenario set would ideally cover the entire risk landscape. The development of "macro threats" is one of the main research areas of the Cambridge Centre for Risk Studies (Coburn et al., 2014). Even if we expected that none of these scenarios would materialize exactly as prescribed, we could still use them to test the risk management frameworks under dire circumstances. Reverse stress testing is a useful concept. Here the starting point of scenario selection is not the trigger event, but a certain loss amount or impact, which would bring the organization to the brink of destruction.

Complex risk management as described in Section "Complex Risk Management" is an example for the second strategy. To the best of our knowledge, this is the first attempt in the insurance industry to analyze the global risk landscape with trigger-consequence diagrams. We are convinced that transparency in qualitative terms about the risk situation is a benefit even if we are not—and probably will never be—able to exactly quantify the trigger-consequence diagrams. Trying to understand the global risk landscape is an active process, during which management options may be detected. Ignoring the white or gray spots on the risk map is not really an option. Because then even more surprises will occur, and the organization's fate is determined more by fortune rather than by responsible actions.

We also believe that it is crucial to accept uncertainty, rather than trying to manage it with (enhanced) risk management tools. This can remove a stumbling block on the way to completely different concepts. Accordingly, we also refer to a principle-based approach for dealing with uncertainty (Weick & Sutcliffe, 2007). This approach is based on the analysis of high-reliability organizations, which cannot afford to fail under uncertainty. Examples are professional fire-fighting teams and operators of power plants or airlines. A lot can be learned from these organizations, in particular about decision making in complex situations.

Education and training of people, who take decisions under uncertainty, will be a success factor in the risk industry. Awareness of psychological influences on risk assessment is necessary, but not sufficient. There is a need for uncertainty competence, rooted in the belief that uncertainty is to be approached with a positive stance.

Accepting and embracing uncertainty are relevant in particular for large firms. A lot of resources in large organizations are allocated to planning and controlling activities. While this is a plausible method to deal with uncertainty, we believe rising complexity and uncertainty will render long-term planning a futile exercise. Rather than putting more efforts into better planning, one could try with less and free up resources. These would be then available to improve redundancy, for example, extra capacities for task forces or capital buffers in the financial industry. Ultimately, uncertainty is the precondition for creativity and innovation.

Organizations need to find ways to better cope with surprises that will arise from a complex risk landscape. The concept of resilience may be a promising way forward. Resilience means the capability of an organization to recover from adverse events and continue with its operations. Resilience is studied intensively in the academia (e.g., Linkov et al., 2014). Academic and industry initiatives have already started to look into applications (Thoma, 2014).

Conclusion and Recommendation

Enterprise risk management is a continuously developing practice. It has always been influenced by related fields of research, in particular economics, mathematics, and physics. This input from outside was highly relevant and led to the development and implementation of highly sophisticated quantitative models. These models improved transparency and led to better informed decisions.

All models have their limitations though. The global risk landscape is evolving to higher complexity. Uncertainty will be more relevant than in the past. There will be a competitive advantage for organizations, who are capable to deal with both risk and uncertainty. Management of risk alone will most likely not be sufficient.

With emerging risks and complex risks, we have given two examples and also demonstrated how risk management can be improved by using methods from uncertainty management and interdisciplinary cooperation between the insurance industry and psychological research. We feel that we have benefited tremendously by looking outside the obvious quantitative disciplines.

Implementation of new ideas and concepts in organizations will always be a challenge. When we improved our emerging risk management and incorporated ideas and insights from psychology into our processes, we also experienced the gap between the intellectual world and the commercial world. The transfer of psychological research results into risk management applications was far from trivial. Psychological literature is full of extremely important results for risk managers. But while the relevance is intuitively (sic!) clear, the practitioner's question "what can we do better and how?" remains largely unanswered.

There is a need for more bridges between industry and research. The transfer of knowledge into applications needs to be strengthened. There is a growing demand in the risk industry for tools and methods to address uncertainty at various levels: methods, processes, organizational setup, and education.

References

Battison, S., Gatti, D. D., & Gallegati, M. (2008). Trade credit networks and systemic risk. In D. Helbing (Ed.), *Managing complexity: Insights, concepts, applications* (pp. 219–239). Berlin: Springer.

Box, G. E. P., Jenkins, G. M., & Reinsel, G. C. (2008). *Time series analysis: Forecasting and control*. Hoboken, NJ: Wiley.

Casdagli, M., & Eubank, S. (1992). *Nonlinear modeling and forecasting*. Boston, MA: Addison-Wesley.

Coburn, A., Bowman, G., Ruffle, S., Foulser-Piggott, R., Ralph, D., & Tuveson, M. (2014). *A taxonomy of threats for complex risk management* (Cambridge Risk Framework Series). Centre for Risk Studies, University of Cambridge. Retrieved from http://cambridgeriskframework.com/getdocument/4

Eller, E., Lermer, E., Streicher, B., & Sachs, R. (2013). *Psychological influences on the individual assessment of risks* (Emerging Risk Discussion Paper). Munich. Retrieved from https://www.munichre.com/site/corporate/get/documents/mr/assetpool.shared/Documents/0_

Corporate%20Website/1_The%20Group/Focus/Emerging%20Risks/2013-09-emerging-risk-discussion-paper-en.pdf
Gardiner, C. (2002). *Handbook of stochastic methods: For physics, chemistry and the natural sciences*. Heidelberg: Springer.
Gigerenzer, G. (2007). *Gut feelings: The intelligence of the unconscious*. London: Penguin.
Harvey, A. C. (1989). *Forecasting, structural time series models and the kalman filter*. Cambridge: Cambridge University Press.
Kahneman, D., & Tversky, A. (1979). Prospect theory: An analysis of decision under risk. *Econometrica, 47*(2), 263–292.
Kahnemann, D. (2011). *Thinking fast and slow*. New York, NY: Farrar, Straus & Giroux.
Kantz, H., & Schreiber, T. (1997). *Nonlinear time series analysis*. Cambridge: Cambridge University Press.
Lermer, E., Streicher, B., Eller, E., & Sachs, R. (2014). *Psychological influences II: Risk assessment in groups* (Emerging Risk Discussion Paper). Munich. Retrieved from https://www.munichre.com/site/corporate/get/documents_E1286451571/mr/assetpool.shared/Documents/0_Corporate%20Website/1_The%20Group/Focus/Emerging%20Risks/Emerging-Risk-Discussion-Paper-2014-10-en.pdf
Lermer, E., Streicher, B., Sachs, R., & Frey, D. (2013). How risky? The impact of target person and answer format on risk assessment. *Journal of Risk Research, 16*(7), 903–919.
Linkov, I., Bridges, T., Creutzig, F., Decker, J., Fox-Lent, C., Kröger, W., … Nyer, R. (2014). Changing the resilience paradigm. *Nature Climate Change, 4*(6), 407–409.
Lo, A. W., & Mueller, M. T. (2010). *Warning: Physics envy may be hazardous to your wealth!* Retrieved from https://arxiv.org/pdf/1003.2688v3.pdf
Manser, T. (2008). Komplexität handhaben - Handeln vereinheitlichen Organisationen sicher gestalten. In P. Badke-Schaub, G. Hofinger, & K. Lauche (Eds.), *Human Factors – Psychologie sicheren Handelns in Risikobranchen* (pp. 273–288). Heidelberg: Springer.
McNeil, A. J., Frey, R., & Embrechts, P. (2005). Quantitative risk management. Princeton: Princeton University Press.
Pearl, J. (2009). *Causality—Models, reasoning and inference*. Cambridge: Cambridge University Press.
Sachs, R., & Wadé, M. (2013). *Managing complex risks successfully* (Emerging Risk Discussion Paper). Munich Re. Retrieved from https://www.munichre.com/site/corporate/get/documents_E-1170441588/mr/assetpool.shared/Documents/0_Corporate%20Website/1_The%20Group/Focus/Emerging%20Risks/302-07873_en.pdf
Thoma, K. (2014). *Resilience-by-design: Strategie für die technologischen Zukunftsthemen*. Retrieved from http://www.acatech.de/fileadmin/user_upload/Baumstruktur_nach_Website/Acatech/root/de/Publikationen/Stellungnahmen/acatech_STUDIE_RT_WEB.pdf
Tremper, B. (2008). *Staying alive in avalanche terrain*. Seattle: The Mountaineers Books.
van Kampen, N. G. (1992). *Stochastic processes in physics and chemistry*. Amsterdam: Elsevier.
Weick, K., & Sutcliffe, K. M. (2007). *Managing the unexpected: Resilient performance in an age of uncertainty*. Hoboken, NJ: Wiley.

Chapter 16
Implications for Risk Governance

Ortwin Renn

Abstract Risk perception differs from scientific or statistical assessment of risks. More than reflecting probability and magnitude, risk perception also includes aspects such as voluntariness of risk, possibility of personal control, or familiarity. It is also based on intuitive processes of making inferences, social values, and cultural beliefs. They follow specific patterns of semantic images and facilitate judgments about acceptability. Risk perceptions should not be seen as irrational responses to complex phenomena but rather as indicators for individual and societal concerns that require management and communication action.

Introduction

Within the social sciences and psychology, the term risk perception has a long tradition (Breakwell, 2014; Slovic, 1987). The term denotes the process of collecting, selecting, and interpreting signals about uncertain impacts of events, activities, or technologies (Renn, 2008; Scholz, 2009; Wachinger, Renn, Begg, & Kuhlicke, 2010). These signals can refer to direct experience (e.g., witnessing a flood) or indirect experience (e.g., information from others, such as reading about a technical disaster or a heightened level of pollution in the newspaper). Yet risks cannot be "perceived" in the sense of being taken up by the human senses, as are images of real phenomena. Mental models and other psychological mechanisms that individuals may use to judge risks (such as cognitive heuristics and risk images) are internalized through social and cultural learning and constantly moderated (reinforced, modified, amplified, or attenuated) by media reports, peer influences, and other communication processes (Morgan, Fischhoff, Bostrom, & Atman, 2001). Perceptions may differ depending on the type of risk, the risk context, the personality of the individual, and the social context. Various

O. Renn (✉)
Institute for Advanced Sustainability Studies, Potsdam, Germany
e-mail: ortwin.renn@iass-potsdam.de

M. Raue et al. (eds.), *Psychological Perspectives on Risk and Risk Analysis*,
https://doi.org/10.1007/978-3-319-92478-6_16

factors such as knowledge, experience, values, attitudes, and emotions influence the thinking and judgment of individuals about the seriousness and acceptability of risks. Perceptions also play a major role for motivating individuals to take action in order to avoid, mitigate, adapt to, or even ignore the risk. Different schools of psychological risk perception research have been working on shedding more light into the rationales and structures of individual and cultural patterns of risk perception.

Four different approaches to study risk perception dominate the literature on this subject, and they are summarized here (cf. Renn, 2008). They refer to:

(a) Attribution studies (attention and selection filters)
(b) Heuristics and biases (cognitive distortions)
(c) Psychometrics and semantic images
(d) Cultural theory of risk

The purpose of this paper is, first, to provide an overview of different "schools of thought" and their contributions to understanding the psychological drivers for perceiving and evaluating technological, natural, health-related, or environmental risks. The second part will draw some lessons from the insights of risk perception studies for normative advice on risk governance.

Attribution: Attention and Selection Filters

Today's society provides an abundance of information, much more than any individual can digest (OECD, 2002; Renn & Benighaus, 2013). Most information to which the average person is exposed to will be ignored. This is not a malicious act but a sheer necessity in order to reduce the amount of information a person can process in a given time. Once information has been received, common-sense mechanisms process the information and help the receiver to draw inferences. One example of an intuitive strategy to evaluate risks is to use the minimax rule for making decisions, a rule that many consumers and people tend to apply when making a judgment about the acceptability of a new, unfamiliar activity or technology. This rule implies that people try to minimize post-decisional regret, i.e., a feeling of dissonance or doubt regarding the possibility of having made the wrong choice in a previous decision, by choosing the option that has the least potential for a disaster regardless of probabilities. The use of this rule is not irrational. For example, banning nuclear power in a densely populated area such as Germany may be justified even if the likelihood of a disaster is very small. Yet when the disaster occurs, the consequences are so catastrophic that even a minute probability of this occurring is sufficient to ban the entire activity. The minimax principle (minimize your maximum conceivable loss) has evolved over a long evolution of human behavior as a fairly successful strategy to cope with uncertainty (better safe than sorry) (Renn, 2008).

However, experience with most risks that modern society is exposed to is limited. Individuals rely on information by third parties in order to come to a judgment about the seriousness and acceptability of a given risk. None of the ordinary consumers has a lab in his or her basement to test emissions from technologies or to verify claims of safety or immanent threats by professionals. They have hardly any other choice but to believe one side or another side in a risk debate. Reliance on third parties' information is a typical pattern of modern risk perception. Risk perception is not so much a product of experience or personal evidence, as it is a result of social communication (Luhmann, 1986, 1997; Rosa, Renn, & McCright, 2014).

The main criteria for selecting relevant information about unfamiliar or unknown risks are *ability* and *motivation* (Chaiken & Stangor, 1987). Ability refers to the physical possibility of the receiver to follow the message without distraction; motivation refers to the readiness and interest of the receiver to process messages. If information about uncertain consequences—that could be a risk or a benefit—has passed the initial selection filters, people will draw inferences from the information and compare the content with previously held images and memories. They will evaluate the significance, truthfulness, and personal relevance of the information, construct new beliefs, and form an opinion or an attitude toward the respective risk and/or its source.

Heuristics and Biases: Using Rules of Thumbs

Once information has been received, common-sense mechanisms come most often into play to process the information and help the receiver to draw inferences. These processes are called *intuitive heuristics*. They are particularly important for the perception of uncertainty since they relate to the mechanisms of processing probabilistic information (Breakwell, 2014; Kahneman, 2011; Sunstein & Thaler, 2009). Early psychological studies focused on personal preferences for different compositions of probabilities and outcome (risk aversion, risk neutrality, and risk proneness) and attempted to explain why individuals do not base their risk judgments on expected values (i.e., the product of probability and magnitude of an adverse effect) (Lopes, 1983; Pollatsek & Tversky, 1970). One of the interesting results of these investigations was the discovery of systematic patterns of probabilistic reasoning. People are risk-averse if the stakes of losses are high and are risk-prone if the stakes for gains are high (Kahneman & Tversky, 1979, 1984). Many people balance their risk taking behavior by pursuing an optimal risk strategy that does not maximize their benefits, but ensures a satisfactory payoff and the avoidance of major disasters. Using rules of thumb rather than calculating expected values has been the main outcome of many empirical studies of how people perceive risks (Breakwell, 2014; Covello, 1983; Boholm, 1998).

Exposure and Hazard Perception One important rule of thumb is to overrate exposure and hazard, rather than the probability of harm (Renn, Burns, Kasperson, Kasperson, & Slovic, 1992). This intuitive heuristic is probably the most powerful factor for rejecting or downplaying information on technological, health-related, or environmental risk. If people assume that any exposure above zero can trigger the negative effect such as cancer regardless of dose or concentration, they will attribute any such outcome to the potential cause that happens to be present (Kraus, Malmfors, & Slovic, 1992). They imply that any exposure is regarded as being threatening irrespective of dose and strength of exposure. For most people it is not relevant whether the dose of the substance or agent was low or high. Once a risk source is associated with emissions such as ionizing radiation, electromagnetic fields, chemicals in air, or water pollutants, most people tend to express high concern about this risk even if the concentration is below the threshold of causing harm. One example may be the use of phthalates in toys. All analysts are aware that the substance is potentially carcinogenic, but given the known exposure and the dose-response functions, there is hardly any realistic possibility for young children to be negatively affected. Yet the mere idea of having a carcinogenic substance in children's toys has incited a fierce debate about the tolerability of such an ingredient in rubber toys (Klinke & Renn, 2012). Many NGOs and consumer organizations have opted for a total ban of this material in toys and successfully lobbied the EU Commission to follow their recommendations.

Harmonization of Risk and Benefit Estimates A second example refers to the perception of risks and benefits. In most cases, one would assume that an activity that leads to high benefits may also be associated with high risks (and vice versa). Empirical studies on how people process information about risks and benefits show the opposite effect. For example, the intake of pharmaceuticals or dietary supplements is linked to high benefit and low risks (Alhakami & Slovic, 1994). One explanation for this high reverse correlation between risks and benefits may be that respondents calculate a net balance between risks and benefits and transfer this net result to both risks and benefits (De Jonge, van Kleef, & Frewer, 2007).

Understanding of Uncertainty A third example for a rule of thumb that deviates from the experts' perspective on risk is the public understanding of uncertainty. The distinction that experts perform when conducting a probabilistic risk assessment (PRA) between a probability distribution and the associated degrees of remaining uncertainties (expressed in confidence intervals or in other forms of uncertainty characterization) is not echoed in risk perception studies (Sparks & Shepherd, 1994; Frewer et al., 2002). There has been a basic understanding among most people by now that the preferred deterministic worldview of judging a situation as either safe or unsafe cannot be sustained and that this view needs to be replaced by a mental model that differentiates among different degrees of certainty. The distinction in safe or unsafe gives way to a model of gradual safety where safe or unsafe are the endpoints of a distribution. However, most people perceive the space between safe and unsafe as an indication of bad or incomplete science rather than an indication of

Table 16.1 Selective intuitive biases of risk perception (source: Renn, 2008, p. 103)

Biases	Description
Availability	Events that come immediately to people's minds are rated as more probable than events that are of less personal importance
Anchoring effect	Probabilities are estimated according to the plausibility of contextual links between cause and effect, but not according to knowledge about statistical frequencies or distributions (people will "anchor" the information that is either of personal significance to them or that seems consciously or subconsciously related to the risk source or situation)
Personal experience	Singular events based on personal experiences or associated with the properties of an event are regarded as more typical than information based on frequency of occurrence
Avoidance of cognitive dissonance	Information that challenges perceived probabilities that are already part of a belief system will either be ignored or downplayed. Since people try to avoid dissonances, i.e., discrepancies between their own knowledge and attitudes and the content of an incoming information, they use many strategies to downplay the significance of this dissonance, for example, by discrediting the source of the information, by assuming the communicator did not mean what he or she was saying, or by linking the external dissonant communication with vested interests or ignorance

(genuine) probability distributions. The more people believe that anything between safe and unsafe is a sign of bad science or confusion caused by lobbying groups the nature of risk as a probabilistic concept get obscured. Often uncertainties are seen as indicators of knowledge gaps or incomplete science. So many demand that more funds should be given to science and research in order to reduce or minimize such uncertainties (De Jonge et al., 2007; Frewer et al., 2002; Sparks, Shepherd, & Frewer, 1994). For example, in the case of genetically modified organisms (GMOs) in agriculture, most people are unwilling to accept the risk associated with the consumption of GMOs unless they are convinced that there is little or no uncertainty about the potential side effects.

These rules of thumbs and examples show that deviations from expert advices are less a product of ignorance or irrationality than an indication of one or several intervening context variables that often make perfect sense if seen in the light of the original context in which the individual decision-maker has learned to use them (Brehmer, 1987; Gigerenzer, 1991, 2000; Lee, 1981). However, there is ample evidence for clear violations of mathematical or logical rules in common-sense reasoning when it comes to processing probabilistic information. Many specific studies identified biases in people's ability to draw inferences from probabilistic information (Boholm, 1998; Breakwell, 2014; Festinger, 1957; Kahneman, 2011; Jungermann, Pfister, & Fischer, 2005; Kahneman & Tversky, 1979; Renn, 1990). Table 16.1 lists the most important biases for making judgments on risks. Risk managers and regulators should be aware of these biases because they shape public risk perception and may be one of the underlying causes for the discrepancy between layperson and expert judgment of risk.

Psychometrics and Semantic Images: An Evolutionary Perspective

Basic Responses to Threats

The psychometric paradigm conceptualizes risks as a subjective estimate of individual fears or expectations about unwanted consequences. Such individual strategies to estimate and handle risks have been thoroughly researched in psychology and social psychology (Boholm, 1998; Breakwell, 2014; Knight & Warland, 2005; McDaniels, Axelrod, Cavanagh, & Slovic, 1997; Slovic, 1987; Slovic, Fischhoff, & Lichtenstein, 1986; Sjöberg, 1999, 2000; Rohrmann & Renn, 2000; Townsend, Clarke, & Travis, 2004). People do not use completely irrational strategies to assess and evaluate information about complex risks, but most of the time, they follow relatively consistent patterns of perception. These patterns can be traced back to certain evolutionary traits of hazard deterrence (Marks & Nesse, 1994; Renn, 2014a). In dangerous situations, humans' reactions rely on four basic strategies:

- Flight
- Fight
- Play dead
- If appropriate, subordination or experimentation

These reaction patterns can be visualized by imagining how our ancestors reacted to a predator in the wilderness. In a situation of acute threat, such as coming up against a tiger, the victim would not have had time—it would not have made much sense to conduct a probability analysis as to whether the tiger is hungry or not. At this moment, a person who was threatened had only three possibilities: first, to flee and hope to be faster than the tiger; second, to believe in his strength and fight; or, third, to play dead, believing the tiger could be duped (Bracha, 2004). In this case, the last option—namely, subordination—would not impress any hungry tiger. Subordination makes sense if the more powerful communication partner interprets this as a signal of respecting his or her superior power.

Qualitative Context Variables

In the course of cultural evolution, these basic patterns of perception, flight, fight, playing dead, and subordination were increasingly supplemented with cultural patterns. Cultural patterns can be described by so-called qualitative evaluation characteristics and, in the school of psychometrics, are measured by using numerical scaling techniques. This approach to risk research was originally developed by the Oregon Group (see Fischhoff, Slovic, Lichtenstein,

Table 16.2 List of important qualitative risk characteristics (source: adapted from Renn, 1990)

Qualitative characteristics	Direction of influence
Personal control	Increases risk tolerance
Institutional control	Depends upon confidence in institutional performance
Voluntariness	Increases risk tolerance
Familiarity	Increases risk tolerance
Dread	Decreases risk tolerance
Inequitable distribution of risks and benefits	Depends upon individual utility; strong social incentive for rejecting risks
Artificiality of risk source	Amplifies attention to risk; often decreases risk tolerance
Blame	Increases quest for social and political responses

Read, & Combus, 1978; Slovic, 1992; Slovic, Fischhoff, & Lichtenstein, 1980; Slovic et al., 1986).

By using psychometric methods, researchers were able to demonstrate why individuals do not base their risk judgments on subjectively expected utilities. The research revealed several contextual characteristics that individual decision-makers use when assessing and evaluating risks (Fischhoff et al., 1978; Renn, Schweizer, Dreyer, & Klinke, 2007; Rohrmann & Renn, 2000; Siegrist, Keller, & Kiers, 2005; Slovic, 1987). The following contextual variables of risk have been found to affect people's judgments about risks (taken and expanded from Renn, 1990) (Table 16.2).

These qualitative characteristics can, for example, be applied to the perception of environmental or technological risks (OECD, 2002). First, large-scale technologies such as nuclear power plants, chemical production facilities, and waste disposal installations are associated with negative risk characteristics, such as dread, lack of personal control, and high catastrophic potential. The perception of technological risks is usually linked to an absence of personal control, and the preponderance of dread amplifies the impression of seriousness. These characteristics make people even more concerned about the negative impacts than is warranted by the predicted physical impacts alone.

Second, the beliefs associated with the risk source (e.g., industry) raise associations to greed, profit-seeking, and alleged disrespect for public health. Third, the possibility to be exposed to risks without prior consent touches upon serious equity concerns focusing on a just distribution of risks and benefits among the population. Inequitable distribution of risks and benefits makes the risk appear more severe and unacceptable. Finally, the possibility of catastrophic accidents and the sensational press coverage about such accidents invokes negative emotions and may even lead to stigmatization. Nuclear energy or genetically modified organisms appear already to be associated with strong stigma effects (Renn, 2005). Another option of grouping and classifying contextual variables is to construct typical patterns—so-called semantic images—which serve as orientations for individuals. This topic is explained and discussed in the following section.

Semantic Images: Constructing One's Own Reality

Perceptions have a reality of their own: just like the characters in animated films who, suspended in midair, do not plunge to the ground until they realize their predicament, people construct their own reality and evaluate risk according to their subjective perceptions. This type of intuitive risk perception is based on how information about the source of a risk is communicated and on the psychological mechanisms for processing uncertainty, intuitive heuristics, and the contextual characteristics discussed in the last section.

Research on risk perception has identified a range of perception patterns that constitute discrete manifestations of key risk characteristics depending upon the context in which the risk is embedded. These are called *semantic risk images* (Jaeger, Renn, Rosa, & Webler, 2001; Renn et al., 2007; Renn, 2014a; Streffer et al., 2003). Although these semantic images have not been directly tested in empirical experiments or surveys, they have been deduced from statistical processing of data from studies of qualitative characteristics. In general, five distinct semantic images have been identified (Renn, 1990) (see Table 16.3). In addition to these five images, additional images of risk exist for habitual and lifestyle risks that are, however, less clear in their composition and structure.

The semantic images allow individuals to order risks on the basis of a few salient characteristics. So groups of risks form clusters such as high-consequence, low-probability risks that are normally associated with the emerging danger category. Once new risks have been grouped in this scheme, they will be treated similarly to older risks in the same category (e.g., CCS facilities are mentally associated with nuclear facilities). Reducing complexity by creating classes of similar phenomena is certainly a major strategy for coping with information overload and uncertainty. The five semantic images are powerful guides that help individuals to navigate through an abundance of often contradicting information. They provide an efficient method of balancing the time for collecting and processing information with the personal need for orientation and attitude formation.

Some risk sources evoke more than one semantic image. So driving cars can be seen as an emergent danger when all car accidents are addressed. It could be located in the category of insidious danger if only car exhausts are considered and be grouped in the category of thrill if people use cars for racing. Combinations of the slow agents and pending danger images are particularly interesting. Risks from large-scale technologies are mostly found in the category of emergent danger. Emissions from the use of high-impact technologies are typical for the category of insidious dangers. This has far-reaching implications. Most risks belonging to the category of insidious dangers are regarded as potentially harmful substances that defy human senses and "poison" people without their knowledge. Risks associated with air pollutants, water impurities, and radiation are mostly invisible to the person exposed. They require warning by regulators or scientists. People tend to believe that toxicity depends less on the dose than on the characteristics of the substance. Hence they demand a deterministic regulatory approach when it comes to controlling environmental pollutants.

Table 16.3 The five semantic images of risk perception (source: adapted from Renn, 1990)

1. Emerging danger (fatal threat)
Artificial risk source
Large catastrophic potential
Inequitable risk-benefit distribution
Perception of randomness as a threat
2. Stroke of fate
Natural risk source
Belief in cycles (not perceived as a random event)
Belief in personal control (can be mastered by oneself)
Accessible through human senses
3. Personal thrill (desired risks)
Personal control over degree of risk
Personal skills necessary to master danger
Voluntary activity
Non-catastrophic consequences
4. Gamble
Confined to monetary gains and losses
Orientation toward variance of distribution rather than expected value
Asymmetry between risks and gains
Dominance of probabilistic thinking
5. Indicator of insidious danger (slow killer)
(Artificial) ingredient in food, water, or air
Delayed effects; non-catastrophic
Contingent upon information rather than experience
Quest for deterministic risk management
Strong incentive for blame

Cultural Approaches to Risk Perception

A group of distinguished anthropologists and cultural sociologists such as Aaron Wildavsky, Mary Douglas, or Michael Thompson have identified four or five patterns of value clusters that separate different groups in society from each other (Breakwell, 2014; Douglas & Wildavsky, 1982; Thompson, 1980; Thompson, Ellis, & Wildavsky, 1990). These different groups have formed specific positions on risk topics and have developed corresponding attitudes and strategies. They differ in the degree of *group* cohesiveness (the extent to which someone finds identity in a social group) and the degree of *grid* (the extent to which someone accepts and respects a formal system of hierarchy and procedural rules).

These groups are the entrepreneurs, the egalitarians, the bureaucrats, the stratified individuals, and—added in some publications—the group of the hermits. Organizations or social groups belonging to the *entrepreneurial* prototype perceive risk taking as an opportunity to succeed in a competitive market and to pursue their personal goals. They are characterized by a low degree of hierarchy and a low degree of cohesion. They are less concerned about equity issues and would like the government to refrain from extensive regulation or risk management efforts. This group contrasts most with organizations or groups belonging to the *egalitarian* prototype, which emphasizes cooperation and equality rather than competition and freedom. Egalitarians are also characterized by low hierarchy but have developed a strong sense of group cohesiveness and solidarity. When facing risks they tend to focus on long-term effects of human activities and are more likely to abandon an activity (even if they perceive it as beneficial to them) than to take chances. They are particularly concerned about equity.

The third prototype, i.e., the *hierarchists (sometimes also called bureaucrats)*, relies on rules and procedures to cope with uncertainty. Bureaucrats are both hierarchical and cohesive in their group relations. As long as risks are managed by a capable institution and coping strategies have been provided for all eventualities, there is no need to worry about risks. Bureaucrats believe in the effectiveness of organizational skills and practices and regard a problem as solved when a procedure to deal with its institutional management is in place.

The fourth prototype, the group of *atomized or stratified individuals*, principally believes in hierarchy, but they do not identify with the hierarchy to which they belong. These people trust only themselves, are often confused about risk issues, and are likely to take high risks for themselves, but oppose any risk that they feel is imposed on them. At the same time, however, they see life as a lottery and are often unable to link harm to a concrete cause.

In addition to the four prototypes, there may be a hybrid group called the *autonomous individuals or the hermit* who can be grouped at in the center of the group-grid coordinates. Thompson describes autonomous individuals as self-centered hermits and short-term risk evaluators. They may be also referred to as potential mediators in risk conflicts, since they build multiple alliances to the four other groups and

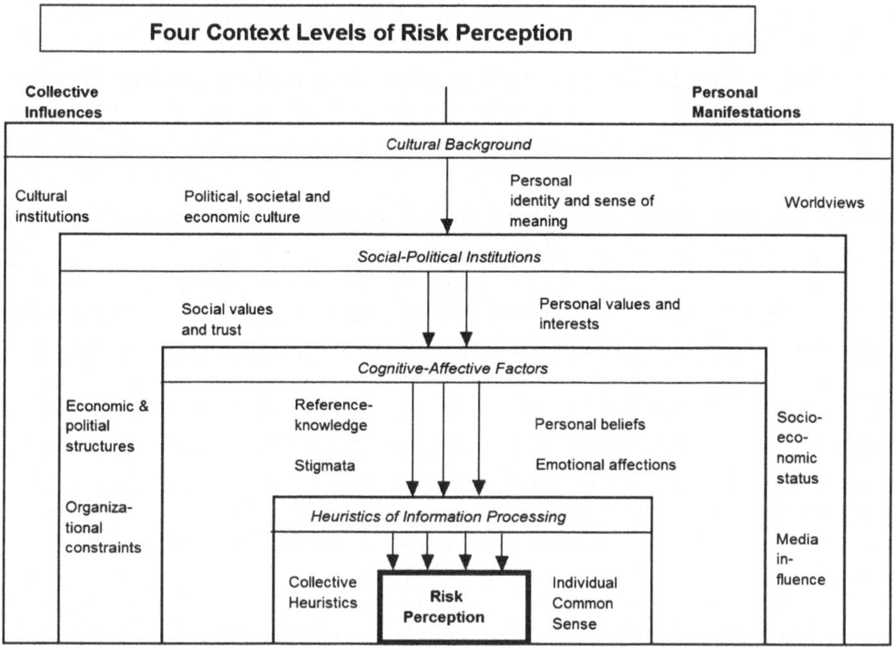

Fig. 16.1 Four context levels of risk perception (adapted from Renn & Rohrmann, 2000)

believe in hierarchy only if they can relate the authority to superior performance or knowledge.

Opinions on the validity of the cultural theory of risk differ widely. Slovic, Flynn, Mertz, Poumadere, and Mays (2000) regard this approach as useful in explaining some of the differences in risk perception; Sjöberg (2001) and Sjöberg (2000) found the variance explained by cultural prototypes to be so low that they rejected the whole concept. Rohrmann (2000) also expressed a skeptical view, mainly because of methodological considerations about the empirical validity of the claims. All authors agree, however, that specific culture-based preferences and biases are, indeed, important factors in risk perception. The disagreement is about the relevance of the postulated four or five prototypes within the realm of cultural factors.

An Integrative Model of Risk Perception

Based on the review of psychological, social, and cultural factors that shape individual and social risk perceptions, Rohrmann and Renn have attempted to develop a structured framework that provides an integrative and systematic perspective on risk perception. Figure 16.1 illustrates this perspective by pointing toward four distinct context levels (Renn & Rohrmann, 2000; inspired by the generic model in Breakwell, 1994).

Each level is further divided into two subsections, representing individual and collective manifestations of risk perceptions, and embedded in the next higher level to highlight the mutual contingencies and interdependencies among and between individual, social, and cultural variables.

Level 1: Heuristics of Information Processing The first level includes the collective and individual heuristics that individuals apply during the process of forming judgments about risks. These heuristics are independent of the nature of the risk in question or the personal beliefs, emotions, or other conscious perception patterns of the individual. Heuristics represent common-sense reasoning strategies that have evolved over the course of biological and cultural evolution. They may differ between cultures; but most evidence in this field of psychological research shows a surprising degree of universality in applying these heuristics across different cultures. Improved knowledge and expertise in logical reasoning and inferential statistics, as well as a principal awareness of these heuristics, can help individuals to correct their intuitive judgments or to apply these heuristics to situations where they seem appropriate. Recent research results suggest that these heuristics as explained in Section "Heuristics and Biases: Using Rules of Thumbs" of this chapter are more appropriate for problem-solving in many everyday situations than previously assumed (Gigerenzer, 2013; Gigerenzer & Selten, 2001). Regardless of the normative value that these heuristics may offer, they represent primary mechanisms of selecting, memorizing, and processing signals from the outside world and pre-shape the judgments about the seriousness of the risk in question.

Level 2: Cognitive and Affective Factors The second level refers to the cognitive and affective factors that are directly related to specific properties of the risk in question. Cognition about a risk source—what people believe to be true about a risk—governs the attribution of qualitative characteristics (psychometric variables) to specific risks (e.g., dread or personal control options) and determines the effectiveness of these qualitative risk characteristics on the perceived seriousness of risk and the judgment about acceptability. The more a risk seems to be voluntarily taken, institutionally controlled, and familiar to society, the more it will be rated as less serious compared to a risk that appears imposed on society, less controlled, and unfamiliar to the observer.

It is interesting to note that different cognitive processes can lead to the same attribution result. In an empirical study, Rosa, Matsuda, and Kleinhesselink (2000) were able to show that for the Japanese sample, the arousal of catastrophic images was associated with the degree of individual knowledge of and familiarity with the respective risk in question, whereas US respondents linked collective scientific experience and knowledge to catastrophic potential. The two samples were, however, identical in assigning the degree of catastrophic potential to a set of technologies, even if they had different mental models about what constitutes catastrophic potential. The fact that individuals, within their own culture or by their own agency, are able to choose between different cognitive routes justifies the distinction between the two primary levels: cognitive factors and heuristics.

While cognitive factors have been extensively explored, emotions have been neglected in risk perception research for a long time. More recently, however, psychologists have discovered that affect and emotions play an important role in people's decision processes (Breakwell, 2014; Loewenstein, Weber, Hsee, & Welch, 2001; Slovic, Finucane, Peters, & MacGregor, 2002). People's feelings about what is good or bad in terms of the causes and consequences of risks color their beliefs about the risk and, in addition, influence their process of balancing potential benefits and risks. Affective factors are particularly relevant when individuals face a decision that involves a difficult trade-off between attributes or where there is interpretative ambiguity as to what constitutes a "right" answer. In these cases, people often appear to resolve problems by focusing on those cues that send the strongest affective signals (see Peters, Burraston, & Mertz, 2004). On the collective level, stigmata referring to risk sources or activities play a similar role in stimulating emotional responses (Slovic et al., 2002). Empirical studies regarding hazards from exposure to technological risks show that emotional and cognitive factors are mutually related (Zwick & Renn, 1998). It is not yet clear whether cognitive beliefs trigger off the respective emotional responses or whether emotional impulses act as heuristic strategies to select or develop arguments supporting one's emotional stance.

Level 3: Social and Political Institutions The third level refers to the social and political institutions that individuals and groups associate with either the cause of risk or the risk itself. Most studies on this level focus on trust in institutions, personal and social value commitments, organizational constraints, social and political structures, and socioeconomic status. One important factor in evaluating risk is the perception of fairness and justice in allocating benefits and risks to different individuals and social groups (Linnerooth-Bayer & Fitzgerald, 1996). Theoretical approaches, such as the risk society by Ulrich Beck, provide plausible explanation of why the debate on equity and justice has become so relevant for risk perception (Beck, 1992; Knight & Warland, 2005). Other studies have placed political and social organizations and their strategies to communicate with other organizations and society at large as the prime focus of their attention (Clarke, 1989; Shubik, 1991).

The media, social reference groups, and organizations also shape individual and societal risk experience. Press coverage appears to contribute substantially to a person's perception of risk, particularly if the person lacks personal experience with the risk and is unable to verify claims of risks or benefits from his own experience. In contrast to popular belief, however, there is no evidence that the media create opinions about risks or even determine risk perceptions. Studies on media reception rather suggest that people select elements from media reports and use their own frame of reference to create understanding and meaning. Most people reconfirm existing attitudes when reading or viewing media reports (Peters, 1991).

Level 4: Cultural Background The last level refers to cultural factors that govern or co-determine many of the lower levels of influence. The most specific explanation for cultural differences about risk perceptions comes from the *cultural theory of risk* (see Section "Cultural Approaches to Risk Perception"). This theory claims that there are four or, in some studies, five prototypes of responses to risk. These prototypes refer to entrepreneurs, egalitarians, hierarchists, atomized individuals, and, as a separate category, hermits.

In addition to the theory of cultural prototypes, two sociological concepts should be mentioned that provide plausible explanations for the link between macro-sociological developments and risk perceptions. The *theory of reflexive modernization* claims that individualization, pluralization, and globalization have contributed to the decline of legitimacy with respect to risk professionals and managers (Marshall, 1999; Mythen, 2005; Renn, 2014a; Rosa et al., 2014). Due to this loss of confidence in private and public institutions, people have become skeptical about the promises of modernity and evaluate the acceptability of risks according to the perceived interest and hidden agenda of those who want society to accept these risks (Beck, 1992). The second approach picks up the *concept of social arenas* in which powerful groups struggle for resources in order to pursue their interest and objectives. Here, symbolic connotations constructed by these interest groups act as powerful shaping instruments for eliciting new beliefs or emotions about the risk or the source of risk (Jaeger et al., 2001).

All four levels of influence are relevant in order to gain a better and more accurate understanding of risk perception. In spite of many open questions and ambiguities in risk perception research, one conclusion is beyond any doubt: abstracting the risk concept to a rigid formula and reducing it to the two components' "probability and consequences" do not match people's intuitive thinking of what is important when making judgments about the acceptability of risks, in particular human-induced risks (Mazur, 1987; Pidgeon, 1997; Wilkinson, 2001). Slovic (1992, p. 150) stated this point quite clearly:

> To understand risk perception, one needs to study the psychological, social and cultural components and, in particular, their mutual interactions. The framework of social amplification may assist researchers and risk managers to forge such an integrative perspective on risk perception. Yet, a theory of risk perception that offers an integrative, as well as empirically valid, approach to understanding and explaining risk perception is still missing."

Implications for Risk Governance

From a normative perspective, knowledge about individual perceptions of risk cannot be translated directly into environmental policies. If perceptions are based partially on biases or ignorance, it does not seem wise to use them as yardsticks for risk reduction. In addition, risk perceptions vary among individuals and groups. Whose perceptions should be used to make decisions on risk? At the same time, however, these perceptions reflect the real concerns of people and include the undesirable effects that "technical" analyses of risk often miss. It is true that laypeople's views of risk are intuitive and less formal and precise than experts' statements. But as has been observed, "their basic conceptualisation of risk is much richer than that of experts and reflects legitimate concerns that are typically omitted from expert risk assessments" (Slovic, 1987, p. 281).

In fact, risk judgments indicate more than just the perception of riskiness. They reveal global views on what matters to people, on technological progress, on the meaning of nature, and on the fair distribution of chances, benefits, and risks. Facing this dilemma, how can risk perception studies contribute to improving risk policies? Pertinent benefits may include (De Marchi, 2015; Fischhoff, 1985; Renn, 2008):

- They can identify and explain public concerns associated with the risk source.
- They can elucidate the context of the risk taking situation.
- They can enhance understanding of controversies about risk evaluation.
- They can identify cultural meanings and associations linked with special risk arenas.
- Based on this knowledge, they can be useful when articulating objectives of risk policies that go beyond risk minimization, such as fairness, procedural equity, and institutional trust.
- They can indicate how to design procedures or policies which incorporate these cultural values into the decision making process.
- They can be useful in the design of programs for participation and joint decision making.
- They can provide criteria for evaluating risk management performance and organizational structures for monitoring and controlling risks.

Social-science research on risk perception has many uses to risk governance. What benefits can scientists and policy-makers gain from the study of risk perception? What guidance can be derived from studies on intuitive risk perception for risk governance and policy-making? Even if there are no recipes to be obtained from analytical studies about risk perception, studies on risk perception can provide some insights that might help policy-makers to improve their performance (Slovic, 2000; Slovic, Fischhoff, & Lichtenstein, 1982).

Implications for Public Discourse: Cooperation Between Experts, Decision-Makers, and the Affected Publics

There is an urgent need for an effective and socially acceptable model of inclusive risk governance. Different knowledge claims, values, interests, and preferences[1] need to be reconciled in order to design and implement collectively binding

---

[1] Knowledge refers here to shared beliefs about the state of the world, values to orientations about how to judge actions in terms of (moral) desirability and ethical norms, interests to personal or

decisions. An integrated governance process, combining risk assessments and perceptions, requires decision making processes that include a multitude of actors and value clusters. On a general level, there is the distinction between the risk producers on the one hand and those who are exposed to the risks on the other hand. It is obvious that, between these two groups, conflicting interests are to be expected. Both groups can be further divided into subgroups with distinct interests of their own, the so-called stakeholders. They are defined here "as socially organised groups that are or will be affected by the outcome of the event or the activity from which the risk originates and/or by the risk management options taken to counter the risk" (IRGC, 2005, p. 49). In general risk issues affect the four main stakeholders in society. These are *political*, *economic*, *scientific*, and *civil society* representatives (as far as they are socially organized). Additionally, other groups that play a role in the risk governance process can be defined, the *media*, the *cultural elites* and *opinion leaders*, and the *general public*, either in their role as non-organized *affected* public or as the non-organized *observing* public (ibid.). So we end up with a four plus two scheme (science, private sector, civil society, politics together with media and the affected public), consisting of four major policy actors and two influential target groups that may become actors themselves.

As governance aims at reaching acceptance of the outcomes of the decision making process, the beliefs, interests, values, and preferences of all these different actors have to be taken into account. At the same time, however, the number of options and the procedures on how they are selected have to be restricted, as time and effort of the participants of the governance process have to be regarded as spare resources and therefore treated with care. Consequently, an inclusive risk governance process, as it is required when facing complex risks, can be characterized by *inclusion* of all affected parties on one hand and *closure* concerning the selection of possible options and the procedures that generate them, on the other hand (Renn, 2014b). Inclusion describes the question of what and whom to include into the governance process, not only into the decision making but into the whole process from framing the problem, generating options, and evaluating them to coming to a joint conclusion (Renn & Schweizer, 2009; Wynne, 2002).

Closure, on the other hand, is needed to restrict the selection of management options, to guarantee an efficient use of resources, be it financial or the use of time and effort of the participants in the governance process (Renn, 2014b). Closure concerns the part of generating and selecting risk management options, more specifically: which options are selected for further consideration and which options are rejected. Closure therefore concerns the product of the deliberation process. It describes the rules of when and how to close a debate and what level of agreement is to be reached (Renn & Schweizer, 2009).

Given the need to include plural knowledge, values, interests, and preferences and still to reach some closure at the end, a governance design is needed that provides enough incentives to invite different perspectives into the governing procedures

instituional net benefits, and preferences to holistic, often socially or culturally embedded, judgments on the personal attractiveness of options.

and includes a deliberation structure that is suitable to produce effective and acceptable outputs.

A report by the American Academy of Sciences on the subject of *Understanding Environmental Risks* concludes that scientifically valid and ethically justified procedures for the collective valuation of risks can be realized only within the context of an analytic-deliberative process (Stern & Fineberg, 1996; US-National Research Council of the National Academies, 2008). *Analytic* means that the best scientific findings about the possible consequences and conditions of collective action are incorporated in the negotiations; while *deliberative* means that rationally and ethically transparent criteria for making trade-offs are used and documented externally. Moreover, the authors consider fair participation by all groups concerned to be essential. It is important to ensure that the various moral and cultural reference systems, which can legitimately exist alongside each other, are organically incorporated into the process.

Depending on the nature of the risk, and the available information about the risk, the analytic-deliberative approach needs to be further specified. In the context of integrated risk governance suggestions for the participation of the public and stakeholders within an analytic-deliberative framework, the IRGC has developed a taxonomy of participatory risk governance approaches depending on the nature of the risk (IRGC, 2005; Renn, 2014b). It includes four types of *discourses*, describing the extent of participation.

In the case of *simple risk problems* with obvious consequences, low remaining uncertainties, and no controversial values implied, like many voluntary risks, e.g., bike riding, over-the-counter drugs, technical safety devices, or health protection standards for acute (non-genotoxic) diseases, it seems not necessary and even inefficient to involve all potentially affected parties to the process of decision making. An *instrumental discourse* is proposed to be the adequate strategy to deal with these risks. In this first type of discourse, agency staff, directly affected groups (like product or activity providers and immediately exposed individuals), and enforcement personnel are the relevant actors. It can be expected that the interest of the public into the regulation of these types of risk is very low. However, regular monitoring of the outcomes is important, as the risk might turn out to be more complex, uncertain, or ambiguous than characterized by the original assessment.

In case of *complex risk problems*, another discourse is needed. An example for complexity-based risk problems is the so-called cocktail effects of combined pesticide residues in food. While the effects of single pesticides are more or less scientifically proven, the cause and effect chains of multiple exposures of different pesticides via multiple exposure routes are highly complex. As complexity is a problem of insufficient knowledge about the coherences of the risk characteristics and functional relationships between agent and effects, it is the more important to produce transparency over the subjective judgements and about the inclusion of knowledge elements, in order to find the best estimates for characterizing the risks under consideration. This *epistemic discourse* aims at bringing together the knowledge from the agency staff of different scientific disciplines and other experts from academia, government, industry, or civil society. The principle of inclusion is bringing new or additional knowledge into the process and aims at resolving cognitive conflicts. Appropriate instruments of this discourse are available, for example, Delphi (iterative assessment procedure) or consensus workshops (experts seek consensus on controversial assessments and evaluations) (Gregory, McDaniels, & Fields, 2001; Webler, Levine, Rakel, & Renn, 1991).

In the case of risk problems due to *high unresolved uncertainty*, the challenges are even higher. The problem here is: How can one judge the severity of a situation when the potential damage and its probability are unknown or highly uncertain? This dilemma concerns the characterization of the risk as well as the evaluation and the design of options for the reduction of the risk. Natural disasters like tsunamis, floods, or earthquakes are, for example, characterized by high uncertainty. In this case, it is no longer sufficient to include experts into the discourse, but policy-makers and the main stakeholders should additionally be included, to find consensus on the extra margin of safety in which they would be willing to invest in order to avoid potentially—but uncertain—catastrophic consequences. This type is called *reflective discourse*, because it is based on a collective reflection about balancing the possibilities for over- and under-protection. For this type of discourse, round tables, open space forums, negotiated rule-making exercises, mediation, or mixed advisory committees are suggested (Amy, 1983; Renn, 2014b; Rowe and Frewer, 2000).

If risk problems are due to *high ambiguity*, the most inclusive strategy is required, as not only the directly affected groups have something to contribute to the debate but also the indirectly affected groups. If, for example, genetically modified foods and their production are targeted for regulation, the problem exceeds a mere risk perspective but touches also upon principal values and ethical questions, as well as aspects of lifestyle or future visions. A *participatory discourse* has to be organized, where competing arguments, beliefs, and values can be openly discussed. This discourse affects the very early step of risk framing and of risk evaluation. The aim of this type of discourse is to resolve conflicting expectations through identifying common values and defining options to allow people to live their own visions of a "good life," to find equitable and just distributions rules for common resources, and to activate institutional means for reaching common welfare so that all can profit from the collective benefits. Means for leading this normative discourse are, for example, citizen panels, citizen juries, consensus conferences, ombudspersons, or citizen advisory commissions (Applegate, 1998; Armour, 1995; Dienel, 1989; Durant & Joss, 1995; Fiorino, 1990; Renn, 2014b).

In this typology of discourses, it is presupposed that the categorization of risks into simple, complex, uncertain, and ambiguous is uncontested. But, very often, this turns out to be complicated. Who decides whether a risk issue can be categorized as simple, complex, uncertain, or ambiguous? To resolve this question, a *meta-discourse* is needed, where the decision is taken, where a specific risk is located, and, in consequence, to which route it is allocated. This discourse is called *design discourse* and is meant to provide stakeholder involvement at this

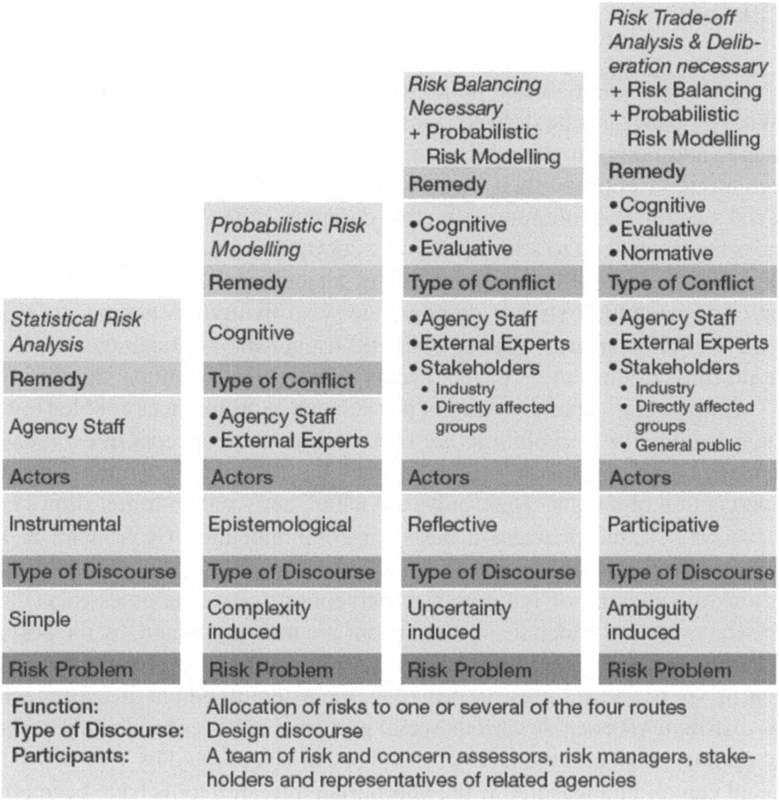

Fig. 16.2 The risk management escalator and stakeholder involvement (IRGC, 2005, p. 53)

more general level (Renn, 2014b). Allocating the risks to one of the four routes has to be done before assessment starts, but as knowledge and information may change during the governance process, it may be necessary to reorder the risk. A means to carry out this task can be a screening board that should consist of members of the risk and concern assessment team (i.e., specialized unit for risk analysis and assessment of stakeholder concerns with the risk in question), risk managers, and key stakeholders. Figure 16.2 provides an overview of the described discourses depending on the risk characteristics and the actors included into these discourses. Additionally it sets out the type of conflict produced through the plurality of knowledge and values and the required remedy to deal with the corresponding risk.

Of course, this scheme is a simplification of real risk problems and is meant to provide an idealized overview for the different requirements related to different risk problems. Under real conditions, risks and their conditions often turn out to be more interdependent among each other and the required measures more depending from unique contexts.

Conclusions

What benefits can scientists and policy-makers gain from the study of risk perception? What guidance can be derived from studies on intuitive risk perception for risk governance and policy-making? Risk perceptions studies can assist risk managers and regulators, to improve their performance when managing, regulating, or governing risks and to become more effective communicators with the different target audiences that they need to address (Slovic, 2000; Slovic et al., 1982; Renn, 2008). More specifically, the following points are of major importance:

First, risk perception studies demonstrate what matters to people. In a democratic society, the concerns of people should trigger the political agenda. Context and supporting circumstances of risk events or activities constitute significant concerns. These perception patterns are not just subjective preferences cobbled together: they stem from cultural evolution, are tried and trusted concepts in everyday life, and, in many cases, control our actions in much the same way as a universal reaction to the perception of danger. Their universal nature across all cultures allows collective focus on risk and provides a basis for communication (Rohrmann & Renn, 2000). From a rational standpoint, it would appear useful to systematically identify the various dimensions of intuitive risk perception (concerns assessment) and to measure the extent, to which these dimensions are met or violated, by the best available scientific methods. Many psychometric variables that matter to people are open to scientific study and scrutiny. In principle, the extent to which different technical options distribute risk across various social groups, the degree to which institutional control options exist, and the level of risk that can be accepted by way of voluntary agreement can all be measured if the appropriate research tools have been applied. Risk perception studies help to diagnose these concerns. Scientific investigations can determine whether these dimensions are met or violated, and to what degree. This integration of risk expertise and public concerns is based on the view that the dimensions (concerns) of intuitive risk perception are legitimate elements of rational policy; but assessment of the various risk sources must follow robust scientific procedures on every dimension.

Second, designing policies about advancing, supporting, and regulating risks requires trade-offs (i.e., relative weights of the various target dimensions). Such trade-offs depend upon both: context and the choice of dimension. Perception research offers important pointers concerning the selection of dimensions for focus. For example, the aspect of fairness that rates highly among people as an evaluation tool for the acceptability of risks plays a significant role in such trade-offs and in weighting the various dimensions. In their roles as risk assessors, experts have no authority to determine which distribution of risks and benefits should be taken as sufficient or legitimate for meeting the criterion of mutual fairness. This is where formal methods such as risk–risk comparisons and other evaluation tools reach their limits. The multidimensionality of the intuitive risk model prevents risk policy from focusing one-sidedly on the minimization of expected impacts. A breach of the minimization requirement, however, implies acceptance of greater damage than is absolutely necessary (although this can be justified in individual cases depending upon the risk situation).

Risk perception studies are crucial for designing and evaluating effective risk communication programs. Without knowing the concerns of the targeted audience, communication will not succeed. In addition, risk perception studies help communicators to identify points of conflict or disbelief. They can diagnose lack of trust or credibility and suggest more effective ways of restoring trust once trust has been lost. The insights from risk perception research will not guarantee the success of risk communication; but they can certainly assist risk communicators in designing more effective and efficient communication programs and informing participatory attempts of including major stakeholders in designing the appropriate risk management strategies. As much as inclusion is a virtue and a functional requirement for improved risk governance, the process of decision making also needs formats and mechanisms to reach closure at the end of the process. A distinction in instrumental, epistemic, reflective, and participatory discourse as advocated by the IRGC risk governance model points to an operational solution to resolve the tension between inclusion and closure.

References

Alhakami, A. S., & Slovic, P. (1994). A psychological study of the inverse relationship between perceived risk and perceived benefit. *Risk Analysis, 14*(6), 1085–1096.

Amy, D. J. (1983). Environmental mediation: An alternative approach to policy stalemates. *Policy Sciences, 15*(4), 345–365.

Applegate, J. S. (1998). Beyond the usual suspects: The use of citizens advisory boards in environmental decision making. *Indiana Law Journal, 73*, 903.

Armour, A. (1995). The citizen's jury model of public participation. In O. Renn, T. Webler, & P. Wiedemann (Eds.), *Fairness and competence in citizen participation: Evaluating new models for environmental discourse* (pp. 175–188). Dordrecht: Kluwer.

Beck, U. (1992). *Risk society: Toward a new modernity*. London: Sage.

Boholm, A. (1998). Comparative studies of risk perception: A review of twenty years of research. *Journal of Risk Research, 1*(2), 135–163.

Bracha, H. S. (2004). Freeze, flight, fight, fright, faint: Adaptionist perspectives on the acute stress response spectrum. *CNS Spectrums, 9*(9), 679–685.

Breakwell, G. M. (1994). The echo of power: A framework for social psychological research. *The Psychologist, 17*(2), 65–72.

Breakwell, G. M. (2014). *The psychology of risk* (2nd ed.). Cambridge: University Press.

Brehmer, B. (1987). The psychology of risk. In W. T. Singleton & J. Howden (Eds.), *Risk and decisions* (pp. 25–39). New York, NY: Wiley.

Chaiken, S., & Stangor, C. (1987). Attitudes and attitude change. *Annual Review of Psychology, 38*(1), 575–630.

Clarke, L. (1989). *Acceptable risk? Making decisions in a toxic environment*. Berkeley, CA: University of California Press.

Covello, V. T. (1983). The perception of technological risks: A literature review. *Technological Forecasting and Social Change, 23*(1), 285–297.

De Jonge, J., van Kleef, E., Frewer, L., & Renn, O. (2007). Perception of risk, benefit and trust associated with consumer food choice. In L. Fewer & H. van Trijp (Eds.), Understanding consumers of food products (pp. 534–557). Cambridge: Woodhead.

De Marchi, B. (2015). Risk governance and the integration of different types of knowledge. In U. F. Paleo (Ed.), *Risk governance. The articulation of hazard, politics and ecology* (pp. 149–165). Dordrecht: Springer.

Dienel, P. C. (1989). Contributing to social decision methodology: Citizen reports on technological projects. In C. Vlek & G. Cvetkovich (Eds.), *Social decision methodology for technological projects* (pp. 133–151). Dordrecht: Kluwer.

Douglas, M., & Wildavsky, A. (1982). *Risk and culture*. Berkeley, CA: University of California Press.

Durant, J., & Joss, S. (1995). *Public participation in science*. London: Science Museum.

Festinger, L. (1957). *A theory of cognitive dissonance*. Stanford, CA: Stanford University Press.

Fiorino, D. J. (1990). Citizen participation and environmental risk: A survey of institutional mechanisms. *Science, Technology and Human Values, 15*(2), 226–243.

Fischhoff, B. (1985). Managing risk perceptions. *Issues in Science and Technology, 2*(1), 83–96.

Fischhoff, B., Slovic, P., Lichtenstein, S., Read, S., & Combus, B. (1978). How safe is safe enough? A psychometric study of attitudes toward technological risks and benefits. *Policy Sciences, 9*(2), 127–152.

Frewer, L. J., Miles, S., Brennan, M., Kusenof, S., Ness, M., & Ritson, C. (2002). Public preferences for informed choice under conditions of risk uncertainty. *Public Understanding of Science, 11*(4), 1–10.

Gigerenzer, G. (1991). How to make cognitive illusions disappear: Beyond "heuristics and biases". *European Review of Social Psychology, 2*(1), 83–115.

Gigerenzer, G. (2000). *Adaptive thinking: Rationality in the real world*. New York, NY: Oxford University Press.

Gigerenzer, G. (2013). *Risiko. Wie man die richtigen Entscheidungen trifft*. München: Bertelsmann.

Gigerenzer, G., & Selten, R. (2001). Rethinking rationality. In G. Gigerenzer & R. Selten (Eds.), *Bounded rationality: The adaptive toolbox* (pp. 1–12). Boston, MA: MIT Press.

Gregory, R., McDaniels, T., & Fields, D. (2001). Decision aiding, not dispute resolution: A new perspective for environmental negotiation. *Journal of Policy Analysis and Management, 20*(3), 415–432.

IRGC (International Risk Governance Council). (2005). *Risk governance—Towards an integrative approach* (White Paper no 1, with an Annex by P. Graham). IRGC, Geneva.

Jaeger, C. C., Renn, O., Rosa, E. A., & Webler, T. (2001). *Risk, uncertainty, and rational action*. London: Earthscan.

Jungermann, H., Pfister, H.-R., & Fischer, K. (2005). *Die Psychologie der Entscheidung*. Heidelberg: Springer.

Kahneman, D. (2011). *Thinking fast and slow*. New York, NY: Penguin Books.

Kahneman, D., & Tversky, A. (1979). Prospect theory: An analysis of decision under risk. *Econometrica, 47*(2), 263–292.

Kahneman, D., & Tversky, A. (1984). Choices, values, and frames. *American Psychologist, 39*(4), 341–350.

Klinke, A., & Renn, O. (2012). Adaptive and integrative governance on risk and uncertainty. *Journal of Risk Research, 15*(3), 273–292.

Knight, A., & Warland, J. (2005). Determinants of food safety risk: A multi-disciplinary approach. *Rural Sociology, 70*(2), 253–275.

Kraus, N., Malmfors, T., & Slovic, P. (1992). Intuitive toxicology expert and lay judgments of chemical risks. *Risk Analysis, 12*(2), 215–232.

Lee, T. R. (1981). The public perception of risk and the question of irrationality. In Royal Society of Great Britain (Ed.), *Risk perception* (pp. 5–16). London: The Royal Society.

Linnerooth-Bayer, J., & Fitzgerald, K. B. (1996). Conflicting views on fair sitting processes: Evidence from Austria and the US. *Risk: Health Safety & Environment, 7*(2), 119–134.

Loewenstein, G., Weber, E., Hsee, C., & Welch, E. (2001). Risk as feelings. *Psychological Bulletin, 127*(2), 267–286.
Lopes, L. L. (1983). Some thoughts on the psychological concept of risk. *Journal of Experimental Psychology: Human Perception and Performance, 9*(1), 137–144.
Luhmann, N. (1986). The autopoiesis of social systems. In R. F. Geyer & J. van der Zouven (Eds.), *Sociokybernetic paradoxes: Observation, control and evolution of self-steering systems* (pp. 172–192). London: Sage.
Luhmann, N. (1997). Grenzwerte der ökologischen Politik: Eine Form von Risikomanagement. In P. Hiller & G. Krücken (Eds.), *Risiko und Regulierung. Soziologische Beiträge zu Technikkontrolle und präventiver Umweltpolitik* (pp. 195–221). Frankfurt am Main: Suhrkamp.
Marks, I., & Nesse, R. (1994). Fear and fitness: An evolutionary analysis of anxiety disorders. *Ethology and Sociobiology, 15*(5), 247–261.
Marshall, B. K. (1999). Globalization, environmental degradation and Ulrich Beck's risk society. *Environmental Values, 8*(2), 253–275.
Mazur, A. (1987). Does public perception of risk explain the social response to potential hazard. *Quarterly Journal of Ideology, 11*(2), 41–45.
McDaniels, T. L., Axelrod, L. J., Cavanagh, N. S., & Slovic, P. (1997). Perception of ecological risk to water environments. *Risk Analysis, 17*(3), 341–352.
Morgan, M. G., Fischhoff, B., Bostrom, A., & Atman, C. J. (2001). *Risk communication: A mental models approach.* Cambridge: Cambridge University Press.
Mythen, G. (2005). Employment, individualization, and insecurity: Rethinking the risk society perspective. *The Sociological Review, 53*(1), 129–149.
OECD (Organisation for Economic Co-operation and Development). (2002). *Guidance document on risk communication for chemical risk management* (Series on Risk Management, no 16, Environment, Health and Safety Publications). OECD, Paris.
Peters, E., Burraston, B., & Mertz, C. K. (2004). An emotion-based model of risk perception and stigma-susceptibility: Cognitive-appraisals of emotion, affective reactivity, worldviews, and risk perceptions in the generation of technological stigma. *Risk Analysis, 24*(5), 1349–1367.
Peters, H. P. (1991). Durch Risikokommunikation zur Technikakzeptanz? Die Konstruktion von Risiko "Wirklichkeiten" durch Experten, Gegenexperten und Öffentlichkeit. In J. Krüger & S. Ruß-Mohl (Eds.), *Risikokommunikation. Technikakzeptanz, Medien und Kommunikationsrisiken* (pp. 11–67). Berlin: Edition Stigma.
Pidgeon, N. F. (1997). The limits to safety? Culture, politics, learning and man–made disasters. *Journal of Contingencies and Crisis Management, 5*(1), 1–14.
Pollatsek, A., & Tversky, A. (1970). A theory of risk. *Journal of Mathematical Psychology, 7*(3), 540–553.
Renn, O. (1990). Risk perception and risk management: A review. *Risk Abstracts, 7*(1), 1–9.
Renn, O. (2005). Risk perception and communication lessons for the food and food packaging industry. *Food Additives and Contaminants, 22*(10), 1061–1071.
Renn, O. (2008). *Risk governance. Coping with uncertainty in a complex world.* London: Earthscan.
Renn, O. (2014a). *Das Risikoparadox: Warum wir uns vor dem Falschen fürchten*. Frankfurt am Main: S. Fischer.
Renn, O. (2014b). *Stakeholder involvement in risk governance*. London: Ark Group.
Renn, O., & Benighaus, C. (2013). Perception of technological risk: Insights from research and lessons for risk communication and management. *Journal of Risk Research, 16*(3–4), 293–313.
Renn, O., & Rohrmann, B. (2000). Cross-vultural risk perception research: State and challenges. In O. Renn & B. Rohrmann (Eds.), *Cross-cultural risk perception: A survey of empirical studies* (pp. 211–233). Dordrecht: Kluwer.
Renn, O., & Schweizer, P. (2009). Inclusive risk governance: Concepts and application to environmental policy making. *Environmental Policy and Governance, 19*(3), 174–185.
Renn, O., Burns, W., Kasperson, R. E., Kasperson, J. X., & Slovic, P. (1992). The social amplification of risk: Theoretical foundations and empirical application. *Journal of Social Issues, 48*(4), 137–160.

Renn, O., Schweizer, P.-J., Dreyer, M., & Klinke, A. (2007). *Risiko: Über den gesellschaftlichen Umgang mit Unsicherheit*. München: Oekom.
Rohrmann, B. (2000). Cross-national studies on the perception and evaluation of hazards. In O. Renn & B. Rohrmann (Eds.), *Cross-cultural risk perception: A survey of research results* (pp. 55–78). Dordrecht: Kluwer.
Rohrmann, B., & Renn, O. (2000). Risk perception research—An introduction. In O. Renn & B. Rohrmann (Eds.), *Cross-cultural risk perception: A survey of empirical etudies* (pp. 11–54). Dordrecht: Kluwer.
Rosa, E. A., Matsuda, N., & Kleinhesselink, R. R. (2000). The cognitive architecture of risk: Pancultural unity or cultural shaping? In O. Renn & B. Rohrmann (Eds.), *Cross-cultural risk perception: A survey of empirical studies* (pp. 185–210). Dordrecht: Kluwer.
Rosa, E. A., Renn, O., & McCright, A. M. (2014). *The risk society revisited. Social theory and governance*. Philadelphia, PA: Temple University Press.
Rowe, G. and Frewer, L.J. (2000): Public Participation Methods: A Framework for Evaluation. *Science, Technology and Human Values, 25*(1): 3–29.
Scholz, R. (2009). *Environmental literacy in science and society. From knowledge to decisions*. Cambridge, MA: Cambridge University Press.
Shubik, M. (1991). Risk, society, politicians, scientists and people. In M. Shubik (Ed.), *Risk, organizations, and society* (pp. 7–30). Dordrecht: Kluwer.
Siegrist, M., Keller, C., & Kiers, H. A. (2005). A new look at the psychometric paradigm of perceptions of hazards. *Risk Analysis, 25*(1), 211–222.
Sjöberg, L. (1999). Risk perception in Western Europe. *Ambio, 28*(6), 543–549.
Sjöberg, L. (2000). Factors in risk perception. *Risk Analysis, 220*(1), 1–11.
Sjöberg, L. (2001). Limits of knowledge and the limited importance of trust. *Risk Analysis, 21*(1), 189–198.
Slovic, P. (1987). Perception of risk. *Science, 236*(4799), 280–285.
Slovic, P. (1992). Perception of risk reflections on the psychometric paradigm. In S. Krimsky & D. Golding (Eds.), *Social theories of risk* (pp. 117–152). Westport, CT: Praeger.
Slovic, P. (2000). Informing an education the public about risk. In P. Slovic (Ed.), *The perception of risk* (pp. 182–191). London: Earthscan.
Slovic, P., Finucane, E., Peters, D., & MacGregor, R. (2002). The affect heuristic. In T. Gilovich, D. Griffin, & D. Kahnemann (Eds.), *Intuitive judgment, heuristic and biases* (pp. 397–420). Cambridge; MA: Cambridge University Press.
Slovic, P., Fischhoff, B., & Lichtenstein, S. (1980). Facts and fears: Understanding perceived risk. In R. Schwing & W. A. Albers (Eds.), *Societal risk assessment how safe is safe enough?* (pp. 181–214). New York, NY: Plenum.
Slovic, P., Fischhoff, B., & Lichtenstein, S. (1982). Why study risk perception. *Risk Analysis, 2*(2), 83–94.
Slovic, P., Fischhoff, B., & Lichtenstein, S. (1986). The psychometric study of risk perception. In V. R. Covello, J. Menkes, & J. Mumpower (Eds.), *Risk evaluation and management* (pp. 3–24). New York, NY: Plenum.
Slovic, P., Flynn, J., Mertz, C. K., Poumadere, M., & Mays, C. (2000). Nuclear power and the public: A comparative study of risk perception in the United States and France. In O. Renn & B. Rohrmann (Eds.), *Cross-cultural risk perception: A survey of research results* (pp. 55–102). Dordrecht: Kluwer.
Sparks, P., & Shepherd, R. (1994). Public perceptions of the potential hazards associated with food production and food consumption: An empirical study. *Risk Analysis, 14*(5), 799–806.
Sparks, P., Shepherd, R., & Frewer, L. J. (1994). Gene technology, food production, and public opinion: A UK study. *Agriculture and Human Values, 11*(1), 19–28.
Stern, P. C., & Fineberg, V. (1996). *Understanding risk: Informing decisions in a democratic society*. Washington, DC: National Academy Press.
Streffer, C., Bücker, J., Cansier, A., Cansier, D., Gethmann, C. F., Guderian, R., … Wuttke, K. (2003). *Environmental standards: Combined exposures and their effects on human beings and their environment*. Berlin: Springer Science.

Sunstein, C., & Thaler, R. (2009). *Nudge. Improving decisions about health, wealth, and happiness*. New Haven, CT: Yale University Press.
Thompson, M. (1980). *An outline of the cultural theory of risk* (International Institute for Applied System Analysis (IIASA) Working Paper, WP–80–177). IIASA, Laxenburg.
Thompson, M., Ellis, W., & Wildavsky, A. (1990). *Cultural theory*. Boulder, CO: Westview.
Townsend, E., Clarke, D. D., & Travis, B. (2004). Effects of context and feelings on perceptions of genetically modified food. *Risk Analysis, 24*(5), 1369–1384.
US-National Research Council of the National Academies. (2008). *Public participation in environmental assessment and decision making*. Washington, DC: The National Academies Press.
Wachinger, G., Renn, O., Begg, C., & Kuhlicke, C. (2010). The risk perception paradox—Implications for governance and communication of natural hazards. *Risk Analysis, 33*(6), 1049–1065.
Webler, T., Levine, D., Rakel, H., & Renn, O. (1991). A novel approach to reducing uncertainty: The group Delphi. *Technological Forecasting and Social Change, 39*(3), 253–263.
Wilkinson, I. (2001). Social theories of risk perception: At once indispensable and insufficient. *Current Sociology, 49*(1), 1–22.
Wynne, B. (2002). Risk and environment as legitimatory discourses of technology: Reflexivity inside out? *Current Sociology, 50*(3), 459–477.
Zwick, M. M., & Renn, O. (1998) *Wahrnehmung und Bewertung von Technik in Baden-Württemberg*. Paper presented at Stuttgart Center of Technology Assessment in Baden-Württemberg, Stuttgart.

Index

M. Raue et al. (eds.), *Psychological Perspectives on Risk and Risk Analysis*,
https://doi.org/10.1007/978-3-319-92478-6

H

I

The manufacturer's authorised representative in the EU is Springer
Nature Customer Service Centre GmbH, Europaplatz 3, 69115 Heidelberg,
Germany. If you have any concerns regarding our products, please
contact ProductSafety@springernature.com

Printed and bound by CPI Group (UK) Ltd, Croydon, CR0 4YY
05/10/2026
02228141-0012